LETTERS
TO LUTHERAN PASTORS

VOLUME II
1951–1956

HERMANN SASSE

Edited by Matthew C. Harrison

Translated by Matthew C. Harrison and Andrew Smith

Foreword by Ronald R. Feuerhahn

Additional translations by Ralph Gehrke,
Fred Kramer, E. Reim, and Norman Nagel

CONCORDIA PUBLISHING HOUSE • SAINT LOUIS

For Ronald R. Feuerhahn, *Doctor Ecclesiae*

Copyright © 2014 Concordia Publishing House
3558 S. Jefferson Ave., St. Louis, MO 63118-3968
1-800-325-3040 • www.cph.org

Wolfgang Sasse, son of Hermann Sasse, has graciously given permission to publish translations of his father's essays and letters for which he holds the copyright.

The English translation of "Sesqui[cent]ennial of Chalcedon" first appeared in *Theologische Quartalschrift*. It is reprinted with permission of *Wisconsin Lutheran Quarterly*. Minor alterations to grammar and capitalization have been made with permission.

The English translation of "The Confessional Problem in Today's World Lutheranism" first appeared in *The Lutheran Layman*, April 1, 1957. It is reprinted courtesy of The International Lutheran Laymen's League; all rights reserved; used by permission. Minor alterations to grammar and capitalization have been made with permission.

Quotations marked AE are from Luther's Works, American Edition: volumes 1–30 © 1955–76 Concordia Publishing House; volumes 31–54 © 1957–86 Augsburg Fortress. All rights reserved.

Most Scripture quotations in this document have been translated from the German. They may in many instances approximate the King James or Authorized Version of the Bible.

Scripture quotations marked RSV are from the Revised Standard Version of the Bible, copyright 1952, © 1971 by the Division of Christian Education of the National Council of the Churches of Christ in the United States of America. Used by permission. All rights reserved.

Scripture quotations identified as ESV are from the ESV Bible® (The Holy Bible, English Standard Version®), copyright © 2001 by Crossway Bibles, a publishing ministry of Good News Publishers. Used by permission. All rights reserved.

Manufactured in the United States of America

Library of Congress Cataloging-in-Publication Data

Sasse, Hermann, 1895–1976.
    [Correspondence. English. Selections]
    Letters to Lutheran pastors / Hermann Sasse ; edited and translated by Matthew C. Harrison ; foreword by Ronald R. Feuerhahn ; additional translations by Ralph Gehrke, Fred Kramer, Norman Nagel, E. Reim, Andrew Smith.
        pages cm
    Includes bibliographical references.
    ISBN 978-0-7586-4155-7
    1. Sasse, Hermann, 1895–1976.—Correspondence. 2. Lutheran Church—Doctrines. I. Harrison, Matthew C. II. Title.
    BX8080.S18A4 2013
    284.1—dc23   2012047167

1 2 3 4 5 6 7 8 9 10   23 22 21 20 19 18 17 16 15 14

CONTENTS

Principal Abbreviations and Works Cited   v

Foreword by Ronald R. Feuerhahn   ix

Preface by Matthew C. Harrison   xi

Letters to Lutheran Pastors

20. Confession and Theology in the Missouri Synod   5

21. The Sesqui[cent]ennial of Chalcedon   33

22. The Deconfessionalization of Lutheranism?   50

23. The Scriptural Basis for the Lutheran Doctrine of the Lord's Supper   76

24. Last Things   98

25. Concerning the Unity of the Lutheran Church   117

26. The Lutheran Understanding of the Consecration   138

27. Worldwide Lutheranism after Hanover   163

28. Altar Fellowship, Church Fellowship, and Ecclesiastical Federation   183

29. Toward Understanding Augustine's Doctrine of Inspiration   205

30. Marginal Notes   227

31. Problems in American Lutheran Theology   244

32. Current Lutheran Doctrinal Discussions   264

33. Toward Understanding the Six Days of Creation   280

34. The Great Schism and Its Lessons   295

35. The Lutheran Church and World Mission   314

36. *Post Festum*   336

37. The Church's Time of Rejoicing   355

38. *Cuius Regio, Eius Religio?*   369

49. Unity and Division within Lutheranism   385

40. Ecumenical Questions   407

41. *Successio Apostolica*   425

42. Word and Sacrament, Preaching and Lord's Supper   451

43. The Confessional Problem in Today's World Lutheranism   475

Indexes   502

Principal Abbreviations and Works Cited

AC / CA	Augsburg Confession
AE	*Luther's Works*. American Edition. Volumes 1–30: Edited by Jaroslav Pelikan. St. Louis: Concordia, 1955–76. Volumes 31–55: Edited by Helmut Lehmann. Philadelphia/Minneapolis: Muhlenberg/Fortress, 1957–86. Volumes 56–75: Edited by Christopher Boyd Brown. St. Louis: Concordia, 2009–.
AELKZ	*Allgemeine evangelisch-lutherische Kirchenzeitung*
Aland	Kurt Aland. *Hilfsbuch zum Lutherstudium*. 4th ed. Bielfeld: Luther-Verlag, 1996. Cited by main catalog number, postil number (Po), or sermon number (Pr).
ALC	American Lutheran Church
ANF	*The Ante-Nicene Fathers*. Edited by Alexander Roberts and James Donaldson. Revised by A. Cleveland Coxe. 10 vols. Buffalo: Christian Literature Publishing Co., 1885–96. Reprint, Peabody, MA: Hendrickson, 1994.
Ap	Apology of the Augsburg Confession
BLP	*Briefe an Lutherische Pfarrer* (*Letters to Lutheran Pastors*)
BSLK or *Bekenntnisschriften*	
	Die Bekenntnisschriften der evangelisch-lutherischen Kirche. 6th ed. Göttingen: Vandehoeck & Ruprecht, 1967.
CHI	Concordia Historical Institute, St. Louis, Missouri.
Christian Cyclopedia	
	Edited by Erwin Lueker. Accessed at http://cyclopedia.lcms.org
CIC	*Codex Iuris Canonici*
Concordia	*Concordia: The Lutheran Confessions*. 2nd ed. Edited by Paul T. McCain et al. St. Louis: Concordia, 2006.
CTM	*Concordia Theological Monthly*
CSEL	*Corpus scriptorum ecclesiasticorum Latinorum*. Vienna: Verlag der Österreichischen Akademie der Wissenschaften, 1866–.
DCSV	German Christian Student Association
DEK	Deutsche Evangelische Kirche (German Evangelical Church)

Denzinger Heinrich Denzinger, ed. *Enchiridion symbolorum definitionum et declarationum de rebus fidei et morum.* 34th ed. Edited by Adolf Schönmetzer. Freiburg: Herder, 1967.

E Erlangen edition of Luther's works. *Dr. Martin Luther's Sammtliche Werke.* 67 vols. Erlangen: C. Heyder, 1826–57.

E^1 = *Luther's sämmtliche Werke* [Erste Auflage] (German works, first series).

EKiD / EKD Evangelische Kirche in Deutschland (Evangelical Church in Germany)

ELC Evangelical Lutheran Church

ELCA Evangelical Lutheran Church of America

ELCA Evangelical Lutheran Church of Australia

Enders *Dr. Martin Luthers Briefwechsel.* Edited by Ernst Ludwig Enders. Frankfurt am Main: 1884–1932.

Ep Epitome of the Formula of Concord

ESV English Standard Version

FC Formula of Concord

Feuerhahn Chronology
See *Hermann Sasse: A Bibliography.* Lanham, MD: Scarecrow, 1995.

HKBP Huria Kristen Batak Protestand

HS Hermann Sasse

Huss number Bibliographic number assigned to Sasse's writings by Ronald R. Feuerhahn in *Hermann Sasse: A Bibliography.* Lanham, MD: Scarecrow, 1995.

Ibid. *Ibidem* (in the same place)

ISC *In Statu Confessionis: Gesammelte Aufsätze von Hermann Sasse.* Edited by Friedrich Wilhelm Hopf. 2 vols. Berlin, 1966, 1975–76.

LC Large Catechism

LCA Lutheran Church in America

LCMS The Lutheran Church—Missouri Synod

Lonely Way Hermann Sasse. *The Lonely Way: Selected Essays and Letters.* Translated by Matthew C. Harrison, et al. Historical introductions by Ronald R. Feuerhahn. 2 vols. St. Louis: Concordia, 2001–2.

LSB *Lutheran Service Book.* St. Louis: Concordia, 2006

Lthtm *Luthertum*

LuBl *Lutherische Blätter*

LWF Lutheran World Federation

MH Matthew C. Harrison

Müller *Die symbolischen Bücher der evangelisch-lutherischen Kirche.* 11th edition. Edited by Johann T. Müller. Gütersloh: Bertelsmann, 1912.

NCCCA / NCCCUS
National Council of the Churches of Christ in the USA

NDB *Neue Deutsche Biographie.* Edited by Die Historische Kommission bei der Bayerischen Königlichen Akademie der Wissenschaften. Berlin: Duncker & Humblot, 1953–.

NKZ	*Neue kirchliche Zeitschrift*
NN	Norman Nagel
NPNF¹	*A Select Library of the Christian Church: Nicene and Post-Nicene Fathers: First Series.* Edited by Philip Schaff. 14 vols. New York, 1886–89. Reprint, Peabody, MA: Hendrickson, 1994.
NPNF²	*A Select Library of the Christian Church: Nicene and Post-Nicene Fathers: Second Series.* Edited by Philip Schaff and Henry Wace. 14 vols. New York, 1890–1900. Reprint, Peabody, MA: Hendrickson, 1994.
ODCC	*The Oxford Dictionary of the Christian Church.* Edited by F. L. Cross and E. A. Livingstone. 3rd ed. Oxford: Oxford University Press, 1997.
op. cit.	*opere citato* (in the aforementioned work)
PG	*Patrologia cursus completus: Series Graeca.* Edited by J.-P. Migne. 161 vols. in 167. Petit-Montrouge: Apud J. P. Migne, 1857–66.
PL	*Patrologiae cursus completus: Series Latina.* Edited by J.-P. Migne. 221 vols. in 223. Paris: Garnier Fratres, 1844–64.
QS	*Quartalschrift* (*Wisconsin Lutheran Theological Quarterly*)
RG	Ralph Gehrke
RGG³	*Die Religion in Geschichte und Gegenwart.* 3rd ed. 7 vols. Edited by Kurt Galling. Tübingen: Mohr (Paul Siebeck), 1957–65.
RSV	Revised Standard Version
RTR	*Reformed Theological Review*
SA	Smalcald Articles
SC	Small Catechism
SD	Solid Declaration of the Formula of Concord
St. Louis edition	See W²
Tappert	Theodore G. Tappert, ed. *The Book of Concord: The Confessions of the Evangelical Lutheran Church.* Philadelphia: Fortress, 1959.
TLH	*The Lutheran Hymnal.* St. Louis: Concordia, 1941.
Triglotta / *Trig.*	*Concordia Triglotta: The Symbolic Books of the Evangelical Lutheran Church.* St. Louis: Concordia, 1921.
UELCA	United Evangelical Lutheran Church of Australia
ULC	United Lutheran Church
ULCA	United Lutheran Church of America
VELKD	Vereinigte evangelische-lutherische Kirche in Deutschland (United Evangelical Lutheran Church in Germany)
Vg	Vulgate
W¹ / Walch edition	*D. Martin Luthers sowol in Deutscher als Lateinischer Sprache verfertigte und aus der letztern in die erstere übersetzte Sämmtliche Schriften.* Edited by Johann G. Walch. 24 vols. Halle: Gebauer, 1740–53.

W²   *Dr. Martin Luthers Sämmtliche Schriften.* Edited by Albrecht F. Hoppe. 23 vols. St. Louis: Concordia, 1880–1910.

WA   *D. Martin Luthers Werke: Kritische Gesamtausgabe.* 73 vols. in 85. Weimar: H. Böhlau, 1883–.

WA Br   *D. Martin Luthers Werke: Briefwechsel.* 18 vols. Weimar: H. Böhlau, 1930–.

WA TR   *D. Martin Luthers Werke: Tischreden.* 6 vols. Weimar: H. Böhlau, 1912–21.

WCC   World Council of Churches

Foreword

RONALD R. FEUERHAHN

HERMANN SASSE WAS A HISTORIAN, a theologian, a churchman, and a pastor. In this remarkable collection of letters—or we might even call them epistles—we meet all of these skills: a historian with a breadth of learning, a theologian of thorough biblical knowledge, a churchman of wisdom, and a pastor of caring words. It is the thorough grasp of the past that has allowed Sasse to be open to a clear perception of the future; E. Clifford Nelson was not alone in his description of Sasse as prescient.[1] Here also we meet a theologian who is able to teach the church from the background of a thorough scholarship of Scripture and confessions and cement them to much of the church of his day. Here is a historian and theologian who speaks the language of lonely pastors throughout the world; thus he also spoke for them and to them as a churchman and as a pastor.

Sasse was also a "teacher of the church," that title that meant so much to Martin Luther. Sasse taught faithfully the doctrine of Scripture and the confession of the church. He applied himself in these letters particularly to the needs of the church of his day. His teaching was respected by churchmen and laity of a very broad, ecumenical spectrum of the church. Yet no one was completely comfortable with this man, least of all the liberal churchmen of his day. They described him as "narrow," a "strict confessionalist." That discomfort is still present today, for Sasse calls all to repentance. He spoke not only to and for "his day," but there is also a certain catholicity to these letters, a wisdom that has prompted many to be grateful for them.

From the very beginning, Sasse intended this to be a series of letters. In the opening sentences of the first letter he stated:

> The following lines and the letters which, God willing, are to follow this one are addressed to Lutheran pastors in totally different churches and nations, in Germany and in the remaining Europe, in North and South

---

1   E. Clifford Nelson, *The Rise of World Lutheranism, An American Perspective* (Philadelphia: Fortress, 1982), 314f.

America, in Africa and Australia. They are addressed to fellow ministers who together with the undersigned know themselves bound by their ordination vow to the Holy Scriptures as the *norma normans* ["norming norm"] of all the doctrinal Confessions of the Evangelical Lutheran Church as the true interpretation of the Scriptures.

Sasse also strikes that note of loneliness facing his many readers:

> They are addressed to brethren whose hearts bleed whenever they see the condition in which the Lutheran Church of our day and of our world finds itself. We know full well: not only we as theologians see and labor under these distressing conditions. Numberless members of our congregations share our experience and sense the reason for the Church's need.[2]

These letters were doubtless intended to address these readers in their distress and loneliness and to bring them comfort.

These epistles, as they may well be called, were intended for a broad distribution; Sasse indicated this to various colleagues.[3] It was with this intention in mind that the editorial staff of the *Quartalschrift*, or *Theological Quarterly*, of the Wisconsin Evangelical Lutheran Synod offered their translations:

> We hope that these letters will also be published in other theological journals[4] of this and other countries, that they will be translated into the languages of all the foreign countries where the Lutheran Church has found a home. Therefore we are placing these letters, as translated by us, at the disposal of those editorial staffs that have not undertaken a translation of their own, or do not intend to do so. For we hold that the content of these letters deserves a careful study on the part of every Lutheran reader.[5]

Such is our opinion today as well.

---

2   These first two citations are from the opening sentences of the *Letters*. See *Letters to Lutheran Pastors*, ed. Matthew C. Harrison, vol. 1, *1948–1951* (St. Louis: Concordia, 2013), 5–6.

3   E.g.: "As I wrote to you, a first letter to Luthern [*sic*] pastors will go out soon. You may translate and circulate it if you deem it useful" (letter to Herman Preus, November 27, 1948).

4   And so they were; this letter was published also, e.g., in *CTM* 20, no. 8 (August 1949): 615–25.

5   The editorial staff, *QS* 46, no. 2 (April 1949): 81n. In all, the *Theological Quarterly* published ten of the letters, ceasing the enterprise, understandably, after the controversial Letter 14, "On the Doctrine *De Scriptura Sacra*," and Letter 16, "What Does Luther Have to Say to Us on the Inerrancy of the Holy Scripture?" Letter 14 was the only writing that Sasse publicly withdrew. See Jeffrey J. Kloha, "Hermann Sasse Confesses the Doctrine *de Scriptura Sacra*," in *Scripture and the Church: Selected Essays of Hermann Sasse*, ed. Jeffrey J. Kloha and Ronald R. Feuerhahn, Concordia Seminary Monograph Series 2 (St. Louis: Concordia Seminary, 1995), 337–423. Various letters would be translated and published in many other journals and in numerous languages.

Preface

MATTHEW C. HARRISON

SOME WOULD WONDER WHAT POSSIBLE benefit might come from the study of half-century old letters of a long-deceased Lutheran theologian. Should not the church be looking forward and not backward? Yet we are confident that you will find these treatises absolutely gripping, especially if Christ has lit in your soul a similar fire for His blessed Word and Sacrament as confessed by the catechisms of Martin Luther. Reading Hermann Sasse is a veritable guided tour through centuries of church history, particularly the history of the nineteenth and twentieth centuries. And no matter how clichéd it might sound, it remains true that charting one's course for the future is aided immensely when one has some idea from whence he has come. And that holds true for churches.

Sasse is prone to see "tragedies" at every turn of church history. He spares no one intense criticism when he thinks it warranted. In this era of postmodernism, or now perhaps post-postmodernism in the wake of the terror of 9/11, Sasse holds out for truth. "The future belongs to those churches which dare to confess their dogma," he loved to say. Sasse was a man once awash in the vague mist of an optimistic and nondoctrinal religion. But shaken to the foundation of his being, he beheld the depravity of man. Then he was shown the blessed truth of the Gospel of Jesus Christ, *vere deus*, as witnessed by the Word of God and as confessed by the Lutheran Confessions. The conviction burned brightly right through the ungodly challenges of the dark night of Nazism, and it burned brightly amid the vacillations and cavillations of well-meaning churchmen who were held captive by much more deceptive and alluring enticements from the truth which is found in Christ and His Sacrament.

Yet amid the failures of men and churches, Sasse was gripped by the fact that because Jesus Christ has a future, the church has a future. *Una sancta ecclesia perpetuo mansura sit!* "One holy church shall ever remain!" (AC VII). And because Sasse was above all else a doctor of the church, a confessor of the church, he was convinced, too, that the church is ever found where the *evangelium pure docetur et recte administrantur sacramenta,* where "the Gospel is purely taught, and the Sacraments rightly administered" (AC VII). *Ubi Christus, ibi ecclesia!* "Where Christ is, *there* is the church" (Ignatius).[1]

May this collection of Sasse's essays cause hearts and lips to burn with the confession of Christ and churches to rise and confess the faith once delivered to the saints, as confessed in the Lutheran Reformation.

ACKNOWLEDGMENTS

I'm deeply grateful for the staff of Concordia Publishing House who contributed to the publication of these volumes of Sasse's *Letters to Lutheran Pastors.* Charles Schaum worked on the project early on, providing his own translation for a significant letter in the collection. I'm indebted to Dawn Weinstock for her editorial work and to Edward Engelbrecht, who managed the process expertly. Finally, Paul McCain has been a constant encouragement in all matters Sasse-related.

We thank the editors of the *Wisconsin Lutheran Quarterly* and Concordia Publishing House for the necessary permission to reprint many of these essays. We thank especially Dr. Norman Nagel for graciously agreeing to translate individual letters and sharing letters translated for his We Confess series. Mr. Andrew Smith has provided numerous letters in English, quietly and capably working for little remuneration other than the love of Lutheran theology. Many have helped here and there through what has suddenly become a twenty-year quest to publish in English Sasse's *Letters to Lutheran Pastors.* We thank Robert Wurst and Jennifer Maxfield for contributing editing skills on this challenging project. Holger Sonntag with Peter Petzling and Paul Strawn provided a burst of effort as the last dozen or so letters were rendered in English. Rachel Mumme graciously searched out the hitherto unlocated first two *Circular Letters to Westphalian Pastors,* and then proceeded to provide wonderful translations of both.[2] Thanks are owed especially to Dr. Ronald Feuerhahn, who, as ever, readily provided needed assistance with this Sasse project and whose published and unpublished works on Sasse are an ever-present help in need! Ron's unpublished "Chronicle" of events in Sasse's life was used to footnote the letters. Also his vast collection of letters and documents was a rich source for the anecdotal details peppered throughout this volume.

Sasse's was a theological life to be sure, but also and in every way a life—with many personal and professional joys and disappointments. I have tried to use some discretion in the use of personal papers, while also revealing historical realities, such as Sasse's simultaneous appreciation and disdain for aspects of Werner Elert's person and work. There are two sides to every story. Sasse himself could be rather difficult, to be sure.

---

1   *Epistle to the Smyrnaeans* 8.2.

2   See *Letters to Lutheran Pastors* 1:435–80, especially pp. 435–51.

THE EDITING

I have slightly revised most of the translations, bringing them into reasonable uniformity of style and expression. In many places in the older translations I have restored theological language where the freight of terms has been diminished (e.g., substituting "office" where the translation of *Amt* slipped into "ministry" with a lowercase "m" and no definite article). Brackets [ ] have generally been used to provide a peek at the original or to add additional bibliographic material not in Sasse's original. Where Sasse or a translator provided both the original (e.g., Latin) and a translation, we have kept the parentheses. I have also taken the liberty to reduce sentence length and to update the language slightly. I have not attempted to make the citation of English Bible passages uniform. In some places translators simply render the German text. Nor are we consistent in quoting a version of the Lutheran Confessions. Often translators simply provide a fresh translation of the confessional text quoted. There is, after all, only so much time in life. And the English-speaking world has waited too long for this collection already. We hope the reader will be pleased with this volume of Sasse's *Letters*.

I have also included anecdotal material from personal correspondence from the general time at which the particular *Briefe* was published as a peek into matters going on in Sasse's life or in the life of the church. These passages favor dealings with the LCMS, but it is also true that Sasse was heavily involved and interested in LCMS dealings. Sasse carried on an enormous volume of correspondence. His son Wolfgang told Ronald Feuerhahn that his father would have four or five typewriters in the house at any given moment, each with a manuscript in process. I only discovered while searching for quotations within Sasse correspondence that by his own admission Sasse had typed "with one finger." What a finger that was!

The publication of this volume is the culmination of twenty years of labor. Kurt Marquart introduced me to Sasse while I was a student at Concordia Theological Seminary in Fort Wayne, Indiana (MDiv 1989; STM 1991). About that time Norman Nagel published his vitally significant translations for the We Confess series, and I devoured them. While an exchange student in Adelaide, Australia (1987), I found everything by Sasse in English that I possibly could, and with the help of Maurice Schild I gained access to the church archives for my first foray into the private papers of Sasse. I developed a warm relationship with Henry Hamann Jr., Elvin Janetzki, Bruce Adams, John Kleinig, and J. T. E. Renner. I came to know Maurice Schild (Sasse's successor at Immanuel Seminary) and met Siegfried Hebart (who had been instrumental in bringing Sasse to Australia) and others. Simultaneously, Ronald Feuerhahn was working on his doctorate on Sasse and was in the process of amassing personal papers. With the help of Robert Preus (under whom I wrote a master of sacred theology thesis on Sasse), I began collecting correspondence for the Walther Library at the seminary in

Fort Wayne (the institution to which Sasse left his vast library) and sharing it with Dr. Feuerhahn. I will never forget sitting in Dr. Preus's office while he dictated a letter to his uncle, Herman A. Preus (then nearly 100 years old), requesting copies of his Sasse correspondence. Dr. Preus also succeeded in convincing Tom Hardt to send his very private correspondence spanning decades. The continued effort brought me into contact and correspondence with Bjarne Teigen, Martin Wittenberg, Ulrich Asendorf, Jobst Schoene, Bengt Hägglund, and even Bo Giertz. It has been an amazing journey.

Despite the amount of Sasse's writings made available in the Lonely Way volumes (Concordia, 2001–2002) and in this collection of letters, there is vastly more to be done. We hope others will take up the task.

✍

As ever, I remain most thankful for my blessed life's companion, Kathy, whose profound Lutheran convictions and living grace make life beyond Sasse projects such a joy. I provide this work for Matthew Martin Luther Harrison, Mark Martin Chemnitz Harrison, and their entire generation and those after, that their hearts might "burn within them" with the confession of Christ as they make their Emmaus journey through life to life everlasting, where we shall—together— know joys supernal. My own translation work is far from perfect. May these letters find their way back to Australia and to many other places around the globe and here, as there, awaken a love for the Lutheran confession of the faith. Above all, may Sasse's ringing clarity on the church and Sacrament be a beacon guiding us to our Confessions and to Christ Himself, who speaks so clearly in Holy Scripture and to whom our Confessions bear incomparable witness.

Matthew C. Harrison
Assistant Pastor, Village Lutheran Church, Ladue, Missouri
President, The Lutheran Church—Missouri Synod

LETTERS
TO LUTHERAN PASTORS

"The only thing I can do is write letters."

HERMANN SASSE

Historical Context

By 1951, Sasse's interests were very much turned toward the Missouri Synod. The talks on church union between the two synods in Australia, which Sasse joined immediately upon his arrival in 1949, brought him directly into dialogue with men who had been trained in St. Louis (such as H. P. Hamann Sr.). Letter 20, "Confession and Theology in the Missouri Synod," demonstrates just how familiar Sasse was with the LCMS. While its criticism is closely linked to views on the nature of Scripture expressed in Letters 14 and 16,[1] Sasse was prescient in noting the danger of American evangelicalism (fundamentalism) for Missouri, a theme he maintained until he died. A significant strength of Missouri, says Sasse, are its genuine Lutheran congregations. But he foresaw a weakness as both major factions in postwar Missouri, in the wake of the 1944 "Brief Statement," took the Lutheran Confessions for granted, lacking the real "joy" in praise to God for the Confession which nineteenth-century Missouri possessed. MH

April 19, 1952

Dr. Hermann Sasse
41 Buxton Street
North Adelaide, South Australia

Dr. Carl E. Lundquist[2]
Lutheran World Federation
Geneva

Dear Dr. Lundquist,

Thank you for your letter .... Since the *Triglotta* is not going to appear again, the original text of the Confessions will soon be unknown to the English speaking Lutheran Churches. What the revised translation will be like, nobody knows. The present text is not free from errors. The most necessary publication is a new edition of the *Book of Concord*, perhaps in several small volumes of the size of the modern editions of the *Summa* of Thomas by the German (Latin and German)

---

1   See "On the Doctrine *De Scriptura Sacra*," and "What Does Luther Have to Say to Us on the Inerrancy of the Holy Scripture?" in *Letters to Lutheran Pastors* 1:240–84, 332–66. MH

2   Carl Elof Lundquist (1908–65) was executive secretary of the LWF (1951–60) (s.v. *Christian Cyclopedia*). MH

and English (only English translation) Dominicans. It should be a book which the pastor can carry along on journeys and at conferences, which was impossible with the big volume of the *Triglotta*. Without a good edition of the Confessions, the Lutheran Church will die. There should also be editions of single books as e.g., the *Augustana* and the Smalcald Articles, with brief explanations for the laymen. I remember the deep impression which the English pamphlets made on other people when at Lausanne (1927) they were distributed to the members of the World Conference on Faith and Order by the delegates of the ULC. A copy of this letter is being sent to Dr. Prenter . . . .

With kind regards,

Yours in Christ,
Hermann Sasse

twenty

Confession
and Theology
in the Missouri Synod

TRANSLATED BY FRED KRAMER

End of July 1951[1]

Prof. Dr. Theol. Hermann Sasse
41 Buxton Street
North Adelaide, South Australia

Dear Brothers in the Office!

It is not meddling in the affairs of another church if we today undertake to speak on one of the basic problems of the Missouri Synod. For the life of a church is not like the life of an individual Christian, a private matter; it is a matter for all of Christendom. Whenever a church, whether it be a small congregation or

---

1 *BLP* 20: *Bekenntnis und Theologie in der Missouri synode* (North Adelaide, July 1951). The original was published in *LuBl* 3, no. 22 (1951). Huss number 289. George Beto first requested that Kramer translate the letter into English. "Some time ago one of your general letters addressed to Lutheran pastors (number 20) fell into our hands. It dealt with the general subject *Bekenntnis und Theologie in der Missouri synode*. It represents—in our opinion—an excellent analysis of the Missouri Synod. In fact, we desire to print an English translation of the letter in the spring issue of our quarterly, *The Springfielder*. May we have your permission to reprint the article? We would be happy to permit you to approve the English translation . . . . Cordially, George J. Beto P.S. I recall with pleasant memory our brief meeting at Oakland and at San Francisco" (Beto to Sasse, December 28, 1960; in the Harrison Collection). "The translation of Sasse, *Letter* no. 20, has been transferred to 15 Dictabelts, and will be given to the faculty secretaries when they return after Christmas. Kramer 12–25–60." The essay was translated but not published. MH

5

a major part of Christendom, confesses her faith before the world, she does so "to those now living and those who shall come after us" (FC SD XII 40 [*BSLK*, 1099.42f.; Tappert, 636]). Therefore the great "We believe, teach, and confess," with which the Missouri Synod, one of the very few great Lutheran Churches which have the courage to make the whole Book of Concord her own, poses a question and an admonition to all churches in the world. The very fact of the existence of this church is a constant challenge to Lutherans throughout the world to understand clearly what the Lutheran Church is, and why there is not complete church fellowship among those who confess allegiance to the Augsburg Confession and to Luther's catechisms. This challenge becomes all the more urgent as we Lutherans begin to realize what light our disunity casts upon our claim to teach Christendom what the true unity of the church is. What does the great *satis est* ["it is sufficient for the true unity of the church"] (AC VII 2 [*BSLK*, 61.7; Tappert, 32]) mean if church fellowship is impossible among those who are one in the doctrine of justification by faith alone and in the Lutheran doctrine of the Sacrament? Therefore no Lutheran theology dare ignore the position of the Missouri Synod. This means, first of all, that it must seek to understand this important Lutheran Church.

1

In connection with the centennial of the Evangelical Lutheran Synod of Missouri, Ohio, and Other States in the year 1947, this church took a new name and thereby took cognizance of the fact that from a union of Lutheran synods in the United States it had developed into a worldwide church which represents a unique type of Lutheranism: "The Lutheran Church—Missouri Synod." Closely linked in the Synodical Conference with her smaller sister churches the Wisconsin Synod, the Slovak Synod, and the Norwegian Synod—and in church fellowship with the Lutheran Free Church [*lutherischen Freikirche*] in Germany and the Evangelical Lutheran Church in Australia—the Missouri Synod, together with her daughter churches and congregations in Brazil and in all of Latin America, in Europe, and on the mission fields of Asia, constitutes one of the largest Lutheran Churches. In America this church embraces almost a third of all Lutherans, with more than one and one-half million members, more than five thousand congregations and preaching stations, and almost four thousand pastors.[2]

Rooted in the agricultural areas of the Midwest, where in some areas Lutheranism is almost more a matter of the people than in many so-called "people's churches" of Europe, the Missouri Synod, like every true mission church, has grown far beyond her historical home. She is a mission church in a sense in which this cannot be said of any other Lutheran Church. This is one of her most

---

2   As of 2010 the LCMS has some 6,100 congregations in the United States. MH

profound characteristics. She is not merely a church of foreign missions, as, for example, the church of Norway, which with her maritime people has retained something of the spirit of the Vikings. Missouri is the church of home missions among Lutheran Churches. While other Lutheran Churches, in harmony with the older Lutheran ethic, see the Christian man in his "station" (*Stand*), to which not merely his nationality and calling but also his religious home belongs, the Missouri Synod sees the individual soul, which is converted to Christ and incorporated into the church. If in the former case there is danger that souls are permitted to perish in their religious home, Missouri is in danger of seeing only individuals and ignoring the blessing which lies in the station, which man has not chosen for himself. Here lies one of the reasons why these two branches of Lutheranism constantly talk past each other.

The Missouri Synod Lutheran cannot understand that a properly called but heterodox pastor, Lutheran in name only, is permitted to lead a whole congregation, a whole generation of the flock that has been entrusted to him, into misbelief and even unbelief, while the ecclesiastical authorities keep silence and even maintain that the congregation is still Lutheran, because the Lutheran doctrine alone has standing, is *publica doctrina*, there. Is he incorrect? Who has the right to forbid the Gospel to be preached to these cheated souls by someone else? But how is it if there is not a clear case of false doctrine, but a mere suspicion? What clear facts must be evident before it is permissible to establish pulpit against pulpit, altar against altar? Is it not understandable that in questions of this kind there have been frequent differences of opinion, misunderstandings, and severe conflicts? What appeared to the one side as Christian missionary duty, the other side saw as proselytizing, that perversion of true mission work, against which Christ Himself warned the church when He held before her in Matt. 23:15 the frightful example of the mission work of the scribes and the Pharisees. Missouri would be no Lutheran Church if she had not asked herself again and again on what her understanding of the missionary duty of the church is founded. Missouri would have no right to call herself Lutheran had she not again and again measured her own actions by the Word of God, and acknowledged and confessed her own sins. However, the errors and sins which were committed in this area do not change the fact that this church has recognized the missionary duty of Lutheranism. The Lutheran Church does not exist merely to preserve the religious home of those people who by historical chance and by the manner in which they were led bear the confessional stamp "Lutheran." Rather, it is her task to preach to all men she can reach the Gospel as it was rediscovered during the Reformation and attested to in the Lutheran Confessions. This is being done today in a particularly effective and impressive way in the all but worldwide radio mission of *The Lutheran Hour*.

Similarly, the school system of the Missouri Synod is a testimony of this will for missions. For a large percentage of the children who prefer the excellent parochial schools of this church to the public schools come from non-Lutheran churches. In the last analysis, each church is in its own way a center of missions and regards itself as such. This explains not merely the steady growth of the Missouri Synod in all parts of America but also the fact that this church more than any other Lutheran Church is able to attract people of other confessions who are without a church home.

These simple facts ought to suffice to move other Lutheran Churches to study the Missouri Synod instead of getting excited over the fact that this church is not asleep in the same measure in which they are.

2

Karl Holl,[3] one of the few German church historians who treated the Missouri Synod in his lectures on more recent church history, always sought to derive all the essential traits and the particular doctrines which are characteristic of the Missouri Synod from Calvinist influences surrounding this branch of the Lutheran diaspora of German origin. That this is impossible is shown by the early history of this Synod, which in consequence of the work of the Concordia Historical Institute of St. Louis and its first director, Prof. Polack,[4] who in our estimation died too young, is better known today than it was thirty years ago. It is certain that the theology of Ferdinand Walther[5] can be explained only from the theology of Luther, of Lutheran orthodoxy, and of the Lutheran revival of the nineteenth century. We now know that the same is true also of the constitution of this Synod, the origin of which has been traced for us by Dr. Carl Mundinger in a beautiful and learned book (*Government in the Missouri Synod: The Genesis of Decentralized Government in the Missouri Synod*, St. Louis, 1947). Mundinger says that the ordering of the relation between pastors and laymen "was not the product of American political thought, nor was it congregationalism after the fashion of Congregational or Baptist churches in America. The polity of Missouri Synod was something apart from anything then known in America." This does not mean that the environment did not influence the developing church. It is not accidental that the name "Missouri" became the name of the church. It was the situation of Lutheranism in the Midwest, which was

---

3   Karl Holl (1866–1926), professor at Berlin, Luther scholar, and instructor of Sasse. Holl led the so-called rediscovery of Luther in the early nineteenth century. That school sought to find the "real" Luther in the earliest Luther and drove a wedge between Luther and the Confessions, and between Luther and the period of orthodoxy. Sasse never overcame the later influence. MH

4   William Gustave Polack (1890–1950), professor of history, hymnology and liturgics at Concordia Seminary, St. Louis, Missouri (1925–50), was a charter member of the Concordia Historical Institute (s.v. *Christian Cyclopedia*). MH

5   That is, Carl Ferdinand Wilhelm Walther (1811–87), first president of the Missouri Synod. MH

suddenly opened to settlement, swamped by immigrants from all European peoples and churches, which made the Lutheran Church a mission church. This church gains her members through mission work. Her churches are—as are all churches in this country—gatherings, assemblies, societies of individuals who consciously decide to belong to the church of their choice. This is the distinctly American trait in the character of the Missouri Synod, resulting from the history of the country. The same trait is found in the other Lutheran Churches of the American West. However, it finds its strongest expression in the Missouri Synod. For this type of Lutheranism possessed that which, given a missionary situation, makes a church a missionary church: the consciousness of vocation and a firm dogmatic conviction, without which missionary preaching is impossible. The consciousness of the Stephanist church as being the remnant of the pure Lutheran Church was refined through catastrophe. Through Walther's preaching and pastoral ministry [*Seelsorge*] was produced the true Lutheran Church consciousness in the sense of a congregation standing in justifying faith and living by the means of grace. This explains the consciousness of vocation found in the Missouri Synod. And this consciousness of vocation is inseparably bound up with the dogmatic conviction of Lutheran orthodoxy.

This is the most characteristic trait of the Missouri Synod. It was in this branch of Lutheranism that the Lutheran revival of the nineteenth century returned most consistently to Lutheran orthodoxy. The beginnings of this revival were still strongly influenced by Pietism, even as the revival after the wars of liberation at first appeared to be a renewal of Pietism. This is plainly evident in the case of Scheibel in Breslaü,[6] and Kavel in Australia,[7] and likewise in the Lutheran revival in Franconia and Pomerania. The awakening Lutheran consciousness in these

---

6   Johann Gottfried Scheibel (1783–1843) was educated at Halle, where Pietism had devolved into rank Rationalism. He found the moral life among the student body appalling. He became a theological professor in Breslau, Prussia (now Poland). As a champion against the Prussian Union, Scheibel was suspended from office in 1830 and took refuge in Saxony until forced to leave. While in Breslau, Scheibel urged a young Martin Stephan (who would lead Walther and the Saxon immigrants to the United States) to study Luther. Scheibel's account of the Prussian Union begs to be translated: *Actenmässige Geschichte neuesten Unternehmung einer Union zwischen der reformirten und lutherischen Kirche: Vorzüglich durch gemeinschaftliche Agende in Deutschland und besonders in dem preussischen Staate* (Leipzig: Fleischer, 1834). Sasse's copy of this book is in the library of Concordia Theological Seminary, Fort Wayne, Indiana. Two doctoral studies were written under Sasse at Erlangen dealing with the Prussian Union and Scheibel's struggle: Martin Kiunke, *Johann Gottfried Scheibel und sein Ringen um die Kirche der lutherischen Reformation* (Göttingen: Vandenhoeck & Ruprecht, 1985), and Walther Geppert, *Das Wesen der preussischen Union: Eine Kirchengeschichtliche und Konfessionskundliche Untersuchung* (Berlin: Furche, 1939). MH

7   August Ludwig Christian Kavel (1789–1860), influenced by Scheibel, joined the Old Lutherans at Posen. In 1838, 250 people left Germany for Adelaide, South Australia (s.v. *Christian Cyclopedia*). MH

areas regarded Spener[8] as one of its great saints. Also in the case of Löhe[9] the pietistic heritage was a powerful influence which helped shape his Lutheranism. In his case, even as in that of Vilmar,[10] romanticism was an added influence, particularly in the doctrine of the church and of the office of the ministry.

Walther, too, passed through a pietistic stage during his student days, but his theology bears the stamp of Luther and Lutheran orthodoxy. With all the limitations which one finds in him, he remains the most Lutheran among the Lutherans of his time. His Lutheranism is limited, not by the theology of Spener, but by that of the orthodoxy of the late sixteenth and of the seventeenth centuries. Luther seen through the spectacles of orthodoxy is the Luther of Walther and of the Missouri Synod. This is certainly not a perfect picture of Luther; nevertheless, it is better than those which are pietistically and romantically colored. And Walther by no means followed the orthodox fathers blindly. He knew Luther too well for that. One is astonished to see how Walther defends the position of Luther in the doctrines concerning the rights of congregations, of the election of grace, and of the last things. He was one of the very few Lutherans of his century who recognized the un-Lutheran character of the doctrine of orthodoxy concerning election *intuitu fidei* ["in view of faith"], and so became the defender of Luther's doctrine of predestination against the orthodox theologians whom he otherwise prized so highly, not because it was against the teaching of Luther, but because he did not find it in Holy Scripture.[11] This is Lutheran! Thus Walther became the instrument for an awakening of Lutheran doctrine and the spiritual father of a church which completely and consciously desired to be the church of the pure Lutheran doctrine.

8 Philipp Jacob Spener (1635–1705), the "father of Pietism." Educated at Strasbourg, Spener's professors included famous orthodox man J. K. Dannhauer (1603–66) and S. Schmidt (1617–96). In 1670 in Frankfurt am Main, Spener introduced the *collegia pietatis* as private devotional gatherings in homes twice a week. He wrote *Pia Desideria* in 1657 and noted the deplorable conditions in the church. The movement he began soon moved in un-Lutheran directions and into various levels of radicalism. Pietism de-emphasizes the objective means of grace and emphasizes the internal religious experience (s.v. *Christian Cyclopedia*). MH

9 Johann Konrad Wilhelm Löhe (1808–72) provided much needed support for the fledgling Lutheran churches of the United States beginning in the middle of the nineteenth century with the opening of a theological school in Fort Wayne, Indiana; through the preparation of his *Agende*; and also through the deaconesses who came to the United States from his Neuendettelsau campus. MH

10 August Vilmar (1800–1868). MH

11 Sasse wrote to Missouri Synod Vice President Roland Wiederaenders, August 10, 1968: "It belongs to the greatness of Walther that he and his synod fought a lonely battle against an error which Luther never would have tolerated. When I came to Australia and joined a church with a strong Iowa tradition, I was criticized for reading with my students *De servo arbitrio*. This was regarded as a bad book. My reply was that Luther at the end of his life declared that all his books might be forgotten, only his Small Catechism and *De servo arbitrio* should be preserved" (Sasse–J. A. O. Preus Correspondence, Fort Wayne, IN). MH

3

The most astonishing thing in the work of Walther and in the history of the Missouri Synod during the nineteenth century is not the re-awakening of the Confession of the church. A new regard for doctrine and confession, a new understanding of church and orthodoxy had been stirring since 1830 in many places within Christendom, in other confessions as well as in Lutheranism. It is, however, doubtful whether another case could be found in the Protestant world in which the doctrine of the church again attained such a high degree of popularity. It is understandable that theologians rediscovered the Confession, even as we have experienced this in our time. But the theologians of the revival did not stand alone. We have in another connection ("The Results of the Lutheran Awakening of the Nineteenth Century," Letter 15)[12] spoken of the fact that the Lutheran Confession was well-known to the common people among the Prussian Lutherans in the years following 1830. But nowhere else has the Confession, the teaching of the church, become so popular, so much a matter of the congregation, as in the Missouri Synod. The understanding and the live interest with which to this day laymen at synodical conventions discuss the doctrinal presentations might shame the theologians of other churches. Whoever desires to get an idea of the extent to which the Lutheran Confession was truly popular in American Lutheranism during the previous century should read the literature published in connection with the tercentenary of the Formula of Concord in 1877, particularly the comprehensive report *Denkmal der dritten Jubelfeier der Concordienformel* (St. Louis, 1877), which in more than four hundred pages describes the celebrations in the churches of the Synodical Conference. One ought to read the sermons and the hymns written particularly for this festival. One ought to see in what large editions the literature preparatory for the festival had to appear; how the churches read the Epitome, which was also explained to them in question-and-answer form; how a translation of the Confession into Norwegian became necessary, though the Formula of Concord had up to this time been unknown to the Norwegian churches.

One positively feels as though he had been transplanted to old electoral Saxony, where the jubilees of the Reformation and of the Augsburg Confession were observed in precisely this manner. In fact, the student of Walther and of the other fathers of the Missouri Synod receives the impression that the Lutheran Church had emigrated from Saxony, from the Elbe to the Mississippi. People in Germany already at that time found it was impossible to believe that the old Confession could mean so much to pastors and congregations anywhere in the world, for educated men (and there were comparatively many academically trained men among the Saxon immigrants) and for simple farmers.

These Lutherans were saddened when they looked back upon their former home and that of their church. "In the Old World, my brethren, the sun of the

---

12   See *Letters to Lutheran Pastors* 1:301–30. MH

pure Gospel which once upon a time rose in Augsburg and at the cloister of Bergen is evidently setting. Therefore many faithful Lutherans in the Old World look with yearning hope upon our young American Lutheran Church, a little flock indeed, but free and therefore called above others to shelter and to preserve the treasure of the pure Gospel entrusted to our church here in the New World in these last times." So Walther himself in his festival sermon in St. Louis (*Denkmal*, 233) expressed the thinking of his church.

Against this background one can understand that during those years the attempt was made to fulfill what was deemed a pressing missionary duty by subsidizing the Saxon separation which took place at that time. Of course, experience taught them that the scion of the Saxon Church could not again be introduced into the soil of the old home; at least the attempt did not meet with the desired success. This experience of Missouri—that it is simply impossible to plant American Lutheranism back into the soil of Europe—leads us to the question: What made possible the development of a church in America in which the Lutheran doctrine was able to become popular in the best sense of that word? Anyone who has come to know congregations of the Missouri Synod in various areas of America—whether it be in rural or industrial areas, whether in the Midwest or in the great cities of the eastern states—must certainly ask himself: What would have happened to these people if they or their ancestors had remained in their old homeland? Had Juern Jakob Swehn, this magnificent embodiment of the Lutheran farmer as he may be found in the Missouri Synod, remained in Mecklenburg, he would have become a disgruntled Social Democratic day laborer or a laboring man without interest in the church. His grandsons would have been Nazis and his great-grandsons Communists. What else could one be in this country in which once upon a time the great Lutheran Kliefoth[13] tried in vain to secure a work-free Sunday for the agricultural workers, in order that they might be able to remain Christians? The Christianity of the Christian nobles simply did not extend this far. For this reason the day came when the patience with which God had borne these gentlemen came to an end. What is the secret of this American Lutheranism, which brings people into the church who in Europe would have been lost to her? How is it possible that a laborer from Stuttgart, who in his homeland had severed his connections with the church, in a Lutheran congregation in America becomes the superintendent of the Sunday school, who sees to it that the children learn Luther's catechism?

After years of thinking about these and other observations, I am able to find no other answer than this: The secret lies in the existence of genuine congregations which are able to attract people and to integrate them into themselves, to stir up their slumbering faith and to draw them into the service of Christ. The secret of the missionary successes of Missouri is the living congregation of the

---

13 Theodor Friedrich Dethlof Kliefoth (1810–95) was a Lutheran theologian, church leader, and liturgiologist (s.v. *Christian Cyclopedia*). MH

Missouri Synod. Whatever objections one may be able to raise against Walther's understanding of the doctrine of the congregation, we find there a measure of understanding of the essence of the New Testament *ekklesia*, and of the congregation concerning which Luther said that it possesses the Office of the Keys. If we ask wherein the congregation in the Missouri Synod is different from that which is considered congregation elsewhere in America, we must answer that here the Lutheran conviction is taken seriously, that not the faith and ethos of men create the congregation, but the means of grace, through which God calls His congregation. It is this Lutheran congregation, as it had never been achieved before and could not be achieved in the national and territorial churches of the Old World, which again made possible this flowering of the confessional Lutheran Church. Here, where the Lutheran Church became popular [*volkstümlich*], the Lutheran Confession also again became popular. It was no longer the property of the teachers of the church, but once again it belonged to the whole congregation. This probably explains why, by and large, the relationship between pastor and congregation is better in this church than in any other. The hierarch, who potentially is present in every pastor, and *Herr Omnes* ["Mr. Everyman"], who is to be found also in the best Christian congregation, cannot gain the upper hand where Luther's doctrine of the means of grace is still taken seriously.

4

The most difficult problem confronting every confessional church is the problem of preserving its doctrine. Insofar as this is viewed as a human task, it is the task of keeping the doctrine pure and transmitting it to others. The Missouri Synod has from its very beginning labored at both tasks with exemplary energy. One may think as he will concerning the doctrinal disputes within the Lutheran Church in America or, in a lesser way, in Lutheranism in Australia during the past century. One may deeply deplore the breaches of the law of love which happened in that connection, as they are today deplored in these very churches, and may find that the Lutheran Churches suffered incurable wounds in these controversies. But there is one thing which cannot be denied. The question of purity of doctrine, and this means of the truth of the Gospel, was taken seriously in a manner not found anywhere else in modern Christendom. The churches which did not do this, which did not fight for doctrine, did not for this reason enjoy greater peace. It happens again and again in political history that nations, despite long wars waged with each other—indeed, in these very wars—grow into unity. So it can happen in the history of the church, that churches which fought hard with each other concerning the truth become one. For the church of God on earth is also subject to the law of secular history that peace is achieved through struggle. In any event, those who themselves surrendered pure doctrine without a struggle have no right to criticize the Lutheran Churches in the Anglo-Saxon world on account of their doctrinal controversies. There simply is no preservation of pure doctrine without the fight against false doctrine, no affirmation of the truth without negation of error, no confession of the church without condemnation of heresy. Therefore condemnation of error can be understood only when one knows which truth is being defended with the anathema. Also in the case of the Missouri Synod, the struggle against error was only the negative side of the effort in behalf of the preservation of the pure Gospel as they understood it. This was expressed in the very name of their theological periodical: *Lehre und Wehre* [*Doctrine and Defense*].[14] For this reason the theological work of this Synod was directed above all to the transmission of Lutheran doctrine.

The development of Concordia Seminary, which was founded in 1839 by the first Saxon settlers and which has grown into the largest theological faculty in Protestant America, and of the publishing house of the Synod with its matchless production of Lutheran literature in the German and English languages, belong to the great accomplishments of the Lutheran Church of the nineteenth century.[15] This, to take just one example, is borne out by the St. Louis edition of Luther, this mightiest literary monument of American Lutheranism during its German-speaking epoch. In what other country could the Lutheran Church have accomplished things like these with no other means save the power of the faith and confessional loyalty of Lutheran congregations! Add to these accomplishments the development of the great system of Christian day schools with its corps of trained teachers, the like of which, at least in the area of primary education, is found nowhere else in America, not even in the Roman Catholic Church. The old Lutheran connection of church and school (cf. the constant placing together of "our churches and schools" in the Preface of the Book of Concord) has here again come to life in completely modern form. No Lutheran Church in modern times has labored so systematically and consciously for the preservation of the purity of the doctrine of the church and for its transmission to the coming generations.

An impassable limit to all human effort in behalf of the preservation of the doctrine and thereby also of the church is set in the *ubi et quando visum est Deo* ["where and when it pleases God," AC V 2] with which the fifth article of the Augsburg Confession expresses the deep mystery of the freedom which the Holy Spirit of God claimed for Himself when He bound Himself to the means of grace, namely, to the Gospel and the Sacraments. Faith cannot be bequeathed by one generation to another. It must be born anew in every generation, must be worked through a miracle of the Holy Spirit. As parents can never guarantee the faith of their children, so the church of the present cannot assure the faith of the next generation. She can lay down her teaching in books. She can establish schools in which this doctrine is transmitted to youth. But what this youth will

---

14   *Lehre und Wehre* was founded in 1855 by Walther, who was its first editor. It merged into *Concordia Theological Monthly* in 1931. MH

15   Sasse here references Concordia Seminary, St. Louis, Missouri, and Concordia Publishing House, also in St. Louis. Both institutions continue to thrive into the twenty-first century. MH

do with the doctrine transmitted to it lies beyond the power of the church. Faith cannot be transmitted. This also constitutes a limit to the transmission of the Confession of the church. For us Lutherans the Confession is the great expression of the continuity of the church. It expresses the great consensus of faith, teaching, and confession which unites the church of all times, the oneness of true faith, which binds us today with the fathers who believed before us and with all coming generations who will believe after us. We transmit this Confession to our children in order that it may become their Confession. Whether it will be their Confession depends solely on the grace of God in the freedom of the Holy Spirit, who through the means of grace, as through instruments, "works faith when and where He pleases" [AC V]. Therefore Luther adds to his admonition to those who shall follow to watch over doctrine—words which are both a warning and a comfort:

> The church will not be preserved by us because we are unable to resist the devil in the pope, sects, and evil men, and so far as we are concerned the church would perish before our eyes, and we with it, as we daily experience, were it not that there is another Man who visibly preserves both the church and us in order that we might grasp and feel it. . . . That which we now say concerning ourselves in these matters our ancestors were compelled to say concerning themselves as the psalms and the Scripture testify, and our descendants will experience it in like manner, so that they together with us and the whole church will sing the 124th Psalm: "If it had not been the Lord who was on our side, when men rose up against us" [v. 2]; and Ps. 60:11: "Give us help from trouble, for vain is the help of man." [*Die angebliche "Vorrede D. M. Luthers, vor seinem Abschied gestellet"* (1548), Aland 754 (E¹ 63:410f.; WA 54:470.15ff.)]

These facts raise what constitutes the real question of life and death for Missouri, as it has for every other Lutheran Church. It is not the question concerning the strength of the external organization, the constitution, the growth of the congregation, or the school system. Nor is it the question with respect to the position of the Confession as the basis for the message and work of the church. Rather, it is the question concerning the strength of the Lutheran faith in the sense of the genuine deep faith of the heart in the saving Gospel, which the Holy Spirit alone can give. It is the question whether and to what extent this strongest confessional church of Lutheranism is a truly confessing church, a church in which the Lutheran Confession is not merely held in honor as the confession of the fathers and therefore in force and unassailable. It is the question whether the Confession is the confession of a living faith of the congregation and therefore the formative life principle of the church. It is the question which Missouri, even as every other church, must ask herself in humility and must answer before the face of God: *Are we still Lutheran?*

5

This seems to be a paradoxical question, for if Missouri is no longer Lutheran, then who is? However, it is not we who raise this question. Recently the venerable Dr. P. E. Kretzmann [1883–1965], one of the most widely known theologians of the Missouri Synod, who has been a member of her ministerium [*geistlichen Amt*] for more than forty years and of the faculty of Concordia Seminary, St. Louis, for more than twenty years, left this church because he believed that it tolerated false doctrines and therefore was no longer the orthodox Lutheran Church. His criticism, which was shared in circles which find their voice in the monthly periodical *The Confessional Lutheran*, is directed against "A Statement," which was published in the year 1945 by forty-four prominent theologians in the Missouri Synod under the leadership of the senior member of the faculty of Concordia Seminary, St. Louis, Theodore Graebner,[16] who has since been called to his reward, as well as against the "Common Confession," a document in behalf of unity between Missouri and the American Lutheran Church. The "Statement" alluded to above was later withdrawn from public discussion, but what it intended is shared by a wide circle within the Missouri Synod, whose paper is the *American Lutheran*. This concern is the great fear that the narrow understanding of church fellowship, which rejects as unionism every *communicatio in sacris* ["fellowship in sacred things," that is, altar and pulpit fellowship] with Lutherans outside the Synodical Conference, is a false and legalistic understanding of the Lutheran doctrine of the unity of the church. We refrain here from judging who is right and who is wrong in these questions, or where in an individual case there is more right or more wrong. It is sufficient to note that in the Missouri Synod itself the minds of men are deeply troubled over the question whether the Synod is still a Lutheran Church in the essential sense of the word, or whether she is in danger of losing her Lutheran character. It is not accidental that this question arose in connection with the problem of church fellowship, the correct doctrine concerning the oneness of the church and of a practice in conformity with this doctrine. For the essence of the Lutheran Church becomes manifest in connection with the question of where the limits of church and church fellowship lie. Basically, it is the same question concerning the self-understanding of the Lutheran Church which today agitates Lutheranism throughout the world. In Germany, in Europe, this question is discussed as the question concerning the true exposition of Article VII of the Augsburg Confession.

What does the great *satis est* ["it is sufficient for the true unity of the church ..."] mean? What does *consentire de doctrina evangelii* ["to agree regarding the doctrine of the Gospel," AC VII 2] mean? What is the minimum of consensus which must be there if church fellowship is to be possible? Is it sufficient that there is a factual agreement in the preaching of the Gospel? Or must this

---

16 Theodore Conrad Graebner (1876–1950) was a professor at Concordia Seminary, St. Louis, Missouri (1913–50) (s.v. *Christian Cyclopedia*). MH

also be expressed by a joint confession? It is no small surprise to the European theologian who addresses these questions to the varied groupings within the Missouri Synod, and tries to understand their discussion, to find that they do not understand our question. They are unconcerned about the understanding of the Augsburg Confession, Article VII, but about the exegesis of a Scripture passage, namely, Rom. 16:17ff. This passage appears to them to be the *locus classicus* for the doctrine concerning the limits of church fellowship. For years the whole debate has revolved around this passage as though there were not a number of other passages in the light of which the Pauline admonition to avoid those who cause divisions and offenses must be understood. The biblical doctrine concerning the oneness and the boundaries of the church, concerning schism and heresy, concerning conduct toward schismatics and heretics must be drawn from many passages, which shed light on one another. One must, for instance, observe that Romans 16 has its parallel in 1 Corinthians 16, where the anathema stands in connection with greetings which indicate church fellowship. Such warnings have found a place in the most ancient Communion liturgies, where they show the limits of the congregation which may attend the Lord's Supper. Into this context belong also the endings of the Pauline letters with which their liturgical formulas (cf. 1 Cor. 16:22f. with Rev. 22:20f.) form the transition to the celebration of the Lord's Supper, following the reading of the apostolic Word. The fruitlessness of the debate which has been waged for many years about Rom. 16:17ff. is explained by the one-sidedness with which this passage has been singled out. This passage cannot give the desired information because Paul does not name the false doctrines for which anathema is intended but assumes that they are known.

But why is it that the Lutheran Confession is not permitted to speak to the question? It is well possible to combine the two. One may examine the teaching of the Confession anew on the basis of the Scripture. One can and should ask whether the condemnations of the Confessions actually correspond to those of the Scripture. One can and must ask whether that which the Confessions say is sufficient, or whether it needs to be supplemented from the Scripture. Why is this not done? Here we must note a fact which at first glance seems hardly believable. *The Lutheran Confessions no longer play the role in the life and in the theological thinking of the Missouri Synod—in fact, for all of American Lutheranism they play nothing of the role—which they played during the nineteenth century.* They are recognized as the self-evident and unassailable foundation of the church. To test them on the touchstone of Scripture is considered unnecessary. Their complete agreement with Holy Scripture is presupposed. Anyone who would deny this would be considered no longer a Lutheran. This is a deep and honest conviction. The idea of an *Augustana variata Americana* after the manner of

Schmucker's Definite Platform[17] is rejected by all Lutherans, though there are those even in the Missouri Synod who play with the idea of a contemporary new wording of the Confession, a new *Invariata*, including modern questions of social ethics (e.g., Wm. L. Young's article, "Missouri Synod and Lutheran Unity," *American Lutheran* 32, no. 10 [October 1949]: 9–10, 22). But practically speaking, the Confession is far from playing the role which it was compelled to play during the nineteenth century in the struggle for the preservation of Lutheranism in the face of the demands of unionism, as we have shown in another connection (*Letters to Lutheran Pastors*, nos. 10 and 15).[18] At that time the Confession was needed to save the very existence of the Lutheran Church. Today the existence of the Lutheran Church is no longer in question (so at least it appears to the Lutheran brethren), and so the Confession recedes in their thinking. The consequence of this has been that considerable parts of American Lutheranism appear to have made their peace with the union, e.g., the great United Lutheran Church or the Augustana Synod.

Even in the churches of the Synodical Conference the Confessions are now the undebatable or no longer debatable presuppositions of the church rather than the expression of the great consensus of faith [AC I 1], from the vantage point of which the great decisions of the church must be made. Even in the case of pressing [*ganz aktuellen*] theological and ecclesiastical questions, which must be answered on the basis of the Confession, it is no longer consulted. The question of the introduction of an epiclesis [*Epiklese*] into the Communion liturgy, as well as certain other questions born of the liturgical movement of our time, must be answered on the basis of the Lutheran understanding of the consecration. However much has been written on this subject in America, I have yet to find an author who adduced the teaching of the Formula of Concord concerning the consecration.

One of the reasons for the astonishing receding of the confessional writings in the Lutheran theology of America during the past generation is probably to be sought in the fact that the Lutheran Churches had to conduct their debates not with the other confessions, but among themselves. Naturally the Book of Concord, which all of them acknowledge, could not constitute the basis for the negotiations in doctrinal discussions which had as their aim a union of the churches. For in these discussions they were seeking the right understanding of the Lutheran Confessions in certain disputed questions, even as after Luther's

---

17　Samuel Simon Schmucker (1799–1873) was infamous for his "Definite Platform," or recension of the Augsburg Confession, which rejected baptismal regeneration, the presence of Christ's body and blood in the Sacrament, and absolution. See Vergilius Ferm, *The Crisis in American Lutheran Theology: A Study of the Issue between American Lutheranism and Old Lutheranism* (New York: Century, 1927; repr., St. Louis: Concordia, 1987). MH

18　See "On the Problem of the Union of Lutheran Churches" and "The Results of the Lutheran Awakening of the Nineteenth Century," in *Letters to Lutheran Pastors* 1:151–81, 301–30. MH

death men in the Lutheran Church disputed the meaning of the Augsburg Confession, which was acknowledged at least theoretically by all, and therefore found it necessary to draw up new documents. It is not to be criticized that Lutherans in a certain situation declare how they understand certain doctrines of the Confession. Yet such formulations can never take the place of the ancient Confession itself. They lack completely the character of the Confession of the church, even when they have been approved by a synod. According to Lutheran understanding, a synod is unable to establish a new confession. This only the church can do—the orthodox church as a whole—by receiving a definite text as her confession. The Augsburg Confession and the Formula of Concord became confessions of the church in the act of reception [*Rezeption*], in which the churches and schools and the individual pastors made these texts their own by means of signature or other pledge. In the doctrinal negotiation during the past two decades within the Missouri Synod itself and between this church and other churches, a document of the year 1932 has played a large role: "A Brief Statement of the Doctrinal Position of the Evangelical Lutheran Synod of Missouri, Ohio and Other States."

This document has been understood both inside and outside the Missouri Synod as the official presentation of the doctrine for which she stands today. Yet despite the importance of this document for theological and ecclesiastical negotiations, it is not a confession of the church. Even if it had been accepted by the pastors and congregations, this would not be the same as the reception of a symbol. If it were to be so understood, this document would have to define its relation to the confessional writings and would have to show clearly why it contains statements (doctrine of the Scripture, of justification, of the church) which go beyond the statements of the Confessions. The "Brief Statement" is, as it were, an epitome, drawn up for practical purposes, indicating how at the moment the chief doctrines of the Lutheran Confessions are understood by the Missouri Synod.

More than this it cannot and does not desire to be. Necessary and useful as such a document is for practical use, it is nevertheless inevitable that also apart from the discussion for which it was intended it will be understood and treated as confession of the Missouri Synod, and that in the life and practice of the church it will for many actually take the place of the Confession of the church which it was meant to support. The same is true of the corresponding documents of other churches, as they have, for instance, been collected in the useful collection published by Concordia Publishing House entitled *Doctrinal Declarations: A Collection of Official Statements on the Doctrinal Position of the Various Lutheran Synods in America* [St. Louis, 1936].

This receding of the Lutheran Confessions in practice in the theological discussions of the churches is perhaps the most astonishing turn in the life of American Lutheranism, which formerly took its stand so firmly on the Book of Concord and lived in it.

The great rediscovery of the Confession of the church, which was the most joyous experience of the German Lutherans in the years between the two world wars, was not shared by our American brethren in the faith. For this reason, even where, as is the case in Missouri, the unshakable authority of the Confession is held in complete earnest, there is nevertheless lacking in the affirmation of the Confession the great joy which should accompany genuine confessional loyalty. "To confess," *exomologeisthai, confiteri* always includes praise to God. Therefore Luther rightly counted the *"Te Deum laudamus, te Dominum confitemur . . ."* among the Confessions.[19]

Are we mistaken if we miss this joy with our brethren in the Missouri Synod when they speak of the Confession? Are we mistaken in believing that their understanding of the doctrine is wholly orthodox, but only in the sense of correct doctrine, while real orthodoxy includes a joyous praise to God? In the case of the old Missouri of Walther, it is still plainly noticeable that here, even as in the classical time of orthodoxy, dogma and liturgy belong together—how greatly St. Louis formerly influenced liturgy in America! If it were still so today, would not then orthodox Lutheranism in particular have something of importance to say to the liturgical movement in America? Christian America, more than many Lutherans sense, waits today for a word from Lutheranism. Members of the Protestant churches in the United States sense the fact that the surrender of the confession of the fathers which has taken place in all these churches during the past century constitutes an irreparable loss of something that is essential for church and for Christianity. The so-called new orthodoxy (*neo orthodoxy*) of Reinhold Niebuhr[20] and of the American adherents of [Karl] Barth [1886–1968] is only a weak substitute for what has been lost. But Lutheranism keeps silence. It appears about to follow the Reformed Churches on the way to confession-less-ness, and with this step to lose its mission to all of Christendom, even as European Lutheranism missed every great opportunity during its history.

6

The question with respect to the character of the Missouri Synod as a Lutheran Church, and therewith the question of what actually constitutes a church that is Lutheran not in name only but in fact, was brought home to this church at the end of the Second World War in the form of the question concerning the limits of church fellowship. For many decades—in fact, practically during the whole first century of her existence—Missouri had held to the old strict position that

---

19 See *Die Drei Symbola oder Bekenntnis des Glaubens Christi* (1538) [*The Three Symbols*], Aland 708 (WA 50:265–66; AE 34:199–200, 205–7). MH

20 Reinhold Niebuhr (1892–1971), born in Missouri, attended Eden Theological Seminary, Webster Groves (St. Louis), Missouri. He became a professor at Union Theological Seminary, New York City (1928–60), where he lectured and wrote on ethics, political liberalism, and dialectical theology (s.v. *Christian Cyclopedia*). MH

made church fellowship dependent on agreement in Lutheran doctrine as it was understood in St. Louis. This did not mean (and this must be maintained in the face of widespread misunderstanding) agreement on all theological propositions. The Wisconsin Synod, for instance, never accepted the narrow concept of church as it prevailed in Missouri, according to which only the local congregation is really church and can act as a church, yet both were in the Synodical Conference. Nevertheless a very extensive measure of agreement on theological questions was the presupposition for *communicatio in sacris*. The result of this strict position was the refusal of the hand of fellowship and of the name "brother" to other Lutheran Churches. In Germany this led to the deep chasm between the Saxon Free Church [*Sächsischen Freikirche*] on the one side and the remaining Lutheran territorial and free churches [*landes- und freikirchlichen Luthertum*] on the other side. The Second World War, during which Missouri had to cooperate closely with the churches of the National Lutheran Council, particularly in the area of military chaplaincy, made necessary a revision of this position. First of all, a *modus vivendi* ["way of living or operating"] had to be found if the Missouri Synod desired to take part in the federal institution of the military chaplaincy. Without this cooperation, she could not have had military chaplains, even as the Wisconsin Synod had none, because she was unwilling to expose her pastors to the danger, undoubtedly present, of unionistic practice and to the conflict with principles held up to this time. The agreements which for the time being had been intended for the duration of the war had to be reviewed and expanded in view of American rearmament. In their latest form, these agreements, on the one hand, recognized the need to organize separately for the time being the pastoral care of two groups of Lutherans which are represented by the Missouri Synod and by the National Lutheran Council. On the other hand, there is the recognition of the fact that in exceptional cases the Lutheran members of the armed forces may, upon confession of the Lutheran doctrine of the Lord's Supper, be admitted to Holy Communion without regard for their synodical membership. It is possible that this agreement of May 1, 1951, may at a later time be considered important in church history. Beyond the question of the care of the men in the armed forces, the later problem of aid to stricken areas after the war demanded a coordination of the work of Missouri with that of other Lutheran Churches of America. Here also the solution was the same: separate organization but far-reaching practical working together. Finally, a third area of work was added: the area of the Lutheran refugees, especially in England. There many thousands of Baltic Lutherans strengthened existing Lutheranism, which up to this time had consisted of but a few congregations of German and Missouri Synod antecedents and who now posed the problem of building a Lutheran Church in England. Here also a working together of the separated groups on practical matters was achieved.

It would, however, be a complete misunderstanding of the development if one were to understand the change in the relation of Missouri to the other

Lutherans only on the basis of the practical necessities of church life and of a change in church politics on this basis. Certainly the changed world situation and the new tasks which faced them in St. Louis did their part. The confessional problem looks different amid the hail of bombs at Pearl Harbor than it does in a quiet parsonage in Illinois. In Nüremberg it looks different than in Korea, and in the migrant camps of Australia than on Broadway in New York, different in the Soviet zone of Germany than in the patriarchal democracy in Wisconsin. How little church politics was the deciding factor is proved by the fact that many opportunities were passed up to further the cause of their own church. It would have been natural to use the rich gifts which were sent to Europe for the furtherance of their own churches, as the American sects did. Naturally also fellow Lutherans received help, but no recipient of help was asked about his faith and confession. This is plain from a perusal of the financial reports of recent fiscal years (e.g., for 1950, *Der Lutheraner* 107, no. 7 [March 1951]: [106]). Even those who desired to bury the Lutheran Church in Germany were unashamed to make use of the charitable spirit of Missouri. And the rich gifts of love, which were distributed without regard to church and confession, won for the name "Missouri" with the common people a regard like that which the name "Quaker" obtained after the First World War. This was the unintended side effect of a great work of Christian love which had not yet lost through [organizational superstructures] the character of fraternal help.

All these practical tasks which Missouri faced during the last decade had a great effect upon the church itself. She had been led out of her isolation in which she had had to live during the first generation of her history. It is possible to find here a parallel to the development of the United States itself, in whose political and social life the center of gravity has moved more and more from the over-civilized Eastern states into the Midwest, with its solid agricultural foundations and its hearty humanity [*gesunden Menschentum*]. Once a German synod with an un-American Lutheran orthodoxy, and thus a foreign body in the American nation, the Missouri Synod has during this century become a highly respected indigenous church. By the very weight of her numbers and by her strong organization she has won a place in public life. Now this other factor was added, that through her chaplains and through her great works of charity she became noticed in other parts of the world. When men and groups of men are suddenly brought out of isolation, there is danger that a spirit of good fellowship may take the place of the former isolationism. Not all theologians of the Missouri Synod were able to escape this danger when the situation in their church suddenly changed. This will explain many an astonishing judgment concerning the condition of the Lutheran Church in Germany or concerning world Protestantism. The reality which they saw did not agree with the patterns in which many had been accustomed to think about matters ecclesiastical. As a result many easily became victims of strange information, the accuracy of which they were unable to check. It is only now that a sober evaluation of things is possible, which will correct many judgments made during the years after 1945.

Yet these experiences do not fully explain the great change which is taking place in the Missouri Synod. They hastened a process which was bound to come sooner or later. The relation of Missouri to the remaining Lutheran Churches was in need of revision, and that not only for the practical reasons above named. The deepest reason lies in the fact that the old theological solution of the problem of church fellowship and of the limits of the church was no longer sufficient. In theory, it is still maintained. The "Brief Statement," which in 1947 was specifically confirmed by the centennial synod, is regarded to this day as an expression of the doctrine for which Missouri stands, as the true scriptural Lutheran doctrine. With him who shares this doctrine it is possible to have *communicatio in sacris*. With him who does not share it, it is possible to have theological discussions after the fashion of the Bad Boll conferences.[21] Or one can enter into doctrinal negotiations with him with the idea of achieving a "common confession," as, for instance, with the American Lutheran Church. But how is it possible to call these documents (in and of themselves wholly necessary) "confession"?! But church fellowship depends on this understanding of the doctrine. In this all parties within the Missouri Synod are agreed, at least theoretically, the authors of "A Statement" of 1945 as well as the circles around *The Confessional Lutheran*, the officials of the church as well as the pastors and congregations. No one desires to abandon the old Lutheran Missourian doctrine as it is expressed in the "Brief Statement."

The difference appears to lie only in the question of how one makes this doctrine effective today. "Speaking the truth in love" was the watchword of the Forty-Four of 1945. They criticized what in the practice of the Missouri Synod they considered legalism and lovelessness. Their criticism moved wholly on ethical, not on doctrinal, grounds. They expressed in a manner which many considered revolutionary, but in any case not wholly disciplined, a feeling which during the past decade has been present in wide circles within the Missouri Synod. The church desired to repent for the mistakes of the past, for the all-too-quick and cocksure judgments, for the tendency to dogmatism in polemics, for the lack of readiness to understand the brethren in the other Lutheran Churches. Here is to be sought the real spiritual experience of this church during the past few years. Here also should be sought the key to an understanding of all her church politics. This appears to be the deepest purpose of her church government, above all things of the wise, pastoral, spiritual leadership of her president Dr.

---

21 That is, the free conferences at Bad Boll, Germany, in 1948 at which representatives of the LCMS and the Lutheran Churches in Germany met for theological discussion. The conferences were enlarged in 1949 to include additional representatives from Germany and America (s.v. *Christian Cyclopedia*). MH

Behnken.[22] The contradiction which arose against this movement, and which found its mouthpiece in the monthly periodical *The Confessional Lutheran*, is not basically directed against repentance on the part of Missouri for sins of legalism and lovelessness where they may have been committed. It is directed against the idea that this repentance includes a quiet change in practice with respect to the limits of church and church fellowship, which up to this time had been considered correct and in harmony with the Confession. This can only mean that the ethical reform has quietly become a dogmatic one. Where formerly it was not considered permissible that pastors of the Missouri Synod officiate jointly with pastors of other Lutheran Churches with which Missouri had no *communicatio in sacris*, this was either right or it was wrong. If this practice was right—that is, if it rested upon a correct dogmatic understanding of what constitutes the oneness of the church—then it must be retained. If it was wrong—if the basic understanding of church fellowship was erroneous—then this must be established and the doctrine revised. At this point *The Confessional Lutheran* has seen more clearly than its opponents. The polemics between these two parties which is so deeply regretted by all members and all friends of the Missouri Synod owes its acidity and its hopelessness above all things to the fact that both sides talk past each other, either because they do not understand the dogmatic side of the problem at all or at least insufficiently. By moving the whole problem into the area of ethics and pastoral theological casuistry (How does the individual pastor or the individual Christian or the individual congregation act in a given case on the basis of Scripture?), the "ecumenical" Missourians overlook the fact that the problem is dogmatic and theological, and therefore cannot be solved with the means of pastoral care alone. *The Confessional Lutheran* men on the other side do not understand why the old solutions have become questionable for many and that they are in need of further examination, which must lead either to new proof or to revision. They consider it self-understood that Lutherans, between whose churches there remain unsolved differences with respect to the doctrines treated in the "Brief Statement," can have no pulpit, altar, and prayer fellowship with one another. Basically, both sides make the same mistake, which is a result of the retreat of the "Lutheran Confession" in the thinking and acting of their church.

It strikes one as strange that "A Statement" of 1945 contains no appeal to the Confession. It spoke of "the great Lutheran principle of the inerrancy, certainty, and all sufficiency of Holy Writ" and otherwise appealed in every article to the

---

22   John William Behnken (1884–1968) served as president of the LCMS from 1935 to 1962, during which time he represented the LCMS at the conferences in Bad Boll. Behnken held Sasse in high regard and encouraged the addition of Sasse to the faculty of Concordia Seminary, St. Louis. However, Sasse departed Germany for Australia in 1949, partially because he found no support among the leadership of the institution, which was already on a course of Lutheran union in America, a course which led to the tragic events of 1974. MH

"historic Lutheran position" in the questions discussed. There is not the faintest trace of understanding for the fact that the question of church fellowship and the limits of the church, and this means the question concerning the essence of the Lutheran Church, has been placed anew before our generation through the events of world history and therefore needs a new answer, whatever that answer may turn out to be.

7

If it belongs to the essence of the Lutheran Church that it is a confessional church, the Church of the Unaltered Augsburg Confession—which in turn means, since the later confessions are all commentaries on the Augsburg Confession, the Church of the Book of Concord—then it is a matter of the very existence of the Missouri Synod that it remain also in the future the church which is loyal to the Confession, rooted in the Confession, and proclaiming the evangelical truth attested by the Confession. It is a matter of her theological, not her physical, existence. For one must assume that this great, to date so healthy, growing church body, one of the most dynamic church denominations in America, still has a great future, even if the contrasts which are visible today should lead to a schism.[23] But the vital question for a church is not so much whether it will continue to live, but whether it will remain that which it has been and which according to its innermost essence it ought to be. The Roman Church actually was, once upon a time, the church of the apostles Peter and Paul before she became the church of Antichrist. The Church of Brandenburg was, once upon a time, the Lutheran Church of a Paul Gerhardt.[24] The Church of Württemberg was at one time the Church of the Formula of Concord, which she repudiates today. In what sense the United Lutheran Church today is still the church of the General Synod and of the General Council is hardly possible to say. There exists also in church history that which in natural science is called pseudomorphosis. As molten rock which enters into available empty forms there crystallizes in a form which is not native to it, so also church forms that have become empty may have become filled with foreign content. It may happen that an un-Lutheran faith seizes control of the forms of the Lutheran Church and that then this church is only externally a Lutheran Church. This indicates the danger which threatens every Lutheran Church at all times. Missouri is no exception to this rule.

---

23 Which did occur in the events of 1974 and the founding of the AELC. MH

24 The greatest German Lutheran hymnwriter, Gerhardt (1607–76) studied theology at Wittenberg and served as pastor at St. Nikolaikirche in Berlin from 1651. He resigned his post in 1666 because he refused to submit to the syncretist edicts of the elector of Brandenburg. The push for union between Lutherans and Reformed was being made in Brandenburg well before it was accomplished by Frederick William III (r. 1797–1840)! See *ODCC*, 667. MH

This danger becomes visible in the case of a notable shift of emphasis which can be observed in the theology of the Missouri Synod. The above-mentioned Dr. P. E. Kretzmann begins his book *The Foundations Must Stand! The Inspiration of the Bible and Related Questions* (St. Louis, 1936) with a statement on the importance of the doctrine of the inspiration of the Holy Scripture:

> We commonly refer to the doctrine of justification by faith alone as the central doctrine of the Christian religion, the *articulus stantis et cadentis ecclesiae*. But even this fundamental truth of personal faith is not a matter of subjective certainty. Rather, it depends, as do all other articles of faith, on the objective certainty of the Word of God as a whole and in all its parts. In this respect the doctrine of the inspiration of the Bible is fundamental for the entire *corpus doctrinae*. (p. 3)

We may assume that any orthodox Presbyterian, Baptist, or Adventist could have written these sentences in precisely this manner. It is, however, our conviction that they can be brought into harmony neither with the theology of Luther nor with the teaching of the Confessions. Reformed Fundamentalism makes the relationship to Christ depend on the relationship to the Bible, as Catholicism makes it depend on the relationship to the church. This is a wrong deduction from the fact that without the Scripture or the oral Word which is based upon the Scripture we would know nothing of Christ. The faith of the Lutheran Church in the Scripture is based on her faith in Christ. It is basically faith in Christ because the Bible, and this is true of the whole Bible, is testimony concerning Christ. Our faith in the Bible as the infallible Word of God is therefore an entirely different faith from the faith of Fundamentalism in the Bible, which at least logically and factually precedes faith in Christ. The conviction that the Scripture from beginning to end is inspired and therefore the inerrant Word of God, whose statements can be trusted absolutely, is not necessarily Christian faith. The orthodox rabbis have the same faith with respect to the Old Testament. The Christadelphians, Jehovah's Witnesses, and other heretics who deny the true deity of the Son and therefore also the true deity of the Holy Spirit, who therefore do not even know what inspiration in the biblical and Christian sense is (Matt. 10:20; John 16:13ff.) but make out of the Scripture a book of oracles after the fashion of the heathen sibyls, likewise teach the plenary inspiration and the absolute inerrancy of the Scripture. This shows plainly that this doctrine is not an absolute defense against false doctrine. Least of all does it guard against unbelief. On the contrary! As it was but a brief step from the orthodoxy of a Hollaz[25] to the Rationalism of a Semler,[26] so also there is but one step from Fundamentalism to unbelief.[27] One

---

25   David Friedrich Hollaz (1648–1713), whose most famous work is *Examen theologicum acroamaticum*. MH

26   Johann Salomo Semler (1725–91), the "father of German Rationalism," was professor of theology at Halle (1752–79). MH

27   For a contrary view on orthodoxy's view of Scripture and faith, see Bengt Hägglund, *Die Heilige Schrift und ihre Deutung in der Theologie Johann Gerhards* (dissertation,

can only respect the seriousness with which earnest Reformed Christians desire to hold to the authority of Scripture. But one must also see the tragic reality when human opinions—for instance, concerning the age of the earth—are proclaimed as divinely revealed truths, with the result that with these opinions the authority of the Scripture collapses. What kind of Christianity is that which can be refuted by a photograph of the depths of space or by the facts (not theories) of radioactivity! No, Luther's mighty faith in the Scriptures as the infallible Word of God has nothing in common with this understanding of the Scripture current in Fundamentalism. One seeks for it in vain also in the Lutheran confessional writings.

If the theologians of the Missouri Synod believed that it was necessary to draw up an explicit doctrine of the Holy Scripture, its inspiration and inerrancy, which goes beyond the brief sentences of the Lutheran Confession, in order to oppose the apostasy from the Word of God which was taking place also in Lutheran Churches, this must be considered a wholly legitimate undertaking. This must be granted, and it is to be regretted that the necessity of such formulation of doctrine was not recognized everywhere. But then Missouri should have formulated a truly Lutheran doctrine of the Holy Scripture, a doctrine which is in complete harmony with the Confession and which takes seriously the principle of the Formula of Concord, that Luther is the foremost teacher of the Church of the Augsburg Confession. Instead, the fathers of the Missouri Synod simply took over the doctrine of the later orthodoxy (Baier, Quenstedt)[28] concerning the Scripture without even asking themselves the question whether this doctrine is Lutheran and whether it can be brought into harmony with the Confession. One need not take this amiss if one considers with what difficulty the fathers of the Lutheran revival also in Germany had to work their way back to the Lutheran doctrine. They were not yet able to see what a deep chasm exists between the understanding of revelation with Luther as compared with the orthodoxy of the seventeenth century. Today this is different.

Historical research in Lutheran theology has shown how deeply orthodoxy was influenced by that same Aristotelian philosophy which Luther had banished from dogmatics. We know now that orthodoxy is a very similar synthesis

---

Lund, 1951), 91. There he notes that for Johann Gerhard (1582–1637) and orthodoxy the testimony of the Holy Spirit is the testimony of Holy Scripture. The Spirit works faith in the Gospel through the Word, and that very faith thus worked recognizes in turn "the voice of the heavenly Father" in the same Scriptures. See also "The Word of God in the Theology of Lutheran Orthodoxy," in *Doctrine Is Life: The Essays of Robert D. Preus on Scripture*, ed. Klemet I. Preus (St. Louis: Concordia, 2006), 79–98. MH

28   Johann Wilhelm Baier (1647–95) was professor and rector at Jena and Halle, and his chief work, *Compendium theologiae positivae*, was especially influential for Walther. Johann Andreas Quenstedt (1617–88) was the nephew of Johann Gerhard and professor of logic, metaphysics, and theology at Wittenberg. He was Francis Pieper's favorite orthodox dogmatician (s.v. *Christian Cyclopedia*). MH

of the natural (reason) and supernatural (revelation) knowledge of God as was the scholasticism of the Middle Ages.

Francis Pieper [1852–1931], the great systematician of the Missouri Synod, could have known this if he had taken cognizance of the results of historical research. But he was so completely the systematician, and so completely imprisoned in the systems of orthodoxy, that he disregarded history. The Missouri Synod of today is beginning to understand orthodoxy historically. Of this, the first publication of the young systematician Prof. Jaroslav Pelikan [1923–2006] in St. Louis, *From Luther to Kierkegaard: A Study in the History of Theology* (St. Louis: Concordia, 1950),[29] bears a testimony which is as surprising as it is gratifying. He shows how the theology of Luther was falsified when Aristotle [384–322 BC] was returned to power in the school of Melanchthon. The writer goes so far as to call the doctrine of justification of the later Melanchthon a caricature of the doctrine of Luther. He sees the rationalism within orthodoxy which made it possible that orthodoxy gave way so quickly to Rationalism (p. 83). He understands the meaning of the criticism of [Immanuel] Kant [1724–1804], who refutes the "proofs for the existence of God which the Lutheran Aristotelianism shared with medieval scholasticism" (p. 92). He shows why the Word of God for Luther was in the first instance not written but oral Word, namely, because it is address of God to man through which man is called by God: "The truth of the Word does not come in the imparting of insights, but in the personal fellowship with God for which man was originally created and to which he is now restored in Christ" (p. 19). He maintains that E[mil] Brunner [1889–1966] learned this existential understanding of the truth from Luther, and the criticisms of Brunner that are voiced by Lutherans, he maintains, "have been informed more by Fundamentalist than by Lutheran theology" (p. 127 n. 93)—though he admits that in other respects Brunner has fallen prey to subjectivism. We quote Pelikan here in order to show that it is quite possible in the Missouri Synod to overcome this un-Lutheran Fundamentalism which today constitutes the great danger for this church.

For as soon as the *sola Scriptura* is superordinated to the *sola fide* we are on the road to a false understanding of the Lutheran Church. It is the Reformed understanding of the evangelical, the Protestant Church, which emerges victorious. For all Reformed from [Ulrich] Zwingli [1484–1531] and [John] Calvin [1509–64] to Brunner and Barth—and all sects which have come out of the Reformed Churches—understand the true Christian, the evangelical church, as the church of the *sola Scriptura* in which there are then, in accord with various ways of understanding the Scripture, various schools. On the basis of this understanding of church, Lutheranism is today being wooed by Modernism and Fundamentalism, by the ecumenical organizations of the World Council

---

29 The great historian Pelikan (1923–2006) left Missouri for the ELCA during the controversy in the 1970s. Before dying, he joined the Eastern Orthodox Church. MH

of Churches and by the fundamentalist International Council of Christian Churches. If it accepts this concept of church, it is lost and will be ground to pieces and will be absorbed by these contrasts. It sounds so enticing that all churches for which the Holy Scripture is still the verbally inspired, inerrant Word of God should stand together. Should not Bible-believing Lutherans, Presbyterians, and Baptists today together and jointly proclaim and defend the authority of the Word of God? Do they not, for practical purposes, already stand together? Is not that which Kretzmann and [Theodore] Engelder [1865–1949] (*The Scripture Cannot Be Broken*, St. Louis, 1944) have published in Concordia Publishing House concerning the Holy Scripture found in precisely the same manner in the writings of the Baptist and Reformed Fundamentalists? But is it possible that a Lutheran should write so much as even one page concerning the Holy Scripture on which all is not dominated by the fundamental distinction of Law and Gospel? Is it possible for a Lutheran to admit in earnest that a Baptist is a Bible-believing man? Luther would not do it. Is it possible for a Bible-believing person to deny that Holy Baptism is the washing of regeneration and the bread which we bless in the Lord's Supper the body of Christ? What kind of faith in the Bible is it that can deny these things? And even though the theologians, when they teach concerning the Scripture in the same manner as the ortho- dox Reformed do, in spirit accompany this teaching with the whole Lutheran doctrine or presuppose this doctrine, the simple Missouri Synod Christian who reads the books of the Fundamentalists and the devotional literature that is based upon them will not even notice the difference. It will not be long before they will find as much edification in a radio sermon which is substantially Baptist as the Southern Baptists experience listening to *The Lutheran Hour*.

One dare not forget that these Christians no longer possess the rich trea- sure of the Lutheran hymnal and of the extensive old devotional literature, since a generation has grown up which no longer speaks the language of Luther and does not even know what a Luther Bible looks like. Even the theologians scarcely still have any conception of a Luther Bible with the Apocrypha (some- thing incomprehensible for Fundamentalists), with the prefaces of Luther and with text which was not yet cut up into verses as is the text in our Bibles, in which the Epistle to the Hebrews no longer appears to be a unified composi- tion but a collection of three hundred Bible passages. Is it surprising that under these circumstances a different type of piety gradually makes its way into the soul? Is it surprising that the process which Lutheranism in the American East experienced already during the nineteenth century now is gradually taking pos- session of the great churches of the West in a different form? When during the seventeenth century the Aristotelian *theologia naturalis* together with a corre- sponding rationalistic understanding of the Scripture worked its way in to the Lutheran Church, the Lutheran hymnal with its sung theology may have pro- vided sufficient antidote. "And if they drink any deadly thing, it shall not hurt them" [Mark 16:18]. What, by comparison, does the church have today?

8

The church today also has one thing which preserves her—only one thing, only one person—Him who has reserved for Himself the task of being the Savior of His Body. One of the most comforting truths which the New Testament teaches us with respect to the church is that the prayer for the preservation of the church is not our prayer alone. The greatest of all prayers which are preserved for us in the Holy Scripture, perhaps the greatest prayer which ever was spoken on earth, is the prayer in John 17 of the eternal High Priest for His church on earth. We know from Scripture that it is not on earth only that prayers are spoken. There is praying also in heaven. The mystery of prayer reaches into the Holy Trinity itself, as the prayer of Jesus shows.

This is our comfort, dear brethren, wherever we may be performing our office in the church in this difficult and sorrowful time, as it was the comfort of our fathers during the "evening of the world," as they regarded their time. This comfort gives us the strength to work while it is day [cf. John 9:4]. The most necessary task we have to perform in the English-speaking world is that we learn again to read Luther and the Confessions as men began to learn to do it in Europe after the First World War. Here lies your greatest theological task, brethren, in the Missouri Synod.[30]

That which your church has done since the days of Walther to preserve the knowledge of Luther, you must now do for a second time. If this can be done together with other Lutheran Churches of your country, and perhaps with the Lutherans of the whole English-speaking world, it will be all the better for all concerned. We need a larger English edition of Luther.[31] Those which have been available to date, grateful as we are for their existence, are insufficient. It is appalling how many writings of Luther are wholly unfamiliar to the theologians of the English world, who no longer understand German sufficiently to read Luther, among them Luther's greatest writings such as *De servo arbitrio* [*Bondage of the Will*] and his great writings concerning the Lord's Supper.

Furthermore, we need a new edition of the confessional writings with a standard English text approved by the churches.[32] We need it so that the pastor may study and know his Confessions, so that we may finally learn again what in reality is the doctrine of the church, so that we may not constantly confuse dogma and theology until we can no longer distinguish between doctrines of the Holy Scripture and statements of Scripture which contain no doctrine.

---

30 We concur. MH

31 The fifty-four volumes of the American edition of Luther's Works began publication some time after the appearance of this letter. Beginning in 2009, Concordia Publishing House is engaged in a significant expansion of the series. MH

32 In 2006, Concordia Publishing House published *Concordia: The Lutheran Confessions*. Intended for the laity, this edition provides a readable English translation as well as a wealth of introductions and annotations intended to aid in understanding the context and application of the confessional documents. MH

Then we shall again know what constitutes the true unity of the orthodox Lutheran Church.

In the bonds of the faith,

Your

Hermann Sasse

Historical Context

Sasse takes advantage of the 1,500th anniversary of the Council of Chalcedon to take to task modern Protestantism. Isn't the Nicene Creed and its confession by Chalcedon exactly the kind of dogmatic Christianity deplored since Pietism and the Enlightenment? But its endurance demonstrates more relevance than any of the pronouncements of modern ecumenism, which are forgotten as soon as they are presented. Sasse was present in Lausanne in 1927 when the Faith and Order Movement confessed the Nicene Creed. But the Ecumenical Movement was not serious. The ancient Christological heresies ever reappear. "Church history of every era teaches that the transition from one heresy to another is very easy." Sasse takes his old teacher Adolf von Harnack to task for his attack on "the bald negative assertions" of classical dogma. "The real tragedy of modern Christendom is this: that together with these ancient confessions it has to a great extent lost the common dogmatic foundation." Perhaps the greatest insight Sasse shares is the conviction that where the church's confessions are lost, the authority of Scripture is lost. MH

April 19, 1952

Dr. Hermann Sasse
41 Buxton Street
North Adelaide, South Australia

Dr. Carl E. Lundquist
Lutheran World Federation
Geneva

Dear Dr. Lundquist,

. . . The [LWF] Theological Commission should help the "younger churches" which are now striving for a new expression of the Lutheran truth without being able to understand every detail of the Book of Concord. It was perhaps a misfortune that our fathers in the sixteenth century have not made a brief statement of the Lutheran faith in analogy to the way the decrees of Trent were epitomized in the *Professio Tridentina* . . . .

With kind regards,

Yours sincerely in Christ,
Hermann Sasse

twenty-one

The Sesqui[cent]ennial of Chalcedon

TRANSLATED BY E. REIM[1]

September 1951[2]

Prof. D. Theol. Hermann Sasse
41 Buxton Street
North Adelaide, South Australia

Dear Brethren in the Office:

In all parts of Christendom, wherever this great Christian creed of the past is still a present force, we are these days commemorating the Fourth Ecumenical Council, which met in the year AD 451 from October 8 to November 1 at Chalcedon, that ancient city on the Asiatic side of the Bosphorus, opposite Constantinople. For the Eastern Orthodox Church this recalls the memory of one of its most splendid synods. As the Synod of the Six Hundred Fathers, it is one of the largest in ancient times, second in importance only to the Council of Nicaea in AD 325.

For the Eastern Church the important thing is the event of the synod as such. For this body considers the ecumenical synod, representing the entire Church, as the instrument by which the Holy Spirit leads Christendom in all truth, bringing about the miraculous consensus of the participating fathers. But for Rome, Chalcedon is the great example of a council in which, as in solemn assembly of the Church and for all the Church to hear, the truth is proclaimed by the successor of Peter and vicar of Christ with the full implications of his official doctrinal

---

1   Dean of Lutheran Theological Seminary of the Wisconsin Synod. MH

2   *BLP* 21: *Zur fünfzehnhunertjahrfeier des Chalcedonense* (North Adelaide, September 1951). This English translation appeared originally in *QS* 48, no. 1 (January 1952): 1–19. Huss number 290. MH

infallibility. Hence the festivities which will be observed in Rome during the coming weeks will be particularly in honor of the great Pope Leo [r. 440–461], through whom this council became a triumph of the Roman Church, albeit not an absolute one. For it was Leo's doctrine which the council accepted as the voice of Peter.

As for those evangelical churches which commemorate the event, particularly the Lutheran, neither the great synod nor the great pope will be invested with a halo. Just as this synod at the gates of Byzantium stood in the aura of the imperial church policy, where concern for the unity of the Church was interwoven with concern for the preservation of the Roman Empire, so Leo was not merely the successor of Peter but covertly also the heir of the Roman Caesars. So only can his church-political moves be understood.

What makes Chalcedon one of the outstanding events in the history of the Church for evangelical believers, and an event worthy of commemoration by the Church, is the single fact that in those days—*hominum confusione et Dei providential* ["in the confusion of men and by the providence of God"], despite all secular and ecclesiastical politicians—a doctrinal decision was achieved in one of the most important articles of Christian faith, one that has not been forgotten as are most of the other decrees of this synod and like so many doctrinal statements of other synods. Rather, it is an article still confessed by the greatest part of Christendom today, an article of which the Lutheran Church holds that it expresses the true doctrine of the Holy Writ, the source of life for the Church.

This doctrine of the Council of Chalcedon, as it is embodied in the *Symbolum Chalcedonense*, the creed of that synod, shall be the subject of the following discussion. We shall not try to analyze the history of this doctrine in all its intricate detail—that would lie beyond the scope of these letters—but we shall try to see what this doctrine means for us today.

1

What turbulent times those four generations were that lie between the outbreak of the Arian controversy (AD 320) and the Council of Chalcedon, the era of the first four ecumenical synods, the era of the formulation of dogma in the ancient Church. Upon the short-lived attempt of the era of Constantine [r. 305–337] once more to unite the empire with the aid of the Church, there followed midway in the fourth century a disintegration that was not to be stayed. When the Second Ecumenical Council assembled in Constantinople in 381, the Goths had crossed the Danube and other Germans the Rhine, and the so-called "migration of the tribes" had begun. At the time of the Third Synod—Ephesus in 431—the Latin Church had from Britain to Africa been partly destroyed, partly reduced to little isolated groups among the conquering Germanic-Arian nations. In the previous year Augustine had died during the siege of Hippo Regius. The year of Chalcedon was a year of new catastrophes. Shortly after Easter, Attila [406–455] had crossed the Rhine with an army of perhaps half a million Huns and made his plundering way through Gaul, until he was brought to a halt in that bloody battle upon the fields of Chalons, where Romans and Germans offered united resistance to the Asiatic hordes. But now Italy was endangered and in the following year was visited by the "scourge," as Leo put it, until there occurred the great miracle that the conqueror departed from Italy after negotiating with the pope, who functioned as a member of the Roman delegation. Do such recollections perhaps play a part in making the observance of the 1,500th anniversary of Chalcedon—coming as it does at a time when Christian Europe and Roman Catholicism are endangered by another great threat from the East—into a jubilee of the great pope of the era of the migration?

This broad historical background must ever be kept in view if one would understand the most profound meaning of the great ecumenical synods and their doctrinal decrees. The great political experiment of the Constantinian era—to preserve the existence of the empire by means of the Church—had failed. The Church had not lived up to the expectations of Constantine. After the sack of Rome, Augustine had felt constrained to dedicate his great work, *De Civitate Dei*, to a refutation of the charge that Rome's transition to Christianity was the cause of its downfall.

But had the Church not really been found wanting? Did it have nothing better to do in those days of world crisis than to engage in theological controversy? Even before Nicaea, Constantine had warned the Church about this. Could the great synods of the empire not have had something more urgent and practical to do than to forge theological formulas? Think of the gigantic mission opportunities with which it was suddenly confronted when Constantine placed a world at its feet. Think of the problems placed before it by the Great Migration. But at that time those resolutions by which modern churches and synods define their position on world issues had not yet been invented. And so "nothing more" came out of the Synod of Constantinople in 381 than the timeless creed which confesses the *homoousia* ["of the same substance/being"] of the Son with the Father.

But is this not actually more than anything else that this synod could have achieved had it issued some timely statement dealing with the situation of the Church, or addressed a message to the world, to the empire, and to the new nations? Is not the Niceno-Constantinopolitan Creed perhaps the very word, the very manifesto, the lack of which modern Christians deplore in the Church of that day? What greater, more important, more pertinent message could the Church have issued to the world, to nations old and new, and to its own members than the message concerning the eternal Son of God, "begotten of His Father before all worlds, God of God, Light of Light, very God of very God, begotten, not made, being of one substance with the Father, by whom all things are made; who for us men and our salvation came down from heaven and was incarnate by the Holy Spirit of the Virgin Mary and was made man . . ."! This confession made by Christians in a dying world became the confession of the new nations and the confession of all coming generations of the Church. Is this not something much greater than any "relevant" and "practical" pronouncement made in the manner of modern church conventions can possibly be? What has become of the many statements with which the ecumenical world conferences have annotated the historical events of our day? The world has never heard them, and the churches have long forgotten them. Not even the textbooks of church history take cognizance of them. But the Creed of that ancient synod is prayed in thousands of churches every Sunday, and probably more martyrs have died for this confession in the twentieth century than in all the past centuries of the history of the Church taken together. And the same is true of the creed of Chalcedon. Everything else that occurred in that eventful year of 451 belongs to the past, even though it may live in the memory of history. But the doctrinal pronouncement of Chalcedon is as vital today as then. As an interpretation of the divine Word, it shares in that immortality which is pictured by that word of Scripture: "The grass withers, and the flower thereof falls away, but the Word of the Lord endures forever" [Isa. 40:8].

2

What biblical truth was at stake at Chalcedon? The first two ecumenical synods had asserted the true deity of the Son, and thereby brought up the problem concerning the relation to each other of the divine and the human natures of Christ. Under the respective leadership of the schools of Antioch and Alexandria, this question was debated by subsequent generations in grave controversies, profoundly affecting the Church. For thus it is the lot of Christendom ever to have its understanding of the truth granted only at the price of a battle for the truth. The vital significance of these great discussions for the Christendom of today can be eliminated neither by the sins which were committed on all sides in this struggle, and particularly by the orthodox Alexandrians, nor by the fact that these controversies were carried on with the intellectual equipment (*Denkmitteln*) of ancient philosophy: Aristotelian in Antioch and Neoplatonist in Alexandria.

If Harnack[3]—and with him the entire school of Ritschl[4]—was of the opinion that the doctrine of the two natures could be evaded by ruling out the concept of the divine or the human "nature" as an inadmissible philosophical formulation

---

3   Adolf von Harnack (1851–1930), the great icon of liberal Christianity, taught at the University of Berlin, where Sasse was one of his students. Sasse's high regard for Harnack did not prevent him from recognizing the end of Christianity in Harnack's rejection of virtually all Christian dogma and the reality of Gospel events. MH

4   Albrecht Ritschl (1822–89) was the son of the bishop of the Prussian Union. From 1864 until his death, he was professor of theology in Göttingen. Ritschl began his career as a disciple of Ferdinand Christian Baur (1792–1860) and the Tübingen School, which posited a radical conflict between Pauline and Petrine Christianity in the New Testament. Faith rests, held Ritschl, not on the intellectual apprehension of a series of facts but on the making of value judgments. The so-called "Ritschlian

(*Philosophumenon*), and sought to understand the divine-human quality in Christ ethically rather than as pertaining to the nature, then he is refuted by the fact that in the process he himself became a Nestorian. The Christology of modern Protestantism is Antiochene-Nestorian: deity dwelling in the man Jesus as in a temple, and the man Jesus standing in an ethical relation to deity. The difference is only this: that the Antiochenes of old still were in earnest about the divine in Christ.

One should consider the Hymn to the Nativity in the Nestorian liturgy, where the mystery of the incarnate *Logos* is proclaimed: "He was in the bosom of His Father from all eternity, before all the world, as true God; He came to us in the fullness of the time and, taking unto Himself our body, redeemed us as true man. . . . For nine months He was in His mother's womb and was born true man. The angels glorified Him as true God. He was laid into a manger as true man. The star proclaimed Him true God." In this manner His entire life is reviewed, and the statements of the Gospel concerning Him are allocated either to the true man or to the true God. The true man increased in wisdom and stature and in favor with God and man. The true God changed water into wine. He prayed as true man. He performed His miracles as true God. "He was nailed to the tree as true man. He rent the rocks as true God." He died and was buried as true man. At this point, the hymn has nothing to say about the deity, but continues concerning the resurrection: "He ate and drank with His disciples after the resurrection as true man. He passed through doors that were shut and greeted the Twelve with the salutation of peace as true God" (quoted according to Fr[iedrich] Heiler: *Urkirche und Ostkirche*, p. 430f.).

One need only omit the statements concerning the true God and one has the liberal picture of Jesus, of the Christ who has been "rescued from mythology" (*des "entmythologisierten" Christus* [i.e., by Bultmann[5] and his followers]). The unity of the person of the Savior which Nestorianism was unable to find, is achieved by this theology of modern Protestantism when with the allegedly philosophical concept of "nature"—which appears in the New Testament in 2 Pet. 1:4—it also eliminates the concept of the divine nature and makes Jesus mere man.

This demonstrates clearly that one cannot get away from the concepts of the divine and the human nature. For nature here is not a physical category, but the word serves to designate the essence, about as the English expression "the nature of the Church" indicates the essence of the Church. The human nature of Christ is His being in substance true man; the divine nature, His being in substance true God. According to His essence, Jesus Christ is true God, and

---

School" was characterized by its emphasis upon ethics and on the community and by its repudiation of metaphysics and religious experience. See *ODCC*, 1400. MH

5   Rudolf Bultmann (1884–1976) taught at Marburg until retiring in 1951. A New Testament scholar, Bultmann was infamous for his program of "demythologizing" the New Testament in an attempt to make the New Testament message intelligible to the modern world. MH

according to His essence, true man. This, and nothing else, is meant by the doctrine of the two natures. "That is why no theology can dispense with it. This explains the relevancy of the old Christological issues. In new forms they turn up again and again. One need only recall how in the sixteenth century the old controversy between the Christology of Alexandria and that of Antioch broke out in new form between Lutheran and Reformed theologians, even on the basis of a mutually recognized creed of Chalcedon, a controversy which really continues to this day.

If we are therefore constrained to speak of a divine and a human nature in Christ, then we cannot escape the question of their relation to each other. After the Council of Ephesus in 431 had condemned Nestorius[6] and thereby rejected the separation of the deity and the humanity of Christ, it now became necessary to defend this truth of the distinction of the two natures against the Monophysitism arising out of the Alexandrian Christology. Monophysitism,[7] which by very unspiritual means had prevailed at the "Robber Synod" of Ephesus in 449,[8] solves the problem of the divine-human person of the Savior, which had proved too much for the Antiochenes, in a most simple and apparently Christian manner. It teaches that the human nature was absorbed by the divine, so that after the union of the natures in the incarnation only a single nature remains: the divine, into which the human has been diffused like a drop of milk in the ocean.

This teaching comes very close to the Docetism of the ancient Gnostics and Marcion.[9] It is incapable of understanding the praying of Jesus. Gethsemane and the "Why have You forsaken Me?" [Matt. 27:46] lose their meaning. The "flesh" of the incarnation is no longer a true flesh. In modern form, this Monophysitism was proclaimed during the German *Kirchenkampf* by members of the German-Christian party—for instance, in this statement of the twenty-eight theses of the Saxon People's Church (*Volkskirche*) of 1933: "The debate whether Jesus was Jew or Aryan simply does not get at the essence of Jesus. Jesus is not a bearer of human nature but reveals in His person the nature of God" (K. D. Schmidt, *Die Bekenntnisse des Jahres 1933*, p. 101). This is an indication that Monophysitism remains a danger for the Church, just as much as Nestorianism and Arianism.

---

6 Followers of Nestorius (d. ca. 451) held that there is no communion of natures in the person of Christ, denied that the Virgin Mary is the "God-bearer" or *theotokos*, and believed that Christ's human nature is only by adoption. Nestorius and his followers were condemned by the Council of Ephesus in AD 431 (s.v. *Christian Cyclopedia*). MH

7 This heresy teaches there is only one nature in Christ, namely, the divine, or one compounded nature. (s.v. *Christian Cyclopedia*). MH

8 By force and with the support of imperial troops, Dioscorus (d. 454) obtained temporary restoration of Eutyches (ca. 380–ca. 456) and condemnation of the orthodox party. The decision was reversed by Chalcedon (s.v *Christian Cyclopedia*). MH

9 Marcion (ca. 100–ca. 160), a native of Sinope and Pontus, was the son of a bishop who excommunicated him because of immorality. An antinomian, Marcion completely rejected the Old Testament and held that the God of the Old Testament had nothing at all in common with the God of Jesus Christ. See *ODCC*, 1034. MH

The answer which Chalcedon gave to this question concerning the relation of the divine and the human nature in the person of the God-man is the simplest one imaginable. The creed of 451 simply sets side by side the three truths which must be taught concerning the person of Jesus Christ, without attempting to explain them. Since the text of this creed is not found in our Book of Concord—its doctrinal content has been incorporated in the *Symbolum Quicunque*[10] and confirmed by the *Augustana* (Art. III) and the Formula of Concord (Art. VIII)—let the chief statements of this lengthy doctrinal decree be quoted:

> "The holy and great ecumenical synod ... stands against those who seek to tear apart the mystery of the incarnation into a duality of sons; and it excludes those from the holy fellowship who dare to declare the deity of the Only-begotten to be capable of suffering; and it opposes those who invent a mingling and flowing together of the two natures of Christ; and it banishes those who foolishly maintain that the servant's form which the Son received from us is of a heavenly substance (*ousia*) or one other than ours; and it anathematizes those who fable that before the union there were two natures of the Lord, but after the union only one.

> "Following the holy fathers, we all with one consent teach men to confess one and the same Son, our Lord Jesus Christ, the same perfect in deity and perfect in humanity, God truly and man truly, of a reasonable soul and body, of one substance with the Father in His deity, and of one substance with us in His humanity, in all things like unto us without sin; begotten before the ages in His deity, in the last days for us and for our salvation born of the Virgin Mary, the mother of God, in His humanity; one and the same Christ, Son, Lord, Only-begotten, to be acknowledged in two natures, without confusion (*asynchytos, inconfuse*), without change (*atreptos, immutabiliter*), without division (*adiairetos, indivise*), without separation (*achoristos, inseparabiliter*), the distinction of the natures being by no means taken away because of the union, but rather the property of each nature being preserved, and concurring in one person (*prosopon*) and one hypostasis (Latin: *subsistentia*). We do not confess (a Son) divided and separated into two persons, but one and the self-same Son and only-begotten God, *Logos*, Lord Jesus Christ; as from the beginning the prophets and the Lord Jesus Christ Himself taught us concerning Him, and the Creed of the fathers handed down to us. Since we have arrived at this decision with great circumspection and care, the holy and ecumenical synod has decreed that no one may set forth any other doctrine, or set it down in writing, or foster it or teach it to others." (Then those who teach otherwise are threatened with removal from office and excommunication.)

This is the faith of the fathers of Chalcedon: belief in the true divinity, the true humanity, and the true unity of the divine-human Person.

---

10 *Quicunque* is the first word of the Athanasian Creed: "And whoever ... would be saved." MH

3

Together with the *Symbolum Quicunque* and the Formula of Concord, the doctrinal formulation of Chalcedon belongs to those confessions of Christendom which were by modern Protestantism considered as horrible examples of an irreligious dogmatism and theological hairsplitting. Especially "the bald negative definitions with which everything is supposed to have been said" (Harnack, *Lehrbuch der Dogmengeschichte* II, p. 397) have rather nettled the critics. Only the reawakening in our day of an appreciation of confession and formal doctrine (*Dogma*) in the Church has tempered this harsh judgment. It is understood once more that negation may have a most positive significance in the dogma of the Church, since there are truths that can be expressed only *in negationis*. Men understand again what the negatives ("unconfused," "unchanged," "undivided," "unseparated") mean by way of limitation. They are like buoys, marking for us the one channel of navigation within which a ship must keep if it is not to be wrecked. And the rediscovery of dialectic and paradox in theology has made the creed of Chalcedon famous even as an example of genuine theological discourse.

Indeed, no serious theologian will today deny that just with its careful limitations against possible errors this confession safeguards the biblical truths that Jesus Christ is true God and true man and at the same time one person. For this reason, and not for the sake of some kind of traditionalism, the churches of the Reformation have declared their adherence. And in his explanation of the Second Article, "the most beautiful sentence in the German language," Luther has succeeded in translating the Chalcedonian creed into a language that even a child can understand and speak: "I believe that Jesus Christ, true God, begotten of the Father from eternity, and also true man, born of the Virgin Mary, is my Lord . . ." [SC II 4]. That is Chalcedon for the children, even as it is probably the criterion of every genuine dogma: that it can be stated so plainly that the simplest person can understand it.

However, our appreciation of the confession of 451 dare not keep us from seeing also its limitations. From a purely formal point of view, it is not a model of confessional writing. It cannot be prayed like the Nicene Creed. Nor does it want to be more than merely a commentary upon the *Nicaenum*, even as the Formula of Concord undertakes to be a commentary upon the *Augustana*. For the fathers of 451, the Symbol of the 150 fathers of Constantinople still remains the Creed—our *Niceno-Constantinopolitanum*, which has been preserved for us in the records of Chalcedon. (Incidentally, this is the evidence that our so-called Nicene Creed is really that of Constantinople.)

Another deficiency must be noted. How is it that the creed of Chalcedon did not attain the recognition which was achieved by the *Nicaenum*? It did indeed preserve the unity of the Greek and Latin Churches, but only a unity of the Church within the empire. Everything that lay beyond the empire—the churches of Armenia, Syria, Egypt, Ethiopia—did not accept it. The churches of the non-Grecian Orient remained Nestorian, like the East-Syrian Church which eventually reached out to China and East India, or they became Monophysites like the rest. There certainly were political reasons for this: these nations and churches wanted to have nothing more to do with the orthodox Christianity of Rome and the Hellenists. This awakening Asia declared its independence of the Church of the empire because this represented "Western Christianity." The Christianity of Asia, both Monophysite and Nestorian, was then either engulfed or overshadowed by Islam. Why? What has Islam in common with Monophysitism, what with Nestorianism?

There is certainly also an anti-Roman and anti-Hellenist spirit (in Islam), the spirit of Asia, which is antagonistic to the Western spirit. But the most important factor is that all three represent Christological heresies, particularly also Islam. And church history of every era teaches that the transition from one heresy to another is very easy, even though these heresies may contradict each other. Thus the fate of the Eastern churches was sealed when they refused to take the step which since the end of the fifth century was taken by the Arian churches of the West, one after another, namely, the transition to orthodoxy. They (viz., the Eastern churches) wished to remain orthodox. The *Nicaenum* remained their confession. But their history shows that one cannot truly preserve the Nicene Creed if one rejects that of Chalcedon as its authentic interpretation—even as no one can hold fast to the *Augustana Invariata* who refuses to accept the Formula of Concord.

But there must be within the confession itself reasons why the creed of Chalcedon did not achieve recognition in all parts of Christendom. It is not yet a weakness that within the limitations defined by the four negative terms there are several possible ways of understanding the Christology. Thus there is also the possibility of understanding the Trinity in the Eastern manner as the Tri-une God (*Dreieinigkeit*) or, like the West, as the threefold God (*Dreifaltigkeit*). But the question is whether more should not have been said on one certain point.

When at the beginning of the sixth century the doctrine of the *enhypostasis* was formulated—that is, the doctrine that the human nature has its *hyposta-sis* in the divine, in other words that the person of the God-man is the person of the *Logos*—then this view came too late to win back the Monophysites. But what course would the history of the doctrine have taken had this thought already been included in the Chalcedonian creed? This doctrine was meant to preserve what was true in the Monophysite contention, even as the concern of Nestorianism for recognition of the two natures had already been unmistakably safeguarded at Chalcedon. The fact that a hiatus remained—and perhaps still had to remain in view of the level of theological understanding of that city—is the chief reason why the council of 451 was unable to bring the Christological controversy to an actual conclusion, but that the antagonism between Nestorianism and Monophysitism flared up in new forms again and again, even within that part of Christianity which recognized Chalcedon.

It is even quite probable that the profound difference between Lutheranism and Calvinism is to be regarded as a revival of the old Christological trends (*christologische Schulen*) upon the soil of the Reformation. That is how the controversy between the Lutheran and the Reformed churches concerning the Lord's Supper became a controversy concerning the interpretation of the creed of Chalcedon. For the question concerning the real presence of the body and blood of Christ in the Sacrament of the Altar leads to the other question: whether the human nature of Christ is united with the divine in such a manner that it partakes of its attributes. Lutheran Christology, continuing the Alexandrian emphasis upon the unity of the God-man, affirms this, while the Reformed denies it, in the sense of the Antiochene version of the doctrine of the two natures and its *finitum non capax infiniti* [the famous dictum of Calvinism: "The finite is incapable of the infinite"]. That is why discussions between the Lutheran and the Reformed church of our day, even down to the practical issues of liturgy and canon law (*Kirchenrecht*), still remain a discussion about the proper understanding of the Chalcedonian creed which, together with the *Nicaenum*, has become the great common doctrinal basis of all Western churches.

4

About one thing we should be clear, no matter how painfully our review of these great interlocking issues reminds us of the calamity of a divided Christendom. The greatest tragedy is not that there are various interpretations of the creeds of Chalcedon and Nicaea, so that there are Christian confessions in the sense of the Orthodox, of the Roman, of the Lutheran, of the Reformed, of the Anglican Church. Rather, the real tragedy of modern Christendom is this: that together with these ancient confessions it has to a great extent lost the common dogmatic foundation. The rift between East and West in the Middle Ages, the schisms of Western Christendom in the era of the Reformation were indeed tragedies beyond words. But they could not entirely destroy the unity of Christendom. How well were not East and West able during the height as well as toward the end of the Middle Ages to speak with each other! What profound understanding of the Eastern Church did not Thomas of Aquinas [ca. 1224/1227–1274] possess! And how constantly he kept all of Christendom in view in his great life-work of theology! And even during the sixteenth and seventeenth centuries, the battling churches of the several confessions still constitute some kind of unity, over and above the chasms that divide them. Only because of their agreement in the great fundamental dogmas of the ancient Christian faith could the theologians of the *Tridentinum* [Denzinger 994–1000] and Martin Chemnitz,[11] could

---

11 Chemnitz (1522–86) was the chief author of the Formula of Concord. He wrote the consummate Lutheran response to Trent, *The Examination of the Council of Trent* (4 vols. [St. Louis: Concordia, 1971–86]). MH

Bellarmine and Johann Gerhard,[12] could Jacob Andreae and Beza,[13] could the Tübingen faculty and the Patriarch Jeremias[14] converse with each other, even though polemically.

Nor is it mere chance that the same confessional document of the Lutheran Church which most emphatically voices the opposition to the Roman Church and calls the pope the Antichrist also in strongest terms declares its solidarity with this church in confessing "the sublime articles concerning the divine Majesty": "Concerning these articles there is no contention or dispute, since we on both sides confess them" (SA I). Only he who takes this seriously knows what the Lutheran Church is, particularly also in its relation to the churches of other confessions. Not until Pietism and Rationalism (*die Aufklarung*) disintegrated the understanding of the dogmas of the ancient Church did the actual unity of the contending confessional churches, which was evidenced thereby, finally break down. Not the sixteenth century but the eighteenth is the real century of church schism. Since then the confessions cease to converse with each other, to know one another, and to believe in their unity.

Now there is a grain of truth in the idea of Calixtus[15] about the *consensus quinquesaecularis* ["the consensus of the first five centuries"] as the basis for a union of churches and in the Anglican counterpart about the Creed of the "ancient undivided Church" as a basis upon which the churches might unite. The point where the syncretism of Calixtus and where the Anglicans were in error is the thought that one could forget the Reformation, re-evaluate its doctrine, and declare the differences and conflicts of the sixteenth century nonessential.

Against this idea of union which today is again playing so important a role in the world, particularly since the Ecumenical Movement has carried it out

---

12   Cardinal Robert Bellarmine (1542–1621) and Johann Gerhard (1582–1637) were contemporary antagonists. Gerhard's *Loci* (translated as *Theological Commonplaces* and published by Concordia Publishing House, 2006–) is filled with references to Bellarmine. MH

13   Andreae (1528–90) and Theodore Beza (1519–1605) attempted to bridge the Lutheran-Reformed gap at the Colloquy of Montbéliard. See Jill Raitt, *The Colloquy of Montbéliard: Religion and Politics in the Sixteenth Century* (New York: Oxford University Press, 1993). MH

14   Andreae and the Tübingen faculty engaged the patriarch of Constantinople in theological exchange, though it was finally rather fruitless. The record of the exchange is available in English: *Augsburg and Constantinople: The Correspondence between the Tübingen Theologians and Patriarch Jeremiah II of Constantinople on the Augsburg Confession*, trans. George Mastrantonis (Brookline MA: Holy Cross Orthodox Press, 1982). Jeremiah's (1536–94) gifts did not include the proper distinction of Law and Gospel. MH

15   Georg Calixtus (1586–1656), professor of theology at Helmstedt, was a seventeenth-century ecumenist and antagonist of Lutheran orthodoxy. See Matthew Harrison, "Abraham Calov on Eastern Orthodoxy," *Logia* 9, no. 4 (Reformation 2000): 5ff. See also Johannes Wallmann's tremendous and readable analysis of the debate in *Der Theologiebegriff bei Johann Gerhard und Georg Calixt* (Tübingen: Mohr, 1961). MH

into all the mission fields, the following is to be said. The Reformation was more than a division of Christendom that one may deplore and forget. It did result in a schism. But essentially it was a new understanding of the Gospel, an understanding that can be accepted, declined, or perhaps even modified, but which at all events calls for a decision. He who refuses to make this decision, who dares to say neither yes nor no to the claim of the Reformation that it is the right interpretation of the ancient creeds with their *propter nos homines et propter nostram salutem* ["for us men and for our salvation"], he is really not taking these old confessions seriously.

In all the attempts at union, therefore, which consider the creeds of the ancient Church a sufficient basis of agreement, these actually are not being taken as a binding expression of Christian doctrine, but rather as ancient and venerable liturgical and canonical texts, which one uses without breaking one's head over what they may mean. Virtue is then made of necessity, and one states that the Creed is derived from the liturgy and that only as a liturgical text can it be used and understood, and one feels oneself at one with the Church of all the ages if it is but heard in the church. But one forgets that for the fathers it was the expression of great objective truths, for which they were ready to die, and that these great trans-subjective truths, as the creeds of Nicaea and Chalcedon testify, are what creates a unity of Christendom that transcends all confessional bounds.

Here lies the greatest tragedy of divided Christendom. During the last 250 years we have lost what was the common possession of all Christians, even during the times of religious wars and of the worst interconfessional polemic. With shocking clarity this has been revealed by the Ecumenical Movement of the previous generation. It was a great moment when at Lausanne in 1927 the World Conference for Faith and Order in the Church confirmed the *Nicaenum* as the common confession of the Church. It soon developed, however, that most of the participating churches had no thought of taking this resolution seriously. The dogmatic foundation of the great ecumenical associations and the World Council of Churches which grew out of this conference of 1947 remained the confession which acknowledges Jesus Christ as "God and Savior." All churches accepting Jesus Christ as their "God and Savior" may participate, whatever this confession may mean for them.

This theologically inadequate and erroneous formula which can cover all kinds of false doctrine has been taken over out of the idiom of the American sects. Never can it take the place of that clear confession concerning the Trinity of God and the God-manhood (*Gottmenschheit*) of Jesus Christ that would have to be the basis for joint church action and for doctrinal discussions between the churches. But it is deeply significant that all efforts of Lutherans and Anglicans to place the Ecumenical Movement on this basis have failed. For the Reformed churches of the world have long since done away with the confessions of the

Church of antiquity, and the "young churches" which they have founded in all mission fields on earth have never possessed them.

But even for the Anglican and the Lutheran churches these creeds actually have largely lost their dogmatic significance and exist only as historical, liturgical, and canonical documents. None of the well-meant Protestant complaints, perfectly justified in themselves, about unscriptural new Catholic dogmas can change the fact that the Church of Rome has at least preserved the old scriptural dogma, even though mutilated by the additions of a later day. One may well ask what would have become of this great heritage of the Church if during the last 250 years, even as in the days of Chalcedon, Rome had not been the guardian of the dogmas of the ancient Church, constantly reminding the evangelical churches of what they either had surrendered or were about to surrender.

5

In conclusion, let me, venerable brethren, say a word concerning the mission (*Aufgabe*) of those who see this distress of the Church and to whom the memory of the Fourth Ecumenical Council is an occasion to declare themselves anew concerning the "sublime articles concerning the divine Majesty" which constitute the great heritage of the ancient Church for the orthodox Church of all time. For there are, praise God, still evangelical churches which know what constitutes true doctrine; and within such churches as have in general become weak in faith, or have fallen from the faith, there are also still Christians and, in particular, faithful servants of the Word who have not gone along in this apostasy and whose daily prayer is that God may preserve them from this temptation.

First of all, we must guard against placing too high an evaluation upon a confession like that of Chalcedon. In his *On the Councils and the Church*, Luther upon one occasion speaks of the scant information which his times had about this council and goes on to say:

> Whither have they gone, the dear saints and Christians who through so many hundred years knew nothing about what this council has decreed? For there must always be saints upon this earth; and when they die, other saints must live, from the beginning until the end of the world. Otherwise this article would be false: I believe one holy Christian Church, the communion of saints. And Christ would necessarily be a deceiver when He says, "I am with you unto the end of the world." Living saints there must always be upon earth, be they where they may; else there would be an end to the kingdom of Christ, and there would be no one to pray the Lord's Prayer, to confess the Creed, to be baptized, to partake of the Sacrament, to be absolved, etc. [*Von den Konziliis und Kirchen* (1539), Aland 382 (E[1] 25:316; WA 50:593; AE 41:107)]

One may be a Christian without knowing the creed of Chalcedon and without understanding its technical terms. But one cannot be a Christian without confessing the faith which it sets forth, faith in the true Godhead and the true manhood of Christ, and the true unity of the person of the God-man. For that is the faith of the New Testament, to believe in the incarnation and earnestly to take to heart the saving message of the Gospel: "The Word was made flesh" [John 1:14].

But as a testimony to this faith Chalcedon has a significance for the Church of all the ages. That is why its doctrinal content has in the second part of the so-called Athanasian Creed become binding doctrine for the Western Church, being subsequently confirmed by the confessions of the Reformation. The experience of Christendom teaches that wherever the authority of these ancient creeds was set aside, this also meant the lapse of the biblical doctrine of the incarnation of the eternal Son. It is impossible to maintain the authority of Scripture while rejecting the authority of the confessions. And this is so because the authority of the confessions is, after all, nothing else than the authority of the scriptural content which is set forth in them. This is why with the *norma normata* ["norm which is normed"] of the confessions there invariably also falls the *norma normans* ["norming norm"] of Scripture.

This has been the sorry experience of Protestant Christianity during the recent centuries. The theory of the Reformed Church and of Reformed biblicism has proved itself to be false, namely, that the authority of the Bible becomes greater and more assured as one lessens the authority of the confessions. While invoking the *sola Scriptura*, Reformed churches from Switzerland to America and to the Far East grant equal recognition to deniers of the God-manhood of Christ and of the Trinity, as well as to those who confess the old doctrines. When in a famed minster of Switzerland, alongside a great preacher who as a friend and pupil of Karl Barth proclaims the Gospel in the sense of the Reformed Church, another can stand in the pulpit who declares himself to be an avowed opponent of the doctrine of the Trinity and who demands of the Church that she be so "catholic" that she have room for Unitarians as well as Trinitarians, and if this condition is legalized by canon law and perpetuated by guarantees for the protection of minorities, then this is but an example for what is today possible and normal in all Reformed churches.

If the church authorities of Hesse-Nassau, under the leadership of [Martin] Niemöller [1892–1984], extend a cordial welcome through an official representative to the congress for "Free Christianity," thereby recognizing it, though at this congress the divine worship of Jesus is assailed as a violation of the First Commandment—what blasphemy toward our Lord Jesus Christ, who Himself asserted His deity!—and if (so that no flesh should glory) Lutheranism was also represented by a guest appearance of Paul Althaus[16] as lecturer, then this is a sign of how little the "Confessing Church" was able to restore the confessions

---

16   Paul Althaus (1888–1966) was a professor at Erlangen from 1925. Sasse was on the Erlangen faculty with Althaus throughout the Hitler years. MH

of the Church to their position of honor. The Church of Bremen—which at first declined to become a member of the Evangelical Church in Germany (EKiD) because it was unable to make even that minimum of confession which is required in the preamble to the constitution—has probably been effectively informed in the meantime that modern churches, even as modern theologians, need not stumble over such threads, just as in the World Council of Churches, church bodies and theologians who do not share the doctrine of the God-man Christ are engaged in cheerful collaboration.

Now, let no one come with the objection that formal confessions and the stipulations of canon law are unable to provide a guarantee of pure doctrine; that it is littleness of faith to seek thus to safeguard the state of the Church; that the Holy Spirit can work also under such circumstances and that it is unbelief not to have this confidence in Him; and furthermore that things are also no better in churches that are theoretically Lutheran. To this we reply that no theologian expects of confessional writings or church orders that they will save the Church. We know that the Holy Spirit moves where and when He will, and that the means of grace are effective wherever they are employed. We have confidence in the Lord of the Church that He who has raised the dead can also bring dying and dead churches back to life, even as He has quickened our hearts that were dead in sins to a living faith. But we declare it to be mere superstition if one thinks that God will by a miracle do what He has assigned to us ministers of the Church, and what in sloth and faintness of heart, in complacency or for fear of men we fail again and again to do.

For the sake of the eternal truth, and for the sake of the souls that are entrusted to them, He has commanded the servants of the Word, the shepherds of His flock, to testify against false doctrine and to exclude it from the Church. We declare it to be blasphemous to expect the Holy Spirit to remove obstacles that we deliberately place in the way of His work. We know that no confession guarantees purity of doctrine—what errors have not crept into churches that, like the Eastern churches and Roman Catholicism, actually have preserved the creeds of Nicaea and Chalcedon—but we also know that the doctrine of the Church must suffer complete corruption, that the Gospel must die, when men forget the confession of the truth.

To say this, to witness it to the Lutheran Church and to Christendom, that is the great mission of faithful Lutherans today. It is a thankless task, for the world—even the Christian world, even the Lutheran world—does not wish to hear this. Today there are only a few groups, and mostly small, who are still saying all this and who do not fear the reproach of confessionalism and orthodoxy. But more depends upon their faithfulness than most of us are aware. At all events, we do not want to be ashamed to belong to them.

⸎

I greet you all with the words that in the liturgy of the Eastern Church introduce the Credo: "Let us love one another, so that we may confess in unity of faith!"

Your
Hermann Sasse

Historical Context

In "American Christianity and the Church" which Sasse published in 1927 after his year of study in the United States, he asserted that in the American context, among Protestants and Catholics, only the Lutheran Church was in a position to pose the question of truth to American Christianity.[1] A quarter century later Sasse beheld the young LWF moving in the direction of the WCC and an ecumenism heavily influenced by Anglicanism's inability to answer the decisive questions of truth, particularly of the Reformation. At Hanover the LWF would fail the test of truth. MH

July 22, 1952

Prof. H. Sasse
41 Buxton Street
North Adelaide, South Australia

Highly Honored Herr Doctor Behnken!

... I would strongly urge you, Herr Doctor Behnken, in Hanover and Uelzen to do everything to hold the German Free Churches together. In the great crisis, which is passing through all of German churchdom, and which, among other things, is resulting in a terrible defection to the Roman Church, Lutheranism [*Luthertum*] stands or falls with the Free Churches. For the EKiD cannot reverse its course.... Without a faculty, the Free Chuch cannot exist, while the Lutheran character of the state faculties is becoming ever weaker. A confessional Lutheran today in Germany can no longer become a professor ....

> Your devoted
> Hermann Sasse

---

1   See *Lonely Way* 1:23–60. MH

twenty-two

The Deconfessionalization of Lutheranism?

REMARKS ON THE PRESENT SITUATION OF THE LUTHERAN CHURCHES

TRANSLATED BY MATTHEW C. HARRISON

New Year 1952[1]

Prof. D. Theol. Hermann Sasse
41 Buxton Street
North Adelaide, South Australia

Dear Brothers in the Office!

Three years have passed since the first of these letters came into your hands. That letter sought to depict, in brief strokes, the situation faced by the Lutheran Churches as it made note of the twofold tendency in the most recent history of our church: a strong external ascendance of Lutheranism, which is accompanied by a threatening diminution of the dogmatic-confessional substance. Most of you will agree with me that the developments of the past three years have corroborated this viewpoint. It is to be feared that the meeting of the Lutheran World Federation in Hanover will not contradict this view. How pleased would we all be, all of us who are so very concerned for the future of our church, if this meeting would prove us wrong, if it shall have revealed something of an ascendancy of the inner spiritual life of the church, of a renewal of the old faithfulness

---

1   *BLP* 22: *Entkonfessionalisierung des Luthertums? Bemerkungen zur Lage der Lutherischen Kirchen in der Gegenwart* (North Adelaide, January 1952). Huss number 208. MH

to the confession of the eternal truth which once found a home in Lower Saxony. But from what one reads in *Lutherischen Rundschau* of the preparations in Hanover, it appears to be much like the massive marches and manipulating demonstrations which the evangelical churches of Germany inherited from the Third Reich, which satisfy a deep psychological need of modern masses. There is no doubt that the Hanover session of the Lutheran World Federation will be just as beautiful and enchanting as the Berlin *Kirchentag* of the EKiD and as the great royal nuptial celebrations of Hanover in previous years. The very same men who in Berlin were so enthused over the unity of the Evangelical Church in German [EKiD] ("We are still brothers!") will be enthused in Hanover over the Lutheran Church. And they will proudly allow the church banners to stream, among which also is the banner of the LWF with Luther's seal, just as at royal weddings the old Hanoverian flags suddenly fluttered again and the old uniforms of the Hanoverian army of 1866 experienced a remarkable resurrection. What a testimony of loyalty that was! Only it was forgotten that it was all merely a beautiful show. The princes no longer rule. The flag of a state which has long since gone under was displayed. The people passionately celebrated a loyalty which had long since been violated. That is the *genius loci*[2] of Hanover. Should it also rule the session of the Lutheran World Federation in August? If not, then it is time to exorcise it. We theologians in any case will remain sober and guard ourselves from the enthusiasm which in every form is the mortal enemy of the true faith. With Lutheran sobriety, which means for us at the same time with constant faith in the reality of the Church of God, we desire to seek to understand the situation of Lutheranism regarding a few essential points at the beginning of this fateful year.

1

The letters, which at Christmastime came from various areas of the Lutheran Church of Europe and America, from territorial and free churches, large and small churches, spoke without exception of the deep inner distress of the churches. They spoke of distressing matters scarcely found in the church papers, matters of which one cannot speak publicly at all, or only in a very limited way. But all these voices give one who resides at a place on the earth outside Europe and America the impression that a single illness threatens the Lutheran Churches of the world. It is the very secularization of the church itself. If twenty-five years ago the secularization of culture was recognized as the great illness of the time, then it is soberly to be asserted today that secularism is now the illness of the church. It is gripping to see that, in order to fulfill the missiological

---

2   The Romans were convinced that everyone born into this world was given a genius, a guardian spirit. They also believed that every house and every institution had the same arrangement—thus *genius loci*. See Eugene Ehrlich, *Amo, Amas, Amat and More* (New York: Harper Row, 1985), 138. MH

goal of calling the peoples of the West back to the Christian faith, the church itself must first be turned back to this faith. "Sweden's people are God's people." That was the solution a generation ago. Today the question is to what extent the Church of Sweden is still the church of God? And so it is in all nations. Great missionary endeavors and evangelization efforts will still be carried out, but it is precisely the most serious evangelists who are coming to the conviction that the Gospel-preaching church must be the first object of their evangelization. This understanding was already once given as a gift to German evangelical churchdom. The consequence of the theology of Karl Barth in the time of his great influence in the first half of the 1930s was based upon this recognition. That was the meaning of his struggle against Otto Dibelius[3] and his "Century of the Church." That was the most profound power of the Confessing Churches of all persuasions in Germany, however they may have differed from one another as Lutherans, Reformed, or United [Churches]. That was really the renewal of the Reformation, for Reformation is indeed the repentance of the church. The end of this repentance meant the end of the Confessing Church. What then followed was mere restoration. Every revolution ends with collapse and the convulsive efforts to restore everything to what it was before. That is an inborn propensity of natural man. From the far southern and eastern portion of the world, one has the impression that the Japanese people have been struck at the very core of their existence in a more profound way and that there are more penitent men, men who have heard the New Testament summons to repentance, than among us Germans. One need simply glance at Lilje's[4] *Sonntagsblatt* [*Sunday Paper*] or the propaganda paper *Christ und Welt* [*Christ and World*] broadcast throughout the world, with the following in mind: What remains here of the Stuttgart confession of guilt which was at least true in 1945? Where the church, however, loses and surrenders the authority to preach repentance, neither can she preach justification. There she loses the Gospel. There she does not experience that repentance which makes the church the church of Christ. There she can still proclaim a Christian worldview; she can train scholars and workers, doctors and philosophers, engineers and journalists at evangelical academies. There her theologians can still proclaim a theory of the forgiveness of sins, but she no longer has the authority to call sinners to repentance. Karl Holl once made an excellent statement regarding the sermons of Schleiermacher[5] from the years after the collapse

---

3   Friedrich Karl Otto Dibelius (1880–1967) was Evangelical bishop of Berlin (1945) and a leader of the Confessing Church at the time of the Nazi struggle. He was president of the EKiD council (1949) and president of the WCC (1954) (s.v. *Christian Cyclopedia*). MH

4   Hanns Lilje (1899–1977), bishop of the Evangelical Lutheran Church of Hanover, member of the council of the EKiD, leading bishop of the VELKD, president of the LWF (1952–)57; see *RGG*[3] 4:378. MH

5   Friedrich Schleiermacher (1768–1834) was a native of Breslau in Silesia, the son of a Reformed army chaplain. His parents converted to the Herrnhuter Brethren, after which he was educated at their college at Niesky and their seminary at Barby. He

of Prussia: "One gets the impression that Schleiermacher, too, perceived the deepening of the understanding of sin in the sense of strict Christianity at that time as a certain hindrance to the necessary ascendance of the fatherland" (*Ges. Aufsätze* III, p. 357). That is Prussian Christianity, the Christianity of the "German Christians" and their kindred spirits in all nations of the earth: one reckons one's own sins against those of others and quickly forgets his own. But God forgets not. He forgives, but only the truly repentant.

Nowhere is the secularization of the Lutheran Church more visible than in the loss of her confessional conscience. In these letters we have often recounted that and why the Lutheran Church is a confessional church *kat exochen*.[6] The confession means for her more than it does for the Reformed—indeed, in many respects even more than for the [Roman] Catholics. The Reformed Churches can survive if the confession is relativized, when it is stated: "We do not know precisely whether next Sunday we will continue to interpret Scripture in the way we do today." Catholicism actually celebrates a triumph when a dogma is proclaimed by the pope, the correctness of which is doubted by many of the best Catholics and which they then in worthy obedience accept, though they themselves know that the proof of tradition is defective and therefore doubtful. Both these groups [Reformed and Roman] lack that ultimate seriousness regarding the question of truth, which was the *proprium*[7] of the Lutheran Reformation. We Lutherans are quite happy to boast about this virtue, but perhaps no longer with justification, just as the Swiss still boast of the bravery which their fathers showed on the battlefields of Europe centuries ago. Indeed, the church does not live on from the faith of the *fathers*. The confession can have a purely historical significance, like the flags and uniforms of Hanover. If it is correct that the *confessio*, the confession of the faith, is indissoluably connected with *confessio* in the sense of the confession of sin and of the praise of God, is not then our lack of repentance and our lack of joyful praise of God in newer hymns a notable parallel to the regression of the dogmatic confession [of the faith]? Allow me to cite the following sentence from the Christmas letter of an American friend[8] as an illustration of this state of affairs:

> I am afraid we have come to a point in American Lutheranism where we no longer dare discuss controversial doctrines. There is a deep concern in all hearts for outward unity, but with that there often goes, as you

---

studied at Halle in 1787 and attempted to reassert Christianity as a religion built upon "a sense and taste for the infinite" over against rationalism. He taught at the University of Berlin from 1810 and had enormous influence on the theologies of the likes of Albrecht Ritschl, Adolf von Harnack, and Ernst Troeltsch (1865–1923). Schleiermacher was "the theologian of the Prussian Union." See *ODCC*, 1465. MH

6   I.e., in the proper sense of the term. MH

7   I.e., the essential point. MH

8   Probably Herman Preus (1896–1995) of Luther Seminary, St. Paul, Minnesota, the uncle of Robert (1924–95) and J. A. O. (1920–94). MH

know, doctrinal differences (read "indifference") and even compromise
on truth. The concern for truth has lost its power in our country, not
least because of the philosophy of goverment and the corruption in government that we have seen for the last two decades. It reaches all the
way down into the church because the young people are educated into
this kind of a philosophy. God help us to be fearless in our presentation
of the truth and in our battle against falsehood.

Thus the great secularization process, which is today passing through all
churches, effects in Lutheranism a troubling regression of confessional consciousness and with this also of dogmatic substance.

And this judgment applies, even in view of the fact that the collapse in other
churches is happening much more quickly and is more imminent than in the
Lutheran Church. I will comment on this in what follows. But no reference to
the great sickness of secularism already farther advanced in other communions
of Christendom can release us from the duty of acknowledging the sickness in
its entire gravity and of reminding ourselves of the means and path to healing to
which the merciful patience of God points us.

2

Allow me to clarify the dogmatic-confessional problem of the Lutheran Church
by noting one of the many ecumenical plans which in our day, especially on the
mission field and in the great lands of immigration such as Australia, are supposed to solve the church's problem. The World Council of Churches indeed
assures us that it does not desire to be a "super church" and that it also refuses
to be, as Dr. Leiper says, a "marriage bureau" for churches. Thus in the theses of
Toronto (III.2), regarding the ecclesiological significance of the World Council of
Churches, it states:

> The task of the Council is not to facilitate union between churches. Such
> negotiations can only be carried out by the churches themselves at their
> own initiative. Its task is to bring the churches into a living perception of
> each other, and thus to promote study and the discussion of questions
> of church unification. [*The Ecumenical Revue* 3, no. 1 (October 1950): 48]

This thesis is explained by the following:

> By its very existence and activity the Council bears witness to the neces-
> sity of a clear manifestation of the unity of the church of Christ. But it
> remains the right and duty of each individual church on the basis of its
> ecumenical experience to come to those conclusions which they them-
> selves believe they must come to on the basis of their own convictions.
> No church, therefore, needs to fear that the Council will necessitate
> decisions from them regarding unification with other churches. [*The
> Ecumenical Revue* 3, no. 1 (October 1950): 48]

It is stated thereby that the World Council of Churches is in fact something like a matchmaker, where the partners are brought together and encouraged to express decisions regarding future marital agreements. The Ecumenical Movement—which a quarter century ago facilitated the encounter of the churches, the new ordering of their mutual relationships, and their common consciousness of the one, holy, catholic and apostolic church as confessed in the *Nicaenum*—has in large measure thereby become a union movement in which the tragedy of all such union movements is repeated: instead of reducing the number of churches, the number is increased through the founding of new churches, just as after 1817 in Germany, out of the Lutheran and Reformed [Churches], something like five union churches of various confessions had been created. And the unification is not unification in faith, but rather unification in doubt, namely, the famous "agree[ment] to disagree."[9] Just what such a church looks like is shown by the plan for a "Reunited Church" of Australia, which on the basis of the Union of South India and the plan for other union churches in the Far East has been worked out by the Commission for Faith and Order with the Australian Council of the World Council of Churches, and in fully official manner set before the ecumenical sessions of this year, especially the Faith and Order Conference in Lund, and commended to the churches of Australia.

The "Reunited Church" is to consist of member churches which, to a certain extent, retain their independence but mutually acknowledge one another's faith and the validity of their respective offices. Each particular church delegates certain powers to the larger church [*Gesamtkirche*]. This has already been realized in Germany in the EKiD, and this is why the EKiD enjoys such great favor throughout the Ecumenical Movement. It is exactly the same plan which is behind the new National Council of Churches of Christ in America (NCCCA), the continuation of the old Federal Council of 1908. According to the view of the present leader of the Ecumenical Movement, this plan shall bring about the solution to the worldwide unification problem, especially on the mission field: unity in diversity, maintenance of the heritage of the individual confessions while setting aside the old absolute dogmatic claims. This is the realization of the Masonic idea so dear to the Western world—the "religion in which we all agree,"[10] making possible further development of the church toward a full realization of the *Una Sancta* "under the direction of the Holy Spirit." The creedal basis in the case of Australia is that which is held to be basic to the Christian faith: *Apostolicum* and *Nicaenum* as expressions of faith in the triune God. How one understands the assertions of these confessions on individual points is, accordingly, unasked. All questions which in these confessions are unanswered remain open, especially all the questions raised by the Reformation. Regarding the Holy Scriptures, for instance, the plan says that the churches accept the writings of

---

9 Sasse's original states this in English. MH

10 Sasse's original states this in English. MH

the Old and New Testaments as "given by God, in order to give us the revelation of Himself in many parts and many ways, which is fulfilled in the Lord Jesus Christ." Not only does it remain an open question whether the Holy Scriptures are God's Word, as the church of all times has believed, but also whether they are the only source and norm of doctrine, or whether there is a tradition also alongside them. New declarations of faith should certainly only be allowed provided "such statements are agreeable to the truths of the Christian religion which is revealed in Holy Scripture." This much of the *sola Scriptura* of the Reformation yet remains. We find here the uniquely flawed position of the present-day Anglican Church regarding the Scriptures. When the archbishops of Canterbury and York in previous years protested against the dogma of the *Assumptio Mariae*,[11] it did not mean, as was understood by Lutherans, that they held that the dogma was false. All Anglo-Catholics celebrate August 15 with the Roman liturgy of the day, thereby confessing their personal belief in the dogma, and thus declare publicly that they accept the *Assumptio*. No Anglican bishop denies them this right. What is contested is only that this doctrine must be believed by all Christians as binding dogma. The Church of England and world Anglicanism see an error not in the belief in the Marian dogmas of [Roman] Catholicism, rather only in the fact of the dogmatization itself. This limitation of the scriptural principle corresponds to the fact that the tradition [of the assumption] again achieved a significance in Anglicanism which was denied it by the Reformation. We have elsewhere already once pointed out the pronouncement of the present archbishop of Canterbury that the highest authority in questions of doctrine is the Holy Spirit, who speaks in the Holy Scriptures, in tradition, and in the present, living experience of the church. One may happily accept a tradition as an article of faith, only one must not ascribe to it general binding force. On the other hand, it is not stated that a binding dogma must be taken from the Scriptures, which is a basic principle of all churches of the Reformation. It just must not contradict Scripture; it must be reconcilable to the revealed truth in Scripture. These basic principles of modern Anglicanism have here been made a norm of faith in the "Reunited Church." Can the *sola Scriptura* of the Reformation be taught within it? Yes, but only as a private opinion of individual Christians or groups of Christians! Can the Tridentine dogma of Scripture and tradition be taught within it? Once again, yes, but only as a private opinion! At first glance it appears to be a remarkable unification of Protestantism and Catholicism, and in this sense its advocates perceived the plan. But upon closer examination, one notes that precisely here is abandoned that which Luther, Calvin, and Trent held in agreement, namely, the recognition of the Bible as the Word of God! But it is precisely the same with all the doctrines of the confessional churches of Christianity. One may

---

11   The belief that Mary, having completed her earthly life, was assumed in body and soul into heavenly glory. Promulgated as official dogma by Pius XII (r. 1939–58) in *Munificentissimus Deus*, November 1, 1950. MH

teach the *sola Scriptura* or the Tridentine doctrine of justification, Calvin's pre-destination doctrine or Arminianism—but always and only as a private opinion. The Lutherans may retain the Book of Concord, the Reformed their confessions, the Catholics the *Tridentinum* [Denzinger 994–1000], provided that they do not absolutize their particular traditions. The *sola fide* of the Lutheran Reformation can be maintained as a private opinion, but it may no longer be asserted that it is the *articulus stantis et cadentis ecclesiae* ["the article by which the church stands or falls"]. The same applies to all the particular doctrines of all confessions.

The union character of this church finds its expression, naturally, most especially in the Sacraments. Both Sacraments based in the Gospel—Baptism and the Holy Supper—are essential for the church. Whether or not there are additional Sacraments remains an open question. Confirmation is regarded as the necessary fulfillment of Baptism. A bishop must administer it. "Baptism is sign and seal of the covenant of grace, the unification with Christ in His body, through which we die to sin and are reborn unto righteousness and through the reception of the Holy Spirit become children of God." Infant Baptism and adult Baptism are looked upon as having equal legitimacy. If parents do not desire to have their children baptized, the parents should make use of a special ceremony to dedicate them to God. "Baptism should thus be imparted as publicly as possible, whereby the essence of the Sacrament is illustrated in appropriate fashion before the assembled congregation, so that the significance of Baptism be quite clearly asserted." Children who die unbaptized should be given a Christian burial. Basing infant Baptism upon its necessity for salvation is avoided. Bible passages are not cited, nor is the necessity of confirmation by a bishop [given scriptural basis]. Of what instruction regarding Baptism is to consist is unsaid. It must contain language at which neither a Lutheran nor a Baptist nor an Anglo-Catholic nor a disciple of the Salvation Army can take offense. The solution to the problem of the Supper is not so complicated. This Sacrament, to be celebrated with bread and wine, with prayer and the Words of Institution, serves for the *remembrance* of the death of Christ, the proclamation of the *sacrifice* of Christ, and the *reception* of the benefits of the Sacrament. Wherein these benefits consist is not stated. The body and blood of Christ are in general not mentioned, which has the great advantage that no controversy regarding the meaning of the Words of Institution can transpire. The doctrine of the Supper is left to the private understanding of individuals. Should anyone think to ask the "Reunited Church" what actually is received in the Sacrament of the Supper, the answer would have to be: "This the church does not know." It is unnecessary here to enter into the stipulations regarding constitution; regarding the offices of the bishop, presbyter, and deacon; how through a mutual laying on of hands a form of reciprocal acknowledgment of offices is to ensue as a replacement for reordination. What interests us is unfortunately the fact that here, under the blessing of the World Council of Churches, a fantastic union church is planned, in which the individual confessional churches are to find their higher unity without giving up their own existence. No words would need to be wasted regarding the plan if the leading circles of Anglican, Presbyterian, Methodist, and Congregationalist Churches of Australia, also the Baptists—not all of them—the Salvation Army and a few other fellowships did not support it, and if this plan did not correspond precisely to what is planned for the great mission fields of the Far East and, in part, has already been realized.

3

It is self-evident—or should it perhaps already no longer be self-evident?—that the Lutheran Church can speak only a decisive no to this and similar plans. Nor can it allow itself to take part in an improvement of such plans. The only thing which the Church of the Augsburg Confession can do here is tell the other churches why such a "Reunited Church" must needs be the end of the Church of Christ. For it would in fact not be a "reunited" church. For such a church has never existed—not immediately previous to the Reformation nor in ancient times. It is the fantasy dreamed up by churchmen who can think neither historically nor theologically. They would tolerate Protestants and Catholics, but what kind of Protestant maintains that the *sola Scriptura* and the *sola fide* are each a nonbinding *theologoumenon*?[12] What kind of Catholic confesses Tridentine dogma without condemning the doctrines of the Reformation? How could such a church attempt to carry out missions in a serious fashion? How can I call men to the faith if I cannot tell them what the Christian faith is? How can I preach justification without mentioning what justification is? How can I exhort men to allow themselves to be baptized if I cannot answer the question of what Baptism gives or profits? How can I dispense the Holy Supper to men if either they or I are unable to say what they receive in this Sacrament? The objection that these questions were not yet answered in the first 1,500 years of the church is perverted. The liturgies of the East as well as the West always stated very precisely what the Sacraments give. And even if all these had been "open questions" before the Reformation, we still could not undo the fact that since the sixteenth century answers have been given, certain answers which contradict one another, answers which one can reject, but answers which one cannot ignore. And indeed, if an unnerved Protestant Christianity no longer will venture to answer these questions, Rome will do it. And despite all its errors, Rome will still have preserved several truths. Shall it actually come to the point that the pope must say to the world that the Bible is the Word of God, that Christ through His death rendered full satisfaction for our sins, that we receive in the Sacrament of the Altar His true body and His true blood, that Baptism actually is the washing of regeneration and is necessary for salvation? Is it really too much to state that that "Reunited Church" would be the end of the Church of Christ? For without these truths of the Holy Scriptures the church cannot live.

12　I.e., a pet theological opinion. MH

But if this is the case, if the *Lutheran Church* must say all of this to Christianity, then it must also say this to the *World Council of Churches*. This means it must protest in every way that such a union plan be propagandized and effected in the name of the World Council or with its consent or indulgence. Should its protest find no hearing, then it must break all connections to this ecumenical organization. It is false to say, "We Lutherans must be present in order to influence developments, in order to avoid something worse." The author of this letter has paid attention to the Ecumenical Movement for twenty-five years, and not merely as an observer. He dedicated several years of his life to it, especially to the Faith and Order Movement. He worked closely with its great leaders, from Charles Brent [1862–1929] to William Temple [1881–1944].[13] He still recalls with thankfulness the conferences where we came together, as Bishop [Dr. Edwin J.] Palmer [1869–1954] of Bombay expressed it, not as negotiators, but as those who sought the truth. "Our conference is about the truth, not about reunification," thus this Anglican bishop began his great address regarding the Office of the Ministry [*geistliche Amt*] at Lausanne 1927.[14] But who today still seriously asks the question of truth? To be sure, serious theologians of all confessions also in the World Council of Churches do this. But who listens to them? The type of "church leaders" who meanwhile have taken the rudder of the churches—the bishops and church presidents in Europe, the presidents of the great churches and synods of America—have entirely different concerns than the concern for the truth, for pure doctrine, aside from a few very outmoded men in remote churches who are not taken seriously because they play no roll in worldwide church politics. This also is part of the secularization of the church, which is apparently the unavoidable fate of Christianity. Where the cause for this development lies is an idle question, whether the failures of men destroy church government, or whether a false church government shatters men. Perhaps it is both. And so today in the history of the church there are no longer men such as Bezzel,[15] Ihmels,[16] and Zoellner[17] in

---

13 On Temple, see below, p. 379 n. 16. MH

14 *Die Weltkonferenz für Glauben und Kirchenverfassung Deutscher Amtlicher Bericht über Die Weltkirchenkonferenz zu Lausanne* (Berlin: Furche Verlag, 1929)], p. 298; compare passages cited in the index (p. 631) under *"Wahrheit und Einheit"* ["Truth and Unity"]. HS [Sasse was editor of this work. MH]

15 Hermann Bezzel (1861–1917) was the second pastor to follow in Löhe's office in Neuendettelsau before becoming head of the Bavarian Church. He was heavily influenced by the Erlangen school, Johann Albrecht Bengel (1687–1752), and Luther. See *RGG*³ 1:1117. MH

16 Ludwig Heinrich Ihmels (1858–1933) was professor of systematics at Erlangen and Leipzig, bishop of Saxony (s.v. *Christian Cyclopedia*). MH

17 Wilhelm Zoellner (1860–1937) served as director of the deaconess institute at Kaiserswerth (1897) and as general superintendent of Westphalia (1905–31). Zoellner also was involved in the German Faith and Order Committee along with Sasse, whom he referred to him as "the young Sasse, whom I certainly treasure very much" (Ronald Feuerhahn, "Hermann Sasse as an Ecumenical Churchman" [PhD diss., University of Cambridge, 1991], 42). However, Sasse became estranged from his former

Germany; Hein[18] in America; Johansson in Finland;[19] Charles Gore[20] in England. Those familiar with Roman Catholicism maintain that a similar situation has, for the most part, also transpired there.

But if the "church leaders," because of wisdom or what they believe is wisdom, are silent, then others must speak. And it is time for such individuals in the Lutheran Churches of the world to finally study the reality of the World Council of Churches. How is it that the World Council, despite its express reserve in the question of actual union, despite its efforts not to injure the dogmatic substance of the churches, has become a sad tool of unionism? For its defenders will also grant this: that at least the champions of ecclesiastical indifference and undogmatic unionism make use of the World Council of Churches to carry out their plans. How is it that such a glaring contradiction exists between the carefully crafted theses of the declaration of Toronto 1950 regarding what the World Council is and what it is not, and the reality, at least at the organizational level, in individual countries? There are two reasons for this: its insufficient dogmatic foundation and the fact that the World Council does not take seriously its dogmatic foundation. The theologically meaningless formula that the churches of the World Council confess Jesus Christ as God and Savior is completely inadequate. Why is there no demand for a clear confession of orthodox Christology, of the *Nicaenum* as explicated by the *Chalcedonense*? Why has it surrendered that which in this regard already twenty-five years ago was achieved at Lausanne in the acknowledgment of the *Nicaenum*? Indeed, the reason is that the ancient confession of the church, which still actually expresses the common inheritance of the faith for all churches, was not taken seriously. This can be a sign of

---

close associate when Zoellner facilitated the participation of Friedrich-Wilhelm Krummacher and Theodor Heckel, who began using their influence to restrict Sasse's participation in Faith and Order activities because of their sympathy with National Socialism. And yet Sasse always retained high regard for Zoellner. "I speak as a representative of a generation which is now slowly dying out. It is the generation of Lutheran pastors who after the First World War, when the churches in Germany were reorganized, tried, under the leadership of great churchman like Wilhelm Zoellner, to restore the Lutheran Church in Prussia; who later started, over against the claims of secular political powers on the Church that movement which has beome known as the 'Confessing Church' in Germany" (Sasse to "'The Participants in the 'Interview,'" *Lutheran Witness* [June 1964]). Sasse contributed "Church and Churches" (*Lonely Way* 1:73–87; Huss number 042) to a *festschrift* for Zoellner (*Credo Ecclesiam* [Gütersloh: C. Bertelsmann, 1930]). "My old teacher Zoellner had an axiom: Let us be concerned for the Lutherans; the Reformed are already concerned for themselves" (Sasse to Leiv Aalen, March 3, 1975; in the Harrison Collection). MH

18   Carl Christian Hein (1868–1937), president of the Ohio Synod (1924) and of the ALC (1930), was active in the Lutheran World Convention (s.v. *Christian Cyclopedia*). MH

19   Gustaf Johansson (1844–1930) was educated in Helsinki and Germany. He was professor of ethics and dogmatics at Helsinki (1877–85) and became archbishop in 1899 (s.v. *Christian Cyclopedia*). MH

20   Charles Gore (1853–1932) became the first bishop of Birmingham in 1905. In his later years he wrote in defense of the Christian faith. See *ODCC*, 691. MH

honorableness. It is certainly more honorable not to mention the *Nicaenum* if one believes neither the virgin birth of the Lord nor His bodily resurrection, just to mention these dogmas of the old *Credo*. But in what sense, then, is Christ's divinity confessed? The confessional formula of the constitution of the World Council of Churches has hitherto prevented no church from joining in which the denial of the divinity of the Lord is tolerated and allowed. The Evangelical Church of Switzerland, for instance, in which the affirmation and the denial of the Trinitarian and Christological dogmas have equal right, was given the express assurance that it need express no objections regarding the confessional formula. But if churches are received which expressly declare that they have no official confession of the divinity of Christ, what sense does it make to maintain the formula? This means there will not and cannot be any examination of the faith or heresy trial. It must be left to the individual member churches whether they are prepared to subscribe to the conditions of membership, and they must be free to interpret them as they see fit. But one must also be clear that the entire confessional basis is, for all practical purposes, suspended when its interpretation is left completely free. This is a theology of the "as though," which Archbishop Fisher[21] of Canterbury or Bishop [Garfield Bromley] Oxnam [1887–1972] of the Methodist Episcopal Church in American can tolerate. But Lutheran churchmen may never go along with this. Indeed, one should expect protest against this from Presbyterians and other serious Reformed [Christians]. He who plays with the confession of the church plays with the Word of God, the explication of which the confession desires to be. Perhaps [Rudolf] Bultmann's critique of the confessional basis of the World Council of Churches will provide the occasion for a thoroughgoing re-evaluation of what alone can be the dogmatic basis for cooperative work of churches. According to the Lutheran Confessions, it can be nothing other than the consensus in "the high articles of the divine Majesty," which according to the *Smalcald Articles* form the point of departure for every dialogue between confessional churches. We once said this in vain during the preparation of the World Conference at Amsterdam (*Bericht über Amsterdam*, Bd. I, *The Universal Church in God's Design*, 1948, pp. 196f.). Perhaps the time will come when it will be understood. This is what the Lutheran Church must say to the World Council of Churches. No Church of the Augsburg Confession can with good conscience belong to the World Council before this demand is fulfilled. A true Ecumenical Movement can and will only exist after the confession of the Holy Trinity and the divinity of Jesus Christ has once again become a confession of the heart and not merely a confession of lips, after the truths of the Apostles' and Nicene confessions of the church are again confessed *magno consensu* [with "great agreement"]. Without this faith, without this consensus, the World Council of Churches is that which it *de facto* is today: an arena for

---

21 Geoffrey Francis Fisher (1887–1972) served as chair of the WCC at its inauguration in 1948. See *ODCC*, 614. MH

power-hungry church politicians and for the thoughtless construction of an illusionary future church. And Lutherans ought to keep their distance. By participation they achieve nothing other than that the public pronouncements are written more dubiously and circumspectly. And because they encumber themselves with the guilt of half-believing syncretism and unionism, they surrender the power to bear witness to the truth. They will slowly, but surely, if one may say it, be "deconfessionalized."

4

Deconfessionalization—that is the model which is taking place today in Lutheranism. For the price of deconfessionalization Reformed Christianity today is—as it has been for the most part since the sixteenth century—prepared to acknowledge the Lutheran Church. No one has anything against the Evangelical Lutheran Church taking up its residence in the great house of ecumenical Christianity. Within this house it may foster its own tradition, preserve its confession, nurse its liturgy, its tradition, and pass on its tradition and inheritance to the next generation. That is the position of Lutheranism within the Ecumenical Movement as represented by the World Council, the position of the Lutheran Churches of Germany within the EKiD, the position which the United Lutheran Church and the Augustana Synod accept within the National Council of the Churches of Christ in the USA, which according to the plans of Stanley Jones[22] and others shall soon develop into an American super-EKiD. It is the position which the Lutherans are to have in the building of conceived or planned union churches on the mission fields of the world or in the "Reunited Church" in Australia. One needs to understand the greatness of this view of the church in order to perceive the power which it has come to have over the souls of Protestant Christianity. We have experienced in the political life of the world, since the nineteenth century, the new type of the federation of states in the USA and its parallels (e.g., Brazil) in the British Commonwealth and in the Commonwealths of Australia, Canada, and South Africa. This is also seen in the form the state has taken in Germany from German Federation through the German Reich to the Federal Republic—and perhaps eventually in a united Western Europe. This is also the case in the east in the USSR and the new forms of the Russian Empire. So also Christianity, at least Protestant Christianity, has begun to develop forms of the church parallel [to these new forms of the state]. As the federated state so also the federated church solves the problem of how to bring into harmony with each other unity and diversity, ecumenicity and confessionalism. It is all so remarkably "obvious" that the advocates of this view of the church simply cannot conceive of anyone opposing it. They can see in an opposing view only the worst sort of reaction, the pointless attempt to repristinate

---

22   Eli Stanley Jones (1884–1973), a Methodist missionary to India. MH

the past. He who dares to swim against this stream appears in the eyes of the world—the Christian and even Lutheran world—as laughable. No publisher, no journal dares to print such an opposing view. Should anyone ever be of the opinion that this should still be discussed publicly, then "Lutheran" bishops are very anxious to censure such attempts so they do not occur. So let it at least be stated here: this view of the church is once again nothing other than the reflection and transference of secular thought [into the church]. Just because the world today seeks a form of communal life in which smaller communities are "united" or "federated," it need not be the will of God that the church also exist in this way. This is all the more so if it appears that thereby motives are coming to bear other than the needs of communal life. It is a definite view of "Christendom" or of the "Christian religion" which is evidenced in this view of the church. The "confessions" [i.e., denominations] are understood as the great forms in which "Christendom" manifests itself. There is a Catholic and Protestant, Lutheran and Reformed, Methodist and Congregationalist "Christendom." Between these forms there are closer or more distant kinships. There are families and familial similarities. There is the family of the Lutheran Churches and the branch of the family of the Reformed Churches. Even Swedish theology, despite all the Luther scholarship, retains so much residue of Ritschlianism[23] and religio-scientific interpretation of the Christian faith that it cannot shake itself of this schema. Even a man such as Nygren[24] thinks in these categories when he speaks of the position of Lutheranism among the confessions of Christianity. But one need only ask what Luther would say to this in order to grasp the untenableness of this treatment of the question of the various confessions. For Luther the Lutheran Church is not the social form of one of the great forms of the Christian religion which was stamped by the religious experience of a gifted reformer, just as Roman Catholicism for him is not a more or less justifiable form or manifestation of Christendom. Of course, one can also seek to understand the Christian faith in a religio-scientific manner. But in so doing one does not come upon the essence of this faith, the essence of the confession of faith, and the essence of the Church in general. Churches are not plants. Therefore there is no morphology of confessions. Neither are churches families, between which one may fix similarities and dissimilarities. The confession [*Konfession*], the confession of the faith [*Bekenntnis des Glaubens*], is not the expression of religious sentiment. Dogmas are not, as Schleiermacher thought (*Glaubenslehre* par. 15), "comprehensions of the pious Christian condition of the heart presented in language." The Lord Christ had no interest in the pious Christian heart of His apostles when He asked: "Who do you say that I am?" [Matt. 16:15]. There are no true or false

---

23 That is, those who, following Albrecht Ritschl, emphasized ethics and the community and repudiated metaphysics and religious experience. See *ODCC*, 1400. MH

24 Anders Nygren (1890–1978) was professor of systematic theology at Lund (1924–48). He also served as president of the LWF (1947–52) and as bishop of Lund (1948–58) (s.v. *Christian Cyclopedia*). MH

plants, no true and false families, and even the difference between the religious condition of the heart of a Hindu and a Muhammadan cannot be expressed in the categories of "true" and "false." But there are true and false churches. There are Christian dogmas to which the predicate of truth is attached, such as the dogma of the ascension of Christ, and there are anti-Christian heresies, such as the heresy of the assumption of Mary.[25]

This false view of the Christian faith as a religion, which arises in various forms, stands behind the modern idea that various churches [*Konfessionen*] complement one another. Every confession is thus a more or less perfect or imperfect attempt to present the true Christian religion, to realize the one Christendom which stands behind them all. Thus they all belong together, and one must bring them together that they may complement one another. Christ, so it is said, is so great that one single man—indeed, a single church—can never completely understand Him. As a mountain viewed from various vantage points presents completely diverse views, and as the scenes which pass by the individual traveler on either side are necessarily diverse but not false, so it is with the Christian church. They should come together. Each shall keep its uniqueness, each render completely its particular contribution, all the while learning to understand its truth as one form of a truth which is multifaceted. Thus the various "values" are preserved, and nothing gets lost. Thus in the planned "Reunited Church of Australia" the value of infant Baptism and the value of believer's baptism are preserved—one wonders just what "value" will come of the rejection of Baptism by the Quakers. Behind this view stands—this may and must finally be stated calmly—the Masonic theory of the "religion in which we all agree" (Ben Franklin). In the Masonic lodges of Europe and America that religion was fostered which for the Deists of the seventeenth and eighteenth centuries was behind the "positive religions." There were the religions of "true humanity," with their belief in God, the architect of the universe, and in human freedom and the immortality of the soul. This is that mystery religion regarding which one really cannot speak in public ("Wise men are but of one religion, but what this is wise men will never tell," as Shaftesbury[26] said). This is that religion cultivated in the secrecy of the lodge and the principles which Freemasonry has advanced in the world. Just as the history of the German unions cannot be understood without knowledge of the lodge and the connections of the Protestant princely houses to the lodge, so also the modern Ecumenical Movement will not be understood without the participation of the English and, especially, the American lodges. One must know that the archbishop of Canterbury and something like half the English bishops are members of the lodge, as well as the leading men of the free churches. The same applies in the case of the great Reformed Churches

---

25　See above, p. 56 n. 11. MH

26　Anthony Ashley Cooper (1801–85), seventh earl of Shaftesbury, was a social reformer. See *ODCC*, 1492. Sasse's original presents Shaftesbury's words in English. MH

in America. The discussion regarding whether a bishop who claims to be the successor of the apostles can simultaneously belong to an organization which is the successor to the Gnostic sects, begun by a few serious Anglican theologians in the monthly *Theology* a short time ago, was not continued. It will have absolutely no practical consequence for the church. A corresponding motion at the Convocation of Canterbury not to allow the matter to be considered is as "bad in form and content."[27] But it must finally be stated that lodgedom is one of the most powerful factors in the process of the dissolution of confessional consciousness—and indeed not in that it is a form of conspiracy against the church, as was earlier thought. Rather, it is so because Freemasonry, by means of its cultus and its communal life, has created an atmosphere in which men who are well-intentioned have lost the sense for confession and dogma. It could be that the change which appears to have transpired in the confessional consciousness of American Lutherans is connected with the fact that the entire Lutheran Church has been brought up through the process of Americanization in the atmosphere of the lodges and has appropriated their ideas completely unaware. Indeed, these ideas play a great roll in the youth organizations (Boy Scouts). America will never overcome the fact that the lodge stood in as "sponsor" at its founding and at the genesis of the formation of its culture [*Volkstum*].

5

With this the question is posed which the Lutheran Churches have to answer in the year 1952: *Shall the process of deconfessionalization, which world Lutheranism is currently undergoing, continue? Will it be stopped? Can it be stopped?* What will the meeting of the Lutheran World Federation in Hanover mean for this? Is the importance of this question absolutely clear?

Many will not understand this question at all. We are Lutheran Churches, Churches of the Augsburg Confession. We hold fast to this. No other doctrine, such as that of the *Variata*,[28] is valid among us. No other catechism than Luther's shall be used for instruction. But precisely as Lutherans we desire to join with the other Protestant confessions and give expression through cooperative efforts to the great Christian and Protestant commonality which binds us together with other Christians. To be sure, we all know that the boundaries of our church are not the boundaries of the *Una Sancta*. The only thing which we desire to lay aside is the old exclusive confessionalism, which pronounced condemnation upon other churches, something only the odd confessional church did. What we desire is an "inclusive confessionalism," as Edmund Schlink [1903–84] has

---

27 Sasse's original states this in English. MH

28 Philip Melanchthon's (1497–1560) later altered versions of the Augsburg Confession. MH

called the new view for which we strive. To this we counter: We also know that the [Lutheran] church does not coincide with the *Una Sancta*.[29] We also confess the one holy, catholic church, which lives in, with, and under the churches of the world [*Konfessionskirchen*]. Nor do we let fall the judgment of condemnation upon other Christians and other churches. We testify with the fathers of the Formula of Concord that the condemnation formulas—the *damnant* ["they condemn"], the *improbant secus docentes* ["they reject those who teach"]—do not mean "persons who err out of simplicity and do not blaspheme the truth of the divine Word, but much less entire churches within or without the Holy Empire of the German Nation" (foreword to the FC, *Bek. Schr.*, anniversary ed., p. 756, Müller, p. 16); rather, [they mean] the heresies and their stiff-necked advocates who force such matters in our churches. We, too, are prepared for every necessary *cooperatio* with other Christians, so far as is possible without denial of the truth. There is one thing we cannot accept. We can under no circumstances view false doctrine, contrary to Scripture, as of equal legitimacy with pure doctrine or tolerate it in the church only as a hypothetical possibility. For this reason we have, as has the orthodox church of every age, no *communicatio in sacris cum haereticis* [literally, "no fellowship in holy things with heretics"]. If this is called intolerance, then we confess that we are intolerant people in the same sense the apostles were (1 Tim. 6:20f.; Titus 4:10; 1 John 4:1ff.) and as was Luther. But we assert that this "intolerance"—which is an abomination to Deists of every age because they know nothing nor can know anything of ultimate truth, because they do not know Jesus Christ as the truth in person—is of the essence of genuine Christian faith. Without this "intolerance" over against heresy there is no real Lutheranism. Without the condemnation formulas at the end of the individual articles, the *Augustana* loses its meaning. Without the "they reject those who teach" [*improbant secus docentes*], there is no Lutheran doctrine of the Supper. Without serious discipline with regard to the Supper, so that only those are allowed to come to the Lord's Table who know what is received there and desire to receive it, there is no Sacrament of the Altar. This is not Luther's discovery. This was ever so in the church since the days of the apostles. The question to world Lutheranism today is whether these principles still obtain [*gelten*]. They do if the Confession obtains. They are an element of the Confession. It is certainly not left to our pleasure whether we would continue to allow them to obtain, for then we would already have fallen away from the Confession.

That is the enormous seriousness of the decision which confronts the Lutheran Churches of the world this year. It is the ecclesiastico-historical decision of Hanover. The men who have convened the World Federation in Hanover need to be clear on just what accountability they bear, not only to their churches as they exist today but also to the orthodox church of all times. [They bear an

---

29 Sasse's original here is certainly an unintentional error: "We also know that the Church of Christ does not coincide with the *Una Sancta*." MH

accountability] to the fathers who can no longer speak to us except through the confessions which they wrote, and to those as yet unborn who cannot yet speak but will finally speak at the last judgment. God grant that when they do speak it will not be as our accusers! Lutheranism desires to speak at this conference as "a responsible church,"[30] a church which is conscious of its responsibility. May it only be conscious of this responsibility! Whether the session is a success or failure will not be decided by what is said by the contemporaries or the world press, the other churches, the great publicity, the politicians, the citizens, the workers, or the church governments and synods to whom the delegates will have to give account. Nor [will its success be determined by] what is said by the congregations and pastors to whom they will report. [The success or failure of this conference will be determined] by what will be said at the last judgment.

The first thing which Hanover owes to the Christian and to the Lutheran world is a clear, unmistakable statement regarding *what a Church of the Lutheran Confession is*. We repeat thereby a question which we posed already last year (Letter 19: "Worldwide Lutheranism on the Way to Hanover").[31] The World Federation owes Christianity an interpretation of its articles regarding its confessional basis. Is a church a Lutheran Church according to the meaning of the constitution if in it there can be a teaching [enjoying the status of] *publica doctrina* other than the doctrine of the *Invariata*?[32] Can a church, or a church federation (such as the *Federacao Sinodal* in Brazil), enjoy the full rights of membership, and thereby render decisions on what is Lutheran and what is not, if this fellowship is just beginning, and has the intent over a given period of time, to establish the Lutheran Confession as the sole legal *publica doctrina* [within it]? Can confirmation [of membership] be imparted on the basis of a confession to be established later? And if the case is made that, on the basis of pedagogical and missiological grounds, they must already be accepted, why, then, with the full rights [of membership]? If one desires to lead churches to the Lutheran confession, which is in fact a worthy and great task, to the accomplishment of which we would all readily lend a hand, why is there not a sort of catechumenate which precedes? Is the situation into which other churches are brought by this practice unclear? But even without reference to the case of the Brazilians, the question must be posed as to what a Lutheran Church is and what it is not in the view of the World Federation. What does appeal to the *Augustana* mean, and what does it not mean?

The *second* thing which must be decided, and which must be answered in connection with the first question, is the relationship of the Lutheran World Federation to *the union churches* which claim to be Lutheran Churches in the sense of the *Confessio Augustana* and the constitution of the LWF. Are they to

---

30 Sasse's original states this in English. MH

31 See *Letters to Lutheran Pastors* 1:404–32. MH

32 I.e., the document presented in 1530 to the Diet of Augsburg. MH

be included in the LWF? The entire problem of the union longs for a solution. It is very simple to determine whether a church's constitution grants it the legal character of a Lutheran or a united church. One hundred thousand Silesians with a few hundred pastors were taken into the Lutheran Church of Bavaria from the United Church of Silesia. In what sense are they now Lutherans? To be sure, they already had Luther's catechism. But they interpreted it, and continue to interpret it today, in the sense of the union, [which grants] fellowship in the Supper with non-Lutherans. The Bavarian Church does not officially grant this. Since it now officially tolerates this—it finally even proclaimed this at the colloquium and even placed a member of the Breslau United Church government into a unique position of church administration—it has *de facto* changed its confession. There no longer is any Lutheran territorial church in Germany in which fellowship in the Supper is not practiced with non-Lutherans—and, indeed, with the full knowledge of the church government. This is so even in Neuendettelsau.[33] With what right does anyone demand of the Christian world that it respect the boundaries which are now only a juridical fiction? What a profound untruth it is to continue to maintain that fellowship in the Supper is demanded by emergency circumstances. Was it an emergency that Communion fellowship in the Christian Student Movement, without respect to differences, was brought about in all evangelical student congregations and made the firm custom of the entire society of young theologians except for the free churches? The German Lutheran territorial churches have placed terrible guilt upon themselves through the profound untruthfulness with which they have dealt with the question of Communion fellowship. May this guilt not become the curse also of the LWF. The Lutheran Churches of the world need a clear directive regarding what is asserted by the Lutheran Confession regarding Communion fellowship and its boundaries. It is a burning question for all Lutheran Churches.

The third thing, which must be decided this year, is the question whether the Lutheran Churches are ready to deal in a worthy manner with the *doctrinal differences* which obtain between them. There is no purpose in resigning ourselves to the illusion that there already is complete unity among the Christian churches which call themselves "Lutheran," and that only a few intransigent, hyperorthodox [churches] are destroying the peace by making their private theology norm for the church and its doctrine. As one who has struggled for many years for the theological unification of Lutheranism, I can only express the conviction that serious and very deep differences of opinion regarding the meaning of the Lutheran Confessions make a complete unification of the Lutheran Churches impossible at the present time. This may be deplored (we all do deplore it), but nothing is helped when we shut our eyes to the reality of this problem. It is an unspeakable problem, a real tragedy, that this Lutheranism, with the seventh article of the *Augustana*, steps before world Christianity and desires to instruct it

---

33　Löhe's church. MH

regarding what true unity of the church is and that it is sufficient that the Gospel be preached unanimously according to a pure understanding of it and the Sacraments be administered according to the institution of Christ. We must say this to the Christian world though we hear the answer: "Physician, heal thyself!" [Luke 4:23]. We must be clear regarding what lack of credibility we Lutherans give to our message regarding the unity of the church. Now, it is indeed the case that the Reformed Churches have no right to boast of a greater unity. Quite to the contrary! But they, too, indeed know nothing of the great *satis est* of AC VII. This distressing situation of Lutheranism, its splintering over doctrinal questions, exists in every part of the earth. Its consequence is that loveless manner of speaking of each other, that complaining of one church over against the other, which is a sickness which results from schism. This circumstance, however, will not be overcome simply by acting as though full unity already exists. The unity of American Lutheranism can be achieved, but only through serious doctrinal discussion—a point regarding which [LCMS President] Dr. Behnken is doubtless correct over against his colleague of the ULC, Dr. Fry.[34] To be sure, this doctrinal discussion cannot simply be the repetition of discussions which, over the course of several generations, were conducted with the same arguments [and] always with the same unfortunate outcome. Today we must move beyond theological schools discussing matters on the basis of the thoughts, categories, and prejudices of the nineteenth century to the doctrine of the Lutheran Reformation and the doctrine of the New Testament, which we in many regards—in no way every way—understand better than our fathers one hundred years ago. By so doing we will then by all means have to consider that in the church only that theology avails which is rooted in the life of the church and is realized in the life of the church. Only the doctrine of the Sacrament is correct and has the power of conviction which is the expression of the sacramental life of the parish. Thus doctrinal statements as such still mean nothing if they are in no way practiced in the life of the church. The theologians of the LWF must work on the basis of this insight. The commission's work on the theological document which will be placed before the full assembly indicates already fortuitous advancement. We repeat once more here what we pointed out already in Letter 19 when we made reference to the Faith and Order Movement and to the Bad Boll discussions.[35] The Lutheran Churches of the world need coordination of the many doctrinal discussions which today are occurring in many countries simultaneously, independent of each other, and under the difficult conditions of the times, often with insufficient personnel and practical means. It would take at least five years' work to begin to deal with the most important differences separating Lutheran Churches. This would take new means and new viewpoints, so that the

---

34 Franklin Clark Fry (1900–1968) served as ULCA president (1945–62), LCA president (1962–68), and LWF president (1957–63). MH

35 See *Letters to Lutheran Pastors* 1:404–32, especially pp. 409, 431. MH

churches would come to a thorough understanding or to a separation into two large groups, which is completely possible. But the unification conferences at which there are only speeches regarding the necessity of unification and regarding the insignificance of doctrinal differences are not worth the cost of travel. They would serve only toward the ever further advancement of the deconfessionalization of Lutheranism and its dissolution into the broth of the substanceless "Reunited Church" of the future. Should it turn out that the theological commission of the LWF attain more than beautiful formulas which only conceal differences, should it produce a document which finds the consensus of many Lutherans, then one might be able to expand it over the span of many years and make it a representative working commission, which is organized so that every Lutheran Church can take part with a good conscience. It would have to possess enough independence that it were not simply an instrument of church governments and have to work under their censure.

The fourth thing which must be clarified in Hanover is the relationship between the LWF and the World Council of Churches. If the LWF is to be done away with, then it should be made the Lutheran department of the WCC. If it is to be maintained, then it should have complete organizational separation from the World Council. One must be clear that there are a series of Lutheran Churches which belong to the World Council, and there are others which under no circumstances will join it. If the Lutheran Churches are to be brought together into the LWF, then this bone of contention must be dealt with. The LWF as such cannot become a department of the World Council of Churches. And it must never give the appearance that it is. A business connection may exist, and this will obtain in many practical matters. But it is unbearable that the LWF already is housed in the WCC building in Geneva, especially when this sharing of living quarters leads also to joint worship [*Hausandachten*]. Also, that the general secretary of the LWF received his salary as an appointee of the WCC was intolerable. With the death of Dr. Michelfelder[36] this will hopefully now cease. It would be best for the LWF to move its headquarters from Geneva to a country in which the Lutheran Church is not merely a foreigner, despite all the advantages Geneva affords for international authorities. It should be left to the individual churches as to how they relate to the World Council, and these developments should be left to them. Indeed, the World Council is today already a *de facto* agent of the Reformed and United Churches, for the fragments of the Orthodox churches which have fled to the West do not really represent orthodoxy. And the Church of Greece, which is the sole larger Eastern church in the WCC, is connected to the World Council more through political interests than churchly interests.

---

36 Sylvester Clarence Michelfelder (1889–1951) of the Ohio Synod was the representative from the Lutheran World Convention at the 1945–46 WCC in Geneva. He played a prominent role in the formation of the LWF (s.v. *Christian Cyclopedia*). MH

The fifth matter which Hanover should bring about is a consideration of the individual Lutheran Churches regarding their connection to heterodox churches. The principle should apply that no Churches of the Augsburg Confession may enter into ties with other churches which would estrange them from their own [Lutheran] sister churches. This applies above all to the Scandinavian Churches, such as the Swedish Church in its relationship with the Church of England. We German Lutherans, who once experienced the comedy of the Prussian-English bishopric of Jerusalem and the attempt to introduce apostolic succession at the back door of Germany, have never taken seriously the attempt of Anglicanism to achieve church fellowship with the Nordic Lutherans. The entire matter, moreover, has a political taste to it like the connections between the churches and states of England and Greece. Apostolic succession has, for a Lutheran Church such as that of Sweden, a completely different meaning than for the Anglicans. For Lutherans it is only one of the human arrangements in the church, and therefore belongs in the realm of *adiaphora*.[37] We Lutherans cannot take a position in the controversy regarding the validity of Anglican ordinations. Whether the archbishop of Canterbury or the cardinal-archbishop of Westminster, together with their respective bishops, are *legitime* successors of the apostles in England we cannot say. In all plausibility neither of these parties can make this claim. The true successors of the apostles in England are those who proclaim the pure doctrine of the apostles, whoever they may be. Neither can we grant our Anglican friends that if today one of the great archbishops of Canterbury of the Middle Ages, such as Anselm [ca. 1033–1109], were to appear that he would find and recognize his church in present-day Canterbury. [We assert this], just as we would not admit that Luther, if he were to return today, would recognize Otto Dibelius, the current bishop of Brandenburg, as his bishop and go to Communion in the City Church at Wittenberg. No Lutheran Church which still takes its catechism seriously can have fellowship in the Lord's Supper in any form, even only in special cases, with the Church of England. We cannot send the members of our congregations to an altar (if an altar can be spoken of in the Anglican Church, for a real altar is indeed forbidden there) where every communicant must read in his *Book of Common Prayer* the words that the natural body and blood of Christ are in heaven and not here, and [where it is asserted] that the body of Christ would not be a true human body if He were to be in more than one place at the same time. So long as this Black Rubric[38] stands in the Anglican Communion liturgy, there can be no Communion fellowship between us and the

---

37 I.e., something neither commanded nor forbidden. MH

38 The name now commonly given to the "Declaration on Kneeling" printed at the end of the service of Holy Communion in the *Book of Common Prayer*. This declaration is first found in the 1552 edition. The expression "Black Rubric" dates only from the nineteenth century when the practice of printing the *Book of Common Prayer* with the rubrics in red was introduced, and because the "Declaration" was not a rubric, it was printed in black. See *ODCC*, 213. MH

Anglicans, not to mention all the other hindrances which make it impossible for us, despite all the great things which it has, to rediscover in the Church of England the church of the Gospel.

The sixth and final matter which we request of Hanover is that Luther's first thesis not be forgotten. The Lutheran Church, the Church of the Reformation, is a church of *repentance*. She renders herself unbelievable when she speaks to the world and to Christianity, when she calls both to repentance, without considering that judgment begins in the house of God. The judgment of God has come upon the Lutheran Church. The millions of Lutherans driven from their native lands bear witness to this. The glorious churches, which lie in rubble and ashes, bear witness to this. Luther once answered the question why lightning had a predilection for striking church steeples. He explained that there is no place, not even a whorehouse, in which so much sin takes place through the transgression of the First and Second Commandments and through impure doctrine which robs the Lord Christ of His honor. We will not recount here all the sins for which our church would have to repent, though it would perhaps be necessary. For the worst sign of divine judgment is perhaps the ease and glibness with which we superficialize the accusations which are raised against our church, which may at least bear a kernel of truth, even where we must rightly counter such accusations. Instead of the many attempts at self-justification and instead of the complaints against others, a serious self-evaluation might occur which could take place under the theme: "The great apostasy—our apostasy." A great and solemn Divine Service of repentance should not be missing among the arrangements at Hanover. It could be the very soul of the entire session, the beginning of a genuine renewal.

6

Finally, honored brothers, allow me to raise a question directed to us all. Who actually represents the Lutheran Churches of the world today? Who is it who speaks and acts in the name of the churches? Whoever it may be, there are two entities in our time which certainly do not do so. It is not the *Christian congregation* [*Gemeinde*]. And it is not the *pastoral office*. Neither will be represented in Hanover. Naturally the parishioners of the Hanover area will flock to the capital and take part by the thousands in the mass events. But they will be represented as little as the many pastors who will come to Hanover for the decisive sessions of the World Federation. Indeed, that would be logistically completely impossible, even if it were the desire of all participants for the pastorate and church membership to take part as much as possible. And here we come up against an important phenomenon of more recent church history, which must be much more carefully noted than has been the case. The development of modern superchurches [*Massenkirchen*] and the application of technical means for bringing together, influencing, and leading men, in regard to the church, has directly and strongly displaced two significant factors which together, according to Lutheran doctrine, fulfill the proper life of the church, the *congregatio sanctorum* ["the congregation of the saints"]. These are the congregation [*Gemeinde*] and the *ministerium ecclesiasticum*, the pastoral office [*Pfarramt*]. Both no longer take part in the great ecclesiastical decisions of our time, at least in Europe. Any knowledge the congregations have obtained of the EKiD and the VELKD is from the ecclesiastical press. Most of the congregational members have no idea what these are. They were not asked. Neither were the pastors asked whether they approved of these decisions. And they were crucial decisions rendered regarding their office and its obligations. They must be satisfied that everything has taken place in a lawful manner. The territorial synods [*Landessynode*] prepared a corresponding resolution. In Bavaria, this synod, if I am not mistaken, consists of some seventy to eighty elected members. These individuals represent well over a million church members. There is no court of appeal against this *ecclesia repraesentativa*. Perhaps there is no other possible way to govern such an enormous apparatus. But then one should not be amazed when the general priesthood of believers dies. Nor are the pastors questioned [regarding what takes place]. They are instructed, schooled, and, if necessary, warned and punished. But a small group of men render decisions for the consciences of thousands of bearers of the office. Is it an accident that in the more recent history of the church the pastoral office in no way plays the role which was self-evident in previous centuries? There are still pastors in Europe: in Scotland, in Holland, in France, in Switzerland. These are men who are still responsible for ecclesiastical decisions, who still represent their churches. In Sweden, in Denmark, and now also in Germany, the church is represented by bishops and the other "church leaders." The individual pastor is nothing. He can obtain something only as part of a large group, such as the pastoral conference [*Pfarrerverein*]. When the bishop has won his pastoral conference for something, then everything is in order. But the pastoral conference has made no ordination vow, thus it cannot break it. And the bishop? We were so proud in Germany when we again had bishops. An entire theology of the office of bishop has been developed. The enchantment with the title of bishop is so great that even the Lutheran Churches of America are playing with the idea of granting it to their presidents occupying chief offices. It has thus far broken down over the episcopal office as an essentially lifelong office. But one must be clear that the essence of the bishop's office encompasses the episcopal functions of ordination and visitation with his legitimate pastoral office. Even to the time of Augustine, "bishop" was the title of the local pastor. The characteristic of the modern territorial bishop in Germany and, on a certain level, the office of a president of one of the churches in America which consist of many synods is, however, this: he exercises neither official pastoral nor episcopal functions or only does so in exceptional cases. In Bavaria the circuit deacons [*Kreisdekane*], and in Hanover the territorial superintendents, are the real bishops. They ordain and visit. The bishop sweeps over the entire church and its affairs [*Kirchentum*] as "church leader." This was perhaps a necessary development. At any rate, such an organism must be governed. The real tragedy, however, is that this [development intended] as a support for the spiritual office has actually served to bring about the broader secularization of the church.

One must have this tragic development before one's eyes in order to grasp what is the duty of the Lutheran pastor. We must, honored brothers, seek to save the office of the Lutheran pastor which threatens to go under in modern ecclesial secularism, so far as this is humanly possible. The highest virtue of the pastor today appears to be silence, even in once-so-democratic America. The modern type of the Lutheran pastor began in Germany in the First World War, when so many theologians became reserve officers. In America it began in the Second World War, when so many pastors became chaplains in the military. Here they learned, along with the virtues of being an officer, also the virtue of silent obedience. But every virtue has its downside, and the downside of mute obedience can be that the pastor becomes a mute dog, that he become silent even where it is of his office, mandated by the Lord Christ, to speak. It appears that much of the difficulty, which has come upon the Lutheran Church has its origin in this false silence. Let us in this fateful year of the Lutheran Church, in view of the threatening deconfessionalization of Lutheranism, fearlessly say what must be said also to the great and powerful in the church. We do not know for how long we will be able to continue to do so.

⟨⟩

In the communion of the faith, I greet you for the new year,

Your
Hermann Sasse

Historical Context

Sasse notes his effort already in 1937 at an apologia for the doctrine of the Lord's Supper.[1] *At the center of Sasse's battles for the doctrine of church fellowship of the Lutheran Confessions was his repeated treatment the Lord's Supper—most thoroughly in* This Is My Body: Luther's Contention for the Real Presence in the Sacrament of the Altar *(Augsburg, 1959). This book remains the greatest defense of Luther's doctrine of the Supper available in English. The following essay is a summary of the book's argument. One comment about how the New Testament and Lutheran doctrine of the Supper had waned struck me as I read this piece again. This warning should be well noted by and for seminaries: "The men in our church who have applied themselves to the New Testament were not well-versed in Luther and Lutheran dogmatics, and vice versa." MH*

February 3, 1952[2]

Prof. H. Sasse
41 Buxton Street
North Adelaide, South Australia

Dear Dr. [Herman A.] Preus,

. . . I am enclosing the script of No. 23 of my *Briefe*: "Der Schriftgrund der lutherischen Abendmahlslehre." This will come out in German in March. I wrote it as a sort of contribution to the discussion on the Lord's Supper in the *Lutheran Outlook*. Papers are coming very slowly from America. Thus I heard of that debate only a fortnight ago. . . . The situation is very much the same as in 1937 in Germany when we Lutherans had to defend the Lutheran doctrine on the Supper . . . .

H. Sasse

---

1   See "Church and Lord's Supper," in *Lonely Way* 1:369–429. MH
2   Feuerhahn/H. A. Preus Correspondence. MH

twenty-three

The Scriptural Basis for the Lutheran Doctrine of the Lord's Supper

TRANSLATED BY ANDREW SMITH

Early February 1952[1]

Prof. D. Theol. Hermann Sasse
41 Buxton Street
North Adelaide, South Australia

Dear Brothers in the Office!

1

The immediate occasion on which I again will say a word about the question of Holy Communion, and thereby finish that which I began to say in Letter 6 ("The Lord's Supper in the Lutheran Church"),[2] is presented by the situation of American Lutheranism. If the indications are correct, the Lutherans in America face a question which is similar to the question which was put to us in Germany in the second phase of the church struggle. At that time, in May 1937, at Halle, the Confessing Synod of the Evangelical Church of the Old Prussian Union, under the leadership of Hans Asmussen[3] and his theological friends of Lutheran

---

1   *BLP* 23: *Der Schriftgrund der lutherischen Abendmahlslehre* (North Adelaide, February 1952). The original was published in *LuBl* 4, no. 26 (1953). Huss number 292. MH

2   See *Letters to Lutheran Pastors* 1:87–99. MH

3   Driven from his pastoral office by the Nazis, Asmussen (1898–1968) became a member of the Confessing Church. He served as president of the EKiD (1946–48). Along with Karl Barth, he was an architect of the Barmen Declaration. See *RGG*[3] 1:649. MH

and Reformed heritage from the school of Karl Barth, proclaimed altar fellowship between Lutherans and the Reformed.[4] They gave it theological basis by noting that both denominations agreed that Jesus Christ Himself is the gift of grace given in Holy Communion, and that the differences existing between them concerned only "the way and manner in which the Lord shares Himself in Communion." First Corinthians 10:16 was cited as a text representing their common conviction. No mention was made of the preceding verses and their meaning. This conclusion corresponded so closely to the prevailing mood in the church and to the general theological convictions of evangelical pastors and professors of theology inside and outside the Confessing Church that the few Lutherans who raised objections at that time to this official renewing of Crypto-Calvinism, verbally and in print, were lonely people. People couldn't believe it. They couldn't understand that there were still theologians who found Luther's eucharistic doctrine in Holy Scripture. They could see it only as a hopeless renewing of a dogmatic view which had finally been conquered, and which had long since been refuted by New Testament scholars. Indeed, they allowed it to be known that they doubted the integrity of the conviction of such theologians. In the fifteen years which have passed since then, a few things have changed. There are more outspoken voices professing the Lutheran eucharistic doctrine, even if essentially only as a theological theory but without its practical consequences, as the Lutheran church, faithful to its Confession, has always maintained them. And perhaps one may at least get to hear about the theological metamorphosis, if the LWF should find time at its meeting in Hanover to discuss the corresponding theses of its theological committee. Then the depth of the differences of opinion which exist within the Lutheran Church, among each individual church regarding the doctrine of the Lord's Supper, will be evident. They became visible when the introduction of a eucharistic prayer into the Communion liturgy, under high church influence, was the object of debate. Anamnesis[5] and Epiclesis,[6] patterned according to the Catholic and the Eastern Church and more or less adjusted, where needed, to the Lutheran doctrine, were

---

4   "The 'Consensus on the Doctrine of the Gospel' that was adopted by the Halle Synod was based upon the preparatory paper given by Asmussen. The Consensus began with the claim that the Barmen Declaration 'bears witness to the indispensable presupposition without which the confessions that are valid among us cannot be rightly taught and truly confessed.' This meant that the Lutheran Confessions should be reinterpreted to make them agree with the Barmen Declaration, which strict Confessional Lutherans rejected" (Lowell Green, *Lutherans Against Hitler: The Untold Story* [St. Louis: Concordia, 2007], 194). MH

5   A Greek word meaning "memorial" that is part of the Words of Institution and is used by liturgists for the commemoration of the Passion, resurrection, and ascension of Christ. Most Catholic liturgies include this in a eucharistic prayer. See *ODCC*, 57. MH

6   A Greek word used for the eucharistic prayer in Catholic and Eastern Churches that invokes the Holy Spirit upon the elements so that they become the body and blood of Christ. MH

suggested and in part already in use. Even in the Missouri Synod, otherwise not inclined to novelties, high church tendencies appeared. But as in Europe, so, too, in America, the rule is valid that liturgical novelties indicate a crisis in doctrine. Where pastors and congregations are no longer in agreement with the classic liturgy of their church, the deeper cause tends to be that the teaching contained in this liturgy is no longer understood. If one still knew what the consecration according to Lutheran teaching means, then one would not call for an Epiclesis, which has its origin in an entirely different understanding of the real presence. And the manifold attempts of the Berneuchen Movement[7] in Germany, and its parallels in other regions of Lutheranism, to renew the Communion service in some sense—in a thoroughly Lutheran sense, as they say—toward the thoughts of the sacrifice of the Mass are the most certain sign that the Lord's Supper of the Lutheran Reformation is no longer understood. So the *representatio* of the sacrifice at Golgotha becomes for many the pattern and practice, substituting for the true, the "real and substantial," presence of that which Christ gave for us, once and for all times (Heb. 7:27; 9:12; 10:10), namely, His body and blood. And that which the human *does*—namely, the thanksgiving, the "eucharistic high prayer," or even the adoration of the eucharistic Christ—becomes the meaning and center of the celebration and overshadows that which the human *receives*. The "for the forgiveness of sins" recedes and is no longer seen as the actual promise of the Sacrament—it is as though the modern human carries his deep aversion to the Reformation teachings about sin and justification even up to the altar of the Lutheran Church. But if that happens already in the green wood of the liturgical movement—whose profound goodness is in this: that it wants to take the Sacrament of the Altar seriously again and regain for it its lost place in the life of the church—what shall we expect from the dry wood of theological halfway education and of the poor, ignorant Christian people, who seem to determine the form of every church in these times?

It is unnecessary to count up here all the sad documents of the lack of understanding about the Sacrament of the Altar, documents which now in our American sister churches are becoming ever more common. An especially crass case was the essay by a retired pastor of the Augustana Church—the earlier Swedish Augustana Synod—which was published by *The Lutheran Outlook* in October 1951 (no. 10, p. 300), the organ of the American Lutheran Conference, which comprises the Lutheran "middle." Under the title "An Inquiry into the Lord's Supper," the author, Olof H. Nelson, seeks to show that the teaching of Luther and of the Lutheran Confessions about the real presence of the body and blood of Christ does not agree with Holy Scripture. He ascertains, as the biblical meaning of the Words of Institution, that

---

7   A high church Protestant liturgical movement in Germany led by Wilhelm Stählin (1883–1975). MH

the broken bread is a symbol of the body of Jesus, broken on the cross, and the fruit of the vine is a symbol of His blood, shed in suffering and death. [p. 301]

Indeed, the author goes yet further than that which Zwingli conceded in Article 15 at Marburg, and which all the Reformed confess, in that he even denies any spiritual benefit [to the Sacrament]: "There is no biblical ground for the belief that anyone receives the body and blood of Christ in the Lord's Supper, either orally or by faith" (p. 303), because, according to Nelson, John 6 does not concern itself with Communion; it remains a purely memorial meal. It does not interest us here how the author comes to this conclusion, especially because new research on this topic is fully unknown to him, and he bases his view on long outdated union writings of the previous century. The discussion, announced by the publisher of *Outlook*, Dr. Dell of Capital Theological Seminary of the American Lutheran Church in Columbus, Ohio, will have in the meantime already taken place.[8] What is important for us here is the fact that such voices are growing ever more common in American Lutheranism. We aren't telling any secrets if we determine that since World War I, which brought such a deep metamorphosis in the American people, in the Lutheran Churches in America, the older traditional teachings of the church have fallen into a process of dissolution. This process began slowly at first and was barely noticeable, but today, frankly, proceeds with frightening speed. That which was at the beginning of the century a clear possession, the doctrinal content of the Book of Concord, is now suddenly placed in question, though, to be sure, not in the same way in all churches. It has become clear that a teaching such as the Lutheran eucharistic doctrine cannot simply be passed on from generation to generation like an old family heirloom. Our American brothers are today experiencing what the European Lutherans in a most painful history have had to experience again and again: that a generation in the church is only firmly founded in the confession of the fathers when it has had to again win this confession in deep scriptural research and in serious wrestling against the errors of the time. This is valid especially, too, for the teaching about the Lord's Supper. So we will best serve today's task if we say something about the scriptural basis of this teaching.

2

Nobody should ever have doubted that the final and deepest reason for Luther's eucharistic doctrine is an exegetical reason. It is not the former Roman priest and

---

8   Sasse later lectured at the seminary in Columbus while teaching in Springfield, Illinois. "In consultation with several of our faculty, we think it would be well if you would give your lecture on 'The Present-Day Roman Catholic Doctrine of the Church' in your morning session and the lecture on 'Peter and Paul' at the faculty group meeting . . . . I will ask Dr. Schuh to come to our seminary for the morning lecture . . ." (E. C. Fendt, president, to Sasse, February 26, 1965; in the Harrison Collection). MH

monk, not the theologian educated in the school of Ockham[9] and of Ockham's consubstantiation[10] doctrine, but rather it is Martin Luther, the researcher of the Scriptures, who recognized that the words "This is My body" cannot be understood as a metaphor. Certainly, Luther had lived in the sacramental piety of the Roman Catholic Church, and the *mysterium tremendum* ["the mystery at which we must tremble"] of the presence of Christ in the host had shaped his belief about the Lord's Supper. But he would have thrown off this Catholic view about the real presence with just as much energy as the thought of the sacrifice of the Mass if the Word of God, which was for him everything, did not force him to hold onto it firmly. The man for whom it was one of his heaviest burdens that he had for fifteen years almost every day held private Mass—and thereby had practiced vain idolatry because he indeed in such Masses had "worshiped not Christ's body and blood, but rather vain bread and wine, and had facilitated others' worship of them" (*Von der Winkelmesse und Pfaffenweihe* [*The Private Mass and the Consecration of Priests*] [1533], Aland 770; WA 38:197 [AE 38:149])— this man would have gladly accepted, as he writes to the residents of Strassburg in 1524, the symbolic interpretation of the Words of Institution, because he thereby could have given the "biggest kick" to the papacy at the beginning of the Reformation. The symbolic interpretation was also made attractive to him by other means and, to be sure, by deeper thinkers than Karlstadt[11]—among them even Cornelius Hoen,[12] from whom Zwingli got it. "But," he continues,

> I have been captured, and cannot escape. The text is too powerful there and doesn't want to be torn out of its meaning with words. [*Ein Brief an die Christen zu Strassburg* (*Letter to the Christians at Strassburg*) (1524), Aland 703, WA 15:394.19 (AE 40:68)]

It wasn't slavish literalness either and his own idea when Luther, in Marburg, wrote the words "This is My body" on the table with chalk. He, who in such discussion was inclined by nature to compromise, wanted to remind himself of the

---

9   William of Ockham (1285–1347) was a philosopher and theologian. "The difference between the biblical use of language and the metaphysical or philosophical terminology is of immediate significance for the general separation of theology and philosophy, which Luther sought to carry through" (Bengt Hägglund, *Theologie und Philosophie bei Luther und in der Occamistischen Tradition: Luthers Stellung zur Theorie von der Doppelten Wahrheit* [Lund: Gleerup, 1955]). MH

10 Falsely attributed to Luther, "consubstantiation" views the bread and body and wine and blood as forming one substance (a third substance) in Communion, or that body and blood are present, like bread and wine, in a natural manner (s.v. *Christian Cyclopedia*). MH

11 Andreas Rudolf Bodenstein von Karlstadt (ca. 1480–1541) was a professor at Wittenberg and supported Luther in his early reforming efforts directed at the indulgence question. Eventually Karlstadt would reject the Sacraments and abolish ceremonies, views Luther opposed. Karlstadt was expelled from Saxony in 1524 and became associated with the Swiss reformers (s.v. *Christian Cyclopedia*). MH

12 Cornelius Hoen (d. 1524) was a Dutch humanist. See Sasse's treatment in *This Is My Body*, pp. 122ff. MH

boundary which was set in this conversation, which was actually conducted in all love and friendliness. In the deciding moment, he lifted the tablecloth and read the words aloud. Then he added:

> Here for everyone is our Scripture. You have not forced it away from us, as you hoped. We need no other. My dearest sirs, because the text of my Lord Jesus Christ remains intact: "This is My body," so I can truly not get past it, but must confess and believe that the body of Christ is there. [Walther Köhler, *Das Marburger Religionsgespräch 1529: Versuch einer Rekonstruktion* (1929), p. 31]

Whoever knows about the Marburg disputation not merely from a summary of church history, but rather whoever has read the old reports openly, he must admit, on whichever side he may stand, that the man who then defended the literal meaning of the Words of Institution did so as an exegete and with exegetical reasons. And this same image arises, if one reads Luther's major writings about the disagreements regarding the Lord's Supper, e.g., *Against the Heavenly Prophets* (1524/1525);[13] *That the Words of Christ, "This Is My Body," Still Stand Firm against the Fanatics [Schwärmergeister]* (1527);[14] and, best of all, *Confession concerning Christ's Supper* (1528).[15] Why these major writings of Luther, perhaps the most significant next to *De Servo Arbitrio [Bondage of the Will]*, are missing in the Munich edition[16] and in the English Holman edition[17] is difficult—or perhaps easy?—to understand. In this way, then, even the pastors in Germany and America who still reach for Luther's works will be unacquainted with Luther's exegeses of the Words of Institution in their context and at their basis. One cannot wonder, then, that the old slogans of Reformed polemics about the dogmatic prejudices of Luther and about the exegetical openness of Zwingli, about the loveless obstinacy of the German reformer and the loving broadheartedness of the Swiss reformer, belong today to the inventory of "Lutheran" studies and editorial offices. It was Luther and his colleagues who, after the collapse of negotiations, at the wish of the duke, still did everything to maintain the greatest quantity of unity which was possible in the discussions about the Marburg articles. It was Luther who suggested a formulation of unification in which the real presence was taught in such a mild form that there was hope that Zwingli could accept it:

---

13 *Wider die himmlischen Propheten*, Aland 588, WA 18:62–125, 134–214 (AE 40:79–223). MH

14 *Das diese Wort Christi "Das ist mein Leib" noch fest stehen, wider die Schwärmgeister*, Aland 679, WA 23:64–283 (AE 37:13–150). MH

15 *Vom Abendmahl Christi Bekenntnis*, Aland 2, WA 26:261–509 (AE 37:161–372). MH

16 Martin Luther, *Ausgewählte Werke*, 3rd ed., ed. H. H. Borcherdt and Georg Merz (Munich: Chr. Kaiser, 1948–65). MH

17 Martin Luther, *Works of Martin Luther*, ed. Henry Eyster Jacobs and Adolph Spaeth (Philadelphia: A. J. Holman, 1915–32). MH

> We confess that the body and blood of the Lord is truly thus: *substantive et essentialiter* but not *quantitative, qualitative,* and *localiter* present and presented. [Bucer, as quoted in Köhler, op. cit., p. 134]

As W[alther] Köhler reports in his biography of the Swiss reformer (*Huldrych Zwingli*, 1943, p. 211) on the basis of [Martin] Bucer's [1491–1551] testimony, it was consideration of the public, which would not have tolerated such a Catholic-sounding formula, that caused Zwingli to reject it. Luther could not compromise any more if he wanted to remain true to the words of Christ as he could not otherwise understand them. He spoke the phrase about the "other spirit," by the way, to Bucer, when Bucer demanded from him a confirmation of his orthodoxy and therewith altar fellowship despite the continuing disagreement. It reads:

> I am not your lord, not your judge, and not your teacher. Our spirit and your spirit are not in sync, but rather it is clear that we do not share the same spirit. For it cannot be one spirit, because in one place they believe simply the *words of Christ,* and at another place they find fault with, attack, bear false witness about, and grab at this same faith with all sorts of wicked and slanderous words. For this reason . . . we commend you to the judgment of God. Teach in the manner for which you want to be held accountable before God. [(Köhler,) *Das Marburger Religionsgespräch*, p. 38, cf. p. 129]

The man who spoke thus was concerned about the words of Christ, and nothing else.

3

But perhaps he understood the words of Christ incorrectly? Perhaps he was a poor exegete in his exegesis of the Words of Institution? Perhaps he was, in his interpretation, without knowing it, prejudiced by dogma! Perhaps his exegetical judgment was shaped by dogmatic biases! That's what the great majority of modern exegetes, even in the Lutheran church, at least in Europe, have in objection to Luther.

One prejudice, we will admit, Luther did have, and here the great chasm immediately becomes visible which divides his exegesis of the Holy Scripture from that of modern Protestantism. It is the dogmatic prejudice, that the eucharistic texts of the New Testament, like all texts of the Bible, are not only historical documents of the past, from which we choose the words and thoughts which we see as normative, but rather that these texts, with no damage to their character as authentic historical documents, are God's Word. This is, we think, a necessary and appropriate prejudice, without which the biblical doctrine of the Lord's Supper, as every other doctrine which is binding upon the church, is not to be found at all. What is meant can be illustrated with an example. In 1947 in Switzerland, I met a German colleague, one of the most respected New Testament scholars, who, coming from an old family of Lutheran theologians, taught in a German Lutheran faculty. He had just preached in a Methodist church, and so the conversation turned to the problem of church fellowship and soon to the problem of the Lord's Supper in the New Testament, a problem which engaged us both. We spoke about his research, and I asked him if he held to his earlier view, that the Last Supper of Christ was to be understood as a symbolic action and accordingly the Words of Institution were to be understood as a metaphor. He affirmed this and confirmed further that the eucharistic understanding of Paul remained thoroughly in line with that of Jesus and that, in any case, in the case of Paul there could be no talk of a real presence in the sense of the later ecclesiastical teaching. The objection that 1 Cor. 11:29, with the phraseology about "not discerning the body," implies realism was deflected with [the acknowledgment] that this indeed was a difficulty, but that he hoped to find some explanation for it. The conversation then turned to John 6, and here my conversation partner admitted that actually the great speech about Christ as the Bread of Life was meant in the spiritual sense, but that the verses from 51b onward (where the Bread is no longer Jesus but His flesh and the speaking is about the eating of the flesh and the drinking of the blood) represent indeed an outspoken realism and are directed to the Lord's Supper. There it is really taught that the bread is the body, that the wine is the blood. To the comment that therefore even he found in one passage of the New Testament the realistic view of the Lord's Supper came the answer: that is correct, but this passage didn't belong to the original composition of the Gospel but was a later addition. To the objection that, as far as we know, the Gospel never existed without this passage, and that it belongs to the New Testament (as the church of all times has recognized it as the authoritative Word of God), and that even the church of the present time acknowledges this New Testament as the source and norm for doctrine—to this objection came the answer: for me, the true words of the historical Jesus are the norm for doctrine! To that I could only reply: that's where theology was fifty years ago, when [Adolf von] Harnack wrote his *Das Wesen des Christentums*.[18] Haven't we learned anything, we, who as the Confessing Church appealed to the *sola Scriptura* of the Reformation? I would not have mentioned this experience if it did not so extraordinarily clearly reveal the crisis of modern Lutheranism in the questions of doctrine. The deepest cause for the decay of the eucharistic doctrine becomes clear here. How can one understand the biblical teaching of Holy Communion when one is unacquainted with any biblical teachings at all anymore? From this it is also to be understood why the discussion at the present time about Holy Communion is so hopeless. If Luther and Zwingli disputed in written and spoken word about the Sacrament of the Altar, then it happened from the common understanding of the Holy Scripture as the Word of God and the source and norm of all doctrine. The acknowledgment of

---

18   *What Is Christianity*, trans. Thomas Bailey Saunders (New York: Harper & Row, 1957).
     MH

the Scripture as the Word of God is the assumption of the great disagreements between all denominations of the sixteenth and seventeenth centuries. One has to be very clear in considering what consequences come from this, that this great common assumption no longer exists for a large segment of the Protestant world. How should I dispute about Baptism with someone who, as soon as I introduce the passage (John 3:5) about the new birth "from water and spirit," decides with Bultmann that "water" is an editorial addition, like the passage about eating flesh and drinking blood (John 6:51b–58), and like the passage about the water and the blood at the crucifixion (John 19:34), and who draws the conclusions from these hypotheses that John is uninterested in sacraments! If that is not a prejudice, what is it? Do these learned ones, who approach the Bible with such prejudices, have the right to criticize the reformers because of their dogmatic prejudices? And is it not perhaps thus, that the allegedly exegetical reasons which make Luther's understanding of the Lord's Supper entirely impossible according to the opinions of modern theologians, when considered seriously, are not exegetical reasons at all, but rather the basis for a worldview, a philosophy, which, according to Luther's opinion, already was determining the exegesis of Zwingli, though Zwingli did not yet doubt the authority of the divine Word?

4

The point of departure for Luther's understanding of the Eucharist is the Words of Institution: "This is My body." This saying of Christ is for him the unshakable basis of his eucharistic faith. He wants to hold up these words before the Lord Christ on Judgment Day:

> My dear Lord Jesus Christ, an argument arose about Your words at the Last Supper. Some people said that they should be understood otherwise than what they read. But because they taught me nothing of certainty, but rather only made one confused and uncertain . . . so I have remained by Your text, as the words read. If there is something mysterious in this, then You have wanted it to be mysterious, because You have given no other explanation about this, nor commanded one to be given . . . If there be a mystery in this, then You will excuse me for not grasping it, as You excused Your apostles when they did not understand You at many points as You spoke of Your suffering and resurrection, and they took the words as they were and did nothing else with them. And as also Your dear mother did not understand, when You said to her (Luke 2): "I must be in that which is My Father's," and she simply kept the words in her heart and did not make them into anything else. Therefore I have remained by these, Your words: "This is My body," etc., and have not wanted to make for myself anything different out of them, nor have allowed such to be made, but rather have commended them to You and have deposited them with You, even if something mysterious be in them,

and have kept them as they read, especially because I do not find that they work against any article of faith. See, no fanatic [*Schwärmer*] will be allowed to speak this way with Christ . . . . [*Vom Abendmahl Christi Bekenntnis* (*Confession concerning Christ's Supper*) (1528), Aland 2, WA 26:446f. (AE 37:305–6)]

Indeed, no fanatic can speak this way, not even now here on earth. Here beats the heart of Luther's eucharistic faith, and whoever understands these words knows why the disagreement about the Lord's Supper was unavoidable and that, for Luther, it was really about the Gospel itself. It was not stubbornness and slavish literalism which caused Luther to remain firm on the plain meaning of the words of the Testament, but rather an extremely tender conscience, which bowed before the majesty of the divine Word, and the faith which trusts the Word against all visible appearances and against all so-called "rational" objections. And perhaps the deepest reason for the decay of eucharistic faith in the Lutheran Church is to be sought in this: that along with such understanding of the Word of God, additionally such seriousness of conscience and such faith have become so rare among us. The sympathy which modern man, even the modern Lutheran, has for Zwingli and Calvin is doubtless bound up with the fact that the Swiss reformers, each in his own way coming out of humanism, are already spokesmen for modern culture within Christianity. Compared to them, Luther seems like a solitary medieval monk. One does an injustice to them by calling them rationalists, and by saying (as happened again and again in the confessional polemics of the nineteenth century) of the old Reformed churches of the sixteenth century that they created their teachings out of two sources: from Scripture and from reason, in contrast to Lutheranism, which created [its teachings] from Scripture alone. It was not difficult for the Reformed [churches] to turn the spear around and to say of the Lutherans that they also had not remained by the *sola Scriptura*, but rather that in their case, tradition, woven into the Confessions, played a role. In reality it was so, that both sides wanted to take the Word of God quite seriously but that their hermeneutical principles were different. Zwingli would have made the sign of the cross on himself [in horror when] confronted with Protestant modernism which denies the authority of the entire Scripture as the Word of God, denies the virgin birth of the Lord and other miracles, and denies, too, the old church dogma of the divine Trinity and the two natures of Christ [so strongly would Zwingli have opposed such things]. But in the principles of his textual interpretation there indeed already lurks—or should we say there still remains? for he never actually was entirely freed from Thomism—a rational-philosophical element, which made for him fully unacceptable Luther's understanding of the Words of Institution.

What are the objections which are raised by Zwingli and the Reformed church—for despite all the separations from Zürich's reformer, Calvin and the theology which followed him stands on his side—against Luther's eucharistic doctrine? They are derived from three main objections: the claim that the identification of the bread with the body is first nonsense or *irrational*; it claims, second, something which is *impossible*; and it claims, third, something which is entirely *useless*. On the basis of these three reasons, Luther must be wrong.

It would be nonsense, *irrational*, so states the first objection, to think that Jesus gave to the disciples His true body as He handed them the bread and that we today receive His true body in Communion. *Deus non proponit nobis incomprehensibilia* ["God does not place incomprehensible things before us to be believed"], as Zwingli offered the classic formulation of this objection (W. Köhler, *Das Marburger Religionsgespräch*, p. 72, cf. p. 71), while Luther thought that all the great contents of faith were incomprehensible:

> If you think that God doesn't set incomprehensible things in front of us, this I cannot grant to you. Mary's virginity, the forgiveness of sins, there is much of such. So, too, "This is My body." As Ps. 77:20 says, "Your way through the mighty waters, though Your footprints are unknown."[19] If we knew His ways, then He would not be incomprehensible, He, the Awesome One! [op. cit., p. 15]

For Zwingli, too, God inspired wonder: *Deus verus est et lumen, non inducit in tenebras* ["God is true and light and does not lead us into darkness"] (p. 67). What would be for Luther a revelation of God which were not at the same time a veiling? "The servant doesn't gripe about the will of his master; one must close one's eyes," he answered Oecolampadius[20] at one point (p. 13), and at another point in the conversation he said to Basel's reformer: "One must let the doctors go their way and believe Christ" (p. 63).

The second objection says: the literal understanding of the Words of Institution claims an *impossibility*. For it is impossible that a body can be at several places at once. God can certainly do all miracles, but He cannot change the laws of mathematics. Zwingli quotes in Marburg the words of Augustine: "If Christ's body is up there, then it is also at a location," and adds:

> If Christ's body is at different places, and we must become similar to Him, then our bodies would have to be simultaneously at several different places too. If He is in all ways similar to us, even being invented [incarnated] in our form, and we cannot be at different places, so He cannot do it either, exactly because He is similar to us ... Christ's body is at a place and cannot be at many places. [op. cit., p. 29]

Luther answers this by making reference to his lengthy treatment of the problem of a nonlocal presence of the body of Christ in his *Vom Abendmahl Christi Bekenntnis* [*Confession concerning Christ's Supper*] of 1528:

> In my book, I wrote about mathematical similarities; you have read this, but not understood it. I don't want to dispute any more about

---

19 This is Ps. 77:19 in English Bibles. MH

20 Johannes Oecolampadius (1482–1531) helped Erasmus (ca. 1467–1536) issue his Greek New Testament. He was influenced by Luther, then Zwingli (s.v. *Christian Cyclopedia*). MH

mathematics, for I can make no prescriptions about how it is in heaven or on earth; we don't want to delve into this. *God is above all mathematicians*; Christ can place His body without location as if it were at a location. He is in the Eucharist not in the manner of being at a location. [p. 29f.]

The deepest motive for Luther's teaching, recognized by the Lutheran church in the seventh article of the Formula of Concord as ecclesiastical dogma—that Christ's body has still other ways of being [present] at a location than the ways which philosophers call "local" or "spatial"—is the understanding of the incarnation which he found in the New Testament. When Oecolampadius demanded of him in Marburg, "Don't cling so much to the humanity and to the flesh of Christ, but rather elevate the mind to the divinity of Christ!" Luther answered, "The only God I know about is the one who became human; thus I want to have no other" (p. 27).

How could any part of creation, how could "space" and "location," divide that which became one in the hypostatic union?

> Wherever you can say, "Here is God," there you must also say, "Then Christ the man is also there." And wherever you would show [us] a location where God would be and not the man, then the person would be divided, because I could then say in truth: "Here is God who is not man and who never yet became man." [*Vom Abendmahl Christi Bekenntnis* (*Confession concerning Christ's Supper*) (1528), Aland 2, WA 26:332 (AE 37:218)]

This is the reason why one must assume that Christ's body participates in this manner of divine presence, which is not a local one, without ceasing to be a natural human body. The philosophical reasons which Luther gives are not to serve the [purpose of] founding or supporting the dogma, but rather only [to serve to] refute Zwingli's objection that the acceptance of a nonlocal presence of the body of Christ is refutable with philosophical reasoning. To this objection, Luther shows that he finds himself in the good company of medieval thinkers—today he could refer to the fact that no modern physicist would recognize Zwingli's concept of space anymore, to say nothing of his primitive idea of the cosmos. But for him, in this connection, absolutely nothing depends on mathematics and physics. "I have simply presented the words of Christ"—namely, "This is My body"—he presses against Zwingli, when Zwingli wants to hold him to a particular idea of space, and comments further

> that I have nothing to do with mathematical reasoning, and simply toss the spatial adverb out of the text of the Last Supper. The words read "this" is My body, not "here" is My body! Whether He is spatially or nonspatially present, about this I want to have said nothing, because God has revealed nothing about this, and no mortal can prove this. [Köhler, op. cit., p. 31]

The third objection claims, relying on John 6:63: "the flesh is of no use," that the oral eating of the body and drinking of the blood of Christ claimed by Luther would be entirely *useless*. "The soul is spirit, the soul is not flesh, spirit eats spirit," says Zwingli in Marburg to Luther, who understands the words of John 6:63 in such a way that only the Capernaitic misunderstanding is ruled out by it, as if the flesh of Christ were to be eaten like other flesh, for bodily satiation. Luther, too, recognizes the spiritual consuming of Christ in faith. But he knows that there is still another [type of consuming]:

> Wherever the Word of God is, there is spiritual consuming: when God speaks with us, then faith is there encouraged and demanded. That is the "eating" (in the spiritual sense). When He adds the physical eating to this, so we must obey. We eat, in faith, this body, which was given for us. The mouth receives the body of Christ; the soul believes the words while it eats the body. [Ibid., p. 15]

> I have already often said that I do not only not deny nor despise such spiritual eating, but rather say and believe that it is especially necessary. But though I say this, it does not follow from this that such physical eating, instituted and commanded by the Lord Jesus Christ, would be useless, first of all to the faithful, who eat not only spiritually but also physically. Still less does it follow—indeed, it does not follow at all—that the true body of Christ could not physically be in the Eucharist at all. It is there and it is beneficial. [Ibid., p. 19]

If one understands the passage John 6:63 as Zwingli does—that is, that even the presence of the body would be useless—then one would have to deny the benefit of the incarnation, which, of course, nobody wants to do. Luther defends himself against the devaluation of physicality which is in Zwingli's exposition:

> If the words may appear physical to you, yet they are words and works of the highest Majesty—nobody can deny this—and therefore not at all physical and inferior. After all, the forgiveness of sins and eternal life and the kingdom of heaven is connected by God's power to these physical and inferior things, that they may be known to physical [people]. And therefore one may not ever empty them and despise them as inferior, but rather one must treasure them as the highest and spiritually superior [things]. [Ibid., p. 11]

And in another place:

> God has some ways and means of creating, building up, and multiplying faith in us: preaching publicly or at home, Baptism, nourishment with the body of the Lord. Whoever wants to can ponder why He has so many and so different methods; that doesn't concern us. He knows what is useful and good for us. [Ibid. p. 24]

5

Against these three objections Luther holds firmly to the simple meaning of the Words of Institution. We have purposefully cited the key points of the Marburg religious debates to show that Luther really took to heart the opposing viewpoint and was familiar with all the objections. Neither the "unreasonable" nor the "impossible" nor the "useless"—the judgments of human reason—could make an impression on him. There could be only one thing which could convince him of this, but which then would also have immediately convinced him that the literal understanding must depart from a symbolic [understanding]. That would have been a single text in the Bible which encourages, demands, or even merely makes possible the metaphorical understanding of the Words of Institution. Zwingli was never able to show him such a passage because the passages which Zwingli introduced as examples of the meaning of "is" in the sense of "signifies" do not confirm at all that which he finds in them. "John is Elijah" does not mean "John represents Elijah." "I am the vine" and the other self-predications of Jesus in John's Gospel do not mean that Jesus represents the vine, the door, the way, etc. Even the text which Zwingli once experienced as a revelation—the sentence Exod. 12:11: "It," namely, the Passover lamb, which one should eat in the haste of breaking out, "is the Lord's Passover"—is not a parallel from which "This is My body" can be understood. Naturally, Luther knows that there is in the Holy Scripture figurative language too. "I do not deny figurative speech, but you must prove that it is *here*," he answers Oecolampadius when Oecolampadius points him to "I am the vine" in John 15:1 (Ibid., p. 10). Everywhere else where figurative speech occurs in Scripture it is marked as such. Even the parables, like those of the prophets, are explained as to their meanings. The actions of the Last Supper are explained, too, by Jesus in the Words of Institution. Luther can rightfully ask why they are unsatisfied only in the case of this explanation, but rather see a metaphor in the explanation, which again only requires explanation. Luther had already alerted us to the fact that his opponents could not agree among themselves about what, then, the Words of Institution, if they are to be understood metaphorically, actually mean. This has always been true of the critics of the literal interpretation, even today. They are united about what they should not mean, but then what their actual meaning is, about this the opinions diverge. What is the *tertium comparationis* ["point of comparison"] in the alleged metaphor? Some find it in the breaking of the bread and the pouring of the wine (e.g., Jülicher[21]), to which Jesus compared the fate of this body—which, however, was not at all broken, according to John 19:36 (cf. Exod. 12:46)—and blood.

---

21 The liberal theologian Gustav Adolf Jülicher (1857–1938) taught at Berlin and Marburg (s.v. *Christian Cyclopedia*). MH

Others (e.g., Heitmüller[22]) reject this explanation and find the point of comparison in the words "for you." Still others find in the separated distribution of bread and wine, as metaphor for the separation of body and blood in death, the meaning of the *verba testamenti*: "You live by means of this, that I die" (Althaus). [Joachim] Jeremias [1900–1979], who otherwise gives us in his learned book *Die Abendsmahlsworte Jesu* (2nd ed., 1949)[23] the historically best discussion of the problem of the Last Supper, finds the *tertium comparationis* for the bread in the fact that it is broken and for the wine in its red color and explains:

> Jesus makes the torn bits of bread into a metaphor for the fate of His body, and the wine into a metaphor for His blood, poured out. "I must die a sacrificial death" is the meaning of the last parable of Jesus. [p. 106]

Lohmeyer (*Das Evangelium des Markus*, 1937, pp. 306ff.) objects to the metaphorical theory, [saying] that the Words of Institution, if they were a metaphor, would have been introduced as such in approximate analogy to Matt. 13:[33]: "The kingdom of heaven *is like* a lump of dough . . . ." He himself blocks his own way toward the correct understanding by the artificial and linguistically impossible assumption that in the sentence "This is My body," "body" is the subject and "this" is the predicate. One may well be eager to learn how this theologian's guessing game will proceed and when the time will arrive at which they, tired of the endless hypotheses which also transform the words of the Last Supper into mere platitudes, return to the assumption that Jesus Himself meant that which He then said, namely, that He gave to His Twelve His body to eat and His blood to drink. In exactly this way, as historical research has returned to the conviction that Jesus Himself considered Himself to be the Messiah and was quite conscious that He was going to His death as the "Servant of God" of Isaiah 53, so it will also return to the view that He Himself is the founder of the realistic interpretation of the Lord's Supper. Who else would it be? The conclusion of human reason, which is expressed in the three words "irrational, unnecessary, useless," attacks essentially every dogma of the church, even the dogma of the incarnation, of the virgin birth, of the atoning death, of the bodily resurrection, and of the ascension. Even the historical-critical method has just now rediscovered and confirmed with its methods that the realistic view of the Lord's Supper is present in [the writings of] Paul and of John. There is no good reason why this development should stop precisely with Jesus. Naturally, that's not to say that the modern Protestants would also believe that which Jesus said and meant at the Last Supper. They do not believe Him on other matters.

---

22   Wilhelm Heitmüller (1869–1926) was a New Testament scholar who taught at Göttingen, Marburg, Bonn, Tübingen. He studied the development of Christianity in light of its historical and geographic environment (s.v. *Christian Cyclopedia*). MH

23   *The Eucharistic Words of Jesus*, trans. Norman Perrin (London: SCM Press, 1964). MH

6

The oldest evidence for the Lord's Supper is [from] the apostle Paul. His report about the institution, which corresponds in all essentials to the report in the Gospels, is more than a decade older than our Gospel according to St. Mark. But this same Paul testifies to the realistic understanding of the Lord's Supper, and not as a novelty in the church, not as something about which the other apostles thought differently than he. It was never even claimed by his Jewish-Christian opponents, who had so much against him, that he had misunderstood or changed the institution of the Lord. We may not understand the words "I have received it from the Lord and transmit it to you" (1 Cor. 11:23) with the older theology and with H[ans] Lietzmann [1875–1942] in this way: that they refer to a special revelation from the Lord. We know today that the expressions which Paul here uses belong to Jewish academic language and mean nothing different than the corresponding formulation (1 Cor. 15:3): Paul passes along the message, which historically goes back to the Lord. This oldest literary witness for the biblical Eucharist says (1 Corinthians 10 and 11) with all desirable clarity how he thought about the presence of the body and blood of the Lord.

> The cup of blessing, which we drink—is it not the participation of the blood of Christ? The bread, which we break—is it not the participation of the body of Christ? For *one* bread—*one* body—are we many; for we have all a participation in the *one* bread. [1 Cor. 10:16–17]

The Württemberg Bible Society, which already has almost a monopoly on printing Bibles, prints the words *blessing* and *break* in verse 16 in italics or bold-face in its German Bibles to show thereby that it is the blessing and the break-ing, that is, that it is the actions which create the communion of the body and blood. But that is, first, an unallowable intrusion into the text—a Bible society is supposed to reproduce the text in its text editions, but not to interpret it— and, second, it is false. For verse 17 says quite unambiguously that the *one* bread makes us into *one* body and gives us a participation in the body of Christ exactly as eating and drinking, food and beverages, create the community in the follow-ing comments about the eating and drinking at Jewish and heathen sacrificial meals. And why is the participation in the blessed bread [equivalent to] com-munion with the body of Christ? Why does the man who consumes the bread consume the body of Christ? To this the answer can only be: because conse-crated bread is the body of Christ! This corresponds exactly to that which we read (1 Cor. 11:27–30) about the unworthy consumption of the bread and wine, which makes the individual concerned guilty of the body and blood of the Lord. So that no one can claim that we are speaking merely out of the prejudice of Lutheran dogmatism, we will quote the judgment of Hans Lietzmann, who is certainly bound by no dogma, who in *Handbuch zum Neuen Testament* com-ments (*An die Korinther I, II*, 3rd ed., 1931, p. 48):

The extent to which the body and blood of Christ is established by means of the eating and drinking arises from 11:27–30, where it is most clearly stated that one consumes the blood of the Lord in the wine and the body of the Lord in the bread. This view, undoubted by ancient Christianity, is stated yet more clearly by John 6:55–56. (See Lietzmann, *Messe und Herrenmahl*, p. 223.)[24]

7

We will content ourselves with these few remarks about Paul, because in this connection we are not dealing with the apostle's entire doctrine about the Eucharist, but rather only with the teaching, undoubtedly contained in the cited passages, that the blessed bread really is the body of Christ and the blessed wine really is the blood of Christ, though bread and wine have not ceased to be bread and wine after the consecration (1 Cor. 11:26ff.; cf. SA III VI on the Sacrament of the Altar, in which Luther refutes the doctrine of transubstantiation with this text). The passage from John 6, introduced by Lietzmann as further evidence for the real presence, still needs a little consideration however.

The great chapter of John about the bread of life, from which Zwingli and the entire Reformed church thought it could take its main arguments against Luther's eucharistic teaching, was left out of the eucharistic debates by the older Lutheran theologians for the reason that it was thought to deal only with the spiritual consuming and not with the Sacrament of the Altar. However, one must understand this chapter, first, in the context of the entire Gospel, and, second, one must grasp its inner construction to see its connection to the Lord's Supper. Why does the Fourth Gospel have no report of the institution, though it portrays the Last Supper of Jesus with such characteristic details? John did not leave it out because he simply wanted to complete the [work of] other evangelists. [If that were so,] he could have left out so much more! It apparently was left out— as in Mark the report about the appearance of the resurrected [Jesus was left out]—because the evangelist considered that it would be good for his purposes to keep it from the readers, who did not belong to the church, perhaps because of expected misunderstandings. As John wrote, there already were rumors spreading through the heathen world about cannibalism at the cultic meals of the Christians, rumors which played such a great role in the [persecution and court-room] trials of Christians. In place [of the Words of Institution], John preserves for us an earlier lecture by Jesus about the bread of life, which acts at first as a sort of commentary on the miraculous feeding with the miraculous multiplication of bread [cf. John 6:1–13], but which then already touches upon the subject of the great miracle of the future—the eating of the flesh and the drinking of the blood of the Son of Man—in anticipating, half-hiding, and half-revealing

---

24 Cf. Hans Lietzmann, *Mass and Lord's Supper*, trans. Dorothea H. G. Reeve (Leiden: Brill, 1979). MH

words. Now, the sayings of the Lord in John's Gospel are not merely historical protocols, written down or memorized by those who heard them, as we must assume about many of the sayings in the other Gospels. On the contrary, historical transmission has taken place in an unusual way by means of inspiration. What John 14:26; 15:26; and 16:13 say about the activities of the Paraclete, the Holy Spirit, has become reality in the composition of this Gospel. In this way, the inner structure of the speeches explains itself. As in John 5, in which the resurrection is mentioned in a double meaning (as the resurrection which already happens when a person comes to faith and as the resurrection which happens on Judgment Day), so also John 6 speaks about Christ as the bread of life and in other verses about the flesh of the Son of Man as the bread of life. He speaks of spiritual consuming, but behind this he points to the sacramental consumption. So there is no reason to deny this chapter's relation to the Sacrament of the Altar, especially because the critique of the world and of rationality against the Sacrament of the Altar is already apparent in the objections of the people at Capernaum. Thus even Lutheran theologians have at all times recognized a relation between John 6 and the Eucharist. But if that is correct, then a light falls from John 6 onto the meaning of the "flesh" and "blood" of the Lord in the Eucharist. Wherever the Fourth Gospel speaks about the flesh of Christ, there the actual flesh is always meant. The true incarnation of the *Logos* is the theme of the Gospel, as it is the great desire of the apostle according to 1 John 4:1ff., whose last days were filled with the powerful struggle against the Gnostics who denied the "flesh" of Christ. For this reason he does not content himself anymore with the word *body*, which still sufficed at the time of Paul. All the heretics admitted that Christ had a body. What they disputed was this: that this body was no apparent body but an actual human body, "flesh." And exactly as the flesh of Christ is taken seriously, so also the resurrection of the body, the "flesh," is taken seriously by John, as by the entire orthodox church. Whoever disputes the reality of the "flesh" of Christ in the Lord's Supper also disputes the "resurrection of the flesh." Here is the reason why, in John 6, the Lord brings His Eucharist into connection with the resurrection. It has often been observed how close the formulations of Ignatius [d. ca. 112] about the flesh of Christ as "the means of salvation to immortality, the means against death and to eternal life in Christ" come into contact with the thoughts of John 6:53 and the rest of the chapter. These old formulations of the Antiochenistic liturgy are an echo of the Lord's words. They show how people at the end of the first century understood the words of the Last Supper. In the oldest church, in New Testament times, there was never any other view of the Eucharist than that of sacramental realism, which recognized in the eating of the bread and in the drinking of the wine the eating of the true body and the drinking of the true blood of Christ.

8

In the framework of this short consideration, we could not say everything which is to be said about the New Testament background to the Lutheran eucharistic doctrine. But that which has been said will make clear that, for Luther, the matter was about the understanding of the biblical Lord's Supper. Even he who believes that he must reject Luther's eucharistic doctrine should not dispute this. And it should also be clear that we Lutherans have no cause to feel inferior to other denominations when the question is raised about the basis of our teaching about the Sacrament. By means of an unspeakably sad lack of development, it has happened that research into the New Testament has been very much neglected in the Lutheran church. A man such as Theodor Zahn[25] founded no school in Germany. And the modern division of labor in the theological discipline has led to this situation: that the men in our church who have applied themselves to the New Testament were not well-versed in Luther and Lutheran dogmatics, and vice versa. But the Lutheran church was born out of research into the Scripture. Luther's teaching assignment was the *lectura in Biblia*. With the Scripture in hand, we have the task of defending the teaching of our church today against Rome and the Reformed, as the fathers once did in the days of the Reformation. In serious study of the Holy Scripture, the wrestling over the Sacrament of the Altar will be decided, a wrestling which today, as in all decisive times in church history, has again become a struggle for the existence of the true church. For as once the church gathered around the Lord's Table in the days of the apostles, so is the Sacrament of the Altar at all times the central point of the church of Christ. A renewal of the Sacrament of the Altar, which in the last 250 years has declined even in Lutheranism, must be one of the foremost tasks of the spiritual office and of the Christian congregation. But how could it otherwise be renewed than that we at once go to the source of the teaching and organization of the church and allow ourselves to be taught by the New Testament about what this Sacrament is? The theories of the theologians do not help us. The treasures of the great ecclesiastical liturgies, as precious as they are to us, can still be only a vague and distant indication of that which they want to witness and preserve. All great liturgists of the church have known that the church can exist, and in some circumstances must exist, without celebrative liturgy. The church remains what it is, even without liturgy. She remains a queen even in the clothing of a beggar (W[ilhelm] Löhe, *Drei Bücher von der Kirche*, vol. 3, p. 9).

Even the Roman church teaches its theologians that its greatest divine services are not the celebrative pontifical offices, but rather the celebrations of Holy Communion, which without all pageantry are secretly held in concentration camps. Therefore there is no renewal of the church by liturgy, but rather

---

25   Theodor von Zahn (1838–1933) was a New Testament scholar who taught at Erlangen as successor to J. C. K. von Hofmann (1810–77). Zahn opposed the radical liberalism of Adolf von Harnack (s.v. *Christian Cyclopedia*). MH

a renewal of liturgy by the faith of the church. Even the ecclesiastical dogmas about Communion are not the last word. How modestly did Luther consider his attempts to express the mystery that the bread is the body with [the words] "in," "with," and "under"! What little value he placed on the theories which were supposed to put forth the possibility of a nonlocal, definitive, or repletive presence of the body of Christ against the claim that such was impossible. For him, the heart of the matter was this which does not fade away with the theories of humans and with the liturgies of the churches, but rather will remain until the end of the world, that which makes Communion Communion, that which is contained in the teaching of the church; it was all about this—about the words of the Lord: "This is My body. This is My blood of the new testament."

∽

I hope, very honored brothers, that this letter reaches you still in the Easter season, in which we all especially have occasion to ponder afresh the mystery of Holy Communion. Perhaps it will help some of you also with new joy to bear witness to the congregation about the miracle of this Sacrament.

In the bonds of faith,

Your
Hermann Sasse

Historical Context

Sasse's correspondence with LCMS President John Behnken is consider-
able. Below he laments the frustration arising within the UELCA because of
its most famous and recently appointed professor. Sasse had no use for an
LWF which failed to confess the orthodox Lutheran faith, and this placed
him in agreement with the ELCA (the Australian LCMS partner) on the
issue. Meanwhile, Pope Pius XII's outrageous Munificentissimus Deus *of*
November 1, 1950, continued to cause Sasse to teach on the nature of the
end times and Antichrist: ". . . the ever Virgin Mary, after completing her
course of life upon earth, was assumed to the glory of heaven both in body
and soul. Therefore, if anyone, which may God forbid, should dare either
to deny this or voluntarily call into doubt what has been defined by Us,
he should realize that he has cut himself off entirely from the divine and
Catholic faith" (Denzinger 2333). "What the Confessions teach is that when
the pope promulgates a dogmatic decision, one which has no basis in Holy
Scripture, and makes men's salvation or damnation depend on their obe-
dience or disobedience toward it, then he is setting himself in the place of
Christ, in the place of God. This is what Luther, with sharp prophetic vision,
saw as the essence of the papacy . . . ." MH

March 22, 1952[1]

Prof. Hermann Sasse
41 Buxton Street
North Adelaide, South Australia

Highly Honored Herr Doctor Behnken!

. . . Our union endeavors have, with God's help, made considerable progress. Dr. Darsow recently called the progress a miracle . . . . On both sides there is considerable distrust . . . . "He [Sasse?] sold us out to Missouri," they occasionally say to me, and I repeatedly find it necessary to emphasize the fact that our churches are not dealing with one another after the manner of negotiations between states or companies, where each party tries to get whatever can be gotten; but, rather, these two churches which once parted ways must now penitently return to the one church which lives by the Lutheran Confessions and by the understanding of Scripture taught by these Confessions, if the Lutheran Church of Australia is not to perish. And this point of view is establishing itself more and more. We are

---

1   CHI Behnken file. Behnken had this letter translated into English. MH

beginning to understand, too, that practical and ethical questions can and must be solved after we have reached agreement in doctrine. But there now arises, as our most difficult question, the problem of our relationship to the LWF . . . .

H. Sasse

twenty-four

Last Things

Church and Antichrist

TRANSLATED BY NORMAN NAGEL

March 1952[1]

Prof. D. Theol. Hermann Sasse
41 Buxton Street
North Adelaide, South Australia

Dear Brothers in the Office!

1
_____

A few years ago, in the time of Germany's collapse, it was reported of a German pastor that he boasted of preaching only on the Revelation of St. John. Probably his poor congregation soon made it clear to him that that would not do. Yet, in his way, he was attempting to make good what had been neglected by the church and by us pastors: *eschatological proclamation.*

In our day the biblical doctrine of the last things has come alive for us as a gift given in the midst of what the church has had to endure. At the beginning of this

---

1   *BLP* 24: *Zur Lehre vom Antichrist* (North Adelaide, March 1952). The original was published in *LuBl* 4, no. 27 (1952). This English translation appeared originally in *We Confess: The Church* (St. Louis: Concordia, 1986), 36–48. Minor alterations to grammar and capitalization have been made. Scripture quotations in this essay are from the Revised Standard Version of the Bible, copyright 1952, © 1971 by the Division of Christian Education of the National Council of the Churches of Christ in the United States of America. Used by permission. All rights reserved. The quotations from the Lutheran Confessions in this publication are from The BOOK OF CONCORD: THE CONFESSIONS OF THE EVANGELICAL LUTHERAN CHURCH, edited by Theodore G. Tappert, published in 1959 by Fortress Press. Huss number 293. MH

century a complacent church regarded the last things as an element of the first Christian proclamation which more or less belonged only to that first period, a form of the Gospel which was for us of only historical interest. Or, alternatively, it was thought of as something that might be of significance for the future, at the end of our lives, or at the end of the world, something we needed to study only in preparation for such an end. That there is for the church no more vitally relevant doctrine than that of the last things was brought home to Christians in Europe by all they were called upon to endure. It was not quite the same for Christians in other parts of the world, though in America some first indications can be observed of a new interest in eschatology.

There was perhaps some dark foreshadowing of what was to come when, at the beginning of the century, historical theology again discovered the eschatological character of the Gospel—much to the discomfort of the "systematic" theologians and the representatives of practical theology. No one can tell us, who have endured the judgments of God's wrath, that the fearful pictures of apocalyptic tribulation shown us in Holy Scripture are but the product of Eastern fantasy. We can no longer read these passages the way they were expounded in earlier centuries. The old expositions seem like the work of a connoisseur who stands before some old paintings as if he had all the time in the world and expounds what he finds so enchanting about them. He is quite at peace with himself and his expert knowledge—or his expert ignorance. The paintings mean absolutely nothing decisive for his existence.

For us these are realities of which we have had some experience. We are like those people in the East for whom Mereshkovski speaks in the introduction to *The Brothers Karamazov* (Munich, 1921).

> They are like men who stand upon some height and looking over the heads of those around them see what is coming upon them, what at the moment is not yet seen by the multitude below. Thus have we, beyond all the coming centuries and whatever could possibly happen, caught a glimpse of the end of the world's history. . . . We may indeed be the weakest of the weak. Our "power is made perfect in weakness." Our strength is in this, that we cannot be won over by any seductions of the most mighty of all devils, by any seductions of the everlasting "normality" of unending "progress." We cannot be bought by any averaged philosophy that is neither hot nor cold. Our faith is set on the end; we see the end; we long for the end. . . . In our eyes there is an expression which never was before in the eyes of men. In our hearts there is a feeling that has not been felt by men for nineteen centuries, not since the vision was seen by that lonely exile on the island that is called Patmos: "The Spirit and the Bride say, 'Come.' And let him who hears say, 'Come.' . . . He who testifies to these things says, 'Surely I am coming soon.' Amen. Come, Lord Jesus!"

It is by living the last things that we are given a new understanding of the fact, and why it is so, that always involved in the Gospel and the proclamation of the Gospel are the last things, the end, Christ's return. There is preaching of the Gospel in the world because we are in the world's evening (Matt. 24:14). The reddening dawn of the daybreak of the kingdom of God is signaled by the lame walking, the blind seeing, that "lepers are cleansed and the deaf hear." Finally, the nearness of the kingdom of God is signaled by the fact that "the poor have good news preached to them" (Matt. 11:5). All preaching is preaching of the last things when it is preaching of the Gospel. And no preaching is preaching of the last things if it is not preaching of the pure Gospel—even if it were the exposition of nothing else but the Revelation of St. John and the other eschatological texts of Holy Scripture. How can anyone proclaim the Lord's death without a thought of His coming again [1 Cor. 11:26]? How can the word "justification" come from our mouths without a thought of His coming again to judge the living and the dead? How can one say "Amen" at the end of the sermon without thinking of that great Amen at the end of the Bible: "Amen. Come, Lord Jesus" [Rev. 22:20]?

2

In the light of the foregoing we shall take up a single part of eschatology, a not unimportant part, *the doctrine of the Antichrist*. In dogmatics it appears, because of its nature, in two places: in the doctrine of the last things and in the doctrine of the church. Yet both belong together, for the doctrine of the church, when seen clearly—that is, when seen in the light of God's Word—is actually only a part of eschatology. There is church only at the end of the world (1 Cor. 10:11). "In these last days," according to Heb. 1:2, "He [the Father] has spoken to us by a Son." At the end of the world the Son calls the faithful from among all nations to the true people of God, the church. All that happens in the church is fulfillment of the prophecies of the end, for example, the whole activity of the Holy Spirit (Acts 2:16ff.; Joel 2:28ff.). The Sacraments of Baptism and the Lord's Supper anticipate what happens at the end and in eternity (Rom. 6:2ff.; 1 Cor. 11:26; John 6:54). So also Holy Absolution and the justification of the sinner anticipate what happens on the Day of Judgment. Even the liturgy on Sunday is an anticipation of the liturgy of heaven (Revelation 4), as every Sunday celebrated as "the Lord's day" anticipates the parousia (cf. the expression "the day of the Lord," Amos 5:18). Only from this vantage point is it possible to understand the church of the New Testament and its hope anchored in the end.

The first Christians were not Adventists. Had they been, they would not have survived the parousia's delay. In fact, the early Christian "Adventists" did fall from the faith (2 Pet. 3:3ff.). Nor were the first Christians Catholics, for whom institutionalization of the church becomes a substitute for the kingdom which has failed to come. Nor were they like some modern Protestants, for whom the kingdom of God becomes a kingdom of this world in social ethics and religiosity. Rather, they lived in the great actuality of the last things, in the church of the living God. They were not a religious association with certain eschatological convictions. They were the holy people of the end time, the saints, who still lived in this world but no longer belonged to it. While for modern Christians, whether Catholic or Protestant, it might only be a matter of pictures and parables, for them it was a reality they actually lived when they designated themselves the people of God, the Body of Christ, the temple of the Holy Spirit.

To the reality of the church, however, belongs the reality of the Antichrist. "Children, it is the last hour; and as you have heard that Antichrist is coming, so now many antichrists have come; therefore, we know that it is the last hour" (1 John 2:18). Because the church lives at the end time of the world, therefore the prophecy of the coming Antichrist is being fulfilled. And because the prophecy of the Antichrist is being fulfilled, the church knows that it is the last time. So the appearance of the Antichrist must run through the whole history of the church. The Antichrist is always coming, and he is already here. Similarly in Paul, who does not use the word "Antichrist," "the man of lawlessness . . . the son of perdition, who opposes and exalts himself . . ." is coming, but in such a way that "the mystery of lawlessness is already at work." But it will only then be fully revealed when "in his time" he comes "by the activity of Satan . . . with all power and with pretended signs and wonders" (2 Thess. 2:3ff.).

Both apostles agree that the Antichrist is on his way, insofar as his appearance belongs to the end time. Both see him active in the present and in the future. While Paul looks more to the future, John focuses more on the present. This matches what they say elsewhere about eschatology. Their unity is not diminished by whether the emphasis is on the present or on the future in an end time that embraces both the present and the future. We must not bend Paul to John or John to Paul. Rather, we must recognize how in them both we have the one harmonious doctrine of the Antichrist.

We may not use our notions of time to make measurements of the last time as we are told of it in Scripture (2 Pet. 3:3–9). There seems to be a contradiction between the fact that the Lord is coming soon and that nineteen centuries have now passed since this was proclaimed. This we simply accept, as we also do the fact that at the time of John it was already "the last hour," in which the Antichrist was in the world, and that the time of his being revealed still lies ahead.

One cannot weaken this apparent contradiction by explaining it away in terms of a development from the comparatively harmless antichrists of the early time to the anti-Christianity which comes to consummation at the parousia. First of all, Holy Scripture does not know our concept of development; it was first read into Scripture by the evolutionistic nineteenth century. Furthermore, what John tells of anti-Christianity is no less satanic, no less dangerous, than what Paul sees. Both derive from the same source: the devil. Both have the same goal: to cast Jesus Christ from His throne and to destroy His true church. Both fight with the same weapons: the power of the lie, and deceptions which seduce to falling away from the true God (1 John 2:22ff.; 2 John 7; 2 Thess. 2:3, 9ff.). The difference is only in the outward appearance. In John the Antichrist appears in the shape of many men who are called antichrists; in Paul, in the shape of "the man of lawlessness." What we are told of is the same, whether in one form of appearance or the other.

The language in 2 Thess. 2:3 is clearly picturesque and apocalyptic. That he "takes his seat in the temple of God" is apocalyptic picture language ever since the desecration of the temple by Antiochus Epiphanes [ca. 215–164 BC], as seen by Daniel. Similarly, that Christ "will slay him with the breath of His mouth" belongs to the picture language of the messianic hope in the prophets (compare 2 Thess. 2:8 with Isa. 11:4 and Rev. 19:15, 20).

Hence it must remain an open question whether the prophecy of "the man of lawlessness" will be fulfilled in the form of one individual man. [Werner] Elert [1885–1954] has a telling comment on the apocalyptic visions in the Bible: "Not the pictures themselves but what is meant by them provides us with what we believe" (*Glaube* [1956], p. 518). In this case the fulfillment can also be in the form of a collective person. This is clearly what John has in mind when he sees the Antichrist in many antichrists. The fulfillment could also be thought of in this way: that the collective person will find his final expression in an individual person.

There are questions here which we cannot answer because Scripture does not give an answer. Scripture tells us that the Antichrist belongs to "the last hour" and is therefore there in some form at all times of the church's history. It is "the last time" ever since Christ, the Firstfruits, rose from the dead and so began the resurrection of all the dead (1 Cor. 15:23). It was already a part of the end of the world when Jerusalem, according to our Lord's prophecy, was destroyed in the year [AD] 70.

Only an utterly unbiblical way of looking at history could suppose that the last things belong altogether to the future, whether near or distant. As surely as the church never ceases to pray "Thy kingdom come" and "Amen. Come, Lord Jesus," so surely it believes what the Lord says: "The hour is coming, and now is" (John 5:25), and also the warning of His apostle: "Children, it is the last hour" (1 John 2:18). Because this is so, the church knows that the Antichrist is in the world.

3

If it did not know about the mystery of the Antichrist, the church would not be able to exist. It would not be able to arm itself against him, to fight against him, to stand against him. When it is taught that the devil does not exist, he has achieved the propagation of his most dangerous triumph. Similarly, there is no greater strengthening of the Antichrist than the view that he is only an apocalyptic figure who will someday later make his appearance—indeed, a most sinister being, but nevertheless a useful warning before the end.

If the Antichrist is not yet on the scene, then the readying alarm has not yet been given. What an assurance of "All's well" is given by such thinking! This is true of the whole system of successive notifications which has been read out of Scripture: conversion of the Jews, resurrection of the martyrs, and so on. Those who think this way don't seem to realize that thereby the signs of the end, for which our Lord commanded us to watch, have been turned into their direct opposite. One may acknowledge that the Lord will come as a thief in the night, but one also knows that it is not yet night, even though it may be evening, and perhaps even late evening. The church will only be at the ready if it knows that the Antichrist is already in the world and that it is at every moment exposed to the full force of his attacks. If it does not know this, then it is hopelessly defense-less against him. That is the meaning of the apostolic warnings.

What, then, is *the mystery of the Antichrist*? What does he want? What does he do? What he wants is to seduce Christians to fall away from the true God, the God revealed in Christ. In the place of the truth of the Gospel he puts the lie, the way of falsehood. Here the passages in John are in full agreement with 2 Thessalonians 2. And there is another point of complete agreement. In con-trast with the devil, the Antichrist is religious. According to John, he comes with a message which sounds quite Christian. He affirms the Gospel, but he falsifies it. According to 1 John 4:3, this falsification is done by denial of the incarnation.

John was clearly writing vis-a-vis emerging Gnosticism. This powerful move-ment in the early days of Christianity was able to win over great numbers of Christians, notably in Egypt and Syria. In the middle of the second century, the orthodox church, the church whose faith was in the incarnate Christ, appears to have been a minority. Yet in its way, how pious was this honoring of Christ as a heavenly being that appeared here on earth with only the semblance of a body! Against this John wrote his Gospel with its central theme: "The Word became flesh" [John 1:14].

The religious character of the Antichrist, as described by Paul, is disclosed in the cult of man. This appears in the church, this religious exaltation of man. The voice of the serpent at the beginning in Paradise is heard again in the message of this Antichrist: "You will be as God" [cf. Gen. 3:5]. This is the oldest heresy in human history, and it appears in ever new forms to the end of the world. This is clearly the sense of the prophecy of the enemy who "exalts himself against every so-called god or object of worship, so that he takes his seat in the temple of God, proclaiming himself to be God" (2 Thess. 2:4).

Whatever forms this divinization of man may take in the future—and cer-tainly such an error always gets worse—one would have to be struck blind not to recognize the appearance of this original heresy ever and again in Christian history. The natural man always has the inclination to use religion for his self-glorification, also the Christian religion. From ancient India we hear: "Atman is Brahman" (the soul is divine). Every missionary to India knows that the greatest hindrance to the Gospel is this divinization of man. This same divinization of man is to be found also in the idealism of the Greeks and of the Germans of the classical period, and it permeates the theology of the Greek fathers, of medieval scholasticism, and of modern Protestantism.

This is what the Antichrist wants. This is what he does. He leads men away from the worship of the one true God, the God who in Jesus Christ became flesh. He leads them to serve the human "I," exalted to the place of God. He does this from the days of the apostles down to the Last Day. This is something that happens in the church. Therefore the Antichrist is more dangerous than all other enemies of the church. No Roman caesar, no modern dictator is so dangerous as the enemy of Christ within the church.

When Pliny [the Younger, AD 61–ca. 112] wrote to Trajan [Roman emperor, AD 98–117], he reported the measures he had taken against the Christians. These went so far as the execution of the "obstinate" ones who refused to recant. In the same letter, he tells of Christians who had fallen away from the church twenty years previously. Such falling away in time of persecution is not the worst thing Christendom has experienced in this regard. This was recognized when the way of repentance was opened for those who had lapsed under pressure of persecution. It was the way the first denier, Simon Peter, had gone. Antichrist's great art is that he can bring Christians to fall away without persecution. When Islam was sweeping over Christian lands, there were Christians who almost clamored to become Muslims. Many of them could give religious reasons for doing so. The Islamic rulers even tried to forbid such conversions to Islam, or at least made them difficult, for the sake of the head tax which Christians were required to pay. The highest art of the Antichrist is that he can make falling away a work of religious piety.

4

In Christian history there is no one who has so deeply probed the mystery of the Antichrist as Martin Luther, no one who so shuddered before it. In Roman theology, even in the greatest teachers of the Roman Church, the Antichrist has always appeared as a comparatively harmless being. This figure of the distant end time may indeed be painted with the most frightening colors, but one need not be too frightened when one knows that this monster will rule for "not too long" a time, that is, three and a half years (Scheeben-Atzberger, *Handbuch der katholischen Dogmatik*, IV, 904). It belongs to the essence of the Roman Church that it puts into a more or less distant future what Holy Scripture says about the events of the end time. For the present, then, Christians need not be much concerned about it.

For Luther, the Antichrist was not so innocuous. Why did the Antichrist loom so large for him? Is this to be explained by the influence of the apocalypticism of the Late Middle Ages, nourished by a mood born of the feeling that a dying world was going under, as well as by the despair of pious people in regard to the ever-more-decadent church? This certainly was an influence upon Luther and upon the whole century of the Reformation. He, along with most of his contemporaries, was convinced of living in the eventide of the world. He never supposed that the world would last much longer. In his *On the Councils and the Church*, he is prompted by Nicaea's Easter canon to speak of the planned reform of the Julian calendar, and he declares it unnecessary.

> What does it matter to us Christians? Even if our Easter should coincide with the day of St. Philip and St. James [May 1] (which I hope will not happen before the end of the world) and move still further, we still celebrate Easter daily with our proclamation of Christ and our faith in Him.

Of the old calendar he says:

> The old garment with its great tear has stayed on and on, and now it may as well stay until the Last Day, which is imminent anyhow. Since the old garment has endured being patched and torn for approximately fourteen hundred years, it may as well let itself be patched and torn for another hundred years; for I hope that everything will soon come to an end. [*Von den Konziliis und Kirchen* (1539), Aland 382; WA 50:557; AE 41:65]

[August] Vilmar once said that it would have been better if Luther had not been so sure that the end of the world was about to happen. He would then have given more thought to the future of the church. Even if this be so, we must remember that Luther was not just captive to the way the Late Middle Ages thought about the world, but that more than any of his contemporaries he had immersed himself in the eschatology of the New Testament. For him, as for the church of the apostles, ecclesiology was a part of eschatology. Unlike the men of the nineteenth century who saw the church as one of the great social constructions of human history,[2] he saw the church as the holy people of God of the end time, attacked by the devil, led by the Antichrist into the great temptation to fall away, and protected and preserved by Christ.

Therefore the Antichrist fills a far different role for Luther than for the men of the Middle Ages. He is not just a frightening figure who announces the Last Day; he is the great antagonist of Christ in the drama of the church's history. No one can know what the church is, what the kingdom of Christ is, who does not know the Antichrist. Therefore the Antichrist can only be understood from the vantage point of the Gospel, and not from that of the Law, as the Middle Ages tried to do. When the twelfth century gave way to the thirteenth in the apocalyptically minded Middle Ages, there were voices to be heard, at first hesitatingly and softly, and then with mounting strength up to the days just before the Reformation, asking "whether the pope is the Antichrist." The reasons given for this thesis were always those of the Law. The pope was the guardian of God's Law on earth, but he did not keep it; he cast it aside. He did not keep the law of Christ,

---

2   E.g., Ernst Peter Wilhelm Troeltsch. MH

for instance, the command of poverty. He is the greatest and most frightful sinner of all because of his scandalous life, because of his greed and his tyranny.

Luther also knew of these sins and blamed the popes for them, but as Hans Preuss[3] has observed: "An utterly scandalous life, no matter how bad, would never have persuaded him that the pope is the Antichrist" (*Vorstellungen vom Antichrist*, 1906, p. 152). Luther always warned the Evangelicals never to claim a higher level of morality than their opponents. We are all of us sinners, and there is no sense in quarreling about who is the biggest one. In his table talk, Luther made a comparison between his battle with the pope and that of [John] Wycliffe [1320–84] and [John] Hus [ca. 1370–1415].

> Doctrine and life must be distinguished. Life is bad among us, as it is among the Papists, but we don't fight about life and condemn the Papists on that account. Wycliffe and Hus didn't know this and attacked [the papacy] for its life. I don't scold myself into becoming good, but I fight over the Word and whether our adversaries teach it in its purity. That doctrine should be attacked—this has never before happened. This is my calling. . . . [T]o treat doctrine is to strike at the most sensitive point . . . . [WA TR 1:294; AE 54:110]

For Luther the pope is the Antichrist because his doctrine is anti-Christian. With his doctrine he casts the Lord Christ from His throne and puts himself there, there in the place which is Christ's alone. Christendom, then, must choose between the Gospel and the doctrine of the pope.

In light of this we can understand why Luther time and again spoke of his lifework as the battle against the papacy.[4] He spoke of his room in the tower in Wittenberg as his "poor little room from which I stormed the papacy, and for that it is worthy of always being remembered." His thus identifying his lifework needs no more quotations, but we may note that he does this whenever he solemnly confesses his faith. So in the *Great Confession* of 1528,[5] in the Smalcald Articles [1537], and in the *Brief Confession* of 1544.[6] For him to confess the Evangelical faith meant also to confess that the pope is the Antichrist. It pained him that this confession was missing in the Augsburg Confession. Hans Preuss has pointed out that just in those hours when it seemed he was about to die he confessed his

---

3 Hans Preuss (1876–1951) was an older Erlangen colleague of Sasse. Sasse contributed "Credo apostolicam ecclesiam" to Preuss's *festschrift* (see Lthtm [= NKZ ns. 47, nos. 8–9] [1936]: 256–68 [*Festgabe zum 60. Geburtstag von D. Dr. Hans Preuß am 3.9.–19–36*]. The text has been translated into English: "I Believe in the Apostolic Church," pp. 88–99 in *We Confess: Jesus Christ*, trans. Norman Nagel (St. Louis: Concordia, 1984). Huss number 157. MH

4 For a penetrating historical study on this topic, see Scott H. Hendrix, *Luther and the Papacy: Stages in a Reformation Conflict* (Philadelphia: Fortress, 1981). MH

5 That is, Luther's *Vom Abendmahl Christi Bekenntnis* (*Confession concerning Christ's Supper*), Aland 2, WA 26:261–509; AE 37:151–72. MH

6 That is, Luther's *Kurzes Bekenntnis vom heiligen Sakrament* (*Brief Confession concerning the Holy Sacrament*), Aland 661, WA 54:141–67; AE 38:279–319. MH

commitment to the battle against the pope as the Antichrist. In 1527, when he was very ill and expected to die, he was sad that he had not been found worthy of martyrdom, but he comforted himself with the fact that so it was even for St. John, who had written a "much harder" book against the Antichrist. Ten years later, when he was grievously ill at Smalcald, he said similar things. Finally, there is the gripping prayer he prayed the night of his death. He thanked God that He had made known to him His Son, "in whom I believe, whom I have preached and confessed, whom I have loved and praised, and whom the wretched pope and all the godless abuse, persecute, and blaspheme" (cf. G. Köstlin, *Martin Luther*, vol. 2, 1903, pp. 170, 632; H. Preuss, p. 146). Also in the wills which Luther made we find the thought expressed that the battle against the Antichrist was the battle of his life.

This battle cannot be explained by reference either to his temperament or to political motives. The former may apply at most to particular expressions which betray the irascibleness of an old man. These the Lutheran Church has rejected, as also have non-Lutheran critics who recognized them for what they were. The battle was not occasioned by moral outrage or by personal dislike. Of these we find more than enough not only in the Late Middle Ages but also among good Catholics at the time of the Reformation. On the contrary, Luther had a sort of human sympathy for Leo X.[7] The recognition that the pope is the Antichrist is for him much rather the other side of the knowledge of the Gospel, and the battle against the pope as the Antichrist is therefore the other side of the battle for the Gospel. To understand this profound connection is to understand what the Gospel is and who the pope is. Here is the reason why the Evangelical Lutheran Church accepts what (not how) Luther taught of the pope as Antichrist and why it proclaims in its Confessions as church doctrine that the pope is the Antichrist.

5

It should never have been questioned that this really is *church doctrine* and not merely a theological opinion of Luther's and of early Lutheran theology. On what grounds could one remove from the Confessions the large article on the Antichrist in the Smalcald Articles (II IV)? The same is true of Apology VII–VIII 24; XXIII 25; XXIV 51 (in all of which the German text uses the word "Antichrist," while Melanchthon's Latin text is content with citing Daniel 11) and in the Treatise on the Power and Primacy of the Pope 39: "It is plain that the marks of the Antichrist coincide with those of the pope's kingdom and his followers." Yet

---

7   Leo X (1475–1521; r. 1513–21). After the expulsion of his family from Florence in 1489, Giovanni de' Medici led a wandering and almost Bohemian life in Germany, the Netherlands, and France. He returned to Rome in 1500 and became a legate in 1511. He sought pleasure, was easy-going, and was liberal with money and offices. Within two years he had squandered the fortune left by Pope Julius II (r. 1503–13). Leo excommunicated Luther in 1520. See *ODCC*, 968–69. MH

if these passages are not in accord with Scripture, they should be removed. First, however, it would have to be shown that they are not in accord with Scripture, and second, if that were shown to be the case, the doctrine expressed there would have to be solemnly retracted before all the world.

One cannot, however, do it the way August Vilmar suggests: "That the pope in Rome is not the Antichrist, as used to be supposed in the Evangelical Church, is now so self-evident that any refutation of such an unclear notion is quite unnecessary and would indeed seem quite foolish" (*Dogmatik*, II, 306). Vilmar himself would likely have revised this statement, and many another which he wrote regarding the Roman Church, had he lived to witness Vatican I.[8] That there may be no doubt about our position, let it be clearly said: A theologian who merely because it happens to be in the Confessions lets the doctrine stand that the pope is the Antichrist and who is not solidly convinced that it is so cannot truthfully be called a Lutheran. He cannot escape the charge of slandering the papacy.

Why did the Lutheran Church accept Luther's teaching on this point? What is the meaning of this doctrine? We must first clearly recognize what the church did not accept. There were items in Luther's view of history which were not accepted, specifically that the end of the world would come not later than within the next century. With such presuppositions Luther could not possibly answer the question as to what new forms the Antichrist might assume in subsequent centuries. The church can have no doctrine which answers such a question. The church can and must teach that all the eschatological prophecies of Holy Scripture come to fulfillment. How that may happen lies beyond its knowing. We can never say with certainty how what Scripture says in apocalyptic picture language will be realized. The fulfillment of all prophecies is greater than could be grasped by those who heard them, even by those who heard them in faith. The Lutheran Church teaches nothing in its Confessions as to how God may let the prophecy of the Antichrist come to fulfillment in the hidden future, that is, what form the Antichrist may take in the final terrors of the end time. What our Confessions can teach and do teach, this and no more, is that in the "last time" which we can see, in the time of the church until the present day, the prophecy of the Antichrist has found fulfillment in the papacy.

Luther himself never supposed that there was nothing to be seen of the Antichrist beyond the papacy. In his *Great Confession* of 1528 he says:

> The papacy is assuredly the true realm of Antichrist, the real anti-Christian tyrant, who sits in the temple of God and rules with human commandments, as Christ in Matthew 24 [:24] and Paul in 2 Thessalonians 2 [:3f.] declare; although the Turk and all heresies, wherever they may be, are also included in this abomination which according to

---

8   Vatican I dogmatized the idea of papal infallibility in *Pastor aeternus* (see below, p. 108 n. 11). MH

prophecy will stand in the holy place, but are not to be compared to the papacy. (WA 26:507)[9]

This always remained his conviction, and Lutheran theology always followed him in this matter.

But why is the pope the "true" Antichrist? The Smalcald Articles give the following answer:

> [He] has raised himself over and set himself against Christ, for the pope will not permit Christians to be saved except by his own power, which amounts to nothing since it is neither established nor commanded by God. This is actually what St. Paul calls exalting oneself over and against God. [SA II IV 10]

It is really unnecessary to quote the passages in which overzealous devotees of the pope have predicated of him what belongs only to God. This they did and were not excommunicated for it. Among them were the medieval canonists Augustine of Ancona[10] and Zenzelinus of Cassanis (d. ca. 1350). (Documentation is given [in Tappert, p. 300, and] in *Bekenntnisschriften*, p. 431.) Among them also were the Ultramontanists of the nineteenth century who so flattered Pius IX [r. 1846–78]. What the Confessions teach is that when the pope promulgates a dogmatic decision, one which has no basis in Holy Scripture, and makes men's salvation or damnation depend on their obedience or disobedience toward it, then he is setting himself in the place of Christ, in the place of God. This is what Luther, with sharp prophetic vision, saw as the essence of the papacy, even though he could not yet know the Council of Trent or Vatican I.

If there was any doubt on the part of some Lutherans as to the correctness of Luther's judgment, then this was removed when Pius IX, with the consent of the Vatican Council, on July 18, 1870, promulgated the constitution *Pastor aeternus*.[11] In it, eternal salvation was denied to those who consciously oppose the dogma that the pope has the exercise of direct episcopal power over the whole church, over the infallibility with which Christ has equipped His church, and that his *ex cathedra* decisions in questions of faith and morals are, "of themselves, and not from the consensus of the church," true and irreformable (*ex sese, non autem ex consensu Ecclesiae irreformabiles* [Denzinger 3074]). And when the first of these new *ex cathedra* decisions was proclaimed—the dogma of the assumption of Mary,

---

9   *Vom Abendmahl Christi Bekenntnis*, WA 26:507 (Aland 2, *Confession concerning Christ's Supper*, AE 37:367f.). MH

10   Augustinus Triumphus (1243–1328), an Italian Augustinian Hermit, lecturer, and preacher. His works include *Summa de potestate ecclesiastica*, the first comprehensive handbook of the papacy (s.v *Christian Cyclopedia*). MH

11   Debate concerning papal infallibility ended on July 4, and voting concerning the constitution *Pastor Aeternus* took place on July 18. Only two members voted no (though others did abstain from voting). Extremists from both sides were disappointed—that his decisions are "irreformable of themselves, and not from the consent of the Church," and that infallibility applied only when speaking *ex cathedra*. See *ODCC*, 1681. MH

in 1950, on All Saints' Day, the day inseparably connected with the Reformation—the shock wave hit all Christendom. Here became visible something of the reality which Luther had recognized with deep dread—the reality of the man who puts himself in God's place and proclaims his fantasies as divine revelation.

The pope is either Christ's vicar or he is the Antichrist. That is the alternative which Luther recognized quite clearly. Either the papacy is indeed instituted by God or it is an institution "instituted by the devil" (Luther: *vom Teufel gestiftet*).[12] This institution is not merely human. It is more than a heretical institution. It is also something fundamentally different from the great non-Christian powers. They launch their attacks against the Christian faith from the outside and will continue to do so. Whatever devilish attacks may be made against the church by the fearful totalitarian powers of the world, no representative of these powers has yet claimed to be Christ's vicar and to speak and act in His name. They set up their temple next to the church and seek to displace it. In the papacy, however, the man who deifies himself has worked his way into the church. This is what is so horrendous in the papacy.

And since 1870 the church, insofar as it has placed itself under the papacy, can never get free of this. Not only are the dogmas which the pope produces irreformable (among them the constitution *Pastor aeternus*), but there is no power above him. "No one shall judge the supreme see." This fundamental law is adduced in the Treatise on the Power and Primacy of the Pope (50) as evidence of the anti-Christian character of the papacy. It is now set in concrete in canon 1556 of the *Codex of Canon Law* (*Codex iuris canonici*). No council can ever judge the pope or in any way stand over him. If the pope dies during an ecumenical council, the council is at the moment of his death interrupted and can only be begun again, or not begun again, by the new pope (canon 229, *Codex iuris canonici*). Both according to [canon] law and according to the doctrine of the Roman Church, this institution can never be removed from the church or be deprived of its claims. Of all the great persecutions which Christianity has endured, those words apply which we hear from the faith of the ancient church: "It is a little cloud; it will pass." Of the sinister temptation which the Antichrist is for the church, it can only be said that he will continue until the returning Christ destroys him.

6

In Letter 13, "Is the Pope Really Still the Antichrist?"[13] we pointed out, over against the position taken by Hans Asmussen, that the papacy today is essentially the same as the papacy which confronted Luther. Responses came also from some Roman Catholic readers of that letter. Among them was a venerable

---

12 See *Wider das Papsttum zu Rom, von Teufel gestiftet* (*Against the Roman Papacy, an Institution of the Devil*) (1545), Aland 550, WA 54:206–99 (AE 41:257–376). MH

13 See *Letters to Pastors* 1:218–38. MH

Jesuit, Father [Cardinal Bea],[14] who for decades has worked for better understanding between our confessions. They sought to persuade the writer that a revision of the old Lutheran judgment of the papacy is made necessary simply by the fact that a common front of all Christian churches is called for against the militant atheism of modern Communism. And it is a widely held notion that the judgment of Luther and the Confessions on this point is only of temporary significance, that it cannot be maintained in the modern world if only because the papacy is not in the hands of such morally vulnerable characters as in the time of Luther. At that time one may have observed the power of "lawlessness" [2 Thess. 2:3], whereas nowadays, on the contrary, the papacy is a stronghold of God's Law and the Christian religion. It has also been said that the first pope to die a martyr's death will put an end to the talk about the pope being the Antichrist. Now we must respond to these objections.

Concerning the morals of the popes, Luther long since put an end to the notion that here are the grounds for recognizing the pope as the Antichrist.

As to the papacy being the guardian of God's Law and the Christian religion in the modern world, it all depends on what is meant by Law and by Christian religion. We have already observed that it is hardly by chance that the great, bloody revolutions took place in Catholic lands. The Catholic countries of Europe and South America have tumbled from one revolution to another. There seems to be only one Catholic king left in the world, in Belgium, and his throne is none too sure. What of Russia? One cannot call it a Protestant country. The mausoleum of Lenin stands next to the Chapel of the Iberian Madonna—a warning as to where the path of giving reverence to men can lead, even if it begins in the refined rites of the cult of Mary. Whoever knows the inner history of Europe's Catholic countries, in particular of the ecclesiastical principalities and above all of the papal states, will recognize the fearful consequences for God's church of not having heeded the Lutheran Reformation's warning against mixing church and state— something that can also be observed in the Lutheran Church itself.

The statement that the papacy is the stronghold of God's Law in the world has its context in the confusion and ignorance of the modern world as to what is law given by God. Is it to be regarded as divine Law that the supposed vicar

---

14 Cardinal Augustin Bea (1881–1968) was a scholar, ecumenist, and leading figure in Vatican II. In 1965, Bea invited Sasse to visit him in Rome. Subsequently, they corresponded (via Bea's secretary, S. Schmidt). See *Lonely Way* 2:330 n. 13. "In Rome I did in one week the work of at least a month, working in the Bible Institute . . . on the problems of Holy Scripture . . . . Cardinal Bea had summoned me *ad audiendum verbu* and opened all doors to me . . . . I had a very interesting conversation with Cardinal Bea. In Geneva the WCC people were so proud that the cardinal had visited them. He told me that this had been the greatest disappointment to him. These people, he said, have nothing learned after all [*sic*]. It is the old liberalism from the beginning of the century. What do these people believe? What does Bishop Lilje believe? We want to dialogue. But where is the church with which we can speak? Wherever I come, I find an individual, a bishop or professor, who can speak only for himself . . ." (Sasse to J. A. O. Preus, July 1965; in the Harrison Collection). MH

of Christ makes the demand that all mankind shall be obedient to him in all decisions concerning faith and morals? Don't people see that here we have the source of the totalitarian systems of our day?

Mussolini and Hitler were sons of the Roman Church. Stalin even got as far as candidate of theology. There have certainly been absolute states before, and they came out of Spain and France. Modern totalitarianism is characterized by its claim to have power over the souls of men. This was not so in the world empires of antiquity. A citizen had indeed to go along with the state cult, but he was left to think about it what he liked. That souls can be compelled to a faith, that was first discovered by Catholicism, and secular imitators of the Roman Catholic church system have made use of this discovery. Without an infallible pope there would never have been an infallible Hitler. The total state was born along with the total church on July 18, 1870.

How deep this connection is can be seen in the history of the last generation, whose documents are now more and more coming out of the archives. Fascism could not have happened in Italy without the pope. The history of the '30s reveals how close was the tie between them, as well as what all was included in the Lateran treaties. The moral responsibility for all the horrors of the Abyssinian war, if it can be called a war, is shared by the Vatican. And it was not only the Madonna of Fatima who rescued the Iberian Peninsula from Bolshevism or what was so called.

We Germans who lived through it, those who had their eyes open in the fateful year of our people, the fearful year 1933, know who it was who helped Hitler to power. Without that help he would not have came to power except by violent revolution. It was not only the foolish Evangelical pastors, not only the decadent German citizenry, but the Vatican that did this. To the horror of thinking German Catholics, the Vatican ordered the dissolution of the Center Party because National Socialism was needed for the struggle against the East. For that the German people were sacrificed. Then, to be sure, when the concordat [between Rome and Hitler; July 7, 1933][15] was broken (that gentlemen's agreement between two parties of whom each was convinced that the other was no gentleman), and it became clear in Rome that the stronger cards were in the other hand, then all of a sudden there was staunch defense of the very holy human rights which had not long ago been betrayed to Hitler.

We mention these things here only to refute the pious legend that the papacy is the stronghold of civil order and God's Law in the world. The Roman Church is the continuation of the Roman Empire with other instrumentalities. It is the empire in the form of a church, at bottom a synthesis of church and world, of

---

15 See "Concordat between the Papacy and the Third Reich, 20 July 1933," and "Ratification of the Concordat, 10 September 1933," in Peter Matheson, *The Third Reich and The Christian Churches* (Grand Rapids: Eerdmans, 1981), 29ff. MH

divine and human, and therefore it is that temple where man has put himself on the throne of God.

The Roman Church is indeed the defender of the Christian religion, but of what sort? In this Christian religion God is not the only Lord who is served. Our Lord Christ said clearly that one cannot serve two lords [Matt. 6:24]. Putting another lord beside Him, or another lady, such as Mary Queen of Heaven, has in it a fatal propensity to displace Him. In theory it sounds fine when it is said that grace is superior to nature and the human will, Christ to His mother, the Redeemer to the coredemptrix, the single Mediator of the New Testament to the mediatrix of all graces. But when Catholic people are taught that the way to Christ is by way of Mary, then she has practically become the savior. Then one has to say of the pope as Luther did in his last confession: "What good does it do him greatly to exalt with his mouth the true God, the Father, the Son, and the Holy Spirit, and to make a splendid pretense of living a Christian life?" (*Brief Confession concerning the Holy Sacrament*, 1544).[16] But we have already discussed this aspect of Catholicism in Letter 13 and so need not repeat what was said there of the organic connection of the institution of the papacy with synergistic doctrine and the cult of Mary.[17]

Only one thing more. A modern pope simply cannot be a martyr for the Christian faith like the old bishops of Rome. He would die not only for faith in Christ but at the same time also for the superstition of Fatima; not only for the doctrine of the Gospel but at the same time also for those errors which have been proclaimed as divine revelations necessary for salvation, such as the dogmas of the immaculate conception and of the assumption of Mary, the universal episcopacy, and the infallibility of the pope. He would die also for the false claim that he is Christ's vicar on earth, to whom every human being, on pain of losing his salvation, owes obedience in all dogmatic decisions, as though to the Lord Himself. This is what has to be said to those who maintain that Luther's judgment on the papacy is no longer current.

7

Among theologians it should not be necessary to spend many words to make it clear that the judgments which the Confessions of our church make about the papacy are statements of theology and doctrine, the opposite of those outbursts against individual popes and against the Roman Church that are produced by human anger and hatred. Luther's judgment against the pope has nothing to do with that of French or Italian Freemasons. It is also quite different from that of German politicians who from time to time tell of the injuries done the

---

16   *Kurzes Bekenntniss vom heiligen Sakrament* (1544), Aland 661, WA 54:160 (cf. AE 38:310). MH

17   See "Is the Pope Really Still the Antichrist?" in *Letters to Lutheran Pastors* 1:218–38. MH

German people from the end of the time of the Staufers [thirteenth century] up to the present. The judgment of the Lutheran Confessions is also something quite different from what was heard from German Protestantism during the *Kulturkampf*,[18] from the Evangelical League in Germany, from the Away-from-Rome movement in Austria [early twentieth century], or from the anti-Rome movement in the United States unleashed by the proposal that the United States have an ambassador to the Holy See. What do any of these movements know of the Antichrist? They can know nothing of the Antichrist, for they do not know what the Gospel is and what the means of grace are, which have been given by Christ.

It was Luther's deep understanding of the Gospel that enabled him, on the one hand, to recognize its fearful perversion in the papacy and, on the other hand, to give a positive evaluation of those elements of the true church of Christ that still live on in the Roman Church. The same Smalcald Articles which so sharply delineate the doctrine of the Antichrist also acknowledge that "the sublime articles of the divine majesty" "are not matters of dispute or contention," and give a considerable list of those matters which they wish to discuss with the Roman theologians. In the eyes of the world, which knows not the Gospel, this is an inexplicable contradiction. To understand it, one must know much about the reality of the church—of the church as Christ's kingdom which must always struggle against the kingdom of the devil in this last and evil time.

It is not only human beings who are engaged in this drama. It was not only Eugenio Pacelli [Pope Pius XII] who proclaimed the false doctrine of the assumption of Mary as a revelation given to Christianity. It was not actually and not alone Giovanni de' Medici [Pope Leo X] who cast Luther out of the church. It was not actually Alexander Farnese [Pope Paul III, r. 1534–49] who repudiated *sola fide* and so also the Lord Christ Himself. Rather, it was the Antichrist who spoke and acted in and through them. For this reason we, as also Luther did, can have some human, sympathetic understanding for those men who bore the fearful office of the papacy. This is especially true in the case of those popes who, as far as human eyes can see, were noble figures in the history of the papacy.

As did our fathers before us, so we, too, know ourselves to be bound together in the one holy church of Christ with all those who live within the true church also in the Roman Church—those who are born of the means of grace, the Gospel and the Sacraments, which have not yet entirely perished in the Roman Church. We Lutherans should also be shamed by the true and living faith in Christ that is present within the Roman Church despite the Antichrist and his seductive wiles. In the Roman Church there are Christians who truly live from the Gospel that is still there, from the Gospel in the prayer in the Canon of the Mass itself, "not judging our merits, but forgiving our iniquities." We know of Christians there

---

18 Otto von Bismarck's (1815–98) attack on German Catholicism in the 1870s. NN and MH

who, when it came [time] to die, knew nothing save Christ and Him crucified, and who died in faith in Him, forgetting about the whole churchly apparatus and the world of saints: "King of majesty tremendous, Who dost free salvation send us, Fount of pity, then befriend us" [*TLH* 607:8]. To recognize this is to see why Luther laid such weight on the fact that the Antichrist would not be the Antichrist unless he were actually seated "in the temple," the church of God.

We are aware, honored brethren, of what a responsibility we take upon ourselves when we today repeat in such a way the old doctrine of the Lutheran Church concerning the pope as the Antichrist. We know that we shall have to answer for this before the judgment seat of Him who someday will judge the claims of all churches, the doctrine of all confessions. His judgment is the decisive one for us, not the opinions of men.

The majority of Western Christians today, and their theologians, including Lutheran ones, show no knowledge of this doctrine of the Reformation. And why is this? Because our generation has to a large extent lost any grasp of the great realities of the faith. One is struck here in Australia, on the edge of the Asiatic world, when meeting Christians from the "younger churches" of the mission fields, by how entirely different is their relationship to the New Testament and to the realities given us there. For them this is all new, fresh, and alive, while for us Europeans or Americans it is covered with a layer of dust centuries thick. The Epistles and Gospels which are read in church on Sunday we already know, or think we know. The hymns we sing once poured out of hearts made glad by the newly discovered Gospel—but that was long ago.

Here lies the deepest reason why Luther's doctrine of the Antichrist has become strange to us. One must know much about the reality of Christ, about His real presence, about His actions, dealings, and sufferings in today's world, in order to see the Antichrist in his manifold appearances, also the most splendid and powerful ones. One must literally live from the Gospel as the message of the sinner's justification in order to know what it means to exclude this Gospel from the church in the name of Christ and to deny salvation to those who teach, believe, and confess it.

God grant us all, pastors and congregations, teachers and students of theology, open eyes and an ever deeper understanding of His Word, and thereby an ever clearer view of the reality of the Antichrist, wherever and in whatever form we may encounter him, even if it be in our own Lutheran Church!

ᔐ

With this wish I greet you, dear brothers in the ministry, in these Easter days, in the unity of the faith.

[Hermann Sasse]

Historical Context

As Sasse calls the Lutheran world back to its own Confessions, he asserts the primacy of the doctrine of the Gospel and its articles, as expressed in the Book of Concord. He attempts to find the middle road. German Lutheranism—thoroughly united with non-Lutheran churches in the EKiD—dominated the LWF and its approach to questions of unity from the very beginning. As Sasse correctly asserted, you can be a Lutheran without the Formula of Concord, but not against it. Missouri was rumbling over the "Common Confession" (adopted by the LCMS in June 1950 and by the ALC in October 1950), which was an attempt to find unity with the ALC. Critics of the effort in the LCMS asserted the official status of "The Brief Statement." Sasse calls for a time-out, as it were, and suggests all parties study the Book of Concord rather than produce new confessions. It's a bit ironic in that Sasse himself was at the time deeply involved in the development of the Australian "Theses of Agreement," which is a confession that became the constitutional linchpin of the LCA. MH

March 22, 1952[1]

Prof. Hermann Sasse
41 Buxton Street
North Adelaide, South Australia

Highly Honored Herr Doctor Behnken!

... Our official representative at Hanover (with our 30,000 souls we have only one delegate) was to be Dr. Stolz.[2] But now he probably will not be able to go. His wife is gravely ill, and he will not travel as long as she is alive. In that case, our representative will be Pastor Doehler.[3] ... He ... is a very faithful man in his way, a man who holds firmly to what he has recognized as right. He will, naturally, be swamped with terrible tales regarding Missouri when he is in the USA, the kind of tales one gets to hear everywhere—just as the segments of the divided Lutheran church here in Australia formerly regaled themselves with such stories. Now everything depends on his getting the right impression of your church when he is in St. Louis. You, my dear Dr. Behnken, must help see to that, and you and the men of your church administration, and above all Dr. Sieck....

H. Sasse

---

1   CHI Behnken file. Behnken had Sasse's German translated. MH

2   John Stolz was president of the UELCA. MH

3   Along with Sasse, Doehler was a member of the Intersynodical Committees discussing the merger of the ELCA and UELCA. MH

twenty-five

Concerning the Unity
of the Lutheran Church

TRANSLATED BY ANDREW SMITH

Pentecost 1952[1]

Prof. D. Theol. Hermann Sasse
41 Buxton Street
North Adelaide, South Australia

Dear Brothers in the Office!

In these weeks, we have all been occupied mentally, and more than a few of us physically, by the pending meeting of the LWF in Hanover and by the theological and ecclesiastical conferences which will follow it. Will Lutheranism succeed—after so many missed opportunities, after so many self-inflicted defeats—in bringing its own house into order and thereby performing for all Christians a service which it owes to them? For the Lutheran churches are indeed the last churches in the Christian world, apart from a small group of Presbyterians and some other Reformed churches, which still have maintained something of the dogmatic heritage of its Reformation. This, however, nobody will expect of Hanover, that it will bring to pass a unification of all Lutheran churches. If ever there was such a hope, that the LWF would bring about a true federation of all churches of Lutheran confession, of all churches which want to be Lutheran confessional churches, then this hope was dreadfully disappointed by the manner in which the meeting in Germany has been prepared. The booklet *Hannover 1952: Handreichung zur Vorbereitung der Tagung des Lutherischen Weltbundes*, which has been distributed throughout the whole world, published

---

1   *BLP* 25: *Über die Einheit der Lutherischen Kirche* (North Adelaide, June 1952). The original was published in *LuBl* [27–]28 (1952). Huss number 294. MH

by the German national committee, shows quite clearly whither the LWF listeth. Next to the Lutheran territorial churches, many union churches in Germany appear in the list of national committees and their leaders, with the exception of the Palatinate, whose union confession is indeed nothing else than the purest Calvinism (cf. Karl Müller, *Die Bekenntnisschriften der Reformierten Kirche*, p. 870). One could understand it, if, as in the old World Convention, those Lutherans in the union churches who reject the union as an injustice and want to reestablish the Lutheran church were brought in for advice and collaboration. But an entire union church council is found among the "national committees," and the church of Berlin-Brandenburg even completed a masterpiece of ecclesiastical politics when it placed Dr. Krummacher, the only one of its general superintendents who is consciously Reformed, at the head of its delegation for Hanover. Article VI of the LWF's constitution, according to which the executive committee has the right to admit for advisory votes representatives of Lutheran congregations in the union churches, offers the legal foundation for these ecclesio-political operations. But where, for example, are Lutheran congregations in Baden? And are congregations which don't at all want to leave the union—but rather merely raise the legal claim to enjoying as union congregations the complete rights of a Lutheran congregation, because in them the Augsburg Confession is still nominally "valid"—really Lutheran in the sense of the LWF? If in Germany the door into the LWF is opened widely to the union, then what sense can there be in expecting additionally the entry of the Missouri Synod and of the Lutheran free churches, which once, because of the union, left the territorial churches on account of conscience? Once again, they proceeded here according to the same recipe, exactly as in the case of Brazil, of setting precedents which one cannot take back. Here again a decision of incredibly broad consequence was made behind the iron curtain of an executive committee. The plenary assembly now merely has the task of legalizing the decision [that has been] already made. How could they, in the presence of the celebratively invited guests, openly discuss the question of whether the invitation was proper or not? Under these circumstances the Lutherans who are true to the Confessions have no other choice than to discuss this question among themselves and to make clear to themselves and to others what actually constitutes the community of the Lutheran Church. They will need to do this without any resentment toward those who think otherwise. Perhaps they also can do it—hopefully they can do it, working together with the LWF, to which so many loyal Lutherans belong who in the simplicity of their hearts cannot imagine that responsible Lutheran churchmen can practice a type of church politics in which *yes* is no longer *yes* and *no* is no longer *no*, and, namely, because they have a thousand considerations to make and are no longer in the condition to work according to the clear reading of the Confession. So the time has come, then, in which all who still wholeheartedly profess the Book of Concord must answer the question: In what does the unity of the Lutheran Church actually consist? The following lines are intended to encourage consideration of that question.

1

The unity of the Lutheran Church may not be confused with the unity of the Church of Christ in general, for we do not confuse, as do the Roman Catholics, our church with the *Una Sancta*. In what does the unity of the one, holy, catholic, and apostolic church consist? The seventh article of the Augsburg Confession teaches that wherever the Gospel is announced so that men can thereby come to faith in Jesus Christ as their Savior and wherever the Sacraments are still administered according to the institution of the Lord, there is the one holy church, the community of saints, that is, the sinners who have faith and who are justified in faith. That can happen inside, and outside, our denominational church. Indeed, Lutheranism has never given up the faith that the true church of Christ is all around the earth, hidden among the historically metamorphosed "churches," wherever the voice of the Good Shepherd can still be heard. Here is the great and authentic ecumeny of our church, which has found its most powerful expression in that which the Apology of the Augsburg Confession, Article VII–VIII, says about the "comforting article" of the *ecclesia catholica*:

> This remains certainly true, that the group and the individuals are the true church which here and there in the world, from sunrise to sunset, truly believe in Christ, which then have *one* Gospel, *one* Christ, one Baptism and one Sacrament, governed by *one* Holy Spirit, even if they have different ceremonies. [Ap VII–VIII 10 (Müller, p. 154)]

This church and its unity are a reality in the world, but a reality which must be believed, as the explanation of the Third Article in Luther's Large Catechism so clearly says:

> I believe that there is on earth a little holy flock or community of pure saints under one head, Christ. It is called together by the Holy Spirit in one faith, mind, and understanding. It possesses a variety of gifts, yet is united in love without sect or schism. [LC II 51 (Müller, p. 457)] [Tappert, 417]

True ecumeny, which sees the one church of Christ wherever the means of grace are yet preserved—through which the Lord calls to His church—even beyond the boundaries of one's own ecclesiology, stands opposed to *false ecumeny*, which treats Christians of all denominations as brothers in faith. This false ecumeny tries to make visible and tangible that which we men cannot see and touch: the church as the people of God, as the Body of Christ, as the temple of the Holy Spirit. This false ecumeny changes the "article of faith" about the church into an "article of sight." It understands the unity of the church, which only the Holy Spirit can create and maintain, as something which we humans can produce. And it tries to produce this unity in that it works to realize the *one* faith, the *one* Baptism, the *one* Sacrament of the Altar as a compromise of various forms of faith, various interpretations of Baptism, and various understandings of Holy Communion. Insofar as it does that, this false ecumeny overlooks [the fact] that the various understandings of the means of grace are not only different possibilities of understanding the truth, but rather that soul-murdering errors and church-destroying heresy also hide among them. True ecumeny sees this. Therefore it is able to recognize the true unity of the church only there where it recognizes the one correct faith, the one correct Baptism, the one Communion of the Lord Christ. True ecumeny asks, therefore, not first about unity, but rather about truth. It knows that where the *true* church is, there, and there alone, is also the *one* church. In this sense it also understands the High Priestly Prayer of the Lord, in which the "that they may all be one" is linked inseparably with "sanctify them in Your truth; Your Word is the truth" (John 17:17, 21).

Does an explicit common confession belong to the unity of the church in this sense? The answer to this must be no. The one common faith of the church will certainly find its expression. The true church of Christ has, at all times, confessed its faith and will confess it until the end of the world. The content of this confession will always be the same; it will be nothing other than an explication of the original confession of the church, that Jesus is the Son of God, the Christ. But this confession can have very different forms, as in the old church very different forms of common confession of faith existed alongside one another until later a few confessional formulas took over in the East and in the West. But is it telling that even the three *symbola catholica seu oecumenica* ["the three ecumenical creeds"] received by the Lutheran church are not, in a strict formal sense, ecumenical, not even the so-called Nicene with the *filioque* ["... proceeds from the Father and the Son"]. The confession of the correct Christian faith belongs to the essence of the church, but not any one confessional formula or confessional document. Even the much-discussed sentence from Article VII of the Augsburg Confession says this about that which is sufficient "for true unity of the Christian church," namely, "that the Gospel is preached clearly according to pure understanding there, and the holy Sacraments are distributed according to the Gospel" (AC VII 1–2 [Müller, p. 40]). The unity of the church depends on this: that the Gospel is really preached purely and in large quantity and that the Sacraments are administered according to their institution. It is therefore a serious misuse of this passage from the Confession when it was said in the German union churches, and when even the so-called "Confessing Church" repeatedly announced through its leading theologians, that a common doctrinal confession does not constitute the unity of the church, but rather the common contemporary announcement of the Gospel; therefore, having a common confessional document is unnecessary. Against this, it is to be said: *Confessional documents as such are unnecessary for the unity of the church but are necessary for that which happens in them, namely, the distinction between truth and error, pure teaching and heretical teaching.* Without this distinction there is, indeed, no pure preaching of the Gospel and no correct administration of the Sacraments. Nobody can know what the *one* church of God is if nobody knows what the *one* Gospel, the *one* faith, the *one* Baptism, and the *one* Sacrament of the Altar are. Every Christian congregation (wherever it is), each part of Christendom (however it may label itself) must have one answer to this and has one answer, even if they aren't quite sure about the contents and implications of their own answer.

2

If a particular historical confession does not actually belong to the essence of the church of Christ, then it does however belong to the *essence of the Lutheran Church*. By "Lutheran Church" we mean that segment of Christendom which accepts as scriptural the great doctrinal decisions of the Lutheran Reformation, as they are recorded in the Lutheran Confessions. As we determine this, so we guard against the misunderstanding which appeared in the Lutheran church of the nineteenth century: that the church be like a type of association and the Confession, the rules of the organization, so to speak, even as a political party has a platform as a type of worldly confession. Such a party or association is indeed held together by such rules, as its individual members declare their joining based on such rules. Hardly any other misunderstanding of the Lutheran Confession has damaged our church like this one. Unlike the rules of an association, the confession of the church is never the expression of the opinions of individuals who link themselves together into a body. It is the expression of the consensus about the correct faith, brought about by the Holy Spirit. It must be noted that the confessional writings are not caused by the Holy Spirit, but rather the faith, to which they attest, and the consensus of faith in the community of the church. The riddle, which is inconceivable to the world, of how the confession of personal faith by the individual Christian—nobody else can believe for me—can be at the same time the confession of the entire orthodox church (and vice versa) is explained by the fact that the Holy Spirit always does both at the same time, as Luther says it so well in the explanation of the Third Article:

> [T]he Holy Spirit has called *me* by means of the Gospel, enlightened me with His gifts, sanctified and kept me in the correct faith; just as He calls, gathers, enlightens, sanctifies, and keeps *all Christendom* with Jesus Christ in correct, unified faith. [SC II, Third Article]

This distinguishes the true ecclesiastical confession from the pseudo-confession of modern Protestant churches, those formulas of compromise which serve more to veil unbelief than to confess belief, formulas in which one attempts to bring the religious views of many individual(ist)s together under a common name. The Lutheran Confessions did not come about in this way. Even the introductory sentence of the Solid Declaration [of the Formula of Concord] may not be understood in such a manner:

> The primary requirement for basic and permanent concord within the church is a summary formula and pattern, unanimously approved, in which the summarized doctrine commonly confessed by the churches of the pure Christian religion is drawn together out of the Word of God.... In the same way we have from our hearts and with our mouths declared in mutual agreement that we shall neither prepare nor accept a different or a new confession of our faith. Rather, we pledge ourselves again to those public and well-known symbols or common confessions which have at all times and in all places been accepted in all the churches of the Augsburg Confession ... and which were kept and used during that period when people were everywhere and unanimously faithful to the pure doctrine of the Word of God.... [FC SD Summary, Rule, and Norm 1–2 (Müller, p. 568)] [Tappert, 503]

Neither the common agreement of the authors of the Formula of Concord, which the signatories approved, nor the determination that the church needed a "summary formula and pattern, unanimously approved" can be interpreted in this sense: as if the Confession were a party platform or an association's rule, arising from the will of individuals who set a norm for themselves. Already the fact that "we believe, teach, and confess" contradicts such a view; the phrase with which the doctrinal decisions of the Formula of Concord begin corresponds to the great "we" which is the speaking subject in all great confessions of the church, from the *pisteuomen* ["we believe ..."] of the Nicene Creed to Luther's hymnic form of the *Credo* ("We all believe in one God") and to the *ecclesiae magno consensu apud nos docent* ["The churches, with great unanimity, teach with us ..."] of the Augsburg Confession. The Lutheran Confession, understood in this sense, belongs indeed to the essence of the Lutheran church. It alone makes it into that which it is. Our church is essentially a confessional church in a sense in which neither the Catholic nor the Reformed churches are—because all these churches have, in addition to their confession, something else which characterizes them in their uniqueness and holds them together: their constitution, their liturgy, their discipline, or whatever else. The Lutheran Church does not have all that. It is part of its understanding of the divine Word, of the distinction between Law and Gospel, that it finds no laws in the New Testament about church constitution, church discipline, and liturgy. It can live with presbyterian, episcopal, or congregational forms of constitution. Its liturgical possibilities reach from Swedish high-churchliness to the absence of liturgy of Württemberg. It has only its Confession. If Gospel and Sacrament are the *notae ecclesiae* ["the marks of the church"] by which we recognize the presence of the church of Christ, then the *notae ecclesiae Lutheranae*, the trait by which we recognize whether a church is Lutheran or not, is the Lutheran Confession. Inasmuch as we determine this, we do not need, after all that has been said, to protect ourselves primarily from the misunderstanding that we would place the *notae* of the invisible church of God on the same level with the traits of earthly historical churches [*Kirchentümern*].

We believe the church of God to be in, with, and under the earthly churches [*Kirchentümern*] because we see the Gospel and the Sacraments there and insofar as we see the Gospel and the Sacraments there. The Confession by which we recognize the Lutheran church is for us nothing else than the "Yes!" to this Gospel and to these Sacraments.

3

According to its content, what is confession which belongs to the essence of the Lutheran church? What belongs in it, and what does not? It has produced new confessions only when it could not possibly do otherwise, but then with great power. The Augsburg Confession wants to confess no other faith than the original faith, which the apostles already had and which the early church symbols expressed. For this reason it begins with a confirmation of the Nicene Creed and does not make an entirely new beginning, in which it would perhaps formulate the principle of Scripture and from that develop a new confession. Even the Formula of Concord wants to confess nothing new, as the cited passage shows.[2] It is a commentary on the Augsburg Confession, insofar as it wants to resolve the disagreements which had arisen between adherents to the Augsburg Confession. It is known how, in the seventeenth century, Calov strove vainly to complete the Book of Concord by adding a confession against syncretism.[3] The mass production of new "confessions" during the German church struggle is explained not only by the need to speak confessionally to the important questions of the era but also by the fact that people were no longer acquainted with a feeling of timidity in the face of new confessions and in the face of the imposing responsibility of a new confession. Luther and the confessors of the Book of Concord submitted their confessions with a continual concern about Judgment Day, when they would be called to account for their affirmations and rejections. It is to be feared that modern theologians, who take such great joy in [the appearance of] new confessions, will now transfer their workspace to the territory of the LWF. Granted, it could be necessary to speak the content of the Book of Concord in a new form to people at the end of the twentieth century; the average student in America and Australia is already so far removed from the German history of the sixteenth century that he can hardly still understand many historical allusions. Even the learned theologians in America have a difficult task in translating the Confessions. What shall we even say, then, about the young churches in the mission field! But such a necessity of "translating" the Lutheran Confessions may never serve as a pretext for replacing the old Confession with a new one. It

---

2   See above, p. 122. MH

3   In 1655, Abraham Calov (1612–86), professor in Wittenberg (1650) and general superintendent (1652), prepared and sought to have approved by the church the *Consensus Repetitus fidei Lutheranae* ("The Repeated Consensus of the Lutheran Faith"). See *RGG*[3] 1:1587. MH

is the old faith, the faith of the fathers, the faith of the correct church from the very beginning, which we have to confess anew as our faith. Nothing of this old faith may be lost.

In this sense, the content of the Lutheran Confession is and remains determined by the Book of Concord. It is true that the Lutheran Church is the Church of the Augsburg Confession. But the Formula of Concord remains a decisive commentary on the Augsburg Confession for the Lutheran Church, even if some churches did not accept the Formula of Concord for historical reasons, as [they did] the Apology, especially in those questions which Crypto-Calvinism of all eras directs toward our church. If one wants to interpret the confessional article of the LWF in such a way that even churches which reject as error the doctrinal content of those Confessions not named in this article—especially the Smalcald Articles, the Large Catechism, and the Formula of Concord—can be members of the LWF, then the LWF is not actually a Lutheran federation, and it should find another name for itself. Moreover, the conscious rejection of the Formula of Concord usually goes hand in hand with the denial of the real presence in the sense of Lutheran doctrine. There should be no doubt about this: that for Luther and for the Churches of the Lutheran Reformation, the article about the Lord's Supper is similar in importance to the article about justification, a fact which Michael Reu[4] has many times pointed out, especially in connection with his works for the Lutheran World Convention. If the article about justification is the *articulus stantis et cadentis ecclesiae* ["the article by which the church stands or falls"] in the discussion with Rome and with the Pelagianizing fanatics [*Schwärmer*], then the article about the Lord's Supper has no less importance for the church battle against the spiritualism of the fanatics and against the spiritualism of the humanists, which destroy the church. Both [articles] belonged inseparably together for Luther in his doctrine about Christ. Already the entire historical context of the Augsburg Confession, with the events of the year 1529, indeed actually show instead that the tenth article of the Augsburg Confession is to be understood in no other way. The tenth article of the Augsburg Confession contains no other teaching than that which the Lutherans had confessed at Schwabach[5] and Marburg. Zwingli also had understood it in this way. The later twisting of the meaning—as if the tenth article of the Augsburg Confession already contained the late Melanchthonian view of a presence of Christ in the celebration and in the action but without being bound to the elements—was made possible only by the fact that one no longer considered the clear words of

---

4   Johann Michael Reu (1869–1943) was born and educated in Germany, studying theology at Erlangen. He came to the United States in 1889 and became professor at Wartburg Seminary (Iowa Synod) in Dubuque (1890). See *RGG*[3] 5:1073. MH

5   The seventeen Schwabach Articles were prepared by Luther and others between July 25 and September 14, 1529, and are reflected in the Marburg Articles. They were first presented at a meeting of the Evangelical princes in Smalcald at the end of November 1529 (s.v. *Christian Cyclopedia*). MH

the German text. *So the Confession by which the church is recognized as Lutheran is the understanding of the Holy Scripture, which is clearly witnessed in the confessional documents of the Evangelical Lutheran Church.*

4

More precisely, what does it mean that this is the confession of our church? *In what does its "validity" consist*, and how far does this validity go? Werner Elert repeatedly drew our attention to the fundamental difference between the Roman Catholic and Evangelical Lutheran understandings about ecclesiastical confessions of doctrine. It consists in this: that the Roman doctrinal confession has the form of an imperative, while the Lutheran has the form of an indicative. Roman dogma is a command of faith; the Lutheran, an expression of faith. There a *credendum* ["something which must be believed"] is presented with a command to accept it. Here is expressed what the church [already] believes: "We believe, teach, and confess." The difference is deeply rooted in the concept of faith. Faith, in the Catholic sense, is the supernatural virtue, by the power of which I hold as true that which the church presents to be the content of revelation: *Fide divina et catholica ea omnia credenda sunt, quae in verbo Dei scripto vel tradito continentur et ab ecclesia sive solemni iudicio, sive ordinario et unversali magisterio tanquam divinitus revelata credenda proponuntur.* "With the divine or catholic faith, everything must be believed which is contained in the written or transmitted Word of God and which is presented by the church as divinely revealed thus as to be believed, whether it be in a solemn decision of faith or whether it be by the orderly and general office of teaching" (Vaticanum, *Const. de fide catholica*, cap. 3, Denzinger 1792). Thus the *objectum fidei*, "the object of faith," is defined. Corresponding to the concept of faith as "holding something to be true," the object of faith is, for a Catholic, always dogma, for example, the dogma about Christ. Corresponding to the Evangelical concept of faith as *fiducia*, as trusting the divine promise of grace in the Gospel, is the fact that, for the Lutheran, the *objectum fidei* is not the dogma about Christ, but rather Christ Himself; not the dogma about the Trinity, but rather the triune God; not the Bible as such, but rather God, who speaks to us in each word of the Scripture. This important distinction was misused by [Albrecht] Ritschl and his school in his time, but then by the entirety of modern liberalism, in order to get rid of dogma in general. What a misuse was created with simply one phrase of Melanchthon's, namely, his famous phrase that recognizing Christ means recognizing His benefits but not His natures and form and manner of the incarnation! As if the benefits of Christ would exist without the mystery of His incarnation, His true divinity and true humanity! As if one could believe in Jesus Christ without believing that He is the God-man! No, the Lutheran church did not set dogma aside, but rather gave to it its proper place, and thereby caused it to be honored as it is honored in no other church. For the *assensus*, which, like the *notitia*[6]—to use the expressions of the old dogmaticians—is indivisibly bound to the *fiducia*, has indeed a very different import when it is not merely the obedience of the intellect to the office of teaching and the documents of revelation—Scripture, tradition, doctrinal decisions—presented by this office, but rather the "Yes!" of the heart and of the spirit to God's own Word. *Ecclesia magno consensu apud nos docent decretum Nicaenae Synodi de unitate essentiae divinae et de tribus personis verum et sine ulla dubitatione credendum esse* [AC I 1]. This beginning of our Confession has only a superficial similarity to the Catholic command to faith, the command to take up the *credendum* in obedience of the intellect and of the will. Melanchthon, as often happened with the theologians of the Reformation—for example, in the *semper virgo* ["ever virgin"] of the Latin translation of the Smalcald Articles (SA I; Müller, p. 299)—simply retained the catholic [Latin] expression and formed a connection between the word *credendum* ["something to be believed"] and the word *decretum*, which Elert (*Morphologie*, vol. 1, p. 178)[7] rightly notes as a mistake. The German text, which in the case of the Augsburg Confession has indeed the same authority as the Latin, contains nothing which reminds one of a command to belief. The normative character—which is here, as in other passages in the Book of Concord, ascribed to the Confession—is explained by its relation to Holy Scripture. Our churches—the plural here, as in the Formula of Concord, is explained by ancient Christian linguistic patterns, in which the church consists of individual churches, local churches—teach in great agreement this or that. They do this because the Scripture teaches this or that. The Confession is, as Edmund Schlink properly states with great emphasis, "the *summa* of the Holy Scripture" (*Theologie der lutherischen Bekenntnisschriften*, 2nd ed., pp. 39ff.),[8] as the catechism is, according to Luther, "a short excerpt and copy of the entire Holy Scripture" (introduction to the Large Catechism, Müller, p. 379). The authority of the Confession is therefore derived from the authority of the Scripture. The Confession is *norma normata* ["the norm which is normed"] for the church's announcement [of the Gospel] and stands thus under the *norma normans* ["the norming norm"] of the Scripture, but within this limitation it has true authority.

From this the question is to be answered, *How far does the validity of the Confession go?* It goes exactly as far as it holds to pure exposition of the Holy Scriptures. The Scripture is God's Word; the Confession is a human word. The Scripture is inspired by the Holy Spirit; the Confession is not, even if it, as is

---

6   The dogmaticians defined faith as "assent" to the truths of Scripture, "knowledge" of the Gospel and its articles, and "trust" in Christ as the central and fundamental element. MH

7   *The Structure of Lutheranism*, trans. Walter A. Hansen (St. Louis: Concordia, 1962; repr., 2000). MH

8   *Theology of the Lutheran Confessions*, trans. Herbert J. A. Bouman and Paul F. Koehneke (St. Louis: Concordia, 1961; repr., 2003). MH

correct preaching, is produced with the assistance of the Holy Spirit. The Scripture is infallible; the Confession is not infallible. Its content needs continual supervision vis-à-vis the *norma normans* of the Holy Scripture. But where the Confession as *summa* of the Scriptures accurately reflects the contents of the Scriptures, then it participates in the authority of the Scriptures, in a similar fashion to correct announcement of the Gospel in preaching. Insofar as the examination of the Confession in relation to the Scripture gives us certainty that it "has been taken from God's Word and is firmly and thoroughly grounded in it," we may—indeed, we must—own it with the *quia* of true doctrinal obligation. As we do that, we give witness that its teaching—that is, its recognition of the teaching of the Scripture—is correct. That does not mean that we own every sentence of the Confession and hold it to be correct, as we must accept every sentence and every word of the Bible. It could be that the exegesis of an individual biblical passage is insufficient—one must say, for example, that in John 6 there is a relation to the Eucharist which Luther and the Lutheran Confession did not see—or that philosophical argumentation or propositions of an older view of nature are no longer intelligible to us, such as the unusual opinion about the effect of garlic on magnets. It is the scriptural exposition of the Confession—that is, the conceiving and portraying of the doctrinal content of the Scripture, the deciding of doctrinal questions based on the Scripture—which we accept, whereby it is of no consequence whether or not such a decision is introduced by the express declaration "we believe, teach, and confess," or whether it happens in a positive development of pure doctrine or in a rejection of a false teaching. As we thus accept the teaching of the Confession, we profess the communality of the church, which in its confession gives the answer of faith to the Word of God.

5

Thus the Confession creates the unity of the Lutheran church. We have no other sign or means of unity and communality for our church. Because the Confession gathers the church, it at the same time draws the *borderline* against everything which does not belong to it. At least, it's supposed to be that way. Is it that way in reality? Or is all that perhaps only a theory which once was correct, but which today is no longer true? There was a time—Elert described it impressively in his *Morphologie des Luthertums*—in which the Lutheran church really from Uppsala and Drontheim all the way to Nürnberg and Tübingen, from Strassburg all the way to Dorpat, from the Netherlands all the way to Hungary, in all the diversity of languages, constitutional forms, and liturgical orders, really was a united [body] in the Confession and by means of the Confession. There was no common organization, but what kind of close community is evidenced in, for example, the reports of the Reformation's 100th anniversary in 1616 and 1617! Never again has the Lutheranism of the world been such an authentic unit as in the centuries of orthodoxy, when there was no other bond of unity than common confession, even if they could occasionally be of very different opinions about the explication of it. By what is a church such as the church of Hanover—with its 3,900,000 souls, of which more than a million were previously members of the Old Prussian Union, and with its more than 1,300 pastors, of which likewise more than 300 were taken over from the Union—actually bound into a unity today? Certainly not by means of [its] confessional status, which is "Lutheran" but is understood differently and determined differently, according to whether or not the Formula of Concord was valid once, several centuries ago, in the individual regions and cities. This same question could be asked in the case of the Scandinavian churches, which have never seriously experienced the problem of the union in their own countries. Certainly in Sweden the Book of Concord is still valid. But is this judicial validity much more than the validity of that Danish imperial law which forbids, as a capital crime, any introduction of the Formula of Concord and which has been left on the books merely because it was forgotten and ignored? Essentially, all these national and territorial churches are held together by very different bonds, and not by means of their confession, by the same bonds which, for example, hold together the Church of England and the Church of Scotland. But even if one considers these large church bodies, historical and bounded geographically, for what they are in reality (organizations in which politics and ecclesiology are inseparably mixed), and if one turns one's eye rather to the spiritual office and the Christian congregation which live in these organizations, is the spiritual unity which exists in this congregation still determined by the Lutheran Confession? That was once the case. There was a time in which the Swedes, the Danes, and the Hanoverians were Lutherans, good ones or bad ones, but in any case formed in their inner lives by the Confession of their church and affirming this Confession. One can say this still today only about a disappearing minority in these once-Lutheran peoples and tribes. One must see this reality in order to understand the hopeless struggle of German Lutheranism against the union. *The Confession has lost the power over souls which it had in the sixteenth and seventeenth centuries.* In the nineteenth century it was still conceivable to gain back this power, at least in a segment of European Christianity; the Lutheran Awakening, the struggle of Lutheranism in the union, and the founding of Lutheran "free churches" witness to this. But the minority who found their way back to the Confession of the church was too weak to make a major impact in the large regional churches and in the modern mass societies. Even the confessional struggle against the [Prussian or Nazi] totalitarian state led in only a few cases to a rediscovery of the *content* of the Confession. Thus one must understand that the large Lutheran Churches of Europe, even in those countries in which there are no Reformed Churches at all, no longer see the ecclesiastical boundary lines against the Reformed or the Anglicans. Lutheran bishops who commune in Reformed and Anglican churches, Anglican bishops who co-officiate with Lutheran bishops in the consecration [of the elements of the Sacrament]: those are the images which one did not see in earlier centuries. How would the Christian congregation of earlier times have reacted to this!

It seems as if a process is completing itself within Lutheranism, a process which the Reformed Churches already have behind them, and a process which one must mark as a dying of the Confession of the Reformation. Certainly the Confession is not entirely forgotten, but it retains only a historical meaning. It is one of the great keepsakes, which every church likes to maintain. But it has lost its original function of collecting and making distinct the difference between truth and error. Can one turn back the wheel of time? Whoever has stood for decades in the vain struggle against the spirit of the current age in the church, and has experienced how German Lutheranism has retreated from one position after another, each time declaring that this would be the position where it would conquer or perish, has no illusions anymore. But what would it mean if the Lutheran church sank into being merely a theological school of thought inside a Reformed-biblicist-liberal-Freemasonic or even a Reformed-fundamentalist world Protestantism? Thereby we would lose that which God gave to Christendom in the Reformation: the understanding of the Gospel in distinction from the Law, and the understanding of Baptism and the Eucharist as means of grace. The real presence would remain with the Roman church. And of all the confessions of the Reformation era, only the confession of the Roman Reformation, the *Tridentinum* [the confession of the Council of Trent; Denzinger 994–1000], would remain. But for the humans at the end of the twentieth century, tired of the secular dogmas of the large political systems, yearning for the Christian dogma and for a firm Christian doctrine, nothing would be left, *faute de mieux*, except for the road to Rome. Consider why in England, but not only there, so many educated people are going this way!

6

The fear that the time of the Lutheran Confession and the Lutheran confessional church could be over is intensified when one considers the churches which, in contrast to the European regional and ethnic churches, base their unity even still today on the profession by the church members of the Lutheran confessional documents. This is the case in the large and small *free churches* [and] above all in *America*. It is worth pondering the question to what degree even in these churches the "Confession of the fathers" has already taken on a historical dimension and become a treasured inheritance, the inner adoption of which is becoming ever more difficult, and how far the *churchly* home has become a "home church," which is more "home" than "church." One does no injustice to the Lutheran Churches of America when one determines that in them this process of deconfessionalization has already largely completed itself in connection with the loss of the old (German, Swedish, Norwegian, etc.) church languages, the advancing assimilation to the Anglo-American surroundings, and the deep spiritual transformation which has occurred in the entire American people since 1917. What especially causes one to think is that the retreat of the old Lutheran Confession is even to be seen in those places in which American Lutheranism passionately professes orthodoxy. We have already indicated this once in connection with the internal developments of the Missouri Synod (Letter 20).[9] We cannot ask our American brothers in faith earnestly enough to turn their full attention to this problem. What is at stake can be made clear by an example.

In September 1951, in Okabena, Minnesota, the "Orthodox Lutheran Conference"[10] organized itself. It is a small circle of pastors and laity from the Missouri Synod—how many congregations or parts of congregations stood and stand behind it is difficult to say, but in any case we're talking about a very small group—whose consciences forced them to believe that they must give up fellowship with the Missouri Synod until it would return to the allegedly ignored orthodoxy. The main point here is not which particular errors were the cause of the rebuke toward the mother synod—mainly it was about the evaluation of the "Common Confession" made between Missouri and the American Lutheran Church—but rather our interest is in the way in which church fellowship is understood and how it is founded. The dogmatic basis of the new conference was expressed in a "confession of faith professed and practiced by all true Lutherans," which consists of two parts: a general section about the confessional foundation and a specific section which considers twelve doctrinal points. In the general section the thesis is established about the authority of the Bible, the symbols, and the "Brief Statement," the doctrinal declaration of the Missouri Synod from 1932.

> We recognize and accept with our whole hearts and without any reservation the canonical books of the Old and New Testaments as the inspired Word of God.—We accept the Lutheran Confessions, as they are contained in the Book of Concord of 1580, as a correct explication of the Word of God in regard to all the teachings discussed therein.—We accept the Brief Statement of the Missouri Synod (accepted in 1932 and confirmed in 1947) as a correct explication of the Holy Scriptures about all the questions discussed therein.

It is telling that the modern doctrinal declarations are no longer understood as a necessary explanation of the Confession of the church, but rather that they receive the status of a confession, as a binding explanation of Scripture, and are practically placed above the old confessions. No decision about the disputed questions is made on the basis of the church's Confession. At one point, the passage from the Formula of Concord (SD X 5, 7, 16) is quoted with its warning

---

9   See above, Letter 20, "Confession and Theology in the Missouri Synod," 5–31. MH

10   The group was led by P. E. Kretzmann and merged into the Wisconsin Synod in 1963 (s.v. *Christian Cyclopedia*). MH

for Christians "not to adapt, even in external forms, to customs which are associated with the enemies of the truth," and added to this is the determination:

> [S]eparation is demanded by God when church fellowship with others,
> even inside Lutheran groups, is equivalent with the toleration of error
> and with the supporting of erroneous teaching.

But what is the church-destroying erroneous teaching which is thereby placed
on the same level with Roman erroneous teaching, which the representatives of
the *Interim*[11] once themselves *de facto* tolerated? What are the false teachings
which, according to the opinion of this document, are tolerated by the leaders
of the Missouri Synod so that one can have no church fellowship with them?
Have these men tossed away some dogma of the church, some proposition from
the Confessions? The only positive error which these "orthodox Lutherans" can
find in the case of the leaders of Missouri is the disputation about the proposition that engagement is actually a marriage vow. This proposition is, however,
not a component of the Lutheran Confession. Beyond that, the matter is about
whether the Missouri Synod, in its negotiations with the American Lutheran
Church and in its behavior toward other Lutheran churches, had made itself
guilty of unionism, and especially whether in the "Common Confession" it used
ambiguous expressions that do not fully give witness to the biblical-confessional
truth. Now, it can happen, naturally—and it has happened often enough—that
a church otherwise loyal to the Confessions denies with the deed that which it
confesses with its mouth. No church is certain against this, as every confessor
can become a denier, as did the very first confessor, Simon Peter. It can be that a
Lutheran Church, by means of its practical dealing, blurs the borderline against
error and finally ceases to be Lutheran. It can be that one will have to separate
one's self from it, for the sake of truth. But to justify that separation, the situation must be so evident [and] so grievous, and irreparable errors—perhaps entry
into a church such as the EKiD, which cannot be reversed—must be present,
such as no sober observer can find them in the case of the Missouri Synod. The
vast majority of all those who do not approve of the "Common Confession" have
also not taken part in this separation. It is as if some severe disease has broken
out in conservative American Lutheranism, when one reads the expressions
with which one speaks about the "teachers of error and false prophets" of the
Missouri Synod in the discussions at Okabena (e.g., *Proceedings*, p. 31).

If we set aside, for a moment, the human and ethical aspect of this matter,
which reminds us very much of certain tragedies in old Lutheran orthodoxy,
what is the theological *sickness* which is here manifested? It is recognizable when
one sees how the unity of the church is here considered. The consensus which

---

11 After the defeat of the Lutheran princes in the Smalcald War, compromising theologians concocted "Interims" (Augsburg in 1548 and Leipzig in 1549) which granted
some popular Lutheran practices (marriage of priests and distribution of both elements in the Supper) but reimposed many Roman Catholic practices. MH

binds the Lutheran church is no longer the *consensus de doctrina evangelii et de administratione sacramentorum* ["agreement in the doctrine of the Gospel and the administration of the Sacraments," AC VII] expressed in the Confessions, but rather it is the *agreement in all and every doctrine of the Holy Scripture*, whether or not it is touched upon in the Confessions. By "doctrine" is understood in this case every doctrinal proposition which one can directly or indirectly take out of the Holy Scripture. Because "everything which was written previously, that was written for us as a teaching" (Rom. 15:4), and this *everything* includes not only the actual dogmatic passages but rather "additionally all other determinations, historical reports, geographic data, and comments made in passing" (*Confession of Faith* II.5; *Proceedings*, pp. 52f.).

But because the Scripture is completely clear in all questions which deal with "life and faith," it is dangerous and misleading to speak of exegetical difficulties, theological problems, and open questions in the exposition of the doctrinal content of the Bible, or so we are further told in the "Confession" (II.7; Ibid., p. 53).

> We reject the claim that it is neither necessary nor possible to be united in all points of doctrine or that complete agreement in details of doctrine and practice is not required. [II.6]

We stand here before a concept of the "doctrine" contained in the Scripture and in the Confession, a form which is unknown to the confessional documents, and which at least in this extreme form was not even shared by the Lutheran orthodoxy of the seventeenth century.

If one wants to understand this hyperorthodoxy—this word is really at home here, because we are dealing with a theology which goes beyond Lutheran orthodoxy—then one must begin with the concept of "doctrine."

> But what was written before, that was written for us as a teaching, so that we may have hope by means of the patience and comfort of the Scripture. [Rom. 15:4]

How can one read from this sentence that even geographic data in Scripture are given to us as "doctrine"? The Greek word *didache*, which the Vulgate renders as *doctrina*, has here the meaning of "instruction." What kind of instruction is meant is shown in the context. It is not the instruction by means of which the extent of our knowledge is expanded, but rather the instruction about the fact that we have a Savior. *Notetur, quam monstrosos vos habeatis articulos fidei* ["It is noted what monstrosities you have as articles of faith"], answered Aegidius Hunnius[12] at the religious debates in Regensburg in 1601 to the Jesuit [Adam] Tanner [1572–1632], as the latter stated with emphasis that it was an article of faith that Tobit took a dog with him on his trip (Tobit 11:9 [11:4]). The orthodox fathers of the seventeenth century often used this example to distinguish

---

12 Aegidius Hunnius (1550–1603) was a professor at Marburg (s.v. *Christian Cyclopedia*). MH

themselves from the Catholic concept of faith and article of faith. Today it is time to remember this again. Even if these fathers still very strongly emphasized the *assensus* in the faith, the faithful acceptance of that which is revealed to us, then they still really never forgot that the actual essence of the faith is *fiducia* ["trust"]. Even if in their case the *credendum* of the dogma was increasingly emphasized, and faith was in danger of finding its object in the doctrine of God instead of in the triune God Himself, then they still express repeatedly, even in their dogmatism, that Christian faith is nothing else than faith in the Lord Jesus Christ. But this truth gets lost if one understands a passage such as Rom. 15:4 in the manner which is found as previously cited above in the "Confession of faith professed and practiced by all true Lutherans." "You have rather odd articles of faith," one is tempted to say to some of our American brothers in faith when they tell us that some historic or geographic item in the Old Testament contained revealed truth and is therefore an object of faith, even if not of justifying faith; that each such truth is an article of faith, if not a fundamental article. Even Luther never doubted the correctness of the biblical history. But this *assensus*, which he expected from every Christian, was for him still not the faith. The Christian faith, for Luther, is always the faith in Jesus Christ, faith in the *deus incarnates* ["God incarnate"], and therefore justifying faith. Therefore an article of faith is, for him, always a proposition in which the faith in Christ is buried, like the sentences of the Apostles' Creed. Because even the faith in God the Creator, in the Holy Spirit who spoke through the prophets, is faith in Christ. Because I confess the one church, the one Baptism, the community of the saints, the real presence of the body and blood of Christ, and the resurrection of the dead, I confess Jesus Christ. Believing in the Scripture as the inspired Word of God means, for him, believing in Jesus Christ, to whom the Scripture gives witness from the first sentence to the last. In this sense, Luther understands the article of faith as a unit, even in the famous passage from his last [formulation], the *Brief Confession concerning the Holy Sacrament*:

> Therefore, the matter is believing everything entirely, completely, and purely—or having believed nothing! The Holy Spirit does not allow Himself to be divided or separated, that he should teach one thing truthfully, and another falsely, or allow it to be so believed . . . for all heretics are of this manner, that they begin by rejecting only one article, but after that, they must all, and all together, be rejected: just as when a ring, if it has a crack or a chink, is of no value to us any more, and when a bell has a fault on one side, it does not ring at all any more, and is entirely worthless. [*Kurzes Bekenntnis vom heiligen Sakrament* (1544), Aland 661, WA 54:141–67 (AE 38:308)]

Luther does not want to say by this that faith is a system, the sum of many individual doctrinal propositions which one takes from the Bible and brings into a systematic ordering, but rather it is a unit because it is always the faith in Jesus Christ, who is the actual *objectum fidei* in all propositions of faith. The divine truth, which we believe in every individual word of Scripture, is not in each case identical with the intellectual content which grammar and logic transmit, but rather this truth can be buried deeply behind the text, which, for example, everyone will agree is the case for the Song of Solomon. Indeed, the clarity which we ascribe to the Holy Scripture does not mean the same thing as the "clarity" of a philosophical book. It does not assert that the full and exhaustive meaning of a biblical passage must be instantly grasped by every Christian reader of goodwill. It also does not assert that we can instantly find the harmony which exists between [various] statements which externally diverge from each other. If the clarity and perspicuity of the Holy Scripture are to be understood in this way, then the history of the church and her doctrinal struggles would be an unintelligible riddle. For this history was not only the history of a fall from the once perfectly given truth and the struggle for the reproduction of the truth, but rather it also was the history of the wrestling by the true church of Christ toward an ever deeper and fuller understanding of the one eternal unchanging truth. Therefore there are not only "*so-called* exegetical difficulties, theological problems, and open questions" in the understanding of the Scripture, as the "confession" of the "orthodox Lutherans" opines, but rather there actually is all of that, from the days of the apostles onward, who also did not all have the same theology and the same interpretation of the Old Testament, until that day of which it is said: "But then shall come completion, then shall the partial cease!" [1 Cor. 13:10].

This is the teaching which American Lutheranism, insofar as it still really takes the Confession of the fathers seriously, must take from the tragic event of the most recent splitting. It must recognize that the consensus which binds the Lutheran church into a unit cannot be a system of exegetical and dogmatic discoveries in which one thinks to have "the doctrine" of the Scripture, which one theoretically identifies with the Confession of the Lutheran church but practically expresses in new confessions. The message which we must send to these churches today is the warning not to consider the Lutheran Confession as an obvious possession which one could lose. *One can lose the Confession of the Lutheran Reformation not only in giving it up but also by believing with far too great a certainty that one possesses it.* Karl Barth once quoted (*Die Theologie und Kirche*, vol. 2, p. 80) the verses of a German Lutheran in the middle of the previous century:

> Our Church, the Church secure,
> Walled about by salvation and defense,
> Augsburg's conquering Confession
> As a bulwark all about her.[13]

What a false security that was! What would Luther have said to this Lutheran! How gruesomely did the judgments of God in Europe sweep away this illusion. We must ask our brothers in America to examine themselves, to what extent

---

13   Translation of hymn text by MH.

they still perhaps live under the illusion of the "certain" confession and of the church "secured" by the Confession. "Back to the 'Brief Statement'!" That is the call which the people around the "Confessional Lutheran" [movement] continually send to their church. The "Brief Statement" is the confession by which the people of [the] Okabena [movement] measure the orthodoxy of the "Common Confession" and other documents. Would it not be appropriate at this time that people on all sides should first pause and study again the Lutheran Confession and honor it? It is, indeed, still a powerful force in the churches of our faith in America. Behind the formulas of the old orthodoxy, which is still vital there, and of modern fundamentalism, which attempts to seep into Lutheranism from the Reformed environment, lies buried the Lutheran faith, which can still distinguish between Law and Gospel and which knows what the means of grace are. But nobody knows what will become of the next generation, if the fleeting agreement of [various] theological schools, with its pseudo-confession made [only] for the [present] moment, takes the place of the consensus of the church which lasts over time, as the Lutheran Confessions express it. It is a false concept of unity in doctrine if a complete uniformity in the explanation of all passages of the Bible with dogmatic content is demanded, and if this demand is justified with the warning of Paul

> that you at all times speak with one voice, and do not let divisions be among you, but rather hold firmly to one another in one mind and in one belief. [1 Cor. 1:10]

It is the same false concept of doctrinal unity if one directs the warning "that you watch those who cause divisions and disagreements contrary to the teaching which you have learned, and avoid them" (Rom. 16:17) toward every brother in faith who has a different theology. The teaching which Paul mentions in both passages is clearly the pure doctrine of the Gospel, the *articulus stantis et cadentis ecclesiae* ["the article by which the church stands and falls"], the doctrine of justification of the sinner, which he announced in Corinth with Peter and Apollos, though he did not come from the same theological school as these men. These passages, and equally the great passage about the unity of the church in Ephesians 4, which are the basis for Article VII of the Augsburg Confession, really assert nothing else at all than that which the Lutheran Church has found in them, the *consensus de doctrina evangelii et de administratione sacramentorum* ["the consensus concerning the doctrine of the Gospel and the administration of the Sacraments"]. But what is here called *doctrina* should really be clear: *not a theological theory about the Gospel* together with a system of theories about all the questions connected with it, *but rather the teaching of the Gospel itself, which happens in the church* in the pulpit and lectern, in the confessional and in pastoral counseling. There, where the unity of the church of Christ is at all, there is also the unity of the Lutheran Church to be sought. Thus the great *satis est* ["it is sufficient"] of the seventh article of the Augsburg Confession is also the foundation of all unity among Lutherans. What this *satis est* includes in particular, what the consensus about the teaching of the Gospel is in detail, this is what the Confessions of our church tell us. Therefore these Confessions are, as they are collected in the Book of Concord, the only means of real ecclesiastical unification for the Lutherans of the world.

It is unnecessary that I discuss with you, dear brothers, why the return to confession, if it is really taken seriously, is no repristination, no romantic attempt to call again the past into life. But because I know that you, as Lutherans loyal to the Confessions, encounter again and again this reproach, and that it has been raised especially these months against us all as we alert the Lutheran world to what the unity of Lutheranism is, for this reason I would like to say to you what we have to reply to this. The "back to the Confessions" is not one of the many romantic calls of this type, which we have heard in our lives since the start of the German youth movement: back to [Immanuel] Kant, back to Thomas [Aquinas], back to the early church, back to Luther, back to orthodoxy, and whatever else. The call to Confession is for us nothing else than the call to the Word of God, which it explains and from which it alone has its authority. No biblicism can be a replacement for that, as the tragic history of all biblicist movements shows, whose end is always in fanaticism [*Schwärmer*], because there is no distinction between true and false interpretation of Scripture without the formation of confession. One can return to the Word of God because it is not the past alone, but rather the present and the future. But this homecoming to the Word is Reformation, the repentance of the church.

∽

My special greeting goes to those among you who are to take part in the convention in Hanover and in the meetings which are attached to it. God bless all the work for the true unity of the Lutheran church, and every witness which is given for the pure doctrine of the Gospel!

Greeting you in the bonds of faith at Pentecost in this fateful year,

Your
Hermann Sasse

Historical Context

Sasse was a persistent critic of sectors of the liturgical movement or "High Church movement," particularly its proponents within Lutheranism, such as Friedrich Heiler (1892–1967), whom Sasse believed compromised the doctrinal content of the Lutheran faith and rejected basic teachings of the Book of Concord, even on the article of justification. Sasse has similar concerns about Missouri's "high church" proponents. But in this essay, he does give the liturgical movement credit for something quite significant— namely, the increased interest in and practice of the Sacrament of the Altar. Sasse unravels the issue of "receptionism" and takes the reader to the teaching of Luther and that of the Formula of Concord, which repeatedly state that the body and blood of Christ are "present, distributed, and received." MH

March 22, 1952

Prof. H. Sasse
41 Buxton Street
North Adelaide, South Australia

Highly Honored Herr Doctor Behnken!

. . . What does the LWF mean by a Lutheran church? And if you are referred to the constitution of the LWF, you must ask: What does subscription to the *Augustana* mean? Does it mean that the CA *Invariata* is the norm of *publica doctrina*? Does it mean that thereby every other public teaching is declared illegal? Our Church Council [UELCA] is insisting on both these points. If that be conceded, what does the mention of the other Lutheran Confessions in the constitution imply? Can one be a Lutheran if one rejects the Formula of Concord? Until now Lutheranism has held to the principle that one can be a Lutheran without the FC but not against it. There must be a clarification of the confessional basis of the LWF . . . .

H. Sasse

twenty-six

The Lutheran Understanding of the Consecration

TRANSLATED BY NORMAN NAGEL

End of July 1952[1]

Prof. D. Theol. Hermann Sasse
41 Buxton Street
North Adelaide, South Australia

Dear Brothers in the Ministry!

Various inquiries from your circle suggest that I say a word about the Lutheran understanding of the consecration in Holy Communion. Among these was the question of a layman from the Prussian Free Church on how one is to understand the connection between the recommendation or introduction of the epiclesis and the withdrawal of the "for the forgiveness of sins" into the background in the recent liturgical movement. This was asserted in Letter 23 ("The Scriptural Basis for the Lutheran Doctrine of the Lord's Supper").[2]

A further inducement came from the fact that the question about the essence of the consecration has become a main issue in the liturgical movement that is going through the Lutheran churches in America and has been the cause of considerable controversy (cf. the article "The Theology of the Consecration in the Lord's Supper" by G. Drach in *The Lutheran Outlook* [March 1952], and

---

1   *BLP* 26: *Zum Lutherischen Verständnis der Konsekration* (North Adelaide, July 1952). The original was published in *LuBl* 4, no. 29 (1952). This English translation appeared originally in *We Confess: The Church* (St. Louis: Concordia, 1986), 36–48. Minor alterations to grammar and capitalization have been made. The quotations from the Lutheran Confessions in this publication are from THE BOOK OF CONCORD: THE CONFESSIONS OF THE EVANGELICAL LUTHERAN CHURCH, edited by Theodore G. Tappert, published in 1959 by Fortress Press. Huss number 295. MH

2   See above, pp. 76–95. MH

the quarrel between this publication and the *Una Sancta* of the circle around Dr. A. C. Piepkorn [1907–73], St. Louis). It could hardly be otherwise. Nowhere do dogmatics and liturgics affect each other more profoundly than in the question of the nature and function of the consecration. The answer to this question makes quite clear whether the Lutheran doctrine of the real presence has been grasped or not.

1

Let me begin with a word about the *liturgical movement* in the Lutheran Church. It is a part of a large movement that goes through all of Christendom and perhaps also touches humanity outside the church, as the political pseudoceremonies and pseudoliturgies of our time suggest. It came about, as its origin in the years just after the turn of the century indicates, with the end of the dominance of rank individualism and rationalism. Where the liturgical movement appeared in the churches, it had something revolutionary about it—not without good reason was it tied up with the youth movement in Germany. It was a kind of revolution when in Catholic churches suddenly the table [*mensa*] of the early church replaced the high altar, while at the same time in Presbyterian churches in Scotland the Reformed Communion table gave way to the medieval high altar. So church governments, from the pope to Methodist church assemblies, had much trouble, the salutary kind of trouble that church governments need so that custom and thoughtlessness do not rule the church exclusively.

If one today in the middle of the century looks back to the results of the great movement, then one would have to say that only *one* church has dealt with it, has set aside its revolutionary excesses, and has put it in its service. That is the Roman Church, which in many countries, especially in Germany and Austria, derived a real inner renewal from this movement. This has happened. The fruits will only become completely clear when languages such as German and English have been raised to the level of liturgical languages and when a Catholic German Mass [*Deutsche Messe*] will remind Lutheranism that it was once a German Mass that led the Lutheran Reformation to victory. If one compares the success of the liturgical movement in the Roman Church with the failure of all efforts to renew the liturgical life of the evangelical churches in our time, one could have serious concerns about the future of these churches.

Where does the difference lie? What is evident immediately is that the liturgical movement in the Roman Church affected all of the people from the Catholic scholars to the most unsophisticated country congregations. All efforts on the Protestant side remain limited to pastors, some church-minded laypeople, and very small, sometimes almost sectlike associations. The second immediately obvious difference is that the liturgical movement in the Roman Church has remained on the foundations of Roman dogma despite some difficult conflicts with dogma and church order—it happened that liturgical

scholars out of genuine enthusiasm for its liturgy joined the Eastern Church—
while on the other hand the liturgical movement in the area of the evangelical
churches of Germany, including the Lutheran, has lived in continuous conflict
with the church's confession. This has been all the more ominous since, besides
the liturgical movement, the confessional movement in which Lutherans and
Reformed were beginning to discover anew the confession of the Reformation
and the doctrine of the church had been going on since the '20s. That this confessional movement has scarcely any relationship with the liturgy is in part to be
explained by the fact that it received the strongest impulses from the Reformed
side. Karl Barth has never understood what church liturgy is—and how should
he ever know it? On the other hand, leaders of the liturgical movement were
men who had never experienced the rediscovery of the Reformation and the
doctrine of the church: Heiler,[3] whose supposed conversion to Lutheranism in
Uppsala was a misunderstanding, as though revolt against the pope were already
Lutheranism, and Wilhelm Stählin,[4] who came from the Nürnberg church, influenced by Melanchthon and the Enlightenment, and from the Gnostic movement
of Rudolf Steiner's "Anthroposophy."[5] It is significant that these two men have
never understood the *sola fide*. For Heiler the authentic doctrine of justification
has always been that of Trent, while Stählin is a latter-day disciple of Osiander.[6]
He has always dismissed the doctrine of justification in the Formula of Concord
with strong words, even though his literary statements are somewhat more
cautious. One should read over his book *Vom göttlichen Geheimnis* (1936), now
translated into English [*The Divine Mystery*], putting the question: What happens
here to the basic doctrines of the Reformation? His criticism of the doctrine of
forensic justification, p. 67 [p. 106], no longer leaves any room for the idea that
God's forgiving and absolving verdict is our righteousness. That we have no
other righteousness than the righteousness of Christ, that our righteousness is
always an alien righteousness—this humbling and gladdening truth no longer
has a place in a theology that regards man's "transformation" as his redemption. As a result, the *sola fide* disappears. This book speaks of faith only in the
sense of the devout appropriation of the divine mystery, no longer in the sense
of confidence [*fiducia*] in God's mercy in Christ. *Sola Scriptura* also disappears.

---

3   Friedrich Heiler (1892–1967) is a frequent target of Sasse. Influenced by Nathan
    Söderblom (1866–1931), in 1919 he joined the Lutheran church in Uppsala. Heiler
    taught at Marburg and was a proponent of the German High Church movement,
    though absent confessional Lutheran dogma. See *ODCC*, 747. MH

4   Stählin taught at Münster and served as bishop of Oldenburg (1945–52). He
    cofounded the Berneuchen Conference (s.v. *Christian Cyclopedia*). MH

5   Rudolf Steiner (1861–1925) left Roman Catholicism for Anthroposophy, a spiri-
    tual and mystical doctrine according to which higher knowledge may be attained
    through concentration and meditation (s.v. *Christian Cyclopedia*). MH

6   Andreas Osiander (1498–1552) reacted against what he believed was an overempha-
    sis in Lutheranism on forensic justification. His position was rejected by the Formula
    of Concord (FC SD III 4) (s.v. *Christian Cyclopedia*). MH

What's the good of all the beautiful words about the "mystery of the Word," pp. 32ff. [pp. 55ff.], and about the character of the Bible as revelation if there are also additional sources of revelation: tradition and the mystical experience? Or is it not the Catholic tradition out of which it can be said about the Sacraments among Lutherans: "What we in the Evangelical Church call 'Sacraments' is all that is still left from a world of mystery that once embraced and filled the whole life of the Christian Church in its breadth, length, depth and height" (p. 49 [79])? And what else is that "meditation," without which we cannot grasp the depths of a Bible passage or other matters, than a Gnostic-mystical experience ("How does one achieve knowledge of higher worlds?" as we are reminded of Steiner's book)? Not the straightforward hearing of the Word with the assistance of the Holy Spirit but "meditation" should disclose "the divine secret" to the person. So we hear that

> practice in meditation is an inestimable aid to really hearing the word, to penetrating into the secret meaning of a Bible phrase, or to experiencing in ourselves the power of a sign or of a melody." (p. 75 [p. 118])

What a combination: Bible, sign, melody!

> All meditation originates a union, perhaps not to be dissolved, between my psychical experience and certain spiritual contents, words, pictures, signs. Every genuine meditative experience is conscious of that very strange occurrence, that I become one with the object contemplated, not so that I pass over to it, but rather that it comes to me, pulls me by the body; indeed, enters into myself so that I experience its presence even in bodily sensations. (p. 75 [p. 117])

This meditation, whose origin from Gnostic sects is well-known, should find its "most beautiful example" in what the Christmas story tells of Mary: "She kept all these things, pondering them in her heart" (p. 75 [p. 118]). To that is added: "Luther often pointed to this." Really? He certainly did not mean this "meditative experience." He spoke in another way about the Word, about faith, and about the Holy Spirit, who works in us faith in the Word.

It is an unspeakable tragedy of German Protestantism that behind such out-and-out pathological and heretical movements there was a genuine longing for the renewal of the Lutheran liturgy and the Sacraments in line with the Lutheran Church. It is this yearning that has led so many Lutherans in Germany into the High Church movement, above all that of the Berneuchener [led by Heiler]. Here they thought they could find what was no longer offered in the churches that no longer understood their own liturgy, neglected the prayer of the church, the daily prayer, and let the Sacrament of the Altar deteriorate. From this one must understand the success of the Berneuchener [Movement]. They did something. They did much that was wrong, but at least they acted. And who would deny that they have also accomplished something good in the area of liturgical prayer and authentic church music? This is the reason that W[ilhelm] Stählin also enjoys respect among those who object to him theologically. But it remains a tragedy of the German church in the past generation that the confessional movement and the liturgical movement did not find the way to each other.

Confession and liturgy belong inseparably together if the church is to be healthy. Liturgy is prayed dogma; dogma is the doctrinal content of the liturgy. The placement of liturgy above dogma, for which one calls in the liturgical movements of all confessions with the well-known saying *lex orandi, lex credendi* ["the law of what is to be prayed is the law of what is to be believed"] (*ut legem credendi lex statuat supplicandi*, Celestine I [r. 422–32], Denzinger 139, called to remembrance by Pius XI [r. 1922–39] in *Divini Cultus*, Denzinger 2200), has been opposed in the Roman Church by the present pope [Pius XII] in his encyclical *Mediator Dei* [Denzinger 2297ff.],[7] in which he points out that one can also turn this saying around and that in all circumstances dogma should be the norm for the liturgy. If that is already known in Rome, how much more should it be known in the church that makes or would like to make the right understanding of the Gospel also be the criterion for the liturgy.

We Lutherans know nothing of liturgy that is prescribed by God's Word. We know that the church has freedom to order its ceremonies and that it can therefore preserve the liturgical heritage of Christendom, as long as it is consistent with the Gospel. Indeed, our church in the Reformation placed the greatest value on preserving as much as possible this heritage that binds us with the fathers. But these ceremonies do not belong to the essence of the church or to the true unity of the church, as Article VII of the Augsburg Confession and Article X of the Formula of Concord teach. Löhe knew this when in his *Drei Bücher von der Kirche* [*Three Books on the Church*], right where he speaks of the beauty and greatness of the Lutheran liturgy, he protests against overestimating it: "The church remains what she is even without liturgy. She remains a queen even when she is dressed as a beggar" (Book 3, chap. 9 [trans. James Schaff, p. 178]). Even the pope has reminded his bishops that the Masses that are secretly celebrated in prison camps, without any pomp, in utter simplicity, come very near to the Mass of the ancient church and are not inferior to a pontifical Mass. In Lutheran Germany, however, one can today hear theologians—even some who come from unliturgical Württemberg—say that there is a form of the Divine Service that belongs to the essence of the church, even that Gregorian chant belongs essentially to the Christian liturgy. It is high time that the liturgical movement in the Lutheran church wakes up from its romantic dreams and subordinates itself to the norms to which the whole life of the church must be subject: the *norma normans* ["norming norm"] of Holy Scripture and the *norma normata* ["norm which is normed"] of the church's confession. And this applies

---

7   Eugenio Pacelli, upon becoming pope, took the name Pius XII. *Mediator Dei*, promulgated November 27, 1947, expressed sympathy with the desire for the use of the vernacular in liturgy and gave conditional support to the liturgical movement. See *ODCC*, 1296. MH

to all the Lutheran churches in the world, for the Scandinavian, in which the Anglican influence is so great, and for the American, in which the ideas of the European liturgical movement have now gained a footing. If this serious reflection does not take place, then the liturgical movement will become what it has become already for many of its adherents: the end of Lutheranism and the road to Rome.

2

On one point the liturgical movement is right absolutely without a doubt, and here it is irrefutable. It has called attention to the fact that the Lutheran Church has more or less gone the way of Reformed Protestantism in being without the Sacrament, and thereby it has lost what belongs to the essence of the Lutheran Church. A part of the essence of the church in the Lutheran sense is the *Sacrament*, and that in a different sense than the Reformed Church claims that about itself. Lutherans and Reformed do not mean the same thing when they use the word "sacrament." For the Reformed, sacrament is always only a sign of divine grace, a sign that can remain empty, that is, when it might please God to have it so, a sign of a grace that also exists without the sign. They are actions that Christ has commanded and that man must carry out; by fulfilling them we show our obedience to the Lord of the church. For Lutherans sacrament is more than a sign; it is a means of grace in the strict sense. In Baptism we receive the forgiveness of sins, rebirth, and the gift of the Holy Spirit, no matter what we may do with this grace later. In Holy Communion we actually receive with the mouth the body and blood of our Lord for the forgiveness of sins or, if we do not believe this, to our judgment.

This difference in the understanding of sacrament, however, must also work itself out in the celebration of a sacrament. So in the Reformed church every Divine Service is a "sacramental Divine Service" [*Sakramentsgottesdienst*] in which one of the two sacraments that exist according to Reformed belief is celebrated, either Baptism or the Lord's Supper. What matters is that the congregation carries out Christ's command. This explains the remarkable custom in modern Reformed churches of performing Baptism before the assembled congregation in the Divine Service. This is probably an influence of the Baptist churches, where the baptismal tank replaces the altar and Baptism is performed as an actual bath with as much water as possible, so that the poor person being baptized has to rush out of the church in order to change clothes on the outside.

The early church did it just the other way around. It had the Baptism performed outside in front of the church by the deacon—just as the apostles themselves seldom baptized but entrusted it to their helpers (Acts 10:48; 1 Cor. 1:14ff.)—after which the newly baptized came into the church. For this reason the baptismal font according to ancient custom had its place at the entrance of the church. If it were not so hopelessly dreary to witness the thoughtlessness and ignorance of modern Lutheranism, one could smile over the eagerness with which the German and American Lutherans are now also taking over the custom of performing baptism in the congregational Divine Service—which from experience is thereby interrupted—from the Reformed churches. The Rhenish Church, the most Reformed among the provincial churches of the Old Prussian Union, has elevated this custom or nuisance [*Sitte oder Unsitte*]—it depends entirely on the outlook—to the level of church law. That is the same church in which, despite the Union, despite Barmen, despite the EKiD [*Evangelische Kirche in Deutschland*]—in which according to its constitution one should "listen to the testimony of the brothers"—one controversy over candles after another broke out because the Lutherans want to have their candles on the altar and the Reformed forbid them because they are not necessary for salvation, as W. Niesel was not ashamed to report in the Reformed church paper.

Naturally, the question of the place of the baptismal font and the time of day at which Baptism is performed, as well as the question of the size of the congregation that is present, is just as much an adiaphoron as the question of whether and how many candles should burn on the altar. The Lutheran Church has the freedom to transfer Baptism into the Divine Service, provided it would not be the occasion to smuggle the Reformed concept of sacrament into our congregations, as if Baptism were a sign that must be seen by as many spectators as possible, a sign that we men may discard, and not the means of grace through which a human soul is born again to eternal life. The instant the Lutheran congregations, as in the Rhineland, have to submit to a Reformed law, the new custom ceases to be an adiaphoron. Then the *casus confessionis* ["case of confession," FC SD X 1] exists, in which there is no more adiaphoron according to Article X of the Formula of Concord.

But assuming that the *casus confessionis* does not exist and that our church, in the exercise of the freedom that it has in all matters of ceremony, introduces Baptism into the Divine Service, this service would not thereby become, as Karl Barth thinks, a sacramental service [*Sakramentsgottesdienst*]. The only sacramental service in the Lutheran sense is the Divine Service in which the Sacrament that belongs in the Sunday Divine Service is celebrated, *Holy Communion*. For the Lord's Supper is still for Luther simply "the Sacrament," as his usage that again and again puts "Baptism and the Sacrament" together shows (e.g., in the Short Preface to the Large Catechism, Müller, [*Die symbolischen Bücher der evangelisch-lutherischen Kirche*], 380: "yet they come to Baptism and the Sacrament and exercise all the rights of Christians, though those who come to the Sacrament ought to know more..." [LC Pref 5]). Others follow him in this, for example, Justus Jonas [1493–1555] in the translation of the Apology (at AC VII–VIII, Müller, 154: "they have one and the same Baptism and Sacrament," which corresponds to the Latin text: *habent... eadem sacramenta*).

As is well-known, the term "sacrament" is never totally, precisely defined in the Lutheran Confessions, and that is because the concept of sacrament is not found in Holy Scripture and is only a way of thinking of later theology in order to summarize the actions instituted by Christ (Baptism, Lord's Supper, Office of the Keys) into categories. Lutherans should never have gotten involved in the polemics regarding the vacillation of the confessions on the question of what all are sacraments. Christ did not institute "the sacraments" but each particular rite. Whether one calls absolution—which does not exist in the Reformed church—sacrament or Gospel is a question of terminology and nothing more. Among these rites, however, is one that belongs to the Divine Service, without which there is no proper Sunday Divine Service in the church of the New Testament and in the Lutheran Church of the sixteenth and seventeenth centuries, even though Holy Scripture lays down no law about when and how often the command of Jesus, "Do this . . ." (Luke 22:19f.; 1 Cor. 11:24f.), should be followed. This is what the fathers of the early church called the Sacrament of sacraments [*sacramentum sacramentorum*] and what Luther simply called "the Sacrament," the Sacrament of the Altar. To restore this Sacrament, which under the influence of Reformed Protestantism and the modern world has also declined in Lutheranism, and give it its proper place in the Divine Service dare not be an interest only of a liturgical reform movement. It is a matter of life and death for the Lutheran Church.

3

Among the great teachers of the church there has probably been none who has understood the inner connection of *Word and Sacrament, of Gospel and the Lord's Supper* as profoundly as Martin Luther. The church, of course, has always known that the means of grace belong together and thus far form a unity. It is very remarkable that even for Catholicism it is the Word added to the element that first makes the sacrament a sacrament. The Word is the *forma* without which the *materia* can never be a sacrament. But what Roman dogmatics has never seen is the connection between the Sacrament of the Altar and the proclamation of the Gospel. If it had understood this, there would never have been the neglect of the sermon, which even there remains a mark of Catholicism, where one has outstanding preachers and the obligation of preaching every Sunday is impressed on the priests. In the Catholic sacrament of ordination, the priestly office, the authority to offer the sacrifice of the Mass for the living and the dead and the Office of the Keys, the authority to forgive sins, are conveyed, but not the authority to proclaim the Gospel. Now to be sure Holy Communion is a particular form of the proclamation of the Gospel ("For as often as you eat this bread and drink the cup, you proclaim the Lord's death until He comes" 1 Cor. 11:26 [RSV]), but it is not the only way.

The Lord's Supper without the sermon would be a misunderstood rite, just as the sermon, if it were not regularly accompanied by the Lord's Supper as our Lord instituted it, would very soon cease to be proclamation of the Gospel. Those are statements that the experience of Christendom confirms. An Abyssinian Mass and a preaching service in many a prominent, modern Protestant church in New York have in common that they are religious ceremonies from which one can no longer hear the Gospel of the crucified and returning Lord. Before this fact all other differences for theology fade away.

For the Crucified One becomes a figure of the past if His true body and His true blood, what He sacrificed for our sins on Golgotha, are not present in the Sacrament of the Altar and given to us. And the One who is coming again becomes a figure of a distant, unforeseeable future that lies beyond the scope of our life unless the church's prayer, "Maranatha," "Come, Lord Jesus," is already fulfilled now in every celebration of the Lord's Supper. There is no Gospel without the real presence. *The Lord's Supper is a component of the Gospel; the Gospel is the content of the Lord's Supper.* That is what Luther saw. Therefore for him the struggle for the Gospel was at the same time the struggle for the Sacrament of the Altar.

The connection between the Gospel and Lord's Supper becomes perfectly clear in the Lutheran doctrine of the *consecration*, as it is fully set forth in Article VII of the Solid Declaration §§ 73ff. (Müller, 663ff.). There the decisive sentences state:

> No man's word or work, be it the merit or the speaking of the minister, be it the eating and drinking or the faith of the communicants, can effect the true presence of the body and blood of Christ in the Supper. This is to be ascribed only to the almighty power of God and the Word, institution, and ordinance of our Lord Jesus Christ. For the truthful and almighty words of Jesus Christ which He spoke in the first institution were not only efficacious in the first Supper, but they still retain their validity and efficacious power in all places where the Supper is observed according to Christ's institution and where His words are used, and the body and blood of Christ are truly present, distributed, and received [*corpus et sanguis Christi vera praesentia distribuantur et sumantur*] by the virtue and potency of the same words which Christ spoke in the first Supper. For wherever we observe His institution and speak His words over the bread and the cup and distribute the blessed bread and cup, Christ Himself is still active through the spoken words by the virtue of the first institution, which He wants to be repeated. Chrysostom says in his *Sermon on the Passion*: "Christ Himself prepares this table and blesses it. No human being, but only Christ Himself who was crucified for us, can make of the bread and wine set before us the body and blood of Christ. The words are spoken by the mouth of the priest, but by God's power and grace through the words that he speaks, "This is My body," the elements set before us [*proposita elementa*] in the Supper are blessed. Just as the words "Be fruitful and multiply and fill the earth" were spoken only once but are ever efficacious in nature and make things grow and multiply, so this word was spoken only once, but it is efficacious until this day, and until His return it brings it about that His

true body and blood are present in the church's Supper [*usque ad hodiernum diem et usque ad eius adventum praestat sacrificio firmitatem*]. [FC SD VII 75–76]

4

If one wants to understand these statements, one must comprehend what they have in common with *Roman doctrine* and what separates them from it. At first glance it might appear that the Roman Church is done an injustice here. Does it not also teach, referring to the fathers of the fourth century, above all Ambrose [340–397] but also referring to the word of Chrysostom [ca. 345–407] in *De prod. Judae* 1.6 (Migne PG 49:380), that the priest performs the consecration *ex persona Christi* and that it is not human words but the words of Christ that bring about the miracle of the real presence? In *Summa Th.* 3, q. 78, Thomas quotes the words of Ambrose from *De sacramentis*: "The consecration happens by the words and statements of the Lord Jesus" [*Consecratio fit verbis et sermonibus Domini Jesu*]; everything else that is said in the way of prayers is a human word and does not have the effect of Christ's words. "Therefore, what Christ says, this it is what makes the sacrament" [*Ergo sermo Christi hoc conficit sacramentum*] (Migne PL 16:440). Yes, even the comparison between the Words of Institution and the words of creation, as Chrysostom offers it, is readily repeated in Catholic dogmatics (cf. *Deutsche Thomas-Ausgabe* 30:429).

Are the fathers of the Formula of Concord, above all is Luther, who knew Roman doctrine well, not guilty of a sin against the Eighth Commandment when they contend that that church teaches consecration through the word of the priest? Could the Reformed not say the same thing about the Lutheran view of the consecration? What sort of basic difference exists for a strict Calvinist between the Catholic priest and the Lutheran pastor, who both maintain that the Words of Institution that they speak as the words of Christ bring about the miracle of the real presence?

In fact, the Lutheran doctrine has a true kinship here with the Catholic. It is no accident that the Formula of Concord here appeals to the teachers of the ancient church, who are the fathers for the Roman as well as the Lutheran Church. Both churches are churches of the real presence; both churches believe that in every valid Lord's Supper the same miracle takes place as at the first Lord's Supper and that then as now it is the Lord's Words of Institution [*verba testamenti*] that bring about this miracle of the real presence. And yet there is a profound contrast between them. Where does this contrast lie?

It does not lie, as many simply assume, in the question of *transubstantiation*. The doctrine of transubstantiation is condemned by Luther and the Lutheran Church because it is not consistent with Scripture—which speaks of the consecrated bread as still bread in 1 Cor. 11:26ff.—and therefore is a false philosophical-theological theory that tries to describe the miracle, which mocks every description and explanation. But the doctrine of transubstantiation does at least want to hold firmly to the real presence. For this reason Luther always judged it more mildly than the Enthusiasts' and the Zwinglians' denial of the real presence. In this matter, despite the deep chasm that exists, the Lutherans stand closer to Rome than to the Reformed, even to the Calvinists.

And one may not, as still happens, attribute a doctrine of consubstantiation to Lutheranism and try to understand the contrast on that basis. If Luther early in his career appealed to the consubstantiation taught by the Occamists against transubstantiation, he only did it to show that even within the Roman Church the doctrine of transubstantiation was not the only option. But the doctrine that two "substances" exist alongside each other, the substance of the bread and the substance of the body of Christ, is also a philosophical method of explanation, which is not the teaching of our church. Selnecker,[8] the contributor to the Formula of Concord, protested explicitly against this misunderstanding when he wrote in 1591:

> Even if our churches use the ancient little words that in the bread, with the bread, or under the bread the body of Christ is received, no *Inclusio* or *Consubstantiatio* or *Delitescentia*—inclusion, dual essence, or concealment—is thereby fabricated. [*Vom Heiligen Abendmahl des Herrn* (1591), fol. E2]

And similar protests have been made again and again.

Even the "in, with, and under" with which the three expressions were later summarized is not a Lutheran doctrinal formulation. The prepositions "in," "with," and "under" are grammatical devices to express the miracle that the bread *is* the body and the wine *is* the blood. Everything depends on this *is* being maintained. For this reason the Lutheran Church did not criticize the old word "change" among the fathers. For *mutare* ["to change"], which Melanchthon still cites in the quotation from Vulgarius (i.e., Theophylact [1055–1107], who in his commentary on Mark at 14:22 speaks of *metaballein*[9]) in Article X of the Apology, is accepted as an expression of the ancient church and is not put on the same level with the Roman Church's *transsubstantiare*, which indeed it is not. That some had doubts about this is suggested by the omission of the quotation in the German translation of Justus Jonas as well as the translation of *metarrhythmizei* in the Chrysostom quotation in the Formula of Concord with *consecrare*. Meanwhile, the Lutheran Church, though it rejected the doctrine of transubstantiation, has never found the primary catastrophic error in this or any other doctrine of change.

---

8   Nikolaus Selnecker (ca. 1528/1530–92) studied at Wittenberg under Melanchthon. He served as professor at Jena (1565) and as court preacher at Wolfenbüttel (1570) (s.v. *Christian Cyclopedia*). MH

9   "Vulgarius, who does not seem to be an unimportant writer to us, says clearly that 'bread is not a mere figure, but is truly changed into flesh'" (Ap X 55; *Concordia* 154). MH

The antithesis lies at another point. Rome's error is not that the words of the consecration effect the real presence but that it understands the consecration as a sacrifice. Here, in the doctrine of the *sacrifice of the Mass*, not in the doctrine of transubstantiation, lies the grievous error that devastates the church for Luther. This is clear from a comparison between the article on the Mass in Part II and the article on the Sacrament of the Altar in Part III of the Smalcald Articles. "The Mass in the papacy must be regarded as the greatest and most horrible abomination because it runs into direct and violent conflict with this fundamental article"—that is, the *articulus stantis et cadentis ecclesiae* ["the article by which the church stands or falls," i.e., the office and work of Jesus Christ and our redemption]. "Yet, above and beyond all others, it has been the supreme and most precious of the papal idolatries" (SA II II 1; Müller, 301). That was from the beginning of the Reformation until the end of his life the conviction of the same man for whom transubstantiation was a "clever sophistry," a false speculation contrary to Scripture. Luther did not impute guilt to himself for the fact that he had believed in this theory when he was a monk but for the fact that for fifteen years he had said private Masses almost every day and thereby had committed idolatry "and worshiped not Christ's body and blood but only bread and wine and held them up for others to worship" (WA 38:197).[10] That was one of the most severe anxieties of his life. That the sacrifice of the Mass, the most holy rite not only of the Roman Church but of all the churches of the East, the center of Christian piety for so many centuries, should be a violation of the First Commandment! One must understand this in order to comprehend the deep chasm between the Lutheran Lord's Supper and the Catholic Eucharist, between the Lutheran and the Roman Mass, between the Lutheran and Roman understanding of the consecration.

What does it mean that the Mass is a *sacrifice*? Already quite early, perhaps already at the end of the first century, the Eucharist was called a sacrifice, even though the New Testament significantly did not adopt this usage. For the comparison between the Lord's Supper and the sacrificial meals of the Jews and the Gentiles in 1 Cor. 10:18ff. says nothing more than that the Lord's Supper is a sacrificial *meal* in which we receive what Christ once sacrificed for us on the cross. Hebrews 13:10 also says no more if one wishes to apply the verse to the Lord's Supper, as Catholic theology does.

The New Testament knows of the sacrifices of Christians, the *spiritual sacrifices* (1 Pet. 2:5) of praise and thanksgiving and of confession (Heb. 13:15), of the *koinonia* of the gifts of love (13:16), of the surrender of one's whole life in the service of God (Rom. 12:1). Generally here the word *sacrifice* is used in a figurative sense according to the pattern of Old Testament usage (e.g., Ps. 50:14; 51:19).

---

10 *Von der Winkelmesse und Pfaffenweihe* (*The Private Mass and the Consecration of Priests*) (1533), Aland 770 (AE 38:149). MH

When one considers that Christianity, as a religion that did not involve the offering of sacrifices, came into a world of religions that did offer sacrifice, that the Christians were accustomed to sacrifice and the Jewish Christians in Jerusalem still participated in the sacrificial worship as long as there was a temple, then one can probably understand that they sought a replacement for the sacrifices that men do and found it above all in the prayer of praise and thanksgiving. So it was with the Jews of the diaspora and with all Judaism after the catastrophe of the year 70. Was it then such a big step to speak of the Eucharist, the church's great prayer of thanksgiving, also as a sacrifice?

In his great controversy with Trent, Martin Chemnitz answers the question of whether one may call the Lord's Supper a sacrifice in this figurative sense in the affirmative. But a limit is placed on this designation. The moment the Lord's Supper becomes an atoning sacrifice, then one has left the ground of the New Testament. For there we find only one sacrifice for sins: the sacrifice on Golgotha, which was offered once for all at a particular moment in history and is therefore unrepeatable and eternally valid. There in the New Testament there is only the high priesthood of Jesus and the priesthood of the whole people of God, the church (1 Pet. 2:5, 9), of which every Christian is a member (Rev. 1:6). To this day no exegesis has been able to find there a distinctive priestly office besides the universal priesthood of all believers. The passage where the Roman Church believes it has found its priesthood, the office of the priest who offers the sacrifice of the Mass, is the words of our Lord at the Last Supper: "This do in remembrance of Me" [Luke 22:19]. Where is there anything about sacrifice there? Where is there even a hint that this was an ordination? How can one understand Jesus' command to repeat in such a way that from now on the apostles and the priests to be ordained by them should sacrifice the body and blood of our Lord for the living and the dead? Something is being read into the New Testament that is not there.

What is the novelty that has invaded the church with this notion of the priest who sacrifices the body and blood of our Lord? It is nothing else than what has found its expression in the idea of Mary, who as the second Eve takes her place beside the second Adam, participating in our Lord's work of redemption. It is nothing but the notion of man sharing in his redemption, a notion that has found its expression in the different types of the Catholic doctrine of grace in the East and West. It is the claim that man has a part to play in what belongs to God alone. It is the secret pride [superbia] of man who cannot bear that he is dependent only on grace, only on the sacrifice that another offers for him, only on an "alien righteousness." This is the terrible tragedy of church history, which is not to be understood only as resulting from human error but from seduction by a superhuman power, that the holiest celebration of the church, in which Jesus Christ is present according to His divinity and humanity, has been ruined by the claim of man also to be something.

No beauty of the ancient liturgies can gloss over the fact that in them a human priest treads beside the eternal high priest, a sacrifice done by man beside Christ's sacrifice. None of the finely worked out theories about the identity of the sacrifice of the Mass with the sacrifice of the cross—for example, Trent's idea that the Mass is a *repraesentatio* of the sacrifice on the cross, a making present of what happened once on Golgotha—eliminates the fact that in the Mass man is also offering a sacrifice: "We Your servants, but also Your holy people . . . offer to Your illustrious majesty . . . a holy victim, an immaculate victim" [*Nos servi tui, sed et plebs tua sancta . . . offerimus praeclarae majestati tuae . . . hostiam sanctam, hostiam immaculatam*]. Thus states the Canon of the Mass in the prayer that follows the prayer with the Words of Institution, and then God is asked graciously to accept the sacrifice as He did the sacrifices of Abel, Abraham, and Melchizedek. At the end of every Mass, the priest implores the Holy Trinity "that the sacrifice that I, though unworthy, have offered before the eyes of Your majesty may be acceptable to You, both for me and for all for whom I have offered it; may it move You to pity and *propitiate* You" [*ut sacrificium, quod oculis tuae majestatis indignus obtuli, tibi sit acceptabile, mihique et omnibus, pro quibus illud obtuli, sit te miserante propitiabile*]. Even if one stresses that the priest acts and speaks *ex persona Christi*, that in the sacrifice of the Mass Christ offers Himself to the Father and thus "re-presents" the sacrifice of the cross or makes it present, the fact remains that the priest makes the offering not only in the name of Christ but also in the name of the church, in the name of the faithful who are present, and even in his own name.

How can man take part in Christ's sacrifice? One must then go as far as modern Catholic theologians, who see in the sacrificing church the body of Christ, so that Christ and the church, the head and the body, do the sacrifice together. But then it is still a working together of God and man, and one even comes to a dangerous deification of man.

Concerning the relationship between the sacrifice of Golgotha and the church, Holy Scripture says: "Christ loved the church and gave Himself up for her, that He might sanctify her" (Eph. 5:25–26). It is characteristic of Catholic synergism that Mary under the cross is now no longer understood only as the church, for which Jesus died, but that the present pope [Pius XII], in the conclusion of the encyclical *Mystici Corporis* [promulgated June 29, 1943; Denzinger 2291ff.], can say of her that Mary also sacrificed her Son there. In the doctrine of Mary as the "coredemptrix," the final consequence of that synergism becomes clear that finds expression throughout the life and thought of Catholicism and also in the doctrine of the sacrifice of the Mass—the deification of man, the obliteration of the line between Creator and creature. This is what one comes to if one, in the words of Karl Adam,[11] teaches "the wondrous fact that not only

---

11 A Bavarian Roman Catholic theologian, Adam (1876–1966) was considered liberal, modern, and orthodox. He was a popular author, especially with the Catholic laity. See *ODCC*, 16. MH

God but also creaturely powers—according to the conditional elements of their creatureliness—have a causative role in the work of redemption" (*Das Wesen des Katholizismus*, 6th ed. [1931], 141).

5

Only from this profound contrast between the Roman Catholic view of the creature's cooperation in his redemption and the Reformation's conviction that there is no such cooperation and that *Christ alone* is the one "whom God made our wisdom, our righteousness and sanctification and redemption" [1 Cor. 1:30 (RSV)] can the difference in the understanding of the consecration be grasped. It is still true, despite every appeal to the word of Chrysostom and despite the contention that the priest speaks the consecration *ex persona Christi* ["in the person/place of Christ"], that he also still acts in his own name and in the name of the faithful. "We Your servants but also Your holy people" offer to the Father the sacrifice of Christ's body and blood—not just the sacrifice of praise and thanksgiving, not just the gifts of the offertory. It is no accident that the Words of Institution are fitted into the prayers of the Canon of the Mass in the form of a relative clause and thereby become a part of a *human prayer*. However beautiful these Mass prayers may be, as not only the Roman Mass but also the liturgies of antiquity and of all the churches of the East have them, they remain human prayer and take the Words of Institution into human prayer. It is characteristic of the predominance of the human prayer that since the fourth century in the Eastern Church, the epiclesis, the invocation of the Holy Spirit to change the elements, has been understood as the actual consecration in place of the *verba testamenti* [i.e., Words of Institution]. But even if one, as was probably the case in the earlier Masses, understood the whole series of the prayers, including the Words of Institution, as the consecration, it would still be the prayer that consecrates. That is confirmed by the fact that in the Roman Mass the whole Canon is prayed inaudibly so that the congregation does not get to hear the Words of Institution and has to be alerted by the ringing of a bell to the moment when they are spoken. The elevation of the consecrated host for all practical purposes replaces the hearing of the Words of Institution. One must consider once what it meant for the German people, after more than 700 years of Christian history, to hear the Words of Institution for the first time in the Lutheran Reformation, and that the same is true of the other nations who accepted the Reformation at that time. Then one will understand what the Lutheran Mass in the mother tongue meant for these peoples.

Long before he created this Mass after years of the most careful theological and liturgical work, *Luther* had recognized where the decisive error in Rome's understanding of the words of consecration lay. In *The Babylonian Captivity* he declared that what makes the Mass a proper Mass in the sense of the institution of Christ is the Word of Christ [*verbum Christi*] alone, that is, the Words of Institution. "For in that word, and in that word alone, reside the power, the nature, and the whole substance of the Mass" (WA 6:512 [Aland 120; cited from AE 36:36]). Everything else is "accessory to the word of Christ" [*verbo Christi accessoria*]. A year later, in *The Abolition of Private Masses*, he interpreted the Words of Institution as the heart of the Sacrament of the Altar. In this Sacrament is the whole sum of the Gospel (*est enim in eo summa tota evangelii*, WA 8:447 [Aland 503]), as Paul says with the words: "As often as you eat of this bread and drink of this cup you will be proclaiming the Lord's death until He comes" (Luther is quoting the Vulgate [cf. 1 Cor. 11:26]). In the German version of the writing (*The Misuse of the Mass*) of the same year he says:

> For if you ask, What is the Gospel? you can give no better answer than these words of the New Testament, namely, that Christ gave his body and poured out his blood for us for the forgiveness of sins. This alone is to be preached to Christians, instilled into their hearts, and at all times faithfully commended to their memories. Thus the godless priests have made words of consecration out of them and concealed them so secretly that they would not reveal them to any Christian, no matter how holy and devout he has been. [WA 8:524 (cited from AE 36:183)]

Hidden deep in the Canon of the Mass among purely human prayers and in such a way that the Christian people can no longer hear them, the words of the Lord's Supper, the Gospel pure and simple, are stuck. By no longer permitting them to be heard and clothing them in human prayer formulas, they have made out of this Gospel a "benediction" [*Benedeiung*], a *verba consecrationis*, as the Latin wording says. That is, they have robbed the words of consecration of their real meaning. For in the Mass they are no longer good news to the believing sinner but only a consecration in the sense in which there are other consecrations, for example, the consecration of churches or bishops, a rite of blessing with a particular effect. In view of all this we can understand why Luther, when he began to reform the Mass, immediately made two liturgical changes: the *words of the Lord's Supper* were to be chanted *aloud* by the liturgist, and the framing of Christ's words with a whole series of prayers was completely set aside. The only prayer that Luther left in this position was the *Lord's Prayer*, which in the Roman Mass follows the Canon, while Luther put it before the Words of Institution. For him no man-made prayer seemed tolerable beside the *verba testamenti*.

Theodor Knolle[12] has shown the profound doctrinal and liturgical meaning of the old Lutheran Mass in several works (*Lutherjahrbuch* [1928] and in his contribution to the volume *Vom Sakrament des Altars* [1941][13]) and raised a warning voice against the introduction of epicleses and eucharistic prayers, which bring

---

12 Theodor Knolle (1885–1955) was pastor at Wittenberg and Hamburg and served as bishop of Hamburg territory (1954). He was a cofounder of Luther Gesellschaft and led the Lutheran Liturgical Conference. His article for *Vom Sakrament des Altars* addressed Luther's rejection of the eucharistic prayer. MH

13 Edited by Sasse. MH

the Words of Institution again into a relative clause between purely human words, even if they are beautiful and venerable human words. Even when one makes the utmost effort to speak of sacrifice only in an indisputably evangelical way, what is Lutheran still becomes a Roman Mass. The pious man again puts himself alongside Christ, and the Words of Institution are no longer the Gospel. The congregation edifies itself with its beautiful prayers, but it no longer hears the Gospel in the Lord's Supper. The forgiveness of sins recedes. It is no longer seen as the great and joyous gift of the Sacrament.

Is there some connection here with the fact that confession, which according to Lutheran teaching should precede the reception of the Sacrament of the Altar, is no longer taken very seriously? It is then either a General Confession without the complete seriousness of self-examination, which was a matter of course for our fathers, or it becomes in many High Church movements a poor imitation of the Roman auricular confession. But the deep inner connection that exists between absolution and the reception of the Sacrament is no longer understood. It can only be understood when one knows that both *absolution and the Sacrament of the Altar* are two sides of the same thing, that both are the *Gospel* for sinners. But if anyone wonders why we should receive forgiveness twice, what it means that one should be absolved of sins and then still receive the Sacrament for the forgiveness of sins, to such a one we may answer—Luther caught the spirit of it—"You have not yet pondered how great is the weight of sin" [Augustine].

6

Although Luther understands the consecration in Holy Communion as something more than the consecration itself, more than the dedication of elements, it remains *consecration* in the strict sense. The Formula of Concord says it in this sense in its doctrine of consecration, as we quoted it above. It is the doctrine as our church developed it in the struggle against the Enthusiasts, after the doctrine of the consecration determined by the sacrifice of the Mass had been overcome in the struggle with Rome. Precisely because the Words of Institution may no longer in any way be blended with human words or be hidden among the words of men because they are the words of the Lord Christ Himself, they are as powerful as God's words in creation and accomplish what they say. So the Word of the Lord in every celebration of His Supper makes the bread to be the body and the wine to be the blood of the Lord. "For as soon as Christ says: 'This is my body,' his body is present through the Word and the power of the Holy Spirit" (*The Sacrament of the Body and Blood of Christ* [1526], WA 19:491 [Aland 658, cited from AE 36:341]). "How that comes about you cannot know" (Ibid., 489 [cited from AE 36:340]). "We are not bidden to search out how it can be that our bread becomes and is the body of Christ" (WA 18:206 [*Against the Heavenly Prophets* (1525), Aland 588, cited from AE 40:216]).

In accordance with the principle that theology should speak where God's Word speaks and should be silent where God's Word is silent, Luther and the Lutheran Confessions make no dogmatic statements about the how of the real presence. The philosophical lines of thought that are found here and there have a purely apologetic character. They do not try to explain the real presence but only to confront the reproach that the Lutheran doctrine is nonsense. *The Lutheran Church does not know a dogma about the how of the real presence that corresponds to transubstantiation.*

This restraint on the question of the how is also observed when it comes to dealing with *practical problems*. When does the real presence begin? When does it end? Is it limited to the moment of reception? What is the difference between a consecrated and an unconsecrated host? Is a second consecration necessary when the consecrated elements are not sufficient, and if so, why? What happens with the elements that are left over?

When one considers Luther's statements, one notices a very realistic "Catholicizing" attitude that is downright offensive to later Protestants of all confessions. First of all, it is determined that the real presence begins with the Words of Institution, which effect it. "There the words make the bread to be Christ's body given for us. Therefore it is no more just bread, but Christ's body wears the bread" [*Ergo non est amplius panis, sed corpus Christi hat das Brot an*] (*Sermon on the Catechism* [1528], WA 30/1:53 [Aland Pr 925]). This notion is no different from the ideas of the *Formula Missae* (WA 12:214 [Aland 510, AE 53:30]) and the *Deutsche Messe* (WA 19:99 [Aland 156, AE 53:81]). It would "accord with the Lord's Supper to administer the sacrament immediately after the consecration of the bread, before the cup is blessed." For Luther is weighing whether it might not be best to follow Luke and Paul here. In this case, the consecration would also remain a consecration and would not become a formula of distribution as has happened in many modern churches.

It is unnecessary here to go into the fact that for Luther only the celebration of the Lord's Supper that corresponds to Christ's institution is a proper sacrament; therefore a private Mass in which no congregation communes is not one. The consecration spoken in this Mass is ineffective, while even in the Roman Mass with Communion—even though only under one kind—Christ's institution is still there, though badly deformed. *Extra institutionem Christi* ("outside of Christ's institution") the Sacrament is not there; consequently, the real presence ceases when the celebration is over. There is no reservation of the Sacrament, no procession with the Sacrament, and naturally no veneration of the reserved host. Such a practice would be veneration of a created thing, for then only the bread is there. But during the celebration the sacramental union of the body and blood of Christ with the elements exists. From this perspective alone is Luther's discussion of the *consecrated host* to be understood. This finds expression above all in his advisory statements in the cases of Pastors Besserer in Weida and Wolferinus in Eisleben.

On January 11, 1546, Luther expressed himself in a letter to [Nikolaus von] Amsdorf [1483–1565] regarding Besserer, who had been imprisoned because he had given a communicant an unconsecrated host in place of a consecrated one that had fallen on the floor (cf. Enders 17:7 n. 2 on no. 3599). Luther opposes his imprisonment but favors his dismissal from office: "Let him go to his Zwinglians!" (Ibid., line 11). "As a mocker of God and of the people he has publicly dared to regard consecrated and unconsecrated hosts as the same thing" [*hostias consecratas ac non consecratas pro eodem habere*] (lines 9f.).

The case of Wolferinus, which happened three years earlier, had to do with the fact that a controversy broke out among the pastors in Eisleben because Wolferinus had put the remaining consecrated elements back with the unconsecrated, referring to the fact that the sacraments are actions [*actiones*], not static facts [*stantes factiones*—things remaining done]. In Luther's first letter to Wolferinus of July 4, 1543, which is also signed by Bugenhagen[14] as one who agreed with Luther's judgment (Enders 15, no. 3285), the Eisleben pastor is urgently admonished to give up this dangerous practice that could lead to Zwinglianism; besides it is against the custom existing in the other churches. The elements that are left over should be consumed by the pastor and the communicants "so that it will not be necessary to raise such objectionable and dangerous questions about the cessation of the sacramental action" (line 46). This demand corresponds with the repeated advice of the reformer that what remains [*die "reliquiae"*] should be either consumed or burned. In a second letter of July 20, Luther warns Wolferinus against a misunderstanding of Melanchthon's statement "There is no sacrament outside of the sacramental action" (Enders 15, no. 3291). Wolferinus is so limiting the sacramental action that he is about to lose the Sacrament. His definition threatens to limit the real presence to the consecration, which is indeed the most potent and the principal action in the Sacrament, and would lead to a renewal of the scholastic question: At which of the words does the presence begin? The action of the Sacrament is not limited to a moment, but actually extends over a period of time. Luther then gives his definition of the *sacramental action* [*actio sacramentalis*]. He expresses it thus: "It starts with the beginning of the Lord's Prayer[15] and lasts until all have communed, the cup has been drunk empty, the hosts have been eaten, and the people have been dismissed and have

---

14 Johann Bugenhagen (1485–1558), the pastor at Wittenberg, was the first Wittenberger to oppose Zwingli. He is considered the great organizer of the Lutheran Church (s.v. *Christian Cyclopedia*). MH

15 The original here is *ab initio orationis dominicae. Oratio dominicae* is most commonly translated as "Lord's Prayer." However, Bjarne Teigen has shown that since Cyprian [ca. 200–258] a part of the tradition has used "Oratio" for the Words of Institution. Luther himself uses "Oratio" in this sense (WA Br 4:367). So while Luther does not fix a precise moment in the sense of a specific word or syllable at which the real presence begins, nevertheless it is the Words of Institution which bring it about. See Teigen, *The Lord's Supper in the Theology of Martin Chemnitz* (Brewster, MA: Trinity Lutheran Press 1986), 215–16. MH

gone from the altar" (line 34), and he adds: "In this way we will be sure and free from doubts and from the offensive, interminable questions" [*et scandalis quaestionum interminabilium*].

These written answers of Luther correspond to his personal conduct as communicant (on that subject see Hans Preuss, *Luther als Kommunikant: Festschrift für Friedrich Ulmer* [1937], 205ff.) and as celebrant. In many churches in which he celebrated the Lord's Supper there remained for a long time memories of his conduct, for example, in the Church of Our Lady in Halle during his last journey to Mansfeld. Long afterward they were still telling of this celebration, one of the last, if not the last of his life.

> The great number of communicants had wearied his aged arms; at one point his quivering hand caused him to spill a little of the consecrated wine on the floor. Luther put the chalice down on the altar, fell to his knees, and sucked up the wine with his mouth so that it should not be trodden under foot, whereupon the whole congregation broke out in sobbing and weeping. [K. Loewe, quoted by K. Anton, *Luther und die Musik* (1928), 59; G. Kawerau offers another report, quoted by Hans Grass, *Die Abendmahlslehre bei Luther und Calvin* (1954), 115–21; Grass's careful treatment of the whole question is emphasized here]

One may not simply explain these notions of Luther as echoes of his Catholic past. How profoundly he had freed himself from this past we have seen in the discussion of the Sacrifice of the Mass.

It all comes down to the question of whether we are here dealing with private views of Luther and his colleagues and the majority of the Lutheran pastors of the sixteenth century or whether the doctrine of the consecration that is involved in these views is to be regarded as *doctrine of the Lutheran Church.* For this is what must concern us here above all, not what falls under the heading of liturgy and ritual.

Against the hypothesis that the Formula of Concord confesses this doctrine the Saliger controversy over the Sacrament has repeatedly been cited. In Lübeck and later in Rostock, *Saliger*[16] had maintained that the real presence is there before the *sumptio*, the receiving of the elements, and he and his followers appeal to Luther. The fact that Saliger was condemned has repeatedly been brought forward to show that according to Lutheran doctrine there is only a real presence at the moment of the reception of the consecrated bread and wine. But other factors played a role in his condemnation, above all the way in which he pursued his cause and the expressions that he used (see on that J. Wiggers, *Zeitschrift f. hist. Theol.,* 1848, 613ff.; H. Frank, *Konkordienformel* 3:66f., 146f.;

---

16 Johann Saliger (or Beatus, d. after 1571) was in Antwerp around 1566, was removed in 1568, and fled to Rostock to promote his views (see Carl Meusel, et al., *Kirchliches Handlexikon* [Leipzig: Naumann, 1894], 5:752). "Salig evidently follows Melanchthon in denying the power of the consecration to achieve the real presence" (Teigen, *Lord's Supper,* 210 n. 73). MH

Grass, 111f.). "In this controversy those who were not followers of Saliger, even those who opposed him, did not maintain a real presence only in the reception. Wigand[17] shows in his expert opinion, after he has set aside the case, that if the sacramental action is interrupted and there is no reception, there is a presence before the eating and drinking" (Grass, 111).

In the decision, the Wismar Recess written by Chytraeus,[18] one of the authors of the Formula of Concord, which was partially incorporated into the Solid Declaration [VII 83–85; *BSLK*, 1000 n. 4], papistic expressions that let the Sacrament exist beyond its use [*extra usum*] are forbidden, but the teaching is also specifically rejected "that the body and blood of Christ are not present in the Lord's Supper until the consecrated bread and wine are touched with the lips or taken into the mouth." Here precisely that view is rejected that later orthodoxy regarded as correct. So it is also not the teaching of the Formula of Concord that the real presence is there only in the *sumptio* [i.e., the eating], in the reception of the elements. This view is explained by the misunderstanding that the *usus*, the use of the Sacrament, is the same thing as the *sumptio*, the reception. Thus the Formula of Concord, making use of the Wismar Recess, decides the question of the effect of the consecration in this way:

> But this blessing or recitation of Christ's words of institution by itself, if the entire action of the Lord's Supper as Christ ordained it is not observed (if, for instance, the blessed bread is not distributed, received, and eaten but is locked up, offered up, or carried about), does not make a sacrament. But the command of Christ, "Do this," which comprehends the whole action or administration of this sacrament (namely, that in a Christian assembly we take bread and wine, consecrate it, distribute it, receive it, eat and drink it, and therewith proclaim the Lord's death), must be kept integrally and inviolately, just as St. Paul sets the whole action of the breaking of bread, or of the distribution and reception, before our eyes in 1 Cor. 10:16.

> To maintain this true Christian doctrine concerning the Holy Supper and to obviate and eliminate many kinds of idolatrous misuse and perversion of this testament, the following useful *rule* and norm has been derived from the Words of Institution: Nothing has the character of a sacrament apart from the use instituted by Christ or apart from the divinely instituted action [*Nihil habet rationem sacramenti extra usum*

17　Johannes Wigand (1523–87) was preacher at Mansfeld (1546), superintendent and pastor at Magdeburg (1553), professor at Jena (1560, though deposed in 1561). He returned to Jena in 1568, was deposed again, and became bishop of Pomerania in 1575. With Matthias Flacius (1520–75), Wigand co-authored *The Magdeburg Centuries* (s.v. *Christian Cyclopedia*). MH

18　David Chytraeus (1531–1600) studied at Wittenberg under Melanchthon and Luther. He lectured on Melanchthon's *Loci* at Wittenberg (1548) and served as professor at Rostock (1551). He was integrally involved in the process which led to the Book of Concord (s.v. *Christian Cyclopedia*). MH

o Christo institutum oder extra actionern divinitus institutam]. [SD VII 83–85; Müller, 665]

The definition of *usus* as *actio* is then repeated:

> In this context "use" or "action" is . . . the entire external and visible action of the Supper as ordained by Christ: the consecration or words of institution, the distribution and reception, or the oral eating. [SD VII 86]

The reception [*sumptio*] is therefore only a part of the use [*usus*]. The teaching developed here by the Formula of Concord matches exactly the one that we found in Luther. For him also the *usus* is the entire *actio*, and the real presence, effected by Christ's Word in the consecration, is bound up in the whole *actio* and can therefore not be restricted to the moment of reception. The consecrated bread is the body of Christ also when it lies on the altar or when the pastor holds it in his hand. This is the Lutheran view.[19]

This view certainly does not allow one thing that the Roman teaching knows: the precise *designation of the moment* at which the real presence begins and the moment when it *ceases*. We have observed that Luther in one place takes into account that the Lord's Prayer, which precedes the Words of Institution, belongs to the *actio* that is attended by the real presence. When we say that the consecration brings about the real presence, we are not making a statement about what Roman theology identifies as the moment of consecration. When we say that after the celebration the consecrated bread is no longer the body of Christ, that is not a statement about the moment when the sacramental union ceases, corresponding to the Roman teaching that the real presence ceases when the forms decay.

The designation of these moments was the work of scholastic theology, above all of Thomas. But even Thomas could not give a scriptural basis for it. He simply concludes from the use of the present tense *est* in the statement "Hoc est corpus meum" that the effect of the consecration takes place at the moment in which the statement has been fully spoken. The same applies to the words about the cup—while his doctrine of concomitance allows him to assume a presence of the blood together with the body *ex reali concomitantia* (*S. th.* 3, q. 78, art. 6). But this is only a rational argument. Until the middle of the fourth century, the

---

19 "So they hold and teach that with the bread and wine the body and blood of Christ are truly and essentially present, offered, and received" (FC SD VII 14; *Concordia*, 564). "Jesus Christ's true and almighty words, which He spoke at the first institution, were effective not only at the first Supper. They endure, are valid, operate, and are still effective. So in all places where the Supper is celebrated according to Christ's institution and His words are used, Christ's body and blood are truly present, distributed, and received, because of the power and effectiveness of the words that Christ spoke at the first Supper. Where His institution is observed and His words are spoken over the bread and cup ‹wine›, and the consecrated bread and cup ‹wine› are distributed, Christ Himself, through the spoken words, is still effective by virtue of the first institution, which He wants to be repeated there through His word" (FC SD VII 75; *Concordia*, 574). MH

early church never knew anything of a "moment of consecration." It turns up in Cyril of Jerusalem [ca. 315–ca. 386] and in Serapion (Egypt [d. after 362]) and in the West for the first time in Ambrose (cf. Gregory Dix, *The Shape of the Liturgy* [1947], 240). But to this day the Eastern Church has not arrived at complete clarity about the "moment of consecration" (Words of Institution or epiclesis), while the influences of Latin scholasticism, from which the question was posed to the Eastern Church, are fading. Influence of the scholastic tradition was also involved when Lutheran theologians sought to designate the moment when the real presence begins and the moment when it ends. Here lies the theological error of Saliger, and Chytraeus was absolutely right when he said in his criticism that for the devout heart it is enough to know from the Words of Institution that the body and blood are given to us, and it is useless to argue about the bread on the paten or the bread that is left over (cf. the Latin wording from Wiggers in Grass, 112). The same thing must also be said to the later orthodox theologians, who for logical considerations denied a duration of the real presence and confined it to the *moment* of the reception, such as Aegidius Hunnius (quoted by F. Pieper, *Christian Dogmatics* 3:373 n. 118, from C. F. W. Walther, *Pastorale*, 175), who tried to show the logical impossibility of a duration of the real presence that begins with the consecration. He points to the hypothetical case of a celebration of the Lord's Supper that is interrupted by fire breaking out after the consecration but before the reception. To that we can only say that here exactly the same mistake is made as in scholasticism. One tries to answer questions that Holy Scripture neither knows nor answers and that therefore the church also cannot answer with rational efforts. We cannot determine the moment of the beginning and the end of the real presence of Christ's body and blood in the Sacrament of the Altar with watch in hand, just as we cannot fix temporally the presence of Christ when two or three are gathered together in His name and therefore the promise of Matt. 18:20 is fulfilled for them. We may never forget that the presence of Christ, His divine and human nature, is always an eschatological miracle in which time and eternity meet.

7

The Lutheran doctrine of the consecration assumes that every celebration of the Lord's Supper is an unfathomable miracle, just as the first Lord's Supper was not, as the Reformed Church supposes, a parabolic action but also a miracle. Every Lord's Supper that we celebrate is a miracle, no less than the miracles that Jesus did during His days on earth. The same is true, though in another way, of Baptism. As the preaching of the Lord was accompanied by His signs and wonders, so the proclamation of His church is accompanied by the Sacraments. And as the deeds of Jesus were the dawn of the coming redemption (Luke 4:18ff.; Matt. 11:4ff.), so in Baptism and in the Lord's Supper we are already given what belongs to the coming world. As often as the church gathers around the table of the Lord it is already the "day of the Lord," that is, the day of the Messiah (cf. Amos 5:18), the day of His return. This is the original meaning of Sunday as the "day of the Lord," on which John (Rev. 1:9ff.) in the Spirit could participate in the heavenly Divine Service, while the churches of Asia were gathered for the Lord's Supper (cf. 3:20). Sunday is an anticipation of the parousia. It is this because on that day the Lord comes to His church in the Word and in the Sacrament of the Altar. For this reason the church greets Him before the consecration with "Blessed is He who comes in the name of the Lord. Hosanna in the highest." The old Lutheran Church of the sixteenth and seventeenth centuries still celebrated the Divine Service in this sense, which Article XXIV of the Augsburg Confession defends with the words: "We are unjustly accused of having abolished the Mass. Without boasting, it is manifest that the Mass is observed among us with greater devotion and more earnestness than among our opponents." This honor is long past, since late orthodoxy neglected the liturgical instruction of the people, Pietism destroyed the Lutheran concept of sacrament, and rationalism nullified faith in miracles.

Will the Lutheran Church recover the Divine Service to which its Confession bears witness? It cannot be a matter of repristinating an unrepeatable past but only of understanding anew the teaching of the Holy Scriptures about the Sacrament of the Altar as confessed in the Confession. Everything else will come of itself. It is an experience of the history of Lutheranism in the nineteenth century that generally, wherever Luther's doctrine of the real presence is again understood and believed, hunger for the Sacrament of the Altar wakens afresh, and the liturgy is renewed. We see beginnings of such an experience even today. No liturgical movement can help our church unless it is inspired with Luther's profound understanding of the consecration. In the consecration Jesus Christ is speaking and no one else. He speaks the Word of divine omnipotence: "This is My body," "This is My blood," and of divine love: "Given and shed for you for the forgiveness of sins." And this Word creates what it says: the true presence of His body and blood and the forgiveness of sins. So both forms in which the Gospel appears meet in the consecration, the spoken and the acted Gospel, the Word and the Sacrament. In this sense the consecration is the Gospel itself.

ᗱ

These pages have been written while in Germany the great vital questions for the Lutheran Church are considered in the convention of the Lutheran World Federation in Hanover and in smaller conferences. Whatever the outcome of these meetings may be, let us never forget, esteemed brothers, that the decision about the future of our church and the preservation of the Lutheran Confessions is made in the individual congregation. For there, in the church at a particular place, stands the altar around which the church gathers.

[Hermann Sasse]

Historical Context

In Letter 27, "Worldwide Lutheranism after Hanover," Sasse chronicles the admission of union churches to membership in the LWF. By accepting such churches from its inception, the LWF demonstrated its intent not to take seriously the Lutheran Confessions. The blurring of the line between Lutheran and Reformed churches—the rejection of the Formula of Concord—proceeded in German Lutheranism with the formation of the EKiD (1948) and now continued to envelope world Lutheranism via the LWF. MH

April 19, 1952[1]

Dr. Hermann Sasse
41 Buxton Street
North Adelaide, South Australia

Dear Dr. [Carl] Lundquist [LWF],

Thank you for your letter to Prof. Prenter. This gives me the opportunity of expressing my thoughts on the future of the Commission on Theology. I would like to recommend to form the commission anew at Hanover with the following main tasks. 1. This commission should continue the theological discussions on a broad scale. What the Lutheran Churches need is a clearinghouse where the doctrinal discussions (*Lehrgespraeche*) which must go on between them in future find a center. The whole future of the Lutheran Church in the world depends on the question whether or not we shall be able to find again the lost *consensus de doctrina evangelii et administratione sacramentorum* ["agreement in the doctrine of the Gospel and the administration of the Sacraments," AC VII]. Much patience is needed . . . . 2. The commission should help the "younger churches" which are now striving for a new expression of the Lutheran truth without being able to understand every detail of the Book of Concord . . . . 3. The third task would be to establish contacts between the theological faculties of the Lutheran World and to help the smaller churches get the necessary theological literature . . . .

Yours sincerely,
H. Sasse

---

1   CHI Behnken file. MH

twenty-seven
Worldwide Lutheranism after Hanover

TRANSLATED BY ANDREW SMITH

Reformation Day 1952[1]

Prof. D. Theol. Hermann Sasse
41 Buxton Street
North Adelaide, South Australia

Dear Brothers in the Office!

You have had to wait for this letter longer than is preferable to me. But I really wanted to get into the question (although still other important questions await discussion) which is especially on all of our minds, and for the answering of which I had to await the printed matter from Germany and America: *What does the Hanover convention of the LWF mean for the Lutheranism of the world*, for the churches who belong to the LWF, and the others who experienced from near or far only as guests and observers that which Hanns Lilje's *Sonntagsblatt* (no. 33, August 17, 1952, p. 16, column 1) calls "the largest rally of Lutheranism since the Reformation"? This is a question which can be answered not only by eyewitnesses, but rather which, on the contrary, can be understood and answered in a particular way, especially [from] there, where the spatial distance allows [one] to perceive only the big lines.

1

The reports about the celebrations in Hanover emphasize how impressive the view was, in which one considered the 5,000 who wanted to come from the East

-----

1   *BLP* 27: *Das Weltluthertum nach Hannover* (North Adelaide, October 1952). The original was published in *LuBl* 4, nos. 29–30 (1952). Huss number 296. MH

Zone [behind the Iron Curtain] and who were prevented from participating, and beyond that [all] the brothers in faith in the East in general. It would have perhaps been good, if one had not entirely forgotten, beyond the human and ecclesiastical fate of the brothers in the East, the question about what type of a *judgment* has come upon the Lutheran church, especially in its homeland—in Thüringia and east of the Elbe—and what this judgment has to say to Lutheranism in the entire world. Certainly, God's judgments, when they come upon a land or geographic region, impact all denominations simultaneously and indifferently. As the Monophysites[2] and the Nestorians[3] shared the fate of orthodoxy in the storm of Islam, as not only the orthodox but also the Lutherans and all other confessions were impacted by the ecclesiastical persecution of Bolshevism, so today all Christian churches on the far side of the Iron Curtain stand in the solidarity of suffering, which has often become a brotherhood of the cross. And yet the fate of the Roman Catholic Church in Poland is still somewhat different than the fate of our church in the old home of Lutheranism, and this again is a different [fate] than the destruction of Baltic Lutheranism in conjunction with the destruction and scattering of the Baltic peoples. Not only the insane politics of Hitler's empire and the defeat in World War II are responsible for [the fact] that in Wittenberg and Leipzig, in Rostock and Greifswald, in Jena and Erfurt dialectical materialism reigns.[4] If the churches had been honest enough to keep statistics about attendance at church services, then we would know what the empty churches in Schleswig-Holstein and Mecklenburg, in Braunschweig and Brandenburg, in Vorpommern [Western Pomerania] and in both parts of Saxony have been announcing for generations already. Then one would have the most serious thoughts about the future in Sweden, instead of comforting one's self with the national church's illusions of the past. Where people no longer go to church, because the church's proclamation has no more power over spirits, other spiritual powers must, with an inner necessity, take the place of the church in such a region. Where the preaching of the church is no longer the announcement of the pure Gospel, then worldly messages will take the place of the Gospel: at first perhaps very religious, even "Christian" messages, such as that which was preached by the followers of Schleiermacher and Ritschl; then later a "Christian" patriotism, in which already the seeds of a heathen nationalism lie; and, finally, the naked heathenism of the "faith in Germany," the cult of the Führer, Marxism, and the nihilism of disappointed people. Is it a coincidence that this all happened in the old regions of the Lutheran church, and that both the convention in Hanover as well as the Luther conference in Berlin were possible only with the protection of the military power of America, as once the Vatican council could meet only with the protection of French bayonets? We do not know how

2   See above, p. 38 n. 7. MH

3   See above, p. 38 n. 6. MH

4   That is, the philosophy of Karl Marx [1818–83] and Friedrich Engels [1820–95]. MH

many participants in the great festive events heard the call to repentance, which the decline of the Lutheran Church in other parts of its former home must signify for the entire Lutheran Church of the world. Certainly there were some who remembered Luther's words, that God's Word and grace are a passing rain shower, which does not return to where it once was.[5] But have we Lutherans in West Germany and Scandinavia, in America and Australia heard the warning words of the Lord: "If you do not improve, you will likewise be destroyed!" [Luke 13:3]. Are we clear about this, that the fate of Breslau and Königsberg, the fate of Wittenberg and the Wartburg can tomorrow be our fate, the fate of the entire Lutheran Church of the world, and [it] will be [our fate], if He does not hold His hand over us, He who is the Savior of the repentant sinner? Nations do not repent. History teaches us that, and whoever didn't know it already learned it in 1945. But even churches have a fatal disposition toward nonrepentance. In the case of the Catholic Church, that is their nature. In the case of the Lutheran Church, the Church of the Reformation, it should be different. Because the Reformation is nothing else than the repentance of the church.

2

All reports about Hanover, at least those from serious theological observers, emphasize the two-sidedness of the impressions. They all speak of the grandness of this convention, of the moving and overwhelming portrayal of that which today still exists in the world of Lutheranism. The Lutheranism of the world has awakened and for the first time has become aware of its significance. On the other side, its great weaknesses have become apparent. *Hanover destroyed the legend of the dogmatic unity of Lutheranism.* This two-sided impression corresponds to the facts of development in church history, which are even worth studying in their own right. Lutheranism grows to be one of the great denominations of Christianity. Already in large-scale world church politics it has perhaps overshadowed Anglicanism. Even in theology its effects are becoming noticeable. The surrender of the classical Reformed doctrine of predestination by Karl Barth will perhaps later be seen one day as the decisive turning point in the history of modern Protestantism: Calvin, who, a generation ago gained such a large significance, begins to step back behind Luther. The legal understanding of the Gospel in the "social gospel" of America, and in the churches influenced by America, gives way to a new search for the distinction between Law and Gospel, after all hopes for a new ordering of the political and social world according to the New Testament have failed. Even the liturgical movement of our time and the new interest in the Sacrament benefits Lutheranism. Fifteen years ago, whoever represented Luther's eucharistic doctrine was seen as an oddball, not

---

5 For the description of the Gospel as a "passing rain shower," see *An die Ratherren aller Städte deutschen Lands* (*To the Councilmen of All Cities in Germany*) (1524), Aland 676, WA 15:27–53 (AE 45:352–53). MH

to be taken seriously, with whom the good theological community would have nothing to do. Today, the voices [of those] who recognize the biblical doctrine in Luther's teaching of the real presence and who profess it are multiplying. Even in England, where Luther was until now completely unknown—and where only a few years ago it could have happened that Lutherans were denied access to the radio with the reasoning that Lutheranism did not belong to the "mainstream of Christian traditions"—suddenly an interest in Luther is growing, above all in the younger generation of the Methodist theologians. This awakening of *Lutheranism* has, however, a different side. The "collapse toward Lutheranism" of which one speaks in Germany is much different than a conversion to the *Lutheran Church*. On the contrary, the "Yes!" to Lutheranism as a type of Christianity, as the inwardly richest type of Protestantism, binds itself with the decisive "No!" to the Church of the Lutheran Confession. The "Yes!" to the Lutheran denomination is a "Yes!" to a theology determined by Lutheranism, but not the "Yes!" with which the fathers of the sixteenth century and the Lutheran Church of all times have adopted the Unaltered Augsburg Confession and the entire Book of Concord. Where today are the pastors who, with the fathers, "before the face of God and of all Christendom, by those now living and those who will come after us, bear witness that the Lutheran Confession and no other is our teaching, belief, and confession, in which we, too, by the grace of God, with fearless hearts, appear before the judgment seat of Jesus Christ and about which we will give account, and against which we want to say or write nothing, secretly or publicly"?[6]

If such men were supposed to have been in Hanover—aside from the guests— why did they not issue some public confession of the Lutheran Church? But perhaps in such gigantic conventions, despite all progress in negotiation techniques and communication technology, that is not at all possible, for purely technical reasons. So the twilight, in which all of modern Protestantism lives, lay over the convention of the LWF. It is that dim light of which one does not know whether it signifies death of the old faith or the breaking forth of a new time of faith.

3

The deepest need of modern Lutheranism revealed itself in Hanover in the fact that the convention was in no condition to issue a common *doctrinal statement*. The document *The Living Word in a Church Aware of Its Responsibilities*, which was prepared by the theological commission and which was sent back largely by pressure from the Swedish side, was already far too long, longer than what could have been thoroughly discussed by the full assembly. But even if that had been possible, the result would have been no different. It remains unclear who

---

6   From the Conclusion of the Formula of Concord (FC XII 39–40; *BSLK*, 1099–1100). MH

is speaking in this document. If it is not only the theological commission, but rather the full assembly of the LWF, would that mean that it speaks in the name of the Lutheran Church? If so, how does this new doctrinal declaration relate to the Confessions of the Lutheran Church, which the LWF proclaims as its basis? Should this declaration be a sort of explication of the old Confessions, a translation into the language of our time? But then it would have to be in full agreement with the Confessions, which is not the case if, for example, in the section about Holy Communion not only is the rejection of the opposing doctrine muted, but rather even such a disjointed assertion as "that the true body and the true blood of Jesus Christ as a blessing is only received in the sacrifice of thanksgiving by the congregation" (according to the English text, which is the only one available to me). Or is the matter here an addition to the old Confessions? Then these [old Confessions] first would have to be recognized as a [foundational] assumption, as the Formula of Concord assumes the Augsburg Confession, and the Augsburg Confession assumes the early church symbols. [But] that doesn't happen in this document. Or is the old Confession to be replaced by a new one? Even in this case, one would have to speak clearly, and it would have to be said, for example, why the rejection of the Reformed eucharistic doctrine can no longer be maintained today. It is, in any case, a sign of the inner distress of Lutheranism that a doctrinal declaration could be presented in Hanover which was not only unclear in itself and which had to arouse opposition, but rather about which nobody could even tell what it was actually supposed to be. The best which could be done with it was this: that the convention "received" it, and with the comments of the theology commission referred it for further work. In 1927 at the World Conference for Faith and Order at Lausanne this is the way they dealt with the internally unclear and disputed commission reports about the church, the sacraments, the spiritual office, etc., because the various denominational churches had very different views about these questions. But here one denominational church was gathered, and on top of that, the one which, as it thinks of itself, keeps its Confession purer than other churches. But what this Confession actually is and means, that they apparently didn't know how to say, as indeed then even the "Church of the Word" apparently has no consensus any longer about what actually is the Word of God to which it refers. For the continual talk about the "living" Word veiled only in a makeshift way the dissent about the sense in which the Holy Scriptures is God's Word. But how can one then make a common confession?

4

But for what reason, then, [would one want to make] a doctrinal declaration, if the old Confession allegedly still stands? Is that not already a more powerful consensus, *not* to be surpassed by *any* new confession, if the many churches bound together in the LWF profess the Unaltered Augsburg Confession and Luther's

Small Catechism? Yes, if only they would do it! But for many of these churches, isn't the "Yes!" to these Confessions still merely an ecclesio-judicial fiction? [To this question] one answers us: that may be, but the LWF is not responsible for this. It cannot peer into hearts and also cannot hold any doctrinal hearings to reveal possible doctrinal errors. It must accept the declaration of a church in good faith, if it in its constitution names the Augsburg Confession and catechism as [a] doctrinal basis. That sounds very plausible. But what is the case with such churches which have absolutely no doctrinal discipline? What about the admittance of such churches which do not at all have that foundation? The executive committee does, after all, examine the applications for admission. It has, or so one hears, rejected a number of applications for admission. But—entirely aside from the question of why it does not submit some accounting about its decisions to the full assembly or to the member churches—why does it admit churches for which the Augsburg Confession and the catechism are, according to their constitutions, in no way binding Confessions, not even a binding norm for the *publica doctrina*? A year-and-a-half ago, in Letter 19 ("World Lutheranism on the Way to Hanover," pp. 17f.), we indicated the unusual confessional status of the Federacao Sinodal in Brazil.

> This church is confessionally determined by the Augsburg Confession and Luther's Small Catechism, and belongs to the *family* of churches stamped by Luther's Reformation, and will express this in its name.

Further, it is said about this synodical federation, which understands itself to be a church, that it

> stands in the *community* of churches which have entered into the ecumenical council which allow the Gospel of Jesus Christ, as it is given to us in the Scripture, as the only rule and norm of their service in the Gospel and of their teaching.

And

> The federation of synods fosters the *ties of faith* with the mother church, the *Evangelical Church in Germany*, which according to its foundational prescriptions allows the *community of evangelical Christendom* in Germany to become visible and stand in the ranks of world Christianity [*Oekume*].[7]

We indicated that the Lutheran Confession is here no longer seen as foundational to church fellowship, and has therefore only historical meaning and no dogmatically normative significance. The understanding of the Lutheran Confession is approximately the same as in the Brandenburg provincial church of the Evangelical Church of the Old Prussian Union, which also understands itself as a church of the Lutheran Reformation and which recognizes the Lutheran Confession as justifiably existing in the old Lutheran congregations, but which simultaneously proclaims altar and pulpit fellowship with the Reformed

---

7   See *Letters to Lutheran Pastors* 1:410–11. MH

[Churches] and thereby nullifies the tenth article of the Augsburg Confession. The Federacao Sinodal, too, expressly proclaims church fellowship and bonds of faith with the "evangelical" [churches], with the churches of ecumeny which stand upon the *sola Scriptura*, and with the EKiD as a whole. Whoever knows the history of these Brazilian synods, of which only *one* was confessionally Lutheran by means of its heritage from Neuendettelsau, then that person knows also that, even with the best will and most charitable reception, one can expect no more from them. But who of the men who had to decide this matter undertook even the small task of looking into the protocols of the Prussian general synods, into the church yearbook, or into the writings of the Gustav-Adolf Association concerning Brazil? In September 1951 there was a meeting in Brazil with representatives of the LWF and the VELKD. The result was that all the participants expressed their satisfaction with the results. But nothing was changed. Indeed, that was not even at all possible, because for that purpose the four synods, of which the united body consists, would have had to have been called together. Chairman Schlünzen of the Lutheran (Neuendettelsau) Synod gave information in no. 9 of the *Evangelisch-Lutherischen Kirchenzeitung* on April 30, 1952, about the current confessional status of these synods in a longer essay: "The Lutheran Church in Brazil." After he tells about the background history of the unification, and the ecclesiastical need which brought it about, he says about the confessional question:

> The first requirement was to see if this unification was at all possible, i.e., if all four synods had the same Lutheran confessional basis; for only upon the same confessional basis is it possible to build up a church. It became clear that all four synods professed, on the basis of the Holy Scripture, the symbols of Dr. Martin Luther, mainly the Augsburg Confession and the Small Catechism. Our synod names, in its constitution, all the confessional writings by name; but for the determination of a confessional basis of a Lutheran Church, the shortened version, as it is mentioned above, suffices. [p. 116]

That indeed must have been a pleasant surprise when The Lutheran Church in Brazil with its 73,000 souls discovered all at once that the Rio Grande Synod (265,000 souls), the Evangelical Synod of St. Catherine and Parana (72,000 souls), and the Mid-Brazilian Synod (30,000 souls) were not at all union churches, as they themselves had always thought and as the Lutherans had called them. Either a great error had gone on for many decades, or there was a miraculous conversion. Yes, the joy must be even greater when suddenly even the Book of Concord appears as the confession. For so writes Chairman Schlünzen further:

> Regarding the confessional basis of the four synods, there was from the beginning no doubt, not even about this, that clearly the *Unaltered* Augsburg Confession was meant and that *all confessional writings of the Lutheran church were binding.*

He writes very clearly in this connection in the Mid-Brazilian Synod's *Cross in the South* (Sao Paulo, 1951, no. 6):

> That we are here called Lutherans is clear; we have received the Reformation from Luther, not from Calvin or Zwingli. We unite ourselves, based on the Holy Scripture, on *Luther's Small Catechism*, and we do actually have the confessional writings, such as *The Augsburg Confession (unaltered), the Large Catechism, the Smalcald Articles, and, in short, everything which one calls the Book of Concord*. [Ibid., my emphasis]

This is not so clear to us Europeans or Australians. "That which one calls the Book of Concord"—to say nothing of the "symbols of Dr. Martin Luther"—once the simple pastors whom Neuendettelsau sent into the American prairie, into the Brazilian jungle, and into the Australian bush knew it well. That was during the time in which those in Neuendettelsau still dared to profess the Lutheran faith even before the important people of the world and of the church. If such ambiguity and ignorance reigns in Brazil today, then that may well be as it is, but that the LWF owns this ambiguity and [based] upon this theological dilettantism makes the decision, with broad-ranging consequences, which allows the admittance of this church federation, that can only be understood from [the fact] that here one is dealing with church politics and not with the truth of the Lutheran doctrine. Nobody would have any objection to the Federacao Sinodal's joining the LWF in a sort of federated or annex relationship, as the Brother Congregations were once annexed onto the German Evangelical Church Federation. Every Lutheran would greet that with joy, if an evangelical-union church desired to return to the Lutheran confession. Every assistance should be granted in such a case. But not only to admit a church which finds itself on the way to Lutheranism, but rather even to allow it to be immediately represented in the executive committee by its until-recently union chairman—this cannot be made to jive with the constitution of the LWF, one reason being that the Federacao is indeed not at all a church yet, and therefore according to the constitution cannot be a member. *Here the violation of confession has become a violation of what is right.*

5

A different and perhaps more striking case of the injury to confession is the admittance of the Huria Kristen Batak Protestand [HKBP], the Christian-Protestant Church of *Batak* on *Sumatra*. Here, too, let it be firmly emphasized that we believe it to be the job of the LWF to take unto itself such a church, which desires annexation, and to help it, so that it becomes a church in the sense of the Lutheran Confession. Such a church, additionally, should have the opportunity of a loose association and close cooperation until the way is clear for full membership. That is the way which truthfulness and love offer. For how can one demand from a church which itself does not profess the Augsburg Confession that it encourage other churches to hold firmly to the Augsburg Confession? What does the doctrinal foundation of the LWF—the profession of the Augsburg Confession and Luther's Small Catechism—even mean if one admits churches which do not have the Augsburg Confession and which regard the catechism not as a confession, but rather only as a textbook, and ascribe to it in any case no dogmatic binding power? It can very well be that a "young church" in the mission field sees itself forced to pour the doctrinal content of the Lutheran confessional documents into a new form, so that all members of the church can understand the Confession. But it must then be very clearly stated that it is the doctrine of the Lutheran confessional documents which one is confessing in this new form. If it is thereby necessary to give confessional answers to questions which were not yet handled in the Book of Concord, then it must be said that the new teaching assumes the old Lutheran Confession and to what extent the new teaching relies upon the old Lutheran Confession. But now look at the new confession, as it has been published in the official German translation by mission inspector H. F. de Kleine in the publishing house of the Rhenish Mission Society[8] in Barmen in 1952. An introduction, not belonging to the confession itself, speaks about the formation of the new confession:

> The formulation of a confession of faith is urgently necessary for the edification of our faith and for the struggle against error. In the ancient church they made ecumenical confessions of faith in order to combat error. In the time of the Reformation there were confessional writings in order to disagree with the doctrine of the Roman Catholics. In this manner they have continually stood firm when errors arose which caused an uproar in the church. Again and again new confessional writings arose. But one did not forget about the old ones because of the new ones, in order to fight new errors. The church needs, therefore, again and again, a new confession for the struggle against new errors. . . . In Germany, starting in 1933, new errors made themselves manifest. At that time, the congregations there awoke and felt that the earlier confessions were no longer sufficient for the struggle against [these] errors. They put together a new confession, the "Theses of Barmen." They put emphasis upon [the fact] that Christ Himself is sovereign. . . . Even in Holland they worked to make a new confession. This confession was based upon the old confessions but had a new tone for the current modern time. . . . Occasioned by those who press against our church, we must now consider the different religions and doctrines, which surround us.

There follows an overview of these opponents. Here one hears the voice of the Rhenish Mission. The new confession is, then, a sort of Batakian Barmen, a renewing of the confessional writings of the Reformation and the symbols of the early church. It is not stated which Reformation is meant; [it is] in any case not

---

Formed in 1799 at Elberfeld, the Rhenish Mission Society was associated with the mission institute at Basel. The society has been for the most part a union mission effort (s.v. *Christian Cyclopedia*). MH

only the Lutheran [Reformation], for this one could have really said openly, since the church uses Luther's Small Catechism as a textbook. But this confessional writing is not at all mentioned in the listing of confessions with which the actual document begins, for the "Introduction" begins thus:

1. This, the confession of faith of the Huria Kristen Batak Protestand, is the continuation of the confessions of faith which have already been, namely, the three confessions of faith which were acknowledged by the fathers of the church: (1) the Apostles' Creed, (2) the Nicene Creed, (3) the Athanasian Creed.

2. This confession of faith is the formulation of that which we believe and hope in this life and for the future life.

2. This confession of faith is the basis of the HKBP, which must be preached, lived, and taught.

4. This confession of faith is the basis of the HKBP in order to turn away, and to struggle against, all false teachings and errors, which are not in accord with God's Word.

Why is there silence about the Lutheran Confessions? Why is Luther's Small Catechism not mentioned even once? Certainly the congregations of Batak know it, and certainly one cannot say that about the Athanasian Creed [i.e., that the congregations know it]. And if one demands this confession of late antiquity from them, why not the main articles of the Augsburg Confession, which they can understand much better? Apparently because the Rhenish Mission Society has transferred its deep antipathy to Lutheran "confessionalism" even to the mission field. It belongs to the missionary societies which grew out of the pietistic awakening—such as Basel and Bremen—which considered it incorrect to carry the opposition of "Lutheran" and "Reformed" out onto the mission fields. In the first half of the nineteenth century, they were convinced that this was possible, that one could simply bring to the heathen instead of the Lutheran and the Reformed view of the sacraments that [teaching] which they considered to be "biblical." Now, as the Batak must deal with Catholics, Adventists, Pentecostals, and similar churches and sects, it becomes clear that one must know what the Holy Scripture teaches concerning sacramental doctrine. For even the Baptists and Adventists, the Catholics and the Pentecostals indeed make appeals to the Scripture for their understanding[s] of the sacraments.

And now consider what this *confession of the Batak* teaches *about Baptism and the Lord's Supper*. Much of it is good Lutheran [teaching], but other [propositions], which belong to the essence of the Lutheran sacramental doctrine, are missing. *About Baptism* it says:

We believe and confess: Holy Baptism is the means of the grace of God for humans. For through Baptism, the believer attains the forgiveness of sins, the new birth, redemption from death and the devil, and he receives eternal blessedness.—With this teaching we confess: even children are to be baptized. For through Baptism, they are given over to the collection of those who have suffered for Christ, [and] at the same time, the children are accepted by the Lord Jesus (Mark 10:14, Luke 18:16). It is unnecessary to submerge [the person] in water at [the time of] Baptism.

A rejection of the opposing teaching, as in the ninth article of the Augsburg Confession, is not present. And there is a deeper reason for this, for apparently a distinction is made between the baptism of the "faithful" through which forgiveness of sins and life and blessedness are given and the baptism of children which signifies admission into the church and acceptance by Jesus Christ (in the sense of Mark 10). What does the proposition that even children are to be baptized mean in the light of this distinction? In the Augsburg Confession it is entailed by the discovery that Baptism is necessary for salvation. Here Baptism is not dogmatically founded, but rather as a matter of church order. Thereby the boundary against the Reformed Church has fallen. Even Baptists could own the first sentence, and [then] reject the second sentence with the reasoning that it in no way follows from the first one.—The article about *the Lord's Supper* is similarly [troublesome]:

> We believe and confess: in Holy Communion the eating of bread transmits the body of our Lord Jesus Christ and the drinking of wine transmits the blood of our Lord Jesus Christ (1 Cor. 11:7; Matthew 26; Mark 14; Luke 22).—With this teaching we reject the doctrine which says that only bread is to be given to the members of the church and not also wine. For our Lord Jesus Christ said such at the institution of Holy Communion: "All of you drink from it!" The first congregation did, indeed, follow this [instruction].—The Mass is not based on God's Word when it says that our Lord is sacrificed every time in the Mass. Therefore we reject this teaching decisively.

Here, too, the building of ecclesiastical boundaries against the Reformed is missing, which is particularly noticeable in the face of the specific rejection of Roman errors. If we look more carefully, then we [notice that] a clear profession of *unio sacramentalis* ["the sacramental union," i.e., the bread/body and wine/blood], of *manducatio oralis* [i.e., the oral eating of Christ's body and blood], and of *manducatio indignorum* [i.e., the teaching that all receive body and blood whether or not they believe] is missing. What does it mean, that the eating of the bread "transmits" the body of Christ? Is the emphasis on the eating, and therefore on the action, or on the bread, and therefore on the element? According to 1 Cor. 10:16f., the bread is the communion of the body of Christ. And what is "transmit"? Is the body of Christ eaten, or do we come into communion with Him in some other way? The absence of the rejection of Reformed doctrine seems in this way to indicate that a mediation was sought. In any case, this article is no equivalent [substitute] for the tenth article of the Augsburg Confession. One wonders whether the Batak-Christians understand that which they have here confessed—or, more correctly, that which their missionaries have given to them as a substitute for Lutheran doctrine. Why isn't Luther's catechism simply

cited with the classically simple and theologically exhaustive definition of the
Sacrament of the Altar:

> It is the true body and blood of our Lord Jesus Christ, under the bread
> and wine, for us Christians to eat and to drink, instituted by Christ
> Himself. [SC VI 2]

The Batak-Christians have certainly all learned this! A ten-year-old child can
understand this! Why, then, this beating around the bush with ambiguities like
modern-day followers of Martin Bucer? No, though we are assured that this confession is a "result of theological reflection by Batak theologians" independently
formulated without the help of Europeans, this confession is actually in reality
the loyal echo of that which the Batak have learned from their missionaries from
Barmen. It is not the confession of a young independent Lutheran Church. It is
not the Confession of the old Lutheran faith in the language of a new people. It
is one of the many modern confessions, as the Reformed Church desires them
for every locally limited church congregation as a substitute for the lost confessions of the Reformation. It reveals the entire tragedy of the modern world missions, which is to be seen on all mission fields: the missionaries want to bring
nothing to the heathen except for the Gospel of Jesus Christ. But because they
do it, they necessarily bring along not only the home confession but also powerful errors. That is true also of Lutheran missions. How Neuendettelsau, to point
the finger at ourselves for a change, carried along with Löhe's Lutheran faith
also contemporary errors in his doctrine of the spiritual office, as well as his
pietistic chiliasm (which was thought to be Lutheran in the middle of the previous century), to America and Australia, and thereby did untold damage to the
Lutheran Church! The large English and American churches made corresponding [mistakes] in great style in India and China. Who knows if it is not better for
the path of the Gospel in China that the American missionaries must pull out
of China for at least a generation? If it goes farther with the Lutheran mission
in India as it goes now, as the "Doctrinal Statement of the Lutheran Church in
India" (*The Lutheran World Review*, April 1950, pp. 222f.) indicates, then one will
not need to wonder when the Lord closes this mission field to our church as well.
For even here, His Eucharist is being taken away from the Lord Christ because
the real presence is limited to the personal presence according to the promises
of Matt. 18:20 and 28:20, probably because that which the Holy Scripture and
the catechism say about this matter belong to the "antiquated theological formulations and slogans." Consider what it means that, in a doctrinal declaration
about the Lord's Supper, the body and blood of Christ are mentioned only when
[the document] is speaking about the memory of the death by crucifixion. Of
a presence of the body and blood of Christ there is no mention anymore. Have
we already gone so far that the Words of Institution by the Lord are "old-fashioned jargon"? Hence, the confessions which arise in the "young churches" in
our time are all two-faced. In them, the young Christians confess not only their

faith, but rather they also confess simultaneously, in moving dependence upon their spiritual fathers, the unbelief and error of their missionaries. Far be it from us to minimize the faithful and blessed work of a mission such as the Rhenish Mission Society among the Batak since the days of the unforgettable Ludwig Nommensen (1834–1918).[9] We do not make any personal reproaches to any of the missionaries in Indonesia and India. They have done what they could, and they have taught that which they themselves have learned. But this result can change nothing of the fact that even the Lutheran missions participate in the tragedy of the modern world mission. They have not always and not only proclaimed the pure Gospel. It would be a job for the LWF, instead of legitimizing such dilettantism and theologically impossible substitute confessions, [rather] to help the young churches to a true Lutheran confession and to an authentic understanding of the Gospel.

6

The *great decision*, which was made *in Hanover* itself shows that the decisions in the cases of the Brazilian church federation and of the Christian-Protestant Church of Batak are not to be explained only by the special situations of need of the diaspora and the mission fields, to which some believe special consideration is due. This was already visible at the great pontifical office [*Pontifikalamt*] with which, as we correctly predicted, the convention was opened. The *old* Lutheran World Convention held no common eucharistic celebrations because there was no *altar fellowship* between its members. That was honest, and it corresponded to Lutheran teaching, because for Lutheranism altar fellowship has meant, since time immemorial, the completion of church fellowship, the communion [*Gemeinschaft*] of the Body of Christ, which is always both at once: communion of His body in the Sacrament and communion [*Gemeinschaft*] of His spiritual body of the church (1 Cor. 10:16). That was even expressed in the negotiations of the theological commission—as far as we know, by Prof. [Werner] Elert—but in vain. Since the influential convention at *Lund* [1947], in which the Lutheran World Convention was transformed into the LWF, the common eucharistic celebration

---

9   Ludwig Ingwer Nommensen, the "apostle of the Batak," was sent by the Rhenish
     Mission Society to Sumatra in 1861. Today the HKBP numbers several million. Inter-
     estingly, with the assistance of friends in the Lutheran Church of Australia, the entire
     Book of Concord has been translated by a Batak man into the Batak tongue (2004):
     *BUKU KONKORD: Konfesi Gereja Lutheran, translated by Mangisi S.E. Simorangkir,
     PT BPK GUNUNG MULIA, Jakarta.* Also, there is a stirring among Batak church lead-
     ership for genuine Lutheranism as the church has through the years accepted the
     influences of general and liberal Protestantism in the place of its saner Lutheran and
     Reformed beginnings. The LCMS *Small Catechism with Explanation* has been trans-
     lated and put into the hands of some 1,000 Batak pastors. The two kingdoms doctrine
     of Luther is of great interest to the Bataks as they face the one kingdom doctrine of
     Islam. See *"My God Told Me to Stay Here": The Life and Work of Missionary Ludwig
     Ingwer Nommensen, "The Apostle of the Bataks"* (n.d.). MH

belongs to the style of these conventions. The Lord's Supper in Hanover was no longer the Lord's Supper, for the maintenance of which the Lutheran Church has fought since the days of the reformer. For it is said of this Lord's Supper, even if it is celebrated as a Mass, in the twenty-fourth article of the Augsburg Confession: *nulli . . . admittuntur, nisi antea explorati* ["No one is admitted unless they have been examined," AC XXV 1]. That means: before Communion, there must be the most serious warning and confession of sins. When, at the great festival service for the 200th anniversary of the Reformation on October 31, 1717, in the Church of the Cross at Dresden, nearly 1,000 people went to the Lord's Table, pastors had on the previous day "sat all day long taking confessions" (E. S. Cyprian, *Hilaria Evangelica*, 1719, pp. 102f.). We in the Lutheran Church are in great danger that the warning and the confession of sins comes too short, or is practically omitted, and that the Sacrament of the Altar becomes a showpiece for the masses and a tool for the union, which in the Reformed Churches it sadly has already become. By orchestrating this showpiece, one has brought serious theologians into serious reservations of conscience, namely, those theologians who, according to the rules of their church, the old Lutheran Church, are not allowed to participate in such a celebration, especially as even the liturgy itself was not immune to objections. True, they didn't use one of the "eucharistic prayers" which are so often recommended these days, which in some places have been introduced into the Lutheran liturgy and which give the consecration a different meaning. The order for the opening service on July 25, 1952, printed in two languages in a 32-page booklet (*Opening Service of the Assembly of the LWF*), carries on its title page the express notice: "The regulations of the Evangelical Lutheran Territorial Church of Hanover will govern the celebration and participation in the Lord's Supper." Despite this, one reads on p. 24 about the "distribution" the following:

> The dispensing occurs with these words:
> [Pastor:] The body of Christ, given for you
> Communicant: Amen.
> [Pastor:] The blood of Christ, shed for you
> Communicant: Amen.
> [Pastor:] Go in peace. Amen.

This is one of the modern distribution formulas, influenced by the Eastern Church, which appears, among other places, in the new "Agenda for Evangelical-Lutheran Churches and Congregations" (cf. the "working draft" for the first volume, 1951, p. 87) produced by the *Vereinigte Evangelische Lutheranische Kirche Deutschlands* [VELKD] along with two other distribution formulas. But— as far as we know—it has never yet existed in the "regulations" of the Hanover Territorial Church. In the case of this distribution formula, used on July 25, 1952, in the Marktkirche in Hanover, it remains doubtful whether "the true body" of the Lord is dispensed, as the Lutheran distribution formulas express it. One must consider that, on the title page of the order of service, not only the complete assembly of the LWF was officially named but in addition to that another sentence read: "The distribution of Holy Communion takes place for the delegates and the alternate delegates," whereby the possibility was not excluded, however, that from among the great number of "official visitors" present, some of them also (e.g., Lutherans from the union churches) could commune, which in fact actually occurred. Gustav Stählin[10] (from Erlangen), in his large presentation "Lutheran Ethics and Mission Practice," appealed for the admission of members of other denominations to Lutheran Communion—not without arousing some opposition, but in such a way that he had a large portion of those gathered in Hanover behind him. The words which he spoke to justify this surrender of the Lutheran viewpoint [actually] direct themselves against himself and against [Hanns] Lilje's grand pontifical office:

> Holy Communion is the gift of inconceivable love in the world. Do we want to make it into a celebration which injures and divides, and in such a way that it does not edify, but rather destroys?

The destroyers of the unity of the church are not those who accept the significance of the Lord's Supper which the Lord Christ Himself gave and which His apostles confirmed. Those who organized such a celebration and thereby made the Sacrament into a tool of church politics are responsible for the split which occurred in Hanover between those who participated in that Eucharist and those who, for the sake of their Lutheran consciences which are bound to the Word of Christ, did not so participate. If the LWF is a federation of Lutheran Churches between which today there can yet be no church fellowship or altar fellowship, then it may not plan such celebrations in its agenda. That does not belong to its tasks. And if it wants to excuse itself by saying that the organization and order of service for such celebrations must be left to the hosting church, then to such we reply that then the church in question alone must invite [participants] to [such a celebration], and that such a celebration cannot belong on the agenda of the LWF. *Perhaps it will later be said that in the Marktkirche in Hanover the Lutheranism of the world was finally split forever.*

7

But all of these—the decision about Brazil and the mission churches, as well as the decision which was made with the celebration of the Lord's Supper in Hanover—are indeed merely symptoms of the *deep crisis in which the Lutheranism of the world finds itself.* This crisis began with the founding of the Prussian Union in 1817, and it continues since then like a creeping disease through the Lutheran Churches of the world. We have spoken often about this disease in these letters, about the deconfessionalization of Lutheranism, about

---

10 Gustav Stählin (1900–1985) was a professor at Erlangen and at Mainz. See *RGG*[3] 6:234. MH

the death of Lutheranism not as a theological-ecclesiastical school of thought, but as a church. Our hope that Lutheranism would be spared the fate of the other Protestant churches is, at least for the great majority of Lutherans in the world, gone. As the Reformed Churches have long since lost the confessions of its Reformation, as the Anglicans have surrendered their *Thirty-Nine Articles*, so the confessional substance of Lutheranism is evaporating quickly. For the LWF, exactly as for the United Lutheran Church in America and for the territorial churches in Germany which are still *de jure* Lutheran, the Confessions are merely working hypotheses. The same is true of the Church of Sweden. One asks in vain how Swedish bishops, who are Luther researchers and Luther experts like no bishop in Germany, could seal the altar fellowship of their church with the Church of England, in whose *Book of Common Prayer* every communicant, after the consecration, reads the words that the body of Christ is not here but rather in heaven, because it is against the nature of a body to be at more than one place at the same time. That has nothing to do with theology, but rather only with politics, exactly as the honor shown the "Lutheran bishop" Dibelius in Berlin. Nobody had any objection to honoring a loyal union man. But that the savior of the old Prussian Union, who sees in his union church the great tool for uniting Germany, is celebrated as a Lutheran by the Nordic and American Lutherans, as was done by [Anders] Nygren in his role as president of the LWF on the occasion of Dibelius's seventieth birthday, we simpler minds don't understand. As we then also don't understand that, after the convention at Hanover, they brought the Lutherans to Berlin, so that they could there, at a union chancel, bear witness to the citizens of Berlin about not only their human bonds, but rather additionally their ecclesiastical bonds. In this connection, finally, the choice of territorial Bishop Lilje as president of the LWF is to be seen. Why the Americans refrained from this office, for which it was their turn, has not become known. Probably because of the difficult internal crises of American Lutheranism and the lack of a top-notch personality in the middle [of the continuum of theological views]. But now consider what it means that Lilje, the acting director of the council of the EKiD, who has repeatedly and solemnly assured his loyalty to this unionistic church type and who is a leader of the Christian Student Movement, with his ties to the Reformed, [now] stands at the head of world Lutheranism, and that Dr. Franklin Fry [1900–1968], the president of the ULC and instigator of the National Council of the Churches of Christ in America has the most important office after him. From Hanover, Lilje traveled to Stuttgart and was there happily and enthusiastically further celebrated. Whether it's the LWF or the German evangelical convention, it makes little difference. The church is the church, and the same people who in Hanover went to the "Lutheran" Lord's Supper went here to the no-longer-Lutheran Communion of the Württemberg church. Perhaps these events are more important than all the resolutions and official proclamations. Perhaps this is the most important decision of church history to be made in this year. Fr. W. Hopf [1910–82], in no. 29 of the *Lutherische Blätter* (p. 7), formulated it this way:

> All those who are chiefly responsible, and those who helped them, for the unionistic ties in their churches received, so to speak, through the so-called world Lutheranism an official confirmation of their decisions. The complete affirmation of the EKiD or membership in one of the old union churches is, in the framework of world Lutheranism as it was understood in Hanover, completely possible.

The falsehood of the German Evangelical Church [DEK] and the so-called national synod in Wittenberg in 1933; the falsehood of Barmen, where they gave a confessional foundation to this German Evangelical Church by means of a joint declaration, which could not be made to square with the Lutheran Confession, of Reformed and Lutherans about what is true and false doctrine in the church; the falsehood of Treysa in 1947 and Eisenach in 1948—all of this monstrous amount of guilt which was upon German Lutheranism and which this Lutheranism will pay to the last penny is now the guilt of world Lutheranism. *Kyrie eleison!*

8

As we express this, we in no way lift ourselves up above the people who bear responsibility for these decisions. On the contrary, we acknowledge our *share of the guilt*. We should have confessed more and said yet more clearly what was at stake, even if our voice was not heard. The most shocking thing about the fate of Lutheranism is the failure of the American churches. At the meetings of the old [Lutheran] World Convention, there were still enough American theologians who knew the history of German Lutheranism. It was, after all, their churches which stood for a long time in battle against unionism and for the Lutheran Church. There were also still scholars who knew what was theologically at risk. But one no longer called to them. In the preparations for the world convention which was planned for 1940 in Philadelphia, the unforgettable *Michael Reu* from Dubuque [Iowa] wrote to the members of the commission about the topic "the Church and churches" and argued against the document which had come from Germany and in which the consensus about the doctrine of justification was presented as sufficient for church fellowship. With his deep understanding of the Sacrament of the Altar—a part of his Neuendettelsau heritage—and with his thorough knowledge of the dogmatic and historical background to the Augsburg Confession, he showed that Articles VII and X of the Augsburg Confession could be understood only on the basis of that which had taken place in Marburg in the previous year [1529], and why, for Luther, the real presence and the doctrine of justification belonged together as the focal point of an ellipse. But this generation of theologians seems to have died out in America. Could it really happen that the theological leader of one of the large Lutheran churches in America, a leading member of the commission of theologians in the preparations for

Hanover, published in the days of Hanover in the most respected academic periodical of American Lutheranism an essay about the Lord's Supper in which he quite seriously made a "Colloquy at the Wartburg" out of the "Marburg religious discussions"—a certain sign, not only for an ignorance of German geography which is excusable for an American, but rather additionally for his not at all knowing anymore what actually happened in Marburg. But even in the case of the leading churchmen among the American Lutherans, a lack manifests itself compared to what their predecessors still had twenty years ago. The things which the dearly departed Carl Christian Hein, president of the Ohio Synod [1924–30], could still say in Copenhagen in 1931 about the Holy Scripture had to be said this time by the president of the Missouri Synod, Dr. John William Behnken [1884–1968], who was present [only] as a guest, and these things were perceived by many as a strange and unfamiliar message. What will happen in twenty or thirty years when, along with the knowledge of the German language, the knowledge of Luther and the Lutheran Reformation will have still further disappeared in different parts of the world? If we did not know in whose hands the fate of the Lutheran Church lies, and that these hands are exactly as powerful now as in the time of the Reformation, then we could well doubt the future of our church.

ᔥ

Ne desperemus. Let us not despair! The comforting article about the church is given to us in the Creed, as the Apology to the Augsburg Confession says (VII–VIII 9; Müller, p. 153). We do not want to forget this, when our heart grows heavy in regard to the decisions of Hanover. *He who believes the church cannot doubt the church.* So let us, dear brothers, pray and work, as we have done until now. If a task has become apparent, then it is this one: to gather those who stand for the confessional Lutheran Church in the old sense. An attempt, and we hope a first beginning, at this has been made in Uelzen, as the German Lutheran free churches met with the churches around the world who stand near to them. The thought of this convention was and should remain, if its work is to be advanced, that it does not understand itself as a competition to the LWF, but rather quite the opposite, that it should work together with the LWF wherever this is possible without injury to its conscience. We may indeed never forget how many true Lutherans in the churches in the LWF do not at all want to go the way of deconfessionalization. But they are not being asked, they have no voice, as it perhaps in such a gigantic organization cannot be otherwise. Some will ask us, why don't we go along [with the LWF], why don't we make our influence felt. To this we answer: we are ready to *work* together. But to *be responsible* together for that which a small executive committee decides, and to which every five years a full convention assembly is forced to say yes, for that we are not ready. We know what kind of a great solidarity binds together all those who, in today's world, profess the Augsburg Confession. We will not pull ourselves out of this solidarity.

We want to help and advise wherever we can. But we cannot accept the fiction that the thing is already there which we all desire and for which we all want to work: the consensus of Lutherans about what the Lutheran Church is.

Greeting you at the new liturgical year and at Christmastide, honored brothers, in the bonds of faith,

Your
Hermann Sasse

Historical Context

"The Holy Scriptures simply teach that church fellowship is altar fellowship." This conviction of Sasse's is also that of orthodox Lutheranism from its inception. Therefore it also has been the consistent conviction of the Missouri Synod. "Altar fellowship is certainly brotherly fellowship in the faith or 'church fellowship.'"[1] Sasse is convinced that this view of the Lutheran Confessions waned because of a loss within Lutheranism of the understanding of the true meaning and significance of the Lord's Supper. The views on church fellowship of Martin Bucer and Ulrich Zwingli have conquered Lutheranism since the beginning of the nineteenth century. The Reformed always viewed the differences on the Supper as not church dividing. Karl Barth gave powerful impetus to the Reformed view in the Kirchenkampf. And in the 1960s even at Concordia Seminary, St. Louis, it was taught that Lutheranism is a confessing movement within the church catholic. For the Lutheran Confessions, the Lutheran Church is the catholic church gone right. MH

November 21, 1952[2]

Prof. H. Sasse
41 Buxton Street
North Adelaide, South Australia

Highly Honored Herr Doctor Behnken!

. . . If we can give our brothers in the office no alternative to the exit from the LWF, then it will be difficult if not impossible to come to unity in Australia. Our general president was so impressed by Hanover and so influenced by the leaders of the VELKD that for him the alternatives are clear: with Missouri in the LWF, or with the European territorial churches in the LWF while forsaking Australian unification . . .

H. Sasse

---

1 Francis Pieper, *Christian Dogmatics* 4:448, quoting C. F. W. Walther's *Pastorale*, 145. MH

2 CHI Behnken file. MH

twenty-eight

Altar Fellowship, Church Fellowship, and Ecclesiastical Federation

TRANSLATED BY MATTHEW C. HARRISON

Christmas 1952[1]

Prof. D. Theol. Hermann Sasse
41 Buxton Street
North Adelaide South Australia

Dear Brothers in the Office!

The events of this year now passing in the church, particularly the great ecclesiastical sessions of Willingen (World Mission Council), Hanover (Lutheran World Federation), Stuttgart (German Evangelical Kirchentag) and Lund (Third World Conference for Faith and Order), have with great urgency directed anew to us Lutherans the question of what the theological conditions are for altar fellowship, church fellowship, and ecclesiastical federation. The question is certainly not new. It had already been thoroughly dealt with in the nineteenth century—so thoroughly, in fact, that one is amazed at the thoughtlessness with which the theology of our time dismisses the answers given then, though these answers still today have significance at least for canonical law. But perhaps it is asking too much of our generation, whose experience of church history began with Barth's *Römerbrief* of 1919,[2] or even only first with the German church struggle

---

1   *BLP* 28: *Abendmahlsgemeinschaft, Kirchengemeinschaft und kirchliche Federation* (North Adelaide, December 1952). The original was published in *LuBl* 5, no. 30 (1953). Huss number 297. MH

2   *The Epistle to the Romans*, trans. Edwyn Clement Hoskyns (London: Oxford University Press, 1933). MH

of 1933, yet to understand the struggle and work of the fathers of the previous century, upon whose shoulders we stand. Still less can this be expected of the American Lutherans who since 1917 together with their nation have undergone a transformation the depth of which can only be compared to the transformation which the Russian nation has undergone since 1917. The American of 1952, even if he should belong to the Lutheran Church, is an entirely different man than the American before the outbreak of the First World War. If Lutherans at the beginning of the century could read their church and synodical newspapers of today, they simply would not recognize their church in them. Thus it appears senseless to appeal to the faith and decisions regarding matters of the faith of the fathers when the great question of the relationships of the churches is the matter under discussion. We must go back to the Confessions of the Lutheran Reformation and to the teaching of the New Testament.

1

The decision regarding the relationship between the Lutheran and the Reformed Church, as is well-known, was rendered at the Marburg Colloquy [1529] and dogmatized in the Confessions. All attempts to reinterpret the meaning of *Augsburg Confession* Article X have ended in failure and have only led to the forsaking of the Lutheran Church. The *improbant secus docentes* ["they reject those who teach," AC X 2] of this article is only a mild form of the *anathema* which precludes church fellowship with the deniers of the real presence as it is taught in the catechism. *The Wittenberg Concord* of 1536, too, by which the South Germans and the Lutherans were united, can be understood in no other way than as it was interpreted and taken up by the *Formula of Concord*. The decisive question is whether Luther was justified when at the conclusion of the Marburg discussions he refused to the Reformed altar fellowship and the recognition as brothers which they had sought. It was not that he was not basically inclined to oblige Christians who thought otherwise. This is shown by the *Marburg Articles* themselves, in particular by the formalization of the article on the Supper, and also by the last offer for union which he made and which the trustworthy [witness] [Johannes] Oecolampadius has preserved for us:

> We confess that, by virtue of these words "This is My body," "This is My blood," the body and the blood of Christ truly, that is, substantially and essentially, not, however, quantitatively or qualitatively nor locally, are present and offered in the Supper. [Cited according to W. Köhler, *Das Marburger Religionsgespräch 1529, Versuch einer Rekonstruktion*, 1929, pp. 131f.]

Luther was satisfied with the mildest form of the doctrine of the real presence in the sense of a substantial and essential [presence], though not a local and quantitative presence of the body and blood of Christ under the elements. But where this was not acknowledged there could be no altar and church fellowship for him. The denier of the real presence was for him no Christian brother, and he well knew what he did when in Article XV he maintained that each side ought to show Christian love to the other, then added the words: "so far as every conscience can allow" (WA 30/3:170.30f.).[3] While the Zwinglians and the later Reformed have always declared that the Lutheran doctrine of the Supper is indeed false but not church dividing, Luther and the Lutheran Church, as long as they took their Confessions seriously, have always viewed the difference on the Supper as church dividing and the Reformed doctrine on this point as a heresy precluding church fellowship. For more than four hundred years the right hand of fellowship of the Reformed has remained outstretched. For more than four hundred years we Lutherans with our reformer have had to hear the accusation of unbrotherliness and lovelessness, because we have refused this hand.

This fact must give us serious cause ever and again to examine whether or not Luther's conscience was perhaps on this point an erring conscience. Woe to us if we would base the denial of altar fellowship on the tradition of our church or the example of Luther. If we did this, we would no longer be Lutherans. Perhaps our opponents have not been totally incorrect if they have often felt our standpoint were essentially only traditionalism. With many Lutherans this is actually the case. This renders their position dubious and explains the defection of so many Lutheran Churches from the position of old Lutheranism. In Sweden today it is declared without concern (as it happened only a short time ago with the World Conference on Faith and Order) that the old rules of church order are a holdover [from the past]. Those who come to the altar are not questioned concerning their confession; rather, one is prepared to give the Sacrament to anyone because the Lord does the same thing at our altar that He does at the Reformed and Anglican altar, namely, He gives Himself in the real presence. Thus open Communion is advocated. In fact, if we have to do here only with a human tradition, then the Swedes and their Nordic and German neighbors are entirely correct when they defect to the practice of open Communion which has been advocated by the Reformed since Marburg. But before we follow their example, the Swedish Luther scholars must explain to us then why Luther so firmly held to the literal meaning of the Words of Institution and what these words meant for his faith. Why, for instance, did he demand from the Bohemians, whom he so kindly addressed in *On the Adoration of the Sacrament* of 1523,[4] the acceptance of the doctrine of the real presence as a condition for church fellowship? Indeed, he did so for exactly this reason: the Words of Institution are the Gospel, which one must simply accept and may not change:

---

3   *Marburger Gespräch und Marburger Artikel* (*Marburg Colloquy and Marburg Articles*) (1529), Aland 452 (AE 38:88). MH

4   *Vom Anbeten des Sakraments des heiligen Leichnams Jesu Christi*, WA 11:431–56 (Aland 664; AE 36:275–305). MH

On these words rests the matter completely. Every single Christian should and must know them and not allow them to be taken from him by any other teaching, even if it were an angel from heaven. They are a word of life and salvation, so that to him who believes through such faith all sins are forgiven, and he is a child of life, has overcome hell and death. The greatness and power of this word cannot be expressed; *for they are the sum of the entire gospel.* (WA 11:432.19ff.)[5]

Luther was convinced that no one can understand the entire consolation of "given and shed for you" who does not believe "This *is* My body," "This *is* My blood." The question upon which everything depends is whether this is biblical or not.

2

The Holy Scriptures simply teach that church fellowship is altar fellowship.[6] "The cup of blessing which we bless is the *koinonia* of the blood of Christ, the bread which we break is the *koinonia* of the body of Christ" (1 Cor. 10:16). The apostle connects this participation in the body and blood of the Lord immediately with the assertion that, as the bread is one, so we who are many are one body because we partake of one bread (v. 17). The *Corpus Christi sacramentale* and the *Corpus Christi spirituali sive mysticum* ["the sacramental body of Christ" and "the spiritual or mystical body of Christ"], *as our dogmaticians say, belong essentially together. Ecclesia,* "church" in the strict sense of the New Testament, is there where the people of God come together at one place and celebrate the Lord's Supper. There the body of Christ in the double sense is reality, though it is of course not only there. From this view of the New Testament—that altar fellowship is church fellowship and church fellowship is altar fellowship—it follows that the boundaries of both coincide. Where does the boundary of altar fellowship in the New Testament lie? It is significant that all our documents concerning the oldest Christian Supper, insofar as they bear a liturgical character, describe a boundary for altar fellowship. "The doors! The doors!" cries the deacon before the Creed yet today in the liturgy of the Eastern Church. With this the liturgy of the "believers" begins, reminiscent of the first Sunday of the church, when the Lord came to His own behind closed doors (John 20:19). "No catechumen, no hearer, no unbeliever, no heterodox" shall be present at the Supper according

---

5   *Vom Anbeten des Sakraments des heiligen Leichnams Jesu Christi* (*Adoration of the Sacrament*) (1523), Aland 664 (AE 36:277). MH

6   So also C. F. W Walther and the LCMS. "Members of heterodox fellowships are not excommunicated by their non-admission to the celebration of Holy Communion in fellowship with the Lutheran Church, much less are they (declared to be heretics and) condemned, but only suspended until they have reconciled with the orthodox church by leaving the false fellowship in which they stand" ("Communion Fellowship," Thesis XI, in *Essays for the Church*, vol. 1: *1857–1879* [St. Louis: Concordia, 1992], 225). MH

to the liturgical cry of the Antiochene liturgy in the eighth book of *The Apostolic Constitutions* (ch. 12), and among the believers no one should have anything against another, nor should a hypocrite approach (cf. the text of Brightman, *Liturgies Eastern and Western*, I, p. 13). *Santa sanctis*, "Holy things for holy ones," sounded the warning call before the Communion. And so that no one thereby understood that the church was a union of Pharisees, the response of the holy people of God sounded: "One is holy, one is the Lord, Jesus Christ, to the honor of God the Father." (Cf. Brightman, p. 24 *et passim*.) The fact that all liturgies of the old Greek Church contain such a cry by which a fence was placed around the Supper points to the fact that this is a very ancient practice. The way in which Justin [ca. 100–ca. 165] (*Apology* 1.66) in his account concerning the origin of the Supper emphasizes that Jesus at the institution of the Supper gave bread and wine *to the disciples only*—who else could He have given it to?—shows that the "to them alone" is essential to his understanding of the Supper. The admonitions and warnings of the *Teaching of the Twelve Apostles* [*Didache*] corresponds to this. "No one is to eat or drink from your Eucharist unless they are baptized in the name of the Lord. For concerning this the Lord has said: 'Do not give that which is holy to dogs'" (*Didache* 9.5). Thus follows the "rubric" in the liturgy: "He who is holy, come; he who is not, repent" (10.6). This same writing prescribes confession and absolution before the Sunday celebration of the Supper in the same way the later liturgies and church orders do:

> But every Lord's day do gather yourselves together, and break bread, and give thanksgiving after having confessed your transgressions, that your sacrifice may be pure. But let no one who is at variance with his fellow come together with you, until they be reconciled, that your sacrifice may not be profaned. For this is that which was spoken by the Lord.[7]

Here follows the citation from Mal. 1:11 and 14, which in this passage for the first time is applied to the Supper, though not yet in the sense of the later theory of the sacrifice of the Mass. For the "sacrifice" is here still the sacrifice of praise and thanksgiving in the biblical sense, applied to the "Eucharistia" (*Didache* 14). When we look at the New Testament in this light, then we see immediately several passages containing the early Christian concept of the "closed Supper," namely, that the Lord's Supper is celebrated behind closed doors, to the exclusion of those who do not belong at it.

First, it is certain that wherever in the New Testament there is the demand for the holy kiss (Rom. 16:16; 1 Cor. 16:20; 2 Cor. 13:12; 1 Thess. 5:26; 1 Pet. 5:14), the "kiss of peace," the later *Pax* which preceded the Communion is in view. The demands for this kiss occur as they do at the conclusion of these letters of Paul because they were read before the gathered *ecclesia*, which then proceeded to celebrate the Supper. Thus the letters conclude with the "apostolic blessing" in its simple form: "The grace of our Lord Jesus Christ be with you," or in the

---

7   English text cited from ANF 7:381. MH

developed Trinitarian form such as we find in 2 Cor. 13:[14]. Is it mere coincidence that in the Greek (the liturgy of Chrysostom) and in the Syrian (e.g., in the liturgy of Theodore of Mopsuestia [ca. 350–ca.428]) Churches they do not begin the preface with "The Lord be with you" but with the formula of greeting from 2 Cor. 13:[14]? The conclusion of the Book of Revelation should also be compared with the Pauline letters. Is it merely coincidental that the "*Maranatha*! The grace of the Lord Jesus Christ be with you!" of 1 Cor. 16:23 is repeated in Rev. 22:20 with the words: "Come Lord Jesus! The grace of the Lord Jesus be with you all"? Was not Revelation written to be read in the liturgy (1:11; 22:18) as much as the letters of Paul? Even if it is impossible for us to know all the details of the liturgy of the first century (Pliny [the Younger] gives us the responsories for the time immediately before the turn of the century; the *Sanctus* is verified for the first century through Clement of Rome [bishop, 92–101]) the letters of Paul certainly show us this much: besides the Words of Institution, which belong to the celebration of the Lord's Supper, there is the demand for the kiss of peace; and then follows immediately the warning against schismatics and heretics, the anathema (Rom. 16:16f.; 1 Cor. 16:20, 22); then the ancient petition of the congregation for the coming of the Lord (still spoken in Aramaic in the Pauline congregations); and finally the benediction. The similarity of the letters of Paul with Revelation and the *Didache* show that these were fixed liturgical usages.

What interests us here is the close connection between the Pax and the Anathema, the kiss of love and peace, which expressed the unity and fellowship of the church, and the inflexible exclusion of schismatics and heretics from the Supper and thereby the church. At the conclusion of 1 Corinthians, which is directed against the divisions in the church of Corinth, it is the stubborn schismatics to whom the Anathema is directed: "If anyone does not love the Lord, let him be anathema" (16:22). For the one who arrogantly splits the congregation, which is the body of the Lord, cannot love the Lord. In the Letter to the Romans, the admonition to greet one another in peace with the kiss of love, and the assurance that the church of Rome is in this kiss bound together with all churches of Christ, is followed by the express warning over against heretics:

> Now I urge you brethren, note those who caused divisions and offenses, contrary to the doctrine which you learned, and avoid them. For those who are such do not serve our Lord Jesus Christ, but their own belly, and by smooth words and flattering speech deceive the hearts of the simple. [16:17f.; cf. 1 Cor. 16:20]

The fellowship of the church, the deepest and most intimate fellowship which there is, presupposes an inflexible separation from heresy (1 John 4:1–7; 2 John 9ff.; 2 Cor. 6:14) because it is at the same time both fellowship between believers and fellowship with the triune God (1 John 1:3). And this separation finds its essential expression in who does and who does not receive the Supper (*Abendmahlszucht*). The fundamental axiom of canon law that there can be no *communicatio in sacris cum haereticis* [literally, "no fellowship in holy things with heretics"] comes directly from the early church and has its dogmatic basis in the New Testament.

3

Luther's view of church fellowship and altar fellowship can be understood only on this basis. It is not true, as is heard time and again, that Luther no longer correctly understood the fellowship character of the Supper. One need only read his sermons on the Supper to realize that the opposite is the case. The following passage from the work cited above from 1523 shows how deeply the reformer understood the relationship between the sacramental and the spiritual body of Christ:

> Thus it is now true that we Christians are the spiritual body of Christ, and altogether *one* bread, *one* drink, *one* spirit. Christ does all this, who through His body makes us all one spiritual body, and we all alike partake of His body, and so among ourselves are alike and one. Likewise, because we partake of one bread and drink, this also makes us one bread and drink. And as one member serves the other in such common love, he thus also eats and drinks the other, that is, he partakes of him in all things and is indeed the food and drink of the other, so that we thus are pure food and drink for each other, in the same way Christ is for us pure food and drink. With these words, St. Paul has laid out the riches and nature of faith and love. In the same way natural bread and wine also signify as much. For out of many kernels which are ground up, there comes *one* bread, and each one forsakes its form and becomes the flour of another. Also, many berries become *one* wine, and each berry gives up its own form and becomes juice to the other. So also Christ has become everything to us, and so among ourselves each has become everything to the other. This is how we are Christians; what one has, belongs to the other, and if one lacks, this affects the other as though he lacked it himself. . . .[8]

One must have such passages in view in order to understand the "no" with which he denied the hand of brotherhood and the fellowship of the Supper to [Ulrich] Zwingli. This *Anathema*, too, can only be understood against the background of the *Pax* which for Luther belonged to the Sacrament of the Altar. And for him the body of Christ in the Supper is a reality such that he knows that the fellowship of the church rests upon the participation in this body. The church is more than a fellowship of the Spirit and spiritual people, as the humanists Zwingli and Calvin thought. It *is* the body of Christ, because the consecrated bread *is* the body of Christ. "There is one body and one Spirit, just as you were called in one hope of your calling; one Lord, one faith, one Baptism; one God and Father of

---

8   *Vom Anbeten des Sakraments des heiligen Leichnams Jesu Christi* (*Adoration of the Sacrament*), WA 11:440.34ff (Aland 664; AE 36:286–87). MH

all …." (Eph. 4:4ff.). This fundamentally important passage of the New Testament on the unity of the church, upon which also the doctrine of the one church in *Augustana* VII is based, says with perfect clarity that the church is not merely what we men call a "spiritual fellowship." As according to 1 Cor. 6:19 our body is a temple of the Holy Spirit; as our body is baptized and thereby at once on the Last Day will become "like unto His glorified body" (Phil. 3:21; cf. Rom. 6:4f.), so the church is also *one* body (notice that the "one body" precedes the "one Spirit"). We do not know *how* the church *is* the body of Christ, just as we do not know how the consecrated bread is the body of Christ. The later theological distinction between the *corpus Christi mysticum* and the *corpus Christi sacramentale* ["the mystical body of Christ" and "the sacramental body of Christ"] is an attempt to formalize [a solution to] this problem. But there is no solution, as the Greek fathers also occasionally designate the sacramental body as the "mystical" body. Thus the Lutheran church must avoid turning the *est* into *significat* in both cases. Just as we reject every figurative meaning for the Words of Institution, so also we reject as unbiblical every understanding of the church which sees in the church only a fellowship of pious souls, a society of believers, who join together in common prayer and for the fostering of their faith. Thus we must also reject the encyclical *Corporis Mystici*[9] and Roman theology which sees in the designation of the church as "body of Christ" only an image for the social character of the church, which is compared to "corporate participation" in one body. Certainly no one can conceive of a comparison which adequately describes the fact that the church is the body of Christ, just as indeed reason cannot understand or describe the relationship between the body of Christ in the Supper and the body of Christ in the church. For Scripture says nothing of this. What we have to accept in faith is the simple truth of the Bible, that the *ecclesia* is the body of Christ as certainly as it is the people of God, whatever the relation of the body of Christ which is the church to the true body [of Christ] which we receive in the Sacrament.

Accordingly, if a deep correspondence obtains between the Sacrament of the Altar and the church, then the destruction of this Sacrament must of necessity lead to the destruction of the church. Here lies the basis for which Zwingli and the other "Sacramentarians" were for Luther destroyers of the church, with whom there can be no ecclesiastical fellowship. If the apostle only acknowledged that spirit as legitimate which confessed "Jesus Christ come in the flesh" (1 John 4:2), and then treated the denial of the incarnation as a manifestation of the Antichrist, then Luther found himself in an entirely similar situation over against the deniers of the flesh and blood in the Supper. For him incarnation and real presence belonged so closely together that he believed the incarnation was no longer correctly taught where the real presence was denied, and

---

9   This appears to be a reference to Pius XII's *Mystici Corporis Christi* (1943) (Denzinger 2290). MH

in making this point he called upon the Gospel of St. John, the apostle of the incarnation. In view of the Christological controversy which in the sixteenth century was directly connected to the question of the Supper, it cannot be denied that the doctrinal difference regarding the Supper stretched deep into the Christological [question]. Luther perceived the Reformed denial of the participation of the divine nature of Christ in the attributes of the human, and vice versa, as a destruction of the biblical Christ. When Zwingli called it an *alloiosis* when it was said that the Son of God died for us, because only the human nature could die, Luther called this separation of the person of Christ "the most horrible heresy that has ever existed." And he asked, "What Christian heart can hear or suffer such [teaching]? Indeed, thereby the entire Christian faith and the salvation of all the world [and] all things are taken away and damned. For he who is redeemed by humanity alone is certainly not redeemed." And Luther continues:

> I confess for myself that I regard Zwingli as non-Christian with all his teaching, for he maintains no part of the Christian faith correctly and has become seven times worse than when he was a Papist. . . . I make such a confession in order to be exculpated before God and the whole world, since I have no part in Zwingli's doctrine nor indeed ever will.[10]

This can be understood only when one conceives of the abyss Luther must have glimpsed when he saw behind the theology of Zwingli and [Martin] Bucer (who would become Calvin's teacher) that theology emerging which has effectively conquered modern Protestantism; a theology in which the incarnation is no longer taken seriously. For the incarnation of the eternal Word becomes mere words where the eternal Word remains also outside of the flesh and where the God-man since His exaltation is no longer present with His church according to His human nature. Where this is the case, the Sacraments fall to the wayside. Baptism, in which the entire man, soul and body (cf. Luther, LC IV, *BSLK*, 700.5ff.; *Trig.*, p. 475) has been buried with Christ into death (Rom. 6:4), so that the entire man may rise, body and soul, becomes a symbol of a psychical transaction [*seelischen Vorgangs*]. And the Supper without the real presence of the true body and blood of Christ ceases to be the Sacrament of the New Testament. It becomes a celebration in which nothing else happens than that which according to Matt. 18:20 occurs wherever two or three are gathered in His name. But where the Supper falls away, so also does the church. Even if it retains its outer organization, still it ceases to be the church of the New Testament, the people of God, the Body of Christ, and remains only a religious society. Thus it was for Luther, and is for the Lutheran Church of all times, that altar fellowship is church fellowship. And precisely because it rests upon the fellowship of the body and blood of Christ, which is impervious to reason, church fellowship is thus not a fellowship which we men can create, and for this reason neither can we arrange it.

---

10 *Vom Abendmahl Christi* (*Confession concerning Christ's Supper*) (1528), WA 26:342.13ff. (Aland 2; AE 37:231). See FC SD VIII 21, 38–45. MH

4

Thus if Supper fellowship and church fellowship are essentially one, then it is self-evident that any change in the practice of Supper fellowship demonstrates a change in the concept of church and in the understanding of the Sacraments. There is absolutely no doubt that the *decline of the Lutheran understanding of the Sacraments*, in particular the Lutheran doctrine of the Sacrament of the Altar, is the deepest reason that so many Lutheran churches have given up the old boundaries over against the Reformed, and thereby Lutheran principles of church fellowship. This happened in the nineteenth century in the form of lawfully constituted unions of various types [*regelrechter Unionen verschiedenen Typs*]. As varied as these may be—there were in Germany some five or six various types of union, which deviated so much from one another that up to the present it has proved impossible to unify these unions—they all had this in common: they all accepted Zwingli's and Bucer's view that altar fellowship and thereby church fellowship is also possible where there are differing doctrines regarding the Supper. The Lord Christ, so it is said, instituted the Supper for His disciples to celebrate in common, not for them to fight over. An Anglican slogan which has been influential in the more recent Ecumenical Movement stated: "Although we may not be united in the definition of the Supper, we can indeed be united in its celebration." Indeed, here we are directly informed that by first experiencing altar fellowship we can be helped to correctly understand the Sacrament. Thus the united celebration of the Supper has even become a means to achieve union. But also in this case the following applies: all this is only possible if the doctrine of Luther and the Lutheran Church are surrendered *de facto*. At the Third (and perhaps last) World Conference for Faith and Order at Lund in August 1952, only an insignificant minority of Lutherans advocated the Lutheran view of closed Communion (indeed, one each from Hanover, Saxony, and the ULC in America). All other Lutheran members of the section which dealt with the question of "inter-Communion" advocated open Communion. Thus one can see how grave is the situation of the Lutheran Church as *Church*, and this all the more since the few who advocated the old Lutheran practice in regard to altar fellowship either were immediately disavowed by members of their own church, or they advocated a law which in their churches obtains only today *de jure*. It has hitherto been impossible to check the movement which has passed through the Protestant world since the beginning of the nineteenth century and which has also brought Zwingli's and Bucer's views on altar and church fellowship to victory even in the Lutheran Church. Even those churches of the Lutheran Confession which have held themselves far distant from the union are themselves influenced by it more than they know or would want. Here lies the deeper reason for why in Germany the EKiD has become a matter of concern for the "evangelical" populace, while the thought of a "United Evangelical Lutheran Church" gains ground only with great difficulty, and this only among theologians. There is only one thing which can again bring to the Lutheran view of altar and church fellowship recognized validity: the real renewal of the Lutheran understanding of the Sacrament. There is no doubt that this understanding has slowly grown among theologians in recent years. But just how far we still are from a rediscovery of the real presence in the Lutheran sense is shown by the otherwise so influential lecture of Peter Brunner[11] of Heidelberg on "The Nature of the Church's Liturgy" delivered at Hanover. In this paper we first read with joy concerning the Words of Institution (preliminary printing of the manuscript, p. 15):

> They say what the food in this celebration is. The relationship which the word of Jesus establishes between bread and body, wine and blood, is not "a connection by analogy . . . , rather a connection by identity" (Lohmeyer). Bread remains bread; wine remains wine. But in the power of the instituting words of Jesus, this bread is His body given up for us, and this wine His blood, shed for us.

But our joy is immediately shattered by the definition of "body" which then follows.

> Jesus' body, which we receive in the Supper, is the embodied *humanity* of Jesus [*leibhaftige Menschsein Jesu*], in which He worked redemption for us. Jesus' *work of salvation*, Jesus' *salvation-suffering*, Jesus' *salvation-victory*, Jesus' entire corporeal *life* lived for us and *death* suffered for us, and the *victory* won for us is in His body and *is His body*, which we receive under the form of the bread in the Supper. Jesus' body is above all His sacrificial body. *This body and His sacrificial death are one.*

Can this really be said? What Brunner goes on to say is indeed correct: "In this sacrificial body we have His sacrificial death. Also in Jesus' blood of the covenant Jesus' covenant-sacrifice for us is present." But this is only the case if we have the essential, the substantial, body [of Christ], as the fathers put it. But do we actually receive the true, essential, substantial body? Or is "body" used here only to designate the true humanity, life, death, and victory of Jesus? This is what the cited passage says plainly enough. Is this not a repetition of what we have seen previously in Paul Althaus, for whom the gift of the Supper can under no circumstances be the glorified body of the Lord as it is for the Catholic Church, for Luther and indeed—according to his peculiar understanding—for Calvin. Rather, Althaus understands the Words of Institution as though Jesus speaks "of 'body and life' . . . thus as the life as the one dying in the sacrificial death" (*Die Lutherische Abendmahlslehre in der Gegenwart*, 1931, p. 40). We read again in Brunner:

> The duality of bread and wine, of body and blood points to this: that the sacrificed body and the covenant-effecting sacrificial blood of Jesus, and *thereby His sacrifice on the cross* itself, are *present* under the eucharistic

---

11   Peter Brunner (1900–1981) taught systematics at Heidelberg beginning in 1947. MH

food and presented and received through the distributed bread and the distributed cup.

It can certainly be said that where the gifts offered up for sacrifice are, there also the sacrifice itself is present. But can it also be said that the *action of the sacrifice* [*Handlung des Opfers*] is present? This is what we read in Brunner:

> The Supper is the finally fulfilled form of an action of signs [*Zeichen-handlung*] in which Jesus' *salvific deed is rendered present in the power of its eschatological freedom. That one-time final salvific happening* which is concentrated in the cross of Jesus *becomes present in the Supper through effective representation.*

Again, there is a deep truth in what is here said. The cross of Christ does in fact have the eschatological meaning which is here ascribed to it. The cross of Christ is a one-time happening (Heb. 9:12, 26, 28) at the end of the world (Heb. 1:2), and yet it is a reality which existed already at the beginning of the world (Rev. 13:8), and the Crucified One (*estauromenos* ["the one who has been and remains the crucified"], not only *staurotheis* ["the one who was crucified"] in the New Testament) is a perfect present. But where does the concept of effective representation come from? It does not come from the New Testament, but out of Catholic dogmatics. With the help of this concept, this dogmatics seeks to define the relationship of the one-time sacrifice of Golgotha and the sacrifice offered in the Mass in connection with the doctrine of the Council of Trent on the sacrifice of the Mass as the representation, remembrance, and application of the sacrifice of the cross (Trent, Session 22, ch. 1). The real presence which Peter Brunner teaches is the realization of the death of Jesus on the cross, acquired through effective representation and thereby the realization, representation, [the] actual, sacramental presentation of Jesus Christ, His life, death, [and] victory. But it is indeed no accident, if I understand correctly, that with Brunner there is no mention in the context of Supper of the risen and glorified Lord. It is indeed also no accident that what is said in the brilliant lecture of this profound and honorable theological thinker on the eschatological nature of the celebration of the Supper has been most strongly influenced by Catholic writers such as Erik Peterson [1890–1960] (*Das Buch von den Engeln*, 1935),[12] but nothing is said of the fact that also for the Lutheran Church the Supper is heaven on earth. It is certainly no accident—rather, intent—that Brunner does not mention the name Luther nor the word "Lutheran." No one in Heidelberg can accuse him of "confessionalism," and it also has a pedagogical significance if at a session such as that at Hanover, where the word "Lutheran" is on everyone's lips, the point is made that in the Lutheran Church the concern is for the Gospel and not for human or historical recollection. But if one borrows from Catholic theology, then why not borrow from the theology of Luther? And when one speaks before Lutherans of

---

12 *The Angels and the Liturgy*, trans. Ronald Walls (New York: Herder & Herder, 1964). MH

the body and blood of Christ in the Supper, should he not publicly state, in order to avoid misunderstanding, that he does not mean thereby what Luther meant and what the Lutheran Confessions teach? [Should he not state] that he does not mean the glorified body of the Lord, the true body, which participates in the attributes of the divine nature? Why is this distinction kept silent? It sounds indeed like a miraculous rebirth of Lutheranism when suddenly in places where this had hitherto not been the case—the old Heidelberger [theologians] would roll over in their graves if they heard it: that the words "This *is* My body" are again understood in the sense of the *est*. But there will be a lot more water over the dam before we again recognize what *corpus* means here. Perhaps we will also learn this from the Catholics if not from Luther. Much can be learned in this regard, for instance, from [Matthias Joseph] Scheeben's [1835–88] *[Die] Mysterien des Christentums*.[13] The Eastern Church also has something to say about this. Perhaps we will take from there what we no longer believe in Father Luther. Everywhere modern Lutheranism vacillates back and forth between the doctrine of Trent and Calvin, seeking but not yet grasping that which is taught in Luther's catechisms. And thus it is absolutely clear that modern Lutheranism carelessly enters into the various unions and ecumenical conferences and is impressed with the views of altar fellowship of every possible denomination, Protestant and Catholic, but does no longer, or does not yet again, understand what the Lutheran Church teaches on church and altar fellowship.

5

If we confessional Lutherans firmly hold to the old principle that church fellowship is altar fellowship, and that there can only be a common celebration of the Lord's Supper where there is the "consensus on the doctrine of the Gospel and on the administration of the Sacraments" (the meaning of which for the present we have spoken in our Letter 25, "Concerning the Unity of the Lutheran Church"[14]), then the question is immediately posed to us: "How do you, then, conceive of *the relation of the churches to one another*?" Should they exist as in the sixteenth and seventeenth centuries, every one claiming absolutely to have the pure doctrine, every church hurling the *anathema* against every other church, each seeking to damage the others? Before we answer this question, we should perhaps point out that the Lutheran Church never declared itself to be the only true church of Christ. This it expressly declared in the Preface to the Book of Concord. The condemnations, that is, "the rejections of godless doctrines, and especially of that which has arisen concerning the Lord's Supper," should in no way mean "that hereby those men who err from a certain simplicity of mind, but are not blasphemers against the truth of the heavenly doctrine, much less, indeed, entire

---

13 *The Mysteries of Christianity*, trans. Cyril O. Vollert (St. Louis: Herder, 1946). MH

14 See above, pp. 117–36. MH

churches, which are either under the Roman Empire of the German nation or elsewhere; nay, rather has it been our intention and disposition in this manner openly to censure and condemn only the fanatical opinions and their obstinate and blasphemous teachers (which we judge should in no way be tolerated in our dominions, churches, and schools)" ([Preface to the Book of Concord 20], *BSLK*, 11; *Trig.*, p. 19). The orthodox fathers constantly made reference to this authoritative explication of the condemnations. The Lutheran Church has never declared that all other churches are sects and no longer churches of Christ. This misunderstanding of the condemnation formulas was held constantly before the enlightened eighteenth and nineteenth centuries, which no longer understood the deep seriousness of the question of truth. This view was taken over by those during the church struggle [at the time of Hitler] who attacked the Lutherans because the latter still took seriously the boundaries of the Supper. Hans Asmussen, for instance, wanted to inform us that according to the Reformation there can be only one church: either the church of Christ or Satan's church: "The Word of God knows of no three-quarter church" (*Abendmahlsgemeinschaft? Beiheft 3 zur Ev. Theologie*, 1937, p. 19). Our church has never denied that the church of Christ and thus true children of God are found also in other denominations where the means of grace are yet effective. Herein it followed the model of the ancient church, which in the controversy over the validity of the Baptism of heretics and in the Donatist controversy opposed Cyprian's understanding of "Outside of the church there is no salvation" [*extra ecclesia nulla salus*] (*Epist.* 73.21; the order in which the four words stand expresses: "If the baptism of public confession and blood [i.e., martyrdom] cannot help the heretic himself for salvation because *there is no salvation outside the church*, how much less will it benefit him if he has allowed himself to be sprinkled and polluted with impure water in secret and in a den of thieves . . . Thus it is impossible for us to have Baptism in common with heretics"). If one asks which of the confessional churches of the sixteenth and seventeenth centuries in practice exercised the most tolerance, the answer must be the Lutheran Church. It was also the case with the Lutherans that a false teacher was not tolerated, and the "whose rule, his religion" [*cuius regio eius religio*] applied also for Lutheran territories in the same way it applied for the Puritans in America. But there is in Lutheran lands no parallel to the bloody persecutions of the Protestants by French Catholicism or to the equally horrible persecution of the Catholics by the Anglican and Puritan state in England. It is comprehensible from a psychological standpoint that in those lands of the West the fanaticism of religious persecution changed to its complete opposite: a tolerant indifference toward all dogma, whether of religious or enlightenment complexion. But to charge the Lutheran Church with intolerance because it still took the question of truth seriously and thus rejected the union plans of the seventeenth, eighteenth, and nineteenth centuries means to misunderstand fundamentally the intention of the Lutheran Confessions. The problem of how the varying denominations should exist side by side and what their mutual relationship should be was not yet understood and thus could not yet be solved in the sixteenth and seventeen centuries. This is shown by the historical fact that for the first time only in the second half of the seventeenth century was there general conviction that the division of Western Christianity was final. It was not until the time of Leibniz[15] that the hope of the reunion of the separated confessional churches in the West was finally shattered. The problem of how Christian churches of various confessions can and shall exist side by side has only been defined as such since that time.

6

It is very instructive to see how in the seventeenth century the denominations [*Konfessionen*] began to order their relationships along firmly fixed boundaries. Naturally the Reformed immediately advanced their union plans so as to at least bring together the Lutherans and the various types of the Reformed. But still several more generations were needed until Pietism and Rationalism had so displaced the confessional consciousness of the Lutherans that in wide areas of Germany the accomplishment of the union was possible. Confessionally conscious Lutheranism offered *doctrinal discussion and cooperation in externals [cooperatio in externis]* in response to the Reformed plan for union, which declared that the doctrinal differences had to do with unessential matters. It is moving to see how the Lutheran theologians, even after the failure of the religious colloquies of the seventeenth century, did not give up the hope that a union in doctrine on the basis of the correct understanding of the Holy Scriptures would be possible. Valentin Ernst Löscher, whose *Peaceable Address and Admonition to the Reformed Congregations in Germany* (appendix to part three of *Historia Motuum*) is the most humanly stirring document of the voice of late orthodoxy for the unification of Christianity, was the last representative of the "doctrinal discussion" method in the eighteenth century, which method then later was applied to the unification of Lutherans by Ferdinand Walther and the present Missouri Synod.[16] Along with doctrinal discussion as a means toward unification, there arose already in the seventeenth century the fixed and organized *cooperation*

---

15 Gottfried Wilhelm von Leibniz (1646–1716). MH

16 Löscher (1673–1749) lived in the great period of struggle over Pietism. He was the last great proponent of Lutheran orthodoxy in the eighteenth century. As superintendent at Dresden, he led the Saxon Church with tremendous fidelity despite the fact that the royal family had converted to Roman Catholicism. He preached at the cornerstone-laying of the famous Frauenkirche in Dresden, which has been reconstructed. Löscher was also an ancestor of Sasse. See Hans Martin Rotermund, *Orthodoxie und Pietismus: Valentin Ernst Löscher's "Timotheus Verinus" in der Auseinandersetzung mit der Schule August Hermann Franckes* (Berlin: Evangelische Verlagsanstalt, n.d.). Paul Schreyer wrote a dissertation under Sasse (which also begs translation): *Valentin Ernst Loescher und die Unionsversuche seiner Zeit* (Schwabach: J. G. Schreyer, 1938). MH

in externals between the denominations. The question whether and to what extent Luther would have approved of the denominations working together is falsely posed. In the first place he was convinced that he lived in the end times, so that even something like calendar reform appeared completely unnecessary to him. Second, he did not yet know of denominations in the later sense—rather, only of the one church of Christ, which stood in a struggle against the power of Satan and the Antichrist. It was the necessities of life of the seventeenth century which first led to a very remarkable form of cooperation among Lutherans and Catholics and between Lutherans and Reformed. There were cathedral chapters and convents [*Stifte*] in which some of the canons were Catholic and some Lutheran, and nevertheless a fellowship obtained for external reasons which came just short of [*bis zur*] *communicatio in sacris*. The demands of canon law on both sides were reckoned with only later. The most important institution of this nature which the seventeenth century produced was the *Corpus Evangelicorum* at the permanent imperial diet at Regensburg since 1653. It stood until the elimination of the old constitution of the empire in the year 1806 and was the forerunner of all later alliances of larger German Protestantism. It was the first federation of Lutherans and Reformed. Indeed, churches were not allied—there were as yet no independent churches in the age of church government by the princes. Rather, those sent by their rulers as Protestant imperial representatives united to form a standing board. In regular sessions they dealt with problems of concern to all the evangelical churches (such as complaints regarding the violation of the legal rights of the minority), and they represented the interests of Protestantism at the imperial diet, the organ of imperial governance. And so it was inevitable that not only questions of imperial canon law would be dealt with, but even questions which cut deeply into the life of the church, such as the reform of the Gregorian calendar. At the beginning of the eighteenth century the *Corpus Evangelicorum* was stormed with the demand from all over that it become the means to bring about the union of both churches. So it was entirely unavoidable that occasionally doctrinal questions arose which the Lutherans did not believe belonged to the sphere of competence of the *Corpus*. None of the theologians of late orthodoxy had taken offense at the establishment of this board, though it was known that "theological matters are smuggled in which are disguised however one wishes" (thus the electoral Saxon delegate who thereby based his case that the board of directors should not be open to the Reformed Palatinate; cited by Ernst Sal. Cyprian, *Abgetrungener Unterricht von kirchlicher Vereinigung der Protestanten*, 2nd ed., 1726, p. 250). Thus the problem of the relationship of the various denominations [*Konfessionskirchen*], which did not yet exist at the time of Luther and which of necessity first emerged in Germany as a result of the splintering of territorial churches, found its first solution. The nineteenth century then further developed this solution: a Lutheran Church can never enter into a union with a church of another confession without surrendering its own confession. It may, however, enter into temporary or permanent federations, if the intent of such federations is only cooperation in externals and theological discussion.

7

The *ecclesiastical federation* rests upon the acknowledgment that one can believe that the church of Christ is still found in another church, even though it be heterodox in essential matters. The church of Christ is present if and insofar as the means of grace, the Word of God and Holy Baptism, are present. The question whether or not in such a church the Sacrament of the Altar is still present was affirmed in the case of the Eastern Churches and the Roman Church by Luther and the Lutheran Church. With respect to the Reformed Churches, this question cannot be definitely answered. Federation excludes any *communicatio in sacris*, as well as pulpit and altar fellowship. The question of when and under what circumstances joint prayer is possible is difficult to answer. But this much can be said: the solemn prayer of the church's liturgy as prayer of the Body of Christ has since ancient times belonged to the *communicatio in sacris*, as is shown by the use of the ancient church in which this prayer as also the corresponding Eucharist was held behind closed doors (which practice was based upon Matt. 6:6). The goal of the federation is first *cooperatio in externis*: for instance, joint dealings with the state on questions of the free exercise of religion [*Fragen der Glaubensfreiheit*], the rights of Christian schools, and the like. But also common churchly tasks may be accomplished through joint effort, such as the way the revision of the Luther Bible in Germany was always a common undertaking by churches, or as in America today the new wording of the Revised Standard Version has been the joint task of various churches. When in the church external matters and internal matters are not clearly distinct, there naturally always remains a certain lack of surety regarding the competence of an ecclesiastical alliance or an otherwise joint organization such as a Bible society [to deal with the issues involved]. This uncertainty is to be tolerated as long as everyone is clear and unanimous on the principle that everything which is a confessional question for one of the churches concerned can be answered only on the basis of its confession and must be answered by each of the churches on this basis alone. The mistake of the Barmen Theological Declaration lies not in the fact that the evangelical churches spoke a common word against the threat of a totalitarian state, but rather that they said it in the form of a joint confession of doctrine. "No, they confessed at Barmen," responded Karl Barth to a Lutheran territorial bishop when the latter posed this question: "Is it not the case that Barmen was indeed only a theological declaration and not a confession?" A mixed synod, at which one party cannot acknowledge the other as orthodox, can never dogmatically answer questions of doctrine. This has always been the viewpoint of Lutheran canon law. The Reformed have a different view on this matter because for them the Lutherans are erring brothers, but not heretics. So it was in Marburg 1529, so it is today. The tragedy of all modern attempts at union between Lutheran and Reformed Churches is explained by these varying understandings of the boundaries of the church by Lutherans and Reformed. For the Reformed the Lutheran church is a part (a sort of backward part) of the Reformed Church, which must be helped to complete the Reformation. Where the Lutherans have in view federation, the Reformed have in view union. This is the case with the EKiD; this is the case with the new American church alliance, the NCCCUS; this is the case with the Ecumenical Council. At the fervent pleas of the Lutherans, these organizations are called federations, and it is denied that their intent is to be a sort of "super church." The constitutions are "improved" as it happened in America where the United Lutheran Church was downright boastful that they had achieved more than forty changes in the constitution of the National Council of Churches. The most important of these changes was that the goal of the alliance was defined in this: that it should manifest "the common spirit" of the member churches, instead of "essential oneness," as the draft read. The word "devotional" was also dropped from the sentence "to encourage devotional fellowship." Does anyone believe that the Reformed Churches and groups of America consequently changed their concept of church and unity of the church and their understanding of the NCCCUS? Great ecclesiastical structures everywhere in Christendom are arising in this manner. They are called federations, but in reality they are churches. They grant each individual church its private confession, but this confession is relativized in that its claim to speak the truth, bindingly and for all, is taken away. And every one of these great organizations claims to teach and preach the Gospel. But that is the function of the church, not of the alliance of churches. An alliance of churches cannot evangelize, just as neither can it administer the Sacraments. But that means it can have no joint celebration of the Supper. An alliance of churches can indeed concern itself with doctrine, but only as a forum for serious doctrinal discussion among member churches.

8

These are the basic principles of the Lutheran Church concerning altar fellowship, church fellowship, and ecclesiastical federation. They have universal validity because they are based on the Lutheran Confession. They also apply in the case of the *relationships of Lutheran Churches to each other*. That a church calls itself "Lutheran" (churches such as that of Württemberg, Sweden, and Norway do not call themselves Lutheran, and, indeed, this does not belong to the essence of the Lutheran Church) or that the Lutheran Confession was once in history the real confession of this church may be of great human and historical importance. But it has no theological meaning. These basic principles apply in the case of a federation of Lutheran Churches such as the Lutheran World Federation. It can only be acknowledged as a federation of Lutheran Churches if these churches are truly Lutheran in the sense that the doctrine of the *Unaltered Augsburg Confession* and the catechisms stand *extra controversiam*. If this is not the case, then the Lutheran World Federation is in no way different from any other alliance of churches. One cannot say: "If we Lutherans can join a federation with Reformed or United Churches with the understanding developed above, how much easier can we enter into an alliance with other churches which call themselves Lutheran and also wish to be Lutheran!" In reality it is not easier, but more difficult. With the Reformed and Catholics I can operate together in external matters on the common basis of the ancient ecclesiastical confessions. I can also enter into a doctrinal discussion with them on the basis of the ancient confessions and the Holy Scriptures (e.g., on justification or the Supper). But if I speak with or operate together with Lutherans, then I have to be certain that we are at least unified on these questions.

If the Lutheran World Federation and its possibilities are viewed from this standpoint, the question must be asked: Is it in a position to call upon its member churches to again take the Lutheran Confession seriously? If it can do this, then it has a great task, and we will happily help it in this regard. If it is not in the position to do this, or if it will not do this, then the cooperation of any truly confessional churches is senseless. We trust that within world Lutheranism there are still strong forces which heartily affirm the Lutheran Confession. If they can be advanced in the Lutheran World Federation (hitherto this has been impossible), then they will have our assistance. The decision on this matter will be made in the context of the great *crisis of the Ecumenical Movement* which became evident at the session of the World Conference for Faith and Order in Lund when the Orthodox Churches of the East politely but unmistakably distanced themselves from the Ecumenical Council as it has developed in the last decade. It is understandable that the churches behind the Iron Curtain did not take part. But the fact that anti-Communist churches closely tied to the West from Greece, Alexandria, and the Russian Church in exile were no longer present but allowed themselves to be represented by a small delegation of the ecumenical patriarch cannot be explained on merely political grounds. The true reasons became evident when the London exarch of the ecumenical patriarch delivered a declaration in which he stated that the Orthodox Church maintained the right to decide what is false in the religious sphere and to make known that which agrees with their faith and that which does not. They allow their theologians and representatives at conferences only to make positive and definite statements regarding Orthodox doctrine, but do not allow them to become involved in fruitless discussion or take part in voting on matters of faith, the liturgy, or church government. When this is compared with the address of the late Archbishop Germanos[17] at the

---

17 Archbishop Strenopoulos Germanos is described in the list of "conference participants" as archbishop and metropolitan of Thyatira, representative of the ecumenical patriarch in Western Europe, doctor of theology and philosophy. See Sasse, *Die Weltkonferenz* (1929), 588. MH

beginning of the World Conference of Lausanne in 1927, in which he pointed out the broad areas of doctrine which the Orthodox Churches could discuss because they had not been defined by any of the Ecumenical Councils, then the change the Ecumenical Movement has undergone within the past forty years becomes evident. The simplistic dreams of union have been exhausted. The Ecumenical Council has increasingly become an organization of Reformed and Union Churches together with a portion of Lutheranism which has forsaken the Confession of the fathers. Is it not time, instead of dealing further with the unattainable union of all churches, to work toward that which truly is attainable: the upbuilding of the great confessional churches and the restoration of a Christian relationship among them? Is it not time to be done with ecumenical fanaticism and return to belief in the *Una Sancta*, which exists as a reality in, with, and under the confessional churches, whose unity we cannot see, just as we cannot see the people of God, the Body of Christ, with our earthly eyes? As one who has participated in the Ecumenical Movement for fifty years and worked within it to the extent that a Lutheran who strives to take the Confession of his church seriously can do so, I see no other possibility for the future. In his great lecture in Lund, Edmund Schlink spoke of the walls which separate the great confessional churches, [walls] which have now become transparent in the apocalyptic events of our century. This is certainly correct. But is the time of the church not always the end times? Was not the end of all things near when the Lord died on the cross? Did not God's new world already break forth on Easter morning? Was not the Reformation an eschatological event, and not only because Luther and his followers thought they lived in the end times? Are not the walls between the confessional churches always transparent for those who believe in the church of God and know that it is holy wherever this church is? Even there, exactly there where we must speak the *Anathema* over false teaching, there can still be the *Pax*, the peace of God which truly passes all understanding, the peace between children of God, the saints of the entire world, even though they see their unity as little as they perceive their holiness itself!

⁓

For the new year I greet you, honored brothers, with the wish that God bless your work in His church, wherever you may occupy the office. Let us be certain of this in faith, that no work which is done for God's church is done in vain, even if our eyes do not see the results. And also that grief which, as I know, many of you bear for the sake of the church belongs to that which builds the church in a way that is unimaginable to us, though it mean for us, in Luther's words, "the dear, holy cross."

In the bond of the faith I remain,

Hermann Sasse

Historical Context

This is a significant transitional piece by Sasse. He uses a study of Augustine as the means to struggle past his previously expressed view that the Scriptures contain errors.[1] By the end of this letter, he states: "For what in the Scripture appears to our reason as error and contradiction is not, because of that, error." Behind this letter one can hear the intense discussions which had taken place on the Intersynodical Committee in Australia in the years immediately prior to this letter. Sasse would grant absolute inerrancy, but not in the sense of the Bible as a "divine book" whose perfection could or must be proved to unbelievers, as the apologist of the second century and Augustine, according to Sasse, attempted to do. While Sasse's limitations never allowed him to appreciate fully the doctrine of inspiration as understood by the orthodox Lutheran fathers, or move past caricatures of it, nevertheless he ends this essay on a vitally significant point: "The Bible, however, and the church of the Reformation know that no one can see the Deus nudus. *For that reason He 'hides' Himself, as Luther puts it, in the flesh. God's revelation is always at the same time concealment. That is what God's revelation in the Scripture also is. It is this reality which Augustine ran up against when he perceived the clashes which the Scripture presents to human reason and which he could not get rid of by means of his reason. He was entirely correct when he denied that the Scripture contains errors." MH*

July 13, 1953

Prof. H. Sasse
41 Buxton Street
North Adelaide, South Australia

Dear Dr. [Herman A. Preus],

. . . I do not know how many years God will still give me. My state of health is, indeed, much better than it was in the years about 1948. But I am facing a similar situation which takes a heavy toll. We have finished our intersynodical negotiations, which meant a lot of work for me. Doctrinal agreement has been reached. But now the Lutheran World Federation creates difficulties. We are

---

1   See Letter 14, "On the Doctrine *De Scriptura Sacra*," and Letter 16, "What Does Luther Have to Say to Us on the Inerrancy of the Holy Scripture?" in *Letters to Lutheran Pastors* 1:240–84, 332–67. MH

a member; our sister church is not and cannot be as long as the LWF is that unionistic body which it is. Our idea was a consultative membership. Now Dr. [Franklin Clark] Fry, answering a letter of our president general, criticized our union and warned against a union with Missouri, if Missouri would not join the LWF. He went so far as to suggest that a third Lutheran Church would be established in Australia consisting of the two German Evangelical congregations here. But Dr. Fry regards Australia as a field of church politics, just as [Hans] Meiser [1881–1956] and [Hanns] Lilje do. They do not know the consequences. Our two churches are the two parts of one church which has broken asunder more than one hundred years ago. The schism paralyzes our church life. Both churches are so poor (they have with their 70,000 members to care for a continent the size of the USA) that they cannot pay a decent salary to their pastors. If I should die, my wife would receive about one pound a week, that means about two dollars, if she were so lucky as to get a pension at all. I never saw such poor pastors' families. In this situation, American (not Dr. Behnken, who encourages the union even if it should mean a loss of influence on their part) and European church leaders advise us to postpone the union until the rest of Lutheranism is united. Thus I do not know what will happen . . . .

Sincerely,
Hermann Sasse

twenty-nine
Toward Understanding Augustine's Doctrine of Inspiration

TRANSLATED BY RALPH GEHRKE

Beginning of February 1953[1]

Prof. D. Theol. Hermann Sasse
41 Buxton Street
North Adelaide, South Australia

Dear Brethren in the Office:

The great doctrinal discussion which should begin between the churches that earnestly want to be Lutheran will have to deal with especially two doctrines: the doctrine concerning the Word of God and the doctrine concerning the Sacraments. Indeed, both doctrines will have to be treated alongside each other, for the means of grace cannot be sundered. Just as they belong together in the life of the church, even so they belong together also in theology. A person cannot at one and the same time have a Calvinist or Crypto-Calvinist doctrine concerning the Lord's Supper and a Lutheran doctrine concerning the Word. When recently a pastor (with whom I am unacquainted and who hails from a North German Lutheran territorial church) let it be known that I should ponder the fact that the Lord Christ had not at all spoken the word "is" in the Words of Institution, since Aramaic does not use a copula in that sort of sentence, I do

---

1   *BLP* 29 (marked no. 28 on the original): *Zur Inspirationslehre Augustins* (North Adelaide, February 1953). The original was published in *LuBl* 5, no. 31 (1953): 15 S. Huss number 299b. The German text was reprinted in *Sacra Scriptura: Studien zur Lehre von der Heiligen Schrift*, ed. F. W. Hopf (Erlangen, 1981). Permission to print this English translation has been granted by the Gehrke family. MH

not know what it is at which I should marvel the more: the erudition which does not know how to translate an Aramaic sentence in keeping with its meaning or this broken relation to the Holy Scripture. God's Word is, for the church of Christ in all ages, not an original text [*Urtext*] which is to be discovered by scholars behind the Greek and Hebrew words of the New and Old Testaments; rather, God's Word is the Bible itself as it was given to us. I adduce this example only in order to show how closely the doctrine of the real presence in the Lord's Supper is connected with the doctrine that the Holy Scripture is really [*realiter et essentialiter*] the Word of God. Corresponding to the *est* in "*Hoc* est *corpus meum*," there is an *est* in the doctrine of the Scripture. "*Hoc est verbum Dei*" is what the church must be able to say concerning the Holy Scripture; otherwise it has no Holy Scripture.

It is with the understanding of this *est* that we have been concerned in several of these letters,[2] and, in response, we have encountered both assent and dissent—dissent which was partly justified and partly based on misunderstandings.[3] We must all be aware of the fact that our Confessions contain no extended doctrine concerning the Holy Scripture and that we therefore are dependent on what the Holy Scripture teaches about itself. This and nothing else is the church's dogma. Whatever is not in Scripture, even if it is a theological exposition worthy of note, is but a more or less successful attempt to explain the Scripture; it is not an article of faith. "The rule is: 'The Word of God shall establish articles of faith, and no one else, not even an angel'" (SA II II 15; *BSLK*, 421.23ff.; *Triglotta*, 467 [Tappert, 295])—not a church or a council, nor theology, and most certainly not philosophy. If Luther's Reformation was the rediscovery of the Holy Scripture, it was at the same time a mighty [struggle over the liberation of the church's doctrine from philosophy, as the] young Württemberg theologian who died so prematurely, Wilhelm Link, has shown so forcefully in his book *Das Ringen Luthers um die Freiheit der Theologie von der Philosophie* (Munich, 1940). There is no article of the Christian faith which philosophy has not attempted to take over. Plato [ca. 428/427–347 BC] and Aristotle have penetrated into all Christian articles of faith, from the doctrine of God to the doctrine of the Sacraments. The doctrine of the Holy Scripture is no exception. We wish to show this process at the hand of an example from ancient church theology which found its culmination in Augustine, and we want to ask what lesson there is for us to learn from this.

---

2   Sasse is referring to Letter 14, "On the Doctrine *De Scriptura Sacra*," and Letter 16, "What Does Luther Have to Say to Us on the Inerrancy of the Holy Scripture?" in *Letters to Lutheran Pastors* 1:240–84, 332–66. RG and MH

3   Insight into the discussion carried on may be had from the documents and annotations in *Letters to Lutheran Pastors* 1:240–99, 332–66, especially "Sasse's Footnotes to Letter 14" (1:292–99) and "Theses on Scripture and Inspiration" of the Lutheran Church of Australia (1:288–91). RG and MH

1

The Holy Scripture contains no extended exposition concerning its nature and origin. It is only in a few places, which are not much more than parenthetical remarks, that the Scriptures explain what needed no closer proof and what lay there as an unexpressed, self-evident foundation for the entire Bible from first to last word, namely, that notwithstanding the human-historical process of its origin (Josh. 10:13; 2 Sam. 1:18; Jer. 30:2; 36:2ff.; Luke 1:1ff.), it is given by inspiration of the Holy Spirit (2 Tim. 3:16; 2 Pet. 1:19ff.) and hence is God's authoritative (John 10:35) and nondeceptive [*untrügliches*] (John 17:17) Word. It is understandable that the people who wished to explain the Scripture wanted to know more. They wanted an explanation of *how* the Bible could be God's Word. Naturally it was *Jewish theology* which first busied itself with that. Hence the rabbis, following the concepts of pagan antiquity (concepts about a book or books in heaven) developed the theory of the preexistence of the Torah in heaven, an idea which later was applied by Islam to the Qur'an. Christian theology never adopted this theory. Early Christian theology, however, appropriated another theory which the synagogue had developed under the influence of pagan antiquity: *the psychological understanding* of the *inspiration* of the Holy Scripture. A classic example of this is the presentation of the Apocalypse of Esdras that comes from the time of Domitian [r. 81–96] concerning Esdra's replacement of the Holy Scriptures which had been destroyed by fire. Esdras receives the command to come before God's presence with five stenographers: "I will light the lamp of understanding [*lucernam intellectus*] in your heart and it shall not be put out until the things you are to write are finished" (4 Esdras 14:25). This promise is God's answer to his plea "*Inmitte in me spiritum sanctum*" ("Impart unto me the Holy Spirit," 14:22). And thereupon the process of inspiration is described: "*Cor meum* cruciabatur *intellectu, et in pectus meum increscebat sapientia. Nam spiritus meus conservabatur memoria, et apertum est os meum et non est clausum amplius*" (14:40 Vg: "My heart was overwhelmed by understanding; and wisdom grew in my breast, for my spirit retained its memory, and my mouth opened and was no longer closed"). Endowed with this superhuman understanding, wisdom, and power of memory, Esdras dictates to his scribes in forty days the entire Holy Scripture, that is, the twenty-four books of the Hebrew canon and, besides them, also secret apocalyptic writings. The same concept of inspiration is found in Philo [ca. 20/30 BC–ca. AD 50]: Inspiration is the working of the divine Spirit upon a person, or, to be more precise, upon only that person who is good and wise. It is enthusiastic ecstasy. The following is the way in which that great Jewish thinker explains the inspiration of the Old Testament:

> The Holy Scripture bears witness of prophecy to every wise man. A prophet, however, does not proclaim his own thoughts, but *thoughts which are foreign to him, which someone else bestows upon him*. A fool is not permitted to be God's *interpreter*, so that no morally wicked person

actually ever goes into the state of *enthusiasm*; that is fitting only for the wise man, since he alone is a sounding *instrument of God*, invisibly played and *struck by Him.*

Thus H[ans] Leisegang (*Der Heilige Geist*, Bd. I, 1, 146) translates the famous passage concerning the nature of inspiration in "*Quis rerum divinarum heres*" ["Who is the their of divine things?"] (§ 259, Mangey, 510), and then rightly adds: "With these words Philo shows a complete misunderstanding of Old Testament prophecy," which does not speak of any attachment of the Holy Spirit and of the gift of prophecy to any special level of education. And we will also have to note that the main point in which Philo differs from the Bible consists in this: that in the Bible enthusiasm, ecstasy, the state of being out-of-oneself (so essential to all pagan "prophecy") does not belong to the essence of biblical prophecy. It is this pagan pseudo-prophecy against which Amos declared in the name of all the biblical prophets: "I am no prophet, nor son of a prophet" (Amos 7:14; cf. Jer. 23:25ff.; Ezek. 13:2ff.). These are only a few examples to show how Judaism, Palestinian as well as Alexandrian Judaism, in the age of Jesus and of the apostles clarified for itself the nature of inspiration. We could cite other examples. For Aramaic Judaism we could cite, for instance, much of what that industrious researcher Paul Billerbeck [1853–1932] has collected in his great *Kommentar zum Neuen Testament aus Talmud und Midrasch* (Bd. IV, pp. 415–51; excursus 16, "*Der Kanon des AT und seine Inspiration*"); for the Greek synagogue we could cite the Letter of Aristeas with its legend concerning the origin of the Septuagint,[4] of which we will still have to speak. At this point, however, it is sufficient to state that Judaism of that day did not content itself with the simple belief that the Old Testament is God's Word because it claims that God speaks in it; but Judaism tried to find a solution to the insoluble riddle of how God speaks through the spoken and written word of men. Since the Bible does not explain this secret, there was nothing else to do but to seek information and explanation from outside the Scripture. And it was found in Oriental and Greek paganism. Pagan theories concerning the nature of pagan "inspiration" and "prophecy" were used to explain biblical prophecy and therewith the character of the Bible as God's Word. It is clear, however, that thereby the true understanding of the Holy Scripture was lost. The workings of the Holy Spirit became psychological phenomena; the prophets became mantics or wise men in the sense of Hellenistic philosophy; the Word of God became one of many oracles that exist in the world.

2

We do not want to go into the question here as to how this misunderstanding, this failure to correctly understand the divine Word (a failure that was characteristic of New Testament-age Judaism) is connected with Judaism's failure to

---

4   I.e., Greek translation of the Old Testament. MH

recognize the *Verbum incarnatum* ["the incarnate Word"], the rejection of the Messiah. What must concern every Christian theologian is the unspeakable tragedy of the ancient church which adopted from Hellenistic Judaism, without criticism and without objection, that theory of inspiration which had originated in paganism, the theory which viewed inspiration as a mantic-enthusiastic phenomenon. At the end of the first and in the second century, Clement of Rome and Irenaeus [ca. 130–ca. 200] bear witness to the fact that the church could content itself, in all simplicity and without asking about the "how," with the fact that the Scripture is inspired by the Holy Spirit and is therefore dependable [*glaubwürdig*]. Thus in 1 Clement 45:[2], the Holy Scriptures are called "the authentic writings which are given by the Holy Spirit" and Irenaeus speaks in a similar vein when he asserts: "*Scripturae . . . perfectae sunt, quippe a Verbo Dei et Spiritu eius dictae*" ["The Scriptures . . . are perfect; in fact, they are spoken by the Word of God and His Spirit"] (*Adversus haer.* 2.28.2 [ANF 1:399]). In this manner faith speaks on the basis of the Word itself and is silent where God's Word is silent. But then those theologians come along who want to know more than the Word tells. The "scientific" theology of the *apologists* comes along, and it is their sad occupation to excuse the dear Lord Himself [*den lieben Gott*] before "the cultured among His despisers."[5] It is among them that Philo's metaphor of a musical instrument struck by the Spirit of God appears, a metaphor which the Jewish apologist had taken over from the pagan theory of "enthusiasm." Thus Athenagoras [fl. 2nd century] is of the opinion (*Legatio pro Christianis* 9) that Moses, Isaiah, Jeremiah, and the other prophets spoke what was given to them "by working of the Holy Spirit, in ecstasy, a process in which the Spirit used them as a flute player uses the flute on which he blows." On the same basis the same apologist argues (in ch. 7) for the "necessity" of accepting such revelation; for it is, he says, "unintelligent [*logon*] to abandon believing surrender to the divine Spirit who touches the mouth of the prophets like a musical instrument [*rganon*, as with Philo] and to guide oneself according to human opinions." Things had progressed so far in the year AD 177 that the refusal to have faith in the Bible is a sign of the lack of intelligence! What becomes, then, of the Gospel which always at all times remains "foolishness to the Greeks" [cf. 1 Cor. 1:22–23]? This self-same explanation of inspiration we find in Ps.-Justin's (Justin himself moves in the thoughts which we find in Irenaeus) *Cohortatio ad Graecos* 8 [PG 6:255–58; ANF 1:276]: the divine Pneuma descends from heaven and uses the holy man—he must be holy, just as he must be wise in the case of Philo, and no sinner and fool like Paul—as an instrument [*organon*), something like the plectrum, the little stick which sets the zither or lyre resounding. That this metaphorical picture not only belongs to the terminology of the learned scholars but also is deeply rooted in the religious consciousness of enthusiastic paganism is shown by the

---

5   A reference to Friedrich Schleiermacher, *On Religion: Speeches to Its Cultured Despisers*, trans. John Oman (New York: Harper & Row, 1958). MH

Montanist movement. A reputed word of the Holy Spirit according to Montanus [fl. 2nd century] is: "Behold, the man is like a lyre, and I have flown hither like a plectrum" (recorded in Epiphanius [ca. 315–403], *Panarion haer.* 48.4.1). The difficult struggle the church had with Montanist heresy ended with the rejection of this intrusion of pagan enthusiasm into the faith of the church. It was a healthy reaction against the pagan misunderstanding of prophecy when the Asia Minor theologian Miltiades[6] brought, in one of his writings, proof "that a prophet dare not speak in the state of ecstasy" (Eusebius [ca. 260–ca. 339], *H. E.* 5.16f.). But Christian apologetics took no notice of this. Rather, it remained with the metaphorical picture of the musical instruments, of the zither, lyre, and flute that were made to sound by the divine Spirit. It stayed with the enthusiastic-mantic understanding of inspiration, which led, of necessity, to a placing of biblical and pagan "revelation" on the same level in principle. Judaism had led the way with its Sibylline Books, in which Jewish prophecies of doubtful character were placed into the mouths of the heathen sibyls in order to win Gentiles for the synagogue. Now Christian theology followed the lead with that juxtapositioning of *prophets and sibyls* which found its highest expression in Michelangelo's art and which even today sounds forth in the line *"Teste David cum Sibylla"* ["By the witness of David with the Sibyl"] in the *Dies irae* in every Mass for the dead in the Roman church. And so it is that Ps.-Justin (*Cohortatio ad Graecos* 37 [PG 6:305–10; ANF 1:288–89]) and Theophilus[7] see that the revelation in the prophets and the revelation in the sibyls stand next to each other "in the most beautiful harmony" (*Ad Autolycum* 2.9). The fact that this conception of inspiration does not do justice to either Old Testament prophecy, which most decisively separates itself from pagan ecstaticism, nor to what the New Testament says in great sobriety about its own origin (cf. Luke 1:1ff.; John 21:24; the Pauline Epistles)—that is something which those old theologians of the end of the second and of the third century did not notice. To explain their failure we must keep two facts in mind. First, they all came from pagan religion and brought along such categories of thought, and, second, they were apologists who had to develop their doctrine of the Scripture and of its inspiration while confronting alien religions, just as the Jewish apologists had already done in Alexandria. The danger of all apologetics, however, is that the apologist not only allows his opponent to dictate the questions, but that already along with that the formulation in which the question is put (a necessarily false answer!). In this way it is understandable that the doctrine of the ancient church concerning the inspiration of the Scripture, as the apologists first developed it, is, to a great extent, nothing more than a pagan theory taken over by way of the synagogue, a theory which was Christianized only externally, if at all.

---

6   This second-century rhetorician and anti-Montanist died in 314 (s.v. *Christian Cyclopedia*). MH

7   Bishop of Antioch in Syria (169) who wrote against Gnosticism. He died ca. 181/186 (s.v. *Christian Cyclopedia*). MH

The tragedy which lies at the rise of this false understanding of Scripture in the ancient church can be compared in its effect on the church only with two other tragedies: the disfigurement and deformation of the New Testament Lord's Supper by the intrusion of the same age's conceptions of sacrifices and priests, and the growth of Mariolatry in the fourth and fifth centuries. All these happenings are connected. They are only various aspects of the re-intrusion [*Wiedereindringen*] of the religion of natural man which had once been pushed aside by the Gospel. For the essence of paganism is that it is the religion of the natural man. Nothing is more characteristic of the great misunderstanding of Christianity in apologetics than the phrase of the great apologist and later Montanist Tertullian [ca. 155/160–ca. 220/230] that speaks of the *anima naturaliter Christiana* ["the naturally Christian soul"].

We cannot here trace the development which the doctrine of the Holy Scripture and of its inspiration underwent in the following centuries on the foundation of the apologetic theory, especially in Alexandria where Clement [ca. 150–215] and Origen [ca. 185–ca. 254] completed in the church what Philo had once begun in the synagogue. Rather, we wish to study the result of the development as we see it in that man who guided the ancient church's view of the Holy Scripture to its completion and transmitted it to the coming centuries of church history as a basic problem of all theology. It is *Augustine* whose thoughts and whose formulations have become normative, also at this point of Christian doctrine for all churches of the West, for Catholics and Protestants in the same measure.

It is only on the background of the older apologetics that Augustine's doctrine concerning the Holy Scripture and its inspiration can be understood. It is no accident that the most important thing that he, the last great apologist of the ancient church, said on these questions was said (except for his letters to the Bible translator and exegete Jerome [ca. 345–420]) in two apologetic works: in the mighty work *De civitate Dei* [*The City of God*] and in the work which, by comparison, is poor and weak [*kleinlich*], though its effects continue to the present, his attempt at a harmony of the Gospels, *De consensu evangelistarum*. The shadow of the great pagan critics of the Christian religion and of its claim to revelation—Celsus,[8] Porphyry,[9] and Julian[10]—pops up behind these works. Augustine's work on the Gospels is directed, above all, to the criticism of Porphyry and his disciples. How far Augustine, following the older apologists, ventures on to the territory of the enemy is shown by the fact that he also puts the prophets together with the sibyls. He attempts to prove the existence of the

---

8   A second-century Platonist and opponent of Christianity. MH

9   A Neoplatonist, Porphyry (ca. 232/233–ca. 304) was born in Syria and studied under Plotinus (ca. 205–270). He wrote *Adversus Christianos* (s.v. *Christian Cyclopedia*). MH

10 Julian (called "the Apostate") was born in Constantinople and raised a Christian, though he eventually embraced paganism. He was Roman emperor (361–363) (s.v. *Christian Cyclopedia*). MH

true God to the heathen by comparing the prophetic and sibylline prophecies in
the following manner:

> If they (the pagans) call *him* God by whose inspiration the sibyls sang
> of the future destiny of the Romans, how should he not be God who
> predicted that the Romans and all nations would, through the church's
> Gospel, believe in him as the only God and that he would destroy the
> idols of their fathers, and, who, on top of that, fulfilled what was proph-
> esied? Finally, if they call *those* beings gods who never dared, through
> their prophets [*vates*], to say anything against this God, how should
> not he be God who not only commanded them to destroy their idols
> but who also beforehand predicted that these images would have to be
> destroyed in all nations by those to whom the command was given to
> abandon their gods and worship the *one* God and who were also obedi-
> ent to this command? Let them read to us, if they can, that one of their
> sibyls or one of their prophets [*vates*] predicted this . . . . [*De consensu
> evang.* 1.19 (CSEL 43:26.1ff.; NPNF[1] 6:88)]

Biblical prophets and pagan seers and sibyls are, to be sure, still contrasted, but
the Erythraean or Cumaean Sibyl is reckoned as a member of the *civitas Dei*
because of the purity of her prophecies. For this sibyl, who proclaimed Jesus
Christ as Savior beforehand (what is referred to is a Christian forgery which
Augustine considered genuine, since, after all, the promise of a world savior in
Virgil's Fourth *Eclogue* appealed to the Cumaean Sibyl), in her entire poem does
not bring a single word which might refer to the worship of false, fabricated
gods; on the contrary, she clearly speaks against them and their worshipers, "so
that it is possible to reckon her among those who belong to the city of God"
[*ut in eorum numero deputanda videatur, qui pertinent ad civitatem Dei*] (*De civ.
Dei* 18.23 [CSEL 40.2:299.16; NPNF[1] 2:373]). Although Augustine naturally otherwise distinguished sharply between the genuine revelation in the Scripture and
doubtful or perverted prophecies of pagan seers and sibyls, still the single exception of the Cumaean Sibyl shows that genuine prophecy and genuine inspiration
can exist also outside of the Bible. The same phenomena of inspiration wrought
by the Holy Spirit which happened among the biblical prophets can happen
and has happened also outside of biblical revelation. That is the logical conclusion that follows from the apologists' concept of inspiration, a concept which
Augustine simply and uncritically adopts. And even if he contests the existence
of genuine, God-wrought prophecy in the vast majority of all pagan "prophets," nevertheless a relationship between biblical and pagan prophecy remains.
Both are prophecy—predictions beforehand of events whose realization or
nonrealization in actual fact can be determined by reason. Every thinking pagan
must see that the predictions of the biblical prophets, in contrast to those of
the sibyls and seers of paganism, have actually come to pass. He can conclude
from that by the light of his reason that the God of the Bible is the true and only
God. That, however, the prophecies of the Bible are something quite other than

predictions of specific events which can be recognized by every man, that it is not the eye of reason but only faith in Jesus Christ, faith wrought by the Holy Spirit, which is able to recognize in Jesus Christ the Messiah promised by the prophets—all that had to remain hidden to this way of looking at things. That it is not the manner of origin but solely the content that makes a word a genuine prophecy, a word of God, and that this content, seen in its deepest nature, is Jesus Christ—all that was something which Augustine and the entire church that he represents was unable to see. It was Luther who first understood this. Throughout the millennium and a half from the apostles to the Reformation, the church had God's Word and lived from it. But what this Word really was, that its theologians did not know, and therefore again and again they opened the door to paganism. The great Augustine was also no exception. And the church of the Reformation ought to think twice before following him in the doctrine concerning the Holy Scripture. How can a man who does not at all know the *sola Scriptura* be a guide to the understanding of the Scripture?

3

There are two thoughts which Augustine inherited from the late Hellenistic, Jewish, and apologetic doctrine concerning inspiration and which he applied to the word of the Bible: (1) the view that the author of a biblical book, as an inspired man, is only the *instrument*, the *organon*, of the speaking, that is, dictating, deity; and (2) the understanding of inspiration as a *suggestio* of thoughts, words, and sentences. Thus the activity of the evangelists as the writers of the message about Christ is understood as a copying of what Christ, the Head, dictated to the evangelists, His members, or, more precisely, His hands: "Since those" (i.e., the evangelists) "wrote what He" (i.e., Christ) "showed and said [*ostendit et dixit*], it dare not be said that He Himself did not write. For His *members* wrote down what they learned from their *dictating* Head [*quod* dictante *capite cognoverunt*]. That means: what He wanted us to read about His deeds and words He commanded those, His hands, to write [*scribendum illis suis manibus imperavit*]" (*De consensu evang.* 1.35.54 [CSEL 43:60.17ff.; NPNF[1] 6:101]). If the thought of the writer being an instrument—similar to the apologists' metaphor of a lyre or flute or similar to the picture of the writer as the *calamus* ["pen"] of the Holy Spirit, a picture which is found in Gregory the Great [r. 590–604] and which ever since has played a great role in theology—is emphasized in this case to such an extent that we can hardly speak anymore of an independent activity by the biblical authors, this independent activity does not seem to be entirely extinguished in the other case where the activity of the divine Spirit is understood not as *dictare*, but as *suggerere* ["suggestion"].[11] Employing this metaphor, Augustine

---

11   See *Moralia Praef.* c.1. n.2 (PL 75:517), where Gregory expresses the opinion that it is
    as senseless to ask who the author of a biblical book is—he was speaking of Job—as

explains the difference of the biblical accounts in their handling of sequences of events, saying "that each one of the evangelists believed he had to narrate in the sequence in which God wanted to supply to his memory [*recordationi suggerere*] what the evangelist narrated, naturally only in the things in which a difference of sequence does not diminish the authority and truth of the Gospels" (*De consensu evang.* 2.21.51 [CSEL 43:153.1ff.; NPNF[1] 6:127]). The only aspect of human authorship that is left is memory, which is guided by the Holy Spirit, the decision concerning what was to be narrated being made freely (according to human perception) but actually being governed by God; that and nothing more is left to human authorship. Little as that appears to be at first glance, it is, however, very much in comparison to the theory that in inspiration the human spirit is only a dead tool, like a musical instrument or a scribal apparatus. Augustine's doctrine of inspiration is not a unified whole. It is disturbed by the tension between the *dictare* which makes man a will-less instrument and the *suggerere* which leaves a certain part of the human spirit. In this tension is revealed the contrast, the opposition between what the Bible is in fact and what it would have to be according to the apologists' pagan-Jewish concept of inspiration. Augustine saw that there was something like individuality in the various biblical authors. He could not cut himself off from the fact that the evangelists narrate in various, different ways and that for that reason at least differences of memory must remain. His mistake was the same as that of the preceding apologetics. Instead of taking as his point of departure what the Bible is and what it says about itself, and setting up, from that starting point, a *Christian* doctrine of the *theopneusta* (cf. 2 Tim. 3:16; 2 Pet. 1:19ff.), he began with what the religions of late antiquity understood by inspiration and "divine" scriptures, even as it is also no accident that Augustine and other fathers substitute for the simple biblical terms "Scripture," "Scriptures," "Holy Scriptures" (Rom. 1:2; cf. 1 Macc. 12:9) terms which were originally pagan, *scriptura divina* ["*divine* scripture"; Greek, *dea grafa*; also in the plural). At the moment it seemed to be a great advantage that Christian apologetics was in this way in a position to smite the pagan opponents with their own weapons, by *proving* to them that the Holy Scripture of the Christians possesses all the marks of a perfect book of superhuman origin, and therefore is, among all the other scriptures that were designated as divine, the only truly "divine scripture." These weapons, however, had to turn themselves against the church the moment this proof lost its probability. There is no other proof for the Bible's claim to being God's Word than the *testimonium Spiritus Sancti internum* ["the internal testimony of the Holy Spirit"]. In practice the ancient church lived from that Word of God, just as the church of all ages has done. For, after all, the men who were converted to the Christian faith were overwhelmed by the power of the Holy Spirit who came to them in the Word

---

it would be to ask with what kind of a pen (*quali calamo*) a letter was written. The author of the Bible, he said, was the Holy Spirit; the writers were only "reed pens." HS

of the Scriptures and in the scriptural [*schriftgemäß*] preaching; they were not won by the artful proofs of the apologists who attempted to make the "divinity" of the Scripture clear to reason. Theology, however, remained under the influence of the religious and philosophical thinking of ancient pagan culture and was not in a position to push off the rationalism which therewith intruded into the church from this surrounding world. After all, the theologians had been pagan philosophers before they became Christian theologians, as was the case also with Augustine. When he was baptized by Ambrose, the pagan Augustine became a Christian; but he remained a Neoplatonist. Augustine contends for the "divine" Scriptures with the disciples of the pagan Neoplatonist Porphyry. A person must understand this destiny from which there was no escape in order to comprehend the tragedy of church history that occurred when Christendom, instead of confessing in all simplicity only what the Bible itself says of itself, had to drag along for centuries—because of the authority of the greatest of the church fathers—a *theory* concerning the Holy Scriptures which is only a crudely Christianized form of a heathen doctrine concerning inspired writings.

4

The understanding of the inspiration of Holy Scripture is connected with an understanding of its *inerrancy*. Already Clement of Rome, as we have seen, calls the Holy Scriptures "the *true* writings, which are (given) by the *Holy Spirit*" (1 Clement 45:2); and the chorus of Eastern and Western fathers, in unison in this regard, bears witness to the ancient church's faith that the Holy Scripture, because it is inspired by the Holy Spirit, is true, and that means free from errors. Hellenistic Judaism's doctrine of inspiration, as it is most clearly set forth in the legend concerning the genesis of the Septuagint, owes its origin to the desire to possess a guarantee for the correctness of a text, for the truth of its content. In the Old Testament, as in the Bible in general, a word is legitimized as a word of God by its content; in Hellenistic Judaism it was by the manner of its origin, its genesis, that it was legitimized. In the former case a conclusion is drawn from content to author; in the latter, from author to content. A prophet proclaims God's Word and demands *faith* in it. In this sense he says of his message: "*Haec dixit Dominus*" ["Thus saith the Lord"]. The Jewish and the Christian apologists do not attribute to the Word anything more than that it presents itself to the hearer as God's Word. That is why they attempt to prove that a specific message is not of human but of divine origin and therefore must be believed by every thinking person. Nothing is more characteristic of Augustine's apologetic understanding of inspiration and the completely uncritical naivete [*die Kritiklosigkeit*] with which he adopts the Septuagint legend in its late form. According to it the seventy-two translators translate the entire Old Testament independently of one another, each by himself, whereupon, "a remarkable and astounding, indeed, God-wrought agreement [*mirabilem ac stupendum planeque divinum in eorum verbis . . . consensum*] in the very wording offers the proof that *one* Spirit, the Spirit of God, was working in all" (*De civ. Dei* 18.42 [CSEL 40.2:335.30; NPNF[1] 1:386]). Augustine did not let anything shake his belief in this legend, though he was apprised of the fact that in this form it said the very opposite of what its older formulation, the Letter of Aristeas and Josephus, had meant, namely, that the translators had collaborated and had come to common wording by comparison (*Aristeas*, ed. Wendland, § 301). The erudition of Jerome (with whom Augustine was in correspondence concerning the Septuagint for a long time) was also unable to accomplish anything, even though Jerome showed that the older tradition had not allowed the translators to work as "prophets." "I should like to know who first invented the fiction about the seventy cells in which they all separately wrote the same thing" (*Apologia adv. libros Rufini* 2.25 [PL 23:470; NPNF[2] 3:516]). But Augustine would not let anyone take his seventy-two prophets away from him and criticized Jerome sharply because he translated his Latin Bible from the Hebrew and not from the equally inspired Septuagint! The deeper theological reason for Augustine's high evaluation of the Septuagint is to be found in the fact that the New Testament cites the Septuagint as Holy Scripture, also when the Greek text varies from what is in the Hebrew text. To this extent the great church father did call attention to a problem that exists also for us. If the New Testament cites an Old Testament passage in the Septuagint version or in one of the very similar translations that varies from the Hebrew text (e.g., Isa. 25:8 in 1 Cor. 15:55), then it must be assumed that both versions of the passage in question—the Old Testament version and the version which was taken into the New Testament—come under the inspiration of the Holy Scripture, no matter how the difference is to be explained.

If Augustine understands inspiration in such a way that man is only the tool of the Holy Spirit and that this alone determined content and form of what was written, then for him the rule must hold that the Bible is free of mistakes, errors, and contradictions, also in the smallest matters. In Letter 82 (written to Jerome; in Jerome's epistolary corpus, Letter 116), which presents a great discussion concerning the doctrine of the Holy Scripture, Augustine presents his fundamental position on this question:

> It is only to those books of the Holy Scripture which are designated as canonical that I have learned to show such reverence and respect that I believe that no error ever crept into any of their authors as they were writing [*ut nullum eorum autorum scribendo errasse aliquid firmissime credam*].

If there is anything in these books that appears to contradict the truth [*contrariam veritati*], there is no doubt, he says, of the fact that either the *manuscript* is corrupt, or the *translator* did not hit the sense of the words, or that *I* did not understand the meaning (*Epistle 82* 1.3 [CSEL 34:354.4ff.]). Let this passage represent many others in which Augustine confesses the complete inerrancy of the Holy Scripture as a self-evident corollary that follows from the fact of inspiration.

5

It is very revealing to observe how Augustine is at pains to harmonize his conviction concerning the fundamental [*grundsätzlichen*] inerrancy of the Bible with the realities of the biblical text. We choose as examples the two most difficult problems that he had to solve in this respect: the relation between the *Septuagint* and the Hebrew Old Testament and the differences among the [*Gospels*].

That the Septuagint is the inspired Word of God, just as the Hebrew Bible, was the common opinion in Augustine's day, even though he later abandoned his negative judgment concerning the Vulgate which had been translated from the Hebrew and declared it helpful and even used it himself, for example, *De doctrina christiana* 4.15 [CSEL 80:129–30; NPNF[1] 2:579–80] where he cites Amos 7:14f. from the Vulgate and gives his reasons. The point here is not that Augustine in this case found himself in deep error, but only that he "found a solution" for the superhuman task which he had posed for himself. To harmonize these texts was an apologetic *tour de force*. Let one example suffice. According to the Hebrew text of Jon. 3:4, the prophet announced the fall of Nineveh in forty days, whereas the Septuagint reads three days. Augustine establishes (*De civ. Dei* 18.44 [CSEL 40.2:338–40; NPNF[1] 2:387]) that the prophet obviously did not say both at the same time, and explains that he personally prefers the forty days of the Hebrew Bible. The seventy translators who came much later had, according to Augustine, been able to say something else with their divergent designation, something which is equally *apropos* and which had the same meaning, though using another metaphor; and Augustine warns the reader against despising either of the two authorities and lifting himself up and away from the historical content to the experience of *what the historical occurrence meant* and what was the purpose of its being reordered. The things that happened in Nineveh refer to what is experienced by the Gentile church, symbolized by Nineveh. Jonah is the type of the Savior who lay "for three days" in the grave and associated with the apostles after His resurrection "for forty days." For that reason both numbers could mean one and the same thing, the one number which was spoken by the Spirit through the prophet Jonah and the other number which was spoken by *one and the selfsame Spirit* through the prophesying of the seventy translators [*per septuaginta interpretum prophetiam*]. Augustine was able to find a solution to the problem of harmonization in this case only by going back to a meaning that lay deeper than the actual wording. *The truth of Scripture was hidden for him behind a seeming contradiction.* When in his youth he first turned to Scripture, he was, he tells us, unable to understand its truth because it was veiled: "And behold, I find what was closed to the proud and hidden to childish sense; what at its entrance was unimpressive [*incessu humilem*] was, as it proceeded on its way, exalted and enwrapped in mysteries [rem . . . *successu excelsam et* velatam mysteriis]" (*Conf.* 3.5 [CSEL 33:50.6; NPNF¹ 1:62]). But this veil fell when, just before his Baptism, Ambrose opened the Scripture [*remoto mystico velamine*] by teaching him to understand the passage: "The letter kills, but the Spirit makes alive" [2 Cor. 3:6].

In actual fact, any other explanation except the allegorical-mystical was impossible if both texts, the Hebrew and the Greek, should pass as inspired and errorless. The question, however, as to what, in this and similar cases, became of the absolute dependability of what was reported in the Bible—that question was a question which Augustine was unable to answer. The question of the historian as to "what actually happened," the problem of historical research, was still more pressing in the case of the Gospels, which cannot be approached by an allegorical-mystical explanation, such as is at least possible in the Old Testament in places where the New Testament itself gives this explanation. That is why the great attempt at a harmony of the Gospels is the most unsatisfying of all that Augustine wrote. Here his effulgent spirit becomes cold and calculating, and a shrewdness which looks for artful ways of avoiding the real question in order that he may still somehow bring his theory (that there dare never be anything in the Gospels that must appear to human understanding as contradiction, even if it is only in things of secondary importance) into harmony with the reality of the differences of the Gospel traditions. Not being in a position to solve the problem with a clear teaching about the nature of the Gospel and its historical form, he has to seek a harmonization in every case where a contradiction or inexactness seems to be present. Thus he finds that the cleansing of the temple[12] (which according to the Synoptics comes at the end of Jesus' public ministry, but which, according to John, came at the beginning) was undertaken several times (*De consensu evang.* 2.67 [CSEL 43:231–32; NPNF¹ 6:160]). The thought that the Holy Spirit had the *freedom* to give us the Gospel in various forms without violating the truth is a thought which Augustine does not comprehend. The fact that Mark designates the third hour for the crucifixion of Jesus (Mark 15:25) whereas according to John (19:14) Pilate delivered the Lord up to crucifixion at the sixth hour is explained in such a way that the Jews are supposed to have demanded Jesus' crucifixion at the third hour: "Mark shows with keen insight that the tongues of the Jews killed more than the hands of the soldiers" (*De consensu evang.* 3.13.42 [CSEL 43:327.2f.; NPNF¹ 6:199]). Naturally that is no explanation. But do we need an explanation? Where is it written that the Bible is only true when such differences do not occur? That is written in the writings of the pagan Porphyry, but not in God's Word. That is Aristotle's concept of truth, not that of the Holy Scripture. Since when must He, who is Himself the Truth, conform to what philosophers call truth? An especially difficult case for the apologists of

---

12   Cf. Matt. 21:12–17; Mark 11:15–18; Luke 19:45–47; John 2:14–16. MH

all ages is Matt. 27:9 where a citation from Zechariah is attributed to Jeremiah. We saw in another connection how Luther at this point in his Zechariah lectures spoke of a *levis error*[13] and how also otherwise Luther adduces Augustine for explanation. It seems that the problem played a role in the Middle Ages. It was the learned Thomist Cajetan[14] who called Luther's attention to this "error" at Augsburg in order to show that the Scripture could not be the sole authority for faith. It was Origen who—if we dare trust Rufinus [ca. 345–ca. 410]—in his *Commentary on Matthew* first called the use of the name of Jeremiah in the place of Zechariah an "error of the Scripture [*errorem scripturae*]" (PG 13:1709). Jerome expressed himself very circumspectly in that letter which is so important for his attitude toward Scripture, the *Epistle to Pammachus*:

> They may accuse the apostle of untruth [*falsitas*] because, in his citation, he does not agree either with the Hebrew text or with the seventy translators and—what is worse—because he makes a mistake in the name [*erret in nomine*] by putting "Jeremiah" for "Zechariah." Far be it from us, however, to speak thus about an apostle and companion of Christ whose task it was not to cite words and syllables but to transmit dogmatic statements. [*Epistle* 57.7 (PL 22:573; CSEL 54:513.17)]

That means: according to the strict standards of historical science, the apostle erred; but we dare not call that untruthfulness because it was not his office to transmit words and syllables, but doctrine. That is how Jerome helps himself. In his extended and complex discussion, Augustine comes to the conclusion that it could have happened that the evangelist thought of the name "Jeremiah" instead of "Zechariah," as that is wont to happen [*ut animo Matthaei evangelium conscribentis pro Zacharia Hieremias occurreret, ut fieri solet*]. He certainly would have later improved this mistake, if he had not, however, thought that the wrong name had come *to his memory when it was led by the Holy Spirit*, if God had not wished that the text should read thus. The deeper reason why God wanted it thus Augustine sees in the fact that basically all prophets form one unity, because the *one* Spirit speaks through all of them and brings about a *mirabilis consensio*. That is the doctrine which is to be drawn, according to Augustine, from the interchange of names (*De consensu evang.* 3.7.30 [CSEL 43:305f.; NPNF[1] 6:191–2]). What appears to us as a mistake in a biblical writer's presentation was, according to this, something wrought by divine will with special purpose. We must "perceive that this happened by a very secret plan of God's providence, by which the minds of the evangelists were controlled [*hoc actum esse secretiore*

---

13 On this question of Luther and his alleged granting of a "levis error," see *Letters to Lutheran Pastors* 1:360ff., especially nn. 16–19. MH

14 Cajetan (Tommaso de Vio, 1468–1534) taught philosophy and theology at Padua and served as general of the Dominican order (1508–18). He was appointed cardinal in 1517 and became bishop of Gaeta in 1519. Cajetan attempted to rein in Luther in 1518 (s.v. *Christian Cyclopedia*). MH

consilio providentiae Dei, qua mentes evangelistarum sunt gubernata]" (CSEL 43:305.9ff.; NPNF[1] 6:191).

<hr>

6

We shall let these examples suffice and proceed to seek an answer to the question as to what lesson we can learn from Augustine's attempt to prove the inerrancy of the Scripture apologetically. That attempt shows that the application to the Bible of the Hellenistic pagan-Jewish concept of inspiration (according to which the divine Spirit uses a person as a will-less secretary or as a mechanical instrument) is impossible. At the same time that concept of inerrancy also falls which equates the veracity and inerrancy of the Bible with the absence of all that must *appear* to human *reason* as contradiction, inaccuracy, or even as a mistake. Along with the psychological understanding of inspiration the logical-rational understanding of inerrancy also falls. If Augustine, like the entire ancient church, had not stood so much under the influence of ancient Greek psychology and Greek philosophy, he would have noticed that he was trying to harmonize and unite what cannot be harmonized and united. What does the inspiration of the prophets and of the holy writers have to do with what the *world* calls inspiration? Is there any activity of the Holy Spirit which can be understood psychologically? The activities of the Holy Spirit in the heart of a man take place at levels into which no psychology reaches. Just as the process of inspiration withdraws itself from comprehension by our reason, so also its result—the fact that a text is inspired—cannot be grasped by human reason. It cannot be *proved* that the First Epistle of Paul to the Corinthians is inspired and that the letter of the church at Rome to the Corinthians which raises the claim of being inspired ("what we wrote to you by the Holy Spirit," 1 Clement 63:2) is not inspired. That must be decided in *faith*, just as the people in Jerusalem had to make a decision of faith as to whether it was Jeremiah who was a true prophet or whether his opponents, who claimed inspiration, were true prophets. If Porphyry does not wish to believe that the Gospels are the inspired Word of God, then it is of no avail that I get rid of everything that looks like contradiction or inaccuracy by harmonizing and by other logically reasonable explanations. Augustine should have seen this. But at this point his eyes were held, being the eyes of a Neoplatonist of antiquity—something which is not an excuse for him, at any rate, though it is better evaluated if we realize that not only the theologians of the Middle Ages but also those of old Protestant orthodoxy repeated, without change, the formulae of Augustine (*dictare, suggerere, manus*—"dictating," "supplying," "hand"), and of Gregory the Great (*calamus*, "reed pen"), just as suddenly everything had been forgotten that the Reformation had taught about *sola Scriptura* (and not supplementary ecclesiastical tradition) determining articles of faith. The doctrine of the Scripture that is found in Quenstedt and Hollaz was taken—what an irony of church history!—not only from the Bible but also, to a great extent, from the Catholic tradition of the West that was based on Augustine. This tradition was still also a force in the Lutheran and Reformed churches at the end of the sixteenth and seventeenth centuries because in it that ancient philosophy still lived on, a philosophy whose sway over the minds of men had been broken by the Reformation only momentarily. If our orthodox fathers had only also taken to heart, along with many other things that they learned from Luther, what he had said about the abominable pagan Aristotle and, with that, about all of ancient philosophy! If they had only had an inkling [*ahnen*] of how quickly the temple of the Goddess Reason would be erected also in their church—like the temple to Reason which the French Revolution erected in the church of *Nostrae Dominae* in Paris, the very church in which Thomas Aquinas once received his master's degree—how would they, then, have pondered Luther's insight and his recognition of the fact that not only the Second but also the First and Third Articles of our Christian Creed are foolishness for the wise of this world. If a person searches the great works of the age of orthodoxy to see what became of the passage concerning the foolishness of the cross (1 Cor. 1:18–25), the passage which was so important for Luther, he will find v. 21 at least in Johann Gerhard's discussion of the doctrine of the Office of the Ministry; Hollaz no longer makes mention of it!

7

But that is not all that is to be said about Augustine's doctrine concerning the inspiration and inerrancy of the Scripture. He himself says more, when he has arrived at the end of his harmonization attempts. When it came right down to it, he was unable to bring *proof* for that type of biblical inerrancy that was derived from the Hellenistic idea of a divine scripture. *Either* he persevered in the very unsatisfying attempts at harmonization, as in the case of the cleansing of the temple or of the hours of the crucifixion, attempts which convince no one and which are historically impossible. *Or* he had to take refuge in the *res velata mysteriis* ["the matter veiled in mysteries"] in the Scripture or in a *secretius consilium providentiae Dei* ["a more hidden plan of God's providence"] which governed the composition of the Bible. The question arises as to why he makes this step his last recourse. Can the Christian doctrine concerning the Word of God, which is inspired by the Holy Spirit, even though it appears in the form of human word, be based on anything else than faith in the *res velata* ["the matter that is veiled"] and in the secret counsel of God, whom it pleased to give us the Bible as it is? Augustine had to capitulate before the reality of God's Word which is not even "revelation" in the sense in which pagans speak of revelation. For them revelation is *revelatio* in the sense that the veil is drawn aside from in front of the divine, so that it may be seen as it is: *Deus nudus*. For the Holy Scripture, however (as Luther saw so clearly), revelation always is at the same time revealing and concealing; it is *revelatio* in the double sense of an unveiling and of a reveiling, so to say. That God cannot be seen (1 John 4:12) is something no pagan understands. If no one can see God, how, the pagan asks, can there be such a thing as revelation? Hence the pagan attempts to take possession of God by way of ecstasy, mysticism. The Bible, however, and the church of the Reformation know that no one can see the *Deus nudus*. For that reason He "hides" Himself, as Luther puts it, in the flesh. God's revelation is always at the same time concealment. That is what God's revelation in the Scripture also is. It is this reality which Augustine ran up against when he perceived the clashes which the Scripture presents to human reason and which he could not get rid of by means of his reason. He was entirely correct when he denied that the Scripture contains *errors*. He was entirely correct when also he saw the *secretius consilium providentiae Dei* ["secret counsel of the providence of God"] at work in such an apparent error as Matthew's interchange of Zechariah and Jeremiah, and *we shall have to follow him in this and give up speaking of "errors" in the Scripture*, even if we only mean such visible human inaccuracies as that to which Luther applied, without hesitation, the expression *levis error. For what in the Scripture appears to our reason as error and contradiction is not, because of that, error.* In dealing with Matt. 27:9, Karl Barth calls attention to the inner connection of the passage with Jeremiah and remarks: "Here we are again dealing with an instance that shows that the Bible is accustomed to being wiser in its misunderstandings and in its 'getting things mixed up' than other books in their correctnesses" (*Kirchl. Dogmatik* II, 2, p. 519 [*Church Dogmatics* 2.2:468]). All this holds true especially concerning the historical narratives of the Bible, which, if measured by the yardstick of logic, do contain contradictions. May we call attention to what we carried out in our Letter 16 ("What Does Luther Have to Say to Us on the Inerrancy of the Holy Scripture?")[15] concerning Luther's statements about difficulties which he found in the Holy Scripture? He could, to cite a further and an especially vivid example, refer to the differences in the presentation of the patriarchs in Genesis, on the one hand, and in Stephen's speech (Acts 7), on the other hand— difficulties which cannot be dismissed by any harmonization attempts. Luther attempts to understand this in the following manner: "About Stephen's narrative this can be said: that it is not his own assertion but is a story which was taken from folklore [*aus dem Mund des Volkes*]; such a tale usually is confused and obscure." This explanation is impossible because the speech of the proto-martyr is in itself, according to Matt. 10:19f., inspired—aside from the fact that it has been taken into the inspired Acts of the Apostles. Furthermore, this explanation fails in this: that the references which Stephen makes agree with the tradition of the Greek synagogue in the Septuagint. This precludes Luther's opinion "that this passage was corrupted in more than one way by some smart alecks." Luther gives his reason for such a judgment by saying: "For that is a plain error [*error perspicuus*] (WA 53:179.12 [Aland 706]) when he says that the Lord appeared to

---

15　See *Letters to Lutheran Pastors* 1:332–66. MH

him (Abraham) in Mesopotamia, before he lived in Haran" (cited according to the text of the *Supputatio annorum mundi* in the St. Louis edition, W² 14:719ff.). In this and other cases it is not a question of errors or contradictions,[16] but of the fact that it pleased God the Holy Spirit to give us the holy history in several forms that vary one from another—all significant events are transmitted in the Bible in several versions!—not to lead us astray, also not to put our faith to the test, but because that is the manner of His revelation. In the manifold forms of His Word, in the priestly and in the prophetic view of Old Testament history, in the fourfold Gospel, in the manifold witness of the apostolic age there appears, as in the various colors of one prism-broken light of the sun, the *one* Word of God which we hear and believe in all of these forms. It is the *one*, sole truth, which we believe, also in the case of what must be believed contrary to external appearance, as Luther says, "*Dei sapientia abscondita est sub specie stultutiae et veritas sub forma mendacii . . . verbum Dei, quoties venit, venit in specie contraria menti nostrae, quae sibi vera sapere videtur*" ["God's wisdom is hidden under the form of foolishness; His wisdom is hidden under the form of falsehood . . . God's Word, when it comes to us, comes in a form which runs right smack against our mind, which imagines that it understands wisdom"] (*Lectures on Romans* [1515–16], at 12:2 [WA 56:446.31ff. (Aland 646; AE 25:438–39)]). Augustine could not yet know what the great Augustinian Martin Luther knew. No one in the ancient church could understand it. One of the fathers, a contemporary of Augustine's, came close to this understanding. That was Chrysostom with his doctrine of the *sugkatbasis, condescensio*, the gracious "condescension" of God to us men in His Word. If it please God, we shall speak of that, when we speak of the six days of creation in these letters.[17] One of his statements concerning God's revelation in the Bible may, however, be cited, an explanation of Hosea 12:11: *in manibus prophetarum assimulatus sum.* "That means," the great Greek father says, "*I came down (sugkatben), and I did not appear as that which I was*" (Fifteenth Hom. on John [PG 59:97f. (NPNF¹ 14:52)]). *Neque id, quod eram, apparui*—thus God speaks to us, concealed in the simple words of the Bible.

↭

I have purposely, worthy brethren, brought more material from the fathers than may seem desirable to some of you. We should, however, not forget that the doctrine of the Word of God concerns every pastor and that the doctrinal discussion

---

16 Sasse arrived in Australia in 1949 and almost immediately joined the UELCA team of the Joint Intersynodical Committee working to reunite the two Australian Lutheran church bodies. By 1951 the committee had agreed upon "Theses on Scripture and Inspiration" (see *Letters to Lutheran Pastors* 1:288–91). Here Sasse is refraining from calling difficulties in various accounts "errors." Facts from a letter of Kurt Marquart to Professor Leigh Jordahl, Decorah, Iowa, of June 2, 1978. See Sasse-Robert Preus Correspondence file in the Harrison Collection. MH

17 See below, Letter 33, "Toward Understanding the Six Days of Creation," pp. 272–84. MH

about it must be carried on in all circles of the Lutheran church, and not just by a few professional theologians. That is why I wished to offer you some material that is otherwise not readily available. Answers to some questions concerning earlier letters will have to be postponed for the present.

With hearty wishing of blessings for the Easter season, there greets you in communion of faith,

Your
Hermann Sasse

Historical Context

In this letter, Sasse continues several themes reflected in correspondence regarding previous letters. By 1953 it was already quite clear that confessional Lutherans within the German (de jure) Lutheran territorial churches had a very lonely path ahead of them. Today there are almost no confessional Lutherans remaining in the state churches. In Bavaria (Sasse's church while he was teaching at Erlangen), only a handful of aging men bear the torch of Wilhelm Löhe's legacy of fidelity. A few years ago the question of the need for the continued existence of the VELKD (those eleven constitutionally Lutheran Churches within the union EKiD) became acute. The VELKD continues, but all member churches remain members of the EKiD and in communion with all. Recently, it was suggested that the whole EKiD should subscribe to the Augsburg Confession. The suggestion failed. The remedies Sasse points to are vital today for the world's Lutheran Churches that do and are again taking the Confession seriously. The Confession is only meaningful if it actually has force in the church. Those who swear to the Confession must be familiar with the Book of Concord and accept it. Anything else is sin. And Lutheran Churches who confess the faith must hold one another accountable to the Confession. The LWF failed to do this from its inception, and it cannot and will not do it now. MH

April 6, 1953[1]

Prof. H. Sasse
41 Buxton Street
North Adelaide, South Australia

Dear Mr. Martinsen,[2]

I thank you very much for your letter of March 26. If *Here We Stand* is to be republished, it should by all means be carefully revised and brought up to date. The first English edition, masterfully translated by Dr. Tappert [1904–73], was prepared on the advice of the late Dr. [Michael] Reu, who wanted to have put in a chapter on Barth, which now is obsolete since the development of Barth has gone on with the appearance of the long series of the volumes of his *Dogmatik*. The book was written during the German *Kirchenkampf,* and its outlook is determined by this fact. The development of world Lutheransim during the

---

1   Feuerhahn/Preus Correspondence. MH
2   Paul T. Martinsen of Augsburg Publishing House. MH

last twenty years must also be taken into consideration. Finally, the author has learned something during that period . . . . If you need advice, please contact Dr. Herman Preus at Luther Seminary, St. Paul. He was always interested in my work . . . .

Yours sincerely,
H. Sasse

thirty

Marginal Notes

TRANSLATED BY ANDREW SMITH

Misericordias Domini (April 19,) 1953[1]

Prof. D. Theol. Hermann Sasse
41 Buxton Street
North Adelaide, South Australia

Dear Brothers in the Office!

Let's use the thirtieth letter in this series to answer a few individual questions, some of which have arisen from your circles, and some of which present themselves from the current situation of the Lutheran church.

1. About Baptism in the Chief Divine Service

I am very thankful to my brother in the office Hans-Otto Harms for drawing our attention, in no. 30 of the *Lutherische Blätter*, to the fact that infant Baptism had already moved into the main service of the Lutheran Church much earlier than I had assumed, namely, in the second half of the sixteenth century. That was the case, however, only in Lower Saxony and northwest Germany. The Lüneburg church order could have been an influential example here. Before I knew about the essay by Brother Harms, a church order which recently came into my possession, printed in 1590 in Lübeck for a small northwestern territory, seems to me to indicate this. It is, at the moment, inaccessible to me, but I will pursue the question further. The peculiarity of this order, like the Lüneburg one, is that the Baptism follows the reading of the Gospel, while the Lower Saxon order places it immediately before the sermon. But here is a practice which in no way was common to the Lutheran Church outside of the Lower Saxon and northwest German areas. We don't want to get too close to our Lower Saxon brothers and their great loyalty to the heritage of the fathers, but the Lüneburgers have here allowed themselves a liturgically false autonomy, which is not to be approved. Brother Harms also commits the mistake of seeing the other Lutheran church

---

1   *BLP* 30: *Randbemerken* (North Adelaide, April 1953). The original was published in *LuBl* 5, nos. 31–32 (1953). Huss number 300. MH

orders through Lower Saxon eyeglasses. When they generally prescribe that the Baptism should take place in front of the congregation, before the gathered congregation, that does not mean in the main Divine Service. In the case of Luther, who always emphasizes that the congregation should be there to pray for the child, Baptism *in* the main service does not come into question, already for the reason that the first part of the baptismal ceremony, which contains the exorcism, according to the *Baptismal Booklet* of 1526 which indeed belonged originally to the Small Catechism, should occur at the church door (cf. *Bek. Schr.*, 1930, p. 540: "Thereafter, lead the child to the Baptism"). The only trace of a connection between Mass and Baptism is the reading of John 1:1–14 after the Baptism, which is found in the Breslau *Baptismal Book* of 1524 (P. Graff, *Geschichte der Auflösung [der alten gottesdienstlichen Formen]* ... vol. I, 1937, p. 308). Because this pericope is the closing Gospel of the Mass, the Baptism in Breslau must originally have been at the end of the Mass, that is, at the end of the main Divine Service, before the congregation left the building. This is, then, the normal place of Baptism in the old Lutheran Divine Service, if it is not done in connection with an afternoon or weekday service. In Strassburg, for example, in 1534 it was ordered that the Baptism in the nearby parishes be done on Sunday after the sermon or at Vespers, [or] in the cathedral "at the children's address or afternoon sermon, when the congregation is together." "After the sermon" means, of course, immediately at the end of the Divine Service. The quotations from Höfling,[2] which Harms cites, may not be understood otherwise. Where the Divine Service did not have the form of a Mass, as was often the case in southwest Germany—or in Württemberg [where it] arose from the medieval sermon service on Sunday afternoons—there the Baptism followed immediately after the sermon, which was the core of the service. But where the sermon followed the celebration of the Sacrament—as was the case in the rest of Lutheran Germany and above all in the area of the Wittenberg order—then the Baptism, if one was to occur, was placed at the very end of the service. The order of service from Braunschweig-Wolffenbüttel (1543) prescribes thus:

> but the Baptism should be done on Sunday mornings after the completion of Communion, and afternoons shortly after the sermon, and on workdays also immediately after the sermon, before the people leave the building. [Quoted according to Höfling, vol. II, p. 293][3]

The [phrase] "after the sermon" is explained by the Pomeranian church order, which—like that of Braunschweig—arose under the powerful influence of [Johann] Bugenhagen, thus:

---

2 Johann Wilhelm Friedrich Höfling (1802–53) was professor of practical theology at Erlangen (1833) (s.v. *Christian Cyclopedia*). MH

3 *Das Sakrament der Taufe nebst den anderen damit zusammenhaengenden Akten der Initiation* (Erlangen, 1846–48). MH

when the child has been brought into the church, the Baptism shall not occur during the ceremonies, when there is preaching or organ music or singing, so that prayer is not disturbed, but rather after the sermon, when the ceremonies have come to an end. [Höfling, vol. II, p. 295]

The desire of Luther and of the old Lutheran Church is consistently that a congregation be present, which with its prayers accompanies the candidate to the Baptism. Therefore, the Baptism was held in conjunction with a Divine Service whenever possible, or at least one rings the church bells on workdays without a service to call the congregation. But it does not belong to the essence of Baptism that it occurs during the Divine Service or even only before a gathered congregation. Even Johann Gerhard does not claim anything beyond this, though the manner and type of his justification for the public setting of Baptism contains a serious misunderstanding. Like many fathers of orthodoxy, he projects the ecclesiastical arrangements of his time back into the church of the New Testament. As he understands—this is an old error of the theologians of the sixteenth century—Justin's monographs about Baptism, the Baptism was at that time done before the congregation, so he concludes that in the early church the preaching of the Word, the celebration of the Lord's Supper, and Baptism were all done in the same way: openly, in front of the gathered congregation. As is well-known, this was not at all the case, as the "baptismal registry" (a very deficient one, measured by later standards) of Paul at 1 Cor. 1:14 shows. The thought that the apostles themselves often did not baptize (1 Cor. 1:14, 17; Acts 10:48) was hardly intelligible to the orthodox fathers. Johann Gerhard makes another mistake when he opines that what is proper for one means of grace is correct for the other. If publicity is appropriate for the proclamation of the Word, then it is additionally for the administration of the Sacraments, whereby Baptism and Communion are again placed in the same category. How far we are here already removed from Luther's Reformation, which did not yet know this concept of sacrament from Reformed scholasticism (no more and no fewer than two Sacraments, exactly as the Roman scholasticism taught—no more and no fewer than seven) and which allowed itself the freedom to still teach three Sacraments in the Augsburg Confession (cf. Articles IX–XIII about Baptism, about the Lord's Supper, about Confession, about repentance, about the use of the Sacraments), as indeed the Lord did not institute abstract "sacraments," but rather instituted the individual actions and left it to His church to name them. In any case, nobody will want to ascribe the same openness to the sacrament of penance, as it still existed in the old Church of the Augsburg Confession, which one considered obvious for the other means of grace, because in the orthodox era, one lived in a world which was still at least nominally Christian, in contrast to the early church.

So much about the historical side of this question; for practical purposes, the Lutheran Church will continue to baptize in the Divine Service there, where it is an old custom. Whether this custom is today still good depends upon the circumstances. It may under no circumstances become a requirement. It may not disturb the character of the service or prevent the replication of the old Lutheran Mass. It may additionally not be forgotten that things which could be assumed in the old churches of the Lüneburg area, and can still be assumed in the congregations of our free churches, are no longer today obvious everywhere to Christians, that is, that the participants know about the essence and the gifts of Baptism. A Baptism in today's congregational Divine Service in a large parish—at the first Baptism which I was to do, there were seventeen children to baptize, and at that no longer candidates in the tender age of earlier years—must necessarily refrain from the baptismal address. The Gospel of the Baptism, which was in earlier centuries a firm possession, can no longer at all be recalled to the memory without a baptismal address. The Baptism then becomes exactly what the involvement of the congregation is supposed to prevent it from being: an *opus operatum*. We must not forget, too, that there are Baptisms which do not belong in the visibility of the world, and that is now the same as the openness of the larger churches. The church of Christ must recognize a remainder of the private [sphere], and it has at all times recognized it. The Baptism of President Eisenhower was indeed done not in *facie ecclesiae*, even if in *conspectu mundi*. So one will take care to defend the practice of the Lüneburg church order today. What was an adiaphoron in the old Lutheran Church is now no longer such where people, under the pretense of a return to that which they consider to be true to the Reformation, make a congregational celebration out of a sacrament, in the sense of a demand which Drews already raised at the beginning of the century:

> [T]he less one can ascribe to Baptism a sacramental significance in the catholic sense, the more urgently must the demand be made to perform the Baptism as a congregational celebration. [RE f. *Prot. Theol. u. Kirche*, 3rd ed., vol. 19, p. 446, sec. 25ff.]

We Lutherans profess Luther's understanding of the sacrament of Baptism, which is "catholic" for all Reformed and neo-Protestants. We can only give the urgent advice to the Lutherans of the Rhineland, who are forced to baptize as a congregational celebration, that they so preach the Gospel of Baptism in the sense of the Lutheran catechism at these congregational celebrations that it becomes clear to all listeners what the Sacrament is according to the Holy Scripture, even if all the Reformed, Barthians, and Crypto-Calvinists take offense at this.

2. Confessing Lutherans in Braunschweig

There are in the Lutheranism of the German territorial churches still many who are loyal to the faith—more than the media tell us. For one mostly sees those who are certainly Lutherans and who would like to renew the Lutheran Church in Germany, but without paying the price for this. The price is the fearless, open confession of faith, and corresponding to this confession, the rejection of error. Without this price of a fearless witness for the truth and against error, the church has never yet been saved, neither in the times of the apostles nor in the days of the Reformation nor in any other critical time of its history. Organizing, discussing, and theologizing alone won't do it. Certainly, one must attempt to organize the ruins of the Lutheran Church, to gather the Lutheran pastors and the laity who are still loyal to the Confessions. Certainly, the theological conversation may not grow silent, and the silent theological work at the desk may not stop. But all of that wins souls and gains real import only when it is accompanied by the witness of the living Lutheran faith, the witness of the Word and of the deed.

We must be thankful to the loyal Lutherans in Braunschweig who have gathered around the altar of the "Brethren" church[4]—Where else does the church really gather, than at the table of the Lord?—for giving such a clear witness in their congregations, in their territorial church, and beyond that in all of Lutheran Germany through the newsletter *Brethren* (published by Pastor Max Witte [1909–55], the Evangelical Lutheran Parsonage of the Brethren, 20 Schützen Strasse, Braunschweig), which has been appearing for four years, for the Lutheran Church and against the unionism of the falsely so-called "Evangelical Church in Germany." This is something which we have not seen since the church struggle in Germany, that in one of the internally weakest territorial churches in Germany a fine group of consciously Lutheran pastors and lay members could gather and confess in word and deed. It is an honor to the territorial bishop, Bishop Erdmann, that in this case even he professes himself to [belong to] these Lutherans, and it shows that this is a serious movement, but it does not explain the power of the movement; for, according to the Braunschweig church constitution, the territorial bishop does not have many rights in the church. It says nothing against this Lutheran movement that it is at the same time a liturgical movement, for confession and liturgy always belong together, if they are both taken seriously. Brother Witte explains the assumption of high churchly forms, which is at first surprising, primarily [by pointing to the fact] that in an area such as Braunschweig, in which the true Lutheran Church has so totally been alienated, one must unconditionally strive, even by means of external signs, to mark for the simple people the Lutheran Divine Service as something totally different as compared to the celebrations of those who have surrendered the Bible and the dogma, the church and the Sacrament. The replication of the Mass—that is, the Sunday worship service with sermon and Sacrament—is a legitimate and salutary goal of the liturgical movement in contemporary Lutheranism, and we need the words of Moses not to be taken from us, too, which are cited in the Augsburg Confession (twenty-fourth article) and which belong to the speech patterns of older Lutheranism and still today of the Nordic churches (cf. the "Högmessa"

---

4   Witte's tradition of liturgical practice, which Sasse so often praised, was carried on by Pastor Jürgen Diestelmann at Braunschweig. See his *Actio Sacramentalis: Die Verwaltung des Heiligen Abendmahles nach den Prinzipien Martin Luthers in der Zeit bis zur Konkordienformel* (Gross Oesingen: Lutherischen Buchhandlung H. Harms, 1996). MH

in Sweden). Whether the expression "holy Mass" is unambiguous [enough] in the Braunschweig situation to have a gathering and distinguishing effect only the brothers there can decide. May they always succeed in finding expressions and forms which testify clearly and sharply to the unbridgeable opposition to the Sacrament-less "Protestantism," but which just as unambiguously make clear that they have neither taken the "way toward Rome" nor participated in the liturgical handiwork of so many high churchly movements. But the fact that the liturgy has taken up the fight against the false union of the EKiD, in simple Lutheran loyalty to the Confession, shows that the liturgy has here a service role, in Löhe's sense, and that for this movement, the issue is the purity of the Gospel and nothing else. As far as the attitude toward the EKiD, the decisive matter is, after all, whether one still takes quite seriously the Lutheran Confession of the fathers. And it is a heartening sign of the times that resistance against the unionistic church model of the Evangelical Church of Germany [EKiD] of 1948— in which the unionistic German Evangelical Church [DEK] of 1933 (Hitler) and 1934 (Barmen) found its continuation and completion—is getting louder, though the ecclesiastical governments of Bavaria and Hanover, each in its way and with the means corresponding to its nature, could in 1948 successfully silence it. Whoever, as a Lutheran, acknowledges the EKiD and thereby the right of the EKiD to exercise all the internal ecclesiastical functions which are granted to it by the constitution, from cooperation in fighting against heresy to youth work and to caring for the diaspora in foreign countries, has surrendered the old Lutheran doctrine of the church and its unity according to the seventh and tenth articles of the Augsburg Confession. An additional declaration with reservations does not help in this matter, as the Bavarian church [had hoped], for limitations of a contract must be recognized by both parties to the agreement. It helps still less to institute at the same time a Lutheran parallel to the EKiD, the United Lutheran Church [VELKD], and begin a competition, for example, in the area of ecumenism and overseas work. One accomplishes nothing more thereby than that the declaration of loyalty, which was given by the Lutheran bishops to the EKiD, appears in a dubious light. The confusion which is created in the world by [all of] this is indescribable. One cannot save the VELKD from the reproach that it deliberately gives a false impression to the Lutheran Christendom of the world as if it were the Lutheran Church in Germany, and that only a few territorial churches and free churches abstain from it. In reality, it is not a church. For the church is always the *congregatio sanctorum*. The members of the VELKD are not the faithful, but rather the territorial churches. It is a federation of territorial churches or, more accurately, of church governments. The congregations and their members were not asked. They were taken over into the VELKD, as they were taken over into the EKiD by the same ecclesiastical governments. When the VELKD speaks, for example, through its "general synod," then the representatives of Lutheran Christians and congregations are not speaking, but rather the representatives of church governments and their territorial synods. And when the EKiD speaks, for example, through its synod or through its council, then again representatives of ecclesiastical governments and synods are speaking, among them also the churches of the VELKD. They speak perhaps somewhat differently, but it is supposed to be the voice of the church. If the VELKD is only a segment of the EKiD, why do both of them call themselves a church? If they belong so closely together, as their bishops assure us at every solemn opportunity, why do they compete against each other and deny each other the character of a church? Don't the people in Germany see that one day the world will stop taking this chaos seriously? And don't our German "church leaders" see that even their Christian people do not want to go along with this game of words and letters? What else remains for even the simplest of Christians—who belongs to his congregation and to his territorial church and who one day learns that, without his knowledge and without his will, he has been taken over into the EKiD and into the VELKD, and that these structures, unintelligible to him, are now competing for his poor soul—than to declare that he will have nothing more to do with all of that! Don't [the leaders] in Germany realize that this ecclesio-political game can end in no way other than in a catastrophe?

That is the meaning of the Braunschweig struggle, that here, in a church which belongs among the internally and externally weakest [churches] in Germany, the quiet and loyal [Christians] in the territory gather around the Lutheran Confession and for that reason reject the EKiD. In no. 30 of the *Lutherische Blätter*, the documents surrounding the case of Lieberg were to be read. This young brother in the office, who is still well-known to me from his student days and professional examinations, is an assistant preacher, who awaits his final promotion to the pastoral office. For the sake of truthfulness, after long negotiation, he has broken fellowship with the Ministry of Spiritual Affairs in the city of Braunschweig because it not only tolerated notorious heretics in its midst, but rather also refrained from rejecting as illegitimate the errors announced in its midst. As he communicated this to the church government, he at the same time declared openly why he could not acknowledge the EKiD, as [it] stands in contradiction to the Lutheran Confession. Subsequently, though a number of Braunschweig pastors think exactly as he does and have communicated this to the church government, a permanent position was denied to him, against the advice of the territorial bishop. They'll keep him on as assistant preacher—one can't very well fire a theologian for pure doctrine—but in the parsonage of a Lutheran member church of the EKiD he is intolerable. The publisher of the *Lutherische Blätter* and others—for example, Brother Hans-Otto Harms in the newspaper of the Independent Lutheran Church—have correctly evaluated the situation which has now arisen. How things have further developed since the critical days of Christmas 1952, we don't know. But the meaning of this disagreement is clear. If the situation remains that an open confession of word and deed against the EKiD, as Brother Lieberg and his friends in Braunschweig have given it, is not tolerated in a Lutheran territorial church in Germany, while open deniers of the truth of the Lutheran Confession—indeed, even of the Apostles' Creed—are tolerated, then a new proof has been delivered [to us] that the territorial churches are not at all confessional churches anymore, and perhaps even no longer are capable of being [confessional churches]. It is then once again made clear that appeal to the Confession and its claim to be a church of the Lutheran Confession is an ecclesio-legal fiction. What will the leading bishops of the VELKD now do, who have been telling the Lutheranism of the world that the Lutheran Church in Germany is blooming again? Certainly, the case of Braunschweig does indeed show that there really is a growing Lutheranism. But it also shows that the territorial churches don't know what to do with this Lutheranism, besides silencing it as quickly as possible. So it went also with the Lutheranism of the awakening in Prussia after 1817. [The territorial churches and the EKiD] can, however, use a Lutheranism which quietly accepts every damage to the Confession and which no longer protests against heresy, or in any case protests only quietly and theoretically. But a confessing Lutheran Church is no longer desired.

However the movement in Braunschweig ends, what will be the result for the congregation? When, in 1933, the territorial church received an unworthy man as territorial bishop, there awoke also in Braunschweig a confessional movement. What fruit did it bear after the long years of the church struggle and the Hitler era? And what will be the fruit of this new struggle? Will it be forgotten in twenty years, or will a confessing Lutheran Church in the Braunschweig territory, even if a very small one, give witness that in the years 1952 and 1953 loyal Lutherans confessed with word and deed the faith of the fathers?

3. de jure and de facto

I cannot tell which enlightening ecclesiastical jurist—or was it even a theologian?—distinguished for the first time between churches which are only *de jure* and churches which are *de facto* Lutheran. He fooled us all with this distinction, including me, as I would expressly like to say. It could not have been a good jurist. A good jurist would have known how inexact and ambiguous these expressions are. In common law, for example, the *de facto* recognition is much less [important] than the *de jure* recognition, while in the recognition of churches, the expressions are used in roughly the opposite sense: the *de facto* is more significant than the *de jure*. But it can also not have been a good theologian. A good theologian would have known that a confession which is only *de jure* valid is no confession at all. The validity of a confession is indeed something very different than the validity of a law. Even in the worst times of state ecclesiology with its mixture of ecclesiastical and worldly jurisprudence—one can still study this mixture today in Sweden or England—the "validity" of the Book of Concord has always been something different than the "validity" of an ordinance under penalty of death. For the Confession is not a legal document which humans have made, as they make an ecclesiastical ordinance, but rather it is an exposition of eternal truth, which the church confesses and teaches before God and before all Christendom, based upon the Holy Scripture, because it believes it. Confession is, therefore, as even the modern church constitutions admit, not the object of law-giving. One can change or do away with the Lüneburg order of service. One cannot "do away" with the Book of Concord; one can only "fall away" from it. And when one has fallen away from it, then it has lost its "validity." A church which would call itself Lutheran because in it the Lutheran Confession still has *de jure* validity, perhaps because it binds its pastors to it, is like a man who calls himself Lutheran and demands the rights of a Lutheran Church member only because he has not yet left the church. When a church cannot say: we *believe*, teach, and confess—when it as a church still merely teaches and confesses but leaves it to the individuals whether or not they want to believe that which it regards as legally binding doctrine—then it has ceased to be a Lutheran church. A church is either Lutheran or it is not. It cannot be *de jure* Lutheran if it is not also *de facto* Lutheran.

The answer which one gets to this tends to be the opposite question: Are there churches which are *de facto* Lutheran? Is it not an otherworldly idealism to suppose that some of the Lutheran Churches of the world, from the Reformation until the present, have really been completely Lutheran? Is it not an intellectual "Donatism," an un-Lutheran perfectionism, which expects from a church that it be completely free from error? These questions are then reinforced with quotes from the sermons or other writings of pastors from the Lutheran free churches. Indeed, the bad jokes which Karl Holl (1866–1926) and Reinhold Seeberg (1859–1935) [both professors in Berlin] made about Missouri as a "reformed sect," without really knowing the history and doctrine of Missouri, are today dredged up from old periodicals in order to show that there is no chemically pure Lutheran church, and that there can be none. But they're beating the air.[5] Neither the sixteenth-century Church of the Formula of Concord nor the German free churches nor the large confessionally loyal churches of America have ever considered themselves to be perfect Lutheran churches. They have always known that they have the treasure of the Gospel in clay pots. They have always wrestled for the pure doctrine, so seriously wrestled that they received the reproach, often rightly, that brotherly love didn't get enough attention. As the Gnesio-Lutherans of the sixteenth century did not shy away from getting rid of Matthias Flacius Illyricus (1520–75), so, too, Missouri's theologians have, when necessary, told themselves the truth thoroughly. By saying that a church is really *de facto* Lutheran, we mean a church which, in all human weakness and error, in all sin and imperfection and incompleteness, owns in complete conviction the great "we believe, teach, and confess" of the Lutheran Confessions, raises up its future servants in this Confession, teaches this without exception to the congregations, and works to ensure that this and no other doctrine is

---

5   Literally, they're knocking on a door that's already open. MH

announced in teaching and preaching. It follows that opposing doctrine is not merely theoretically rejected, but rather that one excludes it by means of evangelical doctrinal discipline of the preaching [i.e., parish pastors] and of the teaching [meant here are university and seminary professors]. We expect no more, but also no less, from a church which should be recognized by us as Lutheran, that is, as a Church of the Augsburg Confession. Here alone is the real difference between territorial churches and free churches in Lutheran Germany, between the churches of Hanover's world Lutheranism and the churches of Uelzen's world Lutheranism. If the churches of Hanover and Bavaria would begin to be serious about their confession—in the sense that they would work to see that their young theologians are raised in a confessionally loyal theology, that the errors in their chancels would be turned away, that the pulpit and altar fellowship with those who strive against Lutheran doctrine would end, and that only those ecumenical relations be pursued which do not stand in contradiction with the Lutheran confession—then there would be no reason to refuse church fellowship to them. Constitutional questions and other matters of ordinance need not be a hindrance. But they shouldn't trouble us with their *de jure* confession. That is an invention of the ecclesio-jurists of the nineteenth century, which has no foundation in Scripture or in the Confession. We are sincerely happy when even today young theologians are still bound to the Book of Concord, but we can only [really] be happy about it when they are raised in this doctrine and affirm it wholeheartedly. To obligate them to something which they don't know and don't believe is a sin, [even if] it may be a thousand times over an old honorable ecclesio-legal act. That is the [type of] ecclesio-legalism over which the devil rejoices.

The practical question which arises from this asks: Do the large territorial and national churches of the Old World *want* to be Lutheran once again in this sense, and are they *able*? The question is not whether individual members, above all bishops and pastors but additionally the Christian laity, desire this. Nobody doubts that a growing group of people very seriously wants this. In the middle of the worldly massive churches of our time, God has everywhere His people, the 7,000 who have not kneeled in front of Baal, with whom pious people so readily feel at home. Why should there not be these 7,000 even in the Lutheran Church? But the question is whether *Herr Omnes* ["Mr. Everyman"], into whose hands one has so trustingly placed church government, also wants this, and whether the other can do something against the will of *Herr Omnes*. This is the difficult situation of our brothers in Braunschweig. They are a small minority among the "church people." And even *those* bishops in Germany who in their hearts are Lutheran, like the bishop of Braunschweig (yes, even—what a miracle!— occasionally a bishop in the union), are lonely people.[6] The small groups and

---

6   "We Lutheran theologians must go our lonely way, as Rudolf Rocholl . . . wrote in his memoir. But in this loneliness our great consolation is the *sanctorum communion*, which Apology VII teaches regarding the church, the *regnum Christi*, which in this

the lonely Christians in congregations and in the office have been since time immemorial the strength of the church, but in such organizations of the church they are not allowed to say anything. The only opportunity for the Lutherans of Braunschweig in the framework of their territorial church, as long as it does not revoke its anticonfessional decisions of 1948, is the struggle for a special status, recognized by ecclesiastical law, as we once experienced it in the struggle of the Schwabach Conventicle.[7] Such a special status would, however, only placate the demands of the oppressed consciences if a confessional practice in *every* aspect were guaranteed to the pastors and congregations in question. Included in that would be the right not only to waive the altar and pulpit fellowship bound to the EKiD, but additionally to form an independent church regime which, in addition to the functions of ordination and visitation, could take over the responsibility to aid the congregations in the future in finding confessional pastors. So far no Lutheran territorial church—not even a union church—has been able to rise to the occasion, to create a special status of this type for decisive Lutheran minorities, whose well-founded claims to complete participation in the funding as well as in the ecclesio-legal recognition of the territorial church must be met exactly because they have held firmly to the confessional and constitutional basis of their old church. The territorial churches could, namely, oblige liberal minorities. It was possible that communities whose doctrine flew in the face of the Confession of the Lutheran Reformation [could] freely exist "inside the territorial church." The formerly Lutheran Evangelical Church of Württemberg could even sign agreements with sects. But for Lutherans who want to live and teach according to their Confession there has been until now only the path into the free church. That may well continue to be the case, and probably should be the case, and is certainly better than any attempt which must perhaps inevitably end up as a compromise. But the territorial churches which criticize the free churches, a criticism they have no right to make—just imagine what would happen to these large churches if even for only two years [they] did not so generously provide them with federally raised church taxes and other financial means, with professors and even ecclesiastical colleges—they themselves are guilty that the most conscientious Lutherans saw no other way left except for the sacrificial way into the free churches, in which truth and error do not have equal rights, in which the doctrine of the Lutheran Confession and false teaching

---

aeon is *cruce tectum*" (Sasse to Leiv Aalen, August 26, 1943; in the Harrison Collection). MH

7   "Some of these men [leaders in the Bavarian Church] belonged to the Schwabach Conventicle, a league of pastors opposed to National Socialism, which was founded in 1940 by Christian Stoll. Friedrich Wilhelm Hopf, a member of this group, writes: 'The Schwabach Conventicle brought together theologians who stepped in for the renewal of the Lutheran Church in regard to the pastoral office, life of the congregation, theology and church government.' The members of the Schwabach Conventicle, all stalwart supporters of the Lutheran Confessions, also included Hans Siegfried Huß, Karl Krodel, and Sasse" (Green, *Lutherans Against Hitler*, 363). MH

do not have equal rights. Who would actually benefit if the Lutheran territorial churches of the VELKD succeeded in persuading a segment of Lutherans from the free churches that they could be kept quite well in the VELKD, because there the Lutheran Confession and no other is *de jure* valid, because they're trying to more strongly enforce the Confession and need the help of those who were until now in the free churches, and because even the Lutherans in the free churches aren't perfect, by the way! One would then have destroyed the free churches, and nothing would change in the territorial churches. Or does anybody really believe that a few thousand free church Lutherans would convert the millions in the territorial churches to the faith of the Book of Concord?

4. The Responsibility of Lutherans for One Another

"All of us like sheep have gone astray, each of us has turned to his own way" [Isa. 53:6]—that is true not only of the old people of God at the time of the prophets, it is also true of the new people of God at the time of the apostles, a people who knows its Good Shepherd and yet repeatedly does not listen to His voice, but rather the jumbled mass of voices from the world. So the churches of Christendom go through history, each looking only at its path. What results is seen in the chaos in the mission fields, a chaos which cannot be avoided by declaring all ways as equally good and not at all asking about the correct path anymore. We here in Australia have seen daily the suffering of the so-called "young churches" in southeast Asia, the suffering of daily life in the church, which one does not see in the large world conferences. But about the history of Lutheranism in the last two centuries, one can also write: "Each of us has turned to his own way." What did the Lutheran Churches of the Old World actually do for their emigrants, and thereby for the emerging Lutheran Churches in other parts of the world? Naturally, something was done, but usually by individuals, clubs, and missionary associations. And in the process, these [individuals and institutions] did not always act completely selflessly. Neuendettelsau bore a substantial part of the responsibility for the fact that Missouri and Iowa did not merge. On the twenty-fifth anniversary of the Iowa Synod in 1879, the head of the Neuendettelsau society, Pastor Wucherer,[8] wrote in his greeting (among other things):

> We were happy, especially about the complete agreement with our ecclesiastical direction and our practical church principles, which are expressed so clearly and decisively in this academic publication. (J. Deindörfer, *History of the Evangelical Lutheran Synod of Iowa and Other States* [Chicago, 1897])

The reception of subsidies and other help depended greatly upon this "ecclesiastical direction," to which belonged the theology maintained by the

---

8   Johann Friedrich Wucherer (1803–81), like Löhe, was influenced by Krafft and fought in later years alongside Löhe for the right of the Confession in the Bavarian Church. See Meusel, *Kirchliches Handlexikon* 7:310. MH

followers, epigones, and sycophants of their master, Löhe, regarding the matters of church and ministry, chiliasm and Antichrist, the limitations of confession, and the open questions. If one reads the letters which were written from Neuendettelsau to America and Australia about such doctrinal questions, then one will be reminded of the instructions of a church council which communicates in a friendly but energetic way with its subordinates. All of that was not entirely selfless, just as even the activity of missionary societies does not have only that aspect which is celebrated at mission festivals. Naturally, on the other side, Missouri energetically made its "ecclesiastical direction" felt, too, that is, making, with justifiable dogmatic demands, the acceptance of certain theological propositions into a condition for church fellowship. The deeper cause for the unspeakable hardships which have existed in the Lutheran diaspora during the last two or three centuries is the self-contentment of the home churches, which did not recognize their responsibility toward the Lutherans of the world. In the churches of other denominations, by the way, it was no different.

One would suppose that in our century, in which countries, regions, and churches have, from a purely spatial perspective, grown closer to one another— how would the Lutheran church history of America gone, if Löhe had accepted the invitation to the convention of the Missouri Synod in Milwaukee in 1864, or [if he] had ever even seen the Lutheran Churches in America once!—it would have gotten better. One would suppose that the togetherness of the Lutheran churches in large organizations such as the former [Lutheran] World Convention or the current LWF would have called forth a stronger feeling of mutual responsibility for churches. And that is indeed the case, insofar as the obligation for help in external hardships is being fulfilled as never before. The tremendous help from all American Lutherans for their comrades in faith, and beyond that for all who suffered hardship, in Europe after World War II is the greatest fruit of this Christian and Lutheran solidarity. But what we need now is a stronger feeling of responsibility for the spiritual life of other churches, for their existence as Churches of the Augsburg Confession. If the Church of Sweden enters into altar fellowship with the Anglicans and thereby—*de facto* and *de jure*—nullifies the Seventh and Tenth Articles of the Augsburg Confession, then it is doing something which concerns all the Lutheran Churches of the world.

> The synod of the Anglican bishops in South Africa has decided to recognize as equals the bishop of the Swedish Lutheran Church in South Africa and the pastors ordained by him. In this agreement is contained the altar fellowship of both churches. The recognition of the Swedish Church is based upon its having unbroken apostolic succession in its bishop's office. Native South African pastors of the Swedish Lutheran Church participate in the altar fellowship only insofar as they were ordained by the bishop himself.

This story is going through the religious periodicals of the world (I take it from the *Lutherischen Nachrichten*, which is published by Pastor Dr. Rose of

Wuppertal-Barmen in the service of the Lutheran Working Group in the Union Churches of Germany). Just imagine what this Anglican-Swedish intercommunion, which is already doing enough damage in the world, must mean for the splintered Lutheranism in South Africa. First, what an insult for a Lutheran Church, which by historical accident has apostolic succession, to have this succession recognized by another church whose own succession is at least very dubious and is not recognized even by the churches of the East. Second, how can two churches enter into altar fellowship based upon a rite of ordination which, for one church, belongs to the essence of the church [but] for the other church is an adiaphoron? The fact that the *Book of Common Prayer* rejects the real presence for Calvinist reasons apparently plays no role anymore for the Swedes in the granting or not granting of altar fellowship, just as they have indeed in Sweden itself nullified the Lutheran Confession with the ordinance—*de facto* and *de jure*—of admission. But now imagine how it must affect [the situation] when there will now be in South Africa—as already in India—two types of Lutheran pastors: some with apostolic succession and some without it. Do the Swedes really expect that those Lutheran congregations and pastors who still take the Confession seriously and who have no altar fellowship with the Anglican Church because it teaches contrary to Scripture about the Lord's Supper will still recognize the Church of Sweden as a church of the Unaltered Augsburg Confession? But the Church of Sweden is not thinking about all of this. "Each one looked at his own path." It is no better in the cases of the Lutheran churches in Germany and America. Have the Lutheran territorial churches in Germany that entered into the EKiD, or the United Lutheran Church and the Augustana Church that entered into the American EKiD, into the National Council of Churches of Christ in the USA, considered the delayed consequence which such actions must have upon the small churches of Lutheranism scattered around the world? When will this *sacro egoismo* of the churches stop, who always only ask: What's in it for us? and subordinate this question to the search for truth? In any case, it should not be this way for the churches of the Lutheran Reformation. For them, a question such as whether they should or can enter the Ecumenical Council should be a question of faith, and not a question of utility which one answers based on purely practical calculation—an answer, the dogmatic justification of which is left by the church leaders, after the fact, to the theologians. But it is hopeless to expect anything different from the churches.

The less the church leadership and the ecclesiastical organizations have a feel for the great responsibility which all churches and all Christians who profess the Augsburg Confession have for one another, the more the individuals need to have it, who have to stand up in the congregation and in the office for that by which alone the Lutheran church lives: the robust preaching of the Gospel and the administration of the Sacraments according to their institutions. In the free churches, the concern about the future of Lutheranism in the territorial churches cannot and may not die. For the Lutherans in the territorial churches which are still *de jure* Lutheran, it cannot and may not be a matter of indifference, what happens to their comrades in faith who live without the legal title of a *de jure* Lutheranism in the union churches and who often take the Confession so much more seriously, which they are newly discovering, than the others who have inherited it and have not had to win it for themselves in bitter struggle. For the loyal Lutherans—and there are still some of them in Sweden, too—it may not be a matter of indifference when their church leadership, by means of agreements with the Anglican churches, not only insults the Lutheranism of the world but also simultaneously sets a new ecclesio-legal precedent which *de facto* and *de jure* nullifies the Augsburg Confession. For us in Australia and Europe it should not be a matter of indifference whether what remains of true Lutheran unity in the Synodical Conference (Missouri, Wisconsin, Norwegian Synod, Slovak Synod) fractures or not, just as it is not a matter of indifference for Missouri what happens to the Lutheran heritage in the German territorial churches. We humans cannot create this consciousness of a great mutual responsibility of all of those who seriously want to be Lutherans, and no LWF can organize it. We can't create it in Hanover or in Uelzen. But it will arrive as a gift of the Holy Spirit, if we pray earnestly for it. What would have happened to the poor weak church of the apostolic era without daily prayer [by believers of] one mind? What would have happened to the Church of the Reformation without the powerful prayer of Luther and without the sustaining prayer of the old Lutheran Church: "Oh, remain with us, Lord Jesus Christ . . . for You alone preserve Your church"? Has the church of today forgotten this? Sometimes it seems so, despite all liturgical work. It is therefore all the more necessary that, at least in small circles, apart from all organizations and above and beyond all boundary lines and ecclesiastical divisions, which do indeed exist between Lutherans and which for the sake of truth must temporarily exist, this prayer of mutual responsibility, the intercession inside the church, happens. Then we will understand the hardship and the promise of the Lutheran Church, which is contained in these words: "All of us like sheep have gone astray, each of us has turned to his own way, but the Lord has caused the iniquity of us all to fall on Him" [Isa. 53:6]!

༄

Greeting you at Pentecost in the bonds of faith,

Your
Hermann Sasse

Historical Context

This letter shows Sasse's uncanny prophetic insight. "The decision on the future of the Lutheran Church and her theology will be rendered in America." "Christianity has no future in the world as a European religion." The future of Christianity will be played out, says Sasse, in Asia and Africa. Free church Lutherans in Germany and American Lutherans have had to go their "lonely way" in struggling to remain faithful to the Lutheran Confessions. Isolation from false theological systems, however, meant that "they have not really learned to overcome these systems." "The Lutheran Churches of America are on the verge of losing their character as confessional churches." Sasse did not exclude the Missouri Synod or Wisconsin Synod from this critique. "What will it mean for American Lutheranism that, with the breathtaking speed which characterizes the development of the American people, the old dogmatic inheritance is quickly given up?" In the Missouri Synod we have lived this loss of dogmatic content as we descended into Seminex and still, forty years after, struggle out of it. Meanwhile, just fifty-six years after Sasse wrote, the bishop of the ELCA (not trained in a Lutheran seminary—an issue Sasse emphasizes) leads his church body into the approbation of homosexual marriage. The task for the remaining orthodox American Lutheran Churches is clear: rediscover, retain, and transmit the dogmatic content of Lutheranism—and we have waned greatly in knowledge of dogmatic categories—and share doctrinal Lutheranism with the world as we assist younger churches toward genuine Lutheran confession in the face of contemporary issues and situations. MH

July 13, 1953

H. Sasse
41 Buxton Street
North Adelaide, South Australia

Dear Dr. [Hermann A.] Preus,

...As to my *Briefe*, I do not know how long I can continue them. Could not that one on the doctrine of inspiration of Augustine be translated for your *Quarterly*? You could omit the beginning and the end. It is actually a contribution to a symposion [*sic*] for the old philologian Prof. Dornseiff in Greifswald in the Eastern Zone of Germany. It is being printed in Leipzig in German. But it could be published as well in English. As to your plans, I think Martin Chemnitz's *Examen* and Gerhard's *Loci* should appear in English.[1] This is, however, such a great enterprise that some Lutheran Churches should do it together. We need very badly the great Lutheran literature of the past in English. But this plan has to be worked out very carefully. Luther's *Vom Abendmahl Christi, Bekenntnis*[2] seems to have been translated in America, but not in the Philadelphia edition. There should be a master plan for publishing Lutheran literature. What do you think of the new Luther edition of the English Methodists? I shall write about these questions in a *Brief.* My best wishes for your stay in Norway. You should lecture on the "History of the Lutheran Church in America" and on the great problems of Lutheran theology in the USA, showing especially the implications of the free church system which has made it possible to accomplish some thoughts of Luther on the church (congregation) which the state church system could not accomplish. Let me know your Norwegian address. Otherwise I shall write c/o Menighets Fakultet Oslo. God be with you.

Yours fraternally,
Hermann Sasse

---

1 Chemnitz's *Examen* has been translated: *Examination of the Council of Trent*, trans. Fred Kramer (St. Louis: Concordia, 2009). Concordia Publishing House is in the process of publishing a translation of Gerhard's *Loci* by Richard Dinda under the title *Theological Commonplaces*. MH

2 *Confession concerning Christ's Supper* (1528), Aland 2, WA 26:261–509 (AE 37:161–372). MH

thirty-one

Problems in American Lutheran Theology

TRANSLATED BY MATTHEW C. HARRISON

Mid-July 1953[1]

Prof. D. Theol. Hermann Sasse
41 Buxton Street
North Adelaide, South Australia

Dear Brothers in the Office!

Most of you live either in Germany or in churches where the ecclesiastical language is still German. Still, the future of American Lutheranism presents a question of extraordinary significance for you and your office. American Lutheranism has come into your purview as never before, and not only by means of its benevolent work, which has literally saved the lives of millions of men in Europe. For the ascendance of the United States to a world power of the first rank has, as with all the American churches, also given to American Lutheranism a new position in the world. There have been theological encounters at conferences, such as the discussions first arranged by the Missouri Synod in Bad Boll.[2] And even if these discussions have in large measure only proven that both sides understand something quite different when they speak of "theology"—similar to the first encounters between the European and American theologians of various denominations in the Ecumenical Movement after the First World War—they have at least awakened an interest on each side for a theology which is different from their own. This alone would justify speaking to the problems of modern

---

1   *BLP* 31: *Probleme der lutherischen Theologie Amerikas* (North Adelaide, July 1953). The original was published in *LuBl* 5, no. 32 (September 1953). Huss number 302. MH

2   See above, p. 23 n. 21. MH

American theology. But there is another reason for taking up this topic: as far as we can humanly determine, the decision on the future of the Lutheran Church and her theology will be rendered in America.

Certainly, as long as Europe exists it will always play a role as the home of Western civilization and the Western church. But the final decisions on the future of humanity will be rendered in other parts of the earth, in the Americas, in Asia, and in Africa. This fact may be painful for us who cling to the homeland of our church and our culture with every fiber of our hearts. But one need only question the experts on world missions to know that this is no empty talk. The ecclesiastical decision which will be rendered in Europe is the question whether or not the thin layer of living Christians, which rests over all the Old World, will be able to bring the masses back into the church, and not merely well-educated individuals, who see where a purely secularized culture has lead humanity. It is moving to see how all the church governments—from the pope, who drives his prelates out of the Curia into the secular executive offices of Rome, to the leadership of the EKiD, which plans its "Church Days" with the circumspection of the Old Prussian general staff—are at pains to solve this problem. But the final decisions on the future of humanity will be rendered on other continents, not in the satellite states and political administrative offices of the East and West in Europe. What Europe and the churches of Europe can and, in great selflessness, must do is work so that the outcome of these decisions is in accord with our desires. Christianity has no future in the world as a European religion. On the contrary, as such it will be rejected. But the Gospel in its purity, unmixed with European philosophy and "religion," and the church of the Gospel—these have a future. The church of God always has a future, because Jesus Christ has a future.[3]

1

Lutheranism, as with all other Christian confessions, came to America as a European confession, and it has preserved this European background longer than the others. Only in this century have the Germans of the Midwest, the Swedes, Norwegians, Danes, Finns, and Slovaks—only to mention a few of the main Lutheran groups—fully made the transition to English as their ecclesiastical language, and thereby fully entered the American scene [*damit in das Amerikanertum eingegangen*]. And corresponding to this, it is a fact that also the theology of modern American Lutheranism has not denied its European origins. There is as of yet no real American Lutheran theology. It was in the process of development in the last century when S. S. Schmucker, with his "Definite Synodical Platform" of 1856,[4] sought unsuccessfully to win the General Synod for

---

3   See Sasse's 1938 essay "The Presence of Christ and the Future of the Church," in *Lonely Way* 1:461–69. MH

4   See above, p. 18 n. 17. MH

what he called "American Lutheranism." In retrospect we see that this American Lutheranism—a remarkable parallel to the Catholic "Americanism" of the contemporary founder of the Paulists, I. Th. Hecker [1819–88]—was a Calvinized Lutheranism, which rejected private confession, baptismal regeneration, the real presence, and the Lutheran teaching on Sunday. When the General Synod, despite its persistent elements of Pietism and Rationalism (the inheritance of the eighteenth century), rejected the "Definite Platform," it confessed its adherence to the theology of European Lutheranism. If this was true of the most "liberal" of the Lutheran synods, it was all the more so of the General Council and the great synods of the Midwest: Missouri, Ohio, and Iowa, to mention only a few.

It is quite significant that, from their inception, these synods were different from the Lutheranism represented in Pennsylvania, New York, and the other Eastern states. For they had been influenced by the great confessional awakening of the years after 1830. Indeed, in large measure they were created by it, as was the Lutheran Church in Australia. Missouri is a daughter of the Saxon and Franconian confessional Lutheran awakening; Iowa originally belonged to the Missouri Synod; Buffalo was a synod which had its roots in Prussian Lutheranism (Grabau[5] came from Erfurt). The confessionalism of these churches also deeply influenced the old synods of the East, the General Synod and General Council, which today make up the greater portion of the United Lutheran Church. The same applies to the churches of Scandinavian origin, to the Swedish Augustana Synod and the synods of the Norwegians and Danes. In the nineteenth century, and yet at the beginning of this century, all these churches were more conservative than their mother churches of the European north. American Lutheranism, as was Australian Lutheranism, was strictly confessional in the sense that all the synods based themselves upon the Book of Concord and were anti-unionistic. They all maintained the Galesburg Rule of 1875—or at least affirmed it, though there were exceptions. According to the Galesburg Rule, "Lutheran pulpits are for Lutheran pastors, and Lutheran altars for Lutheran communicants."[6] They all in theory maintained that the Lutheran Church ought not have altar and pulpit fellowship with the adherents of other confessions. The reason more liberal synods and pastors also accepted this as a basic proposition of their church law

---

5   Johannes Andreas August Grabau (1804–79) studied at Halle and served as pastor in Erfurt. He was jailed twice for refusing to accept the Prussian *Agenda* before emigrating to American in 1839 with members of the congregations of Erfurt and Magdaburg. Grabau engaged in a heated debate with C. F. W. Walther and the Saxons over the nature of the pastoral office and its authority (s.v. *Christian Cyclopedia*). MH

6   In fact, the Missourians did not accept the Galesburg Rule as sufficient. They refused fellowship with unionizing Lutherans, but also with the General Council because of persistent aberrations in practice. "It is atrocious and hypocrisy as well as perjury that the men of the 'Church Council' who after all have signed the Confessions, which include also Luther's words just quoted, nonetheless admit to the Sacrament those who believe different" (Walther, "Communion Fellowship," in *Essays for the Church* 1:222). MH

was that Lutheranism represented a tiny minority of American people (today the figure is something like 4 percent; in Australia, less than 1 percent), which would simply be absorbed by the other churches if this boundary where not maintained, and has actually been absorbed where this boundary would not or could not be maintained.

The United Lutheran Church, for instance, has old united congregations which have their roots in the eighteenth century. Rev. Roy L. Winter, in *The Lutheran Quarterly* of February 1953 ("The Union Church," pp. 56–69), has given an interesting account of this. He notes that the Ministerium of Pennsylvania, the synod of this state so significant for Lutheranism, as of today counts 175 union congregations, of which 85 already had existed in 1820 and thus are older than the Prussian Union. Formation of union congregations has not happened for decades, nor, as Winter asserts, are such to be expected. But the reasons for this are more practical than dogmatic. Pragmatically, it is more correct to have Lutheran congregations instead of union congregations beset with difficult problems. Thus the decision of American Lutheranism for confessional limitation, and against the union church, is explained not only on the basis of confessional and theological grounds, though it was finally decided by the confessional awakening of 1830.

The entire tendency of American Lutheranism was toward the right, toward confessionalism. Even the churches of the "left" were confessionally defined. Although the United Lutheran Church was formed after the First World War (1918), it was still more confessional than any German territorial church. It was the Lutheran awakening of Europe and the confessional theology of various stamps which resulted from it which, transmitted by the mission institutions (Neuendettelsau for Iowa; Hermannsburg for Ohio; Kropp and Breklum for the synods which today compose the United Lutheran Church), defined American Lutheranism of that time. Even the Missouri Synod, which for theological and dogmatic reasons broke the European ties very early as a result of the controversy between Walther and Löhe, remains thoroughly German in its theology. Walther's theology is through and through a German theology, and the St. Louis edition of Luther's Works, a reworking of the old Walch edition, is perhaps the greatest literary monument to things German in the United States.

The theological controversies also have their origin in German Lutheran theology, and this includes the controversies over the so-called open questions and the doctrine of election, as much as the disagreement on the doctrine of the church and ministry. Whoever is of the opinion that Missouri demonstrates the influences of Calvinism must prove that Luther did not write *That a Christian Congregation Has the Right and Power to Judge Doctrine, Etc.*, and that *De servo arbitrio* (the book which Luther always regarded as his best, next to the catechism) is un-Lutheran.[7] The particular problems of the home churches affected the Scandinavian churches, especially the Norwegians and Danes, but their theology remains European and confessionally Lutheran.[8] There is no real American Lutheran theology—rather, only a theology of European Lutheranism, transplanted in America, similar to the theology of other Christian confessions transferred to America. The difference consists in that this theology which emigrated to America did not develop along with European theology in the last decades of the nineteenth century and that it oriented itself to the Confessions.

2

The isolation of American Lutheranism in its own land and away from the Lutheranism of the world has brought it great advantages and disadvantages. If it had not bound itself to the Confessions, American Lutheranism would have been absorbed by the other denominations [*Konfessionen*]. The confessionalism of our American brothers, however, has had a significance also for the rest of Lutheranism, even where it has been more a matter of sentiment [*mehr gefühlsmässig bedingt*] than theological clarity. The confessionally faithful churches of America have saved the Lutheran Confession for the world. For the fate Lutheran confessionalism has suffered in Germany and Scandinavia is very clear. There is in Germany no longer a theological faculty at any university which would be anything more than Lutheran in name only. Since Kolde [1850–1913] softened the confessional requirement of the Erlangen faculty,[9] even this haven of Lutheran theology has succumbed to the fate of all German university theology. That the responsibility for this lies not with the state, because it is a public university, is shown by the simple fact that the "ecclesiastical academies" which were founded after the war are not a hair better. The confessionally faithful Lutherans are as isolated there as in the [university] faculties. And this is not only the fate of German Lutherans. At Uppsala, only the professor of practical theology must be a Lutheran, and one faculty chair, if I am not mistaken, is occupied today by a Methodist. When one considers that also the once Lutheran faculties of the East have all but collapsed and are practically no longer present for the Western world, then a terrifying fact becomes evident: except for the

---

7   See Aland 406 (WA 11:408–16; AE 39:301–14); and *Bondage of the Will* (1525), Aland 38 (WA 18:600–787; AE 33). MH

8   Sasse often recounted the criticism of Missouri as "Calvinist" particularly with respect to the doctrine of election, especially leveled by Karl Holl, his professor at the University of Berlin in the years just before World War I. MH

9   By 1971 the confessional requirement was suspended altogether and the great Lutheran century and a half of Erlangen was over. Lowell Green—a student of Paul Althaus, Werner Elert et al., at Erlangen in the early 1950s—has written a tremendous book: *The Erlangen School of Theology: Its History, Teaching, and Practice* (Fort Wayne, IN: Lutheran Legacy, 2010). MH

free churches and their academies, confessional Lutheranism no longer has any sanctuary in Germany.

If American Lutheranism did not exist, or had this Lutheranism made its peace with the Union in the nineteenth century, as all Lutheran territorial churches of Europe have done, the situation would be even worse for our church. Then the Lutheran Church would no longer exist—rather, only a Lutheranism which, as Harless[10] warned when he prophesied in 1870, would be tolerated as a viewpoint, as a theological school within a general Protestantism. We have our American Lutheran brethren to thank for maintaining the Lutheran Church as a confessional church.

They have paid a great price for this, just as have the free churches in Germany. It has meant, above all, isolation. As the free church Lutherans in Germany have had to go their "lonely way," so the Lutherans in America have long been a lonely people within their culture [*in ihrem Volk*] and in the great Christendom of their land. And this remains so even today where they have remained true to the Confession of their fathers, even where English has become the language of the church. Moreover, there was a more difficult ecclesiastical fate. They were forced by circumstance and their faithfulness to more or less distance themselves from the theology of Europe. They have quite correctly left Ritschl and Harnack to other churches. Who would have been served if this theology had also flooded the Lutheran faculties of America? But the result of this isolation was that they have not really learned how to overcome these systems. They were able to guard the heritage of the fathers, to pass it down undisturbed from generation to generation, but they were unable to fight for it anew, to earn it in order to make it their own.

But if there is anything in the church which cannot be inherited, it is its confession. Each generation must appropriate it in order to confess the faith in the great consensus of the church of all ages, with the fathers and future generations of the faithful. Parents cannot will the faith to their children; rather, the Holy Spirit performs His work anew in the younger generation. So, too, the Confession of the church cannot simply be passed on from generation to generation. It must be appropriated in living faith. Can I make its condemnation of heresy my own if I have never seen this heresy? The fathers fought against rationalism. For the sake of the Sacrament of the Altar, they rejected the Union and sacrificed their home and earthly possessions. But that has now become a part of church history and is learned from books. Where is the Confession in the present day? How

---

10   Gottlieb Christoph Adolf von Harless (1806–79) came under the influence of neo-Lutheran F. A. G. Tholuck (1799–1877) while a student at Halle. As professor of exegesis at Erlangen (1833–45), he founded *Zeitschrift für Protestantismus und Kirche* (1838–86). He served as professor at Leipzig (1845–50), court preacher at Dresden (Saxony) (1850), and president of the Supreme Consistory of the Bavarian Church (1852). Harless was one of the most influential representatives of Lutheran orthodoxy of his generation. See *ODCC*, 736. MH

could it have happened that none of the great churches of the New World, which were born of the struggle against the Union, raised their voice to express criticism when this same Union recurred in 1933 and 1948 in the form of the German Evangelical Church [DEK] and the Evangelical Church in Germany [EKiD]? It was not merely Christian tact which wished to avoid interfering in the internal circumstances of other churches. It was a deficiency of understanding. It was not only a deficiency in understanding of the facts and the theological principles according to which these facts are judged, it was blindness, that terrible spiritual blindness which fails to see the reality of the church and which belongs to the terrible sickness of modern Christianity. And in this case it was a consequence of the great isolation and transmission of the Confession as a doctrinal tradition.

But with this American Lutheranism has fallen into a serious crisis. The sword with which the fathers once fought for the Lutheran faith appears to have become blunt. The Confession, which was for so long uncontested and which remains even today the theoretic basis of all these churches, appears in large measure to have lost its authority. There are great church bodies in which it is nothing more than a mere presupposition [*Arbeitshypothese*] by which a man identifies himself, just as in the Lutheran territorial churches of Europe. Thus American Lutheranism has fallen into a severe crisis, in which it stands in danger of abandoning that which was once its boast—in the sense of Gal. 6:14 and 2 Cor. 11:30. "Lutheran" has become a denominational designation like "Anglican" or "Methodist." Lutheranism, as in Swedish theology, is understood as one of the great families of Protestantism, one of the many expressions of the Christian religion. More and more it has been forgotten that what binds Lutheran Churches together is not familial similarity, not the common characteristics of a denomination, but rather the common Confession. It has been forgotten that there is properly speaking no "Lutheran Church," rather only a Church of the Unaltered Augsburg Confession. In a word: *the Lutheran Churches of America are on the verge of losing their character as confessional churches.*

3

This process, signs of which were already evident before the Second World War, came into play during the war. In recent years this process has led to open crisis. The crisis naturally revealed itself first where the confessional consciousness was weakest, in the United Lutheran Church. Since its founding in 1918, there had been a struggle between the orientation of the two synods which formed its largest component, the General Synod (Gettysburg) and the General Council (Mount Airy). During the time of President Knubel,[11] the conservative forces of the old General Council were still most influential in the leadership of the

---

11 Frederick Hermann Knubel (1870–1945) studied at Gettysburg Seminary and Leipzig. He served as the first president of the ULC (1918–44). Sasse met Knubel while studying at Hartford Seminary in 1926 (s.v. *Christian Cyclopedia*). MH

church. After he was gone, the liberalism of the General Synod, which had never been completely conquered, began to gain ground. It was a process which simply could not be stopped. Within twenty years one could find students from the ULC studying under the great Reformed faculties of the East, who had fled the narrowness of their home seminaries, or what they perceived as such. Some of the them left their church altogether; others were counseled by Reformed [theologians] to remain and await the time when their church would cast off the old confessionalism. Twenty-five years ago I once heard such an admonition from the mouth of an honorable, and in his own way very pious, president of Scottish origin, directed at the Lutheran students at his seminary. He was completely serious, and what he had to say was not in the least some church-political tactic. He was a man who knew that America needed Lutheranism.[12]

When one compares the demeanor of the delegates of the ULC at the World Conference for Faith and Order in Lausanne (1927) and Edinburgh (1937),[13]

Sasse wrote to F. W. Noack on May 9, 1968: "When in 1925/26 I spent a year of postgraduate studies at Hartford Conn[ecticut], I was at that time closely linked with Pres. Knubel of the ULC. It happened that students came from M[ount] Airy who could no longer stand that old-fashioned orthodoxy taught in their dogmatics class. The wise old pres[ident] of Hartford Seminary, Douglas McKenzie, sent them all back to their church. You go back to your church and go into its ministry. In thirty years time your church will be where we are now. He was a Congregationalist. He was right. What would the faithful confessor of the Lutheran faith Michael Reu in Dubuque, [Iowa,] what would Franz Pieper say about the changes that have taken place in their churches?" (Sasse–J. A. O. Preus Correspondence, Fort Wayne, IN). E. Theo. Bachmann many years later related to Ronald Feuerhahn more detail about Sasse's 1925 U.S. visit. Bachmann: "Well, there were three persons who came over in the year 1925, all of whom amounted considerably in the future of the Church. One was Peter Brunner, one was Hermann Sasse, and another Wilhelm Pauck [1901–81]." Feuerhahn: "Oh, they all three came at the same time?" Bachmann: "And went to different places. And Sasse really wondered whether there were any Lutherans at all in America since he landed at Hartford, Connecticut" (from a November 9, 1990, Feuerhahn interview with Bachmann; used with permission).

Sasse visited Bachmann while in the United States in 1948. "I shall go to Valparaiso and Chicago, where a former student of mine, Professor Bachmann, was to see me" (Sasse to Sieck, July 13, 1948; in the Harrison Collection). MH

12 The anecdote is recounted in the previous footnote. MH

13 On January 30, 1932, the Executive Committee of the Continental Committee of Faith and Order met in Geneva at the Hotel Richemond. (1) Sasse listed as present "representing the German Committee" (only five members present). (3) "The General Secretary [Brown] was instructed, in collaboration with Pastor Sasse, to issue invitations for the appointment of thirty representatives of the German Churches to attend the 1937 Conf. and help set it up" (Feuerhahn Chronology). Although the Nazi's prevented Sasse from attending Edinburgh, Hodgsen wanted both Barth's and Sasse's papers on the German Confessing Church published in English. Hodgsen explains to Prof. Wobbermin (April 14, 1936) his reason for printing these papers: "... it seems worth while to let our delegates in general know something of the extreme positions which they must be prepared to hear advocated when we meet at Edinburgh" (Feuerhahn Chronology). MH

then the development becomes clear. In Lausanne they were confessors of Lutheranism, who even distributed portions of the Lutheran Confessions which treated of the unity of the church. They confessed their Lutheran faith before the representatives of Christianity and did not practice altar fellowship with other confessions. In Edinburgh (1937) it was already completely different. Then came the great change of course which can be seen so clearly in the publications of the great publishing house of the ULC (Mühlenberg Press). One need only compare the old Lutheran dogmatics text of the older Jacobs with the new standard dogmatics text of this church (and apparently also other churches), the translation of [Gustaf] Aulén's [1879–1977] dogmatics, *The Faith of the Christian Church* [1948]. In this work of the theology of Lund, all dogmas of the church, from the *Apostolicum* to the confessions of the Reformation, vanish in the cloud of a subjective Christianity which is stuck deep in the theology of Schleiermacher and Ritschl, and in neo-Kantian philosophy. One need only compare the solid chapter on "The Miracle of Christmas" in the *Kirchlichen Dogmatic* of K. Barth (Bd. I, 2, pp. 187–221) with its clear confession of the virgin birth of the Lord, or also the brief but valuable treatment in Elert's dogmatics (*Der Christliche Glaube*, 2nd ed., pp. 378ff.) with the propositions in which Aulén, appealing to Schleiermacher, simply abolishes this dogma (p. 222). Note the "history of religions" dilettantism with which the church's dogma *Qui conceptus est de Spiritu Sancto, natus ex Maria virgine* ["who was conceived of the Holy Spirit, born of the Virgin Mary"] is viewed as "analogous to the widespread view of the ancient world regarding the origin of famous persons." The theological dilettantism with which this teaching based upon Holy Scripture is rejected as a "rationalistic theological explanation" is simply incredible.

But what is Holy Scripture for Aulén? What Luther or the Lutheran Confessions understand as scriptural proof is for Aulén legalistic misuse of Scripture. It is "legalism" when one asserts that a doctrine is Christian because of the fact that it is in the Bible. "It is this same legalism whether one appeals to verbal inspiration or the teaching of Jesus" (p. 83). So it is not then surprising that in this dogmatics the Lutheran doctrine of the Sacrament of the Altar—to mention only one critical doctrine—vanishes. That we receive the body and blood of the Lord is "a serious aberration, which stems from inherited problems and concepts" (p. 396). The meaning of the Supper is this:

> that Christ is effectively present with the one who is His, in the power of His Spirit, and so in the believer He realizes that fellowship with God which He has established with His word and gives "forgiveness of sins, life and salvation." The consecrated bread and the consecrated cup are the instruments which He has availed Himself of in this transaction. They point back to that which once occurred, and they portray the inner correspondence which obtains between the work once completed and that which continues. If a presence in the physical sense is spoken of, this indicates no higher grade of presence . . . . The spiritual presence is

for faith the highest form of presence, and in its unfathomable mystery it is the only "real," regenerating and life-giving presence. (pp. 397f.)

Now the Lutheran students of theology also in America, overwhelmed by the profound learning of the Swedish bishop, learn this doctrine of the Supper which stands somewhere between that of Zwingli and Calvin. And the consequences of this on the understanding of the church and Christian denominations [*Konfessionen*] are absolutely clear: "The denominations are the heterogeneous forms of the one ecumenical church, which has its origin in Christ and his apostles, and which bases itself upon the Word and the Sacrament" (p. 430).

These examples will suffice. Whoever has read the unfortunate study document of Section I of Hanover, "The Living Word in an Accountable Church [*verantwortungsbewussten Kirche*]," knows where the Swedish theology of Lund leads world Lutheranism. Of what use is all the study and understanding of Luther, for which we have the Swedish theologians to thank, if the faith of the Lutheran Church is lost? Here we do not wish to deal with the question of just what was false and wrong with modern Luther studies, in the north as much as in Germany, when it doesn't even mention absolutely basic doctrines of Luther. How was it that the great Karl Holl[14] himself could appropriate the judgment of Tholuck[15] that Calvin was the real disciple and successor of Luther, or that in Johann von Walther's [1876–1940] posthumously published lectures on "The Theology of Luther" (1940) he does not even refer to the doctrine of the Supper. We ask only: What will it mean for American Lutheranism that, with the breathtaking speed which characterizes the development of the American people, the old dogmatic inheritance is quickly given up? What consequences will this have for the life of the church and congregation if this theological development continues?

4

The clock of world history cannot be turned back, and the great developments of church history are irreversible. The romantic attempts of the VELKD in Germany to return the great, once Lutheran, territorial churches back to the Confession of its fathers failed as decisively as corresponding attempts in northern lands would. All these attempts live on the cultural-ecclesiastical fiction that the "churches" of today (in which a small if also very earnest remnant still confesses the faith of the fathers) may be identified with the churches which once accepted the *Augustana* and Book of Concord as the confession of their faith.

---

14 "My main teachers in Church history [at the University of Berlin] were Harnack and Holl" (Sasse, "Reminiscences of an Elderly Student," *Tangara* [Luther Seminary, Adelaide] 9 [1976]: 4–5). MH

15 Tholuck studied at Breslau and Berlin under J. A. W. Neander and Schleiermacher. A proponent of the union, he was a professor at Berlin and Halle (s.v. *Christian Cyclopedia*). MH

In America, too, the churches which have sacrificed the Lutheran Confession to a liberal theology and have joined the National Council of the Churches of Christ in the USA (the American EKiD) in order to there cultivate the famous "religion in which we all agree," such as the United Lutheran Church and the Augustana Church (of Swedish origin)—these churches will follow this chosen path to the bitter end. The question which must move us all is this: What will come of the genuine Lutherans who find themselves in these churches? And what will become of the churches which have hitherto been able to hold on to their Confession? What council can we give them based upon the experiences of the one church and the experiences from the history of Lutheranism in the last generation?

The first thing our American brothers have to learn from their own as well as our history is this: that the maintenance of the ecclesiastical Confession is not self-evident. A church lives not from the "faith of the fathers"—rather, from the faith of the present generation and its descendants. Therefore the Confession cannot simply be "tradition," and every church must examine itself on how much of its Confession is mere tradition and no longer the answer to the Gospel given in living faith. If this question is seriously posed, then it will become a question concerning life and death, and this directly for the most conservative churches, for whom their orthodoxy is self-evident. And we have in mind here not only the churches of the "middle," such as the American Lutheran Church (formerly Ohio and Iowa), the Evangelical Lutheran Church (the formerly Norwegian wing, whose right wing has remained independent and is a member of the Synodical Conference), churches in which men dream of a great Lutheran Church in America which would stretch from Missouri to the ULC. The churches of the Synodical Conference are also endangered, above all Missouri and Wisconsin.

We spoke of the Missouri Synod in an earlier letter, and there made the unchallenged assertion that the Lutheran Confessions, precisely because they are challenged by no one, no longer have the living significance they once had for the fathers.[16] All of American Lutheranism confesses the Lutheran Confessions— some more, some less emphatically. And so modern doctrinal statements have acquired a position of greater practical importance than the Confessions, which are *extra controversiam*. This is also true of all the churches on the right. They themselves see the danger that after they have given up the old ecclesiastical language—which was an unavoidable fate—they may be overrun by Reformed fundamentalism as much as the churches of the "left" by Reformed liberalism. They are aware of the great danger that the Lutheran Church in America will remain as an external organization, but in actuality become something quite different. The fate of old [Lutheran] orthodoxy, which vanished in one generation and degenerated into its very opposite, stands before their eyes as a warning for the church of all ages. For that which has happened once is repeated in the

---

16   See above, Letter 20, "Confession and Theology in the Missouri Synod," pp. 5–31. MH

history of the church, just as it is in the personal history of families and individuals. It has happened in the Reformed churches of America. Why should it not happen in the Lutheran churches?

For that which maintains pure doctrine among us is not our good intention to hold fast in all circumstances; it is not continued maintenance of the Confession as legally binding; it is not the scrupulous passing on of its content to the next generation; nor is it the exercise of doctrinal discipline. Rather, it is the miracle of divine mercy for which the church, just as every individual Christian, must pray day after day: "Lord, keep us steadfast in Your Word!" This, of course, does not mean that on our part there is nothing to be done to prevent this falling away. Where the Confession is carelessly abandoned, there the Lord does not perform the miracle of keeping the church steadfast in His Word.

Thus follows the practical demand that the Lutheran Confession, where it is in danger of becoming an "incontestable" inheritance, is afforded high honor, but in practice is no longer in use and no longer viewed as having any essential significance for the life of the church. Our American brothers in the faith have not yet had to experience what we were forced to live through in the years of the church struggle. For it was then that the old words of the Confession, first Article XXVIII of the *Augustana* and Article X of the *Formula of Concord*, again came to life for us and the fathers began to speak to us once again. Their suffering and struggles for the sake of the church became more for us than mere historical recollections. How significant was it then, that we suddenly were called out of the great isolation in which most of us stood, into the great fellowship of the "We believe, teach and confess" of the confessing church of all ages! The Confession ceased to be a mere number of [isolated] dogmatic assertions [*Summa von dogmatischen Aussagen*], appropriated with greater or lesser difficulty. Rather, it became once again the sum total of the Holy Scriptures [*Summa der Heiligen Schrift*], the joyous "Yes!" of the church to the Gospel, the praise of God: *Te Deum laudamus, te Dominum confitemur.*

Have I been deceived, or is it true that I fail to see this praise when our American brothers speak of confession? Am I mistaken if I find that their theology lacks the great joy which is part and parcel of all genuine theology? For the lowly *theologia viatorum* of this life is bound together with that which the old liturgies of the Eastern church called the "theology which is never silent" (*asigetoi theologiai*), later the word *doxologiai* was used of the angels and archangels, the cherubim and seraphim, the *Sanctus*, which is sung in heaven. Is not perhaps the flight away from the dogmatic and into the liturgy, and indeed away from Lutheran dogmatics into an un-Lutheran, half-Anglican and half-[Roman] Catholic theology (which has happened in Germany in the Berneuchen Movement), also the fate of American Lutheranism? And is it not proof of this that the moment the Lutheran dogma of the Supper has been given up, the cries for the eucharistic prayer, sacrifice, and even the priesthood become audible? Entire Lutheran churches appear to have introduced the eucharistic prayer with a slightly veiled concept of sacrifice at the same time that the limitations on access to the altar, established by the Galesburg Rule, began to fall away. No church government, no theological faculty appears to protest in the churches affected by these changes. The solitary voices of this or that pastor or professor are the only thing heard. But they are fading away unnoticed, just as in the Lutheran churches of Europe. It is truly high time that what remains of a true confessing church in America again lets itself be heard.

5

One of the worst failings which has occurred in American Lutheranism was that the training of Lutheran theologians did not begin promptly. A. R. Wentz [1883–1976] in *The Lutheran Church in American History* (2nd ed., pp. 139ff.) describes the unsuccessful attempts of the American Lutherans since [Henry Melchior] Mühlenberg [1711–87] to establish an institution for training future pastors. Congregations did not have, or believed they did not have, money for this purpose. We hear of one pastor who trained no fewer than twenty-two pastors, of others who trained their own sons, and of others who trained four or five. It was only after some eighty years of unsuccessful attempts that the first seminary was begun in Gettysburg. It is remarkable how the same precedent has been repeated in our own day. In addition to the training of pastors, every great church needs to train teachers of theology as well. Even in Bolshevik Russia it was possible to establish a theological academy above the diocesan seminaries. But a great church such as the United Lutheran Church has until today not been able to accomplish this. It leaves it to its districts to support its smaller or also few larger seminaries for training future pastors. They are quite satisfied to send those young theologians who would go on to a higher level of education to one of the great Reformed faculties (Union Seminary in New York, Yale, Princeton, Chicago). And even if they return as Lutherans, which is not always the case, they still have not learned what an advancing young theologian in such circumstances should have learned: a deeper knowledge of Luther and Lutheran dogmatics, an exegetical method which is defined by the Lutheran understanding of the Word of God, a deeper knowledge of the history of the one church, and a practical theology which knows what Lutheran preaching is. "I am thankful that I am only a New Testament man," a professor of a well-known Lutheran seminary said to me, "since the entire field of Lutheran dogmatics does not interest me." When one considers that Martin Luther held the exegetical chair for his entire life, that the Lutheran Church was born out of study of the Scriptures, then the consequence of the following viewpoint becomes clear (and I have heard the same thing in various churches of the East and West): We want to develop pastors, not professors! As though there could still be Lutheran pastors even if there were no longer Lutheran professors. Today the "liberal" Lutheran churches appear to be satisfied to solve this problem by sending advanced students to Europe for a period of study. But preparation to teach theology takes years of fundamental development! Or they look to the alone-saving Lutheran World Federation, which solves all problems in its Theologian Commission [*Theologen=kommission*]. [After all], America is no haven for serious theological study. This must come from Europe (behold Aulén). But this is not true. America also has Luther studies—at Yale and Chicago with the Reformed! America also has patristic studies, but with the [Roman] Catholics and Anglicans. In the area of American systematic theology, it appears that Aristotle is about to be overcome with Kant, just at the point in time in which not only Kant's metaphysics has been shattered, but also his theory of knowledge [*Erkenntnistheorie*] has been overturned by modern mathematics and physics, which is pulverizing everything. That Reformed "neoorthodoxy" (which could just as easily be called "neoliberalism") has turned to [Sören] Kierkegaard [1813–55] has not improved the situation at all.[17]

The American Lutherans, perhaps because they do not study church history, have not yet learned that theologies cannot be exported. At the time of the first ecumenical councils there existed a blossoming theology in the Syrian and Greek languages. Over against them the theology of the Latins, before Augustine, was weak. The West at that time—as always—had "more important matters to deal with." Its problems had to do with the construction of a church and a church law which could survive the fall of Rome. How easy it would have been to have left theology to the Greeks and to translate their work into Latin. But then the Latin church would not have been able to do the work it did. Translated theology can never compensate for a permanent indigenous theology. Instead of exporting books, the European churches should have sent Europe's theologians into the world, who could have helped the American brothers in the faith to construct their own theology. There are theological questions which can only be solved in America, for example, all the questions which deal with the congregation. The man in Europe (except for those in the free churches) does not know what distinguishes a congregation from a parish, simply because there has been no experience [which has brought this issue to the fore]. This is one of the limitations of our great Lutheran fathers in Germany of the nineteenth century, and it is just as much the case in the northern churches. Just as the canonical law of the Roman Church does not know of the concept of the congregation— nor even the term—so the European continent, whose ecclesiastical structure stems from the Middle Ages, knows nothing of the congregation—rather, only the parish. What Luther wrote on this matter out of his deep understanding of the New Testament has never been realized in our churches in the Old World, and only partly so in the New World. This is only one example of the fact that an

---

17 A reference to Jaroslav Pelikan, *From Luther to Kierkegaard: A Study in the History of Theology* (St. Louis: Concordia, 1950). MH

indigenous American Lutheran theology would find enough problems to occupy the most capable of all of world Lutheranism.

Among the Lutheran Churches of America, as far as I can tell, there is only one which has seen the need for an independent American Lutheran theology. That is the Missouri Synod. By remarkable circumstance there were more studied pastors, and more academicians in general, among the immigrants from Saxony who came to St. Louis than in other groups of immigrants. They immediately saw the need for a school. Whereas the Lutherans in more cultivated Pennsylvania had to wait eighty years, just a few months after their arrival in "the wild West" the Saxon Lutherans established the institution [1839] which would later move to St. Louis and be named "Concordia Seminary." The significance of the founding of this institution for Lutheranism in America and the world can scarcely be overrated. Perhaps American Lutheranism would have long ago been swallowed up by Reformed denominations had not Missouri and Concordia Seminary stood guard, often as an irksome monitor. On the other hand, the unavoidable isolation in which the theology of Missouri arose influenced its character.

It is not so much the "narrowness" which Missouri has often been accused of which has defined its theology. Ferdinand Walther was not "narrow"—in any case, no more narrow than other Lutheran theologians of his day. What gave form to the theology of Missouri is old orthodoxy and its understanding of Luther. Other forms of Lutheranism were dependent upon a more pietistic understanding of the Reformation, be it the Halle Pietism of the eighteenth century or the Pietism of the period of awakening, which also influenced confessional Lutheranism. The harshness and rigidity for which Missouri has often been criticized, and from which modern Missouri may free itself, are explained in part by its inheritance of orthodoxy and in part by the necessity of establishing a boundary over against a unionistic Lutheranism. These, however, are all more ethical than dogmatic marks of Missouri, by which we, under the category of "ethos," come to understand the behavior of the Christian or the church on particular questions. It is not so, as many churches believe, that the behavior of Missouri in certain practical questions, such as prayer fellowship, is inferior and unethical. On the contrary, narrow-mindedness can often be ethically more justifiable than liberality. We Lutherans should be guarded from these reciprocal condemnations of churches by the example and warnings of Luther. "My doctrine is the main thing; that is what I boast about. . . . The other part, my life and person, I know that it is for the most part sinful and nothing to boast about" (WA 23:29.5ff.). "Insofar as my person and life is concerned, I will humble myself before everyone" (WA 23:33), said Luther to the king of England.[18] He knew that he was sinner, just as much as the pope and Henry VIII [r. 1509–47]. Lutheran

---

18 *Auf des Königs zu England Lästerschrift Titel, M. Luthers Antwort* (1527), Aland 194. MH

Churches should never forget this when they conscientiously separate from one another for the sake of doctrine. In this matter there has been sin on all sides, and this includes the opponents of Missouri who think they must criticize, no less than the church they criticize.

What really characterizes the dogmatic theology of Missouri should not be sought in this sphere. It lies in the inheritance of the old orthodoxy, which in a remarkable way was blind to history, in a way similar to the scholastics of the Middle Ages.[19] The Lutherans of the period of orthodoxy were the continuation of the scholastics of the Middle Ages. Luther had not only a comparatively thoroughgoing knowledge of church history, but above all a deep understanding of history in general. For him the history of the world was the struggle between God and the devil, between Christ and the Antichrist, a drama which spanned the ages and hastened toward its end, the blessed Last Day. His view of history was defined by biblical eschatology. This eschatology lost its authority in the age of orthodoxy, and with it dwindled also Luther's view of history. In order to render a correct opinion, one must consider that the seventeenth century (in hindsight, perhaps the most learned of the modern era) distributed its tasks among the various nations. The great historical investigation began at that time in French Catholicism, biblical scholarship among the Reformed, while the Lutheran world created the edifice of orthodox dogmatics. This dogmatics was, for necessary reasons, one-sided. Aristotelian philosophy was used for assistance without a historical understanding of how consequential it had been for the Middle Ages.

Also the great knowledge of patristics, which appears at first to speak in the dogmaticians of the Middle Ages and the period of orthodoxy, upon closer inspection shows itself to be the transmission of tradition, created by the great assemblage of citations which were passed on from generation to generation, and later from church to church. The age of orthodoxy did not and could not possess a real and thorough knowledge of the fathers. But what is worse is that the study of Scripture was also influenced by this historical shortsightedness. The theologians of the period of orthodoxy possessed a great knowledge of the Bible. They literally lived in the Bible. What they unfortunately lacked was the necessary historical perspective which Luther possessed, as his prefaces [to the biblical books] demonstrate. The orthodox view of Scripture and sacred history lacked the deep dimension of historical perspective. All images were flat, as

---

19 A somewhat remarkable statement, given the fact that Flacius—often criticized by Sasse as the proto-orthodox theologian—happens to be the father of historiography via his great *Magdeburg Centuries*. See Oliver Olson's magisterial *Matthias Flacius and the Survival of Luther's Reform* (Wiesbaden: Harrassowitz, 2002), 256: "From 1559–1574, the *Ecclesiastica Historia* of Matthias Flacius, called 'the *Magdeburg Centuries*,' the first comprehensive history of the church in more than a millennium." Page 257: "After the appearance of the *Centuries*, church history could no longer be written in either ecclesiastical camp without documentation." On Protestant church history, Harnack writes: "Flacius being its father" (p. 258). MH

it were, and not viewed stereoscopically. So the Bible, which is really a whole library, became a single book. It was no longer read without chapter and verse interruptions [*nicht mehr in fortlaufendendem Druck*], as was the old Luther Bible, but chopped up into "passages" and "verses." It became a collection of *dicta probantia*, comparable to the collections of the sentences of the fathers. The later misuse of the Scriptures by liberal theology and an untheological, faithless criticism, intent on treating the Scriptures historically, cannot justify the neglect of the genuine history presented in the Holy Scriptures themselves. At the end of the age of orthodoxy the Lutherans left the discovery of "biblical theology" to the Reformed.[20] This, then, worked itself out in the nineteenth century in the theology of Missouri.

It was absolutely correct when Missouri's theologians protested against the misuse of the concept "the entirety of Scripture" by many theologians, which limited the authority of the individual words of Scripture and even eliminated that authority altogether. But it was false when the fact was overlooked that there is in fact an "entirety of Scripture." The doctrine of the church, for instance, is contained in each and every word which speaks of the church. But to understand the fullness of the scriptural doctrine one must not only assemble all such individual passages and draw from every one of them the doctrine therein embedded. One must also see what they altogether, and the Bible as an entirety, have to say regarding the people of God, the Body of Christ, the temple of the Holy Spirit. Does there perhaps lie here, in the false conservation of old methods, the reason why world Lutheranism has thus far awaited in vain for that Lutheran church, which desires to be the church of Holy Scripture more than other churches and whom we have to thank that the doctrine of the inspiration of Scripture has not yet been lost in Lutheranism, to give us a great, new exegetical theology which is equal in this area to the accomplishments of the Reformed Churches? We must never forget that Lutheran theology arose from the exegesis of Holy Scripture. It lives by the correct understanding of Scripture. It dies when it is no longer a living explication of Scripture.

A series of other questions arise regarding related matters. Why, for instance, does Lutheran theology today no longer play the role in the life of the church which it did in the nineteenth century? Men involved in church government— one thinks of Harless, Kliefoth, Vilmar, Walther—were still learned theologians. Since then this has become a luxury which the modern church leader can no longer realize. But there is one thing we theologians must never forget. We do not exist to justify every move of a church government after the fact. We do not exist to provide every church government which comes along with the famous

---

20 A remarkable assertion given Abraham Calov's monumental and insightful commentary on the entire Bible, *Biblia Illustrata*; Flacius's groundbreaking hermeneutics, *Clavis Scripturae* (Olson, *Flacius and the Survival of Luther's Reform*, 55); or Johann Gerhard's *Patrologia* and *Loci*. MH

theology "with which a person can get started at something" (Dibelius).[21] In our office, wherever it may be, we bear the responsibility for maintaining the Lutheran church and her doctrine. But we can only do this if we confess this doctrine ourselves. May God grant us all the strength and fortitude for such confessing, without which no true theology exists.

༄

I greet you in the bond of the faith,

Your
Hermann Sasse

---

21   Otto Dibelius, bishop of Berlin and consistent supporter of the Union, is a persistent target for Sasse's jibes. MH

Historical Context

As I write this, not forty-eight hours ago (September 26, 2013) I was informed that the world's largest Lutheran Church, the Mekane Jesus of Ethiopia (6.2 million members) has formally requested fellowship discussions with the LCMS. It strikes me that precisely what Sasse was suggesting sixty years ago in his letter to Herman Preus and in Letter 32, "Current Lutheran Doctrinal Discussions," is coming to pass with increasing intensity. The discussions with Mekane Jesus will not be what Sasse quips ails the LWF. "This universal medication for the illnesses of the church which can no longer profess a common confession magno consensus is the 'theological discussion.'" When Sasse wrote, Missouri was on the precipice of its fascination with Bultmann's "demythologization" of Scripture, which Sasse rightly recognized (having long known Bultmann) as the "de-dogmatization" of Lutheranism. Sasse states wryly: "However the theological division of the LWF and its work may form themselves, it will be the great task of those still a part of the great 'we believe, teach, and confess' of the Lutheran Confessions to begin for their part and among their acquaintances doctrinal discussion, which must happen between Lutherans who don't want to watch with inaction as the great heritage of the Lutheran teaching which is still left in the world is babbled apart by pseudo-intellectuals. Therefore, come together, brothers in the office, who still have fellowship with others in the magnus consensus of the Lutheran Confession." MH

December 12, 1954[1]

H. Sasse
41 Buxton Street
North Adelaide, South Australia

Dear Doctor [Herman A.] Preus,

. . . Our old churches in Europe have to learn so much from their sister and daughter churches in America, especially in the field of congregational life. Otherwise we are all in the same hospital, the churches in the New as in the Old World. God bless your efforts concerning the maintenance of the Lutheran Confession. These days I shall write also to our common friend Leiv Aalen, who is, I understand, the successor of Prof. Hallesby. I am reading his great book on Zinzendorf [1700–1760] slowly, though with great interest. I think it

---

1   Copy in Harrison Collection. MH

is a mature work and will be very helpful to solve the theological problem of Lutheranism and Pietism which is so important for the Christian people in Norway. Some weeks ago I had to write an opinion on what in Norway is called *verdensrettferdiggjorelsen* for some delegates to the last meeting of the Synodical Conference (I meant the "latest" and hope not the "last") and found Aalen's book very helpful. In reading the *Verhandlungen* of 1872, I came across the name Preus. My idea is that the confessional Lutherans of all churches should form a free theological conference to study anew the great differences and crucial questions still dividing us. We feel the impact of modernism on our young generation very much. Rejection of error is not enough. What we need is a positive presentation of the Lutheran doctrine. This was the reason I wrote, under great difficulties, a book on the Lord's Supper, the manuscript of which is now in the hands of Augsburg Publishing House . . . .

Yours fraternally in *communione fidei*,
Hermann Sasse

thirty-two

Current Lutheran Doctrinal Discussions

TRANSLATED BY ANDREW SMITH

Michaelmas 1953[1]

Prof. D. Theol. Hermann Sasse
41 Buxton Street
North Adelaide, South Australia

Dear Brothers in the Office!

I must test your patience by today continuing in a certain way that which we discussed in the previous letter. But the question of the current status and the future of Lutheran theology is of such practical significance for the existence of our church—indeed, for the life of each of our individual congregations—that even the pastor in the office can now no longer afford to leave the future of Lutheran theology to the wisdom or folly of the teaching faculties and the church governments. At the beginning of this century, those in the pastoral office or in the congregation didn't need to worry themselves about such things, or at least only in exceptional cases, that is, when professors who were finally strangers to the church got carried away [with their ideas] in Germany and elsewhere. Then it could happen that the congregations not only observed but also did something. The theological school at Bethel (1905) and the Congregational Teaching Faculty at Oslo (1908) are, each in its own way, monuments of an awakening sense of responsibility on the part of the Christian congregation about the future of theology. The great change in theology which was introduced by Barth's commentary on Romans (1919) was in large part a revolution of the

1   *BLP* 32: *Lutherisches Lehrgespräch heute* (North Adelaide, September 1953). The original was published in *LuBl* 5, no. 33 (November 1953): 39–53. Huss number 303. MH

pastors against the strictly academic theologians—the pastors, who again took seriously their task of preaching the Word of God, against the representatives of a theology which was no longer capable of telling them what the Word of God actually is. Still today, when the torrent of Barthian theology has long since molded itself into a wide stream, one hears the preacher in Barth's powerful dogmatics, as one uniformly hears the shrewd schoolmaster in the dogmatics of his former comrade [Emil] Brunner. In the years of the church struggle, church and theology then appeared to find each other again, in the face of the common enemy. But this process was not limited to the countries which, like Germany and Norway, had to fight this battle in complete seriousness. One can say of the whole of theology in the Protestant world that it became more churchly. The concept of an "unchurchly theology," coined at the turn of the century by the church historian Gustav Krüger[2] (1862–1940) in Giessen to express the ideal of an academic discipline which follows only its own rules, is now seldom still represented, even in liberal America. There the great turning toward the church was detectable in the years before World War II. So, at first glance, everything seems then to be in order. The liberalism of the turn of the century seems everywhere to have been conquered, and a place has been made for a neoorthodoxy. Church and theology seem to have finally found each other again. And so it seems as if pastors and congregations can again cast off concerns about theology.

And yet, all of that merely seems to be so. In reality, the concerns of those who know the reality of the church and the reality of its theology have only grown larger. Certainly, we want to acknowledge thankfully all that the first half of this century brought in actual church renewal and in actual new theological knowledge, especially in the significant areas of language and the theology of the Holy Scripture, the history of the earliest church, especially its Divine Service, and the research into the Reformation. One needs only thereby to mention the name of Rudolf Bultmann[3] to indicate that the theology of liberalism is not dead, but rather lives on in a modern form. What one today calls the "demythologizing" of the New Testament is, in truth, the de-dogmatizing of the church.[4] The great hope, that the rediscovery of the Reformation among the Lutherans and the Reformed would lead to a new understanding of the church's Confession was not realized, not even in the church struggle, which originally began as a struggle about the Confession. The word "confessionalism" is today still burdened with the same odium as [it had] fifty years ago, perhaps indeed still more, since

---

2 A church historian in Bermen, Krüger taught at Giessen. See *RGG³* 4:82. MH

3 Rudolf Bultmann (1884–1976), professor at Breslau (1916), at Giessen (1920), and at Marburg (1921–51), was a student of Johann Gunkel (1862–1932), J. Weiss, and W. Heitmüller and a follower of the *Religionsgeschichtliche Schule*. Bultmann carried their history-of-religions method (form criticism) to the point at which any historical value in the Gospels was called radically into question. See *ODCC*, 250. MH

4 See Sasse, "Flight from Dogma: Remarks on Bultmann's 'Demythologization' of the New Testament" (1942), in *Lonely Way* 2:93–116. MH

Karl Barth and Alfred Rosenberg, in this case unanimously, have fought against confessionalism. Since the overwhelming majority of the Reformed surrendered the confession of the Reformation already in the nineteenth century, since the Anglicans silently nullified the *Thirty-Nine Articles*, Lutheranism with its loyalty to the Confession was a lonely island in the ocean of the Protestant world. One portion [of it] after another was torn away by the unions of the previous century. Today, the new biblicist theology of Adolf Schlatter's (1852–1938)[5] group, the Christian Student Movement, modern world missionary [movements], and the Ecumenical Movement are flooding the rest of the Lutheran churches. There can be no sense in fooling oneself away from the seriousness of the situation by looking at that which still remains of self-conscious Lutheranism, and by discovering, where possible, with the VELKD and the LWF that Lutheranism is even again on the upswing. The question arises, What kind of a Lutheranism is it which is on the organizational and ecclesio-political upswing? The question arises whether the pastors who remain loyal to the Confessions—and there are some of these in all segments of the Lutheran church—even know what kind of a life-and-death struggle stands before the Lutheran church, and what kind of sacrificial readiness is required to survive this battle? It is easier to confess one's faith in front of a worldly dictator than in front of the important church leaders who don't know whither they lead their churches. And yet all for whom the retention of the Lutheran confessional Church is a matter dear to the heart must now step forward out of their self-restraint and collect themselves into a front, a front which will perhaps go [right through the middle of] all existing Lutheran churches. For the predicament of the Lutheran Church is the common predicament of all churches which still dare to profess the Augsburg Confession. It is not the case as if there were healthy and sick Lutheran churches, and as if the one, perhaps the one of Uelzen, could help the other, perhaps the one from Hanover. Certainly it may make a big difference whether the course of the disease is further or less progressed. The possibility or impossibility of recovery may depend upon that. But we all lie in the same hospital, and we all need the same Physician.

1

As an illustration, let me cite a few sentences which come from a document, of itself insignificant and studied by nobody, which two doctors of theology from

---

5   In 1898 Adolf Schlatter became professor of New Testament at Tübingen. Although not a conservative in the traditional sense, in his investigations of the New Testament and history he more often than not sided with the tradition (e.g., the priority of Matthew's Gospel). See *RGG*[3] 5:1420. Both Adolf and Theodore Schlatter had signed the Bethel Confession in 1933 along with Sasse and some twenty-five others. See Guy Christopher Carter, *Confession at Bethel, August 1933—Enduring Witness: The Formation, Revision and Significance of the First Full Theological Confession of the Evangelical Church Struggle in Nazi Germany* (PhD dissertation, Marquette University, 1987; published Ann Arbor: University of Michigan Press). MH

the VELKD composed to make the LWF palatable to us Australian Lutherans. Regarding the criticisms leveled in Hanover and regarding the refusal of many Lutherans to join the LWF, to which many churches which are only nominally Lutheran and some of them not even that belong, it reads:

> Let's consider the theoretical case in which a complete convention had come together in Hanover of men in [full] theological agreement (which, with a lot of organizational talent, perhaps would not entirely have been impossible). They would have, according to the wish of many friends and critics of the LWF, produced and promulgated an authoritative and "binding" Lutheran dogma for the twentieth century. They would have also thereby, according to the wishes of the critics, not forgotten to hurl powerful condemnations against the heretics of our day. Finally, they would have chosen an executive committee of men whose Lutheran orthodoxy nobody could doubt, and the committee would lead the further work of the LWF unflinchingly and strictly according to the Confession—everything would have really been very, very pretty—*but* would thereby the terrible plight of doctrinal disintegration and inner conflict, in which the churches who belong to the LWF and are represented there sadly and indisputably find themselves (and not only them), *be gone all at once*? Would they [rather] thereby merely be banned?—Would such an "imposing" constitution or portrayal of such a "Lutheran world-church," in reality not there at all, not be a horrid lie? Would that not be wicked unionism, because it would be done "as if" the churches who belong to the LWF had spoken and acted, which would have been in reality not the case?—Every Lutheran thanks God that such a presentation of anti-Christian *theologia gloria* doesn't happen, especially because he suffers greatly from the predicament of doctrinal dissent between our churches, because it is his bleeding wound that we cannot yet have church fellowship among ourselves, because he wrestles, prays, and works toward this: that God in His time may again grant us consensus.

We don't want to pursue the question here where the *theologia gloria* actually celebrated its victory—in Hanover or in Uelzen; what was "unionism," the pontifical office in Hanover or the simple celebration of the Lord's Supper in Uelzen, where only those went to the Lord's Table who profess without reservation the eucharistic doctrine of the Small Catechism and the other Lutheran Confessions. We also don't want to ask whether there is a more horrid lie than the LWF's bold assertion that the Communion which stood in its convention's agenda was not at all its affair, but rather a matter of the Hanover territorial church. These and other questions don't interest us here. What concerns us here is the total misunderstanding of the Lutheran Confession. There was once an era in Germany in which every student of theology learned that in the Lutheran Church no synod has the power to produce and promulgate an "authoritative and 'binding' Lutheran dogma for the twentieth century." Roman and Reformed synods can do that; Hans Asmussen and his synod at Barmen tried to do it. But, praise God, in the Lutheran Church the proposition is still valid: "The Word of God shall initiate articles of faith, and otherwise nobody, not even an angel" (SA II II 15; Müller, p. 303; Tappert, p. 295).

None of our confessional documents was issued by a synod. They became binding dogma through this: the Christian congregation and the spiritual office *received* them, that is, recognized and confessed them as the true teaching of the church because they found that this is the true teaching of the Holy Scripture. Therefore it could never be the task of a convention of orthodox Christians or theologians to promulgate a new dogma. It could be that the church of today [must] respond to new questions, with which the sixteenth century was unacquainted. Then a synod or other convention could put forth propositions. But it remains the task of the congregation to accept these propositions as an extension of the Confession with the great consensus of "we believe, teach, and confess" *because* they express nothing but the doctrine of the Scripture. What a convention, as it was theoretically constructed by the two theologians of the VELKD, could and must do, however, would be to decisively protest against the falling away from the Confession of the Reformation and against the misuse of this Confession. How did it actually happen that the consensus between the Lutheran churches has been lost, [a situation] which we grieve no less than the men of the VELKD? How was it possible that not only this or that theologian, such as the harmless Gustav Stählin, who was entirely undeservingly made into a scapegoat in Hanover, has lost the Lutheran eucharistic doctrine, but rather the overwhelming majority of the members of the Lutheran [theology] departments [in universities and seminaries] and ecclesiastical leaders in Europe? Here, apparently, a falling away from the Confession has happened, conditioned by means of great changes in intellectual history, but still really a falling away. Will this falling away be cured by means of our declaring that the question of the Holy Communion is now an open question, about which we will continue to discuss until the great miracle occurs "that God in His time" may "again give us consensus"? Where is it written in the Holy Scripture that we should continue to discuss with heretics until God converts them by means of a miracle? But it is heresy, the authors of the memorandum for the antipodes will agree in this, to deny the real presence taught in the catechism. I can and should search out the erring brother with all love. I may not—this we are supposed to have learned from Father Luther, if we did not already know it from the words of the Lord about the Pharisees—raise myself above him. He may be a better Christian than [I] in the eyes of God. But I may not tolerate his false teaching. I must struggle against it with the only weapon which is there [for such situations]: the Word of God and the confession of faith in this Word. If all of that does not help, then I must proceed according to the warning of the apostle (2 John 10 and Titus 3:10ff.).

2

But, one will object, why use such a blunt instrument such as Titus 3 right away when we're dealing with differences of opinion between Lutherans? One doesn't call the police right away when a family quarrel breaks out, and we are, after all, one big family, the family of the Lutheran churches of the world. We have already, in an earlier letter, criticized this untheological concept of "families" determined by confession, and can here only once again make clear that it is justified neither by the Scriptures nor by the Confession. The *consensus de doctrina evangelii et de administratione sacramentorum* ["the consensus concerning the doctrine of the Gospel and the administration of the Sacraments"] is something different than a family relationship. It is also not to be understood why we should have a right to take error less seriously in the case of Lutherans than in the case of other people. On Judgment Day we will probably not be asked whether we were Lutherans or Reformed, but rather if we have believed in the Word of God. Even Luther never interested himself in whether people called themselves Lutheran, and our confessional documents do not contain the phrase "Lutheran Church." "Our reformed churches" ([FC] SD, Summary, Rule, and Norm 3; Müller, p. 569; Tappert, p. 504), the "pure evangelical churches" (op. cit., Introduction 6; Müller, p. 566) are the churches which do not more or less honor the Unaltered Augsburg Confession, but rather which confess it wholeheartedly and without reservation, not because it was prepared by our theologians, but rather because it was taken out of God's Word and is well and firmly founded therein (FC SD Summary, Rule, and Norm 5; Müller, p. 569, Tappert, p. 504).

It seems today that a modern concept, arising from the nineteenth century, of the "Lutheran" Church has made itself felt, which has nothing to do with theology but has all the more to do with ecclesiastical politics. It is everywhere present where one declares a church to be Lutheran in which the "Confession" is valid *de jure* without regard to that which pastors, congregations, and ecclesiastical governments believe and confess. It is to be hoped that the nonsensical distinction between a *de jure* and a *de facto* Lutheranism will disappear out of theological discussion, because it is theologically untenable. Either I am a Lutheran, or I am not. Either a church is Lutheran, or it is not. It does not matter that a church such as the one of Hamburg, where out of 1,300,000 nominal members only 30,000 still go to church, maintains about the remaining 1,270,000 that they are members of the Lutheran Church and must accordingly be represented with the corresponding number of delegates in the LWF. Nobody doubts that there are still loyal Lutherans and accordingly Lutheran churches, even in Hamburg. But this is not identical with the masses, whom, after their confirmation, nobody has ever seen in the church again. The same is true of other churches which are still *de jure* Lutheran, but where the Lutheran Christians are lonely little groups, like the stalwarts of the Brethren church in Braunschweig. Should the LWF not finally stop with this soul mathematics, in which numbers are added, numbers which belong to very different systems and which are therefore not at all comparable? Would not the ecclesiastical statistics be much more truthful if one would measure the size of churches by the number of their pastors and congregations? But if we set aside this peculiar territorial system, which has maintained itself until our time, what do we understand to be a Lutheran Church? Really, a church in which one teaches according to the Augsburg Confession and in which, if that does not happen, [the people who have] the jobs, who are responsible to God, work to see that evangelical doctrinal discipline is used, which protects the Christian congregation from false teaching.

It is here, it seems to me, that the deepest woe of contemporary Lutheranism is located. It has found, exactly as the Reformed and Anglican churches, *false teaching in its very own midst.* The territorial churches of Bavaria and Hanover cannot do anything serious at all when their future servants are trained in an un-Lutheran theology. Which territorial bishop can even merely call to account a pastor for preaching the open heresy which he learned in the [courses taught by the theological] faculty [at the university] or [in] the ecclesiastical college of his [own] church? We state this without any resentment. It cannot be otherwise whereby, however, those responsible are not alleviated of their guilt. I once drew upon myself the destructive anger of an honored man in Basel when I asked him why he could tolerate in the church in Basel the same heresy which was intolerable for him in Germany.[6] So it is in territorial churches. What can the church of Denmark do when a theology professor denies eternal life? What can the church of Norway do when a bishop reprimands an honorable professor who dared to say on the radio that there is a hell? What can the Church of Sweden do when its bishops do away with the *condemnationes* of the Augsburg Confession, that is, with an integral part of the Confession? One must consider the entire tragedy of modern Protestantism, of which Lutheranism also has its share, one must have experienced the entire pain of this tragedy in one's own body to understand the situation of our church in the world. Then one will not be placated by the cheap comfort [when some people suppose that] everything will fall into place by itself, that the "collapse into Lutheranism" is entirely unmistakable, and that Christ is still the Lord of His church and will lead it into all truth. To this August Vilmar (1800–68) already gave an answer more than one hundred years ago when he said to the sleeping church of his time:

> Even the lamp of your congregation will be bumped away from its place, as once the lamp of the congregation at Ephesus. For with the general, vague, and silly hopes of foolish nominal Christians and newcomers we cannot comfort ourselves: "Christendom won't really disappear!" The Body of the Lord, His congregation, is founded only upon the office which preaches atonement and forgives sins in the name of the Lord, it is founded only upon loyal confession and living witness, only upon the living members. If the office of the Word, the Sacraments, and the Keys

---

6   Sasse probably refers to Karl Barth, his nemesis at Barmen. MH

is weak, has become worldly, or has even been discarded; if the Confession is an empty profession of words; if the witness has died out; if the members are dead—then the congregation of the Lord will die, too, in its temporal appearance, just as He allowed that those congregations in the East, which were really His, too, congregations of the Lord, to die at the hands of Mohammed and his Islam for the sake of their halfheartedness and self-satisfaction. [*Zur neuesten Kulturgeschichte Deutschlands*, vol. II, p. 47]

No, the church cannot live without confessing the truth, and there is no serious confession of truth without the rejection of error. What would have become of the church of the apostles if it had tolerated the Gnostics, who did believe in Christ, in the hope that the truth would prevail by itself! What would there be of Lutheran faith today in the world if Luther had extended the hand of fellowship to Zwingli and had restrained the Lutheran Confessions from the rejection of heresy?

3

But now one seems to have finally found a process by which the church, at least the Lutheran Church, can painlessly get rid of heresy, and without the surgeries of earlier times. This universal medication for the illnesses of the church which can no longer profess a common confession *magno consensus* ["with great unanimity"] is *the "theological discussion"* as organized by the "theological division of the LWF." Dr. Vilmos Vajta [1918–98], a young theologian of Hungarian heritage, who received his training in Lund and is a docent there, is the director of this division. What he has programmatically written about the tasks of the new division is apparently more than his personal opinion. Otherwise it would not have been mentioned as an official document in the answer of the executive committee to the United Evangelical Lutheran Church in Australia and distributed from Geneva. The German reader finds it in no. 14 of the *Evang.=Luth.=Kirchenzeitung* (July 15, 1953), pp. 209–14.

> After many years of Lutheran cooperation in practical areas, the time seems to have arrived to begin a *conversation* between the Lutherans in the entire world in the midpoint of the Christian faith, *in order to deepen and strengthen the community of Lutheran churches in the unity of the Christian faith in this way.*[7]

The new division is supposed to be an "organ for theological cooperation of world Lutheranism." Such an organ is, of itself, to be happily greeted—for one reason, because the assurance is given, comforting both us and the pope, "that the theological division cannot be, will not be, and does not want to be a Lutheran Vatican, which as the highest authority assigns theological tasks to theologians or presents [final] answers."

---

7   Translator's emphasis. MH

The plan amounts to a great coordination of Lutheran theological work in the world. Research, exchanges of personnel, and the translation and publication of theological literature—those are all things about which one can only be happy. One can only hope that the Lutheran churches here make up that which they have for so long missed and about which we spoke in our previous letter. One can additionally only hope that not too much Geneva water is poured into the fermenting Lutheran wine. The danger is great, especially when one thinks about the financing of such a worldwide program. We Lutherans don't have a Rockefeller, who financed the ecumenical institute in Bossey. If Dr. Vajta is not a man of iron, then his institute will hardly be able to claim itself an institution of the Lutheran Church in the face of the Reformed. But if we assume that Lutheranism is strong enough to affirm its independence, then there remain other questions, which we hereby wish to present to the leading men of the LWF for consideration, not to criticize—it is sad enough that we must always say that which the leading men of the LWF should be saying to themselves—but rather to initiate a discussion of the entire question. In this we speak from the practical experience of almost thirty years in theological dialogue between the Lutheran churches of the world and between Lutherans and other Christians, from the Quakers to the Roman Catholics and theologians of the Eastern churches.

First, we must thankfully recognize that the theology which is here to be nurtured is *theology of the church.* Theology means, in the true sense of the word, the responsibility of the church for announcing the pure doctrine of the Gospel, as well as for the administration of the Sacraments according to God's ordinance.

Now, this is neither logical—theology is not a responsibility, but at most the fulfillment of a responsibility—nor sufficient, as the classical definitions of theology from the great teachers of the church show. Shouldn't we, if we as Lutherans set about such a task, exercise care even in language which since time immemorial has belonged to authentic theology? We make this comment in view of all the many committee reports and ecumenical documents with which we theologians are today flooded, and the lack of clarity which often causes one to think with envy of the Roman church. One of the most important tasks of a "theological division" would be the attempt to coordinate the languages of the church—not even the constitution of the LWF is the same in the various languages—and to somewhat simplify the *glossolalia* of academic theologians in Germany and elsewhere, so that even we simple servants of the Word in the less cultivated parts of the earth can understand them. The truly great theologians of the church have been able to express their deepest thoughts so simply that today, after centuries, the people understand them, Thomas with his hymns, and above all Luther with his Small Catechism. Shouldn't somebody look through the study document from Hanover once with this in mind?

But let's remain with the question of the churchliness of the theology. Which church is it here which is conscious in its theology of the responsibility to pure doctrine? Apparently our church, the Lutheran Church. For we continue to read:

"The responsibility of the church cannot be actualized without thorough study of the Holy Scripture, our confessional documents, and the entire history of preaching and dogma."

This is, as far as I see, the only time that the sources of theology—Scripture and Confession—are mentioned. What a strange mixture: Scripture, Confession, the history of preaching, the history of dogma! Apparently the author thinks that the first two are the source of doctrine. Why does he not say this? And he speaks only of the study of the Holy Scripture and the Confessions—Bultmann is also a researcher in the Scriptures, and the Lutheran Confessions are also studied by Reformed and Catholics. Of a binding of the theological division to *norma normans* ["norming norm"] of the Scripture and the *norma normata* ["norm which is normed"] of the Confessions we hear nothing. Can one practice Lutheran theology—and that's what the "division" wants to be: ecclesiastically bound theology—without ascertaining this binding from the very beginning and exactly defining it?

We are all aware that there are different interpretations of the concept of "Lutheran theology." Lutheranism, theologically seen, is somewhat complicated. By its nature, tensions [between various views] arise. In some cases, these differing *theological traditions* have caused the founding of separate church bodies.— We must keep the difficulties of this situation in the area of theology of world Lutheranism in mind. Sometimes it will be relatively simple to lead a theological discussion, but in other cases it will be impossible to topple the traditional theological opinions and to work one's way to a solution . . . there is, indeed, despite all difficulties, a *foundational unity of Lutheranism*. In one moment, when the different *Lutheran traditions* are set up over against the *non-Lutheran traditions*, this unity must clearly be expressed.

According to this, Lutheranism is a unity in the multiplicity of its theological traditions. This variety will be done away with easily in most cases, for it is merely a difference in opinion, which can be cleared away by means of discussion. We must discuss our differing *opinions* inside of Lutheranism. It would not be a true discussion if we wanted [simply] to repeat *our old traditional opinions* in the same formulations. We must be completely ready to examine that which orthodoxy, pietism, *liberalism*, etc., have given as answers to the questions of our time. What kind of "opinions" or "traditions" are these, which here should come together in conversation with the goal that the existing differences should be overcome? Apparently, the opinions of theological schools are meant, but can these differences within Lutheranism be traced back to those? Certainly, it was the opinions of schools which separated Missouri and Iowa. But was it merely the differences of schools? Was perhaps in this or that point [of contention, or] for a moment with this school and then for a moment with that school, the truth of the Gospel [to be found] or a church-destroying heresy? Was that which, for example, came between C. F. W. Walther and [Wilhelm] Löhe something which by means of serious discussion—and they did discuss—could have been removed easily? And what is the status of the opinions of the schools of liberalism? Here we encounter the same superstition by which the current Ecumenical Movement lives, namely, that the "discussion" in which one "listens to the brothers" must necessarily lead to a unification, because these discussions are the tool of the Holy Spirit: "the theological presuppositions"—Pardon me! What is that? Isn't the dogma of the church one of these "presuppositions"?—must be laid aside and a *theological discussion* without untrusting reservations must be started, as among *brothers*, who have the certainty of belonging to the same *family*. Further, this indicates that *the willingness to listen to our brothers* in different countries with different historical and theological backgrounds is the beginning of our discussion. The theological division must keep its *ear* open *for all voices within Lutheranism*. Of course, it must attempt to bring these voices together in discussion. There is no tendency to consider this or that theological school, personality, or tradition as the official theology of the theological division. *We must believe that God can use the theological division as a tool for the creation of a unity which, however, does not mean uniformity.*

Willem Adolph Visser 't Hooft (1900–1985)[8] believes exactly the same thing about his ecumenical council. Does the author share this belief, or how will he otherwise justify the closest cooperation with the Ecumenical Movement represented by the ecumenical council? He continues:

> uniformity would mean the end of all theological study. We should achieve unity which is seized by the same truth, a unity which seeks the same treasure ....

Naturally, there is in no living church a uniformity of theology. The men who confessed the Augsburg Confession *magno consensu* diverged in several theological views. The confessors who spoke the great "we believe, teach, and confess" of the Formula of Concord came from differing schools and retained their theological peculiarities. In one thing, however, they were united. That was the *dogma* of their church. But that is something which the "theological division" of the LWF and its leader seem not to know. We hear about opinions, schools, and traditions, but we do not hear one single word about dogma, in which the Lutheran Church is one, or should be one, [in] the doctrinal content of the Unaltered Augsburg Confession. Do the people in Lund know nothing about this anymore, or don't they want to know? Certainly there are school opinions, about which one should discuss. Certainly we as Christians and Lutherans are ready to

---

8   See *Lonely Way* 2:323 n. 5. "Even the World Council does not consider itself competent to discuss doctrinal questions in the name of its members. The General Secretary, Dr. W. A. Visser 't Hooft, gave an explicit warning at St. Andrews that to enter into doctrinal negotiations with the Church of Rome would be 'a dangerous deviation from the true task of the World Council.' The report of the Executive Committee then established in precise terms that, in questions regarding the union of churches, 'the World Council, according to its constitution, is not authorized to act for the churches in such matters'" (Augustin Cardinal Bea, *The Unity of Christians* [New York: Herder, 1964], 142). MH

speak with everyone who asks [for] a justification of our faith. We can additionally speak with other denominations, from the Quakers to the Romans, about questions of ecclesiastical doctrine. We can even learn from other confessions. One of the most fruitful conferences which I have experienced was a communal discussion of the Letter to the Ephesians by evangelical and Catholic theologians. Thereby the Catholics did not become Lutherans, and vice versa. There was not even fellowship in prayer. But the encounter was, despite this, enriching, because it led into the Word of God, not into that foggy "living Word" of the Lund school, of which nobody exactly knows what is actually to be understood by that phrase, but rather into the Holy Scripture. If the discussion remains a discussion of theologians and their opinions and "traditions," then the result can be nothing else than that which was formulated under the title "Consensus in Doctrine" in the old bishop's seat of Lund last year by the World Conference on Faith and Order:

> [A]ll accept the Holy Scriptures as either the only authority for ecclesiastical doctrine or as the primary and decisive portion of the authorities to which they refer. The majority accept the ecumenical creeds as explanation of the truth of the Bible or as monuments of a certain stage in the development of the orthodox faith. Some ascribe special meaning to the documents of faith of the early ecumenical councils. A few would say that grounding unity upon confessions of faith at all would mean to ground it upon something human, i.e., upon our understanding of the Gospel and upon our theological efforts to formulate this understanding. A few judge according to the inner light and the leading of the spirit, and feel themselves therefore compelled to issue statements against any use of external confessions of faith, if these are seen as necessary or sufficient.

This confession of absolute disunity under the title "Consensus in Doctrine" continues, then, still further, and concludes with the profession of theological discussion as the great tool of unification:

> We recognize the importance of theological study for intellectual clarification and continual reinterpretation of the Christian faith in the light of the changes of life and thought. Because we, in ecumenical discussion, *listen to each other*, we are moving in the direction of a deeper mutual understanding in faith and teaching. [Translated from the *Report of the Third World Conference on Faith and Order*, p. 19]

The Lutheran theologians in Lund have also accepted this. What will those of the "theological division" accept, which works according to the principles? We ask the bishops and theologians of the executive committee who accepted the program of the theological division: Are you really of the opinion that a theological discussion with no presuppositions, between all who call themselves Lutheran, will create the unity of world Lutheranism? And what is the goal of these efforts? Do they want to create a Lutheran confession of the twentieth century, and if so, what should the relation of such a confession be to the Confessions of our church? Should it add to them or replace them? We publicly ask these men here: Is there for you, worthy sirs, still a dogma of the Lutheran churches which remains *extra controversam*, that is, the doctrinal content of the Lutheran Confessions, as the old Lutheran World Convention in Copenhagen defined the confessional foundation in 1929 in the official declaration of the article concerning the Confession:

> The declaration of the Lutheran World Convention about its confession can contain only one witness, which clearly and emphatically expresses, in front of God and the whole world, *the unconditional and unchanged grasp on the Holy Scripture and on the Confessions inherited from our Lutheran fathers. This witness of the firm and unchanged grasp on the faith of the fathers* may not be mixed with additions and warnings, which are called forth by the current situation, but which divert attention [away] from the actual *confessional content*. [Lutheran World Convention of Copenhagen, statement, 1928, p. 208, emphasis by me. The English text is to be found in the *Lutheran World Almanac*, 1931–33, p. 45]

Is it [something] more than your subjective conviction, which you have presented in your letter to the United Evangelical Lutheran Church in Australia of August 1, 1953, that this is still the valid understanding of the confessional foundation of the LWF? What consequences follow from this for the "theological division"? Could, then, these nonbinding discussions, in which each and every theological opinion which calls itself Lutheran has equal rights, form a substitute for that which the Lutheran churches of the world need now more than ever: a doctrinal discussion upon the firm basis of the Unaltered Augsburg Confession, which stands *extra controversam*?

4

The basic Confession of the Lutheran Church begins: *ecclesiae magno consensu apud nos docent* ["Our churches teach with great unanimity . . ." AC I 1]. The situation of Lutheranism which expresses itself in the document of the "theological division" could be described thus: *ecclesiae magno dissensu apud nos disputant* ["Our churches with great dissensus dispute . . ."]. With this hopeless and irresponsible discussion, which should take place on a worldwide basis between the theologians, professors (which professors? even the *de facto* and *de jure* union ones?), along with the participation of "laity"—against the participation of true Lutheran congregations there would naturally be no objection—and students (who ought to first study, before they speak), we will not progress on the path toward the true unity of the Lutheran Church. What we need instead is the true *doctrinal discussion*. The doctrinal discussion presupposes that the participants have a common basis from which they can speak. Thus we have in common with the Catholic church "the sublime articles of the divine majesty" of which the

Smalcald Articles say that they "are not matters of dispute or contention, for both parties confess them" (SA I I 4–5; Müller, p. 299; Tappert, pp. 291–92).

We have the *sola Scriptura* in common with the Reformed. Such a basis, which is *extra controversam*, is the necessary precondition and makes possible religious discussion, as it was in the century of the Reformation. From this follows additionally the possibility of true ecumenical discussion, which is something different than that which we have quoted from Lund. But from this follows not only this possibility, but rather the possibility of true doctrinal discussions between the Lutherans of the world. A doctrinal discussion between Lutherans, that is, those who accept the Unaltered Augsburg Confession and Luther's catechism as their confession, presupposes a much greater consensus than the parallel consensus in which we may find ourselves with other churches. It presupposes that the doctrinal content of these Confessions is in no controversy or dispute. I can, like Luther in Marburg [1529][9] and Andreae in Mömpelgard [1586],[10] dispute with the Reformed about the Lord's Supper on the basis of the *sola Scriptura* acknowledged by both sides. I can also dispute with the Lutherans about the same topic, but when I do, I must know that the teaching of the Confession about the Sacrament of the Altar stands as firmly for them as [it does] for me. Then we can discuss together the entire inexhaustible riches of the Scripture in its statements about this Sacrament, and attempt to understand the entire content of the eucharistic doctrine still more deeply. The same is true of the other dogmas of our church, in which the Lutheran Church is one or should be one.

Yes, but they are not one, one will object to us. To this one can only answer: churches which only theoretically but not in reality hold the Lutheran teaching as the only *publica doctrina* are not Lutheran and must first again become Lutheran. Even with them we want to speak and should speak, as the Missouri Synod did in Bad Boll and the other conferences in exemplary fashion. But this church never allowed the slightest doubt about what, for it, stands *extra controversam* as the binding doctrine of the church. If its conversation partners believed that it recognized the "equal rights of all views" by participating in this conferences, then it is a terrible misunderstanding of Christian love. Even the friendly expressions about his plans which Dr. Vajta heard in St. Louis do not contradict this. All of us who carry a part of the responsibility for the future of the Lutheran church are ready to help the LWF when we can do it with a good conscience. But if he expects of us that we grant the same rights to errors as to the truth, that we view and treat open deniers of the teaching of the Confessions as brothers in faith, then we can only speak an unconditional "No!"

But however the theological division of the LWF and its work may form themselves, it will be the great task of those still a part of the great "we believe, teach,

---

9   See Sasse's *opus magnum: This Is My Body: Luther's Contention for the Real Presence in the Sacrament of the Altar* (Minneapolis: Augsburg, 1959). MH

10   Raitt, *Colloquy of Montbéliard*. MH

and confess" of the Lutheran Confessions to begin for their part and among their acquaintances doctrinal discussion, which must happen between Lutherans who don't want to watch with inaction as the great heritage of the Lutheran teaching which is still left in the world is babbled apart by pseudo-intellectuals. Therefore, come together, brothers in the office, who still have fellowship with others in the *magnus consensus* of the Lutheran Confession. Study the Confessions, you lonely ones, and preach joyfully and in consolation to your congregations the pure doctrine of the Scripture. Know that you are not alone in the world. And the Lutheran churches, for whom through God's unearned grace the Scripture and the Confession have remained, all have occasion to now come together and in deep doctrinal discussion to confess anew the old consensus. That is the command of this hour for confessional Lutheranism. Let us not waste this opportunity, perhaps the last one after so many wasted opportunities. Let us not think of church politics and ask: What do the others say about that? What will be the result of that? If Luther had so asked, then there would be no more Lutheran doctrine in the world. And the result of confession is nothing in the eyes of the world, even the Christian world. But in the eyes of God, it is much. The Lord Himself told us what the result will be: Matt. 10:32. (Aside from that, a church has never died from its loyalty to confession, but rather from the opposite.) But the great promise of Christ is given only to those who go the way of confessing and the way of confessing doctrinal discussion in all humility, without the aloofness which is the danger of all orthodoxy, but additionally without the arrogance which has already destroyed many an intelligent theologian, because we theologians so easily forget that we are not the midpoint of the world and of the church.

〜

This letter reaches you, dear brothers, as [did] the previous one, in printed form in the magazine *Lutherische Blätter*, with which this [series of] letters has always been closely connected. I hope that they are not any less personal for this. But the subject matter of the *Blätter* and of the letters is one and the same, and I am happy that this can now be expressed also in the external form. It's like a miracle to me that Brother Hopf [1910–82] and I, despite all difficulties, have been able to carry out our common service. God bless our small service, and may He bless every witness which is given by you, in season and out of season, in the congregation and in the church, for the Lutheran Confession.

 Greeting you in the loyal bonds of faith,

Your

Hermann Sasse

Historical Context

This is an amazing piece by Sasse. Engaged in the doctrinal discussions between the two Lutheran Churches which would become the Lutheran Church of Australia, Sasse threads the theological needle between parties who would be prone on the one side to find a cosmology in Genesis or on the other to allow basic truths of the creation account to float toward mythology. Sasse asserts that creation is a "pure article of faith," which simply must be believed. "No human mind can conceive of a creation from nothing by means of the Word, not even a physicist who accepts the idea of an abrupt beginning of the world." And the categories of theology, science, and philosophy must be kept distinct, not unlike Luther's two kingdoms doctrine. MH

December 12, 1954[1]

H. Sasse
41 Buxton Street
North Adelaide, South Australia

Dear Doctor [Herman A.] Preus,

. . . Here in Australia we are still hopeful for the union of our two small churches despite the difficulties which certain big church bosses in Europe and America made by trying to prevent a union between our church which stands in the tradition of Loehe though this has become very weak and Missouri, i.e. the ELCA which is in fellowship with Missouri. The difficulties did never come from St. Louis. On the contrary from there we received great encouragement. But otherwise we have been treated sometimes like certain small ancient churches which became the victims of the church politics of the great patriarchs. We are looking with great interest, and sometimes with concern, at your merger. May God make the year 1955 a real year of grace for our Lutheran Churches. So many years have been wasted. May this year be a year of progress and successful work for our church and for every one of us.

With kind regards,

Yours fraternally in *communione fidei*,
Hermann Sasse

---

1   Copy in Harrison Collection. MH

thirty-three

Toward Understanding the Six Days of Creation

TRANSLATED BY MATTHEW C. HARRISON

Mid-November 1953[1]

Prof. Dr. Theol. Hermann Sasse
41 Buxton Street
North Adelaide, South Australia

Dear Brothers in the Office!

With the scholarship of his era, and the biblicism of then-contemporary English Christianity, the older Lightfoot had reckoned that the world was created on the October 23, 4004 BC, in the morning at 9 a.m.[2] Still today the effect of this explication of Scripture, above all in the Christianity of the English-speaking areas, is remarkable and provides the Catholics a point of ridicule over a "scholarly backward" Protestantism. One might compare this backwardness with the closed nature of the present Roman Church—indeed, it was not always so—with respect to modern natural science. Thus one points perhaps to the speech of the present pope before the Papal Academy of Sciences in the year 1951. The academy had acknowledged present-day astrophysics together with

---

1   *BLP* 33: *Zum Verständnis des Sechstageswerks* (North Adelaide, November 1953). The original was published in *LuBl* 6, no. 34 (January/February 1954): 16–28. Huss number 305. MH

2   Lightfoot's calculation is only one among many. The most influential is the Byzantine calculation from 692, which placed the beginning of the world at September 1, 5509 BC. The Jewish version placed the beginning of the world on October 7, 3761. That Luther (3960 BC) and Melanchthon (3963 BC) in their time tables followed the Jewish reckoning is explained from the influence of the time tables of the synagogues. Naturally Luther's *Supputatio annorum mundi* of 1540 is a private word without dogmatic significance for the church. HS

its view regarding the spacial and temporal expansion of the universe. And there is also the encyclical *Humanis Generis* [1950] with its guarded recognition of the teaching of evolution as a theory discussable within certain limits. "Thus the dogma of church leaves the doctrine of evolution as an open question, so long as it is limited to speculation over the development of the human body from already existing material. That souls are created immediately by God is a view which the Catholic faith lays upon us" [cited according to the English translation of the encyclicals by Ronald Knox]. But also with such positions the Roman Church seeks to win hitherto unheard-of concessions for the modern scientist. Despite that, the theological explanation of the beginning of Genesis remains a problem of first rank for the Lutheran theology today, just as it has always been a problem for Christian theology. Every great theological problem is posed anew in every age and cannot be answered simply by a repetition of earlier solutions. Indeed, it is precisely of the essence of the Holy Scripture as the living and powerful Word of God that it speaks anew in every age, no less or otherwise in the age of atomic physics and astrophysics than in the age of the old Oriental and Aristotelian worldview. Since the Word of God gives one and the same answer to each and every age, it provides an answer which, for all times and all men, has the same validity, for the learned and unlearned, the wise and unwise.

1

It is a great error to think that the problem of "the Bible and natural science" is only a problem which has arisen in the modern world since Copernicus, Kepler, and Newton.[3] The problem is much rather as old as the church—indeed, older. In the third century BC, Eratosthenes of Alexandria[4] demonstrated not only that the earth was a sphere, he now rather famously, on the basis of the observation of the position of the sun in Alexandria and Aswan, calculated the diameter of the earth with an astonishing inaccuracy of only 20 percent. The next century brought the discovery of Ptolemy,[5] that the sun does not revolve around the earth but the earth around the sun. It was a discovery which had to wait

---

3   Elert shows that, in fact, early Lutheranism was quite personally helpful to Nicolaus Copernicus (1473–1543); see *Structure of Lutheranism*, 418ff., 426ff., 431ff., especially p. 426: "If the teaching of Copernicus was fostered at the universities at all, this took place in the domain of Lutheranism." Johannes Kepler (1571–1630) was himself an orthodox Lutheran and had studied theology at Tübingen (Elert, *Structure of Lutheranism*, 427). Isaac Newton (1642–1727) was a professor at Cambridge, England (1669). MH

4   Eratosthenes (276–194 BC) was a Greek philosopher and astronomer. A pupil of Callimachus (310/305–240 BC), Eratosthenes was librarian in the great Alexandrian library. See *Dictionary of Philosophy and Psychology*, ed. James Mark Baldwin (New York: Peter Smith, 1940), 1:339. MH

5   Ptolemy (ca. 90–ca. 168) set forth his system in *Syntaxis*. Its basics were three: (1) The earth is a globe. (2) The globe is at rest in the center of the world, the latter being represented by the celestial sphere. (3) The heaven or world makes a diurnal revolution

1,700 years to be repeated by Copernicus, because the authority of Aristotle with his geocentric worldview was so overpowering that no one could or would contradict the "Philosopher."[6] Alexandrian Judaism, whose Septuagint [ca. 200 BC] was produced in the city of precise natural science, already had to answer the question how the biblical history of the creation could be reconciled with contemporary science. The most meaningful example for this is Philo's book *On the Creation of the World*. His thoughts also with respect to the Talmud found wide dissemination in the Jewish world. The characteristic mark of this explication of the creation history was the attempt to demonstrate apologetically that there was no contradiction between the report of Genesis and a more assured result of science. This proof was provided so that the worldview of the present was read into the old text. And so there was pious astonishment that it was found repeated as divine revelation. The editor of the document on the creation of the world in the German Philo edition (*Die Werke Philos von Alexandrien*, part I, pp. 25ff.), J. Cohn, characterized the manner of proceeding of the great Jewish theologian and philosopher this way: "Philo elucidates . . . in this book the biblical report of the creation with the help of Platonic, Stoic, and Pythagorean doctrines, but in such a way that physics is closely connected with theology, the cosmology with his doctrine of God and the Logos. His doctrine of the creation of the world, or more precisely his worldview, leans toward Plato's *Timaeus* in its essential thrust" (p. 25). Also here Christian apologetics was a continuation of Jewish apologetics. For the church fathers who wrote on the *hexaemeron* ["six days of creation"]—such as Ambrose, Augustine, Basil [ca. 330–ca. 379], Gregory of Nyssa [ca. 331–ca. 396] and Chrysostom—indeed lived in a world which had long overcome the primitive view of the world of the earth as a disk, over which vaults the heavens with sun, moon, and stars. Once Basil criticized the natural scientist who knew so much but did not know the Creator: "One day, doubtless, their terrible condemnation will be the greater for all this worldly wisdom, since, seeing so clearly into vain sciences, they have willfully shut their eyes to the knowledge of the truth. These men who measure the distances of the stars and describe them, both those of the north, always shining brilliantly in our view, and those of the southern pole visible to the inhabitants of the south but unknown to us; who divide the northern zone and the circle of the zodiac into an infinity of parts, who observe with exactitude the course of the stars, their fixed places, their declensions, their return and the time that each takes to make its revolution; these men, I say, have discovered all except one thing: the fact that God is the Creator of the universe and the just Judge who rewards all the actions

---

around an axis which passes through the center of the earth. See Baldwin, *Dictionary of Philosophy and Psychology*, 2:396. MH

6   Thus Thomas, *Summa Theologica* I, question 10, art. 1, rejects Ptolemaeus with Aristotle. For this reason also Nicolaus of Oxerne (d. 1382) was unable to push through his heliocentric worldview. HS

of life according to their merit" (*Hexaemeron*, Sermon 1.4).[7] He complains here about their blindness for the Creator, not their view of nature, which he broadly shares. Thus he remarks on Gen. 1:16 that the sun is not called great because it is greater than stars, but because it appears larger to us. It is this same explanation which the scholastics took over from the fathers, above all from Chrysostom: "Moses accommodated himself to uneducated people (*rudi populo condescendens*) and sticks with things as they appear to the senses" (Thomas, *Summa Theologica* I, question 70, 1; cf. Luther, *Genesis-Vorlesung* on 1:6, WA 42:18.25: *Mose quia scripsit rudi et novo populo*[8]). The apologetic result of the patristic explication of the work of creation led incidentally to deviation from the Genesis account. The most famous instance is the acceptance of Augustine and Gregory of Nyssa that the work of creation happened all at once in an instant and that the division of creation into days only happened in the accounts in order to accommodate them to the ungifted. Only where the contradiction of the Bible over against the scientific view is too great, as in the Aristotelian denial of the beginning and end of the world, do these apologetic views set aside the teachings of philosophy. But otherwise these apologists proceed from the presupposition that between the Holy Scriptures and the scientific understanding of nature no contradiction can exist, because the Scriptures also present knowledge of nature. We notice this view even today in modern Christianity. The knowledge of natural science, so far as it is irrefutable, must be brought into harmony with the truths of Scripture. If the six days of creation are six common days, then nature must be explained such that its phenomena agree with this presentation of the creation. Or if one proceeds from the suppositions of natural science that we are dealing with great periods of time, then Genesis must be explicated such that the days of creation are not days in our sense, but great periods of time. Present-day Catholic theology, on the basis of the decision of the Bible Commission of 1910 (Denzinger 2128),[9] which declared the question open, prefers this latter option. Either the facts of geology are calculated according to the chronology which one believes he takes from the Bible, or the Bible must be interpreted according to the chronology of natural science, and therefore geology and astrophysics. That is the way apologetics old and new has solved the problem of the *hexaemeron*. Fundamentally, it makes no difference whether one has in mind the science of the fourth, thirteenth or twentieth centuries, whether with Gregory of Nyssa and Augustine we collapse the days of creation into one moment or stretch them into

---

7   See NPNF[2] 8:51. MH

8   Cf. *Lectures on Genesis* (1535–45), Aland 517, AE 1:23. MH

9   "De charactere historico priorum capitum Geneseos [Resp. Commissionis de re Biblica 30 Junii 1909] . . . Dubium VIII: Utrum in ill sex dierum denominatione atque distinctione, de quibus in Geneseo capite primo, sum posit vox Yom (dies) sive sensu proprio pro die naturali, sive sensu improprio pro quodam temporis spatio, deque huismodi quaestione libere inter exegetas disceptare liceat?—Resp.: Affirmative." [Denzinger 1911, p. 586]. MH

millions of years. In any case the attempt is made to bring Genesis into harmony with the contemporary worldview. Luther, too, in his *Supputatio annorum mundi* [1541] (WA 53:1ff. [Aland 706]) and in his lectures on Genesis did not escape the danger of attempting to bring the biblical account of creation into harmony with the worldview, which he as philosopher and theologian had learned. In this regard the theological tradition, based upon the material of the fathers, was still too powerful. Luther explained: "We are better off following Moses, the better doctor, whom one can follow with greater surety than the philosophers, who without the Word of God dispute over unknown things" (WA 42:5.30).[10] In and of itself, this is a sound principle, though Moses in this case falls into the realm of philosophy, where he does not belong, and this precisely according to Luther's theology. Are we not indeed again encountering the [old] apologetics and its understanding of Christendom as the true philosophy when he [Luther] says of Plato that he came much closer to the truth of the creation than Aristotle, precisely because in Egypt he apparently assembled "sparks likewise from the sermons of the fathers and the prophets" (WA 42:4.16)?[11] It is not impossible that perhaps in this passage it is not Luther, but the compiler of the Genesis lectures who is speaking. There were continuously men who were Luther's students, such as Veit Dietrich [1506–49], who unknowingly sacrificed to strange gods.

2

This apologetic method of the explication of the six days of creation stands over against a different one, which itself has been a favorite in the modern liberal and history-of-religions theology: the understanding of the creation reports as a myth. In a mild form this view appears in Karl Barth's description of the history of creation as a saga. Yet Barth's explication of the creation history in *Church Dogmatics* (vol. 3, I) is not thus equated with Gunkel's[12] "history of religions" interpretation of the creation account. But myth does have one thing in common with saga, as Heinrich Vogel in his *Dogmatics* (*Gott in Christo*, 1951, p. 424) correctly remarks: "In our ears, what is presented in the form of poetry in the sense of that which is not real remains burdened as something not 'true.'" The essence of all the myths about the origin of the world and the creation sagas is that the human spirit produces on its own an answer to the question of how then the world may have possibly come to exist. Thus we can calmly grant that such myths are full of deep wisdom. Indeed, we cannot completely deny that in such myths there are discernible but perverted reminiscences of an original knowledge of divine revelation before the fall. Indeed, all idol worship, and with

10 *Genesis Vorlesung* (*Lectures on Genesis*) (1535–45), Aland 517. Cf. AE 1:6. MH

11 *Genesis Vorlesung* (*Lectures on Genesis*) (1535–45), Aland 517. Cf. AE 1:4. MH

12 Johann Friedrich Hermann Gunkel, professor of Old Testament at Giessen (1907) and Halle (1920), was an early proponent of form criticism and an adherent of the *Religionsgeschichtliche Schule* (s.v *Christian Cyclopedia*). MH

it all pagan mythology, point to the original relationship of man with his God and Creator. We ourselves should not shy away from seeing this viewpoint in pagan cultus and myths. The same Paul who saw behind pagan religions the horrid reality of the kingdom of demons could approach the paganism of his era preaching: "What therefore you worship as unknown, this I proclaim to you" [Acts 17:23 ESV]. There is in the history of human religion nothing more shocking than the human sacrifices among the old Semites, Germans, and Aztecs. But in their form these sacrifices also indicate the one sacrifice of the Son of Man, just as the bloody sacrifice of the ancient Jewish cultus did in other ways. It is Paul himself, who in 1 Cor. 10:16ff., sets the Christian cultus in comparison with that of the Jews and pagans. What a deep mystery is the parallel between the Christian sacraments of Baptism and the Supper and the rites of other religions, often so externally similar. Justin [Martyr] saw in these rites a mimicking by demons, which would hold men from the Sacraments of Christ. And how will the Christian apologist explain the remarkable communion celebrations [*Kommunionfeieren*] of central America? There is indeed a certain truth in the statement: "Every dogma is as old as the world." From now on we should at least pay attention to pagan creation myths or sagas of the beginning of the world. Only if we have understood their deep gravity, the gravity of paganism trying to wrestle to understand what is to it an impervious riddle, will we be able to say what in these cosmologies is false, demonic, and idolatrous. Then we can begin to understand the entire uniqueness and incomparableness of the biblical report of creation. It alone speaks of the creation in the proper sense. It rests upon the strict separation of Creator and created, which no paganism any longer knows. It alone teaches creation from nothing [*creation ex nihilo*], as the New Testament (Heb. 11:3) correctly understands. In the creation myths and sagas of the pagans there is always something from which the world comes, be it one or more divine beings, from which the world emanates, or a material, a "stuff," from which a "Demiurge" has formed the world as an artist forms his work from a given material. Only the biblical creation history leads back to the moment when there was nothing and almighty God called nonbeing into being. The Bible speaks in a manner different from the myths or the sagas. It speaks of that which actually happened in the creation of the world. It speaks not on the basis of human truth, human investigation, and by means of a religious "divination," which ever remain in the realm of human reason. It speaks on the basis of real, genuine inspiration. God has, in a manner which we do not understand and never will understand, granted this [inspiration] to the writer of these chapters. It is not a human word like the myth and the saga, or like the expression of the deepest human understanding is and remains a human word. Rather, it is God's Word in the strict sense, not in a symbolic [*bildischen*] sense. Therefore it is the word of the eternal Truth.

3

In saying this we delineate ourselves over against another misunderstanding. In addition to the attempts to explain the origin of the world by the creation myth and the saga, we find the philosophical/scientific attempt (rising in part from the saga and myth) to explain the origin of the world. From the Ionian natural philosophers to the great thinkers Plato and Aristotle and the precise natural scientists of the Hellenistic period, from the beginnings of modern physics with Copernicus to its present high point of modern investigation of nature, there stretches the powerful attempt of the human mind to solve the riddle of the origin of the world on the path of science. It behooves us theologians not to pass over this great work, getting back to business with an arrogant smile after we've chosen the results of these sciences by picking and choosing what suits us.

Self-evidently, we as Christians and theologians are compelled to protest when a certain sort of popular author, or occasionally a scientist, otherwise capable in his discipline, makes the attempt with the help of genuine or false science to solve all the "riddles of the world." The older ones among us still remember that Monism[13] which at the beginning of this century in Germany stepped forth as substitute for vanquished Christendom. With its natural philosophical achievements, as though it were a powerful historic discovery, it determined that Jesus had never even lived. "I conclude the first Monist Congress and open the Monistic century." This century did not last long—at least not in Europe. In other countries it appeared under other names still to persist. The man who spoke these arrogant words would have been very much amazed if he were informed that forty years later one of the great physicists of our time, invited to give a guest lecture at a university, began by presenting a Bible study. When we as theologians speak of natural science, then we should have in mind genuine natural science, which has the advantage of differentiating itself from other sciences in that it recognizes its limits. It knows how to distinguish between the facts which one can and must determine with the telescope, the spectroscope, and the microscope, or what experimental research can and must determine. It knows how to arrange these facts in appropriate order and what hypotheses may be made to explain these facts before making scientific acknowledgments. Strict objectivity is the mark of genuine natural science, and in this sense the natural sciences are the high school also of the other sciences. If we theologians can or will learn nothing from a physicist such as Max Plank

---

13   Monism denotes the view of the world as basically one reality. Monism is opposed to any kind of dualism or pluralism that asserts the reality of more than one substance, energy, principle of explanation, or ultimate reality. As a worldview it has the immediate merit of apparent simplicity, since the bewildering manifoldness of nature and history can all be explained in terms of the one reality selected as the "really real." See Julius Bodensieck, ed., *The Encyclopedia of the Lutheran Church* (Minneapolis: Augsburg, 1965), 1662. Of course, in the case Sasse notes there was included the historicism which denied the supernatural doctrinal content of the faith. MH

[1858–1947], then we could at least learn humility from him. The "you shall be as God" (*Eritis sicut Deus* [Gen. 3:5]) is the secret motto of many a dogmatician. But this cannot be written about the quantum theory. Behind the genuine study of nature stands not titanic arrogance, but the command of the Creator, which still applies to fallen humanity, to bring the earth into subjection. This command encompasses not only the vocation of the farmer and the laborer but also the vocation of the natural scientist. And the quiet, self-denying work which the physicist or chemist does in his laboratory, when done correctly, is precisely as much divine service (*Gottesdienst*) as every genuine work of vocation is according to Lutheran ethics. And we theologians must respect this vocation as much as the genuine fulfillment of any vocation.

Only such presuppositionless recognition of genuine science, that is, science which remains within its limits, can enable and empower us to see and express what the purest science of a fallen humanity cannot perform. Science cannot understand creation, just as no philosophy can understand the true and living God. Here Lutheran theology is fundamentally distinguished from that of other churches, particularly Roman Catholicism. One must understand this to calculate the damage done in the church of the Reformation by the invasion of pre-Reformation Catholic thought, both patristic and Thomist. According to Luther and the doctrine of our church, after the fall into sin nothing remains of the original knowledge of God but "a dark little spark of the knowledge that there is a God" (FC SD II 9), so dark that it necessarily leads to idolatry (LC, First Commandment). Thus the Lutheran Reformation understood Rom. 1:19ff. No natural science can know God the Creator from the work of creation which it investigates. We therefore cannot share in the jubilation of the pope, in the essay cited in his speech before the academy, that modern physics, astrophysics, which investigates the macro cosmos, and nuclear physics, which investigates the microcosmos of atoms, have demonstrated the existence of God the Creator: "The concreteness, which characterized the physical proof, established the contingency of the universe and provided the well-founded conclusion regarding the time when the cosmos came from the hand of the Creator" (*The Australian Catholic Digest* 1 [1952]: 18). What has taken place in the last hundred years in the realm of physics is truly astounding. It could be that physicists will come to conclusions, such as that of C. F. von Weizsäcker in his *Geschichte der Natur* (1948) (*History of Nature*) and many others—based on the second law of thermodynamics ("The entropy of the universe tends toward a maximum")—that the so-called "warming death" will bring an end to the world, and which at other times teaches a temporal beginning of the world. And so the biblical conception of creation and time limited by an end [of the world] will again be viewed favorably. ("The entire life of the cosmos is, in its entirety as much as in the individual, a development of ever differentiated forms, enclosed between the chaos of the beginning and the torpor of the end," Weizsäcker, *Geschichte der Natur*, p. 66). Indeed, it could be that precisely the idea of an absolute beginning is achieved again. But who knows what development the investigation of nature will undergo and what new theories may be proposed in the future? For the Roman Church the possibility of proving the existence of God and the facts of creation correspond to their understanding of reason and revelation, knowledge and faith. The pope expressly described in his speech the five proofs for the existence of God which Thomas gives at the beginning of the *Summa Theologiae* (I, question 2, article 5) and finds it confirmed by modern physics. But is the first movement, is the first cause, God? Thomas said of the *primum movens* and the *prima causa*: Everyone calls this God! But have I demonstrated the existence of God if I have demonstrated that there is a first cause? We cannot forget that the existence of God according to Catholic doctrine does not belong to the articles of faith, but to the "preamble" of the faith. From this vantage one can understand how the Roman Church can appropriate modern physics, including the reckoning of the age of our world at something more than five billion years, without thereby giving up a word of Genesis. They can incorporate it all into their philosophic substructure, as the church once did with the system of Aristotle. But it remains philosophy. And "creation," of which this philosophy speaks, is not that which the Holy Scriptures call creation, that creation which no reason can comprehend. It is a pure article of faith, taken from God's Word: "By faith we note that the world through God's Word came into being, that everything which man sees has come from nothing" (Heb. 11:3). So when Lutheran orthodoxy allows Aristotelian philosophy and the proofs of God's [existence], and a philosophical understanding of the creation, to force their way again into the church of the Reformation, Scripture and Confession know nothing of it. We do well to understand creation again as God's Word itself understands it: as a pure article of faith. Just as reason since the fall can no longer recognize the true God, so neither can the greatest and purest natural science any longer understand the creation. "The dark little spark of understanding, that there is a God," corresponds with a dark little spark of understanding that a superhuman mystery lies behind the origin of the world. But what this mystery is the reason of fallen man can no longer fathom. The most learned scientist can say nothing of creation other than as a simple child, hands clasped and before the countenance of God—not before a *primum movens* nor a *prima causa* nor an *ens a se*—confessing: "I believe in God the Father Almighty, maker of heaven and earth." The truly great scientists who "stick to the matter itself" have known this well and still recognize it today.

4

Thus if we avoid in apologetics the mythological and the scientific understanding of the creation, and again see in the article of the creation a pure article of faith, then we are on the right path to understanding the biblical account of creation. It may not be separated from the wider revelation. The Old Testament speaks about creation not only in the first chapter of Genesis but also in the creation psalms, the Book of Job, and in the prophets, especially where they speak of the redemption of the creature and of a new creation. The New Testament continues the doctrine of the Old when it emphasizes before all the participation of the *Logos* in the creation and in doing so teaches us to understand the work as the work of the triune God, which is already indicated in the creation history when in it the Word of God and the *Creator Spiritus* play such a great role. But if the article of creation is so inseparably bound together with the article of the triune God, then it is clear why it is a pure article of faith. Then we understand that the First Article can never be understood or explained without the Second and Third, and certainly not in the instruction of children. For how shall a disabled child be able to speak his "This is most certainly true" to Luther's explanation unless it is in view of the one who opens the eyes of the blind and makes the lame to walk! The question which then arises is what is exactly the doctrinal content of the creation history. Evidently it desires to instruct us on what God has done and on the triune God as He created the world. Its interest lies not in cosmology, as was the interest of many Jewish apocalypses which would purport to instruct us regarding the formation of the world. It lies only in theology. God created. God spoke. God made. God blessed. God saw everything that He had made. God rested on the seventh day. All these deeds and words of God are objects of the Christian faith, even if the clear and perceptible question of "how" is withdrawn. Just as the incarnation of the eternal Word, the work of redemption, the resurrection and the ascension of Christ, His sitting at the right hand of the Father, His coming again, the presence of His body and blood [in the Sacrament] all evade every evidence and perceptibility, so it is with the work of works, creation. No human mind can conceive of a creation from nothing by means of the Word, not even a physicist, who accepts the idea of an abrupt beginning of the world. So also no human can possibly conceive of the individual acts of creation reported in Genesis. We can only attempt to make ourselves clear on the problem of the creation days. What is a twenty-four-hour day when there is no sun? Who can possibly conceive of what it means that God rested for a defined period of time, shorter or longer? Isn't the creation precisely according to Luther's deep understanding a *creatio continua*: "I believe that God has created me and all creatures." And so isn't it tied inseparably with the miracle of preservation (compare John 5:17)? Nothing of this article is visible to the eyes, and still we believe that these words are true, that every sentence of the creation account designates something that actually happened. There really is a "firmament" even if we cannot account for it in our worldview. It is really so that man did not develop from the animal world, but stepped forth into existence through an inconceivable miracle of creation, even if we cannot perceive how this was so. It is really so that in the beginning a pair of human beings existed, and that the first Adam is precisely as much of a reality as the second Adam, even if we, who live on this side of the fall, cannot conceive of those who lived before the fall. Just as the last things which the bible recounts to us supersede our ability to conceive of them, so also the first things exceed our understanding. When the Bible, perhaps in the Revelation of John, speaks of the last things, it cannot help but use biblical language to serve the purpose. Note, for instance, the gripping sentence where the last dealings of God are described: "And God will wipe away every tear from their eyes" (Rev. 21:4). So we will also have to accept that many a statement on the first things is spoken in picture language, which in the case of Gen. 2:7 no one can deny. We must also not forget that the account of Genesis makes no claim to completeness. There has long been a question about how the angels were created or what occurred when they fell. God has revealed nothing to us regarding this, just as He has revealed nothing to us regarding the structure and expansion of the universe. He allowed the biblical writers to speak in the language which their readers could understand. He did not reveal to them a new cosmology (as the Book of Enoch claims for itself); rather, He so revealed to them the miracle of creation in such a way that they could express it with the presuppositions of their view of the structure of the cosmos. As a Catholic theologian correctly noted regarding her view of the heavens: "The grace of inspiration has evidently also here not eliminated the profane knowledge of its time" (Alois Schmitt, *Bibel und Naturwissenschaft, Bibl. Zeitfragen,* 3 Folge, Heft 7, p. 24, cf. *Deutsch Thomas-Ausgabe,* vol. 5, p. 243, and the entire section pp. 237–52). That the Bible speaks thus to us is that *syncatabasis* ("condescension") of which Chrysostom speaks, as a parallel to the condescending of the *Logos* in the incarnation (i.e., Homily on Gen. 2:7): "Behold, with what condescension the Word, which for our weakness' sake He uses . . . in order to instruct us" (Migne PG 53:106 and many other passages with the same thought). This aspect of the Bible should be compared with the religious cosmologies of Hellenistic Judaism (e.g., the travels of Enoch through earth and underworld, aeth. Enoch 17–36) or of Manichaeism. It should be compared with the cosmological, astronomical, and indeed geographic instructions which the authoritative dogmatics of the Eastern Church—*Presentation of the Orthodox Faith* by John of Damascus [ca. 675–ca. 750] in the second book, on the doctrine of creation—brings, and it will be evident what Christianity has been spared. Franz Cumont [1868–1947], the great scholar of the Mithras cult, had once, responding to a statement of [Joseph Ernest] Renan [1823–92], said that the world would have fallen to the Mithras cult if Christendom in the Roman Empire of the third and fourth century had not continued to raise the question of what consequences it would have had for Western culture. Among its answers was that the faith of humanity would have been bound to an untenable physics.—Faith in Jesus Christ as the Redeemer of the world, faith in the triune God, is not burdened with an old cosmology. And the Christian faith in the creation which entails faith in God remains in the realm of theology. And it was never expressed by the church otherwise than in the words of the *Credo*: "I believe in one God, Father Almighty, Maker of heaven and earth, and all things, visible and invisible."

5

But the question arises: Is there, then, a conflict between theology and science? The clear answer must be no. Such a conflict cannot exist, if each of the two disciplines "remains within its sphere of concern." Both the theological and scientific treatments of the world run alongside each other like the rails of two parallel train tracks. Trains travel to and fro upon them, without disturbing each other. A wreck is possible only if a derailment takes place. Such derailments have ever and again taken place and will also occur in the future. Theology is always seeking more knowledge than it has. It seeks, on the basis of the Bible, a Christian conception of the universe and may demand or create a Christian geology or paleontology. And scientists can't deny their origin from medieval scholasticism, in which philosophy and theology were still inseparably bound together in one system. And so it's certainly no wonder that they continually seek to read something into and explain theology. But no authentic scientist will do this, because the concept does not arise in his science. The Catholic scientist who must express his view in a canonization process or by the reporting of an opinion regarding a "miraculous" healing in Lourdes will avoid using the word "miracle," which does not occur in his discipline of science. There are in this case Catholic theologians who use and misuse the concept of miracle. The church has neither the right nor the responsibility to spare her members, or people in general, the challenge which the miracles presented in Holy Scripture provide. But neither has it the right to provide them with an unnecessary offense which, while invoking God's Word, would coerce them into a view of the world which is absolutely not in the Bible. There are cases of overstepping boundaries on both sides, which have wreaked havoc. If there is one church which ought to be free of this problem, then it is the church of the Lutheran Reformation. This church has always fundamentally separated philosophy and theology. A philosopher can certainly be a Christian. He can be a Christian philosopher by vocation. But the faith, which comes from the Word, and philosophy, which comes from reason, remain distinct. For reason does not perceive the truth of the faith, nor can it provide foundation for that truth, ground that truth. And the Word of God does not answer the questions of philosophers. It is like the two kingdoms in which the Christian lives and which must be distinguished. They are the spiritual regiment of Christ and of the Gospel, and the "secular regiment or Law." Luther in *On Temporal Authority* [*Von weltlicher Obrigkeit*, 1523] says: "Therefore one must distinguish both these regiments with diligence and let both remain, one which makes pious, the other which creates external peace and defends against evil acts. Neither is sufficient without the other in the world . . ." (WA 11:252.12).[14] As the Christian in this temporal world cannot live otherwise than in both kingdoms, so can he also as a believer not get rid of the fact that faith is no substitute for fallen reason. Just as the contradiction between the kingdom of Christ and

---

14   Aland 540. Cf. AE 45:92. MH

the kingdom of the world will be completely done away with when the *regnum Christi* ["the kingdom of Christ"] is "revealed" and no longer "hidden under the cross" [*tectum cruce*] (Ap VII–VIII; Müller, 155), so also will the contradiction between the "light of nature" [*lumen naturae*] and the "light of grace" [*lumen gratiae*] in which Christians must live in this age be done away with first in the "light of glory" [*lumen gloriae*] (cf. Luther's doctrine of the three lights [*tria lumina*] at the conclusion of *Bondage of the Will* [*De servo arbitrio*] WA 18:785).[15] The miracles of God, of which we in faith in His Word know, are ever inaccessible to fallen reason. But that does not mean that we should not make use of reason in all things which belong to its kingdom, even if because of the fall reason is clouded and blind in divine matters. Only in eternity, when the spirit of man has become free from sin and its consequences, and faith has become sight, will the "light of nature" [*lumen naturae*], the "light of grace" [*lumen gratiae*], and the *lumen gloriae* ["light of glory"] be one.

These are a few thoughts which I, honored brothers, would like to contribute to the great question of the *hexaemeron*, which has moved Christianity since its beginning and which is also a question for every one of us. We have not touched upon everything which could be said. Among the great thinkers of the Middle Ages, who are known to have made contributions on this subject, I have not mentioned Bonaventure [1221–74], whose *Collationes in Hexaemeron* are the most important elaboration of the creation doctrine of Thomas. Allow me to close with a word from Bonaventure, in which he expressed the essence of the Christian faith in creation over against the highest thoughts of natural man regarding the origin of the world: *Plato commendavit animam suam factori; sed Petrus commendavit animam suam Creatori,* "Plato commended his soul to the demiurge, the builder of the world. But Peter commended his soul to the Creator" (in *Hexaemeron* 9.24). Here in fact lies the difference. He who does not know the Second and Third Articles also does not know the First.

↬

I especially thank those of you who have helped me clarify my thoughts concerning this theme by your questions and other notes to me requesting clarification. I greet you and wish you all "a blessed new year" as,

Your
Hermann Sasse

---

15 Aland 38. Cf. AE 33:292. MH

Historical Context

This is a profound analysis of the great division of Eastern and Western Catholicism in 1054, written for the 900th anniversary of the event. Geopolitical realities then and now have enormous consequences in the church. The ancient Christological heresies and divisions, notes Sasse, weakened Christianity from Syria to China in the face of the ultimate Christological heresy of Islam. "In the decisive moment . . . the eastern Syrians, the Armenians, the Copts, and all the other Oriental Christians listened more to the sound of blood and politics than to the voice of the Good Shepherd." As it was in 1054, so it also was in 1954 with the growing political division between Russia and the West. "It was the world which had made its way into the church." The answer? "Why is healing, by human measurements, impossible? Is there no healing of sick churches? Is there no repentance, no conversion, for churches? We must be clear about this, that the most unrepentant thing in this world is a church." Healing the schism requires repentance (reformation!), which neither Rome nor Constantinople was ready to do in 1954. Unfortunately, the church of the Reformation was in no position to call for repentance. "In all decisive questions, it is no longer the Confession, but rather the real or alleged needs of practical ecclesiastical life which are the norm for all decisions. But thereby one door after another is opened to secularization." MH

September 26, 1954

Prof. H. Sasse
41 Buxton Street
North Adelaide, South Australia

Dear Doctor [Lawrence] Meyer,

. . . There are so many things on my heart. First of all, I want to express to your church my deep sympathy on account of the grave loss which the death of Dr. Fr. Mayer[1] meant to all of us. He has helped us here in Australia a lot by a few letters he wrote in favor of our union. Besides, my family and myself will never forget his visits in Germany. I was just about to write to him to congratulate him for his having finished the great book. I had just found a wonderful stanza such as the old monks of Mount Athos used to write under their manuscripts when they

---

1 Frederick Emanuel Mayer (1892–1954) was editor of *CTM*. The book referenced here was most likely *The Religious Bodies of America*. MH

had finished the work of many years. In this stanza the finishing of a book was compared with the joy of coming home after years of travel. Now our friend and brother has experienced this twofold joy at the same time . . . .

Yours sincerely,

H. Sasse

thirty-four

The Great Schism and Its Lessons

TRANSLATED BY ANDREW SMITH

Pentecost, June 6, 1954[1]

Prof. D. Theol. Hermann Sasse
41 Buxton Street
North Adelaide, South Australia

Dear Brothers in the Office!

You have had to wait for this letter longer than I wanted because I was hindered in my work by ongoing illness. The essay "Fathers of the Church"[2] in the *festschrift* for church superintendent Martin may have been a greeting to you in the meantime. But today, on Pentecost, when all of our thoughts go into the wide world and consider the miracle which stands at the beginning of church history as a divine sign of the *una sancta catholica et apostolica* ("one holy catholic and apostolic church"—the Nicene Creed), I am once again allowed to write to you. The church history of our era reminds us again and again that the one holy church of God is not an article of sight, but rather an article of faith. If we had to judge by visual appearances, then the church of Christ appears so pathetic that instead of the Pentecost narrative, the chronicle of the building of the tower of Babel [Gen. 11:1ff.] could provide the appropriate text for a consideration of the situation of Christendom. We recommend this text to all preachers at ecumenical functions and to all architects of a "reunited church of the future"[3] in Geneva,

---

1   *BLP* 34: *Das grosse Schisma und seine Lehren* (North Adelaide, June 6, 1954). The original was published in *LuBl* 6, no. 37 (July 1954). Huss number 308. MH

2   See *Lonely Way* 2:223–36. MH

3   "'The Future Reunited Church' and 'The Ancient Undivided Church,'" *The Springfielder* 27, no. 2 (Summer 1963). MH

in Evanston, and elsewhere. Does it not sometimes seem as if the judgment against the builders of the tower of Babel, and not the miracle of Pentecost, is the content of the church history of our era? Only he who is acquainted with the tragedy of the ecumenical efforts of our time, who is acquainted with the terrible hardship of the Babylonian confusion of languages, with churches speaking hopelessly past each other, who knows the terrible sins of the theologians who want to "make a name for themselves" and thereby believe themselves to be servants of Christ—only he knows what is the Pentecostal faith in the one church of God, which is a reality in the world, even if our eyes don't see it. *Abscondita est ecclesia, latent sancti* ("the church is hidden, the saints are latent," *De Servo Arbitrio*, WA 18:652),[4] that was Luther's Pentecostal faith. As the Holy Spirit is a reality which no Christian doubts, so is the *Una Sancta* a reality, so is the sanctity of the believing sinner a reality.

In this year, we have special occasion to consider these truths of faith. When these lines reach you, Christendom will be—or should be—pondering an event which is one of the greatest catastrophes of its history, the Great Schism between East and West, which was completed in July 1054. This event concerns not only Rome and the Eastern churches, which separated at that time and which now have been separated for 900 years despite all attempts at unification past and present. Every great event in church history concerns all Christians, even those who are involved indirectly. We can't comfort ourselves by saying wherever possible—and with some glee at the discomfort of others—that this time, we Lutherans, for once, really aren't to be made responsible for this, no matter how you look at it. We can't simply say, to our more-or-less great satisfaction, that the Reformation found an already-split Christendom, [and then walk away from the problem]. For we must ask how the Reformation might have indeed proceeded if it had happened in a unified Christendom, East and West, and if it had not been Rome alone which had to render a decision on Luther's teaching. And finally we must ask whether the sins which were committed in the Great Schism have also happened among us Lutherans, even if in a different form, and how Christendom would look today if we were better Lutherans, if our faith were stronger, our love greater, our hope more living. No, we, too, can enter into July 16 only as a day of repentance for the entire church of God. If we didn't, then we would no longer be the Church of the Lutheran Reformation.

1

It was on a Saturday, July 16, 1054, at nine o'clock in the morning. The Hagia Sophia, the main church in Constantinople, was filled with worshipers, for the preparations of the holy liturgy had just begun. Then the three delegates from the

---

4   *Bondage of the Will* (1525), Aland 38. Cf. AE 33:89. MH

pope who were in the capital city for negotiations—Cardinal Bishop Humbert,[5] Archbishop Peter of Amalfi, and Fredric the deacon and chancellor of the Roman Church—walked through the gigantic church, went through the "imperial door" of the facade into the sanctuary, and laid the bull of ban [Denzinger 350f.] upon the altar, by which Patriarch Michael Cerularius,[6] Bishop Leo of Ochrida, and their followers were excommunicated from the church: "... they are anathema Maranatha"—this word has been misunderstood through many centuries—

> with the Simonists, Valentinianists, Arians, Donatists, Nicolaitans, Severians, Pneumatomachians, and Manichaeans, all heretics—indeed, with the devil and all his angels, unless they accept reason once again. Amen. Amen. Amen.

In this strong, even presumptuous, language of the self-confident papacy in the century of the Investiture Controversy,[7] church fellowship was broken, at first with two men, who had earned nothing better. But for practical purposes fellowship was broken with the Church of the East, which had not deserved it. Why? If we ignore the immediate occasion of this excommunication, then there is no real ecclesiastical or theological reason for such a wide-ranging decision. There had been such excommunications before. It has been calculated that in the five hundred years between Constantine and Charles the Great [Charlemagne, ca. 742–814], church fellowship between Rome and Constantinople had been interrupted for more than two hundred years, if one adds up all the smaller [short-lived] schisms. The tragedy of this break was that it was final. If Humbert had foreseen that, then he might have been a little more restrained with his appeal to divine judgment in the words which he spoke as he turned back from the altar: *Videat deus et iudicet* ("May God see it and judge it") [Exod. 5:21].

What was the cause of this split, which was finally completed after centuries of dispute? To understand that, one must consider the earlier church splits, which had been happening since the beginning of church history. Already Paul, in the First Letter to the Corinthians, complained about *schismata* and *haereseis*, using both words synonymously, in the largest church in Greece. At the same

---

5 Humbert of Silva Candida (d. 1061) was deeply involved with negotiations with Michael Cerularius, patriarch of Constantinople. A reformer, Humbert opposed the practice of simony. See *ODCC*, 802. MH

6 Michael Cerularius (d. 1058) was implicated in a plot against Emperor Michael IV (r. 1034–41), which probably prompted him to enter the monastery. He was violently anti-Latin and intensely opposed to the *Filioque* and unleavened bread in the Eucharist. Latins placed the bull of excommunication on the altar of Hagia Sophia in Constantinople and Cerularius and the Eastern churches replied with their own anathemas (June 21 and 24, 1054). See *ODCC*, 1083. MH

7 The long series of disputes between popes and emperors from the time of the future emperor Henry IV's (r. 1056–1105) withdrawal of obedience to Gregory VII (r. 1073–85) at Worms in 1076 to the Concordat at Worms in 1122. The issue of investiture in the strict sense concerned the kings' right to confer upon bishops and abbots the ring and crosier that were their symbols of office. See *ODCC*, 842. MH

time he speaks of the necessity of such splits: "There must be parties among you, so that those who are righteous will become apparent among you" (1 Cor. 11:19).

This *oportet et haereses esse* ["there must be heresies among you"] are some of the most serious words of the Holy Scripture about the church. Toward the end of his life, the apostle was then forced to direct the warning toward his colleagues (1 Tim. 6:20ff.; Titus 3:9), to avoid any fellowship with the Gnostic heretics. Still more urgently, John, the apostle of love, had to warn his congregations about these false teachers, whom one should not even greet (2 John 10), because in them the Antichrist (1 John 2:18; 4:1ff.; 2 John 7) had appeared. We have no reason to doubt that these Gnostics, like the great Gnostic schools and churches which followed them, considered themselves to be the real Christians, persecuted by a power-hungry orthodoxy. It was exactly this way with the Christendom of the next centuries, as we have shown in an earlier letter. "The old undivided church" never existed, if one understands by this a unified Christianity. It seems that what we would call the rightly believing church was always a minority. What separated this church from the Marcionites,[8] Novatians,[9] Arians,[10] Donatists,[11] and others which competed with it, and what separated these groups from each other, were doctrinal questions, and was finally the question about the correct understanding of the Gospel. But then, in the fourth and fifth centuries, a new cause for divisions suddenly appears. In the case of the Donatists in Africa and then of the Nestorians[12] and Monophysites[13] of the East, it was at first doctrinal

---

8 Marcion (d. ca. 160) was a native of Sinope in Pontus and a wealthy shipowner. According to Hippolytus (ca. 170–ca. 235) he was the son of a bishop who excommunicated him for immorality. Marcion traveled to Rome around AD 140 and at first joined the Orthodox church, but then formed a separate community. He was formally excommunicated in 144. He was an antinomian and posited that the God of the Old Testament was quite different from the God of Jesus. Marcion and his followers presented the church with its greatest dogmatic challenge in the second half of the second century. The movement morphed into Manichaeism by the third century. See *ODCC*, 1033–34. MH

9 Novatians were a rigorous sect in the Western church which rose out of the Decian persecution (AD 249–250). Novatian had been a Roman presbyter. Although doctrinally orthodox, the Novatians were excommunicated. See *ODCC*, 1165. MH

10 Arianism, named after its author, Arius (d. 336), denied the full divinity of Jesus Christ. See *ODCC*, 99. MH

11 A schismatic body in the African Church, Donatists divided from the catholics through their refusal to accept Caecelian (d. ca. 345), bishop of Carthage, because the man who consecrated him, Felix of Aptunga, had failed to confess the faith during the Diocletian persecution. A rival bishop was consecrated and was followed soon after by Donatus (fl. ca. 354). See *ODCC*, 499. MH

12 Named for Nestorius (b. after 351–d. after 451), patriarch of Constantinople and heresiarch, who gave his name to the doctrine that there are two separate persons in the incarnate Christ. See *ODCC*, 1138. MH

13 From μονος ("only one") and φυσις ("nature"), Monophysitism is the belief that in the incarnate Christ there is only one nature, not two (God and man). This is a strict form of Alexandrian Christology and is a term first used after the Council of Chalcedon

questions which caused the conflict and forced the church to break off fellowship with the false teachings. But what made the dogmatic conflicts so bitter
and the divisions so incapable of being healed was something different. As the
Arianism of the Germanic tribes had a political side, so it was the hatred of the
native-born North Africans against the Roman domination which made a resolution of the Donatist schism impossible. It is telling that the "Christian" empire
experienced the splits in which political motives bound themselves to religious
ones. This, then, becomes especially clear in the split of the Nestorians and
Monophysites from the Melchites[14] (the "Imperial Ones"), from the orthodoxy of
that "Rhomaian" empire of Constantinople which the Asiatics detested. As today
the growing national feelings of the Asians turns itself against the European-
American Christianity of Western "imperialism" and "colonialism," so Asia, re-
wakening since the fifth century, could no longer tolerate the Christianity of
the Synods of Ephesus [431, concerning Nestorianism] and Chalcedon [451,
concerning Eutychianism]. Imagine how world history would look if the church
stretched from Syria to Beijing and southern India, if the Arminians, Coptics, and
Abyssinians had remained united with the church of Rome and Constantinople,
and Christianity, which is, after all, an Asian religion, had not been forced to
become a one-sided European religion. It was racial tensions and national hatred
which, in the fifth century, turned the theological and dogmatic differences into
unbridgeable oppositions, across which one could not even talk anymore. But
in the decisive moment, because the eastern Syrians, the Armenians, the Copts,
and all the other Oriental Christians listened more to the sound of blood and
politics than to the voice of the Good Shepherd, who was also still detectable
in the human, far too human, voices of the bishops and theologians inside the
empire, and because they preferred, for political reasons, a Christ who was no
longer both fully human and fully divine or in whom the human nature had disappeared, they were therefore helplessly exposed to the storm of Islam, just as
today the Christianity in China is to Communism. The churches of Europe also
suffered from the fate of the Eastern churches. For not only in the opinion of the
world, but rather also in the judgment of God, Christianity is a unit.

   While all these other earlier splits had not merely political but also still other,
churchly and dogmatic, causes, the actual tragedy of the split of 1054 lies in this:
that it had only political causes. Despite all the tensions between the Greek and
Latin churches, despite all the temporary splits, there remained, at least until

---

(451) to describe all who rejected the council's definition that the incarnate Christ is
   one person "in two natures." See *ODCC*, 1104–5. MH

14   This term was derived from the Greek form of the Syriac adjective *malkaya*, "imperial," which was used of those Christians of Syria and Egypt who, refusing Monophysitism and accepting the definition of faith of the Council of Chalcedon (451),
   remained in communion with the imperial see of Constantinople as "emperor's men."
   See *ODCC*, 1067. MH

the coronation of Charles the Great [Charlemagne],[15] which was seen by the East as the shredding of the empire, a strong sense of unity. The linguistic divisions never had a decisive significance. Not only the Greek churches of southern Italy, but rather even bits of Roman liturgy, such as the Greek Scripture readings in the papal Mass or the bilingual *Trisagion* of the Good Friday liturgy, remind [us] still today of the time in which Rome went from the Greek ecclesiastical language to bilinguality. Until well into the eighth century, Syrians and Greeks sat on the papal cathedra. The tensions between Rome and Constantinople (as the new, second Rome) didn't mean that the entire church of the East and the entire church of the West lived in enmity. In the mission field, too, among the Slavs, there were no boundaries between the churches, and they could honestly say that the Church of Russia was, at first, absolutely unaffected by the split of 1054. But finally the political opposition between East and West, between the ecumenical patriarchs—as the patriarch of Constantinople called himself since 518—and the pope became so large that the unity of the church fractured on it. It was no question of doctrine at first, not even the question of the church's constitution, which was at that time still an open question anyway, which destroyed the unity. It was the world which had made its way into the church.

2

Somebody will object that there are really theological and dogmatic differences between the Eastern Church and Rome. That is true, but these differences didn't cause the split. They were cited after the fact to explain the completed division. Above all it was the Church of the East which searched for heresies with which it could reproach Rome in the proud confidence of theological superiority and of the possession of the old orthodoxy which had been determined at the ecumenical synods. The theologians of the East looked down at those of the West, as today the Swedish and German theologians look down upon their more practically oriented colleagues in America. Where else than in the East were there ecumenical synods? Where else than in the East [was there] authentic theology, compared to which the Latins, even an Ambrose or an Augustine, were upstarts? Whoever was separated from the Eastern Church, for whatever reason, must be a heretic. Already in the schism of Photios[16] in the ninth century, which prepared the way for the Great Schism of 1054, it became clear that the reproach of heresy was secondary. Among the heresies which the great scholar Photios found—he

---

15 Charles was anointed by Pope Stephen III (r. 752–757) in 754 along with Pepin, his father, and Carloman, his brother. On Pepin's death in 768, he and Carloman divided the kingdom between them. The death of Carloman in 771 left Charlemagne sole ruler for the next twenty-eight years. See *ODCC*, 321. MH

16 When Emperor Michael III (r. 842–867) deposed Ignatius, patriarch of Constantinople, in 858, Photius, still a layman, was appointed his successor, thus instigating controversy. See *ODCC*, 1283. MH

probably would have tolerated it, if his noncanonical vote had been recognized by Rome—the most significant, the only one which concerned the topic of doctrine, was the *Filioque*, the Occidental addition to the Nicene-Constantinople Creed, according to which the Holy Spirit proceeds not only from the Father but also from the Son. Perhaps the sentence by John of Damascus[17] in the exposition of the orthodox faith in the eighth century refers already to a border against the *Filioque*, accepted in Toledo in 589:

> [T]he Holy Spirit . . . is from the Father, and we call Him the Spirit of the Father. On the other hand, we do not claim that He is from the Son; however, we call Him the Spirit of the Son. [*De Fide Orthod.* 1.8; *Library of the Church Fathers* 44:27]

Although the *Filioque* was expressly taught even by theologians of the East (Ephraim the Syrian [ca. 306–373], Didymus the Blind [ca. 313–398], Epiphanius), it made itself felt theologically only because of Augustine's influence and became, corresponding to the Augustinian conception of the Trinity, a characteristic doctrine of the Western Church. If you compare both types of trinitarian doctrine, then you must say that the Greek Church here represents an older type which is still strongly determined by the theology of Origen, with its subordination of the Son and the Holy Spirit. Theologically, biblically seen, the Occidental teaching is more correct, even if one must concede to the Orient—even the popes did—that the introduction of the *Filioque* into the creed, the only one which the East and the West have in common, without asking the East was not well done. In the centuries of discussions, above all at the union councils and in the current practice of the Roman Church toward the East, the result has been that the substance of the *Filioque* must be recognized, but that it suffices if one retains the creed in its original form and only interprets it correspondingly. So Rome does not demand from a uniate church[18] that it accept the *Filioque* into the creed, as then in general in these points, as in other points, the Roman Church has been much more tolerant than the Eastern Church. The reproach of heresy has never been raised by Rome against the Orthodox Church, but rather the other way around. It was Photios, the universal scholar, who with his authority justified this charge and stamped it so deeply into the Church of the East that every Oriental Christian, even if he is so weak in his Christian faith that he doesn't even know the main teachings of his church, knows that the Holy Spirit proceeds only from the Father, and that the Christians of the West are heretics because they do not believe this. But the dogmatic reproach was only

---

17 John of Damascus (ca. 675–ca. 750) was a Greek theologian and doctor of the Church. He resigned his position in secular court to become a monk at the monastery of St. Sabas near Jerusalem. He was a defender of images in the Iconoclastic Controversy. See *ODCC*, 891. MH

18 That is, churches that are autonomous and use Eastern rites but are in communion with Rome. MH

a disguise for ecclesio-political claims. Opposing Nicholas I[19] was a patriarch who quite seriously thought about "directly laying claim to the 'primacy' for Constantinople" (Kattenbusch, *P.R.E.* 15:381).

The role which the *Filioque* played in the schism of Photios was played by the question of the *Azyma* ["unleavened bread"] in the schism of 1054. Along with other heresies, such as, for example, the Western practice of fasting on Friday and Saturday, which Photios had already criticized, the worst one for Michael Cerularius and the Eastern Church was the use of "unleavened bread" for the Eucharist, which had been adopted about two hundred years previously in the Occidental church. It is telling that, for the Church of the East, not only a false teaching but also an incorrect (according to its opinion) liturgical practice can be a heresy. As in Raskol,[20] the great ecclesiastical split in Russia in the seventeenth century, such world-shaking questions were decisive as whether in liturgy the name Jesus should be pronounced [in Russian] as "Issus" or "Yissus," whether one should sing the word "Hallelujah" twice or thrice, and whether the cross should be made with two fingers or three, so here the validity of the Eucharist was placed in question if it was celebrated with unleavened bread. To understand this, one must consider that for the Eastern Christians, "orthodoxy" is not only a state of doctrine, that the holy rituals play a very different role and are almost even a means of grace. It is a different [type] of religious thought and feeling, which already then was foreign to the West. The Roman Church then, as always, declared the use of leavened or unleavened bread to be an *adiaphoron* and opined that each church should remain in its custom. But so arose the terrible scenes, which one must keep before one's eyes to understand the entire tragedy of the church's split: the tabernacles of the Latin churches of Constantinople were broken open and the consecrated hosts were trampled underfoot. It was men in high places, not the rabble, who did that. If church fellowship was broken, then the other side must be heretics. To be a heretic at that time—it was the time in which, during the dispute about Berengar[21] [Berenger], the Sacrament of the Altar moved into the center—meant not to have the Sacrament of Christ. Again, dogma was only a facade, as in all the controversies between East and West. There were really no doctrinal differences in the Middle Ages between the two churches. Where there were differences, then it was

---

19 Nicholas I (r. 858–867) was one of the most forceful of the early medieval popes, even involving himself in the controversial appointment of Photius as patriarch of Constantinople. See *ODCC*, 1148. MH

20 "Raskol" was the schism of the Russian Orthodox Church into an "official" church and "Old Believers" brought on by the reforms of Patriarch Nikon (r. 1652–58) in 1653. MH

21 Berengar of Tours (ca. 1010–88) was a pre-scholastic theologian. Much criticized for his teaching on the Eucharist, his case was discussed twice by Leo IX (r. 1049–54) in 1050. He maintained the fact of the real presence but denied that any material change in the elements is needed to explain it. See *ODCC*, 190–91. See Sasse, *This Is My Body*, 33ff. MH

always so, that the Eastern Church represented an older type of theology. Not even the doctrine of the papacy was different in those centuries. For a dogma about this had not even been defined in Rome, and the conciliary movement in the Occidental church of the late Middle Ages, like the Gallicanism in which it was foreshadowed, show what was still possible in the Roman church.

> We have never disputed with the Roman Church about the primacy . . .
> neither have we forgotten the old traditions and the decisions of the
> fathers, by which the Roman church is declared to be the oldest of all
> churches

wrote the scholar Nilos Kabafilas in the fourteenth century.

3

That this matter was really organized only around political and ecclesio-political matters, and not around doctrinal questions, is shown also by the history of the attempts at reunification since the Councils of Lyon in 1274 and Florence in 1439. The terrible debt which Rome brought upon itself toward the East in the era of the crusades and of the short-lived Latin empire of Constantinople could only deepen the chasm and make the schism unhealable. If political reasons, above all the threat posed by the Turks, forced the Byzantine emperor to concede, that didn't help. Even the dogmatic concession on both sides could not remove the schism and will never be able to, because the deeper reason for the split lies on a level at which a dogmatic unification means nothing. It is shocking to see how, after the fall of Constantinople, of the second Rome, the split continued and how now the "third Rome," Moscow, inherited the enmity toward Rome. Not even the Baptism of the Roman Church was recognized, and the conversion of a Russian to the Roman Church was forbidden. It could be done only secretly, as in the case of the great forerunner of a union between the two churches at the end of the nineteenth century, [Vladimir Sergeyevich] Solovyov [1853–1900]. All the sins of old Byzantium were copied and exceeded by Moscow. All attempts of pious Catholics and pious Orthodox to overcome the schism were until now in vain. Neither the prayers for unity—one of the most beautiful is from Bessarion[22]— nor the deep repentance of pious monks of the East as well as of the West, nor the theological work of our century, so great in its way—a worthy parallel to the best which the ecumenical work of the West has accomplished—nor the clever atonement policies of the popes since Leo XIII [r. 1878–1903], above all the current [pope],[23] have had success. The iron curtain which fell in the year 1054

---

22 Bessarion (1403–72) was a Greek scholar and statesman who became a monk in 1423 and was appointed metropolitan of Nicaea in 1437. He accompanied Emperor John VIII Palaeologus (r. 1425–48) to the Council of Ferrara Florence, where in the course of the debates he was persuaded by the Latin's arguments and became an ardent advocate of the union of the Latin and Greek Churches. See *ODCC*, 195. MH

23 Pope Pius XII. MH

has not been, to this day, removed. On the contrary, it seems as if the political division between Russia and the West, which today tears the world and which is also a consequence of the churchly schism, makes atonement impossible. It seems that Christendom must carry this wound until the end.

Why is healing, by human measurements, impossible? Is there no healing of sick churches? Is there no repentance, no conversion, for churches? We must be clear about this, that the most unrepentant thing in this world is a church. Don't we know from the history of our own church how difficult it is for a church to repent, even for the church which began with Luther's first thesis, according to which all Christian life should be repentance? The repentance which would have to precede the healing of this schism would not only be the regret about that which people did to one another out of a lack of love. Not only the regret about the shame which they did to the Lord Christ. It would not help, either, if the churches of the East and of Rome rethink the questions which are divisive between them. It would not be beyond possibility that both churches—despite the Vatican and the claims of the papacy which were elevated to dogma by it— could agree with each other roughly in the way in which Solovyov thought: the Eastern Church recognizes the position of Peter and his successors in Rome in the same way, in Solovyov's opinion, as the great Greek fathers had done it; and on the other side, Rome recognizes the Eastern Church as a church without reservations. Why should it not become the creed of the Eastern Church, as Solovyov says in his famous "credo":

> as a member of the true and most worthy Orthodox, Eastern, or Greek-Russian Church, which does not speak through the mouth of the anti-canonical synods—

that means of the "most holy directing synod," which, after Peter the Great got rid of the Moscow patriarchy, ruled the church of Russia until the rebuilding of the patriarchy after the Kerensky revolution of 1917—

> and not through the bureaucrats of worldly state power, but rather only through the voice of its great teachers and fathers, I recognize as the highest judge in matters of religion the one who was recognized as such by St. Irenaeus, St. Dionysius the Great, St. Cyrill, St. Flavian, the blessed Theodoric, St. Maximus the Confessor, St. Theodot of Studion, St. Ignatius, etc.—namely, the apostle Peter, who in his successors lives, and who heard not in vain the word of the Lord: "You are Peter, and upon this stone I will build My church—strengthen your brothers—tend My sheep."

When Solovyov then refers to [Josip Juraj] Strossmayer [1815–1905], the courageous bishop of the Croats, who for the sake of the union struggled at the Vatican against the dogma of the universal episcopate and against the dogma of infallibility, the Catholics, who despite the Vatican decisions wrestle for the unity of Eastern and Western catholicism, stand before his eyes. Solovyov died young in 1900—that he allowed himself to receive the final Sacrament from an

Orthodox priest because none other could be found does not change anything about his views and does not indicate a "retreat" into the Eastern Church— without therefore realizing that the popes of the twentieth century would go the path of atonement in his sense and would not demand that any Christian or any congregation of the Eastern Church give up any part of its heritage. Why should such atonement, at least with that segment of Eastern Christendom which has preserved for itself the freedom for a decision of this type, lie entirely outside the realm of possibility? But if it came to that, if the deep spiritual efforts of the monks of Almay-sur-Meuse [France] or of Gerleve in Westphalia, to name only two examples, were successful in breaking the stubbornness and pride of hearts, would that then be the repentance of both churches? No. The true repentance of the church is always the return to the Word of God. And neither Western Catholicism nor Eastern Orthodoxy is ready to make this return, to bow before the Word of God. It is telling that when the great Russian thinkers such as Solovyov think about removing the schism, they take their decisive arguments from old churchly tradition and from speculation about the church as the Body of Christ in the sense of a continuation of the incarnation, or even from an almost theosophic speculation about "divine wisdom," a preexisting *Sophia*, which is then further brought into connection with the mother of God. The Holy Scripture comes into the question only insofar as it has to present the *dicta probantia* [the proof passages"], which are to be interpreted in the sense of the consensus of the fathers. And it is telling that the Orthodox, even Solovyov, have in common with Rome the incredibly deep rejection of Luther and the Reformation. Here is the deepest reason why a real turnaround, a real repentance by both churches, is impossible, why even a possible union would not change anything about the situation of Christendom. For the repentance of the church is, if it is a real repentance, a return to the lost and forgotten Word. *The repentance of the church is reformation.*

4

As we say this, we aren't claiming that in the Catholic Churches of the East and of the West the Word of God has disappeared or that it has no power over the spirits. On the contrary. What kind of power the Word of God must have in these churches, if neither popes nor ecumenical patriarchs, neither Roman nor Byzantine emperors, neither czars, sultans, nor Soviet governments have been capable of doing away with it! If it is true that the church of God lives by the Gospel, that it is maintained by Christ present in His Word and in His Sacraments, then this is true also of these large *ecclesias*. Even in them, the *ecclesia abscondita*[24] lives; there live the saints whom no church canonizes but who know the Lord.

---

24 That is, "the church hidden"; cf. *De Servo Arbitrio* (*Bondage of the Will*, 1525), Aland 38 (WA 18:652; AE 33:89). MH

Who has not met people among the Catholics in Germany and in the world who live from that bit of the Gospel which still lives even in their Mass? Their refuge is He who is addressed in the *Canon Missae* with *non aestimator meriti, sed veniae largitor* ["Not weighing our merits but pardoning our offenses"], and to whom one calls in one's dying hour: *Rex tremendae majestatis, qui salvandos salvas gratis, salva me fons pietatis* ["King of tremendous majesty, who in saving does save by grace, save me, O Font of Piety"].[25] Is it a coincidence that the thief on the cross plays such a big role in the Roman liturgy? And whoever in the churches of the Orthodox diaspora in the entire world has experienced the deep meditation with which the priests and deacons, who live the whole week long as simple laborers, and with which the congregations of refugees and their choirs pray and sing their "Gospodi pomilu," "Kyrie eleison," and receive Communion—whoever has experienced this understands something about the true church of Christ, which lives even under the covering of forms and formulas which are so rigid to our sensibilities, because even in them the Gospel is still living. And yet it is not the Gospel alone by which these churches live. Because they place "holy tradition" next to the Word, they carry all that which once entered the church by way of "tradition" in themselves: the religious and political "world" of ancient times. The *cultus* of Mary, saints, relics, and icons as a continuation of the natural religion of ancient heathenism, the philosophy of Origen up to the restoration of all things taught by significant theologians, Platonic and Aristotelian philosophy in Christian clothing, and additionally the evil political heritage of Rome and Constantinople—that is the "world" which formed these churches. So the Roman church is, according to Harnack's accurate characterization, really the Roman Empire, sanctified by the means of the Gospel, living on:

> It still rules the peoples; its popes rule like Trajan and Marcus Aurelius; in place of Romulus and Remus are Peter and Paul; in place of the proconsuls are the archbishops and bishops . . . into the smallest details, into the ecclesiastical justice system, even in the clothing one recognizes the continued effects of the old empire and its institutions . . . the pope, who calls himself "king" and "pontifex maximus," is the successor to Caesar. [*Das Wesen des Christentums*, 1903, p. 157][26]

Indeed, without this connection, the history of the papacy and its politics, even and especially regarding the East, can't be understood.

But what does this giant organism have to do with the church, which the New Testament calls the Body of Christ? What does the *codex juris canonici* [i.e., canon law], this perhaps largest legal book of our time, have to do with the Gospel? And whatever is true about the Roman Church is true also *mutatis mutandis* of the Eastern Church. However, in the East, where the Byzantine

---

25   See *TLH* 607:8. MH

26   *What Is Christianity*, trans. Thomas Bailey Saunders (New York: Harper & Row, 1957). MH

empire lived until 1453 and then was again resurrected in the Russian czardom, there was no room for a world-ruling spiritual caesar, though a man such as Michael Caerularius played with the thought of combining the worldly power with the spiritual power and so becoming that which he criticized in his Roman colleague and competitor. Thus the Church of the East had to settle for the opposite fate. It became a worthless slave of the Caesars. If the church stops being God's people, the communion of the saints, if it becomes instead of that a large institution with pompous ceremonies and impressive legal systems, who would blame the state for then building it into its power structure? So the patriarchs of Constantinople became imperial bureaucrats, whom the emperor, and later the sultan, appointed and fired. In Turkey the ecumenical patriarch was even the political head of the "Romans" under the sultan. And it is well-known the way Russia, from Ivan to Stalin [1878–1953], handled the church, how it oppressed it and exploited it. Because the churches of the East, like those of the West, were formed by the political world in which they lived and by the worldly culture which surrounded them, the world entered into them, and they themselves became a piece of the world, each in its own way. How can they ever get free of this "world"? Can they ever hear the words of the New Testament, in which the command to "reformation" goes forth unto Christendom: *et nolite conformamini huic saeculo, sed reformamini* ["Be not conformed to this age, but be reformed"], or as Luther translates: "*Stellet euch nicht dieser Welt gleich, sondern erneuert euch*" (Rom. 12:2)?

5

Nothing would be more wrong or more un-Christian than if we Christians of the "Reformation" imagined that we are in an essentially different situation because our fathers once heard the *reformamnini* and returned to the Word of God, to the Gospel. Nothing would be more un-Lutheran than if we Lutherans, who have learned from our reformer to see the deep distortion of the Gospel in the papal church, imagined that our churches were any less worldly or were perhaps even protected from becoming worldly. Even in Protestantism, even in Lutheranism, that which happened in 1054 in Catholic Christendom has [now among us] happened [again] on a smaller scale. Certainly not in such an impressive way, but our churches are not really such impressive organizations. There were dogmatic reasons when, in the sixteenth and seventeenth centuries, all attempts to form relations between the Lutherans (Tübingen) and the Reformed (Geneva), on the one side, and the Eastern Church, on the other side, failed. Nothing else was to be expected. But from the viewpoint of the Catholic world of the East and the West, one must really ask why that which we call "Reformation" made so little impression on them, and in any case at that time was not understood by them as a call to repentance. How does it effect the Catholics of the Romantic countries of Europe and Latin American today when, under the slogan of the freedom of faith and in the name of the Reformation which those peoples missed, not only the representatives of large churches born out of the Reformation come to them, but rather at once the craziest American sects and cults? What do the Orthodox Christians of the East say when dilettante "missionaries," whom nobody has sent and who know nothing about the churches to which they come, bring them the Gospel, which they apparently themselves have not understood? Which part of Christendom is capable today of calling other parts to repentance with the authority of reformation? What difference is there, in principle, between the state's enslavement of the church among the Russian and Greek Orthodox, the Anglicans, and the Swedish Lutherans? What type of difference is there between the misuse of the church to achieve national goals in Russia throughout the ages and in protestant Prussia and Germany throughout the ages? The Prussian Union and the EKiD are, in this respect, on the same level as Byzantine church politics. And the political sins of German Lutherans in Hitler's empire are still screaming toward heaven, and forever will be, won't they? If Bolshevist Russia thinks itself able to afford a patriarch in Moscow, why shouldn't the Orthodox archbishop of New York then be elected to [the office of] ecumenical patriarch in Constantinople and be flown thither with a military airplane? If the imperial synods of ancient times had a spiritual and a worldly side, do the German Evangelical Church conventions not have such? What kind of a strategy hides even in the choice of the convention sites: in Berlin—We are brothers, after all!—Leipzig—immediately before Evanston. How much [money] did the United States—and we're not thinking here of the churches of the USA, but rather about the military and civil governments—give out for churchly purposes in Europe and eastern Asia, despite the separation between church and state! And Geneva, the ecumenical council and its meetings: it is really not only the kingdom of God which is being built there. One must really keep these things in mind to understand the criticisms which are heard in the Roman church and in the Orthodox churches as soon as the word "Reformation" is spoken. Is this worldliness not a fate of all churches? And does not the final cause of even the smallest schism lie in this worldliness to which all churches are exposed? Does July 16, 1054, repeat itself over and over again in church history?

In asking this question, we ask what the Great Schism teaches us, the churches who refer to the Reformation, and especially the Lutheran Church. It must teach us above all to understand more deeply what our Confession teaches about the church and the unity of the church, and to act accordingly in the church. The deepest hardship of our churches consists in this: that doctrine and real life aren't consistent with each other; that therefore in all decisive questions, [it is] no longer the Confession, but rather the real or alleged needs of practical ecclesiastical life which are the norm for all decisions. But thereby one door after another is opened to secularization. It is clear to everyone's eyes how this purely worldly ecclesiastical politics has shredded the old Lutheran Churches of Europe. The Confession is no longer a working hypothesis. Which Lutheran church government in Germany or Scandinavia does anything about it, if its Lutheran offspring are being formed in an un-Lutheran theology, for example, regarding the Sacraments? If in Denmark a professor can deny eternal life, and in Norway even bishops can deny the existence of hell, and a governmental commission decides that this is allowed, in what sense is then the *consensus de doctrina evangelii et de administratione sacramentorum* ["agreement concerning the doctrine of the Gospel and the administration of the Sacraments, AC VII] still the unifying bond of the church? What would happen to the bishops of Hanover or Bavaria if they explained that the lectures of the notorious deniers of the Lutheran doctrine would henceforth no longer be acknowledged in their [academic] departments? But what does it mean, then, to erect before the eyes of the world a "United Lutheran Church," which more or less separates itself from the union? What is the unifying bond of this church? Why can they tolerate in Braunschweig churches of all [sorts of] heretics, but not the one congregation which is strictly Lutheran but which has reintroduced a few ceremonies of the fathers? What holds this church together, the *consentire de doctrina evangelii* or the *ritus aut ceremoniae ab hominibus institutae* ["the agreement in the doctrine of the Gospel" or the "rites and ceremonies instituted by men," AC VII]? Just like the union churches of Prussia, Baden, and elsewhere were held together by the organization and not by the doctrine, so it really is today with the large and small churches of the Old World and recently of the New World. For even Dr. Franklin Fry will not want to claim that the United Lutheran Church is held together by the unity of faith, teaching, and confession. And perhaps this is true of most of the Lutheran Churches of America. They have become teachable pupils of European Lutheranism. This is a development which has completed itself in America only in this century. And now it moves on toward the mission fields. In India and Africa we have missionaries and mission bishops who have received, by the Church of Sweden, apostolic succession. They stand in church fellowship with the Church of England, commune there, and stand in Anglican chancels. Their fellowship with the other Lutheran Churches has already become very loose, and some of these Lutherans will not exercise their office or commune in a church without succession. In what sense are they still Lutherans? What does the Lutheran Confession mean to the Church of Sweden, if, at the consecration of its bishops, other bishops participate who freely declare that the *sola fide*, which is the *articulus stantis ec cadentis ecclesiai* ["the article by which the church stands or falls"], is a heresy? From this, one must understand that in the LWF the Confession is only one [of several possible] working hypothese[s]. As the ecumenical council admits every church which endorses the vague confession of the deity of Christ without asking what it means, so the LWF admits every church, and must admit every church, which endorses the constitution [of the LWF] with the confessional article, even if everyone knows that here the faith of the Augsburg Confession is no longer confessed as the norm of [all] doctrine. How could the LWF be even more Lutheran than its member churches?

But thereby the question is placed to the Lutheranism of the world: What is the unity of the church really, if the unity of the faith, teaching, and confession no longer exists? How do the Lutheran Churches think they will answer the Reformed, Anglican, Catholic, and Orthodox when they ask what the true unity of the church is, which we emphasize so much at every Reformation festival?

Where the true unity of the church, the unity in the pure doctrine of the Gospel and in the administration of the Sacraments according to the Scripture, is no longer understood, there it must come to this dissolving of the unity of the church of which the Great Schism is the great, warning example. The Lutheran Church was a unit in the sixteenth and seventeenth centuries as it was one in the faith, teaching, and confession, though it had no unified organization, just as the church of the New Testament was, though it had no common organization, but rather each local church was the church of Christ in that area. In that moment in which the purity of doctrine stops, in which the pure Gospel is no longer preached—and the pure administration of the Sacraments is always a part of this according to the Lutheran understanding—in that moment unity also fractures, as Luther said in that phrase (WA 31:255.5ff.) which is quoted in the FC (SD III 6):

> where this one article (about justification) remains purely on the plan, then Christendom remains pure and quite fine and without serious problems. But where it does not remain pure, then it is impossible that one can deter some errors or problematic spirits. [Cf. Tappert, 540.]

The history of the church has confirmed this. It appears as though now that which today calls itself "Lutheranism" in the world has had this bitter experience. It seems that we are losing today, in the era of the large organizations of Lutheranism in the LWF, that which the Lutheran Churches still had left of unity. It appears as though we Lutherans are following after the Anglicans and the Reformed. But how do we then want to give testimony before the Christian world about that which is the true unity of the church? Can we still want to say this to the Catholics and to the Eastern Churches without making ourselves laughable?

Perhaps this witness can no longer be given today by the large church organizations which call themselves Lutheran with more or less justification. Then the small free churches must do it, the isolated Lutheran congregations and the pastors who still take the Confession seriously. There have been times in church history in which, judged by human standards, a hopeless minority had to preserve and defend the truth of the New Testament about the church and its unity. It may be that this will again become clear in the era of large church organizations on the national and international level. What the large churches, church organizations, and "super churches"—this is what they are, even if they deny it—can no longer do, that is what the small circles and individuals do. What the bishops, archbishops, and church presidents can simply no longer do, even if they perhaps would like to, that is what we pastors must do. That is the incredible responsibility which today is upon us, and may God strengthen us with the Holy Spirit thereto. The gigantic organizations of the church world, which all rest upon a synthesis of church and world, have no promise, in 1954 just as little as nine hundred years ago. The promise of the Lord belongs only to the Word of the Gospel, which will outlast heaven and earth, and to the Sacraments in which Christ is present, and to the office which preaches atonement in that it administers the means of grace, and to the one holy church which is daily commanded anew by Word and Sacrament.

☙

In the bonds of faith, greeting you all who bear the hardship and shame of the church, but who also may participate in the joy and promise of faith in the church,

Your
Hermann Sasse

Historical Context

Sasse reflects on a world in which China had closed itself to Christian missions, millions were being martyred in communist Russia, and, even more shocking, millions were apostasizing from Christianity to the Communist Manifesto. Along with the defection from Christianity evident in the West, this meant Sasse recognized that the utopian dreams of early twentieth-century missiologists that the world would be evangelized during their lifetime was utter folly. "Indeed, the entire world is today a mission field." And particularly in Asia, asserted Sasse, the future of humanity and of Christianity would be determined. Time has proven Sasse's judgment correct regarding the BATAK Church in Indonesia and upon all Lutheran mission efforts in Asia which fail to establish genuine Lutheran churches. "Communism would never have achieved such victories if it hadn't satisfied the hunger for dogma which the churches weren't able to satisfy anymore. But why have we kept from people the true dogma of the pure Gospel? May God strengthen us all for the battle for the true confession and help us, in the power of Christ's love, to call back to the Gospel's truth a Christendom which is sinking into relativism." MH

December 30, 1954[1]

The Rev. Martin Franzmann
St. Louis, Mo.

And the Rev. M[artin] Naumann,
Springfield, Illinois

Very Honored and Dear Brothers!

. . . The end of Oberursel[2] is the end of the witness of Missouri in Germany and Europe. It is the end, so far as we men can know, of the German free churches . . . . For what has preserved these free churches was the fact that the American brothers in the faith stood behind them. And these small free churches were the conscience of the territorial churches. All those who in the nineteenth century left the territorial churches for the sake of the Lutheran altar and pure Lutheran doctrine for reasons of conscience at least had the moral support of the [American] brothers in the faith. I have just read again over Christmas the

---

1   Letter from the Behnken Files, CHI. MH
2   Thankfully, the seminary at Oberursel survives to the present. MH

biography of [Friedrich] Brunn [1819–95]. If someone today does what your fathers did, through which Missouri became great, then in one fell swoop he's ignored by Missouri. I have behind me thirty years' struggle for the Lutheran Church. The church councils and Freemasons of the Union, [Alfred] Rosenberg and the Gestapo, Karl Barth—who forbade my publishing house, which had published the series which I initiated of the Confessing Church, from publishing new editions of my writings—and [Joseph] Goebbels [1897–1945] who confiscated paper to be used for another book, the Luther Academy which did not allow my participation because I was not a member of the [Nazi] Party, the *Kultus Ministerium* which refused to grant me a pass to travel during the Third Reich—all these and still a few other instances were not so horrid as the leaders of your church, who smashed the Schwabach Convent and helped [Hanns] Lilje and [Otto] Dibelius break the opposition to the EKiD. I have overcome all of this, but I cannot conceive that Missouri will now kill the free churches by forcing their rising theological generations to study at state universities, where no one is allowed to hold the teaching office who advocates the old doctrine of Missouri and the Lutheran church on the Lord's Supper and fellowship in the Supper . . . .

Your devoted
H. Sasse

thirty-five

The Lutheran Church and World Mission

TRANSLATED BY ANDREW SMITH

September 1954[1]

Prof. D. Theol. Hermann Sasse
41 Buxton Street
North Adelaide, South Australia

Dear Brothers in the Office!

I will never forget the session in which my great teacher Ulrich von Wilamowitz-Moellendorf (1848–1930) impressed upon us students that an academically educated person should never write about something about which he understands nothing. Wilamowitz was, however, a researcher into ancient things, and I do not know whether many theologians have given their followers the same advice.[2] In any case, it was not followed. Otherwise, the theological discussions of our era would be carried out with significantly less volume and with fewer participants. The youth movements, which have attached themselves to ecumenical organizations for the purpose of forming posterity, would apply themselves to more useful purposes than the discussion of questions about which they yet understand nothing and can understand nothing. And also some other things in the churches would be different. For we want calmly to admit

---

1   *BLP* 35: *Lutherische Kirche und Weltmission* (North Adelaide, September 1954). The original was published in *LuBl* 6, no. 38 (October 31, 1954): 153–70. Huss number 310. MH

2   "I shall never forget what I learned from Ulrich von Wilamowitz-Moellendorf on Plato. Once I had to pass an exam with him on Aristophanes and Menander. With some trembling, I entered his big study and was pleased when he seemed to have forgotten his Greek comedies and instead gave me a private lecture on the style of St. Paul" (Sasse, "Reminiscences of an Elderly Student," 4–5). MH

that the greatest churchly decisions of our time are made by people who perhaps have the best intentions but who do not understand the things about which they are making decisions.

But there are also situations in which even an outsider must speak, even if he runs the danger of speaking about things of which he understands nothing. So I will dare today to speak about a problem which is urgent for all of us—a problem about world missions, even if the brothers among my readers who are or were themselves missionaries, or who have by virtue of their office busied themselves with missiology, will disagree with one or two points. The question which is pressing upon us is that of the possibility of Lutheran churches in today's mission fields, and thereby the future of the Lutheran church in the large mission areas of the earth. Above all, the situation in southeast Asia is before me, which we here from Australia view with special attention, because it affects us indeed in a special way. It is not only our fate which is being decided in this part of the earth.

1

It is necessary that, over and over again, we bring home to ourselves the situation of today's world mission. It was indeed at the most recent conference on world evangelism that the concept was expressed that there is in essence no longer any difference between Christian countries and mission fields. Indeed, the entire world is today a mission field, in the sense that all people need evangelization. There are not churches in India or among the Batak [Sumatra] as there are in Braunschweig and in large parts of Sweden. We have already in these letters recalled the words with which John Mott[3] closed the world mission conference in Edinburgh in 1910, in connection with Archbishop Davidson's[4] speech:

> May God grant that we all in the coming moments make the solemn decision to form our plans and to act and to live in such a way, and so sacrifice in such a way, that those to whom we go will be grasped by the same Spirit. And it may be that the archbishop's words will show themselves to be a glorious prophecy, and that many of us will not taste death before we see God's kingdom coming with power.

For many this meant that, within the present generation, the evangelization of the world—indeed, even the Christianization of humanity—would be completed. The secular faith in progress, which saw in the Euro-American civilization a culture which, because of its internal and external superiority, would

---

3   American Methodist John Raleigh Mott (1865–1955) was student secretary of the International Committee of the YMCA (1888). He chaired the committee which called the first International Missionary Conference at Edinburgh in 1910. See *ODCC*, 1120. MH

4   Randall Thomas Davidson (1848–1930) served as archbishop of Canterbury beginning in 1903 and was a confidential advisor to Queen Victoria (r. 1838–1901). MH

spread out over the entire earth and would become the culture of humanity, found a parallel in Christendom and in this concept of missions. It took two world wars and a series of revolutions and political realignments, such as the decline or transformation of the large colonial world powers, to break this hope, and this optimism is still not entirely dead. But the reality of today's world events speaks far too loudly. Consider the single fact that the vast expanse of China, with its soon to be 600 million people, one of the largest and most promising mission fields of the earth, is now closed to Christian missions, insofar as this is not carried out by brave and faithful Chinese confessors and martyrs. It is a catastrophe as large as the decline of the old Nestorian church once was, which endured from the Near East to the Far East for centuries, until the late Middle Ages. It is one of church history's divine mysteries, which we will never understand in this life, why God leads His church through such declines. Perhaps the martyrdom which is running its course behind the Iron Curtain and other curtains is, in His eyes, much greater than everything which missions have done for building the church. And perhaps, even here, the blood of the martyrs will be the seed of the church.

But what must shock us even more deeply than the fact that the church is led through martyrdom—the Lord did, after all, predict that—is something else. The church is not dying from martyrdom, but from apostasy. How did it happen that a small booklet, which appeared in 1848 under the title *The Communist Manifesto* [1948], has gained such a power over minds? It began in the Christian countries. Karl Marx was the son of a baptized Jew, but his closest collaborator, Friedrich Engels, came from a pietistic factory family in Wuppertal, from one of the many pious families which have always been such loyal supporters of missions. And they found their followers among Europe's workers, Catholic and Protestant. And now this small book, which became the catechism of Europe's workers, has become the confession of uncounted millions throughout the entire world, perhaps the most-used textbook in contemporary humanity, the contents of which even illiterates learn. What does this mean? Does it indicate that the power of the Christian faith has been extinguished or that the Christian message has lost its attractiveness for so many people? Simply compare the numbers of the missionary statistics for the Christian missionaries and the Islamic missionaries in Africa, and you will be shocked, even if you consider that the figures aren't comparable. Consider Islam's power, consider that our mission had its great successes among the primitive people, but that there has not yet been a breakthrough into one of the main high religions of Asia. We do not want to minimize in any way the rich harvest which God has, despite everything, still granted to our mission work. With nothing but thankfulness can we consider the sometimes superhuman work which our missionaries, and not only the Lutheran ones, perform under conditions of unspeakable difficulty. But the big question can't be silenced, whether Christendom as a whole hasn't lost something. It is not only the changed world situation, the awakening of various people groups who now continue the nationalism of our nineteenth century and thence steer straight into Communism, which makes our work so difficult. It must be a deep sickness which has taken from Christendom of all denominations the power which it once had. Such a sickness once destroyed the churches of Africa and Asia, save for a small remnant, as many Christians could hardly wait until they became Muslims and could thereby escape the special tax which they had to pay. A similar sickness is passing through Europe's churches today. It is useless to close one's eyes to it. It doesn't help, if [we renovate] the altar [and make it] higher and prettier, or if more and more clergymen march out in front of it in pompous robes. We have nothing against a good liturgy and a liturgical movement. But if that is supposed to be a substitute for the absent congregation and for the lost Confession, then that is a sign that the church is terminally ill. It won't help, either, if theology becomes more and more subtle, and whenever possible uses a language which an ordinary mortal can no longer understand. Even that can't be a substitute for that from which the church lives. For this type of theology has nothing to do with the authentic theology from which the church lives. That is the theology which can be prayed, like the great theology of the Middle Ages and of old Lutheranism. That is the theology which is a confessing theology like the Nicene Creed [AD 385] or the Augsburg Confession [1530]. That is the theology which even children can already learn, like the Small Catechism [1529]. If we had such a theology, then the church would be helped in many respects. One need only to consider the repulsive vanity and glory-seeking of modern theologians of all denominations in order to remark that something here is wrong, that the secularization of the spiritual life is located in exactly that place from which the cure for it should come.

2

The experience of evangelization's history teaches us that Christianity is adopted in that form in which it appears in the mission fields. The "Arianism" of the old Germanic tribes had nothing to do with Arian convictions. The western Goths [simply] took on that [form of] Christianity which held sway in the eastern part of the Roman empire. Young Wulfila[5] and his parents were Catholics, because at that time there was not yet any other [type of] Christianity. This old lesson is being repeated in the newer evangelization history. Whether an Indian becomes an Anglican, a Baptist, or a Lutheran depends essentially on the accident that

---

5   Ulfilas (Ulphilas, ca. 310/313–381/383), the "apostle of the Goths," was born among the Goths, though he spent his early years in Constantinople, where he was consecrated bishop around 341. Ulfilas returned to his native country and spent the rest of his life as a missionary. He translated the Bible into the Gothic language, omitting the Books of Kings for fear that the deeds recorded there might have a negative influence upon the warlike Goths. Ulfilas was led into Arianism by Eusebius of Nicomedia, and for several centuries the Goths continued in that heresy. An Arian confession of faith by Ulfilas has survived. See *ODCC*, 1654. MH

one or the other missionary society was active in his area. Only in the large cities, where the denominations and confessions exist next to one another, is there a question of a free choice, just as in the Rome of the waning second century a heathen who wanted to become a Christian had to decide between five or more communities, which all claimed to be the only church of Christ. A further lesson is this: that, at least in the first generations, the confession adopted by "coincidence" is truly internalized. The faith in the Savior will be internally taken on in that form in which it came, together with its dogmatics and its liturgy. In the mission fields, where the new mission congregation remains unified and closed for a long time, the connection between the evangelical message and its ecclesiastical and denominational form can maintain itself for a very long time, especially under simple conditions. In this way, truly confessional mission churches can arise. But in many mission fields, the question will sooner or later arise: Why am I a Lutheran or a Methodist or a Catholic? This question, which [has already appeared] in countries which were very early covered by a network of various mission activities—such as China a generation ago, India and Indonesia today—appears sooner or later in every mission field. For Lutheran mission work, this means that it must prepare its young Christians with great seriousness for the day on which they will have to give an account of their Lutheran faith before the world, in the deep conviction that their confession is not the special property of one of the many denominational churches, but rather the profession of the one truth of the Gospel of Jesus Christ. Whether this day comes sooner or later, it comes for every mission church, as it came for the church of the Old World. On this day it is decided whether a church is Lutheran or not. Just as we are not Lutherans simply because our ancestors lived in a "Lutheran" territory in 1624 or because we recently moved from Berlin to Hanover—which suffices, in Germany, to change one's confessional status and to make an atheist *de jure* into a Lutheran—so also a newly converted Christian in the mission field is not yet a Lutheran merely because his missionary society calls itself Lutheran.

From this one must understand that the question about correctness or incorrectness of denominations, and the call for the unity of the church, rings nowhere louder than in the great mission fields, where the manifold Christian denominations stand next to one another and against one another. One can well understand when the Indians ask why the schisms of Europe and America, in which they did not participate and for which they are not responsible, now split Indian Christendom. However, one must accept such reproaches and complaints only with caution. The Indian people has always been split in matters of religion. In how many different forms does Hinduism alone appear? One cannot ward off the suspicion that, in criticizing the ecclesiastical schisms, the Indian Christians have been the good pupils of their missionaries, which is also true of the means toward unity which are today so pressingly recommended. The southern Indian Union, to take the most significant example, is the work of English missionaries who attempted to solve their [own] unification problems in the mission field.[6] For the southern Indian Union was made with an eye toward that which is called the "Home Reunion" in England, the reunification of the dissidents (Congregationalists, Methodists, etc.) with the state church. And yet the call to unity is not to be understood only in this way. Humanity can clearly tolerate the fact that there are different Islamic sects, and that Buddhism divides itself into a series of denominations, among which is the great schism between southern Buddhism and northern Buddhism. But the dividing of Christendom is something else. It is really something else, because all Christians confess, in the Nicene Creed: "I believe in one holy, catholic, and apostolic church." What does this confession mean? That is the question which humanity, Christian and non-Christian, puts to us. In the light of this question, we have to justify our demand that there should be Lutheran churches even in the mission fields of the world.

3

The question whether there should be Lutheran churches even in the mission fields of the world is asked with special seriousness in southeast Asia. For more and more, the mission societies and missionaries who have lost their fields of work in other parts of the world seek new missionary regions in India, Burma,[7] Formosa,[8] Japan, Indonesia, and New Guinea. For the old friends of New Guinea evangelization, it is astounding how this remote mission field, once the most remote part of the world, moves into the center of missionary concern. This is in part conditioned by the fact that, in other parts of the world, the missionaries work "subject to recall" (so to speak). The awakening nationalism of the people of Africa and Asia simply will not long tolerate a missionary system which appears to be inseparably bound to the hated "colonialism" and "imperialism." Indeed, the lifestyle of some American and English missionaries was completely different than the realization of apostolic poverty, for example, when the activity of these missionaries was supported by colleges and other institutions with millions [of dollars]. If all indications do not deceive, the missionary of the future must be a man of his [own] people, an African in the developing areas of the British Commonwealth in Africa, an Indian or Ceylonese in his land, and the main activity of the missionary societies will have to confine itself to the education of the native-born missionaries, as it indeed today already is the case to a large extent. The missionary policies of the Roman church, which everywhere assembles a native-born clergy of bishops and priests, points also in this direction. One must have seen the Indian cardinal of Bombay[9] once, in order to

---

6   See Letter 56, "The Union of South India as a Question to the Lutheran Church," in vol. 3 of *Letters to Lutheran Pastors* (forthcoming in 2015). MH

7   Now known as the Republic of the Union of Myanmar. MH

8   That is, the island of Taiwan, which is known officially as the Republic of China. MH

9   "Another leader was E. J. Palmer, since 1908 bishop of Bombay. It was a great experience for all of us participants in the world conference when this great Anglican

know how the future high clergy in this land will appear: the old Roman heritage melted together with the culture of the Indian subcontinent in a grand harmony. What happens to the Gospel in this case is another question; but we will encounter this question in the case of Protestant missions in a no less serious form.

The questions, which we can only [briefly] touch upon here, are being considered with great seriousness by the missionary societies, by the churches which come into question, and by the International Missionary Council and its various divisions. Nothing is farther from our intentions than to minimize this work. Nobody will forget what these large organizations have done in the area of maintaining mission fields, providing for missionaries, and the technical side of sending [people] out into our world that is shaken by wars and revolutions. Yes, still more: in the research into the primitive or highly developed cultures of the mission field, the languages and linguistic training, and in some other areas of missions (e.g., the pedagogical techniques), the International Missionary Council [IMC][10] has accomplished feats which are entirely unique in church history and which rise above the dilettantism which has so often destroyed true ecumenical work. The incorporation of the Missionary Council into the ecumenical [World] Council of Churches has, despite that, not proved itself to be a good move. For now material cooperation, the *cooperatio in externis*, the mutual help of mission societies, has been built into the program of the World Council. This development has been underway for a long time. What was said in Tambaram in 1938 about the unity of the church and the unification of the churches (cf. the short German report by K. Hartenstein, "The Miracle of the Church among the Peoples of the Earth," 1939, pp. 100 [160]ff., and the official

---

explained to us that the question for unity of the church is the question for the truth. At the beginning of his great speech by which he opened the deliberation of the controversial doctrine of the spiritual office, he said: "Our conference is about the truth, not about reunification. . . . Since we disagree so much on the basic questions, some of us must be in the wrong; in fact, all of us are perhaps to a certain degree in the wrong. We come here with the expectation to learn, and that must mean for us: with the hope of being corrected. We seek the divine truth" (*Die Weltkonferenz*, 298; cited also in Letter 56 in vol. 3 of *Letters to Lutheran Pastors* [forthcoming 2015]). Ronald Feuerhahn has concluded: "It can be argued, as Sasse himself asserted, that no German churchman with the possible exception of his 'Doktorvater' and ecumenical mentor, Prof. Adolf Deissmann, gave more time and commitment to the Lausanne Movement in the 1930s than did Professor Dr. Hermann Sasse. He more than anyone provided the administrative link between the German Church community and those abroad" (Feuerhahn, "Hermann Sasse as an Ecumenical Churchman," 65–66). MH

10 The International Missionary Council, organized in 1921 under the leadership of John R. Mott, Joseph H. Oldham and A. L. Warnshuis, grew out of the World Mission Conference at Edinburgh in 1910. Its purpose was to encourage and assist church and mission societies in their missionary task. Membership consisted mainly of national and regional interdenominational mission organizations. In 1961 the IMC became the Commission on World Mission and Evangelism (CWME) of the World Council of Churches and by the 1990s it been absorbed into Programme Unit no. 2 (Churches in Mission, Health, Education, Witness) of the WCC. See *Evangelical Dictionary of World Missions*, ed. A. Scott Moreau et al. (Grand Rapids: Baker, 2000), 498–99. MH

report in English, vol. IX),[11] that was such a shocking unionism, such a tangible denial of the biblical (Eph. 4:4f.) and Lutheran teaching (Augsburg Confession, Art. VII), that one wonders whether no Lutheran was still there who would have used the teaching of Scripture, the old confessions, and the Confessions of the Lutheran Reformation about the *una sancta perpetuo mansura* ["one holy church will perpetually remain," AC VII 1] to oppose the fanatical [*schwarmgeistig*] efforts to produce unity by means of common eucharistic celebrations and other methods (Hartenstein, p. 103 [163]), and thereby "strive toward the goal of authentic biblical union" (Hartenstein, p. 168).[12] Thus the way into the unionism of modern ecumeny was prepared. According to the opinion of the ecumenical council and its organizations in the mission field, Lutheranism may still exist in the future, but only as one of the [many different] instruments which work together in the large orchestra, to use the old image with which a representative of the church and of the academic department to which Johann Michael Reu (1869–1943) once belonged, traveled through postwar Germany. The Lutheran church in the old sense of the Confessions is no longer desired. The Lutherans themselves have apparently surrendered it—certainly not all Lutherans, but in any case all who are without protest of deed [as opposed to mere protest of words] in the EKiD, in the LWF, and in the ecumenical council. Is it a [mere] coincidence that the "confession of faith" from Tambaram is a modern reformed confession, which actually does talk a lot about the church but which mentions not a single word about the Sacraments?[13] Even the "German declaration to the World Evangelization Conference" doesn't do it. So the world's mission churches are in danger of becoming churches without sacraments, at least without the real Sacrament, which is a means of grace and not a harmless sign which one can, if needed, even omit. The LWF with its mission department can't help either. For the Sacraments, without which Luther couldn't even imagine a church, don't interest it very much, as both its words and deeds show.

4

We want to illustrate the situation of Lutheranism in southeast Asia by two examples. The first is the church of the Batak on Sumatra.[14] It was founded by

---

11 *The World Mission of the Church: Finding and Recommendations of the International Missionary Council, Tambaram, Madras, India, December 12–29, 1938* (London: International Missionary Council, 1939). MH

12 "A similar expression [to Niemöller's call for union of various churches] can be found before the war itself through Karl Hartenstein, Swabian Lutheran Pietist and former director of the Basel Mission, who at the Tambaram 1938 Conference of the International Missionary Council . . . [made the appeal for union in the work of mission]" (Feuerhahn, "Hermann Sasse as an Ecumenical Churchman," 137). Basel, of course, was the mother mission society of the Batak Church in Sumatra, Indonesia. MH

13 See *World Mission of the Church*, 154–55. MH

14 The Huria Kristen Batak Protestant (HKBP). MH

the Rhenish Mission Society in Barmen, which has become, through the life's work of the great missionary Ludwig Nommensen,[15] that which it signifies in the history of missions: the incomparable example of a "young church," independent since 1930, with its 1,000 congregations and 6,000,000 members one of the largest, if not the largest, of the "young churches." From Nommensen it has a Lutheran heritage, and so it attached itself to the LWF to escape the pincer movement of Indonesia's Reformed Churches. Now, nothing is to be said against the LWF's accepting a church [into membership], advising it, and supporting it, if it wants to be Lutheran. But it can only have full membership when it fulfills the conditions for acceptance which the LWF itself has set for its members. The LWF is indeed, according to its constitution, not a federation of churches which call themselves Lutheran—that is not even necessary—nor a federation of churches which, for practical or ecclesio-political reasons, want to be recognized as Lutheran and threaten to join the Reformed if they aren't so recognized—if they feel ties to the Reformed, why shouldn't they do that?—but rather the LWF is a group of churches which accept the Unaltered Augsburg Confession and Luther's Small Catechism as the correct interpretation of the Gospel. If a church can't do that, then one can teach it, one can enter into doctrinal discussions with it in order to make the Unaltered Augsburg Confession and the catechism so clear to it that it says "Yes!" to them with its whole heart. But the LWF has in no case done this, when it has accepted a non-Lutheran church (Federacao Sinodal, Italian, and other cases). It has thereby not only broken its own constitution, but rather, what is worse, shown that it does not take the Lutheran Confession seriously. In the case of a "young church" in the mission field, one can say that it is not in any condition to understand some passages in the Confessions (passages, the understanding of which requires the knowledge of the historical background, e.g., some phrases from the Augsburg Confession's Twenty-Eighth Article, in which the discussion is about the Catholic bishop's office in the sixteenth century), though the main thought, the division between worldly and spiritual power, should be clear to even the simplest Christian. It cannot be understood, then, why a young church doesn't translate the Augsburg Confession into its language and historical concepts.[16] Indeed, nobody will

---

15 Nommensen's work among the Batak began in 1861 in the Lake Toba region. He established schools, hospitals, and a theological seminary and translated Luther's Small Catechism into the Batak language. See Gerald H. Anderson, ed., *Biographical Dictionary of Christian Missions* (New York: Macmillan Reference USA, 1998), 499. While the HKBP is at its core a "union church," nevertheless there is even now a strong internal wind blowing which seeks genuine confessionally Lutheran theology. The church has several million members and more than 1,000 pastors. In recent decades, the church has divided mostly amicably into several different bodies, so there are eleven LWF member churches in Indonesia, all unionistic. MH

16 The entire Book of Concord has recently been translated into Batak by a bishop of a Sumatran partner church of the HKBP, with the assistance of the Lutheran Church of Australia. MH

object that in this way a new confession arises. But such a confession would have to express the doctrinal content of the Augsburg Confession. Let's look, in this regard, at the very famous confession of the Batak, which is understood by the LWF as genuinely Lutheran, but by Karl Barth (*Church Dogmatics* IV.1, p. 789) as a common Protestant confession—one which shames the constitution of his own Reformed church in Basel with its introduction which can only be understood as Arian. What strikes one at first is that not a single word mentions the Confessions of the Lutheran Reformation. They confess, with the fathers, the Apostles' Creed, the Nicene Creed, and the Athanasian Creed (how many of the Batak can understand that?) and state that the present confession is a continuation of the "confessions of faith which have existed until now," that is, these three, as if there were not also the Reformation's faithful Confessions. Then the articles of faith follow, with rejections of contemporary false teachings conditioned by the environment, including the false teachings of Rome, but never a Reformed false teaching. Much is good and incontestable, but the articles in which one seeks the specifically Lutheran teachings leave everything open, if they don't actually teach Reformed [beliefs]. When, for example, in the case of the signs of the true church, church discipline, the goal of which is supposed to be "the suppression of sin," appears on the same level as the preaching of the Gospel and "both" (the number two is always emphasized, in contrast to the Augsburg Confession) of the Sacraments, then it is [clearly] a false teaching of the Reformed. It goes without question that church discipline must be exercised, and that especially the mission congregations in the heathen world must emphasize this—here we can learn from them. But we cannot accept that for this reason the Reformed dogma is adopted, the Lutheran concept of church discipline which serves to save the sinner is silently rejected, and the concept of the church is [thereby] changed. It is also [a symptom of] Reformed [thought] that everything which the Lutheran Confession says about confession and absolution is silenced. "Pastoral care to the members of the church" is substituted. That is Zwingli's teaching, not Luther's. The doctrine of the church is also Reformed: "The church is the collection of those who believe in Jesus Christ, who are called by God by means of the Holy Spirit, gathered, sanctified, and preserved."

This quote from Luther's catechism cannot fool anybody about the fact that, according to Lutheran doctrine, membership in the church is connected to Baptism, which, according to Reformed teaching, would not immediately be accepted as valid, certainly not in the case of the children of baptized parents. Thereby we come to the doctrine of sacraments, which, according to Reformed custom, is begun with an article about the "two sacraments." Now, that may work, though it is not a relaying of the Lutheran doctrine, which knows no article *de sacramentis* and which, at least in the older Confessions, leaves the number of the sacraments open, because it is indeed the business of the church to use this word in whatever way may seem useful to the church.

The article about Baptism seems, at first glance, very proper: "Holy Baptism is the transmission of God's grace to humans. For through Baptism the faithful gain forgiveness of sins, a rebirth, redemption from death and the devil, and receive eternal blessedness." The sentence reminds us of Luther's catechism, and there would not be anything to say against it, if it weren't followed by a sentence about infant Baptism which clearly limits Baptism's gift, as it was immediately previously described, to adults: "Children, also, are to be baptized. For by means of Baptism, they are given over to the gathering of those for whom Christ suffered, and at the same time, the Lord Jesus accepts the children." Here there is no mention of the forgiveness of sins or of the rebirth. Why? Clearly [this document is] in the Reformed tradition, which knows nothing about this effect of the sacrament. Then, an article about the Lord's Supper follows, with the ambiguity of the [*Augustana*] *Variata*: "In Holy Communion, the eating of the bread transmits the body of our Lord Jesus Christ, and the drinking of wine mediates the blood of our Lord Jesus Christ."

[One wonders] if a simple Batak Christian really understands this stilted formulation? What does he receive in the Sacrament? That's what he wants to know. Is the consecrated bread the true body or not? Does he receive the body with his mouth or not? Do all who receive the Lord's Supper receive the body of the Lord, even the unworthy ones? Compare the clear words of Luther's catechism with this "mumble mumble mutter," as Luther called it in his letter to the citizens of Frankfurt.[17] This catechism is the textbook of the [Batak] church, they assured the LWF, and thereby the Christian world. It must have already given cause for reservations, that it was not numbered among the confessions. For if the Athanasian Creed can be understood, how much more so the children's catechism? Naturally, we all know the excuses with which some missionaries want to make us wise, that it is dangerous to announce Luther's doctrine of the Sacraments in the mission field because it could lead to heathen imaginations. But that is, in reality, an old reproach of Zwingli's. We announce this doctrine because it is in the Scripture. It is in reality the unionism of the Rhenish Mission Society and its missionaries which does not want to know anything of Luther's doctrine and therefore forged his catechism. For it is a forgery, if I change the work of a great human and Christian at decisive points which were for the author the heart and center of his faith, [a work] which has moreover become the confession of the church. We are not making reproaches toward the Batak, nor toward the simple missionaries who didn't know any better. But this reproach is well-aimed at the leadership of the Rhenish Mission Society, which is responsible before God and before Christendom about this. In all openness, this mission society declared in a special edition of its "reports" in July 1933 about the confessional character of the Rhenish mission in regard to Indonesia:

---

17   *Ein Brief an die zu Frankfurt am Main* (1533), Aland 225, WA 30/3:561. MH

Some have certainly claimed that the Rhenish Mission Society has brought Lutheranism to a place in which there was until now only the Reformed version of the Reformation faith under the influence of Holland. This opinion is certainly incorrect. The ecclesiastical home territory of the Rhenish Mission Society is the union church, without any particular confessional accent . . . so confessional bonds were not the reason that the Rhein brethren introduced the Lutheran Small Catechism for baptismal and confirmation instruction. Indeed, it can even be proved—for example, in the declaration about the Lord's Supper—that the Batak translation of the catechism weakened the confessional Lutheran character of the catechism to a large extent. It was based upon pedagogical mission decisions, when the Lutheran catechism was chosen over the Heidelberg catechism, not for confessional reasons. It showed itself in the conciseness of its explanations to be more useful than the thought-laden Heidelberg catechism.

About liturgy it is then said:

> The forms of worship were taken over, in the largest part, from the home church. So arose in the Batak Agenda, and later also in the Niassic[18] Agenda, a sort of Indonesian continuation of the Old Prussian Agenda. There weren't any efforts toward the introduction of confessional forms. The same is true of the order of Baptism, confirmation, and Holy Communion, which correspond to the union rites. [Quoted from *Missionsblatt Evangelisch=Lutherischer Freikirchen*, August 1955]

No missionary society is obliged to introduce Luther's catechism and a Lutheran agenda for the celebration of the Sacraments if it does not affirm the Lutheran Confession. But then it should make a union catechism and not forge the Lutheran one. There is no *Catechismus Variatus*.[19] If the LWF now declares that it did not know all this, and had no opportunity beforehand to inform itself, then one can only answer that, if the trip from Hanover to the mission society's headquarters in Barmen, where the files are kept, was too far for territorial Bishop Hanns Lilje (born 1899), then he could have sent one of his younger people. Then one could have given advice to the Batak based upon the facts. But probably everything was known in Hanover.

5

Let it be said once again: the simple Christians of the young churches are not to be held responsible for the church politics of their mother churches. They

---

18 The reference is to the church on the Indonesian island of Nias, famous for the devastation caused by the 2005 tsunami. MH

19 That is, a version of Luther's Small Catechism which was or could be continually altered in the way Melanchthon continued to alter the Augsburg Confession, resulting in interminable controversy with the churches of the Lutheran Confession until the Book of Concord flatly asserted the *Invariata* as the Confession of the church. MH

can, with the best of intentions, not know whether the catechism, which is presented to them in the native language, is authentic or not. They believe they produced the Batak confession themselves. They do not know that it is the echo of that which they have learned from their missionaries, even including the actual wording, which reminds one of the 1934 Barmen Declaration. The same tragedy appears to be underway now in other countries of southeast Asia.[20] The old confessions are replaced by new ones. Of itself, there would be no objection to this, if the dogmatic content remained the same. If now in India a new united Lutheran church would arise from the current church federation, then this church, too, will step into the limelight with a new confession, in which, as H. Meyer[21] (once a Breklumer missionary in India, now missionary director in Hamburg as the successor to D. Walter Freytag[22]) wrote in *The Lutheran World Review* of April 1950, "antiquated theological formulations and slogans are replaced" (p. 222). Naturally, this doctrinal declaration, too, contains many good things according to Scripture and the Confessions, as one can expect from theologians. But as soon as the declaration comes to the Sacraments, one wonders why here the Lutheran doctrine becomes at first unclear, and then is finally given up. The long, obscure declaration about Baptism already allows to be lost the certainty that Baptism gives the forgiveness of sins. Instead of that, we read: "Out of free grace, Christ allows His call to come to us, in order to redeem us from this world of sin and death."

But we hear nothing about forgiveness, especially when it talks about infant Baptism. The article about the Lord's Supper would be approved even by Calvin. There is neither an eating and drinking of Christ's body and blood, nor even a *unio sacramentalis*, a *manducatio oralis*, or a *manducatio impiorum*.[23] The real presence is confined to

---

20   At this point (2007) I do not know of a single nonunion or nonunionistic seminary in all of east Asia or southeast Asia among those seminaries which cooperate with the LCMS and the Lutheran bodies to the left of Missouri. That tragedy must be corrected if confessional Lutheranism is to have a future in east and southeast Asia. MH

21   Heinrich Meyer (1904–78) served as bishop of Lübeck beginning in 1956. He studied at Tübingen, Berlin, and Kiel, before entering the Indian mission field in 1930 with the Breklumer Mission. From 1934 he was president of the Jeypore Evangelical Lutheran Church in Orissa (India), leader of its theological seminary in Kotpad, and superintendent of the mission. While on leave in 1937–38, he prepared a *Lebensordnung* for the Confessing Church. In 1953, Meyer succeeded Freytag as Hanseatic mission director in Hamburg, also teaching theology at Hamburg University. See *NDB* 7:349–50. MH

22   Walter Freytag (1899–1959) was of Moravian background and studied at Tübingen, Marburg, and Halle. Beginning in 1928, he served as director of the Deutsche Evangelische Missionshilfe, as well as in leading positions in the international mission and ecumenical movements. See Anderson, *Biographical Dictionary of Christian Missions*, 228. MH

23   A "sacramental union" (i.e., body and blood united with bread and wine), an "oral eating" (i.e., the body and blood of Christ are eaten in the mouth) over against

the real personal presence of our Lord Jesus Christ as Savior, who became human for us, and who for us gave His body and spilled His blood. He, the entire Christ, God and man, now in glory, gives us Himself in the Lord's Supper under the bread and wine.

This, then, is supposed to be the new Lutheranism of India. Does anybody really believe that the Missouri Synod will join up with this church? What kind of a protest would the old people of Leipzig have made against this, men such as Senior Missionary D. Fröhlich, who struggled so valiantly for the Lutheran Lord's Supper in India, because he knew that the spiritualistic Indians with their incarnations (which are nothing of the sort) needed the real incarnation and the real presence as concrete forgiveness. (Cf. his essay, "Mission and Altar Fellowship," in *Concerning the Sacrament of the Altar*, 1941).[24] It may be that the current Leipzig Missionary Society has at some point spoken [about this confessional concern]. But in the world nobody has heard of it, just as nobody in the world has heard of a protest against the unionism in India. Now this society will send its people to New Guinea. It is not to be expected that Leipzig will demonstrate character there. In 1937, it was still possible to get some Lutheran mission societies in Germany to speak against the results of the so-called Confessing Synod in Halle, which lifted the eucharistic barriers between Lutherans and the Reformed. Today, they don't want to, or aren't allowed to, speak anymore.

6

One of the great decisions of humanity will be made in southeast Asia, not only in the area of politics but also in church history. For here Christendom encounters not only primitive religions but also the great high religions of humanity. The Roman Church understands this. It is arming itself for the great decisive battle of religions. It is building up the front with unheard-of amounts of people and institutions in Australia, not only in order to make good for the territorial losses in other parts of the earth but also because it compares Australia with the Ireland of the very earliest part of the Middle Ages, which sent its missionaries out onto the continent and helped to build up Christian Europe. Even the Protestant churches are beginning gradually to understand what the clock of world history is striking. The International Missionary Council has set its apparatus into motion. But the Missionary Council is not a church and therefore

---

Calvinism, and an "eating of the impious or unbelievers" (i.e., one receives Christ's body and blood no matter if one has faith or not; the body and blood are objectively present). These were the shibboleths of the Luther dogma over against Calvinist and Crypto-Calvinist cavilations. MH

24 Original title: *Mission und Abendmahlsgemeinschaft in Vom Sakrament des Altars* (Leipzig: Doerffling & Franke, 1941), 257–69. Sasse was contributor and editor for this significant volume of essays on the Lord's Supper, published with great difficulty during the war. Fröhlich is listed in the volume as Missionssenior D. Richard Fröhlich, Braunschweig. MH

cannot build any churches. But the Reformed churches, from the Anglicans to the liberal Baptists, know what they want. From Pakistan and northern India, across southern India, Ceylon, and Indonesia, the wreath of the new union churches stretches, which are in part already there and in part still being built. The plans for New Guinea, and even for the "reunited church of Australia"—what a curious idea, as if there ever were a unified church in our part of the earth!— are ready, and the high clerics fly from country to country to make the improved scheme of south India and Ceylon acceptable to Christendom. Every church can remain what it is. Only the ancient Christian confessions are valid; all others are nonbinding and can continue to be used privately. No common doctrine about the Sacraments is necessary. Infant Baptism and adult Baptism are both options, as long as confirmation by the bishop follows as a completion of the "rite of initiation." What one thinks about the Lord's Supper is his own business. What it depends upon is this: that the rite be perform correctly by a clergyman ordained in apostolic succession.

Naturally, the Lutherans will at first decline to enter into such a church. But how long will they be able to do that? When territorial bishop Lilje was in southern India, he gave the Lutheran congregations the advice not to join the Southern Indian United Church, as far as we know with the reason that the Lutherans should first unite themselves, and then "we'll see." In any event, it was not a clear rejection of the Southern Indian Union as a false church. And a differ- ent member of the executive committee, Bishop Eivind Berggrav[25] (1884–1959) from Norway, has already given the opposite advice. With what justification do the Lutherans in India deny their Reformed fellow countrymen pulpit and altar fellowship when they tolerate Meyer's creed concerning the Lord's Supper? Naturally, they will say, the dispute between Luther and Zwingli, which hap- pened centuries ago in Europe, does not concern them. Certainly, but what the Lord Christ said, and what the apostle Paul said by way of explanation about it, certainly should indeed concern them still to some extent. If they no longer take the "is" literally, and if they accept as justified the twisting of the "is" into a "represents," then they are no longer Lutherans, and no power in the world, not even the power of church politics, can stop their path into the Reformed union. The same is true of the Bataks, who still indeed have in their eucharistic article [of faith] a rejection of the Roman but not of the Reformed doctrine. If the Batak church wants to be a Lutheran church, then they must clearly define themselves in sacramental doctrine as apart from the Reformed church. If they don't do this,

---

25 Berggrav was bishop of Oslo from 1937 to 1950. He studied at Oxford, Cambridge, Marburg, and Lund and was influenced by Nathan Söderblom. Berggrav was elected president of the World Alliance for Promoting International Friendship through the Churches in 1939 and was active against the Nazi occupation of Norway. Arrested in 1941, he was imprisoned until 1945. See *ODCC*, 191. MH

then no power in the world, least of all the LWF, can hinder them from one day being a part of the "Reunited Church" of Indonesia.[26]

An essay by Dr. Fr. Schiotz,[27] until now the executive secretary for young churches and unsupported missions in the National Lutheran Council USA (now president of the Evangelical Lutheran Church in America) in the *International Review of Missions* of July 1954 shows how serious the danger is. Here the history of the Batak church's joining the LWF is briefly told by an expert with firsthand knowledge, citing his personal experience and access to files. Since 1947, negotiations were conducted about how one could help the church, which was severely damaged by the war. In 1948, the Huria Kristen Batak Protestant (Christian Protestant Church of Batak), as its official name stands, applied for membership in the LWF. Because there was still no constitution, negotiations were necessary. There was a meeting in Indonesia, in which Bishop (at that time president of the LWF) Anders Teodor Samuel Nygren (born 1890), Bishop Johannes Sandegren (1883–1962), Dr. Schiotz, the president of the Batak church, and a past president of the Batak church took part. To be tactful, they used a Swedish Methodist missionary as secretary at all the meetings. Two Batak students, as well as two German mission directors—Ihmels from Leipzig and Martin Pörksen from Breklum—took part as guests. The representatives of the Batak made it clear that they needed help, but that they actually

> were perhaps not 100 percent Lutheran, but still stood nearer to the Lutherans than to anybody else. Joining the LWF could not mean, for them, withdrawing their membership in the National Council of Churches of Indonesia and the cooperation in the common Protestant college in Djakarta. [Ibid., p. 319]

Bishop Nygren explained that their application should go before the plenary convention at Hanover, but they must give a declaration before then. This was

---

26 The HKBP is in fellowship with all Protestant churches in Indonesia through its ecumenical umbrella organizations. MH

27 Fredrik Axel Schiotz (1901–89) was ordained in the ELC in 1930. He studied at Luther Seminary and received a doctorate in theology from Erlangen in 1952. He served on the Executive Committee of the LWF (1955–71), the Board of Directors of the Student Volunteer Movement for Foreign Missions (1948–54), was a delegate to the LWF meeting in Lund in 1948, served on the Executive Committee of the LCUSA (1967–71), was director of the Department of World Missions for the LWF (1952–54), and served as resident of the ELC (1954–60) and the ALC (1961–71). See Arnold Mickelson and John Martin Jensen, *Biographical Directory of Clergymen of The American Lutheran Church* (Minneapolis: Augsburg, 1972), 815. "You are facing a tremendous task. The present politics of *laissez faire* cannot go on. If Dr. Fuerbringer retires, Concordia St. Louis must be rebuilt. The most imminent danger is that Missouri accepts the view of the late Dr. Fry, which now seems to be the view of Dr. Schiotz, that it is enough if a church accepts *de jure* the Confessions and leaves it to the individual professors to interpret them as they like. This is the *de facto* status of St. Louis, presidency and faculty" (Sasse to J. A. O. Preus, November 3, 1968; in the Harrison Collection). MH

done in 1951 in the form of the confessional declaration of the synod of Batak, quoted by us and acknowledged by the LWF as sufficient.

What comes out of the report of Dr. Schiotz is that all the participants, above all the then-president of the LWF, and therefore president of the executive committee, knew what the faith of the Batak is and is not, and how the confession submitted by them is to be understood. The leadership of the Batak church declared openly and honestly that they cannot accept the doctrinal foundation of the LWF and why they can't. Nobody would ever even dream of denying help to such a church, after they had come into such suffering because of the war. The Missouri Synod didn't ask, either, about the confession of the people whom they helped in Germany. They helped not only the free churches but also subsidized the church in Bavaria and even Niemöller's church for many years, not to say anything of the huge sums of money which went to the aid organization in Stuttgart. So the poor church in Sumatra could have been helped, and if they wanted to become Lutheran, to which nobody forced them, then one could have sent them spiritual help. But thus it will remain what it was—Barmen will see to that—and will be swallowed up by southeast Asia's large union movement. The German Lutherans, who are co-responsible for this, will one day have to answer for it.

7

What is the danger in southeast Asia, assuming that it will be preserved for the time being from Communism and from the fate of the church in China? It is the great danger of the national churches, which will be strengthened by the Reformed principle of the national church councils or church federations. It is astounding with what speed nationalism is spreading in Asia and is gripping even the churches. As the EKiD in Germany, and the NCCCUSA in America, so everywhere national church councils are arising. They claim to be only federations, but they are all (because they practice altar and pulpit fellowship and expect this of their member churches, and indeed even quite consciously train their youth toward this) churches, or organizations on the way to becoming churches. But if the large Lutheran churches of the world in Europe and even, with a few exceptions, in America cannot pull themselves out of this great trend, or don't have the power to do that anymore, what can we expect from the young and weak church structures in the mission field? Why doesn't anybody speak out in Germany, not even in Neuendettelsau, which proclaims its Lutheranism so loudly and now will work hand in hand in New Guinea with the Leipzig Missionary Society, whose leadership has shown that it is not in any condition nor has any desire to protect Lutheranism from sinking into unionism?

One sign of the new union churches in the area of southeast Asia will be the apostolic succession in the Anglican sense. What, then, should hold all the churches together, if they really have no fellowship of doctrine and if altar fellowship no longer presupposes a common understanding of the Sacrament? It is the mutual recognition of their offices, which is possible because they all have bishops, priests or presbyters, and deacons who have received the authority for their office through the laying on of hands by a bishop. In southern India it will still take years until all the clergy have been ordained by a bishop. In Ceylon [Sri Lanka], where the plan has been improved, it's going more quickly. They thought up rituals which are not simply reordinations, but rather in which the members of different denominations successively lay hands on each other, whereby each can think for himself whatever he wants. Already today the Congregationalists in Australia are ready to participate in such a rite. Probably, in the foreseeable future, there will be larger unions, which begin with the uniting of the Methodists, the Presbyterians, and the Congregationalists—the negotiations are already in full progress. Then they will need only an agreement about performance of the "ritual without name," as it is officially called in order to avoid the word "reordination," and then the great "reunited church of Australia" will be ready, which then will also be the church in New Guinea.[28] Thus Protestantism will exist in all of southeast Asia, along with the Roman Church and the Adventists and the Pentecostal sects, which already today play a growing role. And the Lutherans? They will "not yet" enter such a union church, but how long will they be able to maintain themselves, especially when the growing nationalism of Asia spreads to the national churches? Consider a practical example: a short time ago, a leader of Indian Lutheranism traveled through Australia on his way to [the World Council of Churches assembly at] Evanston [Illinois, 1954]. When his grandfather converted, he was baptized by the Leipzig missionaries and stood, like his son, in the service of this mission society. The grandson is the leader of the WCC's division for southeast Asia and has still other high ecumenical offices, even in the LWF. He is the president of the Lutheran church federation in India and will probably one day be bishop of the United Lutheran Church in India. When he was in Adelaide, he preached in the morning at the Presbyterian church, in the afternoon at the Methodist church, and in the evening in the Anglican cathedral—for he indeed has, as a member of the *Tamulenkirche*, apostolic succession. That is the Lutheranism of the third generation in India. If Missouri weren't still there, then one would have to doubt the future of Lutheranism in the Indian mission field. That is the fruit of the unionism with which we became acquainted by means of the *confessio meyeriana*. That is the fruit of the Swedish mission against whose Crypto-Anglicanism and unionism the old generation of Leipzig missionaries fought so hard. Certainly, the hardships of World War I brought the Swedes into a position in India which they would have otherwise never attained, and the Germans had reason to be thankful to them for their

---

28 In 1977 the Methodist Church, most Congregationalists, and a majority of Presbyterians joined to form the Uniting Church in Australia. See *ODCC*, 133. The church's deconfessionalized life has brought diminishing numbers, and it has recently been wracked by controversy over the issue of homosexuality. MH

help. Paul Fleisch [1878–1962], in his instructional anniversary book *Hundert Jahre lutherischer Mission* (1936), described the situation briefly but accurately. What he did not see, and what even the Leipzig Missionary Society didn't notice and even now doesn't notice, is that the Swedish Church was no longer a Lutheran Church in the sense of the Lutheran Confession, however many loyal Lutherans may still have been in it. As long as it considered the apostolic succession to be an adiaphoron, there was nothing to be said against its keeping this old relic. In that moment, however, in which this inheritance was used for forming a brotherhood with the Church of England, the Swedish succession stopped being an adiaphoron. For Anglican consecrations are null and void, not only according to the judgment of all catholic churches except for the Old Catholics, but rather also according to Lutheran canon law. "Bishops," who have a higher spiritual rank than the pastors, the keepers of the *ministerium docendi evangelii et administrandi sacramenta* ["the ministry of teaching the Gospel and administering the Sacraments," AC V], do not exist according to the Lutheran Confessions, and all the baptized are "priests" according to Lutheran teaching. A threefold division of office into bishops, presbyters, and deacons was formed over time in the early catholic church, but the New Testament knows of no such thing. Consequently, the Anglican bishops, even if their office could be recognized from the view of the Catholic canon law, which is not the case (because the Anglican priest is not really a priest, but rather only carries that title, just as the Swedish pastor), would not be "successors of the apostles." It is one of the bizarre things in the church history of our time that at the consecration of Swedish or other "Lutheran" bishops (Finland, India, South Africa), Anglican or other bishops participate in the laying-on of hands, bishops who consider the *articulus stantis et candentis ecclesiae*, the blessed message of the justification of the sinner by faith alone, and therefore the holy Gospel itself, to be heresy. We say nothing against the Christian faith of pious Anglicans, and also nothing against the personal convictions which an Anglican pastor or bishop might have about his office. But what we say with emphasis is this: that every *communio in sacris* [i.e., every act of church fellowship] with the Church of England, wherever it may happen, is a fall from the Lutheran Confession, even if those concerned are not clear within themselves about this. I have never yet met an Anglican theologian—I speak of real theologians—who did not at least understand the seriousness of the Lutheran objections.[29] I have asked some of them upon what should the Christians in India, Ceylon, Indonesia, New Guinea, and other places

---

29 Sasse spent a great deal of time with high-ranking Anglicans as a participant in the Faith and Order Movement in the late 1920s and 1930s. Sasse participated in meetings of German and English theologians in Eisenach in 1928 and was highly valued by others, including Bishop George Bell (1883–1958) of Chichester. See Feuerhahn, "Hermann Sasse as an Ecumenical Churchman," 23ff. The Third British-German Theologians Conference, at which Sasse was a participant, was at Chichester, March 23–28, 1931. See Feuerhahn Chronology. MH

base their conviction that they have the authentic apostolic office? How should they understand the history of England in the sixteenth century? How should they decide whether Rome or Canterbury, or neither of them, is correct? Where the church is no longer founded upon the clear Scripture, but rather upon ecclesio-legal fictions and ecclesio-political claims, there the church of Christ is long gone, even if it decorates itself a thousand times over with the name "Lutheran."

So the time draws nearer when not only the Lutherans in the large churches of the Old World but rather also the Lutherans in the mission field will become lonely people, even lonelier than they have been until now at their widely spread stations. As at home, so today also in the mission field, the Lutheran pastor stands before the difficult, and yet so thankful, job of speaking the Gospel so clearly, as clearly as the catechism and the Augsburg Confession do. The Confession must become alive [in] us again, and we want to begin with ourselves. For, basically, contemporary humanity of all races has had enough of nonbinding chatter. Communism would never have achieved such victories if it hadn't satisfied the hunger for dogma which the churches weren't able to satisfy anymore. But why have we kept from people the true dogma of the pure Gospel? May God strengthen us all for the battle for the true confession and help us, in the power of Christ's love, to call back to the Gospel's truth a Christendom which is sinking into relativism.

ᔕ

Greeting you, especially those among you who are missionaries and who are responsible for evangelization among the heathen, in the bonds of faith,

Your
Hermann Sasse

Historical Context

This letter is a critique of the ecumenical ramifications of the Roman Church's pronouncements of 1950 and 1954 on Mary. "It is really a Marian century which has ended in 1954. The Mariology of the Roman Church is now complete." Letter 17, "Mary and the Pope," should be consulted as the companion to this piece.[1] Sasse laments that while Rome steps beyond Sacred Scripture in creating dogma about Mary, the churches of the Reformation are not even strong enough to reject denials of the virgin birth in their midst. Today's apostasy of the Church of Sweden is a sad end which Sasse prophetically lamented already in 1954. A Lutheran church which cannot confess its doctrine at the altar will finally confess it nowhere. MH

January 20, 1955[2]

Prof. H. Sasse
North Adelaide,

Dear and Reverend Dr. [Lawrence] Meyer:

I have just received your letter . . . . The group in your church which is represented by the *American Lutheran* is unfortunately unable to develop a theological program of its own. They want to lead Missouri out of the "ghetto," but they do not realize the danger to the doctrinal standard with which Missouri stands and falls. They are blind when it comes to Missouri's relationships with other churches. This blindness is lastly a lack of the great gift of "distinguishing the spirits." Thus it can happen that Missouri's archenemies, the leaders of the German *Landeskirchen*, write their reports in that journal. I am shocked when I read the most uncritical remarks on the Ecumenical Movement. Even the *Christian Century* is more sober in its judgment on Evanston. You must realize that this is a sickness which threatens the very life of Missouri. The same development which has gone on in the ULC and in the ALC is endangering you. I remember Dr. Knubel's last visit to Europe in summer 1939. His life's work had been to keep his church at least in the tradition of the General Council. His fight was lost, the dike broke, and the floods of unionism and liberalism destroyed the remnants of the confessional heritage. The same tragedy became apparent from the last letters I received from Dr. Reu when liberalism and Crypto-Calvinism

---

1   *Letters to Lutheran Pastors*, 1:368–83. MH

2   Original in English. CHI Behnken file. MH

made their inroad into Dubuque. These are movements which are perhaps beyond the control of men, great spiritual movements and diseases which capture men like the great political movements of our age. You must not think that Missouri will escape the danger. Such movements are stronger than they seem to be at first sight. If a strong man such as the late Dr. Th. Graebner was infected by this disease, what will happen to men of smaller stature? It is impossible to suppress such movements by way of discipline. Nor can the problems involved be settled by gentlemen's agreements. Dr. Behnken's way of dealing with them *seelsorgerlich* is right, but such *Seelsorge* must lead to a deep insight of what is wrong. They must see the dangers not only to the Missouri Synod but also to the whole church of Christ which needs the undefiled witness of true Lutheranism . . . —

May God graciously bless your work in 1955. With kind regards,

Yours sincerely,
H. Sasse

thirty-six

Post Festum

CHRISTIANITY AT THE TURN OF THE NEW YEAR 1954/1955

TRANSLATED BY ANDREW SMITH

New Year, 1955[1]

Prof. D. Theol. Hermann Sasse
41 Buxton Street
North Adelaide, South Australia

Dear Brothers in the Office!

I greet you all at New Year's, whether you have ended the old year and begun the new year in the cold north or in the hot summer of the southern hemisphere. Even if this greeting comes belatedly into your hands, then the consideration of those things which Christianity has experienced in the fateful year of 1954 will be useful to us all. Just as the political decisions of 1954 will reveal themselves in their entire import only in the future, so it is also with the decisions of church history, and we do well at this moment to bring these decisions, with all their implications, which will be of great consequence even for the Lutheran Church, home to ourselves.

1

We begin with a glance at the Roman Church. Whether we like it or not, Rome is still the center of church history. When all of Evanston's[2] papers and conclusions

---

1   *BLP* 36: *Post festum: Die Christenheit an der Jahreswende 1954/1955* (North Adelaide, January 1955). The original was published in *LuBl* 7, no. 40 (February 1955): 1–16. Huss number 311. MH

2   The Assembly of the World Council of Churches met in Evanston, Illinois, in 1954. MH

have long been forgotten—and they are really already today as good as forgotten—the big announcements and decisions of the "Marian Year"[3] will live on. This is not only because the Roman Church is still the largest in Christendom, it is not only because of its political power and its organization, as one all-too-easily supposes. Without a doubt it is also because it has both intellectual and spiritual powers which are missing in other parts of Christendom. Rome does not live by its errors, but rather it lives despite its errors from the Christian substance, which even under the cover of heresy and heathenism still lives in hiding. Whatever one may say against the Roman sacramental system and praxis—and we agree fully with what the Lutheran Confession says against them—this church really has at least still kept Christ's Sacraments, which one can no longer say about a large segment of Protestantism. And with the Sacrament, it has kept something of the true Gospel, if indeed Luther was correct when he said about the Lord's Supper: "The Sacrament is the Gospel."[4] Even if, in the concept of the sacrifice of the Mass, the human puts himself on a par with Christ, so the Roman Church has really never forgotten that the sacrifice of Golgotha is the foundation of our redemption. How the Protestants must be ashamed, who have left to Rome the foundational truths of the Apostles' Creed and the Nicene Creed, and thereby the truths which were never contested by any of the reformers and on which the Reformation was founded! What right do Lutheran bishops, who say nothing against it when the Christmas narrative is "demythologized" in their churches and seminaries and when the [phrase] "born of the Virgin Mary" is denied, have to complain about certain outgrowths of the Marian cult? Only he who stands firmly on the ground of the Reformation, only he for whom God's Word is the Holy Scripture, who believes in the God-man Jesus Christ and in the real presence of His body and blood in the Lord's Supper—only he has the right to speak with the Roman Church, to direct questions toward Roman theology, the questions which once the Reformation put to it.

On December 8, 1954, that which one could call the Marian century, and which began with the announcement on December 8, 1854, of the dogma of Mary's immaculate conception, ended with the "Marian Year." In an earlier letter, we indicated the historical and theological connection between the dogma of 1854 and the dogma of 1870 [i.e., papal infallibility], between the development of Mariology and the doctrine of the papacy.[5] The dogmatic connection was indicated by no less than the great catholic dogmatician Matthias Joseph Scheeben (1835–88) in volume 3 of his essays about "The Ecumenical Council of 1869" (Regensburg, 1871; it appeared later as an independent publication).

---

3   Rome defined the dogma of the immaculate conception of the Blessed Virgin Mary in 1854. The dogma of the assumption of Mary into heaven upon her death was likewise defined by "infallible" papal decree in 1950. Thus 1954 marked a centenary of the first Marian decree. MH

4   See *Adoration of the Sacrament* (1523), Aland 664, WA 11:442.13 (cf. AE 36:289). MH

5   See Letter 17, "Mary and the Pope," in *Letters to Lutheran Pastors* 1:368–83. MH

From the evangelical point of view, we can see that both dogmas are an expression of that synergism which constitutes the deepest essence of Catholicism: the human puts himself into the place where Christ alone belongs: Mary becomes coredeemer (*coredemptrix*) by means of her *fiat*,[6] and the infallible pope as the vicar of Christ. Historically seen, it was the theology of the Jesuit order which won in the announcement of these dogmas. The bull *Ineffabilis Deus* [Denzinger 1641] in 1854 was the dress rehearsal for infallibility. The bishops actually were asked, and the theologians were heard. But it was not their vote, but rather the will and the decision of the pope himself, not the consensus of the church, which created the new dogma. Basically the decision of 1870 was thereby already made, and one must wonder that none of the leading men, who later spoke against infallibility, noticed it. Döllinger wrote in 1874:

> I myself have already regretted it, that I did not already in 1854 loudly declare my rejection of the new dogma; at that time, I quieted my conscience with the thought that it really was a matter about a small point in the doctrinal system, and that the dogmatization was only the arbitrary act of this pope. [Quoted by J. Friedrich, *Ignaz von Döllinger*, vol. III, pp. 650f.]

It was then, as far as I can see, only one simple Bavarian pastor from the diocese of Passau, Thomas Braun, who did not accept the illegally issued dogma and was subsequently excommunicated and robbed by the Bavarian government of his income. The "Marian century": promoted by means of Lourdes and Fatima, it reached its high point under Pius XII in 1950 with the announcement of the first dogma since 1870, the teaching of Mary's bodily ascension to heaven, and now, four years later, in the proclamation of the new Marian feast as Queen of Creation. This feast, to be celebrated on May 31, was until now already permitted to every diocese which wanted to celebrate it as Mary the Mediator (*mediatrix*) of all graces. The encyclical *Ad caeli Reginam* of October 11, 1954, in which the new Marian feast is directed (the twenty-second Marian feast of the Roman church year, if my missal is complete), determines what is the position of Mary, who has been taken up into heaven. She is queen, not only of heaven, as the old *Salve Regina* calls her, she is also queen of all creation.

> It is certain that Jesus Christ, the God-man, is alone king in the full, authentic, and absolute sense. Thus Mary has a participation in the royal honor, even if in a limited way and in the manner of an analogy, whether as mother of Christ, whether by virtue of her participation in the work of the divine Redeemer, of her participation in His struggle against the enemies and His triumph over them. [from the English text of the encyclical]

---

6   That is, her "Let it be"—"And Mary said, 'Behold, I am the servant of the Lord; let it be to me according to your word' " (Luke 1:38 ESV). MH

Included in this, as it seems, definitive definition of the position of Mary is apparently the teaching that she is the "mediator of all graces" and the "coredeemer," whereby it is distinguished between the sole mediatorship of Christ, who won grace, and the secondary mediatorship of Mary, who in her way collaborated in redemption and who, by means of powerful intercession, makes the grace won by her Son accessible to humans (*dispensatrix*).[7]

2

It is really a Marian century which has ended in 1954. The Mariology of the Roman Church is now complete. It could be that the pendulum of development now swings toward the other side and that the subordination of Mary, the emphasis upon her being a creature, the boundary between God and Mary, which is theoretically retained in the dogmas and in the liturgical texts, will be in the future again more strongly stressed. A revision of the teaching, however, is impossible because of the *irreformabilis* of the Vatican. I had to say this to a Catholic priest in 1930, who, as that lonely Bavarian pastor in 1854 once did, became derailed over the new dogma and asked me what I thought about this matter in European Catholicism. But what is then the deepest essence of this Marian era? Many good things have been said in recent years by Edmund Schlink and other leading evangelical theologians about the theological-dogmatic side of Roman Mariology, and we don't need to repeat it. But perhaps it is good if we consider that Mariology and Mariolatry arose not in the Roman Church, but rather have crept into it from the East. Every visitor to a Catholic church notices the pictures of Mary which at first glance betray their Byzantine heritage by their gold background, the Greek letters, the portrayal of the mother with the child according to the manner of icons. Over the Madonna with the Christ Child two angels float, Gabriel holding the cross and the nails, another angel with the other instruments of torture. From Smolensk to Palermo, from today's Eastern churches to the Catholic churches in America and Australia, one sees these pictures, with varying typologies, but all finally based upon the famous icon of Constantinople, the so-called *Hodegetria* (the name is accidental, after a neighborhood in the old imperial city, but later understood as "she who shows the way"). Allegedly painted by Luke, the author of the Gospel, it was the great relic of the Marian city on the Bosphorus. Temporarily hidden during the dispute about images, the icon existed until the Turks smashed it to pieces. The picture thus symbolizes still today the history of the Marian cult, which began at the end of the fourth century, and specifically, it seems, at first in the Syrian-speaking church. This East-Syrian church retained for a long time, like the Egyptian church, the influences of the great Gnostic movements, which almost caused these churches to

---

7   "*Ad Caeli Reginam*: Encyclical of Pope Pius XII on Proclaiming the Queenship of Mary, October 11, 1954," in *The Papal Encyclicals*, ed. Claudia Carlen (Raleigh: McGrath, 1981), 4:271–78. MH

be destroyed by heresy. In this church, for a long time, Baptism was allowed only for those who took an oath of celibacy, as with the Marcionites. So the virginity of Mary, which was already such a foundational mystery for Ignatius [martyred ca. 112] (*Letter to the Ephesians* 19.1), became especially important for the Syrian Christians, and already in the fourth century, hymns to the holy Virgin were sung in the Syrian language. Here is the root also for the teaching of the perpetual virginity of Mary, against which any disputation, like that of Helvidius in Rome in 380,[8] was already at that time a heresy. This teaching stood so firmly in the Middle Ages that even Zwingli, who rejected the real presence without a second thought, retained it without question. It is not true that this *theologoumenon* is a dogma of the Lutheran Church, as many suppose. For the *semper virgo* ["ever virgin"] in the Latin text of the Smalcald Articles (I I 4; Müller, p. 229; Tappert, p. 292), which came out of the translator's pen by force of habit, founds no dogma because only the German text of the Smalcald Articles is indeed normative and, above all, because a proof-text is missing. The passage from Luther quoted in the Formula of Concord (SD VII 100; Müller, p. 668; Tappert, p. 587) about the *clauso utero* [i.e., that Mary gave birth to Christ with her virginity intact] limited this view expressly as a theological opinion ("as some suppose"). It is a further proof for the Syrian origin of the Marian cult that the dogma of Ephesus in 431, according to which Mary is labeled *Theotokos*, "mother of God," which is of course also the teaching in the Lutheran Church, actually promoted the Marian cult in the Orthodox and Monophysite Churches, but in no way hindered the full blooming of this cult in the East Syrian Church, which did not recognize this dogma and the condemnation of Nestorianism. Friedrich Heiler indicates (*Urkirche und Ostkirche*, 1937, pp. 452ff.) in very informing explanations that especially the Nestorian church fostered the cult of *Mart Mariam*, the Princess Mary, in a significant way. Its Marian songs distinguish themselves from those of the other churches of the East only by avoiding the phrase "mother of God." It is noteworthy that she appears in the Mass as an intercessor and is not directly addressed. For the Mass was originally never the *locus* of Marian adoration, as indeed even today in the Roman Mass, even on the Marian feasts, the prayers are directed only to the persons of the Trinity. But just as since [the time of] Leo XIII and Pius XI the *Ave Maria* and the *Salve Regina* are prayed silently after the Mass, so also in the case of the Nestorians Marian prayer appears as an appendix to the Mass. As the churchgoers leave the building, they receive at the door, that is, in the area of the baptismal font, the eulogies, the blessed but not consecrated bread, and kiss the cross which the priest holds in his hands. Thereby the prayer is uttered:

---

8   The Iconoclastic Controversy concerning the use of icons aggravated the Greek Church from approximately 725 to 842. Monophysites diminished the human nature of Christ and rejected icons. See *ODCC*, 815. MH

O Lord, may the prayer of the holy Virgin, and the intercession of the Blessed Mother, and the pleading and petitions (here Heiler translates "mediation," but that is too strong) of she who is full of grace, of the Princess Mary, of the blessed one, and the great power of the victorious cross and the intercession of the Master John (i.e., the Baptist) be continually with us at all times, O Lord of all, Father, Son, and Holy Spirit, in eternity. [Brightman, *Liturgies Eastern and Western*, 1:304]

In contrast to the East Syrian Nestorian Masses and to all Western Masses which we know, including the Gallican and Mozarabic (in Spain), the direct prayer to Mary is found in the Egyptian Mass. So we hear in the Marcus liturgy—that is, in the orthodox liturgy of the older churches in Alexandria—in the great intercessory prayer, where the perfected saints are considered prior to the mention of "our most holy, untainted, and praised princess, the mother of God, and the eternally enduring virgin," suddenly the *Ave Maria* in the Greek form: "Be greeted, you who are full of grace, the Lord is with you, you are blessed among women, because you have borne the Savior of our souls" (Brightman, [*Liturgies Eastern and Western*], 1:128; German translation from *Library of the Church Fathers: Greek Liturgies*, p. 170).

The liturgy of the Monophysite Copts and the Abyssinian Church has many more prayers to Mary, and no fewer than thirty-three Marian feasts. We quote here a noteworthy prayer, which is found in some manuscripts of the Coptic liturgy (the Coptic texts together with an English translation published by C. Bezold as an appendix to C. A. Swainson, *The Greek Liturgies*, p. 382), and which from there found its way also into the Ethiopic (Abyssinian) Mass (Brightman, [*Liturgies Eastern and Western*, 1:]216f.):

[G]reetings, O pure Virgin Mary, who truly intercedes for humanity: pray for us in the presence of Christ, your Son, that He graciously send us the forgiveness for our sins. Greetings, you pure virgin, you true queen . . . we ask you, consider us, true mediator, in the presence of our Lord Jesus Christ, that He forgive us our sins.

Here we have the titles which in the Marian year have played such a large role: Mary as queen and as mediator (Bezold translates *mediatrix*; Brightman, "mediatress"). The prayer does not, however, go beyond the "pray for us sinners."

The liturgy of Constantinople (the so-called Liturgy of Chrysostom and Liturgy of Basil) goes still farther than the churches which took their point of departure from Alexandria. It was someone very well-acquainted with the Ethiopian liturgy who coined the sentence: "The Byzantine liturgy is, among all Christian liturgies, most strongly Marian; more than others, it is governed by, and permeated with, the thought of the mother of God" (H. Engberding, CSB, in the anthology published by the Abbey of Gerleve in Westphalia, *One Body—One Spirit*, Münster o.J., p. 44).

Along with the many songs of praise to Mary which are sung in the Mass, most telling is the fact that in the Canon of the Mass, the central and most important piece of the liturgy, with the Words of Institution and the appeal to the Holy Spirit, the silent prayer is broken by a hymn to Mary, which is no longer only a "pray for us": "Intellect is confused and incapable of praising you, mother of God, as gracious, accept our assurances. For you know even our inner desires. For you are the leader of Christians; we magnify you" (from *The Library of the Church Fathers: Greek Liturgies*, p. 249).

Even the Roman Church is acquainted with songs of praise to the holy Virgin on its Marian feasts, but always so that they become songs of praise to Christ and are subordinated to Him. In the actual Mass, on the other hand, Mary appears only five times, and always together with the other saints and always so that it never goes beyond the "pray for us."

We'll let it suffice here to look at the Mass and ignore the feasts. Even so, it becomes clear that Marian devotion came out of the Eastern church into Western Catholicism. The Roman Church can correctly claim that it does not teach anything about Mary which is not also believed in the churches of the East, and the Eastern churches can hardly raise any objection against the Roman teachings, as far as the content is concerned. Even if Rome, as some signs indicate, would take Marian devotion more and more out of the sphere of private devotions and lesser ceremonies and into the actual liturgy (cf. Joh. Pinsk, "Mary in the Roman Missal," in the anthology *Mary in the Liturgy and in Doctrinal Pronouncements*, Maria Laach, 1954, pp. 57ff., with a quote from the then-current state secretary Montini), then nothing would thereby be done which old Byzantium hadn't always done. Even the political significance of Mary as the protector of Christendom in its struggles against its external enemies is anticipated in the idea of the Marian city of Constantinople, which is protected by the covering of the Madonna and therefore owes her special honor. What is, then, actually new about the Marian century of the Roman Church since 1954? First, it consists in the Marian cult having gained a shocking geographic expansion. The churches of the East lived, apart from the fate of their emigration in recent times, their own life, closed off from the rest of Christendom. It was considered a forbidden curiosity and tactlessness that Sergei Bulgakov (1871–1944), one of the greatest theologians of the Russian emigration, attempted in 1927 in Lausanne to bring Marian devotion to the discussion. Rome has carried the Marian cult to the ends of the earth. In all the mission fields, the heathen religions encounter this cult, and above all, the great world religions encounter this cult. It was non-Christian Indians who raised a protest against the triumphal journey of Fatima's Madonna statue through their country. In what kind of form is Christendom here appearing? How should the primitive peoples, or the scholars among the Asiatic peoples, who see so many primitive religions around them, be able to understand the fine distinctions between worshipful adoration and devotional invocation, or between *latreia, hyperdulia,* and *dulia*,[9] the honors which are due [respectively] to the persons of the Trinity, to the holy Virgin, and to the saints? And the Madonna is supposed to conquer the Russians? If, according to Karl Marx, religion is the "opiate of the people," if Marxism declares the Christian faith to be a fantasy, does anybody really believe that the pathological visions of Lourdes and Fatima[10] will persuade [Marxists] of the opposite? Certainly, it is explained, that nobody is required to consider such revelations as authentic. But when Bernadette[11] is canonized, when the cult of Fatima is promoted, and when it is explained that the church's recognition does not make the miracles into a dogma but that it would be very undisciplined to deny [these miracles] such recognition, then the credibility of dogma is destroyed along with the borderline between dogma and pious opinion. The Eastern Church has been more cautious than Rome, as it did not dogmatize those things which escape dogmatization, whereby we do not wish to excuse it, for it first allowed into the church again the heathenism which quite certainly lives on in the cult of the Madonna. But Rome's great guilt, since the rejection of the Reformation and especially since the proclamation of the Marian dogma of 1854,[12] is that it is no longer in any condition to distinguish between truth and falsehood. In 1933 in the last pilgrimage to Trier, who among the bishops preaching so beautifully about the undivided garment of Christ as a symbol of the unity of the church believed in the authenticity of the alleged relics? They leave the task of believing in such things to the simple people. What kind of an unimaginable tragedy is this Marian century! What kind of mystery hides behind the development of the largest church in Christendom? The Lutheran Church knows well what it says when it sees in this mystery the end-times secret of the Antichrist, who robs the church of truth as he places people into those positions where Christ alone belongs, the one Mediator between God and man, next to whom there is no *mediatrix*, even if only in a derived sense. For all the fine distinctions between the one Mediator in the sense of the atoner and the subordinated mediators of grace in the church show themselves to be baseless, if it can happen that the last prayer of Pius XI was: "Jesus, Mary, and Joseph, into your hands I commend my spirit" (*Von Pius XI. zu Pius XII.*, published by the bishop's professorship of Berlin, 1939, p. 11).

---

9 These technical Greek terms differentiate forms of worship to be afforded the Trinity, the Virgin Mary, and the saints. MH

10 See *ODCC*, 998. MH

11 St. Bernadette (1844–79) was a peasant girl in Lourdes. At the age of 14 she claimed to have received eighteen visions of the Blessed Virgin Mary at the nearby Massabielle Rock. Bernadette joined the Sisters of Notra Dame at Nevers, where she lived for the rest of her life. She was beatified by Pius XI in 1925 and canonized in 1933. Her feast day in France is February 18. See *ODCC*, 192. MH

12 *Ad Caeli Reginam.* MH

3

If there was ever a time in church history which needed the witness against the Marian cult—which is not to be confused with honoring the mother of God, which even our Confession states,[13] and which in the three Marian feasts of the old Lutheran Church (annunciation, visitation, and Candlemas) found expression, which are at the same time feasts of Christ—then it is the "Marian era" in which we live. But where is this witness to be heard, the witness of the true Reformation? So that no flesh may become proud, the year 1954 has also been a type of *anno santo* ["holy year"] for Protestant Christendom. The pilgrimage was not to Rome or Fatima, but to Evanston, Illinois [the WCC Assembly]. But the effect was about the same. Just as there were many pious Catholics, upstanding Christians, who sought the blessings of the Marian year and came home with the feeling of having experienced something, of having experienced an expansion of Christianity, exactly so went many pious and upstanding Christians also to Evanston, to the meeting of the ecumenical [World] Council of Churches, and came back with the feeling that, despite all the hardships and difficulties, things were moving up with the church. And just as the clever church politicians in Rome have widely exploited their Marian year, so also have the not-so-clever church politicians of the Protestant world attempted to reach their goals. In this regard, there is hardly any difference indeed between the pre-Reformation church and the post-Reformation church. It would be worth it to more carefully investigate the psychological side of the mass processions and the gigantic announcements of modern Christendom and to determine what they have in common with the corresponding demonstrations in the political world. It began with the Trier pilgrimage of 1844, then came all the eucharistic and Marian congresses and Catholic conventions, which on the Protestant side found their counterparts in the church conventions and world church conferences. Somehow, the mass procession and the gigantic announcements belong to the innermost needs of modern mass humanity. They have a fascinating effect. They effect conversions. How many people were won for Hitler by the Nuremberg party conventions—even people who, until then, were convinced opponents [of Hitler]? The same has certainly happened in Moscow, just as it happens on the other side on Peter's square in Rome, and perhaps also at church conventions. Where is the difference? That is a serious question for the church. Where one thinks he has detected the Holy Spirit, where one feels how He moves through a meeting, as

---

13   "Granted, the blessed Mary prays for the Church. Does she receive souls in death? Does she conquer death? Does she make alive? What does Christ do if the blessed Mary does these things? Although she is most worthy of the most plentiful honors, yet she does not want to be made equal to Christ. Instead she wants us to consider and follow her example. The very subject reveals that in public opinion the blessed Virgin has taken over Christ's place. People have invoked her, have trusted in her mercy, and through her have wished to appease Christ" (Ap XXI 27–28; *Concordia*, 205). MH

has been stated by participants in church conventions in the nineteenth century and from the Great Awakening[14] in America, there is needed, in any case, the strictest self-examination. For one can always only believe in the Holy Spirit, not feel Him. God is not in the storm, not even in the storm of the masses. And there are always people there who seek themselves in such storms. The appearance of holiness which lies upon the large synods, conferences, and processions of Christendom needs again and again to be inspected for authenticity. Holy things and very unholy things have happened at synods since Nicaea [325], which are, after all, gatherings of sinners. And it is well-known that Luther said that nowhere in the world is there as much sinning as in church. Werner Elert (1885–1954) liked to quote the words of the Reformed thinker Moïse Amyraut ([Moses Amyraldus], 1596–1664) ("who must have indeed known"): "*In synodus non quaerunt veritatem, sed victoriam,*" "At synods they aren't looking for the truth, but rather for a victory."

Even if thereby not everything is said which can be said about synods, nonetheless it remains a truth, which may be forgotten by no church which attaches itself to the Reformation. Basically, the sin of Barmen was the same as the sin of the 1933 National Synod in Wittenberg. Whether one allowed the DEK (Deutsche Evangelische Reichskirche) [1933] to be officially recognized by Hitler or allowed the EKiD [1948] to be officially recognized by the Allied occupational forces (including the Russian [Soviets]), what real difference is there? Luther would have recognized neither of them.

One must admit that, despite the presence of some representatives of Eastern churches, Evanston was a Protestant gathering. It doesn't matter if the ecumenical council continually assures us that it is truly ecumenical, encompassing Christendom. It is not only the Iron Curtain which hinders the participation of the great Orthodox churches. None of the Orthodox patriarchates were represented, aside from Constantinople, and the political ties of the "ecumenical patriarch" to Washington are known, just as are the political ties of the Greek Church, the only larger church of the East to be represented. The Church of the East has always had such ties. That is part of its fate. The Orthodox churches of the exile were naturally also there, from economical, if not ecumenical, reasons. How Orthodox churches could participate in the National Council of Churches of Christ in the USA, whose concept of the unity of the church strikes the Eastern Church directly in the face, is a part of such *koinonia* which the canon law of the East, in contrast to that of the West, includes. It is a broad interpretation

---

14 This name is given to a widespread religious revival in the United States that began in the Dutch Reformed churches of New Jersey around 1726. It spread to the Presbyterians and Congregationalists in the following decade and reached its zenith in New England in the 1740s. Its most notable preachers were Jonathan Edwards (1703–58) and George Whitefield (1714–70), though both discouraged the excessive emotionalism which marked the revival. Visible evidence of conversion was crucial, and those without visible signs of inner grace were denounced as unregenerate. See *ODCC*, 702. Confessional Lutherans would call it *schwarmgeisterei.* MH

of canon law, which practically ignores this law, simply for the sake of physical existence. The poor church of the East has always had to live this way, externally compromising to its emperors and sultans. In Latin it's called *pia fraus* ["the pious lie"], but the Oriental mind finds fun in such cleverness. The few theologians of the East know what they have to do at such gatherings, and when it came to dogmatic questions, then the Orthodox bravely confessed their faith, an example to other churches. But in the long run, it naturally doesn't work that at such meetings the Orthodox Church professes that it alone is the church of Christ and the others aren't, not even the Anglicans, who will do anything to be acknowledged. You can do that once or twice, but not over and over again. In this point the Roman Church is at least responsible. It is only a question of time until the last of the Orthodox reject any participation in a movement whose method of solving the problem of reuniting [the church] "is completely unacceptable from the standpoint of the Orthodox Church," as it says in the declaration, because such a reunification would only be possible on the basis of the full dogmatic faith of the old undivided church, without exception or change, and on the basis of the true apostolic succession of bishops. (This and the following quotes, where no other source is indicated, are taken from the detailed report of the *Christian Century* of August 25 and September 22, 1954.)

So Evanston was practically a convention of the Protestant world, if not the entire Protestant world. For we would first like to see the 173 million Christians who are allegedly represented by the WCC. Nonetheless, it was a powerful event, especially if one considers that in America, by radio and television, uncounted millions experienced much of it. And this large convention had a truly great and contemporary theme: "Christ the hope of the world." What a counterpoint to the Marian year Evanston could have become if this theme had been handled properly! What a one-time opportunity to set the great and strong Christ faith of the New Testament and of the Reformation against the Mariology and Mariolatry into which the largest segment of Christendom is threatening to fall: *Christus solus*. "There is salvation in no other, is also no other name under heaven given to humanity, in which we are to be saved" [Acts 4:12].

No other name, not even all the wonderful honorific titles by which the church of the East and the West has distinguished Mary. We have no other hope than He, the one Mediator! We don't know whether Mary, or whether the blessed ones in the church triumphant, hear our voices. It may be that they pray for us. But that we should call to them—nothing about that is found in the Scripture, and Luther is correct when he says that we should rather ask the living saints on earth for their intercession than the dead ones, about whom we know nothing. And we should, above all, call to Him who is always with us until the end of the world, and whose return is anticipated in every celebration of His Sacrament. It would have been the task of Evanston to announce this *unica spes* ["one hope"] of Christians. But that was impossible. As Edmund Schlink held his presentation about the main topic, deeply rooted in Scripture and explaining Scripture, the "Lutheran" Bishop Eivind Berggrav[15] made the comment to another delegate: "The Word became theology and did not dwell among us" (*Time*, Pacific ed., August 30, p. 36). While Schlink—whose presentation is certainly known to, or accessible to, each of you—expressed the biblical hope for Christ's coming in all its relevance to the present, the correspondent, Prof. Robert L. Calhoun from Yale, a Congregationalist, developed the "American" version of Christian hope, in a manner which was certainly very significant, discussing the old Social Gospel of a previous era but really essentially rooted in liberalism and American Ritschlianism, according to which the goal of this hope is being more and more realized, even if not entirely perfected, already in this world. It was, in other words, the old contrast from Stockholm in 1925.[16] It was an English lay delegate who declared that he was neither an Adventist nor a German theologian, but he considered it to be the unsurrenderable task of the church to announce the second coming of the Lord. Finally, it centered about this question, and over it the minds were divided. Whoever reads the reports will be reminded of the event which Heinrich Wilhelm Josias Thiersch (1817–85) reports (*Leben*, published by P. Wigand, 1888, p. 42) about his years as a student in Tübingen, where in the first sermon which he heard there, during Advent, Ferdinand Christian Baur[17] (1792–1860) said: "Christ is not coming again." One sees how a man such as Thiersch could be steered into his Irvingian[18] detours by exactly [such a remark]. Perhaps some people experienced similar things in Evanston. The well-prepared draft of a declaration about the great topic was rejected after intense discussion. In the document which justifies the rejection, it states:

> We are not satisfied by the presentation of that which the report calls "rival hopes" (i.e., the hopes of political worldviews offered as a substitute to contemporary humanity). Some believe that they are presented with too much sympathy; others wish for a still more understanding treatment. Many bring it to [our] attention that the list is incomplete and should, in any case, also contain hopes which falsely call themselves Christian. We are not entirely satisfied with the treatment of non-Christian religions, and cannot agree among ourselves about the correct definition of our hope in regard to those who believe in God but who do not recognize His revelation in Christ .... Finally, some are of the opinion

15 Sasse uses the quotation marks because Berggrav was a supporter of Reformed/Lutheran intercommunion, Barmen, etc. MH

16 The Stockholm Conference of 1925 grew out of an appeal for peace and fellowship sent out by Christian leaders in several neutral countries at the outset of the First World War (1914), followed by an appeal by Söderblom in June 1917 for an immediate conference. See *ODCC*, 1544. MH

17 Baur founded the Tübingen School of New Testament study and taught at Tübingen beginning in 1826. He was a student of German idealism and was drawn to modern theology by Friedrich Schleiermacher. See *ODCC*, 171. MH

18 After E. Irving (1792–1834), a Scottish preacher. MH

that the boundaries between the church and the world are drawn too sharply.

A practical example of this was the treatment of the question of the hope for Israel. Here, not only political considerations were raised by those from the Eastern Church, but rather a Mr. Taft (a brother of the senator) declared bluntly, not only in his name, that any mention of the possible conversion of the Jews would be the end of his relationships with his Jewish friends (*Time*, September 6, p. 34). So they did the only thing they could: they forwarded the report to the churches "for study, for prayer, and for exhortation." That means that the attempt to utter a common word about Christ as the hope for the world ended in failure. Certainly, still more was then said about this in the "message to the churches." But for exactly this reason, the rank-and-file voted against the message, as the *Christian Century* honestly reports, which therefore in no way expresses the consensus of faith of the participants and can be understood by each according to his preferences. The *Christian Century* writes:

> Give the world council about four more such theological or dogmatic main topics, perhaps "the essence of the authority of the Bible" for 1960, "the essence of the church" for 1966, "the essence of redemption" for 1972, and "the confessional foundation of the council" itself for 1978—and if the world hasn't exploded by that point, then the WCC certainly will. [September 22, p. 1125]

Note well: it is not an opponent of the ecumenical council who writes this, but rather the editorial staff of the important, serious periodical which has done more for Evanston and for the ecumenical council than any other church newspaper could do.

4

One must grasp this immeasurable tragedy of non-Roman Christendom in order to understand the fate of even the Lutheran Church in the world. If there would be one church which could witness to the Gospel and thereby to the real hope of the church in the face of Rome and of the ecumenical council, then it would have to be the Church of the Lutheran Reformation. But it, apparently, is floating down the stream of an unevangelical ecumenism. Indeed, it is odd that exactly the loudest and least critical endorsements for the WCC are made in those churches which today still carry the name "Lutheran." Among all the gifts which are given to the Lutheran bishops, presidents, and other "church leaders," the gift which is so severely needed for a bishop's office—as well as for the pastor's office—is the great graciously given gift of discerning among spirits. Only so can one explain the coverage by the *Sonntagsblatt* about Bishop Lilje: Evanston [viewed] in a positive light, only vaguely hinting at criticisms, which will therefore hardly be understood by the simple readership, which even the best *Sonntagsblatt* has. What the church publications of the United Lutheran

Church in America (*The Lutheran*) and of the American Lutheran Church (*The Lutheran Standard*) present to their readers, one had best pass over in silence. Only one quote from the periodical of the church which claims Wilhelm Löhe [1808–72] and in which even a Michael Reu [1869–43] taught need be presented:

> A certain tension was present regarding our varied opinions about the Lord's Supper and altar fellowship. These are divisive within our basic oneness in Christ and form a very serious problem. This problem demands further study from the division of Faith and Order. [*The Lutheran Standard*, September 18, p. 11]

Here they have entirely bought in to the concept of the church presented by the modern Reformed Churches. The distinctions between Lutherans, Reformed, Methodists, Baptists, Quakers, and the others among the 163 churches which are represented in the world council should be taken seriously. But they are divisions within the one ecumenical church, to which they all belong if they believe in Christ, however they may understand this belief, whatever they may teach about the Lord's Supper, whether they recognize the *sola fide* as the Gospel or whether they reject it as a false *theologoumenon*, whether they practice infant Baptism or adult Baptism or no Baptism at all (like the Quakers and the Salvation Army). How can you reconcile that with the Augsburg Confession's teaching about the true unity of the church or with the Lutheran doctrine of the *Una Sancta*? You can't. And people don't even understand the question at all anymore, because they have lost the Confession. In Lausanne [1927], the delegates from the United Lutheran Church still distributed printed excerpts from the Lutheran Confessions. At the time, the Lutherans still gave a statement as the Orthodox [did in Evanston]. That would be unthinkable today. Certainly, general altar fellowship was not practiced [in Evanston], or only by a few isolated individuals. Following a common preparatory service on Saturday evening (August 21), there were various Communion celebrations on Sunday, of which the Methodist, Anglican, and South Indian Union were "open" for everyone. The Orthodox celebration was "closed," except for the admission of viewers [who would not commune]. The Lutheran celebration was open only for those "who believe in the real presence," which doesn't mean much, because even the Reformed believe in it, only they understand it differently. Of the Lutheran church's belief in the real reception of the true body and blood of Christ there was no mention, as it has indeed then been given up even by the leading theologians and bishops of the Lutheran churches. But even this mildest form of Lutheran "exclusivity" was already too much for Mr. Berggrav (according to the report of the *Christian Century*, September 22, p. 1158).

But you have to be there if you want to have an influence on the developments. You have to raise your voice inside the WCC, otherwise you won't be heard. That's the way the Lutherans, who have serious reservations against much of what happens in the ecumenical [World] Council, justify their cooperation. To this one answers: exactly the opposite. An institution such as the World Council or the LWF can be influenced only from the outside, because the confessionalists are always a minority and will be outvoted. Lutheranism's witness in the Ecumenical Movement has not been absent. It has been given for decades. It has not been heard. One proof among many for this is the *History of the Ecumenical Movement 1517–1948*, which appeared in time for Evanston, an anthology of more than eight hundred pages (edited by Ruth Rouse and Stephen Charles Neill, SPCK, London, 1954). Published by the ecumenical institute of Bossey, with a foreword by Reinhold von Thadden-Triglaff [1891–1976] (what would have the old Thadden have said to that, indeed!), it presents the Ecumenical Movement as the sum of the union movements of all time until their high point, the founding of the ecumenical council in Amsterdam in 1948. Because a German edition is planned, those in Germany will soon be able to form their own judgment [about this book]. This book, with its censures against Lutheranism which is unfriendly toward unions, shows more clearly than all else that the witness of men such as Ludwig Heinrich Ihmels in Stockholm, Werner Elert and Wilhelm Zoellner in Lausanne, and many others, especially even the American Lutherans, has not been heard. Does president Franklin Clark Fry of the ULC, whom they cleverly made president of the large committee which governs the world council until 1960, really believe that a witness from him will be heard? Everybody knows that he can never give such a witness, after he, in a solemn ceremony in 1950, opened the American National Council of Churches and had to thereby declare that the Quakers, Baptists of all varieties, and the hundred other sects which belong to this council portray the "unity of the church of Christ." Does president Henry Frederick Schuh [1890–1965] of the ALC really believe that he, as one of the ninety in the large committee, can bring the other eighty-nine to change their minds? From this type of Lutheranism we can hope for, and expect, nothing. [If anything were to be expected,] then more likely [it would be from] the few confessionalists among the Anglicans and Reformed who dared to ask questions in Evanston. It was, to my knowledge, an Anglican bishop who asked the question whether the strength of the Christian faith in the world didn't perhaps lie in exactly that in which we don't agree, and whether the cramped attempts to find a unifying formula at any cost must not lead to an emptying of the Christian faith[, leaving it hollow]. And it was the Reformed who asked the decisive question of what sense it makes if each calls upon the Holy Scripture as authority and each understands this authority differently. If Evanston taught us anything, then it is this: that the Gospel in the world ends where one no longer can distinguish between truth and error, pure doctrine and heresy, church and cults. We Lutherans know that Christ's church is hidden under the ecclesiologies of this world. We believe in it, because we believe in the power of the Gospel and of the Sacraments. But to make that visible, which in this life can only be the object of faith, is human *hubris*, whether it happens in Rome or in Evanston. We know that the Body of Christ can't be torn apart by humans; that the *Una Sancta* is already there. But we know, too, that the Lord's prayer "that they may all be one, so that the world may believe that You have sent Me" [John 17:21], is an eschatological prayer. Indeed, the day will come when, together with Christ's glory, the church's glory, His Body, too, will be revealed, and all tongues in heaven and on earth and under the earth will confess that He is the *Kyrios* [Lord] [cf. Phil. 2:10–11]. Until then, we cannot do anything except profess our faith and in true Christian love organize and do with other Christians what is common (in the field of the deeds of love and in the mission fields) and can be done together without injury to the conscience. Everything else is fanaticism [*Schwärmertum*], even if it decorates itself with the name "Lutheran."

5

I cannot end this letter without considering a man whose physical death has moved us all deeply,[19] Prof. Werner Elert in Erlangen.[20] Once he gave a good confession in Lausanne; therefore he was omitted from the *History of the Ecumenical Movement*. A man who stood very near to him theologically and humanly, but who could never understand that this great Lutheran scholar had no feel for Luther's view of the Old Testament, once said of him: "He is unhappily my dear friend." Others could have spoken similarly about him. He was a child of his generation, in which Lutheranism had reached a low point after the great confessional awakening of the nineteenth century. So he had to fight his way, slowly and alone, to the Lutheran doctrine. With this, his heritage from the time in which territorial ecclesiology was still predominate, is connected the fact that he had no understanding for the "confessing church," which actually had an originally Lutheran character until Asmussen and Barth took it over. That was very difficult for many of us. But even those whose churchly paths went in other directions learned thankfully from him, above all from the first volume of his *Structure of Lutheranism* and from the second part of his *Dogmatics*. His last major book about *Eucharist and Church Fellowship in the Ancient Church* (1954) is a wonderful gift to all of Lutheranism. It destroys the entire myth of the "ancient undivided church" from which the modern Ecumenical Movement lives, above all, insofar as it is influenced by Anglicanism. It shows, further, the Swedish speculations and other speculations about intercommunion to be a break not only with the tradition and with the ecclesiastical law of 1,600 years, but rather, what is more, as a denial of the New Testament. May this voice be heard before it is too late. Werner Elert saw with great clarity the breathtaking

---

19 See "Der Ruf zur Einheit: Werner Elert," in *Die Weltkonferenz* (1929), 101f. MH

20 Sasse's relationship with Elert, particularly how the latter as dean of the theological faculty of Erlangen shielded Sasse from the Nazis for the duration of the Hitler period, is detailed by Lowell Green in *Lutherans Against Hitler*. In a letter from Elert to Sasse on February 21, 1933, Elert claims he was first to mention Sasse's name for the position. See the Huss Collection and Feuerhahn Chronology. MH

seriousness of our church's situation during the evening of his life. His journey home reminds us that the church in this world is in a foreign place, and only in heaven will it be at home.

☙

In conclusion, I would like thankfully to remember all of the readers who sent me Christmas greetings and who have helped me and Brother Hopf in the past year to carry on [the work of publishing these] periodicals and letters. God bless, for us all, the year 1955, and especially the Passion season, at the beginning of which my lines should come into your hands.

Greeting you in the bonds of faith,

Your
Hermann Sasse

Historical Context

In this delightful letter, Sasse turns his religionsgeschichtlich *skill toward the development of Easter and the Easter season as a time of joy in the church. It is marvelously contemporary. "What does a Christendom which threatens to be drowned in spiritualism need more urgently than the truth of the resurrection of the body?" Personal correspondence from the early 1950s shows that there was tension among the faculty at the UELCA's Immanuel Seminary in Adelaide, South Australia. Sasse was, after all, a very big fish in a very small pond. This letter is certainly in part an auto-biographical account of Sasse's own reconsideration of Christian joy and its source. MH*

April 10 (Easter), 1955

H. Sasse
41 Buxton Street
North Adelaide, South Australia

Dear and Reverend Doctor Behnken,

I am most grateful for your kind letter. . . . You ask about my book on the Lord's Supper . . . . This book [*This Is My Body*] has taken all of my spare time during three years. Actually, it is the fruit of studies carried on for almost twenty years, since in Germany intercommunion was proclaimed by the "Confessing Church," and since only open Communion was practiced at our university services and the real presence openly denied by the university preacher, which caused me to abstain from that Communion. Two books I could bring out in German: one in 1938 [*Here We Stand*], the second during the war [*Vom Sakrament des Altars*, 1941]. The reprint of the first was made impossible by Karl Barth, who had the same publisher and did not want my publications to reappear at Kaiser Verlag, Munich. The other, a symposium, came out at Leipzig where the publishing house was destroyed. So I should like to see at least this book to appear . . . . A lot of people helped me, not only the people at Minneapolis [Augsburg], but others, too, from the Catholic archbishop of Adelaide who made accessible to me the Greek fathers to a country pastor of your church who knows me from my "letters" and who helped me when he heard that my typewriter had broken down. All these experiences have encouraged me to go on with the book which, as I hope, will help to clarify the whole problem if it can appear. Have you, by the way, read the late Dr. Elert's last book, *Abendmahl and Kirchengemeinschaft in der Alten Kirche* (Berlin, 1954)?[1] It gives the definite proof from the New Testament and the fathers that Luther's attitude toward intercommunion is in accordance with the doctrine of the church since the days of the apostles. A former student of mine heard the lectures which Elert gave on the subject at a large pastors' conference in Hanover. He wrote to me what a shock it was to Elert that nobody seemed to understand what he said against general intercommunion within Protestantism . . . . I am convinced that also in your country the question of the Sacrament will become a grave issue in Lutheran theology . . . .

All of us wish you God's blessings for your work and for you personally in this joyful time of the church year.

Yours, very sincerely,
H. Sasse

1　*Eucharist and Church Fellowship in the First Four Centuries*, trans. Norman Nagel (St. Louis: Concordia, 1966; repr., 1998). MH

thirty-seven

The Church's Time of Rejoicing

TRANSLATED BY ANDREW SMITH

Reminiscere 1955[1]

Prof. D. Theol. Hermann Sasse
41 Buxton Street
North Adelaide, South Australia

Dear Brothers in the Office!

In these letters we have had to speak much about the difficulties of the church and about the suffering which we all bear for the church's sake. That was necessary, and it is not only so in the Lutheran Church, that the servants of the Gospel are filled with serious concerns about the future of the Christian faith. It is also not the case that these concerns exist only in those places in which the Christian faith is threatened externally or in which the church even seems to be dying. For the third time, the church in China is experiencing a collapse. As it was extinguished in the Middle Ages after centuries of flourishing, as the great Catholic missionary work in the sixteenth and seventeenth centuries collapsed, so now the church in China is experiencing a catastrophe for the third time. And nobody knows how it will end. A similar collapse is completing itself in the Lutheran church in the countries around the Baltic Sea, and sometimes it seems that Western Christendom will have a similar fate to Oriental Christendom, where the church did actually remain, but comprised only a fraction of the peoples. This difficulty impacts all Christian denominations and confessions simultaneously. The attempts, great in their own way, to confront this difficulty

1   BLP 37: Die Freudenzeit der Kirche (North Adelaide, [March 6,] 1955). The original was published in LuBl 7, no. 42 (April 1955): 17–28. Huss number 313. MH

by the new means of ethnic mission work only disclose the true situation. The world, the entire world, including the countries which call themselves Christian because in them the entire population once belonged to the church and because their culture still allows the heritage of the Christian past to be recognized, has again become a mission field. The church simultaneously returns to its beginnings even in this: that it is again becoming the church of the martyrs. In our enlightened century, in an era in which all national constitutions guarantee the freedom of faith, more martyrs have died than in all earlier centuries of church history combined. As Johannes Lepsius,[2] the great missionary and friend of the Armenian people, predicted this at the beginning of the century, he was ridiculed. Today, nobody is laughing about this anymore.

But if we thus return to the beginnings of the church, then we don't want to forget that the church of the confessors and the martyrs, the church which stood under the death penalty from the world, was the church of joy. When in the middle of the third century the decline of the Roman Empire became apparent, when the Germanic tribes for the first time threatened its existence, and when a plague decimated the population of North Africa, then the words of the *Te Deum* rang out for the first time in Cyprian's book *On Dying*—the *Te Deum* which led Christianity through the centuries of the decline of the ancient world. The church father from Carthage calls for his Christians to be happy to die, just as our fathers [did] in the time of the Thirty Years' War [1618–48]. He teaches them to look upward toward heaven:

> There is the famous chorus of the apostles, there is the rejoicing group of the prophets, there is the great company of the martyrs, crowned with glory and victory for the sake of their struggle and suffering. (*De mortalite* 26)

One has the impression, when one reads the writings of the fathers and the old liturgies, that at that time the church was a place of joy, just as indeed even in our church it was exactly the time of large-scale death in the Thirty Years' War which was the time in which the great song of praise and thanksgiving rang out as an expression of the joy which the world doesn't know and doesn't understand. How should it be any different in the church of the Gospel?

1

Christian joy always has an eschatological character. No book of the New Testament speaks so seriously about earthly suffering, about unspeakable terror, about people's despair than the Revelation of St. John. But neither is a book so full of the great comfort and of the great joy which has been prepared

---

2   Johannes Lepsius (1858–1926) founded the Deutscher Huelfsbund Mission and served as assistant pastor to the German Protestant Congregation in Jerusalem (1884–86). He started a mission to Armenians in 1895. See Anderson, *Biographical Dictionary of Christian Missions*, 396. MH

for God's people. Over the world's suffering ring the jubilation hymns, which are sung before the Lamb's throne:

> The Lamb which was slain is worthy to receive power and riches and wisdom and strength and honor and praise and adoration. [Rev. 5:12]

> Now our God's salvation and power and kingdom have come, and His Christ's power, because the accuser of our brothers has been rejected . . . and they have overcome him by means of the Lamb's blood and by means of their testimony's Word, and they did not love their life unto death. [Rev. 12:10–11]

Heaven's joy, of which the earthly church's joy is a reflection, is deeply connected with that which happened at Christ's cross. It is noteworthy that exactly in the farewell speech by Jesus in John, joy plays such a very great role—thus the Gospel pericopes for the church's joyful time between Easter and Pentecost are taken from these speeches or from the Fourth Gospel in general.

Although for Occidental Christianity, Christmas has become the actual festival of joy, the Oriental church, which indeed in many respects represents older forms of Christendom, has retained the original Christian joyful time of "Pente-Coste," the time between Easter and Pentecost, but above all Easter as the actual festival of joy. There was, after all, in the first centuries no Christmas celebration. As the Christian festival calendar with December 26 as the festival of the first martyr Stephen [Acts 7] shows, Christmas, as the celebration of the Lord's birth, has "wedged its way in between" [the other already-existing festivals], like its noteworthy twin, Epiphany. Still today, even the Occidental church year shows that the year's liturgical high point is Easter. There is naturally no use in discussing what is greater, the incarnation or the resurrection of Christ, Christmas or Easter, the joyful message of the angel at Bethlehem or that of the angel at the open grave at Jerusalem. Neither is there without the other. The cross and the manger belong together, and we celebrate thankfully all the festivals of the church year. But perhaps we can learn something after all from the Easter jubilation of the Oriental church and of the church of the beginning [of Christianity in the first century]. As the Occidental Christmas festival has influenced all Christendom, just as the Lutheran and the German manner of celebrating Christmas finally gripped even the Reformed Churches, who once despised Christmas as a "Papist" festival and—for example, in London during the years of the Westminster Synod[3]—even hindered the celebration of Christmas in homes by means of police intervention, so it could be that we learn from the early church and from the Oriental church to better and more deeply understand and celebrate Easter's joyful time of the church year. For it is so that even for us Easter is the high point of the church year, the festival of festivals, already by means of the fact that every Sunday is a miniature Easter. It could be

---

3   The 1643 Westminster Assembly began the process but did not result in unity in England, though it did produce the Westminster Confession. See *ODCC*, 1732. MH

that truths which have become alien to modern Christendom, such as the resurrection of the body, become accessible again to many by means of the proper celebration of Easter. What do we need more urgently in this century of mass death, in which the individual human life seems to be worth nothing anymore, than the message that the graves will open themselves and the dead will rise after the Firstborn has risen from the dead? What does a Christendom which threatens to be drowned in spiritualism need more urgently than the truth of the resurrection of the body? Is the noteworthy fact that the Eastern Church has survived all the catastrophes in its history, everything that had to appear as "the final decline" to human eyes, connected to the fact that it retained the early Christian Easter faith with special loyalty? Whoever has read [Nikolaus von] Arseniew's [1888–1977] books about the Eastern Church which have appeared in Germany, his depictions of the Easter celebration, above all even the classical depiction of the "holy Moscow," that reader knows why nobody has ever been able to kill this church. Whatever the errors and sins of the Eastern Church may be, it has retained something in its Easter joy which belongs to the deepest essence of the New Testament faith and which, for example, in the *troparia* ("hymns") of the Easter canon of John of Damascus finds its classical expression, where it is sung:

> Today all is filled with light: heaven, earth, and the underworld. The entire creation celebrates the resurrection of Christ . . . . Every creature rejoices in jubilation today: for Christ is arisen, and hell is bound . . . The holy Passover has revealed Himself to us today, the new and solemn Passover, the mystical Passover, the Passover worthy of all honor, Passover—Christ the Redeemer, the pure Passover, the great Passover, the Passover of the faithful, the Passover who opens the doors of paradise for us, the Passover who sanctifies all the faithful . . . . It is the day of the resurrection; let jubilation shine through us, and let us hug each other; let us, O brothers, say, even to those who hate us, "We excuse everything for the sake of the resurrection," and therefore we call out, "Christ is arisen from the dead, because He overcame death by means of His death . . . ." [according to the translation by N. von Arseniew, *Ostkirche und Mystik*, 1943, p. 18]

These hymns and shouts of the old church belong to the liturgy of the Easter night, as it is so often described in Russian literature. Through the church, lying in darkness, the shouts ring out ever louder and more urgently: "Arise, O Lord, prepare the end . . ." until around midnight, when the Easter message is announced and the candles are lit, a sea of moving candles in the hands of the congregation, and they all answer the words of the liturgist with the "victory song": "Christ is arisen from the dead, after He overcame death by means of death, and gave life to those who were in the graves."

2

It is a noteworthy fact that the ecclesiastical name for the Easter festival in Latin and in Greek, in the Romantic languages and in the Slavic languages, is "Pascha," that is, the "Passa" of the Hebrew language, grecized in the Greek Bible of the Old and New Testaments, while the Jews in Germany took over the Germanic "Easter" for their Passover. This fact indicates that the Christian Easter feast was originally a Christian Passover. As the Jewish Passover is the feast of redemption, the miraculous freeing of Israel out of Egypt, and simultaneously the anticipation of the future redemption by means of the Messiah, whose arrival is expected at the Passover feast, so the oldest church celebrates its Passover as the great redemption feast. Jesus did, after all, die at the feast of Passover. In the New Testament, as is well-known, there is a difference in the dating of His death between the Synoptics and John. While the Synoptics put the institution of the Lord's Supper in connection with the Passover meal, which occurs on the evening of the 14th of Nisan, John does not mention the Passover at the Last Supper. Because he also does not mention the institution of the Lord's Supper, which he well knows, this silence does not prove much. But other passages in the Passion of the Fourth Gospel indicate that he assumes that Jesus did not die on the 15th of Nisan, the great Passover day, but rather on the 14th of Nisan at that time in the afternoon at which the Passover lambs were slaughtered in the forecourts of the temple. This is derived clearly from John 18:28, where it is said that the Jews did not go into the courthouse, in order not to become impure for the coming Passover meal. How this difference is to be explained, we do not know. None of the proposed explanations really satisfies. On the decisive points, there is agreement: Jesus is dead and buried on Friday. On Sunday, the grave was found empty. And "in the night in which He was betrayed," He had the Last Supper with His people and instituted the Sacrament. The connection between His suffering and death, on the one hand, and the Passover feast, on the other hand, was thus historically given. The most interesting aspect is that the oldest church does not, as we do, observe Good Friday, and then "on the third day" Easter, but rather that back then Good Friday and Easter fell liturgically on one day. As the Jews celebrated their Passover as the feast of redemption—beginning on the evening of the 14th of Nisan and then lasting eight days long, with the 15th of Nisan as the high point—so the first Christians celebrated the work of their salvation as the true Passover, of which the Old Testament Jewish feast was only a foreshadowing, a *typos*, in one night or, rather, in a single moment. After a fast of eight days, which later stretched itself to forty days—Sundays not included—they held the nightly Divine Service, mourning and pondering the death of the Lord, until then at a certain point, whether it be midnight or the first crow of the rooster, the mourning turns [suddenly] into joy. The fast is over. The Eucharist is celebrated, in which those participate for the first time who were baptized that very night—buried with Christ in Baptism and resurrected with Him [Rom.

6:1ff.]. Then followed the joyful time, in which there was no fasting and in which prayer was not made while kneeling. It encompassed, at first, perhaps only the week until the Sunday which we call *Quasimodogeniti*, the "White Sunday," on which the newly baptized appeared once again in white baptismal clothing in the church and were addressed with something like the beginning passages of the first letter from Peter, in which the apostle speaks to the newly baptized and indirectly to all the baptized. Later, the joyful time was stretched out to the fifty days until Pentecost, and the [days] after Pentecost were called "[the days of] Pentecost." In the early church this word signified not only "the day of Pentecost" but also the entire seven weeks of the joyful time, which were a foretaste of heavenly joy. The characteristic of this understanding of Easter is that one does not primarily think of the historical date as a day of remembrance, but rather that the great salvation work of the death, resurrection, ascension, and sending of the Holy Spirit (on the day of the Jewish "Festival of Weeks") is understood as a unit. The historical events, which one never forgets as such, are seen simultaneously from heaven, where there are no earthly days. The joyful time of the church is thus a single large feast, which reaches from Easter to Pentecost. This explains the fact that the fortieth day came to be separately celebrated as Ascension Day only relatively late [in church history].

From this also the famous Easter disagreement between Rome and Asia Minor is to be understood. Those in Asia Minor celebrated their Passover together with the Jews on the 14th of Nisan, whereby the reference to John played a great role, whose chronology was perhaps already represented by Paul, as the often-misunderstood Easter Epistle reading (1 Corinthians 5) shows. As in other things, [so] also in the celebration of the Easter feast at first a variety [of observances] apparently existed. Soon it was unbearable to celebrate Easter on any other day but Sunday, the day of the resurrection, the day on which God created light and on which the sun of righteousness ascended in the resurrection of Christ, the "day of the Lord" which (according to Amos 5:18) was understood as the day of the arrival of the Messiah, the day on which the Lord comes to His congregation in the Sacrament, as He came to the disciples on the first Sunday of the church eight days after Easter and converted the doubting Thomas to the Easter faith. How, then, the calculation of the Easter Sunday gradually loosened itself from the Jewish calendar does not need to be retold here.

3

Innumerable texts of the fathers and of the old liturgies show that this was the understanding of the Easter feast and of "Pentecost" in the early church. It has maintained itself in the Eastern Church, while the Roman Church is only today again in the process of moving the very old Easter ceremonies to Easter night, which until now had been done on Good Saturday morning—one of the clever deeds of Pius XII, who in so many ways, for better or for worse, has become a reformer of his church and perhaps later will be considered in history as one of the greatest popes of modern times. Whoever wants to get an overview of the large amount of historical material should be directed to the essay of Odo Casel,[4] a Benedictine of Maria Laach who has since been called to his [heavenly] home: "The Nature and Meaning of the Earliest Christian Easter Celebrations" in the fourteenth volume of the *Yearbook for Liturgical Science* (Münster, 1938, pp. 1–78). Here is mentioned as an example a document, the actual text of which Casel did not have, one of the most treasured papyrus discoveries in the 1930s, a decade which was, in this regard, so fortuitous [because of the many papyrus finds]: *An Easter Sermon by Melito of Sardes*[5] from the end of the second century, the only almost completely preserved work of Asia Minor's great theologian. The clever Egyptian papyrus dealers had taken the book apart and sold the pages individually to those who bought such things, whom they thought crazy. So the work came in fragments in part to England, in part to America, and the happy owners didn't know what to do with the text until it was discovered that the pages belonged to one another, and together they presented us with this lost writing by Melito. In the year 1940 they could appear simultaneously in Philadelphia and London in an exemplary edition by Campbell Bonner at the University of Michigan in Ann Arbor. It is a sermon, preached during Easter night, and therefore according to Asia Minor's custom in the night of the Jewish Passover, on the basis of the narrative of the institution of the Passover. A few quotes may illustrate the content:

> The Scripture of the Hebrew Exodus has been read aloud, and thereby the words of the mystery have been made apparent, as the lamb is sacrificed and the people are rescued. Therefore, listen, dearly beloved: the mystery of the Passover is old and new, eternal and temporary, mortal and immortal, fading away and remaining forever. It is old according to the Law, and new according to the Word. . . . Fading away in regard to the slaughter of the lamb, remaining eternally in regard to the life of the Lord. Mortal, insofar as the Lord was buried, immortal insofar as He arose from the dead. The Law is old, the Word is new (i.e., the Gospel).

Then the Passover lamb of the old covenant is treated as a foreshadowing of Christ:

> Instead of the lamb, the Son came . . . the Law became the Word (i.e., Gospel), the old became the new and went out from Zion and Jerusalem. The commandment became grace, the foreshadowing became reality. The lamb became the Son, the sacrificial lamb became human.

---

4   A liturgiologist, Casel (1886–1948) entered the Benedictine Monastery of Maria Laach in 1905, and from 1922 until his sudden death was spiritual director of the nuns at Herstelle. See *ODCC*, 294. MH

5   Melito (d. ca. 190), was bishop of Sardis. He was virtually unknown until Campbell Bonner in 1940 published *Peri Pascha*, a work preserved in a papyrus shared between the Chester Beatty Collection and the University of Michigan. See *ODCC*, 1068. MH

> The human became God. For He was born as a son, led as a lamb to the slaughter, and buried as a human, but He arose from the dead as God, He, who by nature was God and man. He is everything. As Judge, He is the Law; as Teacher, He is the Word (i.e., Gospel); as Savior, He is grace; as the One who begets, He is the Father; as the One who is begotten, He is the Son; as the One who suffers, He is the sacrificial lamb; as the One who was buried, He is human; as the One who arose, He is God. This is Jesus, the Messiah: to Him belongs honor eternally. Amen.

Naturally, one shouldn't take offense at the undeveloped Christology of this early church father, which is probably the reason that his works weren't preserved. His treatment of the Old Testament corresponds to that of Paul, especially in the Easter Epistle, or at the beginning of 1 Corinthians 10 and the use of the Old Testament in the Letter to the Hebrews. The divine grace which came to the old people of God during the exodus, this miracle of redemption, repeats itself on a higher level in Christ's Passion and resurrection as the redemption of the new people of God. The old event already contained the future one, or, better said, it is a "mystery" of this event. In it is hidden that which will happen in the future, in the blessed end time in which the church lives. That is the New Testament's scriptural interpretation, indeed, by the Lord Himself, for example, in the interpretation of the brass serpent or of the manna in John's Gospel. Thus the church, in following Jesus and the apostles, understood its Bible, the Bible of Jesus. So the Old Testament is the Holy Scripture of the church, as it was indeed also for Luther the Holy Scripture in the authentic sense, while the New Testament is for him actually an "oral proclamation," the living announcement of the revelation already contained in the Old Testament. It does not need to be said that in the course of church history much misuse of typological and allegorical biblical interpretation has been committed. But that may not hinder us from accepting the typology which the New Testament itself contains. One can't say that Melito has gone beyond this. He is a loyal student of Paul and John in the discussion of Exodus. The preacher then continues with a vivid retelling of the Exodus narrative in all details. One notices in this sermon that which we indeed know from so many of the ancient church's books and from the pictures of the earliest ecclesiastical art, how the Christian congregation lived in the Bible of the Old Testament, how deeply the narratives had imprinted themselves upon the hearts, and with what joy they could hear the old histories again and again. The development of basic thought of the typology follows this presentation once more:

> Everything has its time. The foreshadowing has its time, and the object portrayed therein has its time . . . the redemption and the truth of the Lord were exemplified in the people . . . the people became a prototype of the church.

Where the foreshadowing has been fulfilled, there it has lost its content.

Once the sacrifice of the lamb was held in great honor, now it is worthless, because the Lord lives. Once the death of the lamb was honored, now it has no worth, because the Lord has completed the redemption. The blood of the lamb was precious, now it has no more worth for the sake of the Lord's Spirit. The mute lamb was precious, now it has no more worth for the sake of the flawless Son [here is a play on words with *aphonos* and *amomos*]. The temple here below was precious, now it is worth nothing anymore for the sake of Christ, who is above. [Is this a motif from a time before the destruction of Jerusalem?] Jerusalem here below was precious, now it is no longer regarded, for the sake of the Jerusalem above . . . for God's glory no longer dwells in one place in a pitiful form, but rather His grace has been poured out unto the ends of the world, and there the almighty God has taken up His residence by means of Jesus Christ, to whom honor is owed for eternity. Amen.

Thereby it is naturally not said that the Bible of the Old Testament has lost its worth. It does, after all, contain the "mystery" of the coming Christ.

There follows, then, an explanation of the word "Passover," which is derived [according to Melito] from the Greek *paschein* and *pathein*, that is, the word for suffering. This segues to an explanation of Christ's sufferings, which begins with a portrayal of human sin in its various forms and with a presentation about the destiny of death which covers humanity. Even the Christ's sufferings have their Old Testament types in the suffering of the patriarchs and prophets.

If you want to understand the mystery of the Lord, look at Abel who was killed like Him, look at Isaac who was bound like Him, look at Joseph who was sold like Him, look at the prophets who in the same way suffered for the sake of Christ. Look also at Him, who was sacrificed as a lamb in the land of Egypt, who beat Egypt, and who redeemed Israel by means of His blood.

Christ was therefore "mystically," as the fathers said, already present in the first Passover, a thought which is not far removed from the Pauline statement that "the rock was Christ." But then follows a reference to the predictions of Psalm 2, of Jer. 11:19, and above all of Isaiah 53, the most quoted, as far as I know, passage of the Old Testament among the fathers. It continues with the burial of Jesus, and the powerful Good Friday sermon becomes a repentance sermon. The *improperia*[6] of the Roman Good Friday liturgy call forth:

My people, what have I done to you? How have I given you cause for sadness? Answer Me. Because I led you out of the land of Egypt, you have the cross prepared for your Savior. Because I led you through the wilderness for forty years and fed you with manna, you have the cross prepared for your Savior. What else would I have still done for you, and

---

6 *Improperia* or "Reproaches" are the reproofs addressed by the crucified Savior to His ungrateful people, which form part of the Good Friday liturgy of the Latin Church. The use of the reproach as a homiletic devise may go back to St. Cyril of Jerusalem. See *ODCC*, 1385. MH

did not do it? . . . It was I who for your sake struck Egypt together with its firstborn, and you deliver Me to My hostage-takers . . . .

And so forth. There can hardly be a doubt that we here encounter, already in the second century, the original form of the *improperia* which connect to Mic. 3:3ff., God's lament about His people's thanklessness. So we read further in Melito's text:

> Come, He says, Israel, you have killed the Lord. Why? . . . It is He who led you on the path to Egypt and protected you there and preserved you there. It was He who gave you light by means of the column of fire and who gave you shelter under the cloud, who parted the Red Sea and led you through it and destroyed your enemy. It is He who gave you manna from heaven, who gave you water to drink from a rock, who gave you the Torah on Mount Horeb, who gave you an inheritance in the land, who sent prophets to you and raised up kings for you. It is He who came to you, who healed your sick, who raised your dead. It is He whom you have insulted. It is He whom you have tortured, whom you have killed . . . come here, Israel, and present your case against Me because of your thanklessness . . . .

Thus the lament about Israel's unthankfulness continues further. It is still the Jewish people, which is here addressed, while in the *improperia* the church identifies itself with the people, inasmuch as God's laments are always answered in Latin and—a sign of its great age—in Greek: "Holy God, holy Mighty One, holy Immortal One, have mercy on us." Finally, the Good Friday sermon becomes the Easter sermon:

> He arose from the dead and calls to you: "Who is it who is arguing with Me? Let him appear before Me. I have freed those who were condemned, I have made the dead alive again, and I awake him who is buried. Who wants to raise his voice against Me? I," He says, "am the Messiah. It is I who conquered death, who triumphed over the enemy, who trampled Hades underfoot and who bound the strong man, who bring the people safely home to the heights of heaven, I," says He, "the Messiah. Therefore, come to Me, all the nations of humanity, who are covered with sins, and receive the forgiveness of sins. For I am your forgiveness. I am the Passover of redemption, the Lamb who was sacrificed for you. I am your ransom money. I am your light, your Redeemer. I am the resurrection, I am your King. I lead you to the heights of heaven. I will show you the Father who is from eternity, I will awake you with My right hand."

Then the preacher continues:

> This is He who in the beginning created heaven and earth, who was announced by means of the Torah and the prophets, who became flesh in a virgin, who hung on the boards of the cross, who was buried in the earth, who arose from the dead, and who climbed up to the heights of heaven and sits at the right hand of the Father.

A doxology no longer extant seems to have formed the conclusion of this sermon.

4

The Easter sermon by Melito offers many theological problems, for example, the concept of the "mystery," the treatment of the Old Testament, and Christology. We won't deal with those here. It also cannot be seen as typical for sermons of ancient times, for its author was not a great theologian and not a usual bishop. We have presented it as an example of the understanding about the feast of Easter in the old church, in which Good Friday and Easter were celebrated together as the Christian "Passover." The homily shows how seriously Christ's sacrificial death was taken, and if, at first glance, the moment of Easter joy seems to be missing, then it may not be forgotten that this joy found its expression in the Eucharist which followed the sermon. The memory of death and the Good Friday lament belong most closely together with Easter joy. This is indeed true, too, of the understanding about Holy Communion. If Hans Lietzmann [1875–1942] and others have represented the opinion that the Lord's Supper in the first congregation in Jerusalem must not be understood from the Last Supper of Jesus and from the memory of His death, because it was entered "with rejoicing" (Acts 2:46 ἐν ἀγαλλιάσει; cf. the lexicons about this word, which is peculiar to the language of the Bible and of the church, and about the verb which belongs to it), even indeed as the eucharistic prayers of the *Didache* [ca. 120] do not mention Christ's death, then it is to be replied to this that [it is] exactly the death of Christ [which] is the deep reason for Christian joy, for the joy of the redeemed. Exactly as the Sacrament of the Lord's body and blood, Communion, is the "Eucharist," a thanksgiving and simultaneously a foretaste of heaven. The connection between Good Friday's suffering and Easter joy is precisely the essence of Christian joy. Consider the joy about which the Lord speaks in His parting comments: "That My joy may remain in you, and that your joy may be complete" [John 15:11] and "Your sorrow will turn into joy" [John 16:20]. The other thing which constitutes the essence of Christian joy is its eschatological character. It is the joy of heaven, the joy about Christ's return: "I will see you again, and your heart will rejoice, and nobody will take your joy away from you" [John 16:22].

As every Sunday is the Easter of every week, as the Lord's Day is an anticipation of heavenly joy, as every Communion is an anticipation of its parousia, so the church's joyful time between Easter and Pentecost is an anticipation of the joy of heaven, of eternal blessedness. This is what the ancient church, since the days of the apostles, has known. The church of the martyrs lived from this joy. There are hardly any records of martyrdom in which the joy of the confessors and blood witnesses is not mentioned. This joy has remained especially in the Eastern Church, but it lives on in all liturgies of the joyful time.

We need this joy now more than ever. The world needs it, and Christendom needs it. If ever the joyful news was necessary for the world, then [it is] in our century of great wars and mass death. But how should we, servants of the Gospel, announce this joy to the world if we ourselves do not have it? What is missing in the churches of Christendom today is the measure of joy which the ancient church possessed. We all stand in great danger of having the fearful seriousness of our time, the concerns in the church and in the parsonage, even the concerns about the church which are commanded to us, to not allow the great joy to arise, or to kill it. This is especially true of those among us who work in "dead" congregations, who perhaps must preach in empty churches, and upon whom too much work has been placed. But it is true there, too, where the congregations are rich, sometimes too rich, where the ecclesiastical life seems to bloom and the Christian faith [is] in no way attacked from the outside. There it is worldly joy, the secularized substitute for the true joy of the Gospel, which threatens to destroy Christ's joy. In America in the year 1948, I drove with a fellow clergyman by car throughout the land.[7] We spoke about how churchly life had changed in the last generation.[8] Large beautiful churches have replaced the old wooden churches. Large parsonages were built by the willing congregations of the prosperous farm regions. Suddenly my comrade said:

> I don't know if all of that is a blessing; has not the new house, the new car, and everything which has been given to us become more important to our congregation's members and to us pastors than the gift of the Gospel and of the Sacraments?

If one of the large American Lutheran churches named its most recent convention, which bore witness to flourishing churchly life and to the growths of gifts and of the increasing wealth of the church, "The Joyful Convention"—what kind of joy was meant by that? God help us all toward great Easter joy and grant to His entire church on earth this year a proper joyful time.

༄

Greeting you in the bonds of faith,

Your
Hermann Sasse

---

7   Sasse lectured at Concordia Seminary, St. Louis in 1948. MH

8   It had been more than twenty years since Sasse's first visit to the United States. "However, what Lutheranism is, I learned in America 1925/26. I was pastor in Oranienburg and Berlin, a Lutheran within the union" (Sasse to Tom Hardt, June 18, 1958; in the Harrison Collection). See Feuerhahn Chronology. MH

Historical Context

The issue of religious freedom is very contemporary. Lutherans ought to be well aware, according to Sasse, that the route to religious tolerance in the West came through Lutheranism's struggle. Sasse warns prophetically that "such tolerance can change tomorrow into intolerance.... Resistance against the total state can come only from the church, but not the church which lets itself be governed by the state...." MH

[Postmark June 1955][1]

Prof. H. Sasse
41 Buxton Street
North Adelaide, S.A.

Dear and Reverend Dr. Behnken,

I apologize for having not earlier replied to your very kind letter of March 23, which gave me so much valuable information concerning the situation of the Synodical Conference. I thank you very much indeed for your great confidence. Rest assured that I have not spoken to anyone about the information you gave me .... My prayers will be with you.

... One of these days I received from the theological department of the LWF an invitation to attend the International Congress on Luther Research at Aarhus, Denmark, in 1956. A journey from Australia is, of course, financially impossible .... From Germany all faculties will be represented; from America, among others, Prof. Bainton; from England, Methodists and even an Anglican. From your church, Prof. Pelikan, Chicago, and Dr. Schwiebert are named. Otherwise no church of confessional Lutheranism will be represented. The great danger is that the theological side of Luther research will be dominated by the school of Lund, by the German unionists and the more liberal churches in America. Thus a great responsibility rests upon the two scholars of your church, and the question should be raised whether or not a competent member of the faculty of St. Louis should be added. Dr. Pelikan is the successor to Pauck, who once went with me to America in 1925. Pauck has become the leading scholar in the field of Luther research. He is an able man, a representative of the school of Karl Holl, with whom he shares the conviction that the only real Lutheran was Calvin. I do not know whether Dr. Pelikan has a full insight into the European situation.

---

1   CHI Behnken file. Original in English. MH

I have reasons to doubt that. Dr. Schwiebert is a very good historian and would contribute a lot, but he has perhaps not the same qualities as a theologian. Since this congress will determine the future course of all Luther research, St. Louis, which has meant so much for knowledge of Luther in America, must be represented. For Luther research is and ought not to be a privilege of the LWF. They could help organize it, but they should not determine its future course. To invite the Quaker Bainton is quite proper for a scientific congress, but not to invite St. Louis—this is impossible. I do not know who at present is responsible for and active in Luther research in your faculty. But if you let me know a name, I would see that such a representative would be suggested . . . .

In the great distress of our churches,

Yours sincerely,
H. Sasse

thirty-eight

Cuius Regio, Eius Religio?

ON THE FOUR HUNDREDTH ANNIVERSARY
OF THE AUGSBURG RELIGIOUS PEACE

TRANSLATED BY ANDREW SMITH

Pentecost, 1955[1]

Prof. D. Theol. Hermann Sasse
41 Buxton Street
North Adelaide, South Australia

Dear Brothers in the Office!

1

On September 23 of this year, the Lutheran Church will ponder an event which was at first of importance for Germany and for German Lutheranism, but the distant effects of which reach into the Lutheran Churches of the world in our time. The peace, which was sealed four hundred years ago between the Catholic and Lutheran nobility of the "Holy Empire," of the "Empire of the German Nation" and which was signed by Ferdinand[2] "on the 23rd day of the month of September, in the 1555th year after the birth of Christ, our dear Lord; of our empire, the Roman one, in the 25th year, and in the other one, in the 29th year" (i.e., twenty-five years after Ferdinand took on the title of a "Roman king" as a representative

---

1 *BLP* 38: *Cuius regio, eius religio? Zur Vierhundertjahrfeier des Augsburgischen Religionsfriedens"* (North Adelaide, [May 29,] 1955). The original was published in *LuBl* 7, no. 42 (June 1955): 49–61. Reprinted in *ISC* 2:152–62. Huss number 314. MH

2 Ferdinand (1503–64; emperor, 1556–64) was the brother of Emperor Charles V (s.v. *Christian Cyclopedia*). MH

of his brother, Charles V[3]), was at first a political peace, in which the imperial nobility of both confessions refrained from the use of warlike methods for the resolution of the religious division, insofar as both of these confessions were concerned. If the Edict of Worms[4] had once justified the action against Luther by noting that the dissolution of the old ecclesiastical order, effected by Luther, would not only lead the "royal German nation" into "an inhumane division" but also eventually "all other nations," then the imperial congress's statement of Augsburg in 1555 justified the peace agreement thirty-four years later with the necessity of "dissolving" the existing

> insecurity, and of placing the spirits of the nobilities and their under-lings again in peace and trust toward each other, and of protecting the German nation, our beloved Fatherland, from final fragmentation and decline.

It has often been asked who was the winner in this peace agreement and who was the loser. Naturally, this question can only be answered this way: Both parties achieved what they could achieve. Hermann Friedrich Theodor von Kolde[5] opined that a better political leadership among the evangelicals would have achieved more in an era in which seven tenths of the German population were Lutheran, two tenths were members of the various sects and smaller Protestant groups, and only one tenth still professed the papal church (cf. his *Protestantische Realenzyklopädie*, vol. II, p. 233). But it was certainly no coincidence that no better political leadership was present on the Lutheran side. It was, as [Paul] Joachimsen [1860–1930] correctly commented, "a sign of the fatigue of public life" that the reformational movement found "its conclusion in a compromise brokered by national politics" and that "even this [compromise] appeared to the men on both sides as a gift from God" (*Propyläen Weltgeschichte*, vol. 5, p. 208). It was an exhaustion, such as we see again in all of Europe after the large so-called religious wars of the seventeenth century [which often were not "religious" at all, but rather about land and power], and at which point led to the final omission of religious unity in the Occident. In Augsburg in 1555, they

---

3   Charles V (1500–1558) was the grandson of Ferdinand and Isabella and became the most powerful man in Europe when he was elected Holy Roman emperor in 1519. However, Charles was plagued by enemies within and without, including France, the papacy, the Turks and the Protestant princes. Throughout his reign, he alternated between concession and repression of the Lutherans: crushing the Smalcald League after Luther's death (1546), yet at the 1555 Diet of Augsburg (after his defeat) accepting the verdict of *cuius regio eius religio*. To avoid both allowing and persecuting Protestants in different parts of his realm, Charles abdicated in 1556. He died in retirement at the monastery of Yuste in Estremadura. See *ODCC*, 323. MH

4   Issued just after Luther's "Here I stand" speech on April 18, 1521. MH

5   Kolde (1850–1913) was educated at Breslau and Leipzig and served as professor at Marburg and Erlangen. His works include *Luther und der Reichstag zu Worms* (s.v. *Christian Cyclopedia*). MH

had still not given up the hope of unification. But the possibility that the division could be a permanent one had already appeared on the horizon: if an

> equilibrium by means of the general council, national convention, colloquia, or imperial negotiations is not achieved, then this condition of peace should nonetheless . . . exist and remain until some final equilibrium of religion and matters of faith, and should therefore . . . be and remain a continuous, constant, unconditional, eternal peace, set up and finalized forever and ever.

Even if this peace lasted only two generations, until the Thirty Years' War [1618–48] interrupted it and drew Germany again into the large so-called religious wars of Europe, it still really has the great significance for the Lutheran Church that it, despite all the retaliations by the Counter-Reformation, actually made possible the building up of ecclesiology and the extension of theology. The Lutheran church still lives today from the blessings of this peace, so deficient in itself. And this is true not only of German Lutheranism, but rather of the Lutheranism of the entire world.

2

Here we want meanwhile not to speak about the details of the achievement of peace in 1555 and not about its political significance for the German people. What interests us all about the Augsburg religious peace, honored brothers, whether we live in Europe or on other continents, in one of the old territorial or national churches or in one of the free churches, is the great foundational question of the freedom of faith and conscience. This distinguishes the Peace of Augsburg from all earlier and transitory agreements, that for the first time the "old religion" and the "religion related to the Augsburg Confession," and therefore two confessions in the [one] "holy empire," were acknowledged together. The empire was a "holy" empire, insofar as it was the Christian Roman Empire whose emperor had an office in the church as *advocatus ecclesiae* ["advocate of the Church"]. This concession was so great that Charles V would rather lay down his crown than sign his name to such a document. To this extent, the history of religious freedom in the Occident begins with the Religious Peace of Augsburg. It is, however, only a beginning. For the freedom, which was here conceded, was valid provisionally only for the territorial rulers. The thought still seemed unbearable that a territory could encompass two or more denominations, two sorts of Divine Service. Although Luther himself had actually allowed freedom of faith to the individual—"God desires no coerced worship"—he did, however, consider impossible the public exercise of a different [manner of] worship. It was a clear axiom of the national ecclesiology of the sixteenth century that "where there is one ruler, there is also one religion" (*nam ubi unus dominus, ibi sit una religio*), out of which, then, later came the *cuius regio, eius religio* ["whose reign, his religion"], which does not yet appear in the Augsburg Religious Peace.

That was no different in Germany than in any other country in Europe, no different with the Catholics than with the Protestants. The medieval laws regarding heretics, going back to the Christian empire of ancient times (cf. the Edict of Thessalonica, AD 380), are a force even in the centuries after the Reformation. Luther made a notable exception when he opined that heretics should only be executed if they are revolutionaries at the same time, and the thirty-third item in his list of errors, which the bull threatening his excommunication damns as "heretical, or provoking offense, wrong, giving irritation to pious ears, or seducing simple minds against the catholic truth," reads simply: "It is against the will of the Holy Spirit that heretics are burned."

That was a new thing in a century in which even [Ulrich] Zwingli had the first Anabaptists drowned, and [John] Calvin had the Antitrinitarian Michael Servetus,[6] who had escaped the Inquisition, burned. And this is to say nothing at all about the Catholic countries and about the unspeakably sad fate of the English people, whom a worthless king, despite his Catholic convictions, tore away from Rome and who now were treated by their children according to the *cuius regio, eius religio*: Lutherans, Catholics, Anglicans, Calvinists, and Catholics again fell victim to this system, and were naturally celebrated by their followers as martyrs, in part rightly, such as Thomas More[7] (1478–1535), and in part improperly, such as Thomas Cranmer[8] (1489–1556), the official martyr of the Reformed state church. Mary the Catholic [1516–58; r. 1553–58], the daughter of Henry VIII and the sad Catherine of Aragon, received in the official history the nickname "bloody," while the bloodguilt of her successor Elizabeth[9] was cloaked

---

6   Michael Servetus (ca. 1511–53) was a theologian and physician. Educated in France, he attended the coronation of Charles V in 1530. After his arrest in Vienna in 1553 for propagating his Antitrinitarian views, he escaped but was arrested again in Geneva, where he was condemned and burned (s.v. *Christian Cyclopedia*). MH

7   More served as Lord Chancellor of England. His most famous work, *Utopia* (1516), was the description of an ideal community, which was governed by natural law, religion, and reason. In the Lutheran controversy which raged throughout Europe, More emerged as a zealous supporter of Catholicism and assisted in Henry VIII's literary attack on Luther. However, when More refused to support Henry's marriage and secession from the Roman Church, he was executed on July 1, 1535. Pope Leo XIII beatified him in 1886, and he was canonized by Pius XI in 1935. See *ODCC*, 1114. MH

8   Cranmer served as archbishop of Canterbury and supported Henry VIII's divorce proceedings against Catherine of Aragon (during the proceedings, Cranmer secretly married Margaret Osiander, niece of Andreas Osiander!). Cranmer was Henry's chief tool in overturning papal authority in England. After Henry's death (1547), Cranmer invited Peter Martyr (1500–1562) and Martin Bucer to England and pushed forward his plan to unite with the other Protestant churches of Europe. When Mary Tudor assumed the throne, Cranmer was accused of treason, tried, and sentenced. He was burned at the stake in Oxford on March 21, 1556. See *ODCC*, 428. MH

9   Elizabeth I (1533–1603) was crowned queen of England in 1558. The daughter of Henry VIII and Anne Boleyn, she conformed outwardly to Catholicism during the reign of her half-sister Mary, but was often suspected of plots against her. After her elevation to the throne, Elizabeth immediately demonstrated her Protestant

in the mantle of patriotic love. It is a miracle of God that the English people survived this training in untruthfulness and hypocrisy at all and did not entirely lose their Christian substance. It is no mere coincidence that England, after the religious confusion of the seventeenth century, which led to a bloody revolution, became the home of the tolerance movement—which, by the way, already appears in Thomas More's humanistic *Utopia*. But not only the English church history but also that of America shows how long it took until this concept made itself felt. In England it was only in 1828 that the Catholics were granted the full rights of citizenship, because previously, tolerance had seemed possible only between [different types of] Protestants. Nothing is more telling for the power of the *cuius regio, eius religio* than the fact that it was still practiced even in America by those immigrants who, like the Pilgrim fathers, had left homelands with their state churches to live in the freedom of their faith. Only in 1833 did the Congregationalist church in Massachusetts give up its state subsidies, which it still received despite the already long-ago-declared separation of church and state. Pennsylvania was the great textbook example of a territory in which, for the first time, complete freedom of faith was granted for all religions. It was English disinterest, and the Enlightenment, which finally implemented religious freedom in the Occident, though one should not forget that not only in Luther's statements but also in the Religious Peace of Augsburg already significant beginnings are to be seen. In the peace of 1555, there is at least one case in which the coexistence of both confessions is very clearly recognized as possible. We are not thinking about Ferdinand's declaration about a certain tolerance in the ecclesiastical territories, which was not recognized by the Catholic side because it was not a part of the imperial congress's decision, but rather about regulation of conditions in the free imperial cities in which until then Catholics and Lutherans had lived together. The citizens of these cities, of both the worldly and spiritual classes, should henceforth

> peacefully and quietly live together among each other, and not venture to do away with any part of the other's religion, church customs, or ceremonies, or to force them away from such, but rather each party allow the other to peacefully and quietly remain by its religion . . . .

One can only ask: why was this possible only here? The followers of various religions can actually live peacefully together, even in one and the same political structure! And this must also not be forgotten, that at least the right to emigrate was granted to the individuals who, for reasons of conscience, could not follow the religion of the territorial royalty. In the nineteenth century they laughed at this *beneficium emigrandi* as a terrible atrocity. In the middle of our enlightened twentieth century, in which the *cuius regio, eius religio* has again gained an

---

sympathies. See *ODCC*, 540–41. Because she desired a broad Protestant front against Roman Catholicism and the Holy Roman Empire, she worked against the efforts for the Book of Concord among the Germans. MH

unheard-of actuality, we begin to understand again what kind of an unheard-of tolerance there was [in 1555]. Just try to emigrate from a country today because you do not want your children to be raised in the "correct belief" of the authorized officials![10] Compared to our era of the strictly guarded border, of emigration and immigration certificates, of the requirement of so many governments that their citizens provide not only slave labor until they collapse but also that they confess the proper political views and the correct worldview, the era of the Augsburg Peace was an era of tolerance, and the imperial congress's decision of 1555 was the documentation of a freedom which today no longer exists anywhere in the world.

3

We usually don't see this change clearly, because we always see the church and its fate against the background of the nineteenth century, a time of a freedom unimaginable to other eras. All churches owe that which they are today to this freedom, even as limited as it was in the minds of its contemporaries and as limited as it in many cases actually was. Even the Roman Church, which thoroughly denies the principle of tolerance, made use of it wherever it could. The bull *Unam Sanctam*[11] was never repealed—indeed, even the current pope [Pius XII] expressly referred to it in his encyclical *Mystici Corporis* [promulgated June 29, 1943] about the teaching of the church. Rome, which happily raises claims to tolerance in the non-Catholic countries, is not ready to grant the same measure of tolerance to those who according to its opinion are heretics in Spain or in certain countries in Latin America. And yet the Roman Church actually lives by the tolerance which it enjoys in the predominantly Protestant countries. This is true not only of the small Catholic minorities, as in, for example, the Scandinavian countries. It is especially true of the large areas of the English-language territories, such as in the United States and in Australia, into which Rome, with incredible infusions of people, money, and political influence, hopes to make good the losses which it has suffered in the countries behind the Iron Curtain, just as once its missionary work in Asia and America was supposed to compensate for the loss of half of Europe suffered in the Reformation. Those of our readers who live in West Germany see this building up of Catholicism daily before their eyes, but one must always consider that it is progressing with the

---

10 Sasse is no doubt waxing a bit personal here, having emigrated to Australia only six years earlier with his wife, Charlotte, and two sons. At that time he complained of the mountains of paperwork and complexity of the process. MH

11 A papal bull was the most solemn and formal written mandate of the pope. The word "bull" comes from the Latin *bulla*, or "bubble," which was the lead or wax stamped to seal and authenticate documents since the sixth century. *Unam Sanctam* [Denzinger 468] was promulgated by Boniface VIII (r. 1294–1303) in 1302 at the height of the imperial papacy of the Middle Ages. It contained the most sweeping papal claims to churchly and secular power. MH

same intensity in the immigration countries and in the mission fields of Africa and Asia, insofar as they are still open. The modern Catholic Church is that which it has become by means of shrewd use of the tolerance principle once so decisively opposed by it. We may not consider that as insincerity, but rather as the result of its situation in a world which forced it to develop its own tolerance principle. A Catholic author in our time formulated this principle thus:

> [F]or us in the twentieth century, the principle of tolerance is clear. The church never hesitated to judge the errors of other religions. Truth and error, good and evil, are irreconcilable opposites. Therefore intolerance against that which is in itself false or evil is a virtue. But love forbids extending this intolerance to the humans who represent the error or the evil. Another principle stands opposite to the principle of dogmatic intolerance, namely, the axiom "that nobody may be forced, against his will, to accept the Catholic faith, because he cannot believe if he does not want to" (Leo XIII [r. 1878–1903]). The law of love commands consideration of the religious convictions of another person.

In this matter, the Catholic Church really has learned something. Catholic theology finds the theological foundation in the teaching of Thomas [Aquinas] about the conscience, according to which an involuntarily erring conscience is binding (*Summa Theologica, Prima Secundae*, quaestio 19, art. V and especially VI), so that it would actually be a sin if I, convinced of the correctness of the Lutheran doctrine, did not follow it but rather would accept the Catholic doctrine seen by me as false. One may never forget what an important role the conscience plays, even in Catholic teachings. It was not only the Englishman but also the Roman Catholic Englishman John Henry Newman [1801–90] who uttered the well-known saying that he would be ready to raise his glass in a toast to the pope, but first to toast the conscience, and only then the pope. The Augustinian interpretation of "compel them to come in" [Luke 14:23], with which the Middle Ages justified forced conversion, has been given up. Although it could still happen in the nineteenth century in the ecclesiastical state of Pius IX that a Jewish child would be baptized and taken away from its parents so that it would not lose its salvation, Pius XII allegedly allowed the orphans of Jewish parents who had been baptized and raised in a Catholic orphanage to be given back to the parents, whereby the summoning of all papal authority was however necessary, because, as is well-known, mothers superior of all denominations are more infallible than the infallible pope. The justification for not baptizing a child against the will of its parents had already been given by Thomas (*Summa Theological* III, qu. 68, article X): it is a right under natural law that parents raise their children or determine how they will be raised. From this, the view of modern Catholicism about the problem of tolerance is to be understood, which is a different view in the strictly Catholic countries and in the states with religious equality. In contrast to the Middle Ages, today in a Catholic country such as Spain the private exercise of their religion is granted to "heretics," but however not public evangelization or instruction. In the states which grant thorough religious equality—comparable to the imperial cities mentioned in the Augsburg Religious Peace—or in the states in which the separation of church and state has been carried out, the Roman Church allows its members to act according to the government's laws as far as these can be brought into harmony with the Catholic faith. One can be very generous in this case and allow, for example, a Catholic judge to participate in a divorce procedure. Thus the Roman church has been capable in a quite astounding way to accommodate itself to the judicial atmosphere of the modern state and its principle of tolerance. How its justice system would develop if something like a new "Middle Ages" with a Christian "total state" would arise, one can naturally not say in advance. But the example of Spain shows in what direction such development would go.

4

What interests us above all as Lutherans is the situation of the Lutheran Church in the world of freedom of faith. The Augsburg Religious Peace and the stipulations of the Peace of Westphalia [1648] (these and other important documents are collected in the appendix to *Das Grundrecht der Religionsfreiheit . . . in Deutschland* by H. Fürstenau, 1891; the non-German documents are found in Z. Giacometti, *Sources for the History of the Division between Church and State*, 1926) gave our church the right of public existence, which it already had in Denmark, Norway, and Sweden for a long time. This right to exist, however, had to be purchased by a great sacrifice: by the authority of the regional monarch over the church. It is known how decisively Luther protested against the fact that the regional royalty, who in a time of crisis had been called to help as Christians and as *praecipua membra ecclesiae* ["chief members of the church"], were making permanent institutions out of their emergency bishoprics, and it is also still known how the true Lutherans sighed about the *apap*, the reversed papacy.[12] It is true that the regional aristocrats of the sixteenth century, of whom the majority, like the majority of the ordinary people, were deeply moved by the Reformation, faithfully carried out the duty of caring for the church (*cura ecclesiae*). But as the absolute state of the seventeenth and eighteenth century extinguished the last remains of the Lutheran doctrine of state and church, then the territorial system arose, which in Germany corresponds to the state ecclesiology of England, about which we spoke above. To the reader who knows Luther and who knows Henry VIII, we need offer no justification for the statement that this system is not to be explained from the Lutheran Reformation, but rather stands in the sharpest contradiction to it. For according to this ecclesio-legal system,

---

12 For what Feuerhahn called "one of the most thorough discussions of the relation of church and state, not only in Sasse's corpus, but also in any English language literature," see "Church Government and Secular Authority according to Lutheran Doctrine," in *Lonely Way* 1:173–241. MH

the church government—and not only as *ius circa sacra* ["law around sacred matters"] but rather also as the *ius in sacra* ["law in sacred matters"]—is a component part of the territorial power. The regional monarch as such is the bishop of his church, which he allows to be governed by his civil servants. This is also the case in those countries which have retained the episcopal system. We must say this above all about the Church of England, but also about certain churches of the Lutheran north. The king of England is, according to the English national ecclesiastical law, the senior regent of his church and alone has the power—naturally, after the parliamentary system, through the prime minister—to present to the cathedral chapters bishops and archbishops for canonical vote, whereby an old law makes it a duty of the chapters to elect the nominated candidates and none other. Here one can only speak of a papacy of the territorial monarch. The circumstance of this territorialism in Germany was the slow destruction of the ecclesiastical doctrine and of the church as a confessional church. The most telling example of this is Prussia, whose fate has determined the entire history of Lutheranism in the world. It can still be explained from the Calvinist convictions of the Prussian princes and kings that they slowly attempted, ever since the conversion of Johann Sigismund (1572–1619)[13] to the Reformed Church in 1613, to take away the strictly Lutheran character from the Lutheran Church of their territory and to move it toward a union with the Reformed. Calvin and his followers never did, after all, understand why there should be an ecclesiastical boundary between Lutherans and the Reformed. But the fact that the union was introduced and acceptance was forced "voluntarily" on its subjects only in the state in which Prussian territorial law ruled with its broad tolerance indicates that even the state which is thoroughly tolerant can do a good job of being intolerant. Only fifteen years after the beginning of the open church struggle in Breslau, a general concession was granted to the "Lutherans holding themselves apart from the territorial church" [1845], and the injustices and police harassment to which the confessional Lutherans had to allow themselves to be subjected not only in Prussia but also in the other German territories—such as Baden (Eichhorn[14]) and Nassau ([Friedrich] Brunn[15]) and even still in the new German empire in the territories of Kur-Hesse and Hanover, which had become Prussian—show where the boundaries of the freedom of faith were drawn even

---

13   The elector of Brandenburg (1608–19), Johann [John] Sigismund was educated as a Lutheran but after his conversion to the Reformed church, he and his successors followed a union church policy (s.v. *Christian Cyclopedia*). MH

14   Karl Eichhorn (1810–85) was the champion of the Lutheran Church in Baden. Strengthened by his association with Wilhelm Löhe, Eichhorn rejected the union in Baden, leaving the territorial union church in 1850. See Meusel, *Kirchliches Handlexikon* 2:315. MH

15   Friedrich August Brunn (1819–95) severed ties with the Nassau state church in 1846 and organized the congregation at Steeden. C. F. W. Walther's visit to Germany in 1860 gave impetus to opening a seminary at Steeden (1861). Brunn sent many men to the Missouri Synod to serve as pastors (s.v. *Christian Cyclopedia*). MH

in the nineteenth century. *Cuius regio, eius religio*. Even if this phrase was no longer valid in the sense of the sixteenth and seventeenth centuries, so it really remains true in a different sense in the era of the thoroughly tolerant state. One often asked the question whether the struggle of the loyal confessors of the Lutheran faith and the freedom of the Lutheran Church was really worth it. One points to the small amount of success, small when measured by the externals, of these confessionalists and compares the thousands of the free churches to the millions in the territorial church. But apart from the complete untruth of these statistics—for among the "millions" there are the masses who do not go to church at all anymore—it is to be said it is due to the witness of the Lutheran free churches that there are still Lutherans even in the territorial churches. The free churches have gained for German Protestantism the freedom of faith, which neither the centuries of the Augsburg and Westphalian Religious Peace nor the era of enlightened tolerance could give. They have also produced out of the *beneficium emigrandi* ["the right to emigrate"] the right and the possibility of building up the Lutheran Church as a free church on the far sides of great oceans, independent of the *cuius regio, eius religio* of the Old World. It is the great discovery that the freedom of the church is not a real freedom if it is not still accompanied by the freedom of faith, a discovery made by the free churches in the many sacrifices in their struggle.

5

One has often asked why the free church movement in Germany, and in the Old World in general, was not stronger. The number of those who in the nineteenth century went the sacrificial way out of the territorial churches into the free churches was, actually, quite small, taken all in all. But one must then also ask who of the Lutheran theologians in Germany protested against the untruthfulness of the DEK (*Deutsche Evangelische Reichskirche*) of 1933 and the EKiD of 1948, which was not neutralized by the untruthfulness of the VELKD. Every Lutheran bishop in Germany who signed the constitution of the DEK and the EKiD knew that he was damaging the Confession to which he was bound, just as each of the Danish bishops who declared that they did not see why their church should not have altar fellowship with the Church of Scotland knew exactly that he thereby, strictly speaking, broke his vow of ordination. Certainly, each of them had his reasons with which he attempted to calm his conscience. We are also not speaking about the individual person who has to make such a decision, though it is very astounding that not even one of them resigned from his office before taking a step which was not only a sin for himself, but rather which also led countless others to sin. I know of only one church leader in our generation who only under unspeakable torture bowed to the state, in this case to the English parliament, which in 1928 rejected the new *Book of Common Prayer*, and disavowed his own struggle for the freedom of the church. That was William

Temple (1881–1944), who died in 1943 [1944?] as archbishop of Canterbury.[16] What stands behind this collapse? It is not only human cowardice, not only the concern for the estate of the church, and for earthly existence. Why do the bishops, pastors, and congregations in Norway allow themselves to be content when the governmental department responsible for such matters declares that the doctrine about eternal punishment in hell is not a binding doctrine of the church—despite the Seventeenth Article of the Augsburg Confession? The simple answer to all such questions is *Cuius regio, eius religio*. This axiom is so deeply rooted in the post-Christian culture of Europe that hardly anyone can free himself from it. People say they can't voluntarily give up the [concept of the] *Volks* church and its missionary opportunities, but people forget that churches without confessions have no more missionary power, neither in terms of "in-reach" nor in terms of "outreach." People also overlook the fact that one can no longer speak of a *Volks* church there where the citizens scorn the Gospel and the Sacraments. It is essentially nothing else than the hidden power of a thousand-year history which makes the *cuius regio, eius religio* into a foregone conclusion even still today. The state never gives freedom to the church, and no church frees itself voluntarily from the state. This is the experience of our century. At most, revolutionary events can occasion a separation. But even then the separation remains more or less nominal, as in Germany in 1918. Nothing is more telling for the power of the *cuius regio, eius religio* than the fact that the evangelical churches in Germany, when the freedom from the state which they had discussed for more than one hundred years fell into their lap as a gift, had nothing

---

16 Temple was among the leaders of the Life and Liberty Movement who called for a degree of autonomy for the Church of England, which was granted in 1919. His short period as archbishop (1942–44) was overshadowed by ill health and the war. See *ODCC*, 1586. Sasse knew Temple through the Faith and Order Movement, and in fact had consulted Sasse at his home in York on the difficult situation faced by the church under Hitler. "When I visited Temple the last time in York—1936, it happened secretly, for I was already under prohibition of travel, but I had to finish my business as secretary of Faith and Order for the continent" (Feuerhahn, "Hermann Sasse as an Ecumenical Churchman," 57). Temple wrote his wife from a Faith and Order meeting in Hartenstein: "I had a long talk with Sasse, after luncheon—very interesting. Among other things he said—'I gave a lecture lately on the religion of Hitler; but I did not call it that; I called it the religion of Robespierre'" (Feuerhahn, "Hermann Sasse as an Ecumenical Churchman," 76–77). On July 24, 1935, Dr. Molitoris, the "Erlanger Dozentenschaft," wrote to the rector of Erlangen University denying Sasse's request for permission to travel to Paris and Hindsgaul: "At this likewise political organiza-tion/event, I hold Prof. Sasse, considering the church political differences, with his opinions expressed, not suited to be sent to Paris and Denmark as representative. As regards his participation till now, inquiry by our intermediary agents and his church political bias, Sasse appears to us unsuitable to become known abroad (the foreign country), in order there to give a correct report of things in Germany." At the time Sasse was a member of the Faith and Order Continuation Committee and the Execu-tive Committee, serving as secretary (Feuerhahn Chronology). MH

more urgent to do than to seek for new political powers to rule them.[17] True, they did decline the Weimar Republic, though they accepted its money. But the German National Party, whose local chapters in Berlin grew out of the Positive Parochial Clubs and whose party leaders had so much influence in the church that—to name only one example—the majority leader in the Prussian legislature was at the same time the president of the Prussian General Synod (we don't say anything against him as a human or as a Christian, just as we don't personally criticize others among these party and church leaders), ruled the church, and it was only the logical consequence that, later, Hitler and his party assumed this role. At that time a segment of German Christendom gained the knowledge that this dependence upon political powers must be the end of the church. But the church struggle was already, after a few years, politicized—for those who could see, already in 1934 at Barmen—just as it was then widely understood in other countries as political. And nobody will disagree that the great decision of 1948 [EKiD] was politically conditioned: one church, one people, one empire, so it went in the admittedly terrible situation of the shredded German people. With the same arguments the unions of the nineteenth century were founded. The one Evangelical Church bound the Prussian provinces from Aachen to Königsberg and Breslau. The one Evangelical Church was necessary to patch together the grand duchy of Baden. Whoever doesn't want to believe that all of this is still the same today, let him ask and answer the question who in the General Synod of the EKiD in Espelkamp was elected president, and who not, and why.[18] All of these processes in the Christendom of Europe are finally not to be explained by the decision of this or that individual, though certainly each one bears the responsibility for his decision before God and before all Christendom. Its deepest cause lies in the more than thousand-year tradition of *cuius regio, eius religio*.

6

Thus we stand before one of the deepest riddles of church history and of human history in general. Why are we Lutherans? Certainly because of deepest convictions. But these, our personal convictions, have something to do with the fate of history, from which each of us comes. We are Lutherans because we come from a family which once, in the year 1624, the "Normative Year of the Westphalian Peace," lived in a Lutheran territory. Those parts of the family which perhaps lived a few miles away in a formerly ecclesiastical territory, or lived under a

---

17   The defeat of Germany in World War I and the establishment of the Weimar Republic brought an end to the rule of the princely houses throughout Germany. These heads of state, and therefore also heads of their respective territorial churches, were done ruling. The opportunity for getting things right for the Lutheran Church in Germany was lost again. MH

18   Here Sasse is referring to Otto Dibelius, bishop of Berlin (the Old Prussian Union Church), who was elected the first bishop of the EKiD in 1949 and again six years later at Espelkamp. MH

Catholic prince, remained Catholic, and their descendants are perhaps Catholic today by deepest conviction. This historical "accident" stands behind our church membership, and for most people of the old Christian world, this external membership in the church of the fathers remains the only thing which binds them to Christendom. One should not call that church membership. It is the untruthfulness of European territorial ecclesiology that one still does [call it church membership], and acts as if these essentially nonbelieving masses are members of the church and of the Body of Christ and have claims to the rights of the general priesthood of all believers. It can naturally happen, and it does happen, that from this external fellowship, which is not even the *societas externarum rerum et rituum* ["an association of external things and rites," Ap VII–VIII 5] of the Apology (because one can in many cases belong to such a "church" without even being baptized), a real membership in the church of Christ in the sense of *societas fidei in cordibus*, the "fellowship of faith in the heart" [Ap VII–VIII 5], arises. But that is, each time, a miracle of the Holy Spirit, exactly as the conversion of a Jew or a pagan.

The historical "accident" which made people members of these large institutions, which are churches neither according to the Holy Scripture nor according to the Lutheran Confession, though the church of Christ can still live deeply hidden in these social structures—this accident can in some cases be "power." With brutal power, Lutheran territories were returned to the papal church in the era of the Counter-Reformation. And this method was in many cases successful, as successful as the forced conversion of the Saxons to Christianity by Charlemagne.[19] A few generations after this brutal conversion, which brought the sharp criticism of his own high-ranking clergy against the emperor, Saxony was the heartland of Christian Europe. Still today, the *Heliand* [a medieval literary work], the fate of Gottschalk,[20] and the first works of art by the Saxon people witness the living faith which lived in the hearts of those whose grandfathers were "Christianized" with warlike force. *Cuius regio, eius religio.* Again and again, such experiences are had. When Christian Spain regained the Saracen territories in [seemingly] endless wars, many Moors and also many of the Jews who had lived in the Muslim areas were forcibly Christianized. For a long time, these Christianized Jews still carried on secretly the customs of the old faith, for example, as they secretly lit the Sabbath candles on Friday evening, even as in the case of the Saxons the heathen customs were similarly still carried out for

---

19 After Charlemagne assumed the Lombard crown, he sought to conquer the Saxons, taking Bavaria in 778 and moving on to add Avar and Pannonia by 796. See *ODCC*, 321. MH

20 A heterodox monk and theologian and the son of the Saxon count Bern, Gottschalk (ca. 804–ca. 869) advocated the double predestination doctrine of Augustine throughout Italy and the Balkans. He returned to Germany and was condemned at Mainz and again by the Synod of Quiercy. He was sentenced to life in prison. He also participated in the controversy over the Eucharist involving Radbertus (785–865). See *ODCC*, 696. MH

a long time. Out of the forcibly baptized Jews grew faithful Catholics, and even apologists against their old religion. Even the grand inquisitor Torquemada[21] himself is said to have come from such circles, as they also say of the Catholic statesman Salazar in Portugal.

7

The *cuius regio, eius religio* is valid not only in the Christian world. The most fearful riddle in church history is much rather [the fact] that one can, according to this rule, get rid of churches entirely. Of the more than two hundred million Muslims who are in the world today, probably more than half of them are traced back to the forced conversions of their ancestors. The descendants of Christians have become fanatical Muslims. Does the answer to the riddle of why missionary work among the Muslims is so difficult perhaps lie here? The old church in the Roman and Persian empires resisted the *cuius regio, eius religio* with the authentic courage of faith, until the collapse came in the East. Will the Christendom of our century summon up the power of faith with which alone one can offer resistance to the [worldly] powers which threaten today to falsify or destroy the Christian faith with their *cuius regio, eius religio*? We have already had preludes in National Socialism and Fascism of that which can happen. Hitler already knew that one can take an old faith away from people and give them a new one. Eastern Communism knows it much better. It knows that one can even bring a Roman cardinal to deny his convictions. What is truth in an era which can manipulate human souls by means of a refined science, so that they deny the truth which they believed an hour ago, and both times out of conviction? Don't say that this can happen only in the case of the barbaric peoples of the East. It happened in Germany with the highly educated men of the SS. It can happen tomorrow in any other country in the West. How harmless, by comparison, the application of the *cuius regio, eius religio* in the sixteenth and seventeenth century appears. Even the Spanish Inquisition never saw such demonic destruction of humanity and of human worth as we experience them today. That is not supposed to be an excuse for the fact that such evil happened in the name of Christ and His church.

Where is the church, we ask in conclusion, which resists the *cuius regio, eius religio* of our time? In the years of the Hitler government, a few people in Germany and in the world got a new understanding about this, that the church of Christ is the locus of true freedom. The tolerance of the modern world is not the wall against totalitarianism; on the contrary, any such tolerance can change tomorrow into intolerance, as the history of the tolerant Prussian State shows,

---

21 Juan de Torquemada (1388–1468) was a Spanish theologian. In 1417 he attended the Council of Constance (where Hus was burned), and he was active in negotiations with the Bohemians (Hussites) and the Greeks on the question of reunion. He was made a cardinal in 1439. See *ODCC*, 1632. MH

but the history of other states [show it] just as well. Resistance against the total state can come only from the church, but not the church which lets itself be governed by the state, which lets itself be told by the government, or (as can happen in the large free churches of America) by *Herr Omnes* ["Mr. Everybody"], that there is no hell. Not the church which is itself a part of the state, or a religious club of the world, can resist the authoritarian claims of the modern state and the modern world, but rather only that church which in all weakness and poverty, but in the strongest faith in Him, who makes us free, announces the pure Gospel and administers the Sacraments, the means of grace, by means of which Christ builds His kingdom in this world: the kingdom which, as our Confession states, is "hidden under the cross" [Ap VII–VIII 18][22] in this age. Only there is the true freedom of faith. The faith in Christ, in the kingdom of Christ, has there taken the place of the worldly *cuius regio, eius religio.*

༄

In this sense let us, dear brothers, celebrate the anniversary of the Augsburg Religious Peace and remind our congregations of that which is the true church and the true freedom of the church.

Greeting you in the bonds of faith,

Your
Hermann Sasse

---

22 "For Christ enlivens His true kingdom by His Spirit, whether it is revealed or is covered by the cross, just as the glorified Christ is the same Christ who was afflicted [John 17:1]" (Ap VII–VIII 18; *Concordia,* 145). MH

Historical Context

Letter 39 surveys the current state of Lutheranism as it is divided into state church, union church, free church, and church of the diaspora. The Reformation anniversary of 1717 provides a plumb line for Sasse as he rehearses the history of Lutheranism and its struggles for unity since that time. MH

December 12, 1955[1]

North Adelaide,

Dear Brother Oesch,

... One of the deepest [problems] we have is the general phenomenon of our century that we no longer have learned or theologically accomplished bishops and church presidents. They all want a "theology with which a person can start something" (Dibelius). The theologians are there to chime in and demonstrate that the mistakes of the church leaders are no mistakes. So it is in all churches. This also spares them of the trouble of repentance, which would be awkward....

Greet the colleagues.

Your
H. Sasse

---

1   CHI Behnken Correspondence. MH

thirty-nine

Unity and Division within Lutheranism

TRANSLATED BY ANDREW SMITH

September 1955[1]

Prof. D. Theol. Hermann Sasse
41 Buxton Street
North Adelaide, South Australia

Dear Brothers in the Office!

This letter must begin with very hearty thanks to those among you who thought of me in old friendship and brotherly love on my sixtieth birthday, and even surprised and gladdened me with the *festschrift* in an edition of the *Lutherische Blätter*. I can't say [enough] how beneficial was this manifestation of the *communio fratrum*, which is between us who all work somewhere in the broad diaspora which the Lutheran church has become in the whole world.

Fittingly, we should, even in this letter, think of the man whom God has called out of the struggle and out of the work for the Lutheran church, our brother Max Witte in Braunschweig,[2] who in a difficult life and in deep inner experience had ripened into a confessor of the Lutheran truth, the likes of which we have had only a few in German Lutheranism of the last decade. In this letter we will pursue the question of how it happens that the general leveling and equalizing which characterize our era of the masses do not stop even with the churches. Our departed brother belonged to those who were by no means to be made the same, whether by a "special ruling" or by ecclesio-political doctrinal discussions.

---

1   *BLP* 39: *Einheit und Spaltung im Luthertum* (North Adelaide, September 1955). The original was published in *LuBl* 7, no. 45 (November 1955): 129–45. Huss number 316. MH

2   On Witte, see *Lonely Way* 2:244. MH

What he taught us is first this: that even today, a living, believing, praying congregation can still gather itself around the Lutheran Confession, even there, where one did not expect it at all. It is, then, the old truth of church history that liturgy and dogma, preaching and sacrament belong inseparably together, because confession in the New Testament sense is always both: confession of the eternal truth and praise to God. In an era in which the liturgical movements are only all too often a substitute for the lost doctrine of the church, and the high church efforts hide the fallen status of the evangelical faith only with great effort, the congregation arisen out of the rubble of Braunschweig and gathering itself for daily Divine Service, for the service of the Word and of the Sacrament and of prayer, has been for all of us alike a symbol of that which we hope for the Lutheran church of the world. Certainly, the work of Brother Witte was a beginning and was burdened by some of the problems of such beginnings. But at some point, the beginning had to be made—with a revitalization of the old liturgical heritage of our church. May God grant to those who are responsible the wisdom which is necessary to maintain such a work, and [may He grant] to the congregation, and to the circle of brothers of the deceased, faith in the unbreakable promises of the Lord of the church.

1

The coming year, 1956, will be a year a great decisions for world Lutheranism, and the old problem of the unity and the division of the Churches of the Augsburg Confession will be the main point of interest. So it is good if we all remind ourselves what the teaching of our Confession is regarding the unity of the church. The great danger lurks that we, in this age of world organizations, would forget the *satis est* ["it is sufficient"] of Article VII of the Augsburg Confession:

> For it is sufficient for the true unity of the Christian church that the Gospel be preached in conformity with a pure understanding of it and that the sacraments be administered in accordance with the divine Word. It is not necessary for the true unity of the Christian church that ceremonies, instituted by men, should be observed uniformly in all places. It is as Paul says in Eph. 4:4–5, "There is one body and one Spirit, just as you were called to the one hope that belongs to your call, one Lord, one faith, one baptism." [AC VII; Tappert, p. 32]

We quote the exact wording of the article here because it is continually being misunderstood. It intends, as the conclusion shows, to be an exposition of the text of Ephesians 4, so important for the unity of the church and continually misused. The church is a *body*, even according to Paul, not because it is a united organization or, in the language of the Catholic (Möhler) and Anglican and even Lutheran theologians who have been formed by romantic sociology, an "organism," as, in an odd agreement, [both] the encyclical *Mystici Corporis* [promulgated by Pius XII in 1943] and many representatives of modern ecumenical theology think. The Body of Christ is constituted by means of the means of grace (1 Cor. 10:16; 12:13). It belongs therefore inseparably together with the Holy Spirit and is, like the Holy Spirit, a pure article of faith. As we cannot perceive the Holy Spirit, but rather can only believe, so also the church, as the Body of Christ, is hidden from our eyes, recognizable to faith only by the means of grace as the

> sign, by which one knows it, namely, where God's Word goes purely, where the Sacrament is administered according to God's Word, there is certainly the church . . . . And the same church is alone called the Body of Christ in the Scripture. For Christ is its Head . . . . [Ap VII–VIII 5; cf. Tappert, p. 169]

The [High Priestly] Prayer of our Lord, today so wrongly understood, also refers only to this church as the Body of Christ, "that they may all be one, as You, Father, [are] in Me, and I [am] in You; that even they may be one in Us, that the world may believe that You have sent Me" (John 17:21).

How can anyone understand the High Priestly Prayer of the Lord in such a way, as if the world, which does not know God and which persecutes His church, would suddenly come to faith if Christendom existed as a unified organism! There will however be a day on which the world will recognize whom they have crucified (Rev. 1:7), on which the mystery of Christ and His church, the unity of Father, Son, and Holy Spirit, and the community of the saints in the Body of Christ will be revealed. But that will be our beloved Judgment Day, not an earthly day earlier, as even indeed Paul says (Phil. 2:10). The unity of the Body of Christ is recognizable to the eye of faith already now by the pure preaching of the Gospel and the administration of the Sacraments according to their institution. The great *satis est* does not mean, as some have often opined on the basis of the misunderstood Latin text, that a consensus in general about the Gospel must be present, but it really doesn't matter what kind of a consensus. What is meant by *consentire de doctrina evangelii* ["to agree concerning the doctrine of the Gospel"] is shown with all clarity in the German text, which in the case of the Augsburg Confession has the same authority as the Latin [text]. It is the correctly understood Gospel around which the church of Christ gathers. And the administration of the Sacraments according to their institution means more than the correct completion of the holy actions instituted by the Lord, whereby it remains open how they are [to be] understood. The church has from ancient times, however, demanded nothing more for the validity of Baptism than the correct completion. But it is entirely wrong and un-Lutheran to conclude that it must therefore be so in the case of every sacrament. First, one should never forget that there is no doctrine regarding what a sacrament is, because the New Testament knows of no such doctrine. The Lord Christ instituted Baptism, the Sacrament of the Altar, and the Office of the Keys, and [He] left it to His church whether it would choose for these three or for two of them a common name, and which name it would choose. Already the institution shows that they cannot simply be placed on the same shelf. For the institution of Baptism is, according to the views of the ancient and medieval church, views which our church also follows (cf. Luther's baptismal hymn "To Jordan Came the Christ, Our Lord"[3]), accomplished by means of His Baptism. The Office of the Keys was instituted three times (Matt. 16:19; 18:18; John 20:22f.), and in the case of the Lord's Supper it is yet again different. Whether one should add the exercise of the Office of the Keys to the sacraments, with Luther and the Augsburg Confession,[4] or reckon it as [part of] preaching the Word, is a question of theological definition alone, and thus of Christian liberty. Our church should not let this liberty be taken from it, one reason being that even the pre-Reformation church did not yet have a firm doctrine about this. Under no circumstances is it proper that now suddenly in the new doctrinal declarations—which more and more take the place of the old confessions, like the confession of Bataks or the "United Testimony," the foundation for a unification of the Lutheran "middle" in America—the categorical declaration appears that there are two sacraments. Naturally, the church has the liberty to adopt the Augustinian definition, which speaks of word and action as the components of the sacrament, and accordingly to label only Baptism and the Lord's Supper as sacraments. But it may not make a dogma of this, as the Reformed Church does, which rejects the absolution in the sense of the Catholic and the Lutheran Church. It is Lutheran to deal at first with the individual sacraments, like the Augsburg Confession, and only then with the sacrament in general (cf. Articles IX–XIII in the Augsburg Confession). Only in this way can one do justice to the nature of the individual sacrament, to its *proprium*, which it does not share with every other sacrament. Only in this way does it become clear why, in the case of Holy Communion, the mere completion of the action with the proper elements and the recitation of the Words of Institution does not fully constitute the sacrament. Truly, the Lutheran Church does not adopt the Roman doctrine of the necessity of the "intention," the purpose of the priest, to at least do that which the church does, a doctrine which damages the objectivity of the sacrament and which leaves us in uncertainty about whether we have received the correct sacrament. It is not our faith, either, which makes the sacrament. But one needs only to compare the baptismal formulation with the Words of Institution of Holy Communion to see the deep difference which exists here. In the baptismal formula, the servant of Christ speaks about what he's doing naturally as a servant of Christ and thus about that which the Lord does through him. The Words of Institution of Holy Communion are something different. First, they give an explanation, which the baptismal formulation does not do. This explanation was given by the Lord Himself and is part of the institution. Luther was right when he indicated that it is impossible to understand one part

---

3   See *LSB* 406

4   "Absolution can properly be called a Sacrament" (Ap XIIA [V] 41; *Concordia*, 162).
     MH

of this explanation literally [and] another part figuratively. One cannot say "Take and eat" are to be literally understood, [while] "This is My body" is figuratively to be understood, and "for you" is again to be literally understood. These words are a unit; they are the Gospel itself. The explanation by Christ is part of the institution. Wherever one celebrates the Eucharist with another explanation, there it is no longer the sacrament which the Lord instituted. It is indeed also to be considered that there is no Communion in the church without instruction about the Lord's Supper. Otherwise the Sacrament of the Altar would be only a performance of mysteries, in which each person may think to himself whatever he wants. Second, the Words of Institution are the words of consecration for the Lutheran Church, words of the Lord which still do today what they did in the first Communion, as the Formula of Concord so beautifully and forcefully teaches it in Luther's sense. In no Reformed liturgy is there a consecration in the strictest sense, because there is no real presence of the true body and blood of Christ.[5] In all these liturgies, the recitation of the Words of Institution is a report, which is given to the congregation about that which the Lord once did. Some liturgies introduce them again also in a eucharistic prayer, as the Anglican *Book of Common Prayer* does. But then the "Black Rubric" makes it immediately clear that there can be no talk of a real presence of the body and blood, that this is not therefore effected even by that which one still, or again, calls a "consecration."[6] From this it will be understood, when Luther explains in the well-known letter to the citizens of Frankfurt in 1533, that it was for him

> terrible to hear that in some churches, or at some altars, one should receive both parts of the one sacrament and believe one part—that one receives the powerless bread and wine—but not believe another part— that one receives the true body and blood of Christ. [WA 30/3:564; *Ein Brief an die zu Frankfurt am Main* (1533), Aland 225]

and when he gives the "reliable advice" to the Frankfurters, and to all whom it may concern, "to whom, in the sight of God, I owe" [it]:

> Whoever knows about his spiritual caretaker [*Seelsorger*], that he teaches like Zwingli, should avoid him; and he should live his entire life without the Sacrament before he should receive it from him, indeed, he should rather die and suffer in every way about this matter.

---

5   So also Luther's teaching enshrined in the Formula of Concord: "It does not rest on man's belief or unbelief but on the Word and ordinance of God—unless they first change God's Word and ordinance and misinterpret them, as the enemies of the sacrament do at the present time. They, indeed, have only bread and wine, for they do not also have the words and instituted ordinance of God but have perverted and changed it according to their own imagination" (FC SD VII 32, cited from *Concordia*, 568; cf. *Confession concerning Christ's Supper* [*Vom Abendmahl Christi Bekenntnis*] [1528], Aland 2, AE 37:367 [WA 26:506]). MH

6   On the so-called "Black Rubric," see above, p. 71 n. 38. MH

For those who claim that they are not like Zwingli, he adds:

> but if a spiritual caregiver is one of those "with two tongues," who with
> his mouth puts forth [words] as if the body and blood in the Sacrament
> are real and present but is actually suspicious that he is selling a "pig in
> a poke" and thinks differently, that is, contrary, to that which the words
> say: then go tell him, or send a message, and say quite explicitly what
> that is, which he hands to you and which you receive with your mouth
> .... If he's an honest *Schwärmer*, who wants to deal forthrightly with
> you, then he'll say that he hands you [merely] powerless bread and wine,
> and during [that action] you're supposed to think about and believe in
> the body and blood of Christ, etc. But if he's one of the jugglers who
> plays "with his hands hidden under a hat," then he'll say, "Mum, mum,"
> and slosh the mush around in his mouth, and finally spit out, "Oh, it's
> enough that you believe in the body which Christ intends." Then you will
> have gotten your answer and will have given reason for the hope which
> is in us, as St. Peter teaches. (WA 30/3:561)

We have cited these passages from Luther because they are a good commentary to that which the Seventh Article of the Augsburg Confession says
about the correct administration of the Sacrament and about what meaning
lies in the *improbant secus docentes* ["they reject those who teach," AC X 2] of
the Tenth Article. For it already follows implicitly from the fact that the German
text has *verwerfen* ["to reject"], which is used in the other articles—for example,
in the one about Baptism, to render *damnant anabaptistas* ["they condemn the
Anabaptists"]—that this *improbant* ["reject"] is effectively exactly the same
as the *damnant* ["condemn"] of other articles. The bitter words with which
Luther criticizes the "juggling game" of certain *Schwärmer* are directed toward
a conscious dishonesty, against the deceitfulness of those who later as Crypto-
Calvinists would make so much trouble for the Lutheran Church up until the
present day. None of us would make a moral reproach to an honest Reformed
[believer] who by reasons of conscience—for even an erring conscience
demands respect—cannot profess the real presence of the body and blood. We
also don't know what the Lord may grant to a Reformed congregation which
celebrates the Lord's Supper according to its confession. We may assume certainly that a *manducatio spiritualis* ["a spiritual eating"] takes place there, as all
churches understand it, even Rome. But to claim that the authentic institution
of Christ is also there, where one does not want to distribute or orally receive
the true body and the true blood of Christ under the forms of bread and wine,
that is against the Lutheran Confession [FC SD VII 32]. It is also against the conviction of the church in the sixteenth century, a conviction based on Scripture
in 1 Cor. 10:16f., in which church fellowship and altar fellowship are identified
[with each other], because both are fellowship of the Body of Christ. It would
be good, if more theologians would consider the most recent book by Werner

Elert [1885–1954], who showed that our church agrees on this point with the church of the first centuries, back to the time of the apostles.[7] The teaching of the Seventh Article of the Augsburg Confession about the unity of the church is not an invention of the Lutheran Reformation.

2

The actual unity of the Lutheran church of the sixteenth and seventeenth centuries rested upon this teaching of the unity of the church of Christ. One can say, without exaggeration, that our church was never so united as in the centuries in which there was yet no common organization. When, in the year 1617, the head court preacher of Dresden, together with the theology department at Wittenberg, called forth the Lutheran churches of all Europe for the one hundredth anniversary of the Reformation, everybody answered their call. And even the common Reformation anniversary of 1717, which is described in great detail in Ernst Salomon Cyprian's[8] (1673–1745) *Hilaria Evangelica*, a large book of more than twelve hundred pages, still offered a gripping image of a real spiritual unity within Lutheranism. This unity had been won at great cost, as is every authentic church unity. The sixteenth century had its difficult struggle for the heritage of Luther against Philippism and Crypto-Calvinism in the generation after the death of the reformer. It is wrong to say that the theology of the later Melanchthon has exactly the same right to be in the church as that of Gnesio-Lutheranism, because Luther did, after all, tolerate Melanchthon. This patience had purely human causes. It did not indicate any theological decision and would not have been possible in the long run. That as much of Melanchthon's heritage as was tolerable was actually taken up into the Formula of Concord shows that the great disagreement was a purely theological one, in which the issue was, despite all errors and sins, the truth. So the Formula of Concord served the [cause of] unity, and the fact that it was not formally accepted by everybody did not destroy the unity of Lutheranism, because its doctrinal content was not controverted. In the seventeenth century, the humanistic thought of western

---

7   See *Eucharist and Church Fellowship in the First Four Centuries*, trans. Norman Nagel (St. Louis: Concordia, 1966; repr., 1998). "Sasse, with clear vision, saw all of this coming and fought manfully but to no avail to keep the Lutheran Land Church of Bavaria from an entangling alliance with the EKD, an entanglement that would deny the position of the Lutheran Confessions on church fellowship. Sasse, who was out of favor with the other professors on the faculty of the University of Erlangen, received little support. However, Elert attempted to stave off unionistic fellowship that violated the teachings of the Lutheran Confessions in his own way. He wrote a scholarly book titled *Eucharist and Church Fellowship . . .*" (Green, *Lutherans Against Hitler*, 367). MH

8   Cyprian was director and professor of theology at Casimir College, Coburg, and a member of the consistory of Gotha. He staunchly opposed the plans of Frederick William I to unite Lutherans and Reformed (s.v. *Christian Cyclopedia*). See Schreyer, *Loescher und die Unionsversuche seiner Zeit*. MH

Europe brought forth the syncretist movement, but it did not make an impact among the [common] people, as Pietism later would. It is astounding to see how deeply the confessional consciousness was still living in hearts around 1717, twelve years after the death of Philipp Jacob Spener (1635–1705), and in the flowering of Halle Pietism. Even the Pietists in the city of Halle wanted to be Lutherans. One must read the reports about the celebrations and sermons and speeches to have an impression of how the Lutheran Church of Europe, existing in the many small and large territorial churches and national churches or in individual congregations of the diaspora, in all varieties of language and rites and ceremonies, understood itself as a unity. From Dublin and London to Vienna, where the congregation of the Danish embassy staff enjoyed toleration (in a country which was then and still is officially 100 percent Roman Catholic) and whose pastor, who held controversial sermons "with moderate zeal," had large attendance; from Drontheim and Christiana to Hungary and Siebenbürgen, from Reval and Riga to Mömpelgard, from Strassburg to Copenhagen and Aarhus, the great Reformation anniversary was celebrated in thousands of churches. The thousands of documents which Cyprian collected, as a learned consistory councilman in Gotha, are an inestimable treasure for the history of Lutheranism in the early eighteenth century. The Norwegian and Danish comrades in faith find in this work texts which are even in part in their language. Only a few churches are missing, because political situations made correspondence difficult:

> [F]rom Sweden we have, because of the bloody war, been able to get no
> information . . . what our dear brothers, who in the war have fallen into
> the power of Moscow, may have done is equally very little known to us.

As a substitute for Sweden, a moving prayer of thanksgiving is offered in German translation, which was prayed in all churches in the year 1693 at the hundredth anniversary of the council of Uppsala, at which Sweden accepted the Unaltered Augsburg Confession. May our Swedish friends consider the earnestness with which their fathers prayed at that time, asking that God "turn away all heretical, erring, and seducing doctrine and maintain His Word, which alone blesses, which He has ignited among us, that it may give light for us and our progeny until the end of the world" (Ibid., p. 863). There was naturally not unity and brotherly love everywhere, for example, in London, where "the Swedish sailors did not want to pray with the Danes, because the latter had prayed for the blessing and success of the Danish military" (p. 898).

And still, this Reformation festival in 1717 is the evidence of a churchly unity of Lutheranism as it has never again existed, a unity which was based upon the *consensus de doctrina evangelii et de administratione sacramentorum* ["consensus in the doctrine of the Gospel and the administration of the Sacraments"] and not upon any human organization.

3

No song appears more frequently in the festival programs than

> Oh, stay with us, Lord Jesus Christ,
> Because it has become evening-time.
> Your divine Word, the bright light,
> Don't let it go out among us.

There is no longer the feeling of standing at the evening of the world, a feeling which the author of this song shared with all of older Lutheranism. But for us it sounds like a premonition of that which awaited Lutheranism in the next decades. Only a few men, such as Valentin Ernst Löscher (1673–1749) and Ernst Salomon Cyprian, saw the great danger at that time. If one reads the directories of the professors, the names of not only Pietists but also of the first Enlightenment thinkers are already appearing. It is a law of all history, including church history, that great changes take place almost unnoticed by contemporaries. The Roman Empire declined without its contemporaries noticing it. There are always only a few who notice a decline. So it was, too, at that time in the era of late orthodoxy until the death of Löscher and Johann Sebastian Bach (1685–1750) in the middle of the century. But the feet of those who were supposed to carry on the heritage of Luther already stood at the door, or even already in the church. In the festival speeches of the universities and in other expressions, Rome is indeed criticized, in that it had placed Aristotle above the Scripture. One didn't notice that Aristotle, that repulsive heathen, in the meantime had again assumed a position of honor in the Lutheran Church. In the introduction to the *Hilaria Evangelica*, Cyprian struggles against atheism. Atheism is, to him, folly, "so this distressing situation demands that one make the greatest possible severance toward such abominations and certify that their folly has nothing to do with *healthy reason*" (p. 6).

Healthy reason—is it really healthy?—proves that God exists, that He is omnipotent and omniscient, that God created the world *ex nihilo*—which according to Heb. 11:3 can be known only by faith—indeed, even the immortality of the soul is one of the teachings of "natural religion." The tragedy of orthodoxy, which Aristotle cooked up because Luther's great philosophy—for Luther was indeed also a philosopher, even if he never wrote a philosophical book—was no longer understood, becomes clear here. It is noteworthy that even a [noble author such as] Franz ("Francis") Pieper (1852–1931) could still write in his *Christian Dogmatics* in 1924: "As far as the claim that there is not proof for the existence of God, it is to be corrected thus: only for those people who refuse to use reason" (vol. 1, p. 447).[9]

---

9   Sasse appears to be consistently Barthian on this point. He is ever wont to repeat the assertions of the nineteenth century that the orthodox fathers are somehow responsible for rationalism sweeping away Lutheran Christianity. Pieper, like Luther, noted that the existence of God may be posited by human reason. Of course, knowledge of who that God is (Christ) and what He has done is accessible only in the divine

Here we have "healthy reason," which according to the teaching of the Formula of Concord no longer exists since the fall, because the fall has effected "a deep, evil, repulsive, baseless, unfathomable delinquency of the entire human nature and all [human] powers, especially the most advanced powers of the soul in the understanding, heart, and will" (FC SD I 11), so that "nothing healthy or unspoiled is left regarding the body or the soul of the human being, regarding his inner or outer powers" (FC Ep I 8).

The Formula of Concord teaches that the natural human has still only "a dark, small spark of the knowledge that there is a God" (FC SD II 9), as indeed Melanchthon, too, in the Apology of the Augsburg Confession names not only the *contemptus Dei* ["contempt for God"] but also the *ignorantia Dei* ["ignorance of God"] as a consequence of original sin (Ap II 8; Müller, p. 79; Tappert, p. 101[10]), or as the German text has it: "... that we humans, all of us, are therefore born into such a category that we do not know God or God's work, do not see it or notice it, and despise God ...."

How quickly, then, has this "dark little spark" been stoked up to a bright flame by means of the reintrusion of Aristotelian philosophy into orthodox theology— a flame which still shines in Pieper's *Dogmatics* where, in explicit reference to Paul, Aristotle, and Cicero, it is said about the content of the natural knowledge of God that it includes

> not only the knowledge that there is a personal, eternal, and almighty
> God, who created the world, maintains and governs it, but also the

---

revelation of the Word of God. Elert does not see a shift in the dogmaticians away from understanding that any "natural knowledge of God" must only lead to doubt. But he says nevertheless "later dogmaticians also spoke of the knowledge attained by 'natural man.' This it had both a right and an obligation to do—in keeping with the example of Paul" (Elert, *Structure of Lutheranism*, 50). I find it hard to let these criticisms of Pieper go, because it is due in largest measure to Pieper's magisterial *Dogmatics* that the LCMS (unlike most Lutheran Churches of the world) held unqualified commitment to the Book of Concord against unionism. That great accomplishment is due to Walther's and Pieper's familiarity with and commitment to both the theology of Luther and the orthodox Lutheran fathers. It is precisely Missouri's familiarity with the orthodox fathers which has guarded her—even with all her weaknesses—in a way which nearly all other American Lutheran bodies have not been protected from the inroads of de-dogmatized confessionlessness and union (to use a few of Sasse's favorites). On rare occasions Sasse could compliment Pieper: "Pieper's *Dogmatics* which came out since the Reformation Jubilee became the recognized textbook also outside Missouri. When this work was no longer studied, the de-Lutheranization of American Lutheranism could not be stopped. Every textbook on dogmatics is a dialogue. Pieper had to fight and reject not only German theology of the nineteenth century, but he had already to take into account the theology of the Reformed churches in America. But his book could of course not take into account what was going on in European Protestantism, the new discoveries of Luther research and the rise of Karl Barth. So your church was not prepared for the great encounter with the churches of Europe" (Sasse to Robert Preus, January 19, 1975; in the Harrison Collection). MH

10   Instead of "ignorance of God," Tappert mistranslates the latter as "ignoring God." MH

knowledge that God is a holy and just God, who demands and rewards goodness and punishes and forbids evil. [*Christian Dogmatics*, p. 445][11]

In how much more restrained a manner does the constitution of the Vatican council speak about the Catholic faith! This was, therefore, the error of Lutheran theology in the era of orthodoxy in the seventeenth and the beginning of the eighteenth century. The twilight of the old Lutheran Church had come. The terrible night of the Enlightenment broke upon it. What was still left of the Lutheran faith lived on in the liturgy, in the old songs, in Bach's *Passions*. "Healthy reason" had then won, and it seemed as if the prayers of the great Reformation festival for the maintenance of the church of the pure Gospel echoed unheard.

4

The Lutheranism which in the time of the awakening, together with the other denominations of Christianity, awoke out of the night of the Enlightenment and out of the dreams of "healthy reason" was no longer the old Lutheran Church which once had celebrated its last great festival in the unity of faith in the year 1717. After the Reformation anniversary of 1817, celebrated still almost entirely in the sense of rationalism, there began a slow awakening of Lutheran consciousness, announced by the ninety-five theses of Claus Harms (1778–1855) and by the resistance of Johann Gottfried Scheibel (1783–1843) against the Prussian Union in Breslau. At the three hundredth anniversary of the Augsburg Confession, thirteen years later, it was clear that the awakening of the old Lutheran faith, even if in many respects in a pietistic modification, would lead to an awakening of a churchly consciousness, a development which had its parallels in the Roman, Russian, Anglican, and many Reformed Churches. In these pages we have often spoken about this awakening of the Lutheran Church in the nineteenth century,[12] its successes until 1850, its decline until 1870, and its decay since 1870, and therefore we do not need to go into detail. But a few observations are of great importance for our topic. The first is the lightness with which large portions of the Lutheran Church entered into the unions of various types as a foregone conclusion, despite the energetic resistance of not only theologians and laity, people of great character, from the higher ranks of royalty and the middle class, but rather also from the ordinary people, to the extent that they were still Lutheran. That was, however, a disappearing minority even in the times of the struggle for the faith. The Lutheran free churches, above all the Prussian one, are, to be sure, a monument to this loyalty to the faith, but in their small size also a terrible sign for the alienation of not only the masses but rather also of the churchly

---

11 Virtually nothing more or less than what Paul asserts about the natural knowledge of God in Romans 2. MH

12 See, e.g., Letter 15, "The Results of the Lutheran Awakening of the Nineteenth Century," in *Letters to Lutheran Pastors* 1:301–30. MH

circles from the faith and from the Church of the Lutheran Reformation. The territorial churches, which remained *de jure* Lutheran, have also been unable to maintain the heritage. The loyal champions for the Lutheran Confession in Bavaria and Saxony, in Hanover and Mecklenburg, among them some of the greatest churchmen whom Germany ever brought forth, have been able to more or less successfully keep their churches indeed with the Confession as the legal foundation of the church. Like Ludwig Adolf Petri (1803–73) in Hanover, Johann Konrad Wilhelm Löhe (1808–72) in Bavaria, and Jacob Wilhelm Georg Vilmar (1804–84) [and his brother August] in Hesse, they also helped to form a generation of Lutheran pastors behind whom stood again vital lay groups and congregations. But their success was [merely] partial and insufficient. They were able at that time to prevent a general German union, but they did not defeat the union. Therefore practically all the territorial churches have fallen victim to it in this century. The Lutheran "church leaders" of our time have known well that none of their great predecessors in the nineteenth century would have accepted the DEK (Deutsche Evangelische Reichskirche) of 1933 or the EKiD of 1948. What would Gottlieb Christoph Adolf von Harless (1806–79) have said—to say nothing of Löhe—if one had demanded of him that he suddenly accept as Lutherans, with the full rights of church fellowship, several hundred thousand unionized Silesians without any serious instruction and their pastors without colloquium, and at the same time demand that even the members of the Breslau free church enter into this half-unionized territorial church, and thereby should betray their fathers? That happened a few years after they solemnly attended the hundredth anniversary of the death of Scheibel in Nuremberg and decorated the grave of this prophet at the St. Johannes cemetery. No VELKD and no Lutheran church politics can disguise the fact that the consciousness of the Lutheran church, together with the Lutheran faith, has been extinguished in the great masses of the church members and the pastors. Certainly we are happy about the awakening of the Lutheran Confession in many theologians, especially those in the union churches, where they have felt the consequences of confessionlessness on their own bodies. But that is not yet an awakening, and the loyal Lutherans today are as lonely as their fathers a hundred years ago. Whoever soberly considers the realities of churchly life knows what stands behind the facade of the large European national and territorial churches in Germany, among the Scandinavian people, but also in England and Scotland, in the Netherlands and Switzerland, and even large portions of the Roman Church in France and Italy. We must look this reality squarely in the eye. There are no Christian nations or Lutheran countries anymore. That is the great change which has taken place since the eighteenth century.

Along with the developments in the Old World, developments in Christianity outside of Europe were moving along in the English-speaking world of America and the British Commonwealth, in Latin America, and on the mission fields. Eleven years before the Reformation anniversary of 1717, the Lutheran mission in India began. At the same time, there were the first Lutheran congregations in North America, and starting in 1748, the Lutherans of the New World—at that time still limited to the English colonies in the east—began to organize themselves into synods. The large church bodies of the Midwest followed in the nineteenth century, and today the entire North American continent is covered with Lutheran churches, which, taken together, form the third largest Protestant denomination. Alongside the national and territorial churches of Europe with their parochial system, a completely new mode of existence for Lutheranism formed itself: free churches on a grand scale, built upon congregations and synods, in some countries an almost disappearing minority, the diaspora of the diaspora, as in Australia, where the two Lutheran churches, approximately the same size, do not make up even 1 percent of the population, while, if I understand correctly, among every one hundred Americans there are about four Lutherans. If one adds the "young churches" of the Lutheran Confession in the mission fields, then it becomes clear that the question of the unity of the Lutheran Church in the world today is a completely different question than it was in earlier centuries.

5

In what sense can there be a unity of the Lutheran Church under these completely different circumstances? The unity of 1717 was, despite all borders, still the unity of the great consensus of the Confessions, because these Confessions were accepted by the people, by entire ethnic groups, as the confession of their faith, for example, by the Swedish people. It was, despite everything, a spiritual unity, founded on the great *satis est* of the Augsburg Confession. So, then, the unionistic attempts, which came above all from [the city of] Halle, were at that time still almost unanimously turned away, and Halle still wanted to be thoroughly Lutheran in its missionary activity and in its pastoral care for American Lutherans. Friedrich August Tholuck's (1799–1877) great discovery, which was then repeated by Karl Holl (1866–1926)[13] and his followers—that Calvin was actually the one who completed the work of Luther and thereby the greatest Lutheran after Luther—was still unknown to the eighteenth century. But this dissolving of the Lutheran Church into theological schools, in which the loss of the old Confession shows itself most clearly, began with rationalism. It is the tragedy of the Lutheran awakening of the nineteenth century that in the course of the laborious rediscovery of the church's doctrine not only the doctrine of the Confessions became valid again. We do not want to minimize the work of the Erlangen School, the work of Vilmar and Löhe, Petri, Friedrich Conrad Dietrich Wyneken (1810–76) and Carl Ferdinand Wilhelm Walther (1811–87), and others,

---

13 Holl was a favorite lecturer of Sasse's while he was a student at the University of Berlin in 1913–14. MH

as is customary today. These people had no scholarly Luther editions, didn't have the tools of modern research in the history of dogma, also didn't know the "young Luther" who is supposed to have been the correct Luther (probably because he hadn't yet fought against Zwingli)[14] in contrast to the aged reformer or, let us rather say, in contrast to "Luther in the epoch of his completion." But in the theology of these fathers, great for its time, there lurked some anachronisms.[15] The Erlangen School never shook off [the effects of] Friedrich Daniel Ernst Schleiermacher (1768–1834). Non-Lutheran elements of Pietism maintain themselves in many Lutheran Churches. Chiliasm [i.e., millennialism], the unhappy heritage of Johann Albrecht Bengel (1687–1752) and of the Adventism of the early nineteenth century, experienced a flourishing in Neuendettelsau [and] was disrupting and disastrous to Lutheran eschatology. Vilmar and Löhe read the romantic concept of society as an organism into the Lutheran doctrine of the church, while Walther, without knowing it, understood the Lutheran doctrine of the church through the eyes of the Enlightenment's concept of society.[16] If one knows what kind of insufficient tools our American fathers had to use,[17] then one will understand the tragedy, that almost everybody accepted the teaching of orthodoxy about *theologia naturalis*, which is contrary to the Confessions, and that the terrible idea of *intuitu fidei* (the teaching that God has elected us not to faith, but rather with an eye toward future faith) unleashed a fight about the election of grace—a fight which should never have been possible in the Lutheran Church. Even the doctrine of justification did not escape corruption, as conservative Lutherans in America, in order to come against the synergistic doctrine of Iowa, now fell into the error of accepting a doctrine from, of all people, pietistic theologians of the eighteenth century about the justification of the world which threatened the *sola fide*, and which, when it appeared for the first time at the end of the sixteenth century, was expressly rejected by the [theology] departments [at the universities of] Wittenberg and Tübingen, and was for this reason also never taught by orthodoxy. We want to mention here only the older errors as examples, and not go into all the modern heresies which have

---

14 "It is absolutely necessary that we break with the thesis in theology that the young Luther is the entire Luther" (Sasse to Leiv Aalen, December 28, 1944; in the Harrison Collection). MH

15 That is, readings of Luther conditioned by modern circumstances or contemporary ideas read into the Reformation writings. MH

16 Walther viewed the church through the eyes of Luther's main treatises on the same, and he read Luther in light of the tragic experience of the Saxons under the leadership of Martin Stephan (1777–1846) in Perry County, Missouri, and against the attacks of J. A. A. Grabau and other hierarchically minded Lutherans. See Walther's, "Das fruchtbare Lesen der Schriften Luthers. Referat Dr. C. F. W. Walthers nach dem Protokoll der Missouri=Districtsconferenz, auf Beschluss der Letzteren dem Druck übergeben," *Lehre und Wehre* 33, no. 11 (November 1887). MH

17 E.g., no scholarly editions, poor libraries, lack of communication with universities, etc. MH

bothered the Lutheran consensus in the last [few] generations. The sins of the European churches against their overseas daughter churches are unimaginable. They have laughed about their "primitive" theology without asking themselves what kind of firm theological convictions are part of building up the church in the South American jungle and in the Australian bush, often building up from nothing. For this task, one needs more than a little bit of Kierkegaard and an exegesis mired and stuck in a sea of unsolvable historical problems. How many German and Swedish professors have even found it necessary to at least see this diaspora once? A great chapter of Lutheran church history was written in the world, and the church historians in their study rooms didn't even notice it at all. The formation and training of pastors for this diaspora was left to the missionary institutions. It is amazing what these seminaries have accomplished, operating with only half-power, but their work was necessarily insufficient, and similarly insufficient were the institutions which arose on the other continents. The consequence of all of this was that the isolated Lutheran Churches disintegrated into theological schools—just as, indeed, the mother churches disintegrated into parties and schools. One learned one's theology in Neuendettelsau or St. Louis, in Philadelphia or Dubuque, in Gettysburg and in Thiensville, and was now no longer in any condition to distinguish between the doctrine of the church and the doctrine of the school, between dogma and *theologoumenon*. In addition to the natural division of Lutheranism into linguistic groups, which does not negate the unity of the church, there arose division for the sake of doctrine, very often necessary, because serious dogmatic questions were at stake. But in other cases people dissolved church fellowship for the sake of a school's doctrine, which did not concern dogma. Then the words of Rom. 16:17—the "anathema" which follows on the heels of the "pax" in the previous verse—were applied not to the heretics, but to the representatives of another school: "I urge you, brothers, to watch out for those who create dissensions and obstacles in opposition to the teaching that you have learned; avoid them."[18]

For many people, the understanding of the Lutheran Confessions was lost concerning this matter then. Ephemeral doctrinal declarations replaced the Confession, which was allegedly recognized by everyone. So this decay of the living confession, which happened in Europe in a very different form, completed itself. The visible sign of this decay of the confession, even in the American churches, is the view concerning the union—the greatest problem of Lutheranism since the Marburg debate and the Unaltered Augsburg Confession! While the old General Synod was often uncertain in the question about the view concerning the union since the eighteenth century, the General Council was consciously confessional in the sense of the confessionally conscious German

---

18   About the time of this essay, Sasse was penning "Bemerkungen zu Röm. 16:17" (North Adelaide, November 22, 1955; English translation by Ralph Gehrke: "Observations on Rom. 16:17–18" (Huss number 316). He had been asked for this study by Dr. John Behnken, president of the Missouri Synod. MH

territorial ecclesiology. When both synods joined in 1918 to form the United Lutheran Church, it seemed at first that the spirit of the General Council would be successful. But since the retirement of President Frederick Hermann Knubel[19] (1870–1945), it became apparent that the anti-union position was disappearing bit by bit, because the younger generation no longer understood the confessional questions. The Lutheranism of the West—the old synods of Buffalo, Missouri, Iowa, and Ohio—were formed by the Lutheran confessionalism of the nineteenth century and gave this viewpoint also to the churches of Scandinavian heritage. But World War II and the deep changes in the American people have led to the situation that even the churches of the middle, which grew out of those synods, have given up their old view of the union—indeed, especially under the influence of Swedish theology and the Ecumenical Movement. The question of the union is certainly not merely a question of German Protestantism, but rather it has become the existential question of Lutheranism in the entire world, above all in southeast Asia. It appears to be only a matter of time until church fellowship between the South India United Church and the Lutheran Church of South India will be declared. *Lutheran World*, the organ of the LWF, contains an informative report (1955, no. 1, pp. 74ff.) by H. W. Gensichen in Madras about the doctrinal negotiations with important documents, above all, a formula of unification about the Lord's Supper which makes major concessions toward Lutheranism (reception of the body and blood of Christ independent of the faith of the recipient and inseparable from the reception of the bread and wine). This happy departure from Zwingli and Calvin is, however, compromised by allowing the question to remain open about what now the body and blood actually are. The commentaries, which are given by the Reformed side, for example, in a detailed article in the *Christian Century* on May 18, 1955, leave no doubt about the fact that this which Luther meant by "true body and blood" is rejected as Capernaitism by many, if not most, of those who profess this document, with special emphasis from the Swedish member of the commission. In the case of these negotiations, as in the case of similar negotiations [elsewhere], it has become apparent that there is no unity within Lutheranism anymore about the Sacrament. The great consensus of the Lutheran Churches of the world about the pure Gospel and the administration of the Sacraments according to the Scripture has fallen apart. Thereby the door has been opened wide to the unionism of the ecumenical council and its suborganizations. We must come to terms with the fact that the unity of the Lutheran church fell with the authority of the Confession.

---

19 Sasse became personally acquainted with Knubel while studying in America at Hartford Seminary in 1926. MH

6

What is to be done under these conditions? First, we must all guard ourselves against the illusion that the lost unity is to be reclaimed by means of organizations and theological "discussions." It is an illusion, if one thinks that in Germany one day the free churches, the territorial churches, and the union Lutherans could be united in one church, or that the day is not far in which all the Lutherans in America will form one big church. Those are utopian hopes, because [in them] the seriousness of the division is not recognized. Certainly the demand for unity is legitimate, and whatever can happen, must happen, in order to reach true unification. There will even be mergers. But true unification presupposes separation from error. If any of the large church groups of contemporary Christianity can still distinguish at all pure doctrine from false doctrine, then it is Lutheranism, insofar as it still takes the *damnamus* of the Confessions seriously. It doesn't matter if, on the one hand, they stress the biblical warnings against fellowship with error, as in the "United Testimony" of the American churches of the middle, but, on the other hand, recognize as brothers all Protestants, insofar as they teach justification by faith, even if [recognizing them] as erring brothers whom one must teach, as Aquila and Priscilla taught Apollos [Acts 18:26]. What would a man such as Michael Reu have said to this! Can they no longer distinguish between Christian love, which we owe to all men, and the "brotherhood" of the church in the New Testament sense? Why has no loud protest been raised out of these circles against church fellowship between the Scandinavian churches and the Churches of England and Scotland? Why does nobody take offense that union churches, such as the Church of Pomerania, are accepted into the LWF without giving up their membership in the union? It is not to be expected that these churches will change their course. But it should be possible for the people who are [still] loyal to the Confession, people who still really do exist in all these churches, to raise their voices and to remind their own church government about the Confession. Why does that not happen anymore? How is this terrible silence to be explained? It is this single phenomenon, which is to be observed in all the churches of the world since the Vatican council declared not only the infallibility but rather also the universal episcopate of the pope, which is at least as bad. Thereby the nature of the office of the bishop in the old catholic sense was completely changed, as one of the bishops of that time expressed it: we came as bishops and left as trustees. The same process completes itself in the Church of England, where the question is seriously being asked why pious and learned men, who as pastors or professors were independent characters, are suddenly "brought into line" as bishops after the first conversation with the current archbishop of Canterbury and collaborate with the current politics of Lambeth Palace silently or without criticism? It was a revealing scene when, a few years ago, serious resistance against Freemasonry broke out in the church, and the question of whether an Anglican bishop or pastor could belong to the lodge was forever answered by the archbishop of York when he said that the membership of the archbishop of Canterbury (Dr. G. Fisher)[20] in the lodge gave him the certainty that Anglicans have nothing to which to object against lodge membership. Thereby the carefully presented dogmatic objections were resolved. This much freedom does still remain in England: that the rector of a London church could deny access to the chancel to the archbishop as a lodge member. But that changes nothing about the decision of the church, exactly as the protest of many Anglican pastors against the now-declared intercommunion with the Church of the South Indian Union changes nothing about the large-scale politics of the church leadership. The large masses follow the leadership. The acceptance of the Evangelical Church of Pomerania into the LWF must be correct, because the executive committee does, after all, consist of nice and respected people. The executive committee, in turn, bases its decision on the trust which it places in the German national committee, which examined the question for two years. And so it is everywhere, in all churches. The laity follow the pastors, the pastors follow the bishops or presidents, the churches follow the ecumenical council. This is the papalism of the church. So the papacy came to be: the congregations relied on the representative presbyters, the presbyters relied on the episcopate which went forth out of their ranks, the bishops relied on the metropolitans, the metropolitans followed the patriarchs, and the logical consequence was drawn by Rome. All of that was, perhaps, sociologically necessary. It could not be differently. But it was still a fall from faith. For it means that trust in humans steps into the place of the unconditional trust in the Lord of the church, the human authority of interpretations steps into the place of the authority of the Word of God, whereby it is an inconsequential distinction whether this interpreter is an ecumenical conference, the head of a theological school, or the pope. I remember a meeting in Leipzig during the church struggle (1934) at which the Lutherans met among themselves to formulate a certain conclusion, and then had to wait a very long time for the decision of their Reformed friends, because the long-distance phone call from Bonn didn't come through, just as once in Trent they often had to wait a long time for the mail from Rome, until "the holy synod, gathered properly in the Holy Spirit" could say what was now actually correct and what not: "For there is no distinction; all have sinned and are deprived of the glory which they should have before God" (Romans 3).

It is the sin of all of us, the secret sin against the First Commandment, the trust placed in humans, there, where there should only be trust in God and His Word. Here is the deepest cause of the failure of the Lutheran Church as a church which confesses the truth and holds firmly to the faith in the Confession. It is the powerlessness of our faith which leads to the shattering of the Confession

---

20 Geoffry Francis Fisher (1887–1972) chaired the inaugural assembly of the WCC in 1948. In 1960 he became the first archbishop of Canterbury since 1397 to visit the pope in Rome (see *ODCC*, 614). MH

and thereby to the dissolution of the true unity of our church, which cannot be replaced by any external organization. Such organizations are necessary, but they are not part of the essence of the church and cannot create the unity of the church. It is more necessary, if our prayer is to be heard, "that we, in the unity of faith, can teach to all Christendom even Your true witness."

Let me conclude, dear brothers, with the words of Jer. 17:5ff., which once meant so much to us in the church struggle, and under the judgment and promise of which we all stand in this time of the great crisis of our church:

> This is what the Lord says: "Cursed is the one who trusts in man, who draws strength from mere flesh and whose heart turns away from the Lord. . . . But blessed is the one who trusts in the Lord, whose confidence is in him. They will be like a tree planted by the water that sends out its roots by the stream. It does not fear when heat comes; its leaves are always green. It has no worries in a year of drought and never fails to bear fruit." [ESV]

Greeting you in the bonds of faith,

Your
Hermann Sasse

Historical Context

Here Sasse presents an extraordinary critique of the Ecumenical Move-
ment as a "movement." The introductory comments about a shrinking, a
globally linked world, might have been written in 2014 and not in 1955!
Sasse's experience with the worst of mass movements in the twentieth
century renders him doubly suspicious of the Ecumenical Movement,
which had simply devolved into unionism. MH

March 3, 1956[1]

Prof. H. Sasse
41 Buxton Street
North Adelaide, South Australia

Professor Hans Rottman
Seminario Concordia
Porto Alegre, Brazil

Dear Brother Rottman,

. . . Recently at our pastoral conference a pastor, who otherwise is very pious,
expressed the thought that it is our duty to pray that the Synodical Conference
would be dissolved and Missouri would join the Lutheran middle-roaders. You
must therefore not be surprised if the ancient opposition to Missouri comes to
life again also in Brazil.

Let me first say a word in explanation of the fact that the names of Elert and
myself were mentioned in this connection. I remember distinctly the faculty
meeting at which Elert declared that he would take back everything he ever said
in his whole life against Missouri. This statement was not made in view of the
care packages which came from Missouri, but after he had learned to know Dr.
Behnken and other representatives of Missouri. Although he seriously tried to be
just in his *Morphologie* (*Morphologie des Luthertums* [*Structure of Lutheranism*]),
his early judgment (of Missouri) was largely motivated by his experiences with
the Saxon Free Church. But even at a later date Elert did not agree with the theology of Missouri. As his *Dogmatics* shows, of which soon a new edition is to

---

1   CHI Behnken file. This nine-page letter is written in English. MH

appear, his doctrine of Holy Scripture was absolutely un-Lutheran.[2] This caused my old colleague, our Old Testament scholar [Otto] Procksch [1874–1947], deep pain. In this respect, your critic is correct in saying that Elert dare not be regarded as having been pro-Missouri. But what Elert absolutely confessed was the real presence, as this is proved by the excellent chapter in his *Dogmatics*. However, he was limited by the fact that he could not gain the victory in the fight for that which theoretically he had learned to regard as true. At Hanover he valiantly protested against the demand of Gustav Stählin for intercommunion (altar fellowship of those not agreed in doctrine). But at Erlangen, where Stählin frankly advocated intercommunion for many years, he [Elert], for collegiate [*sic*] reasons, kept silence, though we Lutherans since 1938 fought bitterly for the real presence. He did not . . . cooperate with me on my anthology (*Sammelwerk*) *Vom Sakrament des Altars* [1941], though Procksch and [Hans] Preuss joined me in this work. In the last faculty meeting which I attended, we discussed the appointment of a second professor for the New Testament. For this position the Mennonite [Ethelbert] Stauffer [1902–79] had been suggested, who at Bonn had joined the Church of the Prussian Union though he had never changed his doctrinal views. He had just published no less than seven reasons against the Lutheran doctrine of the Lord's Supper. I declared that I could not vote for him until he would recant, since when I was received into the faculty I had solemnly vowed to do all in my power to preserve the Lutheran character of the faculty. Without mentioning it to others, I had hoped that Elert would agree with me, but he was satisfied with the thought that Stauffer, by moving to Bavaria, would automatically become Lutheran. I remained the only one to vote for [Karl Heinrick] Rengstorff, who was known as both a good scholar and teacher. The Catholic Minister of Public Worship and Education informed me that he could not understand how a Lutheran faculty could tolerate the denial of the (Lutheran) doctrine of the Holy Supper. Nevertheless, he would appoint the candidate who would receive the *placet* ("okay") of the state church. Meiser, of course, approved the *placet* for political reasons and so deprived the Bavarian state church of the possibility to subject to church discipline a pastor who taught Calvinist doctrine. These, then, were Elert's limitations, which became manifest already at the beginning of 1934 when I offered him in the name of hundreds of German pastors the leadership of the Confessing Church (*der Bekennenden Kirche*). I can still hear him saying, "Do you know, Colleague Sasse, where this resistance will lead to? Can you renounce your professorship and salary?" I replied: "That I do not know, but I hope that God will grant me the power to do so, should the case become necessary." "By the way, Colleague Sasse, I am sure that you will also be able to do it," [Elert said. I replied,] "Your Breslau fathers

---

2   It is a rather intense irony that Sasse should critique Elert at precisely this point, given Letter 14 (see *Letters to Lutheran Pastors* 1:240–84) and Sasse's continuing criticism of Missouri's *doctrina de Scriptura Sacra*. MH

also were able to do so." To this he replied, "They were altogether wrong, for at that time they should have remained in the state church."

I am not writing you this, dear Rottman, to criticize a man who we all respected highly and of whom I can say with Procksch: "He was my unfortunate favorite (*meine unglückliche Liebe*)." We are not to judge other people and must realize that a genius is not a genius in all areas of life to the same degree. My purpose is only to make it clear to you why later he clung to Meiser's VELKD (United Evangelical Lutheran Church in Germany) and wanted to fight in it in his own way for the Lutheran church, until toward the end of his life he saw that here there was nothing for him to hope for. He last work, *Abendmahl und Kirchengemeinschaft* . . . [*Eucharist and Church Fellowship in the First Four Centuries*], is his last will and testament, which you may point out to all those who desire to claim Elert for the EKiD (Evangelical Church in Germany). I have learned also from *Kirchenrat* Schulz and other members of the Breslau Free Church how during the last months of his life he spoke of the Lutheran Church in utter despair. Missouri was his last hope. He realized that with the fall and apostasy of this church, the Lutheran Church as such would cease to exist. . . . But I must conclude my letter, dear Brother Rottmann. Kindly excuse me for having written so much, but it may give you some food for thought. My spirit is depressed. I fully understand Elert's gloomy forebodings during the last months of his life. . . . May [God] grant to all who must decide the future of Lutheranism the spirit of wisdom, of repentance, and of love. May He grant them also the gift of discerning the spirits. May God guard also the church in your country. Kindly greet your colleagues and your dear wife. In the unity of the faith there greets you,

Your most devoted
H. Sasse

forty

Ecumenical Questions

TRANSLATED BY ANDREW SMITH

Mid-January, 1956[1]

Prof. D. Theol. Hermann Sasse
41 Buxton Street
North Adelaide, South Australia

Dear Brothers in the Office!

From year to year, we all detect ever more clearly that the world in which we live becomes more and more a unit. A unit, [but] not in the sense of internal unity and growing peace, as the utopian faith in progress of the nineteenth century and the beginning of the twentieth century thought. It is gripping, when one hears today the confession from men of the older generation, who occupied positions of leadership a generation ago in the British and American churches, that actually all of their hopes for a better and more peaceful world have crashed. This is similarly true of the hopes of the European peoples and their churches. The world has become a vast arena of war, only that the wars in the meantime are fought with different methods, because everyone has fear of the incalculable effects of modern tools of destruction—you can't really call them "weapons" anymore. The bleeding border which divides Germany; the corresponding division of Korea and other Asiatic countries; the Iron Curtain and all the other "curtains" which divide the Eastern and the Western world, about which each claims it is the world of peace and freedom; and the important and perhaps consequential decision of the last year, the failure of the attempt to unite western Europe—all of that does not seem to indicate that the world is become a unit. Was it not much more a unit fifty years ago, when one could travel unhindered from country

---

1   *BLP* 40: *Ökumenische Fragen* (North Adelaide, January 1956). The original was published in *LuBl* 8, no. 46 (February 1956): 3–18. It was reprinted in *Igreja Luterana* (Brazil) (1956): 97–113. Huss number 317. MH

to country, from continent to continent, without passport and currency difficulties? And yet it is true that this fragmented humanity of the waning second millennium, living in a status between war and peace, represents a unit which the history of earlier times did not experience. Problems which were earlier the problems of an ethnic group or of a continent have today become problems for the whole world. European nationalism has today gripped the peoples of Asia and Africa and is the strongest weapon in the struggle against the "colonialism" of the West. Communism, which a hundred years ago was a movement within the European working class, has become a worldwide movement, whose victorious march can only be compared to the storm of Islam. The race question has become one of the most serious problems in the entire world, not only in America, Africa, and Asia but also in the motherlands of the decaying colonial empires. The Christian churches, Buddhism, Islam, and Communism attempt to give their answers to this. The industrialization of the entire world has raised everywhere the same economic and social questions, and it is noteworthy how the development of technology, the necessities of leading modern mass societies, the development of political institutions, and the necessities of state intervention into the economy even in those places in which one theoretically upholds free enterprise all lead to parallels in exactly those places in which one would least expect them. Siberia is becoming more and more "Americanized," and from American sociologists one can find thoughts about the society of the future which are worse than what Bolshevism and the totalitarian states of Europe have brought forth in this area. Thus John McPartland, in his book *Sex in Our Changing World* (New York and Toronto, 1947), develops the thought that the state of the future, in its regulation of human life, must go even farther than the Soviet Union and the Axis powers and regulate even the sexual life of the individual with all means of medical science, and influence feelings and even the conscience with hormones and medicines, as the interests of society dictate. He asks whether we will like such a world and gives the answer: "That is a question which cannot be answered. Our great-grandparents would probably not like our world of today, but they helped to build it."

Here we have, in the midst of the "free world," not only the idea of an absolutely necessary development, as Marxism teaches, but rather also a program for extinguishing the individual, as another author, whom McPartland quotes in passing, expresses it: "The thought that we are individuals is wrong. The only individual characteristic which we humans have is the ability to suffer. That is the only thing which one can do alone . . . ."

That is the world in which the church today lives. A world of mass societies (Germany had, at the beginning of the nineteenth century, twenty million inhabitants, as many as at the beginning of the seventeenth century; England at the time of the Reformation [had] approximately a tenth of its current population; the United States around 1850 [had] approximately eighteen million [inhabitants]) and the mass church (the Roman Church had, at the time of Napoleon, approximately 100 million members; today it counts approximately 400 million) on an earth whose continents have come closer together by means of modern travel in a way which was only a generation ago unimaginable. One must understand the Ecumenical Movement of the present and its problems against the background of this world; today we want to discuss some of these problems which affect us all.

1

It is clear that, in this modern world, churches and denominations face new problems which did not exist either in the ancient world or in the time of the Reformation. Already in the last century people saw that the migration of the white race over the entire earth, the creation of new peoples out of the migrations of the last centuries, and the spreading of Christianity in its various forms by means of modern world missionary activity would change the mutual relations of historical ecclesiologies, and would force all Christians to rethink and reform their relations to one another. They also foresaw that all of this would lead to a new quest for the church of God. Vilmar said prophetically that modern world travel would not only help the anti-Christian forces, but rather also would form the knowledge base of the one holy church in the future. Indeed, the quest for the church has become the question of theology in our century, as different as the answers may be which this question receives. After all, until now, no segment of Christendom has given a final answer to the question of what the church is. The Roman dogma *de ecclesia Christi* lasted only until the first constitution, which the Vatican announced and which dealt with the papacy. Everyone who knows a little Catholic theology is aware how much of the doctrine about the church is still open. By what does one recognize the church? It is visible, according to the foreword to the twenty-ninth volume of the German edition of Thomas, "only in and by means of its sacraments." The Eastern theologians console themselves about the fact that their church is unable to say what the church that confesses the Nicene Creed actually is, with the idea that indefinability is a sign of its vitality. The fact that what our Confessions say about the *Una Sancta* (above all in the Apology of Articles VII and VIII of the Augsburg Confession) is not exhaustive follows already from the fact that their statements, scattered among many articles, answer only specific questions. It is no accident that today the great topic of New Testament study is everywhere the biblical teaching about the church. And that is not only a development within theology. Just as the church has always been a problem for politicians, so it has become in the twentieth century in a very special manner, even there, and especially there, where church and state are separated, as in America and Russia. It has caused many people who otherwise couldn't begin to think about the church, to deeply ponder that the only real resistance against the totalitarian systems of our time came from the ranks of the churches, and that the churches, as weak and suffering as they may otherwise be, have still had the power to bring forth martyrs. And nobody will be able to write a history of World War II without considering the fact that in this war the solidarity of the churches was not broken, as was the case in World War I, and that the great helping actions of Christendom, which began already in part during the war, saved the lives of millions of people. So the world is placed before the riddle of the church, and Christendom itself stands today as never before in front of the mystery of faith of the *credo ecclesiam*, as it approaches the end of the second millennium of its history. And as every article of faith has a very practical meaning because it concerns the deepest existence of the human—his creation, redemption, salvation, and completion, the decision between blessedness and damnation, eternal life and eternal death—so also [this is true] in a special way [of] the article about the church. For only he who lives in the church and by means of the church can believe in the church. This is true not only of the individual Christian, but it is true also of confessional churches and denominations. Despite all differences and unbridgeable oppositions which divide them, each of them lives from the faith in the church. With this faith in the *Una Sancta*, however one understands it, stand and falls every congregation. And this faith, consequently, has its practical consequences. No confessional church, not even Rome or the Eastern churches, claims that outside of its external trappings the church of Christ does not exist, as is proven by the recognition of heretical baptisms. But thereby the faith in the *Una Sancta* places before each church the question of how its relations to other Christian communities should be organized. If, for Rome and the Eastern churches, the other communities appear to be only recipients for teaching and missionary work, even if of a missionary work done in love, still it is becoming ever more clear in individual examples that they themselves have the feeling that this is insufficient. The evangelical Christians in Germany have often been called "our separated brothers" by the Catholics since the time of the common struggle against the totalitarian state, and the pope himself has allowed in certain cases common prayer between Catholics and Protestants (the Lord's Prayer or another prayer approved by the Roman side), though this is against the text of the canon law (canon 1253 CIC) that admits no *communicatio in sacris* [church fellowship or joint participation in sacred acts] but rather at most a *praesentia passive* ["passive presence"]. So the Ecumenical Movement, in the sense of a quest for the church, for the *Una Sancta*, which all of Christianity's communities confess, is one of the great facts of the church history of our century.

2

The Ecumenical Movement has been, since its origin in the nineteenth century (about which we have [already] spoken in [earlier installments] of these letters), both a great spiritual movement which goes through all of Christendom and the compilation of attempts to solve practical problems which arise from the changed situation [in which] Christianity [finds itself today]. From the beginning, all of these attempts were conditioned by the tension between [individual] denomination[s] and the union. There were the great worldwide mergers of Anglicans, Lutherans, Reformed, Methodists, and Baptists, along with organizations which were indifferent to confessions, such as the Evangelical Alliance (1851) and the YMCA (1855). In the area of missionary work, which has always been interested in this question in a special way, there was the pietistic-unionistic group of mission institutions such as Basel, Barmen, and Bremen, which, to speak about the organization of Bremen, did not see it as their job to carry the opposition of Lutheran and Reformed into the mission field—for which reason the Batak do not know, even today, for example, what is taught in the Lutheran catechism about the Lord's Supper—and again a mission agency such as the old one in Leipzig, which is concerned about the full truth of the Lutheran Confession and which could not conceive of a missionary activity in which the newly baptized are not told what the biblical teaching about the Sacrament is. The same opposition between denominations and union is also to be observed in the case of the English and Scandinavian missionaries; it governed the beginnings of the great ecumenical organizations in this century. It is very interesting to observe how, in the first world conference for faith and church constitution, confessionalism was still a force. Not only the orthodox used their veto against the threatening erasure of denominational boundaries, and thereby against destruction of ecclesiastical doctrine, but rather also the Lutherans. And it was serious Anglicanism which declared through the mouth of the bishop of Bombay (Palmer): "At this conference, the issue is the truth, not reunification," and reunification could only be a fruit of common knowledge of the truth. It is the tragedy of the Ecumenical Movement that this knowledge has as much as disappeared in the course of two decades. The Anglicans and Lutherans have practically given up. And the protest, which regularly comes from the side of the Eastern churches, insofar as they still participate in the movement, has lost its meaning because it has not become a protest of actions. In today's Ecumenical Movement, as it was organized in 1948 in Amsterdam in the WCC, the issue is not the truth, but rather the "reunification," a unification not on the basis of divine truth but on human compromise. The Ecumenical Movement has become a unionistic movement, confessionalism defeated by unionism. What the Orthodox Church wanted (which it called in 1920 the formation of a "federation of churches"), what the conscious Lutherans wanted, what the serious Anglicans and Presbyterians wanted in the beginnings of the movement after World War I—namely, a new ordering of the mutual relations between the great confessional churches of Christendom, Christian cooperation where it was compatible with the various convictions of faith, and a true doctrinal conversation in which the truth was the issue—these possibilities of an authentic Ecumenical Movement have been surrendered to the advantage of a unionism which dissolves the ecclesiastical confession together with the substance of the Christian faith.

3

We have repeatedly spoken about this tragedy of the Ecumenical Movement in these letters, and it is unnecessary to repeat that which we have presented as practical examples about South India and the other unions which are in motion in southeast Asia, all under the patronage of the WCC. We don't need to repeat what was to be said about Evanston [1954], where even the last appearance of truthfulness was destroyed by means of a message which presented the illusion of a unity of faith which was not present. Certainly, this message has already been forgotten, as all these messages from the large world conferences. But the damage which they did to simple Christian souls and congregations because they heard this message about Christ as the hope for the world, a message which, first, was approved only by a majority vote against the opposition of a significant minority (earlier, such documents had to at least be approved *nemine contradicente* ["with no one contradicting," i.e., with the dissenting abstaining]), and a message which, second, cleverly hid the fact that the convention was not united about the catechetical truth that the Lord Christ will come again to judge the living and the dead: this damage is not to be repaired and will have bitter consequences. How is this development to be explained? How is it to be understood that even pious people do not understand this deep untruthfulness, which has crept into this modern "ecumeny," and that no protest is ringing in their own ranks? What is here said of the WCC is also valid about the LWF. It is apparently impossible to make clear to its leading men, bishops as well as theologians, that it is a deep untruthfulness if, in a federation whose foundation is the Unaltered Augsburg Confession—to which the Apology also belongs as the normative commentary—and Luther's catechism—you can't have the Small one without the Large one—people accept [into membership] one church after another which *de facto* is unionized, because it allows the Reformed to have full church fellowship, or even now a church—and there will logically soon be more—which quite foundationally affirms the union and further belongs to it. The same is true of the relations of the EKiD and the VELKD in Germany. One can have an Evangelical Church in Germany to which various territorial churches belong regardless of confession. Or one can have a United Evangelical Lutheran Church which may enter into a federation with the Reformed and, if it must be, with the unionized church. But you can't have it both ways. That is the deep untruthfulness of the Lutheranism of the German territorial ecclesiology, which will be the end of it. We could leave the evangelical territorial churches of Germany, which have now chosen this path, to their internal feud, if only they didn't carry this feud out into the world. The earlier foreign congregations, strengthened by emigration and by refugees from Eastern Europe, attach themselves to churches which use the name Lutheran, but which give to non-Lutherans the full rights of membership. Thus the Evangelical Lutheran Church of Italy professes in its constitution the Augsburg Confession of 1530 as its confession, and then continues: "The confessional status of the church does not exclude Christians of the Reformed confession from membership."

In its bylaws, it determines that its spiritual service is offered to all evangelical Christians, whereby the concept "evangelical" is defined thus:

> as evangelical Christians are: (a) such comrades in faith who call themselves Lutheran, Reformed, or Union; (b) members of other Protestant churches and other Christian communities of faith, insofar as they are represented in the WCC.

This is an example which we quote from the "information service of the VELKD." It is exactly this way in England, in Brazil, Argentina, Chile, Peru, and other countries. Does one wonder, then, that Missouri pulled back from cooperation in such a church in England? And how can one wonder, in Hanover, that the Evangelical Lutheran Church in Brazil, standing in church fellowship with Missouri, declines to join itself to the Federacao Sinodal, as long as the latter has not accepted the Augsburg Confession as the norm for doctrine and stands in church fellowship not only with the EKiD but rather even with the Evangelical Church of the Union, as the Old Prussian Union is now called. What a senseless struggle it is when not only Neuendettelsau trains pastors for the Federacao—and actually for all parts of the Federacao, which consists of three union synods and a Lutheran (in the sense of Neuendettelsau) synod—but rather when now also the Evangelical Church of the Union claims that it must continue the work of the former Berlin district office in Brazil, and has therefore concluded to train pastors for Brazil in conjunction with the other unionized churches and, namely, beginning in Barmen! One should certainly not force a congregation to be Lutheran if it doesn't want to be. But one also should not force a church to accept the union if it doesn't want to. What kind of dreadful power brokering is this, which here rules the German churches! Is this missionary service to those scattered around the world? Doesn't anybody think about the souls which are here made into the objects of church politics? Does the Martin Luther Bund really wonder that in Brazil—and in other places, as we shall see—sects [and cults] are growing in numbers? How is it to be explained that all of this happens without the leading men of the churches, or the theologians, whose job it would well be to speak, raising their warning voices?

4

To understand all of this, one must first consider that the Ecumenical Movement is that which its name says, a "movement," one of those intellectual trends which is not under the control of an individual person. We have experienced in our time great political movements, which were not called forth by an individual, though a seemingly leading person stands at their beginnings, like a raging stream through a people or through all humanity, grasping the masses and leading individuals to goals which they themselves do not know. Even the "leaders" of such movements appear to be more the object than the subject, the tools which a movement forms for itself. World history is full of such movements, but they appear in a special way to belong to our era of the masses. Church history has them too. Pietism, which in less than a generation destroyed orthodoxy, was such a movement. It had power over spirits, until this power went on to its successor, rationalism. Such movements can also have a very positive side, such as the great repentance movements of the Middle Ages. Good and evil can be mixed in such currents, such as in the Hussite movement of the fifteenth century, or in that which one tends to label collectively the "Reformation" and in which a church-destroying enthusiastic trend stood next to the authentic evangelical movement. This fact of all history—church history also—we must keep ever before our eyes in order to understand the essence of the Ecumenical Movement. In it, too, an authentic spiritual movement, the asking and seeking for the *Una Sancta*, is mixed with a church-destroying enthusiasm, and both of them cannot only stand next to each other in the same movement but even in one and the same person, as indeed every human soul is a battleground on which God and Satan wrestle with each other; as even every church is a battlefield between Christ and Antichrist, who sits not only in Rome—even if there in his finest and most charming form—but rather, as the New Testament and Luther teach us, in every heresy, even in that heresy which threatens us today. Therefore the apostle of love encourages his congregations to test the spirits and warns [them] with such seriousness about the antichrists who were appearing in the church of his time, as in the church of all times, in the clothing of Christian piety. Therefore the Church of the Reformation prays continually: "Lord, keep us steadfast in Your Word!" Therefore we prayed in the church struggle, as the evening bells rang, with the fathers: "Ach, bleib bei uns" ["Lord Jesus Christ, with us abide, For round us falls the eventide. . . ."].[2]

Where this prayer grows quiet, where the anxiety about error and heresy ceases, there the Church of the Reformation comes to an end. There the church of Christ dies, and the souls fall victim to "movements" in which they "move and are tossed about by every wind of doctrine" (Eph. 4:14). Even the best and most noble "movement" in the church can end this way. What a promising springtime did the Christian Student Movement seem to be at the beginning, which led so many young academics to Christ and into the service of His church! But what has become of this powerful movement, which has given leaders to the current Ecumenical Movement? We don't want to name names, but we ask: Why have contemporary church leaders, bishops, and theologians who have come out of this movement in Germany and England, in America and in the mission fields,

---

2　　See "Lord Jesus Christ, with Us Abide," *LSB* 585:1. MH

almost without exception, lost the sense for the distinction between church and cult, between pure doctrine and heresy? A secretary of the Christian Student Movement in Germany could be a Baptist or a Methodist. That makes no difference, just as the YMCA was recognized by the church. Could one expect from a Leipzig missionary of the younger generation, who came out of the Christian Student Movement and had learned there to have fellowship with all denominations, that he in India now suddenly would be a confessional Lutheran like his predecessors? In some cases, one can show in the history of families how inside of one generation the enthusiastic "movement" has extinguished the heritage from the old church. Exactly the same thing happened in the Ecumenical Movement. What was great and healthy about it—the authentic seeking for the true church, the search for Christian cooperation inside the borders determined by the variety of confessions—that was destroyed by the enthusiasm of the "movement." This enthusiasm gripped at first the youth groups, which were formed to move the movement forward, because the older generation was still not far enough yet. Today, a youth convention runs parallel to every ecumenical conference, which then presses its stormy demands onto the "old people." Even in Evanston young students of the Missouri Synod themselves fell victim to the ecumenical fever. And how could it be otherwise? It is not thoughts, reasons, or convictions which propel people in such cases, but rather it is the "movement."

5

The second thing which one must understand in order to grasp the Ecumenical Movement and its successes is *the power of the organization in our era of mass culture*. It is a characteristic of the modern world that a large portion of its life is formed by anonymous organizations. In earlier days the economy lay in the hands of the enterprising individual, the farmer and the tradesman, the shopkeeper and the business owner, the laborer and the employee. Today, the unionized working class and the large anonymous corporations are the movers of the economy. These organizations have the tendency to go beyond the borders of the individual nations, so that, for example, a large business concern which has offices in various countries is even more or less beyond the reach of the state's legal system. The consequence of this development is that there is no personal responsibility in the strictest sense. Certainly the individual person is responsible for that which happens in the small area of his life in the economy. But the corporations or the union has no conscience. The same is true of politics. Who is the authority today? Certainly the humans in the authoritative offices, but who put them there? The party, whether it is one of many parties, as in the democracies, or only the single party of the "people's democracies." But the party is exactly that which the organization of the capital or of the workers is to the economy: an artificial structure. And it has no conscience. The development of such structures is necessary in the era of masses. It is an inescapable fate of modern society that it must organize itself so. But what is thereby lost? In what sense does the corporation belong to the "station," instituted by God, of the *ordo oeconomicus*? In what sense does the party belong to the divinely instituted "station" of the *ordo politicus*? The farmer prays for a good harvest and thanks God for his blessings. The craftsman, the shopkeeper, and each individual human in his "station" prays for God's blessing. A corporation cannot pray. And a party can't pray. They have, as social structures, no relation to God, as the guilds and councils of the Middle Ages still had because they were also Christian brotherhoods and therefore a type of congregation. Even a people has a relation to God, but not a party, even if it calls itself Christian and espouses a Christian platform or what it considers to be one. The crisis of modern society rests upon this development, which has cut the society away from God.

A very similar development is completing itself before our eyes in the church. It began with the great formation of churchly associations in the nineteenth century. This was necessary in the era of masses. How could, for example, the work of domestic and foreign missionaries have been done without associations! But more and more the fate of the worldly organizations repeated itself in the formation of these churchly associations. Werner Elert posed the question and denied that a church council can receive forgiveness of sins. We want to leave the question aside, whether the Holy Scripture admits of a collective guilt of a people (e.g., Mic. 6:5) and of the church (Revelation 2 and 3; cf. the use of Mic. 6:5 in the *improperia* of the liturgy)[3] and what that means for the institutions of the church. It is no coincidence that, in Germany, the domestic missionary work, which did so much good for the people and for the church in its almost incomprehensibly large and complex organizations, was the first to prepare the way for the secularizing of the church. In his essay "Power over Spirits" (reprinted in *Zur neuesten Kulturgeschichte Deutschlands*, part II, 1858, pp. 101ff.), August Vilmar already saw this in 1849 with a prophetic look, as he, on the one hand, applauded the domestic mission work organized after Johann Hinrich Wichern's (1808–81) great appeal at the first German evangelical church convention, but, on the other hand, warned at the same time against forgetting the actual job of the spiritual office in the face of all the meetings, the organizing of associations, fund-raising, and distributing books. But what the churches in the individual territories already experienced in the previous century—by the way, including even the Roman Church for its part, above all in the political arena—the Christendom of the entire world is now experiencing in its gigantic organizations. Certainly an organization such as the International Council of Missionaries is necessary to do certain external things which an individual church or missionary society can't do. But why must such an organization begin right away to act like a church, as, for example, the Missionary Conference of Tambaram did in 1938, in that it formulated a confession of faith in the name

---

3   See above, Letter 36, *"Post Festum,"* pp. 336–52. MH

of the "true church," about which it was stated: "Despite all the weaknesses and omissions of our churches, the true church is in them" (German report: *Das Wunder der Kirche unter den Völkern der Erde*, 1939, p. 205).

Is it really in all of them? Even in those which have no sacraments? Even in a church whose representatives so blur the line between the Christian faith and the non-Christian religions, as the respected American theologian W. M. Horton did in Tambaram when he reported about his encounter with a Buddhist priest in Japan, whom he considers as his "brother in Christ":

> He gave me a picture of the Bodhisattva, which is for him a complete symbol of the spirit and of the worldview, which demands his simple confession of faith, namely, "to purify the heart of evil and to make the world into the kingdom of God." A light smile of self-contentment is on the face in the picture, and that reminds me of the deep chasm which forever lies between Buddhist self-discipline and the Christian feel for the grace of God toward the sinner. But when I spoke with the priest who gave me the picture, then the chasm was no longer there. Distinctions of the traditions between us seemed to disappear, as I have often seen them melt away between Christians of different denominations at ecumenical gatherings. Our souls encountered each other at a level which is less to be grasped or defined than are forms of speech and thought, but which are infinitely more real and authoritative. If I belong in some sense to the body of Christ, then he does, too. It would be an insult to the Holy Spirit, to the pneuma of God, which blows whither it wants, if I denied my Buddhist brother his place in that body.

The speaker continues that he had actually wanted to speak the next day to a Christian gathering about the text "there is no other name under heaven given to men by which we should be saved" [Acts 4:12], "but I thought to myself, I would rather have the spirit without the name, than the name without the spirit" (official English report about Tambaram, vol. I, *The Authority of Faith*, pp. 149f.).

We'll not deal here at all with the details of this astounding expression, with its confusion of the love toward neighbor, which we as Christians owe to every human, with the brotherly love which is found inside the Body of Christ, and will only ask: Is this the "miracle of the church among the peoples"? In what sense can a convention in which such opinions are represented speak about the true church? And is the job of the International Missionary Council to publish such blatant heresy without criticism? We have no objections to the great practical work and even the theoretical work about evangelism of this, the best of all ecumenical organizations. But at some point, when speaking about the church, one must speak about the border between church and heresy; and in the case of evangelism, one must speak about the unbridgeable opposition between the Gospel and the message of the great world religions. Who is responsible for this, when it doesn't happen—when, to the contrary, error is given the same rights as truth? Apparently nobody. For an ecumenical organization has no soul which can believe. It has, as a well-known English proverb says of such organizations, no body to hit and no soul to damn.

This is especially true of the WCC, which refrains from being a church or a type of super-church, which rather only carries out, in the service of the churches, the assignments which the churches give to it. It demands unions in southeast Asia and everywhere else in the world and has the plans drawn up for them, it raises Christian youth in this purpose, it represents the thoughts of the organic unity of all churches in its writing. But the responsibility for that which then happens it leaves to others. Let the *History of the Ecumenical Movement, 1517–1948* serve as an example, an anthology which appeared shortly before Evanston, edited by Ruth Rouse and Stephan Charles Neill in London in 1954.[4] The book was published in the name of the ecumenical institute in Bossey, as it says on the title page and as the foreword confirms, written by the president of the commission which leads the institute, Reinhold Thadden-Trieglaff (what Lutheran's heart does not bleed when he finds this name in such company!). The WCC actually planned the book, promoted and distributed it. But we read that the WCC takes no responsibility for the content, with the exception of quotes taken from official WCC documents. Each of the contributors in the more than 800-page book is responsible for his contribution, but nobody takes responsibility for the compilation of the material and the selection of the contributors, not even the institute in Bossey. The Ecumenical Movement is here understood as the unification movement of the church, going through the centuries, according to its four aspects:

> (1) cooperation between Christians of different denominations and church membership, (2) cooperation between various churches and denominations, (3) union or reunion of divided churches, (4) the complete and final replication of the unity of all Christendom.

One can think who in this book the actual heroes of church history are and who are the villains. With this the theological youth are fed. Yes, "every Christian should be familiar with ecumenism; for the entire Christian church must be occupied with the solution to the problems which are presented to our generation by striving toward unity in Jesus Christ," writes Thadden-Trieglaff. But nobody has responsibility for the book and the propaganda which it makes for an "ecumeny" which makes no distinction between truth and falsehood, between church and not-church, and which represents the opinion that the organizational unification of all Christians is the fulfillment of the petition in the High Priestly Prayer "that they may all be one." *Et ad veram unitatem ecclesiae satis est . . .* ["and for the true unity of the church, it is sufficient," AC VII]—the Lutherans of the world seem, too, to have forgotten this, with the exception of the Missouri Synod, criticized on p. 325 as "a serious obstacle to unity, even among Lutherans," allegedly

---

4   Sasse reviewed this book: see *RTR* 14, no. 1 (February 1955): 1–9. Huss number 312. MH

emigrating from Prussia to America,[5] whose intransigent pose expresses itself shockingly in their refusal to join the WCC.

6

Whither does this large organization, burdened by no churchly responsibility, lead the Protestant churches—for we'll ignore the Orthodox, who salve their consciences with declarations and with the cleverness of the East enjoy the advantages of such organizations. At the end of this path stands the destruction of the church, not unity. It is one of the odd facts about church history that the individual churches do not live from that which they have in common with the others, or from that which they believe to have in common with the others, but rather from that which divides them. Take away its baptism from a Baptist Church, as it has happened in many cases in America, and it loses that [aspect] of the church of Christ which was still alive in it. Mislead a Lutheran Church for the sake of unification with the Reformed into not taking the real presence very seriously anymore, and you will see how it dies from this. Similar things are true of all churches, as the history of unions between churches of differing confession shows again and again. Successful unions have occurred, until now, only between churches of equivalent confessions. However that is to be explained, the realization that it is so is dawning today in many different corners of Christendom. As in Germany, where precisely in the union churches a new understanding of the Lutheran Confession is here and there breaking out, so one can see how in the cases of Anglicans and Presbyterians suddenly the realization dawns that the decommissioning of the confession has served not to unify the church, but to crumble it. But until now no church has succeeded in reproducing the lost confession. There are only small minorities in whom it awakens and again becomes powerful. So it was in Germany, so it is in the world. But there, where the confession of the fathers is again taken seriously, in that place the true ecumenism awakens—the ecumenism of those who take the search for the truth of the Gospel quite seriously, even if the answer which they find is not always the same. They know that the *Una Sancta* is not an article of sight, but an article of faith, that we cannot make the Body of Christ visible, least of all through the mass organizations of modern Christianity, which are not the church, but rather the world in churchly clothes. They understand Luther's deep expression in *De Servo Arbitrio*: that *abscondita est ecclesia, latent sancti*, "the church is hidden, the saints are latent" (WA 18:652).[6]

In the same book, Luther directed the serious comment toward Erasmus, which is also valid for the followers of Erasmus in the Ecumenical Movement:

---

5   As Sasse knows, the Missourians were largely the result of the Saxon Stephanite emigration and the Löhe *Sendlinge* emigration (Bavaria et al.). Grabau was from Prussia. MH

6   Cf. *Bondage of the Will* (1525), Aland 38, AE 33:89. MH

tolle assertiones, et Christianismum tulisti. "Take away assertions, and you have taken away Christianity" (WA 16:603 [cf. AE 33:21]). That it really is crucial to the life or death of the church is confirmed by the shocking fact that the churches of the WCC are in visible decline. Henry Van Dusen [1897–1975], president of the large Union Theological Seminary in New York, one of the leading theologians of his country, reported in a much-noted article in *The Christian Century* (August 17, 1955) about a vacation which he made through the Latin American countries around the Caribbean Sea, and through the Caribbean islands, a trip in which he discovered what kind of role the sects which live on the border of the historical churches play today. Along with the Roman Church and the Protestantism united in the WCC, a third group of Christians stands as a growing power, above all Adventists, Pentecostals, groups of miracle healings, free Baptists, the Church of God, and various others.

> In Puerto Rico, a man who could speak knowledgeably about the churches told me that the total number of Protestants on the island was estimated at about 200,000, but that the historical Protestant churches counted not more than 50,000 souls. The phenomenal growth of the "sects" had happened essentially in the last 20 years.

Henry Van Dusen himself indicates that the same phenomenon is to be seen everywhere in the world, especially in the mission fields of Asia and Africa. Indeed, there are in southeast Asia areas in which Adventists or Pentecostals simply are "the" church. In the large cities in Australia, one can make exactly the same observation, and corresponding facts are reported from Germany and other European countries, as I myself experienced it already after World War in my first congregation in Oranienburg, that on Sundays many more people went to the sects than to church.[7] Although Henry Van Dusen sees the eerie danger of these sects, he still thinks that perhaps here a new Reformation is gearing up, an optimism in which we cannot follow him. For along with true piety, as one can find in the cases of some people in the Pentecostal movement, a terrible low point of religious life manifests itself here, for example, in the case of the Jehovah's Witnesses, who not only reject all civil authority, but rather conclude from certain Old Testament passages that lying to outsiders in the interests of preserving the movement is permitted. Add to this that many people wander from one sect to another, just as wandering from church to church—we are not thinking about true conversions—is trademark of our era. Where are the

---

7   "Ordained in the Church of the Old Prussian Union (1920), Sasse served as assistant pastor first in Berlin (1920) and then Templin (1920–21). His first pastorate was in Oranienburg some 20 kilometers north of the capital; it was a parish of some 10,000 in two churches. During this period, 1921–28, he was promoted (1923) to Licentiate under Adolf Deissmann and married Charlotte Margarete Naumann (1924). It was also in this period that he went to the United States for further study. Sponsored by the International Missionary Council he took the S.T.M. at Hartford Theological Seminary, Connecticut (1925–26)" (Feuerhahn, "Sasse as an Ecumenical Churchman," 16–17). MH

hundreds of thousands which the United Lutheran Church, the largest of the Lutheran Churches in America, has lost in recent years? From where have the new members come, who, in the statistics, are partially counteracting this loss? How is the powerful growth of the (conservative) Southern Baptist Church to be explained? But remaining with [the topic of] the dangerous sects, how does it happen that in the areas of South America ignored by the church, not only Protestant churches and the sects imported out of North America but also millions of spiritists—indeed, even African paganism—form the greatest competition to the Roman Church? If one reads the statistics and compares them with the statistics of churchly life in Europe, Protestant as well as Catholic, then one often has the impression that Christianity as such stands in an eerie crisis, and this impression is strengthened by the fact that the national awakening of the Asian and African peoples is accompanied by an awakening of the other world religions, of Hinduism, of Buddhism, and of Islam—to say nothing at all of the progress of Communism.

7

In this world we have the task, honored brothers, as Lutheran pastors and Christians to believe in the *Una Sancta* and to confess. We cannot do this without considering that which our churches have omitted and how they have sinned. Why did the Lutheran Church not promptly recognize that a true ecumenical movement was possible and necessary? Why did our church not punctually gather itself anew around the Scripture and Confession, and call other churches to the cooperation which is possible without injury to the eternal truth of the Gospel? Why did it not become that which it could have been, "the unifying middle of the denominations"? It is easy to find fault with the Reformed Churches and especially with the churches of America, that they acted as they did and surrendered the Reformation. It is easy to criticize the union churches and movements like the "alliance." Why was the union born in Germany? Why didn't the Lutheran Churches put anything in the place of the "Christian communities" of the YMCA and the DCSV (German Christian Student Association)? Why did the dismantling of the Lutheran territorial church begin out of Tübingen and Stuttgart, out of old Lutheran Württemberg? Why did the Lutheran Churches in the Ecumenical Movement not at least make sure that the WCC was set upon a foundation which could bear some weight, that at least the authority of the Holy Scripture and the Nicene Creed was acknowledged? We should place these and other questions before ourselves, if we criticize the Ecumenical Movement which now, like a raging river, threatens also the remains of the Christian confession. Only when we all speak the *mea culpa, mea culpa, mea maxima culpa* from our hearts, only then will we be in a condition to do that which is today most necessary to gather the remains of battered Lutheranism and, if it must be, as a small flock, to testify with word and deed what God's Word says about the *Una*

Sancta ecclesia perpetuo mansura ["the one holy church which shall continue to remain," AC VII 1]. Such confession and such witness never come too late. And it can be given in the smallest congregation and from the loneliest pastor. The Lord Christ never promised that He would be with the millions and with those who have the large political influence in the world. Let us believe anew that where two or three are gathered in His name, the church is present [Matt. 18:20], the church in which He is present—He, to whom all power is given in heaven and on earth. That is not resignation. That is the faith of the New Testament.

Greeting you in the bonds of faith,

Your
Hermann Sasse

Historical Context

The intensification of the Ecumenical Movement in the 1950s brought the matter of the validity of the Office of the Ministry of churches to the fore as Anglicans wrestled with Roman and Eastern Orthodox dogma. The question intensified among Lutherans in the period, particularly because Scandinavian Lutheran Churches had never experienced a disruption in the so-called succession of bishops. As usual, Sasse gets to the heart of the matter. As venerable as the tradition may be, the real "apostolic succession" is a successio doctrinalis, *or the tradition of the doctrine of the apostles. The Office of the Ministry is created by the Word, not the Word by the Office of the Ministry. MH*

June 5, 1956

Prof. H. Sasse
41 Buxton Street
North Adelaide, South Australia

Dear and Reverend Dr. Behnken,

. . . As to liturgical "accessories," we should discourage everything which is conducive to Romanism. But we should exercise the Christian freedom for which Luther stood. Why should we not, as even in the *Haustafel* of the Small Catechism it is suggested, make use of the sign of the cross, even in private prayer? Much wisdom is needed for the Lutheran Churches if they want to get rid of the Puritan destruction of the liturgy which has occurred in the eighteenth century and to restore something of the beauty of the Lutheran service of the sixteenth and seventeenth centuries. But all this must go hand in hand with the restoration of the doctrine and with the doctrine of our church on the adiaphora and, most of all, with the Christian love which is necessary in such things. Unless our churches take in hand wise leadership in liturgical matters, the liturgical movement will grow wild and destroy the precious heritage of our Church with the inseparable unity of Word and Sacrament. This may suffice for today. I shall write as soon as I can, one of my *Briefe* on "Word and Sacrament, Preaching and Lord's Supper."[1] . . . We had Drs. [Franklin] Fry and [Henry Frederick] Schuh[2] here. World Council and LWF are exercising a strong influence. Our hopes for

---

1   See below, pp. 443–64. MH

2   Schuh (1890–1965) served as president of the ALC from 1951–60. MH

a union in the near future seem to fade away. No one in America can perhaps realize what a tragedy this would mean to Australian Lutherans. Until Hanover 1952 everything went well. We would perhaps be one Church already had not Bishop Meiser persuaded our then-President Stolz and our church leaders that the unity of all Lutherans would be reached soon. We were constantly told that Missouri was about to join the LWF . . . . The only man who could present the other point of view effectively to our men would be you. No one else could speak with such authority . . . .

Yours in the communion of the faith,

H. Sasse

forty-one

Successio Apostolica

TRANSLATED BY NORMAN NAGEL

Mid-April 1956[1]

Prof. D. Theol. Hermann Sasse

41 Buxton Street

North Adelaide, South Australia

Dear Brothers in the Office!

This present letter and, God willing, the one to follow quickly shall deal with the questions which are posed to our church by the high church liturgical movement of our times. Today we want to consider the problem of apostolic succession. The next letter will take up the relationship of Word, Sacrament, preaching, and Holy Supper. Both are questions which are immediately pertinent to us all for our understanding of the Office of the Ministry [*geistlichen Amtes*] and thereby also significant in our carrying out of the office. Just how pertinent a question such as apostolic succession is, also for Lutheranism of our day, will become evident from the following.[2]

---

1   *BLP* 41: *Successio Apostolica* (North Adelaide, April 1956). The original was published in *LuBl* 8, no. 48 (June 1956): 61–82. Reprinted in *ISC* 1:188–204. This English translation appeared originally in *We Confess: The Church* (St. Louis: Concordia, 1986), 84–107. Minor alterations to grammar and capitalization have been made. Scripture quotations in this essay are from the Revised Standard Version of the Bible, copyright 1952, © 1971 by the Division of Christian Education of the National Council of the Churches of Christ in the United States of America. Used by permission. All rights reserved. The quotations from the Lutheran Confessions in this publication are from The BOOK OF CONCORD: THE CONFESSIONS OF THE EVANGELICAL LUTHERAN CHURCH, edited by Theodore G. Tappert, published in 1959 by Fortress Press. Huss number 319. MH

2   This first paragraph was translated by MH.

1

Apostolic succession is an ancient concept, and yet the particular implication with which it is used nowadays is, as far as I can see, a quite recent product among Christians. In 1833 appeared the first of the "Tracts for the Times," calling for a renewal of catholic thinking in the Church of England. It was a powerful summons to the Anglican clergy to ponder the responsibilities of their office. The author reminded his brother clergy that the Anglican ordination liturgy contains "the doctrine of the apostolic succession." He was the same John Henry Newman[3] who twelve years later gave up this view and converted to the Roman Church.

His appeal had to be to the liturgy, since none of the confessions of the ancient church, or the *Thirty-Nine Articles*, contain such a doctrine. Noteworthy is also the fact that the Roman Church has no particular doctrinal article concerning the *successio apostolica*. There appears to be only one doctrinal document in which the expression is used, and that, significantly, in what the Holy Office wrote to the Catholic bishops of England in 1864 (*apostolicae successionis praerogativa*, Denzinger 1686).

In the Roman textbooks of dogmatics the matter itself is dealt with in the doctrine of the apostolicity of the church and in the doctrine of priestly ordination. Trent speaks of it, rather in passing, in the doctrine of the priesthood, when it says the bishops succeeded to the place of the apostles (*in apostolorum locum successerunt*, Session 23, ch. 4). In the following canons, in which the doctrines of the Reformation are rejected, there is no mention of any succession at all.

There are two places in the Interim of 1548[4] which approach the way in which the term is used nowadays. The Interim is not a doctrinal statement, and yet it does give a good indication of the thinking of the Catholic reform theologians at

---

3   John Henry Newman (1801–90) led the Oxford Movement in the 1830s and later became a cardinal. His *Parochial and Plain Sermons* had a profound influence on Oxford and upon the whole country. The "Tracts for the Times" (1833–41), twenty-seven of which were written by him, called for a middle way between Protestantism and Romanism, represented by the patristic tradition of the Church of England. In his famous Tract 90 (1841), he advocated the interpretation of the *Thirty-Nine Articles* generally in line with the decrees of the Council of Trent, which caused a violent controversy. From 1839 he had doubts about the claims of the Anglican Church and by October 1945 he had been received into the Roman Catholic Church. See *ODCC*, 1142. MH

4   The Augsburg Interim (June 30, 15480 was drawn up as a stopgap solution to the Lutheran issues by a commission appointed by Emperor Charles V after he had defeated the Lutheran princes and the Smalcald League. It included Julius von Pflug (1499–1564) and Johann Agricola (1499–1566). The doctrinal articles and Romanizing practices were forced on much of Germany, and many pastors (including Johann Brenz [1499–1570]) were driven from office. It was to be a solution until a general council could be called. The Peace of Augsburg 1555 (after the Lutherans defeated the emperor's troops) brought an end to the interims. Unfortunately, the Council of Trent was the ultimate Roman Catholic response (s.v. *Christian Cyclopedia*). MH

that time. Catholicity is said to be a "sign of the true church, that is, that it is universal, poured out through all places and times through the apostles and those who followed them right up to us and in continuing succession to the end of the world." Similarly the article concerning the sacrament of ordination speaks of the succession of the church: "When the bishops lay on hands and ordain to these offices, they are acting in this always continual transmission and succession of the church" [Melhausen, pp. 66, 94].

What nowadays is called apostolic succession is regarded in the Catholic churches as so self-evident that there is scarcely need to talk about it. It is quite simply given with the sacrament of priestly ordination. When the Church of England and its daughter churches (recently also certain Lutheran churches, and union churches such as that of South India) make so much of their apostolic succession, one is prompted to ponder the fact that we are most apt to speak of those virtues which we do not possess. It is hardly by chance that this overemphasis on apostolic succession emerged in a church which indeed claims to be catholic and to possess the three offices of bishop, priest, and deacon, and yet is unable to say what these offices actually are.

We would have no need of engaging the Anglicans and their lack of clarity (the product of the sorry history of their Reformation), if they were not continually beating on the doors of all other churches, demanding from Rome the recognition of their orders and from Protestants the receiving of their "apostolic succession." Prussia repeatedly looked with longing eyes at the Church of England, from the first king, mightily impressed by "no bishop, no king," to romantic Frederick William IV [1840–61][5] and his failed attempt to found a Jerusalem bishopric under the auspices of Prussia and England. The plans for this bishopric were what finally drove Newman to Rome. They contained the thought that the Church of England would help those churches "less fully organized."

In our lifetime we have seen a renewal of this friendly offer. It was made—to the dismay of all serious English theologians—by certain English bishops as Hitler's millennium was breaking upon us. In all seriousness they said to us that our struggle against Ludwig Müller[6] and the other "German Christian" bishops was hopeless. The thing to do was for the German "bishops" to have themselves consecrated from England. That would bring everything into proper order. We

---

5   The son of Frederick William III (who instituted the Prussian Union), Frederick William IV (1795–1861) was crowned king of Prussia in 1840. He issued the *Generalkonzession*, July 23, 1845, which permitted the "Old Lutherans" to form a Prussian Lutheran free church. MH

6   Born at Gütersloh and educated at Münster, Ludwig Müller (1883–1945) was an army chaplain when he met Hitler at Königsberg (1926). He became Hitler's confidential adviser in church affairs in 1933. Under Nazi pressure Müller was elected bishop of the Old Prussian Union and also *Reichsbischof* of the DEK. See *ODCC*, 1124. Sasse often noted how the German Christian movement was strongest in the de-Lutheranized and deconfessionalized union churches, especially Prussia. MH

were invited to consider the example of certain Nordic churches which enjoyed a good standing with the Church of England.

We will speak later about the fateful consequences for Lutheranism through-out the world which resulted when the churches of Sweden and Finland entered upon joint consecrations with the Anglicans. They should have said not only that such consecrations by the Church of England are null and void in the eyes of Rome, but that the notion that something more is given by them than is given to the ministry of Word and Sacrament also runs counter to the Lutheran Reformation, according to the understanding of Article V of the Augsburg Confession.[7]

The baleful consequences are plain for all to see in the mission fields of Africa and India. There we are now blessed with two groups of Lutheran missionaries. The one has "apostolic succession," the other does not. Both are more or less in church fellowship with a whole range of churches, but no longer with each other and no longer with whatever Lutheran Church faithful to the Confessions is still left in the world.

To what extent this matter has become a problem in Germany can be seen by the shocking case of Friedrich Heiler,[8] a professor of theology in the Evangelical faculty of Marburg. He had himself secretly consecrated bishop. Secretly he bestowed priestly ordination on evangelical pastors so that they now secretly (their congregations were not informed) would be able to effect the "change" in the celebration of the Sacrament of the Altar.[9] Were there ever before in Christ's church sacraments and ordinations at which what was given and what

---

7   *Augustana* V reads: "So that we may obtain this faith, the ministry of teaching the Gospel and administering the Sacraments was instituted. Through the Word and Sacraments, as through instruments, the Holy Spirit is given [John 20:22]. He works faith, when and where it pleases God [John 3:8], in those who hear the good news that God justifies those who believe that they are received into grace for Christ's sake. This happens not through our own merits, but for Christ's sake. Our churches condemn the Anabaptists and others who think that through their own preparations and works the Holy Spirit comes to them without the external Word" (*Concordia*, 33). MH

8   Sasse respected some of Heiler's [1892–1967] liturgical study (see above, Letter 36, "*Post Festum*," pp. 336–52), but he finds this leader of the German High Church move-ment a ready target, epitomizing the tendency of such movements to ignore and con-tradict Lutheran dogma. Sasse came to be concerned about Heiler already in 1931; see "Prof. Heiler und die Hochkirche," *Christentum und Wissenschaft* 7, no. 6 (June 1931): 227–28 (Huss number 79); and "Fr. Heiler und die evangelische Theologie," *Christentum und Wissenschaft* 8, no. 8 (August 1932): 307–11 (Huss number 100). MH

9   "Heiler had followed the example of that society in England which in the nineteenth century, when the hope for corporate union with Rome had vanished, provided for valid (in the Catholic sense) reordinations of Anglican priests. . . . When this became known, I asked Archbishop Temple when I stayed with him in York what the attitude of the English bishops was to such a procedure. His answer was that they unani-mously rejected secret ordinations" (Sasse to Piepkorn, Let\CHI56394). See Feuer-hahn Chronology. MH

was received was not clearly stated, but kept secret, not done in the presence of the Christian congregation? The church governments in Germany would do well to keep a watchful eye on such surreptitious Romanizing, as well as on the open Calvinizing of the Lutheran heritage. Instead, they make special laws and take measures against those who are again taking seriously the old heritage of genuine Lutheran catholicity, the only weapon against Romanizing.

2

In any attempt to understand all the talk nowadays about apostolic succession, we must begin with the fact that apostolicity is integral to the church. Therefore any church, any collection of people that claims to be church, claims apostolicity in its own way. Roman Catholic theologians are in the habit of dividing between apostolicity of origin, apostolicity of doctrine, and apostolicity of succession (*apostolicitas originis, doctrinae, successionis*). Every church claims the first two. Every church finally traces its origin back to the apostles and so to Jesus Christ Himself.

So it is nonsense to say that the Lutheran Church and the other Protestant churches came into being in the sixteenth century or even later, while the Roman Church goes back to Jesus and the apostles. The Eastern Church is evidence and protest enough against such an idea. Where was the papal church before there was a papacy? Whether any church has its origin in the church of the New Testament or not is simply a matter of faith. The Baptists and the Disciples of Christ make the claim that their church was the church at the time of the New Testament. Our Lutheran fathers never had the idea that they were founding a new church. They were of the conviction that Christ's one church was being renewed with the pure apostolic doctrine in contrast with Rome, which had fallen away from the Gospel.

These are matters of faith, and one should not try to settle them by appeals to historical proofs. How this goes may be seen in the polemics between the Anglicans and the English Roman Catholics. Both attempt to prove that they are the legitimate continuation of the medieval church in England. We Lutherans have no part to play in that sort of dispute, though it has often been suggested that we should.

To provide the proof for the identity of any historical construction is always enormously problematic. One may, for example, speak of an English nation and of a German nation that continue through the centuries. But if one looks more closely, one notices how great are also the differences. In what sense are the English people of Henry VIII's time identical with the ten times as many English people of today? In what sense are today's German people identical with the people of Luther's time? Was it anything more than a fiction when it was thought that the Holy Roman Empire of Byzantium was living on in the empire of Charlemagne and the German empire of Otto the Great [r. 962–973][10] until it expired in 1806? Is there more of an identity between the Roman Church of today and the church of Peter's day than there is between the Roman Empire of the first century and the Holy Roman Empire around 1800? It has been observed that the difference between the church before Constantine and the church after Constantine is greater than the difference in the Western Church before and after the Reformation. Here the historical proofs of identity simply fail.

The apostolicity of origin, the claim that the church to which I belong is identical with the church of the apostles, is a matter of faith. The answer has to do with whether I consider the doctrine of my church to be apostolic. The claim of the Lutheran Church to be apostolic stands or falls with the claim that it has faithfully preserved the doctrine of the New Testament. For Lutherans certainly everything depends on the question: "Where today is the doctrine of the apostles?"

Naturally, every church claims to be apostolic also in the sense of the apostolicity of its doctrine. Now it is especially worth noting the enormous difficulties the Roman Church has gotten itself into through its development, especially since the Reformation. At the beginning of his work Luther could still—within the Roman Church—appeal to *sola Scriptura*. Beside it there had long been the view of those who regarded tradition as an expansion of Scripture. How old and widespread this was we may observe in the Eastern Church, but it had never been made into dogma. It was first at Trent that tradition was set beside Scripture as a second equivalent source of revelation.[11]

When this happens, when, to speak with the Smalcald Articles (II II 15), Scripture no longer alone sets up articles of faith, then Enthusiasm has forced an entry into the church. It pushes beyond the doctrine of the New Testament, destroys it, and abolishes the church's apostolicity. It is one of Luther's most profound recognitions, also expressed in the Smalcald Articles (III VIII), that Enthusiasm is engendered by scorn of the external Word, the words of Scripture read and preached. Enthusiasm leads to the religion of the natural man, fallen man who puts himself in God's place. Luther saw that this is the great heresy which the Enthusiasts, the pope, and Muhammad—the three forms of the Antichrist known to him—had in common.

All three cited the much-misunderstood words of our Lord in John 16:12–13: "I have yet many things to say to you, but you cannot bear them now. When the Spirit of truth comes, He will guide you into all the truth." These words find welcoming ears with the pope, the archbishop of Canterbury, the Quakers, the liberals, and all sorts of heretics. Not so much, however, the words which follow, the rule by which one can recognize whether it really was the Holy Spirit whom

---

10   Otto I was king of Germany and emperor of the Holy Roman Empire. MH

11   See *Catechism of the Catholic Church*, 2nd ed. (New York: Doubleday, 1995), § 81, p. 31. MH

one has heard or whether it was only the spirit of man or a still worse spirit: "He will glorify Me, for He will take what is Mine and declare it to you" (v. 14), that is, interpret the Gospel of Christ ever more deeply and thus glorify Jesus.

How far things can go when this is not heeded we may see in the history of the Roman Church—Christianity's greatest tragedy. At first tradition is like a tethered balloon, more or less held by the apostolic witness. But with the declaration of two equivalent sources of revelation—Scripture and tradition—the rope is cut and the balloon sails with the wind, no one knows where. The answer came in the course of time. By the nineteenth century it was so clear that the best Catholics were filled with anxiety. Neither in Scripture nor in the tradition of the first centuries can the grounds be found for any of the modern dogmas, from the immaculate conception of 1854[12] through the 1870[13] Vatican Council's papal dogma to the assumption of Mary [1950].[14] None of these were known to the early church.

The doctrine of the Roman Church is no longer apostolic. Even in 1854 and 1870 it was still possible to claim to be reaching back to relatively old traditions, or to what were regarded as such. Passages of Scripture could be interpreted so as to be persuasive for faithful Catholics. With the dogma of 1950 this is at an end. The assumption of Mary is a late legend, and only "conclusion theology" can produce Mary as *mediatrix* of all graces and *coredemptrix*.

---

12 *Ineffabilis Deus*, promulgated December 8, 1854: "We declare . . . that the most Blessed Virgin Mary at the first instant of her conception, by a singular grace and privilege of Almighty God, in virtue of the merits of Christ Jesus, the Savior of the human race, was preserved immaculate from all stain of original sin, has been revealed by God, and on this account must be firmly and constantly believed by all the faithful. Wherefore, if any should presume to think in their hearts otherwise than as it has been defined by Us, which God avert, let them know and understand that they are condemned by their own judgment; that they have suffered shipwreck in regard to faith, and have revolted from the unity of the Church . . ." (Denzinger 1641). MH

13 *Dogmatic Constitution I on the Church of Christ* (Session IV, July 18, 1870). ". . . the Apostolic See and the Roman Pontiff hold primacy over the whole world, and that the Pontiff of Rome himself is the successor of the blessed Peter . . . the head of the whole Church and faith" (Denzinger 1826). ". . . the Roman Pontiff, when he speaks *ex cathedra*, that is, when carrying out the duty of the pastor and teacher of all Christians by virtue of his supreme apostolic authority he defines a doctrine of faith or morals to be held by the universal Church, through the divine assistance promised him in blessed Peter, operates with that infallibility with which the divine Redeemer wished that His church be instructed in defining doctrine on faith and morals; and so such definitions of the Roman Pontiff from himself, but not from the consensus of the Church, are unalterable" (Denzinger 1839). MH

14 *Munificentissimus Deus*, promulgated November 1, 1950: "We pronounce, declare, and define that the dogma was revealed by God, that the Immaculate Mother of God, the ever Virgin Mary, after completing her course of life upon earth, was assumed to the glory of heaven both in body and soul. Therefore if anyone, which may God forbid, should dare either to deny this, or voluntarily call into doubt what has been defined by Us, he should realize that he has cut himself off entirely from the divine and Catholic faith" (Denzinger 2333). MH

At work here has been the "theory of development." This was proposed by J. H. Newman and has been avidly put to use. By the way, one can find it already in Möhler.[15] This theory, which is supposed to justify the modern dogmas, is the product of Romanticism and of the nineteenth century as a whole (the obvious parallels are Darwin and Marx). The picture is that of a seed. At the beginning of the church all its doctrines were contained within the seed, and these then unfolded from century to century. Was not this the case with the doctrines of the Holy Trinity and the person of the God-man?

To be sure, the understanding of these doctrines progressed through generations. They were, however, already there from the beginning in the apostolic witness. The New Testament declares that Jesus Christ is not a creature but the eternal *Logos*. The New Testament declares that Jesus Christ, true God and true man, is one person. What unfolds in the church is the ever deeper understanding of the apostolic words. But nothing can unfold if it is not there in the apostolic words.

In Roman Catholic theology today we find such questions dealt with as, "Did Mary ever die?" Questions do arise which call for answers, such as, "What is the essence and the extent of papal infallibility?" Since Bernadette has been canonized and solemnly exalted "to the honor of the altars," can any good Catholic have doubt about the genuineness of the appearances [of the Virgin Mary] at Lourdes? If we further probe the question of the authority of the papal teaching office, do we not reach the point where, in addition to Scripture and tradition, there appears a third source of doctrine, namely, Christ's regent on earth?

We can only rejoice in all that is done in the Roman Church in honor of Scripture. In all doctrinal explanations attention is given to Scripture and tradition. Many a Protestant church could find much to learn here. But what are we to make of private revelations when they are claimed not by some unknown person but by the pope himself? If he experienced the miraculous sun of Fatima also in Rome, or had a vision of Christ, why does he not keep this to himself, which would be the proper way? Why is it proclaimed through the media to the city and to the world? Why does the believing Catholic accept the pope's every word in questions of faith and morals? Because he has tested it against Scripture and tradition? Certainly not, but because the pope has said it!

"The pope's word is God's word." This could be read during the war on the doors of the cathedral in Salzburg in a Lenten letter of the archbishop. Now Christians all know that human words can at the same time be God's words. "Do you believe that the forgiveness I declare is the forgiveness of God?" At

---

15 Johann Adam Möhler (1796–1838) was a Roman Catholic theologian and historian who studied at Erlangen and Tübingen before serving as professor of church history at Tübingen from 1828. He was the principal representative of the Tübingen Catholic School and emphasized the nature of the church as a living community filled with the Holy Spirit, rather than seeing it as an institution. He was influenced by German Romanticism and Idealism (Schelling and Hegel). See *ODCC*, 1099. MH

Confession this question is put [SC V 27]. But only the Word of God, the Word of the Gospel, the Word of the living proclamation of the apostolic message today—only this can be God's Word.

Into what airy heights does the balloon of supposed tradition float off when the line with Scripture is severed! When *sola Scriptura* is left behind, left behind also are God's revelation and its authority. One can only think with horror of the fearful fate the Roman Church is readying for itself. After all, it is still Christianity's largest and most influential church. Is it still the church in which our fathers lived during the Middle Ages? Is it still an apostolic church? Has it not lost the apostolicity of doctrine? Not as though the apostolic witness had died out within it. That is still there. Otherwise Rome would be no church. Also in the Roman Church there are people who still believe in the Savior, Jesus Christ, as the only Mediator between God and men. Also in this church Christ is still present in the means of grace, to the extent that these are still there. Also in this church people are born again to eternal life. But there is also in this church that horror which Luther saw, the anti-Christian exaltation of man, whether in the cult of Mary or in the revering of the pope.[16]

If we recognize this, we can do so only in the spirit of penitent self-examination. Perhaps the same disease, Christianity's mortal illness, lurks also in us and our church, ever ready to break out. How is it said by Luther at that place in the Smalcald Articles?

> In short, enthusiasm clings to Adam and his descendants from the beginning to the end of the world. It is a poison implanted and inoculated in man by the old dragon, and it is the source, strength, and power of all heresy, including that of the papacy and Mohammedanism. Accordingly, we should and must constantly maintain that God will not deal with us except through his external Word and sacrament. Whatever is attributed to the Spirit apart from such Word and sacrament is of the devil. (III VIII 9–10)

This is an earnest warning to every church. We cannot be discovering this heresy in other churches without earnestly asking also of ourselves, "Is it I, Lord?"

3

The doctrinal locus concerning the apostolic church has, beside the apostolicity of origin and the apostolicity of doctrine, also the apostolicity of *succession*.

---

16 "In fact they remind us of what one brother in the forest of Thuringia did to the other. They were going through the woods with each other when they were set upon by a bear who threw one of them beneath him. The other brother sought to help and struck at the bear, but missed him and grievously wounded the brother under the bear. So these enthusiasts. They ought to come to the aid of Christendom which Antichrist has in his grip and tortures. They take a severe stand against the pope, but they miss their mark and murder the more terribly the Christendom under the pope" (*Concerning Rebaptism* [1528], Aland 768, AE 40:233 [cf. WA 26:148]. MH

This is what looms most largely in Christian affairs nowadays. We must first ask what it actually is, this apostolic succession, which the Anglican churches esteem themselves as having, which the Church of Sweden believes it possesses, and which the Eastern churches and the Roman Church regard as their own possession.

In his famous *Symbolism* [English translation 1906[17]], Möhler attempted to clarify the meaning of tradition for modern Catholicism. He found himself in remarkable agreement with Newman and his friends in England as well as with Russian thinkers such as Chomjakov. Möhler's view of tradition has been traced to contemporary philosophy and Romanticism's understanding of society as an organism. Thus J. Ranft, the dogmatician from Würzburg, in his learned work *Der Ursprung des katholischen Traditionsprinzips* (1931). Other Roman Catholic scholars agreed. (Cf. the collection in honor of the hundredth anniversary of Möhler's death, *Die Eine Kirche*, ed. H. Tüchle, 1938.)

Möhler finds the law of tradition, which binds together the different generations of a people or of a religious society, in the life of all such societies.

> The Divine Founder of our Church, when he constituted the community of believers as his permanent organ, had recourse to no other law than that which prevails in every department of human life. Each nation is endowed with a peculiar character, stamped on the deepest, most hidden parts of its being, which distinguishes it from all other nations and manifests its peculiarity in public and domestic life, in art and science, in short, in every relation. It is, as it were, the tutelary genius; the guiding spirit transmitted from its progenitors; the vivifying breath of the whole community. (*Symbolism*, pp. 279f.)

Just as there is a national spirit for peoples which sustains a people in its peculiar wholeness through the generations, so there is also such a spirit in religious communities. As examples of this we are given not only the Chinese, the Parsees, the Muslims, and Hellenic heathenism, but even Lutheranism:

> Lastly, let us contemplate the religious sect founded by Luther himself. The developed doctrines of his Church, consigned as they are in the symbolical books, retain, on the whole, so much of this spirit, that on the first view, they must be recognized by the observer as genuine productions of Luther (*echt lutherisch*). With a sure vital instinct (*Lebensgefühle*), the opinions of the Majorists,[18] the Synergists[19] and others were

---

17 *Symbolism or Exposition of the Doctrinal Differences between Catholics and Protestants as Evidenced by Their Symbolical Writings*, trans. James Burton Robertson (London: Gibbings, 1906). MH

18 Georg Major (1502–74) compromised with the prevailing powers in the Leipzig Interim. Flacius accused him of denying the Lutheran doctrine of justification. Major denied the charge, but taught good works are necessary for salvation. His phrases are repudiated in FC IV (s.v. *Christian Cyclopedia*). MH

19 The Synergistic Controversy stemmed from Melanchthon's departure from Luther in the second edition of his *Loci* (1535), where he taught three causes in conversion:

rejected as deadly; and, indeed (from Luther's point of view, *Geist*), as untrue, by that community whose soul, whose living principle he was; and the Church, which the Reformer of Wittenberg established, proved herself the unerring interpretess of his word. (pp. 280f.)

What revealing sentences these are! Plain for all to see is the utter distortion of Lutheranism, and so a lot of words are not called for to show that the Lutheran Church is not a religious association founded by Luther, having as its principle the spirit of Luther. What is most significant is that this way of speaking about a church is not put right even if we cross out "Luther" and substitute "Christ"; instead of what was allegedly established by the reformer of Wittenberg, the church established by Christ; instead of the Lutheran Church as "unerring interpretess" of the words of Luther, the Roman Catholic Church as "unerring interpretess" of the words of Christ. In the tradition of doctrine and the succession of teachers there is said to be an inherent spirit at work infallibly revealing things. We hardly needed the specific references to the Chinese, Greeks, Parsees, and Muslims to recognize that such an idea is no product of the Christian faith and the witness of the apostles. Such an idea did indisputably exist throughout the ancient world, Hellenic and Asiatic, and it has certainly not died out. But what has to be decisively disputed is that the idea is a biblical and Christian one, though there are indeed traces here and there of its influence on the *language* used in the Bible, and we may observe how later it infiltrated Christ's church and helped form the idea of the "catholic" church.

The Holy Spirit, who creates unity of faith and confession, is not the collective spirit of the Christian religious association. The church as the people of God is something completely other than the people of Mani[20] or Muhammad. The church as the Body of Christ is not an organism such as a secular association, a family, a nation, or any other kind of "body." Möhler's misunderstanding, and that of the whole Romantic movement, cannot be excused by pointing to the ancient church's use of terms from ancient sociology of religion in speaking of the church of Christ. One must never forget that the church fathers came out of ancient heathenism and continued to carry some of its concepts around with them for a long time, for instance, in their apologetics. The vital distinction to be made is between what is truly biblical and what was brought into the church from that ancient heathen world. Clearly the catholicity and apostolicity of the

---

(1) God's Word, (2) the Holy Spirit, and (3) man's will not resisting God's Word. Like Erasmus, Melanchthon taught that man was able to apply himself to grace. This synergistic view found expression in the Leipzig Interim, but Flacius and company countered. Melanchthon's views were rejected by the Formula of Concord. MH

20 Mani (Manes or Manichaeus, ca. 216–ca. 277), the founder of Manichaeism, claimed to have received divine revelations and to be the last and highest prophet. Mani traveled to India and possibly to China, where he became familiar with Buddhism. Manichaeism is syncretistic, dualistic, and includes Gnostic, Zoroastrian, and Christian elements. Augustine was a Manichaean as a youth. This heresy is frequently condemned by the Lutheran Confessions (s.v. *Christian Cyclopedia*). MH

church are taught in Holy Scripture. The same cannot be said of the way catholicity and apostolicity were understood through the centuries of the development of the Catholic Church.

We have only to look at the sentence Augustine penned to overthrow the Donatists:[21] "When the whole world passes judgment, that judgment is sure" (*Securus iudicat orbis terrarum*). He refers to the church everywhere; the Donatists were to be found only in Africa. This is the sentence that began to shake Newman's faith in the catholicity of the Church of England. Ever and again it has deeply impressed Catholic and high church circles. It does not come, however, from Scripture but from the religious thought of the non-Christian world, perhaps from very early forms of religion which are still alive within us or could become so. "The voice of the people is the voice of God" (*Vox populi vox Dei*).[22] This is Stoic philosophy, and at the same time a piece of ancient wisdom—or foolishness. "My community will never agree in error."[23] Thus from Muhammad the doctrine of *ijmā'*, the consensus of all Muslims.

Möhler is quite right in observing that here we are dealing with doctrines which appear also outside the church. What he failed to observe is that they do not come from Holy Scripture, and indeed cannot be brought into agreement with Scripture.

How useless, indeed impossible, it is to understand the doctrine of the church from such principles is shown by the impossibility of putting into practice the well-known dictum of Vincent of Lerins.[24] According to this dictum, that doctrine is to be regarded as catholic, and thus orthodox, "which has been believed everywhere, always, and by all" (*quod ubique, quod semper, quod ab omnibus creditum est*). Of the geographic catholicity of "everywhere" we have already spoken. It is difficult to say anything better regarding the temporal catholicity of "always," or what is often called apostolicity. Here, however, we come upon the heart of the doctrine of "apostolic succession." What is this heart? It is the conviction of all the great schools of wisdom and established religions of Asia and the Hellenistic world that in the beginning there was truth and that it was handed down in purity from generation to generation, from father to son, from master to disciples, as from hand to hand, without anything being added or taken away. The

---

21   See above, p. 298 n. 11. MH

22   Cf. Seneca the Elder (ca. 54 BC–ca. AD 39), *Controversia* 1.1.10; Homer, *Odyssey* 3.214f. NN and MH

23   *Hadith. Muctamad*, 458–76. Cf. Lammens, *Islam* (1968), p. 93. NN

24   Little is known of Vincent of Lerins (d. before 459) except that he became a monk on the island of Lerins. His main work, *Commonitorium*, was written under the pseudonym "Peregrinus" and was designed to provide a guide to the determination of the Catholic faith. Thus the famous dictum. See *ODCC*, 1699–1700. MH

quasi per manus tradita ["as though passed on by hand"] which appears in the fourth session of Trent (Denzinger 783[25]) is an age-old technical term for this.

Now how much of this can be found in Holy Scripture? In 1 Cor. 11:23 and 15:3 Paul uses the technical terms for the receiving and passing on of a tradition (*parelabon, paredōka*). (We may note in passing that this has no adverse effect on the independence of his apostleship, which he so strongly emphasizes in Galatians.) In the New Testament we do have tradition in the sense of the message of the Gospel, or some particular message, being faithfully kept and handed on (1 Tim. 6:20), without addition or subtraction (Rev. 22:18–19). This "tradition," however, whether it be the oral proclamation of the apostles or whether it was already written down, has nothing to do with a tradition which was later placed in opposition to Scripture. The apostolic witness cannot be divided into what was preached and what was written down. These are one and the same. The authentic doctrinal tradition of the church in the sense of the New Testament is never anything else than the living transmission of this witness in preaching and instruction. It can never be an independent source of revelation. Authentic apostolic succession, then, is always and only the succession of doctrine. It may be known by its identity with the witness of the apostles in the New Testament. In this way the content of what is proclaimed by any and every church is to be weighed.

There is indeed also a succession of teachers who have faithfully proclaimed the apostolic message. But who these surely are only God knows, just as He alone "knows those who are His," who are truly His church [2 Tim. 2:19]. To set down lists of such succession is an understandable desire. It is a human desire which in the ancient world produced lists of teachers, chains of transmitters of a tradition, in many schools and religions. It was therefore a piece of ancient non-Christian religion that penetrated into the church with the setting up of lists of those who held office and were transmitters of tradition. People sought in human books what is written only in the books of God.

4

The problem with these lists of succession may be illustrated by two examples, touching the Old and the New Testament. How rabbinic Judaism understood the handing down of what was taught in the Old Testament is shown by the chain of tradition with which the Mishna tractate *Pirqe Abot* ("Sayings of the Fathers") begins. "Moses received the Torah from Sinai and transmitted it to Joshua, Joshua to the elders, the elders to the prophets, and the prophets transmitted it to the men of the Great Synagogue." The line then continues through Simon the Just (ca. 300 BC or a century later) to the rabbis of the later period.

---

25 ". . . the unwritten traditions . . . have come down even to us, transmitted as it were from hand to hand . . . ." MH

We need not enter upon the question whether the Great Synagogue ever actually existed or whether it was a fiction developed out of Nehemiah 8–10. It is enough to consider the inclusion of the prophets in the list of those who transmitted the Torah to recognize the fiction. This artificial construction was intended to show the transmission of divine truth through the generations. The history of Old Testament revelation is pressed into a scheme whose origin is not biblical and which cannot be brought into agreement with the biblical record.

Our second example is the understanding of New Testament revelation to be found in 1 Clement. There we read in chapter 42:

> The apostles for our sake were given the Gospel as proclaimed to them by the Lord Jesus Christ. Jesus the Christ was sent from God. Christ, therefore, is from God and the apostles from Christ. . . . When they had received their instructions, having been filled with certainty by the resurrection of our Lord Jesus Christ and strengthened by the Word of God, they went out full of confidence in the Holy Spirit, proclaiming the Gospel that the kingdom of God was about to come. Through the country and the towns they preached, and appointed their firstfruits, after testing them by the Spirit, to be bishops and deacons of those who would believe. Nor was this any new thing. For a long time ago there was mention of bishops and deacons in Scripture. For there is somewhere in Scripture a passage which says, "I will appoint their bishops in righteousness and their deacons in peace."

Where is this written? Nowhere. The author probably had in mind Isa. 60:17, where the Septuagint (literally translated) has: "I will give your rulers (*archontas*) in peace and your overseers (*episkopous*) in righteousness." Do we have here only a lapse of memory, or is it a "spiritual" interpretation of the passage? In that case, though, it should somehow be indicated. As the text stands in 1 Clement it is a spurious quotation.

There is much to ponder in the fact that such a falsification or whatever one may call it (perhaps our norms are not applicable to an earlier time) occurs in the first document of the Roman Church, near the end of the first century. The document sets up as a law that those who bear churchly office are undeposable without evidence against them, and this is imposed upon another church with the demand of obedience [59:1] and the claim to be giving a decision given by the Holy Spirit [63:2]. This was at a time when there was not yet a monarchic episcopate in Rome, let alone a papacy. Clement was one of the bishops in Rome, and we learn from the *Shepherd of Hermas* that he had the responsibility of correspondence with congregations elsewhere [Vis. II, 4, 3]. What he gives out as a binding decision has as its basis a falsification. Where this all leads to we may see in its fruition in the *Donation of Constantine* and the *Pseudo-Isidorian Decretals*.[26] We here observe the first instance of that viewpoint which Cardinal Manning summed up in connection with Vatican I and its undemonstrable and untrue historical assertions about the place of the Roman bishops in the ancient church: "Dogma must prevail over history" [*Vatican Council* (1969), pp. 125ff.].

Quite apart from the problem of the spurious quotation, we have to ask, "What is the meaning of the way history is pictured in Clement?" We find a mixture of truth and fantasy. Revelation does indeed have a chain of succession. The Father sends the Son, the Son the apostles. The apostles hand their commission (*Auftrag*) on to those who bear office (*die Amtsträger*) in the church. That is biblical. "As the Father has sent Me, even so I send you" [John 20:21]. And the commission to proclaim the Gospel to every creature, even to the ends of the earth and until "the close of the age," was in fact given the apostles by their Lord. And of this we are told in Holy Scripture that the apostles appointed officebearers, both to help them and to take their place. Thus Paul put Timothy in office. According to Acts 14:23 Barnabas and Paul "appointed elders" for the mission congregations in southern Asia Minor. This historical fact was then dogmatically simplified in 1 Clement, as also by such writers of the second century as Irenaeus and Tertullian—yes, by the whole church of that time.

There is first the fact that it was not always the Twelve who founded and organized the churches—yes, not even apostles in the real meaning of the word. Indeed the greatest of the ancient churches, Antioch and Rome, were founded by unknown Christians. It is simply historically not the case that Peter and Paul were the *founders* of the church in Rome, as Irenaeus claims at the beginning of his list of Roman bishops. It is further simply not the case that the Office of the Ministry [*das geistliche Amt*] always arose in the same way, namely, by being received from the apostles. The *Didache* (15:1) gives admonition to congregations as to what to do in case there are no wandering apostles, prophets, or teachers among them:

> Elect therefore for yourselves bishops and deacons worthy of the Lord, men mild and not greedy for money, truthful, men who have been tested. They do the same service for you as the prophets and teachers. Therefore do not think less of them, for they are the honorable ones among you, along with the prophets and teachers.

What was always at first manifold is later brought into unified forms. This may be observed from the beginning of the church's history (for instance in the liturgy), and it is the case also with polity. It is the simplifying, dogmatic view which leads to such simplified constructions of history as we saw in Judaism's

---

26 Documents important to the power of the medieval papacy, claiming to be produced by Emperor Constantine and giving the authority of both state and church to the pope. They were recognized as forgeries by the time of the Reformation. See Luther's preface, marginal glosses, and afterword to the *Donation of Constantine* (1537), AE 60:158–84. MH

scheme of succession in the "Sayings of the Fathers" and in its counterpart in what Clement of Rome did for early Christianity.

5

It is well-known how the great struggle against the Gnostic sects, which the church had to carry on in the second century, brought toward victory the idea of the apostolic succession of bishops and thereby created the Catholic office of bishop.[27] From the standpoint of the Reformation we may regret that in this struggle the church was not content to trust its defense to the Rule of Faith (the early form of the Apostles' Creed) and to Holy Scripture. However, we must not forget that it was not so easy to stand by *sola Scriptura* at a time when the canon of the New Testament was not yet in existence and when Holy Scripture was the Old Testament. Our New Testament had not yet emerged from the various writings which claimed to include the genuine apostolic witness. We need to consider what it meant in the year 180 for the martyrs of Scillium in North Africa that they were able to recognize the Pauline Epistles only as worthy documents but not yet as Holy Scripture.[28] At that time it was impossible to draw scriptural proof from the Epistle to the Romans. We must consider this situation of the church in order to understand what weight was then attached to the "apostolic" office of the bishops as guardians of the pure doctrine.

To explore the problem of the oldest succession lists, we turn to the work of Erich Caspar [1879–1935], the great historian of the papacy, whose lifework remained unfinished. From the *Schriften der Königsberger Gelehrten Gesellschaft* (1926) we have his *Die älteste Römische Bischofsliste* ["The Oldest Lists of Roman Bishops"]. Although much has been said in criticism of details of this work, its essential result remains, namely, that the names Irenaeus gives in the list of bishops (*Adv. haer.* 3.3.3) are genuine.

---

27   "We see from the warnings of Ignatius how close together the false teachers and the faithful lived. He described the doctrine and practice of dangerous neighbors. He will not name them; everybody knows them. He warns his readers not to associate with them and not even to speak of them publicly or privately. They are to hold to their bishop. Here the faithful are given a clear direction which is seemingly as convincing as it is simple, but unfortunately it did not work. It did not fulfill what Ignatius and his congregations expected of it. One hundred and fifty years later the bishop of Antioch was the archheretic Paul of Samosata. What would have happened if the Christians at Antioch had followed Ignatius' directive? Another century later we find three, and for a time even four, bishops opposing one another for decades in Antioch. These pronounced one another heterodox or schismatic. All claimed the Antiochene apostolic succession which would make them the legitimate successors of Ignatius. This was the time of the Meletian schism. Every Christian in Antioch who remembered Ignatius' admonition to obey the bishop could not help asking, 'Which one? With which one am I to be in fellowship?'" (Elert, *Eucharist and Church Fellowship*, 49–50). MH

28   Owen, *Some Authentic Acts of the Early Martyrs* (1927), p. 72. NN

As Hegesippus[29] traveled among the churches of the East and the West, he made lists of successions. He operated according to a dogmatic viewpoint which had the false presupposition that one could prove the transmission of the pure doctrine by the succession of the bishops, but his researches have given us highly valuable historical material [Eusebius, *Historia ecclesiastica* 4.22.1–3].

The Roman list which Irenaeus brings up to his time has nothing but authentic names. Its age and authenticity are evidenced by the fact that, in contrast with the current official list of popes, Peter does not appear as the first Roman bishop. Peter and Paul are presented as the founders of the church in Rome. They are said to have committed the episcopate to Linus. The whole following list with its numbering of the third, sixth, and ninth bishops is constructed on the presupposition that Linus was the first bishop, and that Peter and Paul put him in this office. In Rome in the third century Peter and Paul were still always named together as of equal rank.

It is clear from 1 Clement, as also from Ignatius' Epistle to the Romans, that at the beginning of the second century in Rome there was still no monarchic bishop, but rather a college of bishops. It would appear that it was the incursion of the great Gnostic sects into Rome which produced the need for a unified government of the church by one bishop. Pius, the brother of the author of the *Shepherd of Hermas*, seems to have been the first monarchic bishop in the chief city of the world.

Also here the rule proves true that things moved from East to West, not only the Gospel but also church institutions. Already in the Revelation to John we see that toward the end of the first century every church in the East had its own bishop ("To the angel of the church in . . . write . . ."). What then were Linus, Anacletus, Clement, Evaristus, Alexander, Sixtus, [Telesphorus], and Hyginus, who appear in the list prior to Pius? They were, as Harnack already saw, obviously outstanding members of the college of bishops, men who were renowned as teachers of the church. The list, we must judge, indeed has nothing but genuine names, and yet it is an artificial construction, similar to the succession list in the Mishna tractate.

And what was the list intended to prove? Nothing except that in Rome there was a tradition of doctrine, that the apostolic message was faithfully handed on from generation to generation. The point of the list is that there was a succession of teachers and therefore of doctrine. Others could have been named, for all these "bishops" had colleagues associated with them. These names may have been chosen because of the reputation of these men, but a "succession" in a strictly historical sense it was not. Without historical foundation are also the

---

29 Hegesippus was a second-century church historian and, according to Eusebius, a converted Jew. He wrote five books of *Memoirs* against the Gnostics. Only fragments survive. It appears (Eusebius, *HE* 4.22.1–3) that he drew up a "succession list" (*diadochv*) of the early bishops of the church at Rome, which is likely the earliest witness to the names of the first Roman bishops. See *ODCC*, 746. MH

"years of reign" with which they were later supplied. There is no solid evidence for dates until the middle of the [second] century.

6

The greatest difference between the old Roman list of bishops and other lists of bishops, on the one hand, and what is today understood by "apostolic succession," on the other hand, is the following. These lists, such as the official Roman list of popes, and the list of the archbishops of Canterbury or of Cologne, give the names of the incumbents of a particular bishop's seat, one after the other. They do not speak, and do not intend to speak, of a succession of *consecrations*. The incumbent of a bishop's seat is not consecrated by his predecessor. Succession of office must be strictly differentiated from succession of consecration. This latter only gradually began to play a part in the church. Yet today this is the idea of apostolic succession that is so insisted upon: a bishop receives his consecration from another bishop, whose consecration goes back to other bishops, right back to the first bishops who were consecrated by the apostles.

How historical is this succession? In later times it can certainly be demonstrated or accepted with confidence, for after the year 200 the old usage stood firm that a bishop was chosen by the clergy and people of his church but that he could receive consecration only from one or (very soon) several bishops.[30] It also became settled practice that only a bishop could ordain presbyters and deacons [Council of Ancyra, Canon 13], as also that ordination was done with the laying on of hands. But does this tell us that all consecrations go back to the apostles? Timothy was ordained by Paul with the laying on of hands (2 Tim. 1:6). In 1 Timothy 3 and 5 he was given instruction for appointing bishops, deacons, and widows (deaconesses), where the laying on of hands is explicitly mentioned. But were bishops everywhere ordained in this way? How were things done in Rome in Clement's day? We do not know.

The historian may regret a gap in our knowledge of what went on, but for one who believes Scripture to be God's Word there is a deeper meaning in the fact that we nowhere have a mandate of our Lord to carry out an ordination, let alone instructions as to how it should be done. We have the mandate to baptize. We have the mandate to repeat the Lord's Supper, and there is the institution of the Office of the Keys. This last, we do well to note, in threefold form: Matthew 16 to Peter, Matthew 18 to the assembled congregation, and John 20 to the Twelve (more precisely the disciples who were gathered on the evening of Easter Day). But no one has been able to show when Jesus ordained the Twelve. The Catholic churches have to resort to the command to repeat the Lord's Supper. With the words "This do in remembrance of Me" Jesus is said to have ordained the apostles to be priests.

---

30 A presbyter might consecrate a bishop (*Canons of Hippolytus* 2.10). NN

It cannot be without significance that we hear of no laying on of hands. Jesus laid His hands on children and on the sick, but not on the Twelve. Where we might most expect it, when He gives them the Office of the Keys, there at John 20:21ff. we read: "Jesus said to them again, 'Peace be with you. As the Father has sent Me, even so I send you.' And when He had said this, He breathed on them, and said to them, 'Receive the Holy Spirit . . .'" One almost gets the impression that here, as whenever He sent out the apostles, Jesus intentionally avoided the laying on of hands. Such an avoidance may have been due to the fact that ordination by laying on of hands was rabbinical usage. That is how a rabbi ordained his disciples. Pondering what Jesus said against the scribes in Matthew 23 may suggest why Jesus did not follow their usage. Does He not say that among those that are His the title "rabbi" is not to be used, "for you have one Teacher (*didaskalos*), and you are all brethren" (v. 8)?

This did not prevent the title "teacher" from being used in the church for the great office of expounding Holy Scripture, at first the Old Testament. This office, along with that of the apostles and prophets, was foundational in the beginnings of the church, recognized not only in a particular congregation but throughout the church. And, after all, the title "teacher" was not directly prohibited by the words of our Lord. (Cf. also "master" (*kathēgētēs*, v. 10.)

However that may have been, it was certainly bad that, under the pressure of age-old Eastern custom, and against the express will of Jesus, the church again took up the title "father" in place of "teacher" and first of all addressed the bishop thus (*pappas, papa,* cf. *abbas* in monasticism). (Cyprian of Carthage was still addressed thus; today the title is restricted to the bishop of Rome and the patriarch of Alexandria.)

The suggestion that Jesus was acting in deliberate contrast and opposition to the rabbis when He avoided the laying on of hands in what we might call ordination is strengthened by the noteworthy fact that the rabbis no longer followed the usage of the laying on of hands when in the second century it had become a characteristic of Christian ordination. So the laying on of hands is an early usage in the church (Heb. 6:2), with an Old Testament background (Moses laid his hands on Joshua, Deut. 34:9; cf. Num. 27:18), but it cannot be said to be something that Christ commanded us to do, let alone be called a sacrament. It was a way of bestowing a blessing, and that it certainly did.

It is also clearly not something that was reserved to the holder of a particular office. Beside the laying on of hands done by the apostles was also that done by the elders. Elders were men of special standing, not incumbents of a specific office. Thus it was in the synagogue, in the church of Jerusalem, in the Pauline congregations, and still so in Rome at the time of Clement. Elders were elected by the congregation as "honored ones," as *prōtokathedritai* ("having the first seats"), as they are still called in the *Shepherd of Hermas* [Vis. III, 9, 7; cf. 1 Clement 1:3; 21:6]. Because of their age, because of what they had done for the congregation, or for some other reason, they occupied the first places in the Divine Service. They represented the congregation. From among them the bishops were chosen, the group of officers who led the congregation, in particular to perform the office of preaching the Word or of saying the liturgical prayers, especially during the Eucharist. They did what was otherwise reserved to the prophets. Elders who then also performed such offices were to be "considered worthy of double honor, especially those who labor in preaching and teaching." What is said in 1 Tim. 5:17 matches perfectly what is said of the situation in Rome in 1 Clement. The elders as representatives of the congregation participated in the ordination of Timothy. They laid their hands on him (1 Tim. 4:14), as also did the apostle [2 Tim. 1:6].

How free was the usage of the laying on of hands in the early church we may see from the noteworthy passage Acts 13:1–3, where the church ordains an apostle. Here in Antioch we find prophets and teachers officiating, among them Barnabas (from the sound of the words, a prophet) and Paul (the schooled scribe) as "teacher," that is, as one who expounds the Scriptures. During the liturgy the Holy Spirit by way of prophetic statement (as in the case of Timothy) instructs them to send out Barnabas and Paul on a special mission. "Then after fasting and praying they laid their hands on them and sent them off" (v. 3). In the early church there are more examples of a teacher becoming a missionary. There was Pantaenus,[31] who gave up the office of teacher in Alexandria in order to go as a missionary to "India" [Eusebius, *Historia ecclesiastica* 5.10.2].

Who laid on hands here? The congregation, perhaps through its elders. I have never been able to understand how learned Catholics, such as Tixeront in his well-known work on ordination [*Holy Orders* (1928), p. 142] can read Acts 13:3 in such a way that the laying on of hands by the congregation could be taken as little more than a sort of godspeed for a good journey. The problem here is that the later Roman Catholic idea of ordination is being read back into a time when it had not as yet developed, or to say the least, into a time when there was greater diversity of forms in the life of the church. One has only to study such forms as they have survived on the fringes of ancient Christianity, in Ethiopia or in old Ireland, to see how at the beginning there was always diversity, which under the influence of the great metropolitan centers was reduced to unified forms.

7

What emerges from the foregoing? Here so much could only be pointed to, and yet what help have we found for dealing with the problem of the "apostolic succession" today? From a doctrinal point of view it can only be seen as a soap bubble, on which no church can be built. The Roman Church has the wisdom to put the whole matter in its doctrine of the priesthood. Rome knows that

---

31   Pantaenus (d. ca. 190) is described by Eusebius as head of the catechetical school of Alexandria and one of the teachers of Clement. A convert from Stoicism, Eusebius states that Pantaenus preached the Gospel in India. See *ODCC*, 1215. MH

apostolic succession, in the double sense of a sequence of bishops and a succession of consecrations, has never guaranteed what the ancient church wished to have guaranteed, namely, purity of doctrine, the apostolicity of the church. Rome also knows how many bishops, consecrated with every proper rite, have fallen away in persecutions or into heresy. The church in the East knows this too.

Bishop Lilje, then, is crashing through open doors when he charges that it is heresy to affirm that the apostolic succession guarantees pure doctrine. Rome does not affirm this. For Rome the purity of the doctrine, the apostolicity of the church, is guaranteed by the office of Christ's infallible vicar as successor of the "Prince of the Apostles." The significance of the succession of consecrations/ordinations for Rome is simply and only that which is expressed in the liturgy of ordination to the priesthood: the power to offer the sacrifice of the Mass for the living and the dead (*potestas ordinis*) and the power of the Office of the Keys (*potestas iurisdictionis*).[32] The silken thread upon which the Roman doctrine of office hangs is the notion that when our Lord said, "Do this in remembrance of Me," He wanted to ordain the apostles to be priests. If these words are to be understood differently, namely, in the sense that the Twelve here as in other passages are the representatives of God's people as a whole, then the entire special priesthood simply collapses. The New Testament knows that in the new covenant there is only one high priest, Jesus Christ, and the priestly people of God, whose members are kings and priests.

If the reformers—indeed, also the fathers of the Reformed churches, including the Anglican—saw one thing clearly, it is that it is quite untenable to hold this interpretation of our Lord's bidding that His Supper be repeated. In addition Matt. 18:18 makes it clear that the Keys are not the sole prerogative of the clergy. Evidence of their belonging to the whole church may be found in the early church and for a long time thereafter. There is the lovely story related by Melanchthon in the Treatise on the Power and Primacy of the Pope (67f.), ascribed to Augustine and to be found also in Gratian's *Decretum*, where it appears as an illustration for a point of canon law.[33] Two shipwrecked Christians were together in a boat. One was a catechumen. Him the other baptized, and then by him was absolved. The view of the Lutheran Confessions that the Keys have been given to the whole church is in harmony with Scripture and the ancient church.

If one accepts the Roman view, then the apostolic succession makes some sense: the power to make the sacrifice of the Mass and the power to absolve is

---

32 "Ecclesial communities derived from the Reformation and separated from the Catholic Church, 'have not preserved the proper reality of the Eucharistic mystery in its fullness, especially because of the absence of the sacrament of Holy Orders.'... '[W]hen they commemorate the Lord's death and resurrection in the Holy Supper... profess that it signifies life in communion with Christ and await his coming in glory'" (*Catechism of the Catholic Church* [1997], § 1400, p. 392). MH

33 *Decr. Grat.* P. III D. 4 c. 36 as a letter of Augustine to Fortunatus. The Latin is available in *BSLK* (1998), 491 n. 2. MH

bestowed. If one does not accept this view, then there is no apostolic succession. Leo XIII was then quite right in declaring Anglican orders to be null and void because their form, that is, the words of ordination, was invalid and because the right intention was lacking.

The words of ordination of the Anglican ritual are indeed ambiguous. One must probably be an Anglican in order not to see that they are therefore impossible.

> Receive the Holy Ghost for the office and work of a priest in the Church of God, now committed unto thee by the imposition of our hands. Whose sins thou dost forgive, they are forgiven; and whose sins thou dost retain, they are retained. And be thou a faithful dispenser of the Word of God, and of his holy sacraments.

These words can mean ordination to the Gospel office of proclaiming the Word and administering the sacraments. "Priest" then means presbyter, in the general sense which was the usage for a long time in North Germany and is still the usage in Scandinavia, where the parson is called "priest." This is the way the formula is understood by evangelically minded Anglicans. Among the High Church and Anglo-Catholics, however, "priest" means *sacerdos*, one who offers sacrifice at the consecration in Holy Communion. As to right intention, what the ordaining bishop may be thinking he is doing is left up to him. This is also the case with what is meant by the formula for consecrating a bishop, whose office is said to be "the office and work of a bishop in the Church of God." What is essential to this office is not said.

This way of doing things is characteristic of Anglicanism. We may look for its roots in the character of the English people, as well as in the inexpressibly sad story of the English Reformation, which was at first an event of national politics rather than a religious event. This is not to deny all that has been and is great in this church; there is much for us Lutherans to learn from it. Its "apostolic succession" we cannot, however, acknowledge; it is an empty form.

For us there are different grounds than those of Rome for rejecting Anglican "apostolic succession." For us the matter is not decided by whether the consecrating of Archbishop [Matthew] Parker[34] [in 1559] was adequately done: Two bishops with Roman Catholic consecration (but without office), plus two Reformed bishops participated. This is also not the direction of the Roman arguments against the validity of Anglican orders. As we have seen, these attach to the faulty formula of ordination and the lack of the intention to make the one ordained into a priest in the Roman Catholic sense. Against these considerations the laying on of hands, be it ever so canonical, is of no avail. When our

---

34 Matthew Parker (1504–75) was archbishop of Canterbury. Treated well under the reign of Henry VIII and Edward VI (r. 1547–53), he went into obscurity during Mary's reestablishment of the Roman Church in England. Under Elizabeth I, Parker's fortunes again changed when she chose him for the vacant archbishopric of Canterbury. See *ODCC*, 1222. MH

Anglican friends would make us in our "less fully organized churches" into successors of the apostles by their laying on of hands, we will have to teach them that the genuine succession of the apostles is that which lives by the pure proclamation of the Gospel and celebration of the Sacraments, and not by the myth of an unbroken chain of consecrations going all the way back to the apostles.

8

Not to see this clearly is for Lutherans a grievous failure. Of the offered "apostolic succession," we must ask what is its nature and what are the consequences of accepting such an ecclesiastical myth. The sooner the answers, the better. We may recall the answer given by Archbishop Söderblom at the World Conference for Faith and Order at Lausanne in 1927. Whatever else may be said of his limitations, it was surely a piece of his Lutheran heritage which came to sober expression when he said that the Church of Sweden has preserved the apostolic succession together with other things inherited from the ancient church, but that such a succession is according to Lutheran doctrine an adiaphoron. This he did quite unforgettably. He threw aside the printed text of what he had intended to say, for he felt compelled to speak even more clearly.[35] For that all Lutherans were grateful.

If one looks more closely at the Swedish succession, it is really much better than the Anglican one. The critical link was a man who had just been consecrated by the pope himself in Rome, or, as Luther might say, the succession was received directly from the Roman Antichrist. But just this circumstance shows what nonsense it is to regard succession as more than time-honored custom and to consider it as theologically necessary or important. As an old ecclesiastical form, as an adiaphoron, it can be borne with that humor with which Söderblom carried his bishop's staff. Once, during a visitation, he realized that he had forgotten to pack it. It was quickly replaced by one cut from a birch tree. Is it possible for a Swedish Lutheran seriously to suppose that a pope who rejected the doctrine of the Lutheran Reformation as heresy could be the one to guarantee that the Church of Sweden has indeed true bishops and pastors?

Yet even there the old, healthy view of succession, the view in harmony with the Lutheran Confessions, seems to be losing ground in influential circles. In the official statement about itself in the handbook of the Lutheran World Federation, *The Lutheran Churches of the World*, ed. A. R. Wentz (1952), p. 171, we read that the Church of Sweden accepted the Unaltered Augsburg Confession in 1593 and that since 1686 the Book of Concord is the church's confession. Then on p. 174 we read: "Sweden's apostolic succession has opened the way for intercommunion with the Church of England," an intercommunion that has meanwhile been raised by both parties to the level of church law.

---

35 Sasse was present at Lausanne. MH

About the consequences of all this for Lutheranism around the world more than enough has already been said in these letters. We can only ask why others did not raise their voices while there was still time. Where was the voice of the bishops of Norway and of Denmark? Where was the voice of the Lutheran churches of Germany and of America? Where was the voice of the Lutheran missions? They looked on complacently when Lutheran bishops were consecrated with the assistance of Anglican bishops and archbishops. They were silent when it was up to them to raise their voices in warning; they owed this brotherly service to the Lutheran churches of the world. The old Archbishop Johansson of Finland was the first to see where this path would lead. His voice died away unheard.

We all reassured ourselves at first with the fact that the "apostolic succession" is an adiaphoron—and that it is, if it is understood in the Lutheran manner as simply a form from the ancient church. But there comes a time when an adiaphoron ceases to be an adiaphoron. This is said with all necessary clarity in Article X of the Formula of Concord. This article was a beacon and banner for us in the church struggle in Germany, and we were privileged to experience that it is still a weapon with which one can fight for the church of God. "In a case of confession or scandal nothing is an adiaphoron." Where the pure doctrine of the Gospel is at stake, there toleration of adiaphora ceases. There it is the duty of "the entire community of God . . . and especially the ministers of the Word as the leaders of the community . . . to confess openly, not only by words but also through their deeds and actions . . ." (FC SD X 10).

We are not in a position to tell the Lutherans in Sweden who hold to the old heritage of their church (it is a truly great heritage) what they should do in order to preserve the pure Gospel of justification by faith alone and the pure administration of the Sacraments, to which pure proclamation about the Sacraments also belongs. We can pray for them. What we cannot do is acknowledge the Church of Sweden as a church of the Unaltered Augsburg Confession when it has altar fellowship with Anglicans and has Anglican bishops who reject "by faith alone" participate in the consecration of Swedish bishops. The same must be said of other Lutheran churches when they put themselves into a similar situation.

Here the Lutheran World Federation would have a great task, the task of saying clearly what the Lutheran Confessions still mean for our day and wherein the true unity of the church resides. But can we expect anything else from it than that it simply offers justification for what has already been happening? Can we expect that it will commit suicide? It is at the outset committed to the principle that churches which are in church fellowship with the Reformed and the Anglicans are to be recognized as churches of the Unaltered Augsburg Confession, despite the latter's Articles VII and X, not to speak of the Formula of Concord.

The witness of the Lutheran Confessions will then have to be heard outside the Lutheran World Federation. May this happen only in humility and love! However conscious we may be of our poverty and weakness, this is the great service that is ours to do for those who have lost the confession of the Lutheran Reformation or are in danger of losing it. It is the task of those whose ordination to the Lutheran ministry gave them the authentic apostolic succession. This is no mysterious something that rests on a myth of consecrations. Rather, it consists in the clear commission which our Lord gave to His whole church, to proclaim the pure apostolic doctrine and administer the Sacraments according to the Gospel.

That is the great responsibility which today is given to the Lutheran pastor. It cannot be taken from him by any bishop, any church government, or any ecumenical organization. We may and can confess, also if those remain silent who are in the first instance called to do this. In faithful confession lives the whole glory of our office, even when this glory is hidden under the cross.

ᑐᑐ

In the bond of the faith and the ministry, I greet you,

Your
Hermann Sasse

Historical Context

"We have to beware of liturgical experiments, both the serious and the silly." Sasse's advice is significant when churches are tempted with the silly (worship as entertainment) and the serious (incorporating rites which popped up somewhere in the ancient church but which are foreign to Lutheranism). In the mid-twentieth century, the liturgical movement was an ecumenical force. In that context Sasse takes the opportunity to elucidate the Lutheran view of the Sacraments in the context of worship, over against ancient Augustinian problems and modern equivocations on both the essence and effect of the Word and Sacraments. MH

July 24, 1956

Prof. H. Sasse
41 Buxton Street
North Adelaide, South Australia

Dear and Reverend Behnken,

During the next weeks I shall be unable to attend to my correspondence due to the fact that we have to shift into another house, about a mile from here. This means a lot of work, since my wife's health is not as it ought to be. Everything must be done slowly, especially since our boys are preparing for their degrees. So I am writing to you in view of your forthcoming visit.

... Our "Theses of Agreement" are partly made by men who are now dead, and the younger generation takes them only as a means to practical ends without taking their content as seriously as they were taken when they were drafted. It is a similar development as that which has taken place in the ALC. The younger generation no longer realizes what unionism is .... The last words which my old colleague Karl Mützelfeld [1881–1955] spoke to me, suddenly awakening from a state of coma, were: "Sie sind zu spät nach Australia gekommen, Bruder Sasse" ["You came to Australia too late, Brother Sasse"]. Perhaps he was right. I tell you this in order that you might have my view of the situation before your arrival ....

With best regards from my family,

Yours sincerely,
H. Sasse

forty-two

Word and Sacrament, Preaching and Lord's Supper

TRANSLATED BY NORMAN NAGEL

Beginning of July 1956[1]

Professor Dr. Theol. Hermann Sasse
41 Buxton Street
North Adelaide, South Australia

Dear Brothers in the Office!

There is probably no question that leads so deeply into our office, its essence and its task, its necessity and its promise, as our present subject. Whenever theology becomes quite practical, it engages this problem. The profoundest Christian thinkers have pondered it, and it has affected all the churches of the world, the "Catholic" no less than the "Protestant." It is a problem not only for Protestantism or for Lutheranism in particular. The Catholic churches of the East and West also have their problems with preaching and the Lord's Supper. The Eastern Orthodox Church, for example, which has gained a firm foothold in the West because of the massive migration of Orthodox Christians from Eastern

---

1   *BLP* 42: *Wort und Sakrament, Predigt und Hl. Abendmahl* (North Adelaide, July 1956). The original was published in *LuBl* 8, no. 49 (August 1956): 103–24. Reprinted in *ISC* 1:73–90. This English translation appeared originally in *We Confess: The Sacraments* (St. Louis: Concordia, 1985), 11–35. Minor alterations to grammar and capitalization have been made. Scripture quotations in this essay are from the Revised Standard Version of the Bible, copyright 1952, © 1971 by the Division of Christian Education of the National Council of the Churches of Christ in the United States of America. Used by permission. All rights reserved. The quotations from the Lutheran Confessions in this publication are from The BOOK OF CONCORD: THE CONFESSIONS OF THE EVANGELICAL LUTHERAN CHURCH, edited by Theodore G. Tappert, published in 1959 by Fortress Press. Huss number 321. MH

countries, cannot be satisfied with continuing to celebrate its "Holy Liturgy" in the liturgical languages when it is no longer understood by the younger generation. They have to make use of their principle that the liturgy be celebrated in the language of the people. So an English translation has already been completed. But the liturgy must also be explained. Can the Eastern Church ever forget that its greatest preacher was John Chrysostom and that it is not enough to venerate his icon—that his example must also be followed?

Similar questions arise for Roman Catholicism, as the liturgical movement indicates. It was born before the First World War out of a deep dissatisfaction on the part of the best young Catholics with the situation in their church. After 1918 it pointed out the shortcomings of the common Catholic worship so candidly that it had to be curbed and in part shut down by Rome. But the Curia had absorbed its great desire to elevate the major European languages to the position of liturgical languages with such vigor that we can still expect a major reform of the Roman liturgy in this century.

Is it a coincidence that the liturgical movement in Germany and other countries went hand in hand with a "Bible movement" and that the modern Roman church has produced masterpieces of biblical translation? Is it a coincidence that the Roman church in the age of radio and television has again produced popular preaching that recalls the classical period of popular preaching in the Middle Ages?

But the encouragement of Bible reading and the special popular preaching are no substitute for the every Sunday parish sermon, especially if the latter is only a short lecture on a question of dogmatics or ethics. Truly, the problem of "Word and Sacrament, Preaching and the Lord's Supper" is not only our problem but that of all Christendom. Strictly speaking, it has been a problem throughout the history of the church, ever since Paul had to deal with the problems of the Lord's Supper (1 Corinthians 10 and 11) and preaching (1 Corinthians 14) in the church at Corinth.

1

Old as the problem of Word and Sacrament is, it was first put as a theological question and given a theological answer by Augustine. Here, as in other matters, this great church father of the West is not always helpful, and we may not follow him as blindly as did the theology not only of the Catholicism of the Middle Ages but also of the Reformation. This can even be said of Luther himself, though he was able to break through the constructions of Augustine's sacramental doctrine at decisive points by bringing to light the witness of Scripture, a witness that was better maintained by the Eastern fathers. Since we have been reared in Augustine's sacramental teaching and even see Luther's teaching on the Sacrament through Augustinian spectacles, it is not easy. But should we just leave it to Roman Catholic theologians to recover something of the rich resources of the Greek fathers, who have such a great role to play in the Catalog of Testimonies at the conclusion of the Formula of Concord (*BSLK*, 6th ed. [Göttingen, 1967], 1101–35) as witnesses of scriptural truth, just as they frequently appear also in the earlier Confessions?

Wherein lies the weakness of Augustine's sacramental doctrine? This may first of all be found in his attempt to establish *sacramentum* as a universal idea or category that applies to all religions [*Contra Faustum* 19.11]. The Christian sacrament is then only a specific instance of a universal phenomenon common to all religions, both the true and the false. Now it is true that the Christian sacraments, such as Baptism and the Lord's Supper, have their parallels in many religions, as the apologists of the second century, and even Paul in 1 Cor. 10:18–21, have observed. No one denies that heathen rites and the myths they follow have echoes of the original knowledge of God, but through sin they have been perverted into the service of idols [Rom. 1:19–23]. In this sense, even the human sacrifices of the Teutons, the Aztecs, and the Syrians could be regarded as demonically perverted hints pointing to the sacrifice of the Son of Man. "Every dogma is as old as the world."

But to try to understand the Christian Sacrament on the basis of a concept of sacrament derived from the history of religions is totally impossible. What constitutes the church's Sacrament is something unique; it has no parallels. All the honor and love we owe Augustine as a great father of the Western Church may not obscure the fact that he had lived too long and too deeply in heathen religion and philosophy. He was unable to banish the old man from his thinking in the same way that he was from his life and faith. That is what it cost him to have "loved so late."

We may find something similar in what Augustine taught on Holy Scripture. Here also he has a universal idea or category of what "divine scripture" is and must be. This he applies to the Bible and shows how it matches his ideal instead of simply starting with what Holy Scripture has to say about itself. Had he done this, he would not have been able to put the Sibylline Oracles on a level with the prophets because they apparently correctly prophesied the coming of the Redeemer [*De civitate* 18.23]. As the Bible is not just a specific instance of what may be called "divine scripture" in the religions of the world, so also the Christian Sacrament cannot be understood from a universal idea of *sacramentum*. The Christian sacrament is what it is because it was instituted by Jesus Christ and so is inextricably bound up with the incarnation of the eternal Son of God.

The theological tradition of the West has shown a remarkable stability through the Middle Ages into modern Catholicism. The same may be said of Lutheran and Reformed theology in the Reformation and through the period of orthodoxy. In doing theology, we simply may not spare ourselves the labor of differentiating between what the Bible says and the human mode of thinking. This is so even for so central a doctrine of the Christian faith as the doctrine of the Trinity. With the East one can think of it as three in one [*Dreieinigkeit*], with

Augustine and the West as threefold [*Dreifaltigkeit*], without in any way diminishing the truth of the impenetrable mystery.

It was one of the mistakes of our fathers in the age of orthodoxy that they all too often identified the thought form with the biblical content of a doctrinal statement. As a result they unconsciously and unintentionally clothed the eternal truth of Scripture in the transitory garb of a theological tradition. It should not be necessary to point out that this observation has nothing to do with the attempt of the Ritschlian School, above all of Harnack in his *History of Dogma*, to rob Christian dogma of its biblical content by replacing what were taken to be the categories of Greek metaphysics with those of Kantian ethics. Nor does it have anything to do with the modern "demythologizing" of the New Testament by translating the biblical statements into existential philosophy. What we have in mind here is what Luther did when he confronted the falsification of the biblical faith by Aristotelian and Thomistic philosophy and when he told the Swiss, who so energetically appealed to Augustinian metaphysics in the Marburg Colloquy, where the limit of the authority of the church fathers is:

> We would indeed show the beloved fathers such honor that we read what they have written, which is so helpful to us, with the best understanding of which we are capable, insofar as they are in harmony with Holy Scripture. But where their writings are not in harmony with Holy Scripture, it is much better that we say they are mistaken than that because of them we depart from God's Word. (According to Osiander's report, which is confirmed by the reports of others, that Luther appealed to Augustine's own rule, according to which only the canonical books of Scripture have unqualified authority; see the texts, WA 30/3:144–45, and W. Köhler, *Das Marburger Religionsgespräch: Versuch einer Rekonstruktion*, where several sources are cited on p. 177.)

It would have been better for the Lutheran Church if its theologians had always held to this rule in more rigorous self-criticism.

The practical consequence of the foregoing is that we must claim our freedom from the Augustinian school's universal idea of the *sacramentum*, as our Confessions essentially do when they do not first set down a definition of the nature of a sacrament and even leave the question of the number of sacraments open, in contrast with Rome (not more and not less than seven) and the Reformed Church (not more and not less than two). The way of the Confessions is in harmony with teaching of the early church, which was innocent of any such idea of sacrament. They spoke of particular "mysteries," using the word *mystery* quite broadly. In the eleventh century the Latin *sacramentum* was still being used so broadly that Hugh of St. Victor,[2] besides his other dogmatic works, wrote a dogmatics with the title *De sacramentis*, in which even the Trinity is

---

2   Little is known of Hugh of St. Victor (d. 1142) beyond his entry into St. Victor, the house of Augustinian Canons founded in Paris by William of Champeaux (ca. 1070–1122). According to one account, Hugh came from Saxony. See *ODCC*, 800. MH

called a *sacramentum*, that is, a mystery, something known only to faith. The classical dogmatician of the Eastern Church, John of Damascus, also knows no doctrine of the sacraments as such. He has chapters on "The Faith and Baptism" and on "The Holy Spotless Mysteries of the Lord," that is, the Eucharist [*De Fide* 4.9.13]. In harmony with this, when Luther uses the word *Sacrament* in the singular, he usually means "the Sacrament of sacraments," as the Sacrament of the Altar was first called by the fathers of the Greek church. There is an echo of this Lutheran usage in Justus Jonas's German text of the Apology when he renders Melanchthon's *eadem sacramenta* as "the same Baptism and Sacrament" (Ap VII–VIII 10). In this way also the Lutheran Church retained the freedom to call absolution a sacrament. Whether the Office of the Keys is called a sacrament or not is purely a matter of terminology, in which the church has and must have complete freedom if it wants to remain on the foundation of Scripture. Christ did not institute some abstract *sacramentum*. He instituted the Office of the Ministry, Baptism, Holy Communion, and the Office of the Keys. Only if we regain this freedom of the Lutheran Reformation will we be able to go all the way to the heart of what is uniquely referred to by the term "sacrament," whose essence is not to be found in any phenomena from the history of religions or in any human speculation about what God must do to redeem us. It is in the institution of the Lord that eludes every human why and in the incomprehensible wonder of the incarnation. If we take that seriously, then the problem of Word and Sacrament takes on a completely different appearance.

2

Augustine has left behind another difficult question for all the churches of the West in his definition of a sacrament as the "sign" [*signum*] of a divine "thing" [*res*].[3] What we have here must first be recognized as a man's theological theory. It is quite noteworthy that the Eastern Church, which here, as always, represents an older form of Christianity, developed no such theory of sacrament as a sign of something divine. In the late Middle Ages and the century of the Reformation (Cyril Lucarius and his Calvinism),[4] the Latin Scholastic doctrine, and with it the doctrine of sacrament as sign, did gain some entry into Eastern theology, but this private teaching today enjoys hardly any recognition, least of all by the Russian theologians. To be sure the sacraments (mysteries) are spoken of as symbols, as "the outward means of the unfathomable, hiddenly laden working of grace by the Holy Spirit through which the sanctification of man is again

---

3   "Signacula quidem rerum divinarum esse: visibilia, sed res ipsas invisibiles in ies" (*De Cat. Rud.* 26.50; *Contra Faustum* 19.11). "Ista, fratres, ideo dicuntur sacramenta, quia in eis aliud videtur, aliud intelligitur" (*Serm.* 272; *Ep.* 138.17). "Aliud est sacramentum, aliud viruls sacramenti" (*In Joh. Tract.* 26.11). NN

4   As patriarch of Constantinople, Cyril Lucaris (1572–1638) essentially adopted the doctrines of Calvinism. He was condemned by several Orthodox synods. MH

brought to completion" (Stef. Zankov, *Das Orthodoxe Christentum* [1928], 102).[5]
What is characteristic, however, is that even Dionysius the Areopagite sees what
is termed sign and symbol more in the details of the celebration of the sacrament, the particular rites and ceremonies, the gestures and actions of the priest,
than in the sacraments as such. That is also to be understood when he speaks of
the Eucharist in the plural: "the mysteries."

Thomas [Aquinas] understands Augustine's definition of sacrament as a
sign in such a way that it is spoken of as an effective sign (*signum efficax*). This
is applied only to sacraments in the New Testament; the "sacraments" of the
Old Testament have only a significative meaning. In the Eastern Church what
is central is what they do. God works on man in a sacrament. "A Mystery or
Sacrament is a holy act through which grace, or, in other words, the saving power
of God, works mysteriously upon man." So Philaret[6] in the *Christian Catechism*
[284]. In such a doctrine of sacrament it can never come to that tearing apart of
"sign" and "thing," *signum* and *res*, that since Berengar [ca. 998–1088], Wycliffe
[1320–84], the radical Hussites, the *Devotio Moderna*[7] in the Netherlands, the
humanists, Zwingli, and Calvin has reduced sacrament to being only a *sign* of
grace. This is probably not what Augustine had in mind. There are two levels in
his sacramental doctrine—one, as presented in the liturgy, catholic realistic, the
other spiritualizing. This split is the tribute he pays to Neoplatonic philosophy
and is a burden that the churches in the West bear to this day. We in no way
want to glorify the teaching of the Eastern Church here or excuse its serious
errors, but on this one point it stands nearer to the New Testament than what
Augustine and those who followed him taught. *The New Testament does not know
of the idea of sacrament as sign.* Perhaps the whole idea of sign originated in the
designation of circumcision as a "sign of the covenant" [*signum foederis*] (Gen.
17:11). But despite the parallel drawn in Col. 1:11ff. between Baptism and circumcision—Paul was addressing Gnostics with a Jewish background—no one
has ever found a place in the New Testament in which Baptism or the Lord's
Supper or even the "elements" of water, bread, and wine are understood in the
sense of the "sign" theory. None of the words that could be interpreted as such
a "sign," such as *eikōn* ("image"), are used of Baptism or the Lord's Supper in
the New Testament. Nowhere is it written that Baptism is an image or a sign
of regeneration. It *is* the washing of regeneration (Titus 3:5). "We *were* buried

---

5   Cf. *The Eastern Orthodox Church* (1929), 113. NN

6   Philaret (Vasili Mikhailovich Dorzdov, 1782–1867) was born near Moscow and
     became a monk in 1808. He was a professor at St. Petersburg (1808), a member of
     the Holy Synod (1818), bishop of Jaroslav (1820), archbishop of Moscow (1821), and
     metropolitan of Moscow (1825) (s.v. *Christian Cyclopedia*). MH

7   The term for the revival and deepening spiritual life which from the end of the four-
     teenth century spread from the Netherlands to parts of Germany, France, and Italy. It
     found its classic spiritual expression in Thomas a Kempis's (ca. 1380–1471) *Imitation
     of Christ*. It placed great emphasis on inner life and methodological devotion. See
     ODCC, 475. MH

therefore with Him by Baptism into death" (Rom. 6:4). "You *were* buried with Him in Baptism, in which you *were* also raised. . . . And you . . . God *made* alive together with Him" (Col. 2:12–13). Also the word *tupos* in the sense of model or image is not used of Baptism and the Lord's Supper or of their elements. There are "types" of the sacraments in the Old Testament, as when Paul in 1 Cor. 10:1ff., where we find Baptism and the Lord's Supper arranged together for the first time in the New Testament (cf. 12:13; John 19:34), points to certain experiences of the old people of God as "typological" [*tupikōs*] (1 Cor. 10:11, which the Vulgate accurately translates *in figura* [Tertullian, *figurate* (*Idol.* 5)]) of the sacraments of the new people of God. So the "baptism" of the fathers in the cloud and in the sea, the "spiritual food" of the manna, the bread from heaven (cf. John 6:31ff.), and the "spiritual drink" of the water from the rock are types, prefigurements, of Christian Baptism and the Lord's Supper. But Baptism and the Lord's Supper are not "types," not prefigurements or parables. They do indeed point to the future, but it is a future already present with its gifts of grace. More will be said later on what it means that the future is present in the sacraments.

Here is where we find the heart of the Lutheran confession of the sacraments. Certainly Luther made much use, especially in his early period, of Augustine's idea of sacrament as a "sign." Here as in other patterns of theological thought he was bound by the theological schooling from which he came. We should not overlook the fact that until 1522 he had to carry on the struggle against Rome for the *sola fide* also in regard to sacrament according to the old formula: *Non sacramentum, sed fides sacramenti justificat* ("Not the sacrament, but the faith of the one receiving the sacrament justifies").[8] To that Luther always clung, with special emphasis at the point where he had to join the "through faith alone" in Baptism with the objectivity of the sacrament. "My faith does not constitute Baptism but receives it." This is from the Large Catechism, where Luther is defending the Baptism of infants (LC IV 53); it is sure for them too. If the unqualified adherence to the *sola fide* is one side of the sacramental teaching of Luther and the Lutheran Church, the other is the insistence on the objectivity and reality of the sacrament, which was necessary over against the Enthusiasts. How serious this was for Luther is shown by the fact that he went beyond Thomas in his insistence on objectivity. Thomas stated, "An adult who lacked the intention [*intentio*] of receiving Baptism should be rebaptized [*esset rebaptizandus*]" in order to receive Baptism validly and without question. But if the lack of intention is not certain, in case of doubt it should be conditional (*Summa theol.* 3.68.7.3). Luther regarded the Baptism of a Jew who "should come today deceitfully and with an evil purpose" as a true Baptism (LC IV 54), which under no circumstances is it to be repeated if the sinner should come to faith. This objectivity of the sacrament was settled for the reformer from the very beginning, just as he always held

---

8   See *De captivitate Babylonica ecclesiae praeludium* (1520), Aland 120, WA 6:466.26f. (cf. AE 36:66). MH

fast to the real presence, even when he finally gave up transubstantiation in *The Babylonian Captivity*.[9]

But the more he had to urge the objectivity of the sacrament against the "Sacramentarians," the more cautious he became in using the word *sign*. They were misusing it in a way that made of sacrament only a sign. In the catechism he avoids the word *sign*, and we need only look at the Heidelberg Catechism[10] to understand what that means. Here the sacraments (Question 66) are understood only as "signs and seals" [*Wahrzeichen und Siegel*], and no other effect is ascribed to them than of reminding believers of the actual salvation event and assuring them of it. This actual event is independent of the sacrament. Question 72 asks, "Is the outward washing with water itself actually the washing away of sins?" to which the answer is given: "No, for only the blood of Jesus Christ and the Holy Spirit cleanse us from all sin." The following question, why the Holy Spirit calls Baptism the washing of regeneration and the washing away of sins, is given the answer that He wants to teach us "that *just as* the filthiness of the body is taken away, so are our sins taken away by the blood and Spirit of Christ" and "that He wants to assure us through this divine *pledge* and *sign* [*Pfand und Wahrzeichen*] that we just as truly have been washed of our sins spiritually as we are washed with physical water." In the Lord's Supper bread and cup are "*signs* [*Wahrzeichen*] of the body and blood of Christ" (Q. 75). Only "according to the nature and usage of sacraments" is the bread called the body of Christ (Q. 78). The bread *is not* the body, and so the body and blood of the Lord are not taken orally (Q. 76 and 77).

Under the pressure of such spiritualizing Luther more and more stepped back from the conventional word *sign* and also *pledge* [*pignus*], which was much beloved in the theology of the Middle Ages and had meant much to him in his early years. He was profoundly aware that sacrament has another side, the "external thing," which the Enthusiasts scorned (LC IV 7), the "gross, external mask," that is, outward form [*Erscheinungsform*] (LC IV 19). However, as it is of

---

9 See *De captivitate Babylonica ecclesiae praeludium* (1520), Aland 120, WA 6:497–573 (cf. AE 36:11–126). MH

10 The Heidelberg Catechism was compiled in 1562 by Zacharias Ursinus (1534–83) and Caspar Olevian (1536–87) at the insistence of Elector Frederick III (1515–76). It was accepted in the following year as the standard of doctrine in the Palatinate. In fundamentals its theology is Calvinist. See *ODCC*, 747. Today the Heidelberg Catechism is, along with the Lutheran Confessions, an official confession of the Saxon *Kirchenprovinz*, the church body of Saxony-Anhalt. Luther's congregation, St. Mary's in Wittenberg, is a member of this body. It is union church in every sense of the word and has been since the Prussian Union. The *Kirchenprovinz* is not even a member of the LWF, nor is it one of the eleven churches which make up the VELKD, which is also in full communion with the Reformed and Union churches via the EKiD, of which all these churches are members. On May 20, 1930, Sasse lectured to candidates of theology in the "Predigerseminar," a meeting of pastors and laymen in Wittenberg. See Feuerhahn Chronology. As of the publication of this volume, the *Kirchenprovinz* had merged with the Evangelical Lutheran Church of Thuringia. MH

the nature of divine revelation that God comes to us veiled, as the incarnate one ("In our poor flesh and blood, enclothes himself the eternal Good"), so is it of the nature of divine action "that God will not deal with us except through His external Word and sacrament" (SA III VIII 10). In this recognition of the indissoluble unity of "sign" and "object" [*Zeichen und Sache*] the danger of spiritualizing is overcome—the danger that lay in what Augustine taught and that since Berengar and Wycliffe captured so many Catholics of the late Middle Ages and since Zwingli and Bucer a large part of the Reformation movement. In this sense what Luther taught on sacraments is the great overthrow of Augustinianism in the church and the return to the essence [*est*] of the New Testament.

3

The third problem, which Augustine never fully found his way through, is the question of "Word" and "element." He first of all gave the solution that is quoted again and again in the Middle Ages, in modern Roman theology, and by the reformers: "Take the Word away, and what is the water but simply water? The Word is added to the element, and there results a sacrament, as if itself also a kind of visible Word" (*In Joh. Tract.* 80.3). Of first importance here is the emphasis on the Word as that which constitutes the sacrament. It was a serious error to try to explain sacrament from the natural side [*Naturseite*], as was done in the nineteenth century under the influence of theosophical speculations, which even infiltrated Lutheran theology, and in the twentieth century in the Berneuchener Movement influenced by Rudolf Steiner.[11] The most impressive attempt to understand sacrament from nature was made by Paul Tillich [1886–1965] in his early writings and in his dogmatics. He presents the view that in a sacrament an element from nature becomes the "bearer of the holy" [*Symbol und Wirklichkeit* (1966), 50; *Systematic Theology* (1963), 3:123]. That is supposed to be the essence of the Lutheran idea of sacrament. It is significant that Catholic theology must be brought to bear against him. It is not some mysterious quality of the water in Baptism or the bread and wine in the Lord's Supper but only the institution of the Lord that has designated just these elements, and His almighty Word alone makes them sacraments. Later as Scholasticism spoke of "Word" and "element" as "form" and "substance" and this was taken into Roman dogma, the constituting significance of the Word for a sacrament was underscored because the "form," the "idea," is always regarded as higher than the "substance." We should never forget that nor misunderstand it, as though the sacramental word in the Catholic sacrament is a kind of incantation with a magical effect, as Protestant

---

11 Rudolf Steiner founded Anthroposophy (1913) and assisted in the production of the Weimar edition of Goethe's works. His aim was to develop the faculty of spirit cognition inherent in ordinary people and to put them in touch with the spiritual world from which materialism had long estranged them. He taught the nobility of the human spirit and claimed clairvoyance. See *ODCC*, 1539. MH

polemic has often understood it. Johann Gerhard (Locus 21.13) emphatically repudiates the Reformed understanding of the Roman and Lutheran consecration as a magical incantation [*magica incantatio*]. There may be a suggestion of "magic" in the Roman view that at ordination a power to consecrate [*potestas consecandi*] is given to particular men as a *virtus*, a power in them. But even we would not acknowledge that, because today "magic" is generally understood as exercising coercion over the deity. In any case we must grant that the Roman Church also puts the Word above the element. What, then, is the relation of Word to element? What may be said of the element in the sacrament?

The answer that emerges may at first surprise us. The "element" does not at all belong to the essence of "sacrament." This follows from the fact that the medieval church had to abandon the idea of element and replace it with "substance" [*Materie*] which does not have to be an element, a thing of nature [*Naturding*] at all. So in the sacrament of penance what was done by the penitent (contrition, confession, satisfaction) was understood as the substance, while the absolution was its form. (Time will not allow us here to explore the magnificent attempt of Hugh of St. Victor, the first dogmatician of the medieval church, to construct a doctrine of the sacraments without the apparatus of Aristotelian philosophy. Despite his beginning with Augustine's definition of sacrament as the "sign" of a holy "thing," he tries to keep clear of any philosophical system; *De Sacramentis* 1.9.) Also the Augsburg Confession and its Apology do not know the idea of element with sacrament as such. This is shown by the inclusion of absolution among the sacraments (AC XIII): "The genuine sacraments, therefore, are Baptism, the Lord's Supper, and absolution" (Ap XIII 4). In Gospel freedom the Apology (Ap XIII 11) declares that even ordination may be called a sacrament because Christ has instituted the Office of the Ministry and given it the promise of Isa. 55:11. This freedom in speaking of sacraments in the Lutheran Church includes the freedom to regard the formula "Word and element" as what it is, a theological attempt to describe sacrament. The concept of *elementum* is dubious because of its ambiguity (consider the manifold meaning of the word in the New Testament) and vagueness, and we might well ask whether the reformers have done well in taking it over from Augustine's sacramental doctrine without more reflection.

4

What is *our task* in view of this state of affairs? As Lutheran theologians we should follow the example of the Augsburg Confession in our theological thinking as in our teaching and preaching and never start from one common doctrine of the means of grace or the sacraments but deal with each of the means of grace by itself in its own particularity: preaching the Gospel, Baptism, confession and absolution, the Sacrament of the Altar. Only then will we be able to understand the fullness of God's dealing with us, the different ways by which He comes to us, and the whole uniqueness of every single means of grace and so come to the proper use of each (consider the order of the articles of the Augsburg Confession and the arrangement of confession between Baptism and the Lord's Supper in the Small Catechism). Already with Baptism and the Lord's Supper it only causes confusion if we always try to draw parallels between them and to assert that what is true of the one sacrament must be said of the other. So it has been argued recently in the Ecumenical Movement even by Lutherans: Since the churches recognize one another's Baptism, they must also have reciprocal recognition of the Lord's Supper. As they put it, "altar fellowship" follows of necessity from "baptismal fellowship." But Baptism and the Lord's Supper, as immeasurably great as each of these sacraments is and as much as they cohere (1 Cor. 10:1ff.; cf. also the baptismal practice of the early church on Easter Eve and even the custom of the medieval church of giving infants the Lord's Supper, at least in the form of consecrated wine, right after Baptism), are simply not the same.

What the Sacrament of the Altar is was told to us by the Lord Himself; what Baptism is we learn from His apostle. We know when the Lord's Supper was instituted from the account of the institution. The *institution* of Baptism, according to the common notion of the early church, and also of Luther ("To Jordan came the Christ, our Lord"), took place as a result of the Lord's letting Himself be baptized by John ("There He established a washing for us") and is not identical with the *command* to baptize. Baptism was performed in the apostolic age "in the name of Jesus" (e.g., Acts 2:38; 10:48; 19:5; cf. the command to baptize of Matt. 28:19 according to Eusebius in the apparatus of Nestle; 1 Cor. 1:13), later with the Trinitarian baptismal formula. The apostles often left the administration of Baptism to others, and it is no devaluation of the sacrament for Paul to say that the Lord did not send him to baptize but to preach the Gospel. Baptism remains, with all the freedom and diversity of administration, the washing of regeneration, the full, complete sacrament, needing no completion in confirmation, as Anglican theology today says, not without effect on the Protestant churches.

We cannot go into the question here of what we would have to say today in our individual congregations about Baptism. It seems to me that the so urgently necessary instruction about the sacrament in Bible classes and sermons on the great texts of the New Testament that deal with Baptism should be taking place. Beyond that, the fourth chief part of the Large Catechism should be treated in lectures and discussions. That applies especially to the question of infant Baptism. We have to be aware of how ignorant the modern generation is, even in the Lutheran Church. We recognize far too seldom that religious and confirmation instruction and the Sunday school can in no way give what previous generations knew from home through Bible reading and what was learned from pious parents. Today the need of the hour for the Lutheran Church is to become a teaching church again. The success of Rome, of the sects, and of Communism is based substantially on the fact that what they teach, they teach unflaggingly. And our congregations hunger more than we know for teaching. Why don't we give them the bread that they want? How often we have given the impression at the administration of Baptism in the congregation or with a small baptismal party that an *opus operatus* has been administered. Who of those present knows what a miracle has happened here under the insignificant veil of the external sacrament? Who is aware that here a decision is made between the life and death, salvation and damnation of a person because this sacrament reaches *into* eternity? Are our congregations aware that they must pray in all seriousness for the newly baptized? Luther maintained that so many of the baptized are lost because this intercession has been lacking (WA 19:537f.; *BSLK*, "Taufbuchlein," 536:20ff.). If this intercession were taken seriously, would it not also mean the beginning of a renewal of the office of sponsor that has become so secularized? Do we really believe that the members of our congregations take so much with them from a few hurried hours of confirmation instruction, in which something is said at the end about the sacraments—though they should really determine the whole content of confirmation instruction—that they are able to live on it throughout their whole lives as people who daily return to their Baptism?

5

Where Baptism is rightly taught, there the Gospel is rightly proclaimed, for the whole Gospel is contained in this sacrament: Christ's death and resurrection, our dying and rising with Him in repentance and faith, the bestowal already now of future heavenly treasures, eternal righteousness, innocence and blessedness. The same applies to the Sacrament of the Altar. Of it Luther once said: "This Sacrament is the Gospel"[12] ("Concerning the Veneration of the Sacrament of the Holy Body of Christ" [1523], directed to the Christians in Bohemia with a powerful emphasis on the real presence against every symbolic explanation). This is one of the reformer's most profound theological perceptions. Because this Sacrament is the Gospel, the struggle over the Sacrament was at the same time the struggle for the Gospel, and vice versa. That alone can explain what the world calls Luther's stubbornness and obstinacy in the controversy over the Sacrament, his inflexible seriousness on just this question. Neither for Zwingli nor for Bucer was the struggle for the Sacrament so important.

Why is the Sacrament of the Altar the Gospel for Luther? First of all simply because the Words of Institution contain the whole Gospel. To attack them is to attack the Gospel itself.

> Everything depends on these words. Every Christian should and must know them and hold them fast. He must never let anyone take them away from him by any other kind of teaching, even though it were an angel from heaven [Gal. 1:8]. They are words of life and of salvation, so

---

12 "Just as you cannot make out of the gospel a sacrifice or a work, so you cannot make a sacrifice or a work out of this sacrament; for this sacrament is the gospel" (*Adoration of the Sacrament*, Aland 664, AE 36:289 [cf. WA 11:442.22]). MH

> that whoever believes in them has all his sins forgiven through that faith;
> he is a child of life and has overcome death and hell. Language cannot
> express how great and mighty these words are, for they are the sum and
> substance of the whole gospel. (WA 11:432.19 [cited from AE 36:277])

It must be called an attack on these words if part of them is taken literally and
another part figuratively, as when "Take and eat" and "Drink of it, all of you" are
taken literally, "This is My body" and "This is My blood" figuratively, and then
"which is given for you" and "which is shed for you" literally again. It is characteristic of Luther that right in the cited passage, as usual, he regards faith in the
"for you" as most essential. It is what brings the blessing of the Sacrament. At
the same time he stresses that this "for you" is inseparably bound with faith that
the words "This is My body" and "This is My blood" are true and must be taken
as they stand.

> Now beware of such a view. Let go of reason and intellect; for they strive
> in vain to understand how flesh and blood can be present, and because
> they do not grasp it they refuse to believe it. (WA 11:434.17 [cited from
> AE 36:279])

With this understanding of the Sacrament, the relationship between Word
and sacrament is no longer a problem. They go together. The sacrament is the
verbum visibile ("visible Word"); the Word is the *sacramentum audibile*, the
audible and heard sacrament. The spoken and heard Word of itself is a thing of
nature, sound waves that come from the voice box and are received by the ear.
And yet we hear "in, with, and under" these sound waves the Word of the eternal
God Himself. The natural word becomes the Word of God, *is* the Word of God.

The Gospel comes to us in this twofold way, as Word and as sacrament. Thus
absolution can also be counted among the sacraments: "Do you also believe that
my forgiveness is God's forgiveness?" [the confessor asks]. As Christ's body and
blood are hidden under the forms of bread and wine, so God's Word is hidden
under the form of the human voice (and also Holy Scripture under the form of
human writings). What the Word means for the Sacrament of the Altar becomes
clear from the fact that nothing made such a profound impact on those who
came from the Roman to the Lutheran Mass as the Words of Institution, which
the German people had never heard before because they were spoken softly in
the Roman Mass. Now they were chanted aloud at the altar in their own mother
tongue. "Word" and "element" became one. In both God comes to us to give us
one grace in different forms. This is surely the way of divine revelation. God does
not come to us as *Deus nudus*, as Luther says, not naked, but always veiled. Thus
in Christ divinity was veiled under His humanity and could be recognized only
with the eyes of faith. This is the mystery of the incarnation, in which the sacraments are rooted: "And the Word became *flesh* and dwelt among us, full of
grace and truth; we have beheld His glory" [John 1:14]. "We," that is, the "witnesses chosen beforehand," the apostles and all those who by the Holy Spirit are

to come to faith on the basis of the apostolic testimony. In faith they all are to see Christ's glory, which is hidden to the world until that day when it will be revealed to all people when He comes to judge the living and the dead.

6

"This sacrament *is* the Gospel." Luther's recognition matches perfectly what the New Testament teaches. "For as often as you eat this bread and drink the cup, you proclaim (*kataggellete* is to be taken as present, not as imperative) the Lord's death until He comes." Thus Paul writes at the end of the first and oldest account we have of the institution of the Lord's Supper. Several of the ancient liturgies quote these words of 1 Cor. 11:26 as if they were a part of the account itself that Paul is quoting here [*Ap. Can.* 8.12]. For the passage at 1 Cor. 11:23ff. belongs to the "traditions" that the apostle "received" and had faithfully passed on, just as the passage at 15:3ff., which reminds us of the Second Article of the Creed. That Paul received his Gospel directly from the Lord and not from men (Gal. 1:12) does not at all preclude his coming to know of details in the life of Jesus and the texts used in the liturgy by way of the church, probably in Antioch. The words "I received [*parelaban*] from the Lord what I also delivered [*paredōka*] to you" contain the same technical terms that we find in 1 Cor. 15:3 and probably mean no more than that what Paul hands on goes back to Jesus' Last Supper and what He Himself said and did there. Evidence of the utter reliability and great age of this account may be seen in the fact that it records an item that is no longer found in Mark. It was no longer regarded as essential that at the institution Jesus distributed the bread during the meal while the cup came at the end. Whether verse 26 belongs to the ancient account itself or is an authoritative commentary of the apostle, it does say with incisive brevity that the Lord's Supper is the Gospel itself.

Baptism is the Gospel because the whole Gospel is contained in it, not only in words but also in what our Redeemer does in His mighty rescue of us from sin, death, and the devil. Absolution is the Gospel, the forgiveness of sins, the anticipation of the verdict of justification that will come in the last judgment. The Lord's Supper is also the Gospel, and indeed in quite a special way. The Gospel is the Good News proclaimed in all the world in these last days (Matt. 24:14; Acts 2:17; Heb. 1:2). It is the message of the incarnation of the eternal Word, of His redeeming death, His resurrection and ascension, His sitting at the right hand of the Father and His return in glory for the final judgment and to complete our redemption in our own resurrection.

It is the will of Christ that this Gospel be proclaimed to all peoples. But this proclamation is not only to be the message of what God has done in the past and what He will do in the future. The proclamation of this "eternal Gospel" (Rev. 14:6) is always to be accompanied by the celebration of the Sacrament that our Lord instituted, by which His death is proclaimed until He comes. Without the

celebration of this Sacrament, the proclamation of the Gospel could be understood as just one of the many religious messages in the world. This does indeed
happen where people are ignorant of the Sacrament. Without the continual
proclamation of the Gospel this Sacrament may be understood as just one of the
many fellowship rites that exist in the world of religions or as an unintelligible
action of a mystery religion. But the Gospel is more than a religious message;
the Sacrament of the Altar is more than a religious ceremony. Both the Gospel
that is preached and the Gospel that occurs in the Sacrament contain one and
the same gift, though in different forms: the forgiveness of sins. This is not some
doctrine about the possibility of a forgiveness of sins, not an illustration of such
a possibility, but the actual forgiveness itself, this unfathomable miracle of God's
mercy that blots out our guilt and gives us everything that comes with forgiveness: life and salvation, redemption of the whole person, both soul and body.
Both the Gospel and the Sacrament bring this forgiveness, for in both the Lamb
of God who died for the sin of the world is present.

7

And so we come to the question of the *real presence*, which we must touch on
here at least briefly. Why was this, for Luther, the question about the Gospel
itself? The Lord Christ is present in all the means of grace. He comes to us in the
preaching of the Gospel, in Baptism, and in absolution. In these He is present in
His church, which is His Body. Also where two or three are gathered in His name,
gathered around His Word and Sacrament, there is the Body of Christ, the whole
Body. For the Body of Christ is not some sort of organism. It cannot be separated into pieces. It is always completely present, just as the sacramental body is
always completely present in each part of the consecrated bread.

> Whether one this bread receiveth
> Or a thousand, still He giveth
> One sure food that does not fail.[13]

Luther and our Lutheran fathers loved to quote these words from Aquinas's
Lauda Sion salvatorem. They ring on in the Communion hymns of our church.
They can and must be applied in an analogous way to the "mystical Body," the
church, in order to avoid the unbiblical, romantic theory of the church as an
organism. The presence in the Sacrament of the Altar, however, is not the same
as the presence in the other means of grace.

There is today a most earnest struggle going on to understand this presence.
There are Catholic and Protestant theologians who speak of it as making Christ's
death, Christ's Passion, contemporary, a re-presentation of His sacrificial death.

---

13   *Sumit unus, sumunt mille/ Quantum iste tantum ille/ Nec sumptus consumitur.* From
     Lauda Sion Salvatorem written in approximately 1264 by Thomas Aquinas for the
     Mass of the Corpus Christi festival. MH

Among Catholic theologians such theories emerge from the effort to clarify the doctrine of Trent that identifies the sacrifice on the cross with the sacrifice in the Mass. According to the doctrine of Trent, the sacrifice of Mass is to be understood as *memoria, repraesentatio*, and *applicatio* of the sacrifice on Golgotha. It was the late Benedictine monk Odo Casel who propounded the mystery theory that has engaged so much discussion. The point of departure for his exposition of the "cultic mystery" was the Hellenistic mysteries. These are then seen as "shadows" of the future mysteries of the church, corresponding to the relationship between nature and supernature [*Übernatur*].

> The *Kyrios* of a mystery is a God who has entered into human misery and struggle, has made his appearance on earth (epiphany) and fought here, suffered, even been defeated; the whole sorrow of mankind in pain is brought together in a mourning for the God who must die. But then in some way comes a return to life through which the God's companions, indeed the whole of nature, revives and lives on. This was the way of pious faith and the sacred teaching (*hieros logos*) of society in the earliest mystical age. But the world, society, is always in need of life; so the epiphany goes on and on in worship; the saving, healing act of God is performed over and over. Worship [*Kult*] is the means of making it real once more, and thus of breaking through to the spring of salvation. The members of the cult present again in a ritual, symbolic fashion, that primeval act. . . .
>
> The mystery, therefore, embraces in the first place the broad concept of ritual "*memorial*"—*anamnēsis, commemoratio*—the ritual performance and *making present* [*Gegenwärtigsetzung*] of some act of God's, upon which rests the existence and life of a community. (*Das Christliche Kultmysterium*, 2d ed. [1935]; emphasis added [*The Mystery of Christian Worship* (1962), 53]).

Justin and the early church could never have dreamed up something like this, certainly not if they remained in agreement with Paul, who did not regard these mysteries as earlier stages of Christian worship but as demonic perversion of divine truth. This whole theory falls to pieces before the simple fact that while the Hellenistic mysteries rest on myths, the Sacrament of the Altar is a matter of history. When did Attis and Osiris live? When did they die? The question is senseless because the myth does not tell of historical events. Jesus Christ, however, is a historical person. His death is a historical event that happened outside the gates of Jerusalem "under Pontius Pilate." The women who went to find His body did not have to wander all around like Cybele and Isis in the myth. They knew the place of His grave. And His resurrection was also a historical event: "On the third day He rose again from the dead" [cf. 1 Cor. 15:4] The whole theory was constructed to provide a foundation for the dogma of the identity of the sacrifice on the cross and the sacrifice of the Mass as defined by Trent. But where is there any such foundation in the New Testament? Is it by chance that the passage in the New Testament putting the high priestly work of Christ at the center has the word "once" [*ephapax*] right at the crucial place? He "entered *once* for all into the Holy Place, taking not the blood of goats and calves but His own blood, thus securing an eternal redemption" (Heb. 9:12). Who dares to interpret away this "once" in view of the words that conclude this great chapter: "Just as it is appointed for men to die once, and after that comes judgment, so Christ, having been offered once to bear the sins of many, will appear a second time, not to deal with sin but to save those who are eagerly waiting for Him" (Heb. 9:27).

Casel's theory is therefore untenable. It can be accommodated in the Roman Church because, for one thing, it has a different relationship with heathen religion than we do, and for another, because its doctrine of the real presence is not in any way challenged by it. That is not the case with similar theories that have sprung up in Protestant soil and today even make an impression on Lutherans. Casel betrays a very significant uncertainty regarding the biblical concept of remembrance, as is shown by his opinion of Passover.

> God's prescriptions were carried in exact ritual: the paschal lamb eaten in traveling clothes; *the history read recalling* how they left the land where they were slaves. So Israel's salvation and the founding of God's people was celebrated each year in ritual. . . . But the passover use was not properly a mystery because it was related first of all to human events and a *human deliverance.* (Casel, 60 [*Mystery*, 311])

What a misunderstanding this is of *salvation history* [*Heilsgeschichte*] and *salvation facts* [*Heilstatsachen*] in the biblical sense!

In his thoughtful study "The Salvation Event in the Proclamation of the Word and in Holy Communion" (in *Grundlegung des Abendmahlsgesprächs* [1954], 35-79 [for the English, see *Worship in the Name of Jesus* (St. Louis, 1968), 141–96]), Peter Brunner points out the realization of the presence of salvation history in the cultus that was first propounded by Rudolf Otto [1869–1937] and developed by Old Testament scholars such as Mowinckel,[14] von Rad,[15] and Weiser. It is expressed in the words of Moses in Deut 5:1f.:

> Hear, O Israel, the statutes and the ordinances which I speak in your hearing *this day*, and you shall learn them and be careful to do them. The Lord our God *made a covenant with us* in Horeb. *Not with our fathers* did the Lord make this covenant, but *with us*, who are all of us *here* alive *this day*. The Lord spoke with you face to face at the mountain, out of the midst of the fire, while *I stood between the Lord and you at that time, to declare to you the Word of the Lord.*

The interpretation that von Rad gives of this "actualization of the redemptive events" in the cultus and in God's holy Word that is part of the cultus is found in

---

14   Sigmund Olaf Plytt Mowinckel (1884–1965) was an Old Testament scholar who taught for his entire career at Oslo. He regarded the Psalms as yearly enthronement liturgies for Yahweh. See *ODCC*, 1121. MH

15   Gerhard von Rad (1901–71) taught Old Testament at the University of Heidelberg (s.v. *Christian Cyclopedia*). MH

P. Brunner, p. 38 [*Worship*, 145]. It is really true that those who eat the Passover, in which they remember a historical event, are present at this event, because it is "salvation history," the history of what God had done, for which there is no temporal time. In addition to the way in which a past event is made a present reality through the Word, the Old Testament also has parabolic actions by the prophets, such as in Ezekiel 4 and 5, something still seen in the New Testament in the action of Agabus in Acts 21:10f. This *oth* [Hebrew], a holy sign (the word is also used of God's miraculous deeds), for the people of the Old Testament is really more than just a parable. R. Otto has called it "an effective representation" [*The Kingdom of God and the Son of Man* (Boston, 1957), 302]. He and others have used this, then, as the way to explain the Lord's Supper. The sacrifice of Christ's death, anticipated at the Last Supper, is re-presented in the celebration of the Sacrament, just as also, from the opposite perspective, the messianic banquet in heaven is anticipated in it. This has been used by Anglican theologians, and even by some Lutherans, to take the hazardous step of seeing in the Sacrament the "re-presentation" of Christ's sacrifice and in this way seeing the Sacrament itself as a sacrifice. There was indeed a reality inherent in a prophetic sign, as also in the prophetic Word. It makes no difference whether the fall of Jerusalem is proclaimed by Jeremiah by "word" or by "action." But the category of parabolic action or of *oth* simply cannot explain the Lord's Supper. This is indicated by the fact that those theologians who explain it in this way no longer have any appreciation for the actual presence of the body and blood of Christ. Their doctrine of the real presence is Calvinist, and that of the sacrifice is Roman Catholic. When it happens that they become Roman Catholic, they then have no difficulty in accepting transubstantiation.

There must be something else that is unique about the real presence in the Lord's Supper. The death of Christ is indeed a unique historical event. As with every actual event in earthly history, it is unrepeatable. But at the same time, like the exodus from Egypt commemorated in the Passover, it is also God's redemptive act, something that stands outside of earthly time, which does not exist for God. Revelation 13:8 calls Christ "the Lamb slain from the foundation of the world" [KJV]. He is the Crucified not simply as *staurōtheis* (aorist, which signifies a single event) but as the *estaurōmenos* (perfect, which means that what happened continues in effect). We note how Paul uses the aorist and perfect, comparing, for example, 1 Cor. 1:13 with 1:23; 2:2, 8; 2 Cor. 13:4 with Gal. 3:1; etc. From this we may see that with God a "temporal" event can be "eternal." But as a general principle this may be said of all God's deeds. What applies to Golgotha applies also to Sinai according to Deut. 5:2. However illuminating may be the recognition that in the Bible God's deeds in the past have also a present reality, this does not explain what is the *proprium* of the Sacrament. Brunner acknowledges this when he says that re-presentation and the real presence go together. "Through the real presence of Jesus' body and blood the *repraesentatio* carried out in Holy Communion receives its real and present concretion" (*Grundlegung*, 64 (*Worship*, 177]). The question that Brunner leaves open is what the actual "body" and "blood" are that are received under the forms of bread and wine. This is where I must part company with him, even though he quotes my statement in *Vom Sakrament des Altar*[16] (p. 69) in support of his view (*Grundlegung*, 64 [*Worship*, 178]). The context of my statement shows that we are not in agreement.

Brunner says (p. 63 (*Worship*, 177]) "that the *sacrificed* body and the atoning and covenant-effecting *sacrificial* blood and, with this, Jesus' sacrifice on the cross, are present to us under the eucharistic food and presented [*dargereicht*] with the bread and the wine" (Brunner's emphasis). Why is sacrifice stressed so much? There is no doubt that we receive the *sacrificed* body and the *sacrificed* blood. But why is it not said that the sacrificed body is at the same time the glorified body? It is certainly true that, along with the Christ who was sacrificed for us, His sacrifice on the cross is present—along with the one who suffered [*Christus passus*] comes also His suffering [*passio Christi*]. But can the sacrifice of the cross be *distributed* [*dargereicht*, that is, to the communicants]? If I have misunderstood Brunner, I would ask him in sincere friendship to clear up the misunderstanding. And I would put to him the question, What do unbelievers receive, that is, with the mouth? And how can something be possible today that the church regarded as impossible for 1,700 years and that is still today regarded by most of Christendom as impossible, namely, that there can be fellowship at the Lord's Supper between those who confess that the consecrated bread *is* the body of the Lord and those who confess no more than that the bread is a *sign* of the body, as is the case with those who hold to the Heidelberg Catechism. In his careful and conscientious investigation of the question (*Grundlegung*, 11–33), Brunner concedes that his approval of altar fellowship between Lutherans and those who confess the Heidelberg Catechism would not have been shared by Luther, had he known of this catechism (*Grundlegung*, 32 n. 25). But does this disagreement between Brunner and Luther perhaps relate to a deeper disagreement in understanding the essence of the real presence?

8

Here we must break off the discussion of the real presence. Our intention was to substantiate Luther's statement: "This Sacrament is the Gospel." If this is so, then it is clear that the church cannot exist without it. It had such vital place in the Divine Service in the time of the apostles, in the ancient church, in the Middle Ages, and also in Lutheranism before the incursion of Pietism. The Divine Service was the "Mass," a service of the Word and at the same time a service of the Sacrament. There is a growing conviction in all Protestant churches that, with the conscious dissolution of the Mass among the Reformed churches and its decline in Lutheranism, something has been lost that is essential to the

---

16 *Vom Sakrament des Altars: Lutherische Beiträge zur Frage des heiligen Abendmahls* (Leipzig: Dörffling & Franke, 1941). Huss number 226. MH

church. There is something of the truth to the saying often heard in America: "If a Protestant goes to church, he finds a preacher; if a Catholic goes to church, he finds Christ." Preaching can only decline, can only lose its essence as the proclamation of the *Gospel*, if the Sacrament of the Altar no longer gives us the objective presence of the incarnate Christ, if we no longer receive His true body and His true blood. On the other hand, in the Roman Church the decline in the proclamation of the Gospel has changed the character of the Sacrament. It is something marvelous to behold in a Cistercian abbey when the monks, after choral prayer together early in the morning, go into the sacristy, take off their cowls, put on their chasubles, and each goes by himself to his altar in the great church to celebrate his Mass, to offer the holy Sacrifice, as they say. But is this impressive celebration still the Mass of the early church, not to mention the Sacrament of the New Testament? No one has more effectively criticized this development of the Mass, in which the praying church [*ecclesia oralis*] disappears, than the leaders of the liturgical movement in the Catholic Church. I know an Anglican monastery, which is also a theological seminary, where the students go to Communion every morning but for months on end hear no sermon. Can the Gospel survive in such churches? The early church was a preaching church, as was also the church of the Middle Ages at the high points of its history. Certainly the juxtaposition of preaching—in the early church there were often several sermons—and the Eucharist has always presented a practical problem, even in the East where there seems to be plenty of time. The pressure of time led either to the sermon's being cut short, as in today's Catholic High Mass on Sunday, or to the establishment of special preaching services without the Sacrament on Sunday afternoon as in the late Middle Ages or as is still the case today with Vespers. It is by no means the case that only we Lutherans are plagued with the problem of finding the rightful place for both preaching and the Sacrament of the Altar in the Sunday Divine Service.

Another question is closely related to this one, namely, the congregation's Communion. In the ancient church all who took part in the Mass of the Faithful received Communion. This later came to an end when masses of people came streaming into the church, and Communion was often replaced by the distribution of bread that was blessed but not consecrated at the end of the service. In the Middle Ages, Communion was very infrequent. To receive Communion four times a year—at the three high festivals and at one lesser one—was a sign of the highest piety. Even of monks no more was required. I once greatly astonished a Dominican when I explained that Thomas certainly did not celebrate Mass every day. Receiving Communion was replaced by adoration of the host, a practice unknown in the ancient church and still not practiced by the Eastern Church.

Just as customs changed in the early church in connection with Baptism (the baptizing of infants and adults), so there was also a change in church customs with regard to the Lord's Supper. Over many centuries pastoral care has wrestled with the problem of whether frequent or less frequent but more devoutly prepared-for

Communion is preferred. There were already debates about this in the Middle Ages. Later the Jansenists[17] and the Jesuits were in controversy about it, until at the beginning of this century the decision came down in favor of frequent and, where possible, daily Communion. But this was at the cost of not taking sin seriously, since according to Catholic doctrine no one may receive the Sacrament who is in a state of mortal sin. This same problem arises in the Lutheran Church when frequent Communion, going to the Lord's Supper at each Divine Service is urged, or when the participants in church gatherings are more or less morally compelled to go to the Table of the Lord without a serious confession preceding it, as our Confessions encourage it. For the *exploratio* of Augsburg Confession XXIV is expressly described in the Apology in such a way that it includes confession: "In our churches Mass is celebrated every Sunday and on other festivals, when the Sacrament is offered to those who wish for it after they have been examined and absolved" (Ap XXIV 1 [XXV 1; XV 40]). This confession previously took place on Saturday and still does in many a congregation. To give this up or to let it rise or fall in the general confession of sins of the congregation would be a corruption of the Lutheran Sacrament and would open the door to a false understanding of the Lord's Supper. If appeal is made to the Catholic liturgy, then it must be remembered that there also confession is to precede Communion, though it does so differently because of the different understanding of sin.

If we ask ourselves what we as pastors can do about these questions, we should take comfort from the fact that we are not the first to have to struggle with the problem of "Word and Sacrament, Preaching and Holy Communion." The church has always faced the needs indicated by these questions. So we have to beware of liturgical experiments, both the serious and the silly. The latter do exist, as when Bishop Lilje's *Sonntagsblatt* recently published a letter that reported a new way to celebrate the Lord's Supper. When the congregation sat around a table for the Lord's Supper, they left one place empty for the coming Lord. That is a Jewish custom practiced in all pious Jewish homes in the East. At the festive Sabbath meal or some other festival, a place is always kept open for the coming Messiah. What ignorance about the meaning of the Lord's Supper and the liturgy is to be found in our congregations! The need is not met by the artificial liturgical constructions of some High Church people. The great learning of modern liturgics is of no help either unless its fruits are translated into the plain language of the people, as Pius Parsch [1884–1954] of Klosterneuberg on the Catholic side has done in splendid fashion for German-speaking people.

Why do we not explain the liturgy to our congregations, especially to the youth? That naturally presumes that we know the teaching of our church

---

17 A reformatory movement in the Roman Catholic Church inaugurated by Cornelius Jansen (1585–1638) as a means to counteract the Jesuits. The movement sought to revive Augustine's doctrines of sin and grace in the church. Jansen's book on Augustine was condemned by the church in 1641. Dutch Jansenists left Rome for the Old Catholics in 1723/1724 (s.v. *Christian Cyclopedia*). MH

regarding the Divine Service, that we ourselves study the old church orders with their liturgical treasures, that we understand the Lutheran way of combining loyalty to the old liturgical heritage with the great Gospel freedom of which Article X of the Formula of Concord speaks. We do not mean liturgical arbitrariness, but authentic Gospel freedom. We have to face the fact that a heritage that has been lost over 250 years cannot be restored quickly. We must have several forms of the Divine Service, just as the Roman Church has and practices in the preservation of unfamiliar rites. We need small circles and congregations in which the old liturgical heritage is preserved along with *confession—confessio* always means confession of the faith, confession of sins, and praise of God—all in one, as is done in such an exemplary way, a way that puts us all to shame, in the "Brethren" congregations in Braunschweig. Moreover, in the large congregations we need extensive instruction in the liturgy. We need preaching services and special services of Holy Communion. We particularly need the Divine Service in the sense of the Lutheran Mass with both preaching and the celebration of the Sacrament. The sermon will then need to be short, but above all it must be authentic proclamation of the Gospel. There can be no renewal of the Lord's Supper without renewed preaching, preaching that is not just the pious talk of a man but disciplined exposition of Holy Scripture that strikes the heart. Such preaching grows out of serious study of Scripture, plumbing the depths of the divine Word. It should not be that the hearer of the text will always know exactly what is coming next because he has already heard it a hundred times.

Such are the tasks set before us, and no one can relieve us of them, neither hierarchy nor synod nor theological faculty. From the inner renewal of our office, the *ministerium docendi evangelii et porrigendi sacramenta* ("ministry of teaching the Gospel and administering the Sacraments," AC V), the primary office of the church, the only one that the Lord Himself has instituted, can the renewal of our church come. *Veni creator Spiritus!* ["Come, Holy Spirit!]

☙

This letter has become longer than I had planned. But I wanted to fulfill my promise before a planned move to another suburb of Adelaide and other necessities which burden me had delayed it even further. Please regard it as a replacement for all the personal letters which I have not been able to write. My address from mid-August will be 63 Clifton Street, Prospect, South Australia.

In true unity, I greet you,

Your
Hermann Sasse

Historical Context

In Sasse's letter to Behnken, it is shocking to read that he had attempted to obtain employment with the Australian Post Office to supplement his meager church wages. We rejoice he did not did not find such work, and I suspect (though I have not verified it) that Behnken provided some occasional cash. Behnken had provided Sasse with care packages after the war. As Sasse's son Wolfgang reported, his father had five or six typewriters about his study at any given time, with letters and books and essays in process. In this Letter 43, Sasse reprises language from "Union and Confession" (1936)[1] to describe the apparent rise of Lutheranism. "An epoch-making development of incalculable consequences for the Church is approaching its consummation in our days: the dying of the great confessional churches which were born out of the Reformation. As in every historical process of that type, the issue is one of the gradual development extending through generations. And like every other decline recorded in history, it is regarded by those who participate in it as an ascent, as the promising dawn of a new day . . . ." Whether Sasse's LLL readers comprehended his warning is hard to say, but it's amazing such an essay appeared first in English where it did. MH

November 1, 1956[2]

Prof. H. Sasse
63 Clifton Street
Prospect, South Australia

Dear and Reverend Doctor Behnken,

Thank you very much indeed for your kind letter of October 15. I am sorry that I could not answer earlier, but I had an attack of arthritis after the overstress connected with my removal to Prospect. In this country, as you have come to know, we have to follow the "do it yourself" method. But I am improving . . . .

Time is running out for confessional Lutheranism. Think what it means that all Scandinavian and German churches have entered altar fellowship with Reformed and Anglican bodies and that the same is true of Holland and the younger churches in Asia and Africa. Thus I ask you once more to act or to advise

---

1   See *Lonely Way* 1:265–305. MH
2   CHI Behnken file. Letter in English. MH

us how to act. It seems that the decision of the ELC to join the WCC has definitely broken the last conservative resistance in the churches belonging to the LWF.

Copies of my last letters, continued in the *Lutherische Blätter* ("*Successio Apostolica*" and "Word and Sacrament, Preaching and Lord's Supper")[3] have been ordered for you and Dr. Meyer. Another *Briefe* on "The Remembrance of the Dead and Prayer for the Dead" is being written now.[4] I have found a lot of interesting material on that subject with Martin Chemnitz and Johann Gerhard. I still have to write the *Briefe* in German, because they are being read by the pastors of the German Free Churches, the last service I can render to my old country. They need them badly. As to the financial side, everything paid by the subscribers has so far gone to the printer. . . . I was planning this year to get some job with the post office, as others must do, too, but my application was declined on account of my age. So I must leave it to you to see whether you can add a little sum to the mere expenses. I shall send always a copy of the manuscript of the letters to you, even before they can appear in print, which might be delayed by the present political situation . . . . I had a very friendly reply from Dr. Piepkorn, and I hope we can work together in many ways . . . . My wife and I shall always gratefully remember your visit to our home. She and our boys send their best regards. Once more I want to thank you for what you are doing for my manuscript [*This Is My Body*]. With best regards,

Yours sincerely,
H. Sasse

---

3   See above, pp. 425–49 and 451–72. MH

4   See Letter 45, "The Remembrance of the Dead in the Liturgy," in *Letters to Lutheran Pastors*, vol. 3 (forthcoming 2015). MH

forty-three

The Confessional Problem in Today's World Lutheranism

November 1956[1]

Prof. Dr. Theol. Professor Hermann Sasse
63 Clifton Street
Prospect, South Australia

Dear Brothers in the Office,

It was my intention to greet you at the close of the church year with a letter concerning the remembrance of the dead in the church.[2] Various circumstances

---

1   *BLP* 43: *Das Bekenntnisproblem im heutigen Weltluthertum* (Prospect, November 1956). The original was published in *LuBl* 8, no. 51 (1956/1957): 149–72. Huss number 323. This translation is from *The Lutheran Laymen* 27, no. 4 (April 1, 1957), courtesy of The International Lutheran Laymen's League; all rights reserved; used by permission. Permission has been granted for minor alterations to spelling, capitalization, and punctuation. The article was published with an introduction by LCMS President John W. Behnken:

> I am deeply grateful to the executives of the Lutheran Layman's League, who recognized it as a scholarly presentation of the very vital problem, and decided that it should be made available not merely to all our pastors but also to all laymen of our Synod. Herewith I desire to encourage and urge every pastor and layman to read and study it thoroughly. If you have opportunity, discuss it with others. This will be decidedly beneficial. Do not throw it away. By all means keep it for future reference. Things are happening in world Lutheranism. Things are happening to the Lutheran Confessions. Some strange winds are blowing. Storm clouds are appearing on the horizon. The day may soon come when all who bear and love the name Lutheran must squarely face some important doctrinal issues, yes, must take a definite stand on such doctrines as inspiration, fellowship, unionism, even the Lord's Supper and others. We shall need to be thoroughly informed. Both pastors and people will need to recognize the Lutheran Confessions as the correct exposition of the Word of God and, by God's grace, remain loyal to them. Our beloved synod, most highly favored of God with pure doctrine, bears a tremendous responsibility. We can meet our obligations only if we remain faithful and loyal to God's Word and our Lutheran Confessions. May this scholarly Letter 43 help to convince us of the urgency and the importance of this matter! Yours in Christ, John W. Behnken" (*The Lutheran Laymen*, 1). MH

2   See Letter 45, "The Remembrance of the Dead in the Liturgy," in *Letters to Lutheran Pastors*, vol. 3 (forthcoming 2015). MH

made it impossible for me to finish the letter which I had already begun (I hope to mail it at the beginning of the new year), and the state of affairs in the Church as well as a few questions from your midst impel me to speak once more about the confessional problem. Even at the risk of repeating some of the things which have been said in previous letters, I wish to speak on the question of the Confessions as the vital question of the Lutheran Church against the background of the political and church situation in the world, which is constantly growing more serious.

1

An epoch-making development of incalculable consequences for the Church is approaching its consummation in our days: the dying of the great confessional churches which were born out of the Reformation. As in every historical process of that type, the issue is one of the gradual development extending through generations. And like every other decline recorded in history, it is regarded by those who participate in it as an ascent, as the promising dawn of a new day. The decline of the Roman Empire was scarcely noticed by its contemporaries. It was even regarded by the last Latin poets, insofar as they were not believing Christians who knew of God's judgment, as a time of progress, because Rome had never had so many great poets and orators. Never did the people of Europe so fervently believe that they were progressing as at the beginning of this twentieth century, when the storm clouds of the approaching world wars and world revolutions were already hovering in the skies.

It is a law of all history that the meaning and import of the history experienced by its contemporaries remain hidden from them. Profound psychologists may attempt to explain this phenomenon, which exists in the history of Israel and in the history of the Church in a particularly serious form which is no longer accessible to the probing of human psychology. The people in Jerusalem in the days of Jeremiah simply could not endure the genuine prophecy, the Word of God which revealed to them the full seriousness of their situation, and turned to the more comforting promises of the false prophets who assured them that Jerusalem would not go under.

There was no lack of great Christian teachers in the nineteenth century to whom God had given a "prophetic gift of grace," *charisma*. Read [August] Vilmar's essays on Communism and on the fate of the Church in Germany. Think of [Wilhelm] Löhe's dream of the burial of the Lutheran Church, which is carried to the grave with great ceremony by its own pastors. But instead of hearkening to such voices and inquiring what truths could perhaps be contained in such prophecy, since 1848 they joyfully celebrated the *Kirchentag* at which the mighty rushing of the Spirit was heard more plainly in the same measure that the Confession of the fathers were forgotten. Commensurately with the local genius, the *Kirchentag* at Berlin in 1853 had adopted the Unaltered Augsburg Confession "with heart and mouth" as the confession of the entire evangelical Germany, with the addition that the members of the *Kirchentag* could individually hold to the particular confessional writings of their churches and that "the differing position of the Lutherans, Reformed, and United churches with respect to Article X of this Confession should not be prejudiced" (quoted from R. Rocholl,[3] *Geschichte der evangelischen Kirche in Deutschland*, pp. 505f.) Only three Lutheran faculties (Erlangen, Leipzig, Dorpat) still protested against this abuse of the Lutheran Confessions. Step by step the Lutheran church in Germany was pushed back by the Union, and the Lutherans in the Union churches were deprived of their rights.

Some courageous battles were fought in the period between 1830 and 1872, ranging from the struggle of the Silesian Lutherans under [J. G.] Scheibel to the struggle of the Hessian Renitence, the solemn protest which Harless, the president of the Lutheran High Consistory in Munich and presiding officer of the General Evangelical Lutheran Conference, voiced in 1870 in a letter to Bismarck, in which he showed what it would mean if the new constitution of the *Reich*, in contradistinction to all constitutional documents of Germany since the Peace of Augsburg and Westphalia, no longer guaranteed the right of existence to the Church of the Lutheran Reformation, and if the Lutheran Church became either a separate communion or a mere school of thought within an all-Protestant evangelical church of Germany: "Only with deepest anguish can one pursue the thought that the Lutheran church, which was the best fruit and noblest adornment of Germany, should have her candlestick taken from her" (cf. *The Documents of Th. Heckel*, Adolf von Harless, 193, pp. 482f., in the Appendix). That, too, was prophecy in a decisive hour of church history. It died away unheard.

The world, also the Christian world, calls a thing like that "unfruitful pessimism" by which nothing has ever yet been gained in the world. Or it curtly speaks of "unbelief," which just cannot imagine that God would allow the Church of the pure Gospel—"the temple of the Lord"—to go under. "I would rather hope myself to death than to perish in unbelief." They did hope themselves to death, these Lutherans in the state churches, because that faith was secret unbelief. For it is unbelief when one no longer bows to God's judgment. It can be God's judgment that He takes away from us what our fathers in the Reformation once achieved by way of deep understanding of the Word of God and defended at the risk of their lives.

Who does not recall at this point Luther's statement concerning the Word of God as a pouring rain which does not return where it once has been?[4] Why,

---

3   Rudolf Rocholl (1822–1905) was a Lutheran theologian who served as the superintendent of Göttingen. He left the Church of Hanover to join the Old Lutherans in 1878 (s.v. *Christian Cyclopedia*). MH

4   See *An die Ratherren aller all Städte deutschen Lands, dass sie christliche Schulen aufrichten und halten sollen* (*To the Councilmen of All Cities in Germany*, 1524), Aland 676, WA 15:27–53. The "passing rain" or *farender platz regen* statement of

even the reformer himself reckoned with the possibility that the fate of the Gospel could be the same in Germany as it has been in the lands of ancient Christendom. Hence it could be that also our Church could be drawn into, or has already been drawn into, the great dying of the confessional churches which were born out of the Reformation.

2

The dying of the confessional church began in the Reformed Churches. In an opinion concerning the "desirability and possibility of a general Reformed confession of faith for the Alliance of the Reformed churches holding the Presbyterian system," Karl Barth in Cardiff (1925) defined a Reformed confession of faith as "the statement of the insight granted provisionally to the universal Christian Church concerning the relation of God to Christ Jesus, witnessed only in the Holy Scriptures, formulated spontaneously and publicly by a *locally circumscribed* Christian fellowship, decisive *for the present* for its character toward the outside and directive *for the present* for its own teaching and living" (*Gesammelte Vorträge*, Bd. II, 1928, p. 76; emphasis ours).

What this definition has in common with the Lutheran understanding of the Confessions is the designation of its contents as an interpretation which is correct and has therefore been given to the whole Church. What distinguishes both is the stronger emphasis placed on the normative significance of the Confessions among Lutherans over against the "pious relativism" (Ibid. p. 79, 83), which expresses itself in the terms "locally circumscribed," "for the present," "temporarily."

It is actually true that the Reformed Church knows no common confession, but that the Augsburg Confession, which unites the Lutheran Church, faces a multitude of Reformed confessions, the *Helvetica*, the *Gallicana*, the *Belgica*, the

---

Luther is found at WA 15:32.7, cited here from AE 45:352–53: "Let us remember our former misery, and the darkness in which we dwelt. Germany, I am sure, has never before heard so much of God's word as it is hearing today; certainly we read nothing of it in history. If we let it just slip by without thanks and honor, I fear we shall suffer a still more dreadful darkness and plague. O my beloved Germans, buy while the market is at your door; gather in the harvest while there is sunshine and fair weather; make use of God's grace and word while it is there! For you should know that God's word and grace is like a passing shower of rain which does not return where it has once been. It has been with the Jews, but when it's gone it's gone, and now they have nothing. Paul brought it to the Greeks; but again when it's gone it's gone, and now they have the Turk. Rome and the Latins also had it; but when it's gone it's gone, and now they have the pope. And you Germans need not think that you will have it forever, for ingratitude and contempt will not make it stay. Therefore, seize it and hold it fast, whoever can; for lazy hands are bound to have a lean year." Sasse also references this above in Letter 27, "Worldwide Lutheranism after Hanover," p. 165, and in Letter 12, "*Ecclesia Migrans*," in *Letters to Lutheran Pastors* 1:211. MH

Scotica, the *Anglican Articles*, etc.[5] Also confessions which thereafter not only achieved local standing, as, for example, the Heidelberg Catechism and the Westminster Confession, never were adopted by all Reformed Churches.

Now of course no objection can be raised if a locally circumscribed church, be it a regional or state church, confesses its faith. On the contrary, it *must* do that. The only question is, why the same faith should not be confessed by *all* in the same words, as we do in the ancient creeds of the church. Isn't there perhaps a connection between the localizing of the confession of faith and "for the present," between the renunciation of local ecumenicity and the renunciation of temporal ecumenicity? It is essential for the Lutheran Confessions that they wish to give expression to the truth which unites the entire orthodox church of all times and places, the believers presently living with the brethren in the whole world, with the fathers since the beginning and with those who will confess the true faith unto the end of the world. That, then, leads to this: that the confessor confesses the faith in which he wants to persevere and with which he wishes to step before the judgment seat of God.

Barth and the whole Reformed church of today assures us that this is *hybris*, that we are seeking an unattainable safeguard and thereby actually destroying the character of the Scriptures as the only norm. We intend still to enter upon the relation of the Scriptures and the Confessions, of the *norma normans* (the guiding principle) and the *norma normata* (the guided principle). At this point we should like, first of all, to call attention to the fact that confessions existed also in the old Reformed Church, to which the relativism of "for the present" was still foreign, for example, the Confession of the Church of Scotland of 1560, which was rightly valued so highly, edited, and commented upon by Karl Barth. Here as in the Lutheran Confessions—from Luther's confession of 1528 (*Vom Abendmahl Christi Bekenntnis*, WA 26:490 [Aland 2; AE 37:161–372]) to the conclusion of the Formula of Concord—one finds the same view of judgment and the resolve to abide by this confession. The Preamble of the *Confessio Scotica* concludes with a reference to the judgment which according to Matt. 10:33 is to descend upon the deniers of the truth of the Gospel, after which these words follow: "Therefore it is our definite resolve, through the mighty Spirit of this our Lord Jesus Christ, to abide in the confession of this our faith as it is expressed in the following articles" (quoted from Barth's Gifford lectures of 1938, *Gotteserkenntnis und Gottesdienst nach reformatorischer Lehre*, Zollikon, 1938, p. 11; the Preamble is missing in the edition of the Reformed Confessions by E. F. K. Mueller). With respect to the readiness to permit themselves to be corrected by the Word of God, there is therefore no difference between the Old Reformed and the Lutheran view of the Confessions.

---

5   For more information on each of these confessions, see the respective entries in *Christian Cyclopedia*. MH

The "certain pious and free relativism" which according to Karl Barth is suited to the Reformed Confession was doubtless prepared in the sixteenth century. But it achieved its triumph only gradually in the *latitudinarianism*[6] of the Anglicans, in the independent Puritanism and in the syncretistic movements of the seventeenth century ("syncretism" is the term commonly used in the sixteenth and seventeenth centuries for what is later called "union" and "unionism"). At this place we would mention only the second of these phenomena, which has become of immeasurable importance for modern Protestantism in Europe (through Pietism) and America.

In his famous farewell sermon preached to the Pilgrim fathers who were leaving Leiden for America, J. P. Robinson[7] said: "The Lord will let still additional truths burst forth from His holy Word. I cannot sufficiently express my regret over the Reformed churches which have arrived at a frontier in religion and are not now willing to go forward, as the instruments of the Reformation.—Luther and Calvin were great shining lights in their days, but they did not penetrate the whole counsel of God." And he even hazarded this statement: "All pious people, though they are themselves outside the true visible church, are by faith members of the mystical body of Jesus Christ—common reason as well as Holy Scriptures teaches that." In these words, by the way, the future church history of America is prophesied.

What are the confessions to these Congregationalists? Since the local congregation, which assembles here and now for the worship of God, is the Church of Christ, its confession can actually be only a local one. There can be no confession which binds all Christendom. Within a year the local congregation [has changed and] is not the same as it is today. Consequently its confession can only be a provisional one. How can I say that a congregation whose composition (membership), as we know, is continually changing will abide by one particular confession? Yes, how can I myself say with Luther and all the confessors of the church that I desire to step before the judgment seat of God with this, my confession? I can do that only, and a congregation can do that only, on the basis of the firm conviction that this confession teaches nothing else than the truth of the Word of God. Also the Pilgrim fathers of 1620 knew that. But they were told that the

---

6   This term was applied in the seventeenth century to a group of Anglican divines who, while continuing to conform with the Church of England, attached relatively little importance to matters of dogmatic truth, ecclesiastical organization, and liturgical practice. In general the sympathies of Latitudinarian divines lay with Arminian theology. Their views did much to prepare the way for the religious attitudes of England in the eighteenth century. See *ODCC*, 956. MH

7   John Robinson (ca. 1575–1625) was pastor to the Pilgrim fathers. Little is known of his early life, though he probably studied at Cambridge. He was ordained in the Church of England, but became a Puritan. As a result of the extreme measures against nonconformity, in 1608 Robinson and his congregation fled to the Netherlands, where they settled in Leiden. Although not a passenger on the *Mayflower*, Robinson assisted in the preparations. See *ODCC*, 1403. MH

churches of the Reformation had stood still; that God would still let new truths burst forth from His Word; that, to say the least, a completion of the Reformation by means of a new Reformation, the completion of the old confession by means of new confessions, was necessary. And who would find these new truths, formulate these new confessions? That would be done by the individual local congregation out of the *hic et nunc* ("the here and now") of its confessional situation. A host of new confessions would thus come into existence.

And that has actually been the case. Karl Barth himself points out that the same renewal movement of the nineteenth century, which in Lutheranism led to the revival of the *Book of Concord*, resulted in the drafting of ever so many new confessions in the orthodox free churches in the Reformed area (*Gesammelte Vorträge*, Bd. II, p. 80). The pressure for new confessions, the emergence of new confessional forms for a more or less limited area, which we observe in modern Lutheranism, is a criterion of the Calvinizing process through which our churches are passing, all the more since this movement goes hand in hand with a growing lack of understanding of the old Confessions of the Lutheran Reformation and of the meaning of the confessional pledge in our Church.

Here, with respect to our confessional pledge, opinions are divided even as the churches themselves part company at this point. Here it also becomes clear why the Reformed Churches have not been able to preserve their Confessions. The "pious relativism" of the Reformed Confession finds expression in the *quatenus* (the "insofar as") of the doctrinal pledge. Whereas the Lutheran pastor assumes the responsibility of teaching according to the Confessions "because" (*quia*) they are in harmony with the Holy Scriptures, the Reformed pastor does this only "insofar as" (*quatenus*) it is scriptural, and because he regards the Lutheran pledge with the *quia* as presumption, yea, as an elevation of the Confessions above the Holy Scriptures.[8]

What shall we say to this? First, that the properly understood *quatenus* ("insofar as") is self-evident for every church which appeals to the Reformation, since no church wants to teach anything which is not Scripture doctrine. It is so self-evident that one does not need to articulate it. Men can and must accept also the Talmud or the Tridentinum [creed of the Roman Catholic Council of Trent] *quatenus*, "insofar as," they interpret Scriptures correctly. The *quatenus* pledge is really no pledge at all. Second, the question which comes into consideration in connection with the confessional pledge is simply and solely the question whether the Confessions are scriptural, whether they are the substance of the Holy Scriptures, as the Formula of Concord expresses it. Only if I am unshakably convinced, and that on the basis of most earnest searching in the Scriptures, can I accept it and promise that "I will neither privately nor publicly

---

8   See Sasse's "*Quatenus or Quia*," in *Lonely Way* 1:455–60. Originally published in *AELKZ* 71, no. 7 (February 18, 1938): 152–54. Huss number 201. MH

speak or write anything contrary to it, but by the help of God's grace intend to abide thereby" (Conclusion of the Solid Declaration).

Later on we shall have to answer the question whether the Lutheran Church of today still desires and is able to abide by this attitude, and that means whether she desires and is able to remain a confessional church. Here we are speaking only of the tragic fate of the Reformed churches which have lost their confession because along with the *quatenus* they also lost its meaning. It was a logical consequence of the *quatenus* that the great Reformed Churches of the world in fact, and frequently in theory, know only of a pledge upon the Holy Scriptures. The understanding of the Holy Scriptures must be left entirely up to the individual; hence one need not marvel that very soon, in accordance with the above-quoted prophesy of Robinson, common reason took its place at the side of Scripture as a source of truth and eventually as *norma normans* (the guiding principle or "norming norm") in its place.

In the church at Basel, to which Karl Barth belongs, every pastor may teach trinitarian or unitarian doctrine, may confess or deny the fundamental truths of the Apostolic Creed, such as the virgin birth and the resurrection of our Lord, according to his preference. The same is true of all great Reformed and Presbyterian Churches of the world. That is the final result of the "pious and free relativism" which according to Barth belongs to the essence of the Reformed Confession. Only a few small groups have succeeded in salvaging remnants of the Reformed Confession. Aside from that, the Reformed Church as a confessional Church has foundered.

3

The same fate has overtaken the Anglican churches. The Anglican revival of the nineteenth century was a revival of the Roman Catholic heritage. Its result was the destruction of the Reformation heritage, which had found its dogmatic expression in the *Thirty-Nine Articles*. In the last of his "Tracts for the Times" (1840), John Henry Newman made the vain effort to interpret the articles so ingeniously that they did not contradict the Roman Catholic doctrines. Since the controversy over Newman's tract (no. 90) and his secession to the Roman Church, the conviction has prevailed more and more that the claim of the Church of England to the unbroken continuation of the "ancient, undivided Catholic Church" is irreconcilable with the Reformed doctrine contained in the *Thirty-Nine Articles*.

Nor are these articles regarded today as the official doctrinal confession of the Anglican Churches, though every candidate for ordination in the Church of England and in the majority of her daughter churches must solemnly subscribe to them. How can they do that? We Lutherans do not understand—or have we, too, perhaps come that far? The more silent things became with respect to the *Thirty-Nine Articles* in the nineteenth century, the stronger the significance of the ancient church confessions, the Apostolic Creed and the Nicene Creed, which the Lambeth Quadrilateral of 1888[9] recommended as the basis of a general church union. Also the Athanasian Creed, as we know, has its place in the liturgy, where it is prayed on high festivals and on apostle's days in place of the Apostolic Creed. Now even the archbishop of Canterbury is silent on the Nicene Creed, and entire dioceses do not dare to declare it to be a doctrinal confession, because its adoption in its Western form with the *filioque* (the doctrine that the Holy Spirit proceeds from the Father *and the Son*) would hinder the hopes for union with the Eastern Churches, while the Oriental form without the *filioque* would, on the other hand, hinder the union with Occidental Catholicism.

I did not want to believe my ears when a competent Anglican theologian explained this to me. Only the doctrinal content of the *Book of Common Prayer* is to be regarded as binding doctrine of the church, whereupon I could merely ask whether the *filioque* was not included in the Athanasian Creed which is expressly designated as "this Confession of our Christian Faith" in the *Prayer Book*.

It is necessary to have read the great Anglican theologians of recent times—from Pusey to Gore—in order to estimate the incalculable tragedy which is occurring in the Church which more than others claimed to be the unifying center of the confessions (various churches). What keeps it alive, now that it has dispensed with its confessions? Its age? Its alleged succession? The ancient Scottish Confession already (Article 18) gives the correct answer to this question: "Cain has preeminence of age and dignity over Abel and Seth. Jerusalem had preeminence over all places on earth, and its priests stood in direct Aaronic succession. All this one finds more readily in Rome than in Canterbury; and, in addition to all the errors and heresies, one also finds there 'the high articles of the divine Majesty'" [S.A. I], which since Luther are neither in dispute nor controversy between the papal Church and the Church of the Reformation. The Anglican Church merely appears to cling to it, for it is unable to say what it really thinks about the Trinity and about the incarnation. There are simply solemn words, concerning which everyone may think as he will.

4

From the Reformed and Anglican Churches we now take a look at the modern Ecumenical Movement, which has its origin in both groups. To avoid misunderstanding, it should be said at the outset that we do consider a sound Ecumenical Movement to be necessary. In a world, in which the most distant nations have become neighbors, in which the great problems of political and agricultural

---

9   Sometimes called the Chicago-Lambeth Quadrilateral, a slightly revised version of the four articles agreed upon at the General Convention of the Episcopal Church in the United States in Chicago in 1986. The four points are (A) the Holy Scriptures, (B) the Apostles' and Nicene Creeds, (C) the two sacraments ordained by Christ, (D) the historic episcopate. See *ODCC*, 946. MH

life must be solved on an international basis, also the churches are confronted by problems which they must solve jointly. One needs but to think of the problems in the mission fields and of the great relief projects in a century of world catastrophies.

Vilmar already brought up the question whether the modern means of communication—how modest these were in the middle of the nineteenth century!—should benefit only the unbelievers. More than that! The relation of the churches to one another also must undergo a change at a time in which they are no longer separated by the boundaries of countries and continents, but have become close neighbors and are learning to know one another in a manner as never before. Just consider what it means that the Eastern Church has a following in all parts of the world. And what a change has come about in the relation of Rome to the "separated brethren," who, after all, according to dogma and church law, are heretics. Cooperation of the churches in all areas in which this is possible without violating conscience, including the serious discussion of doctrine, cannot be disputed by anyone.

However, we must be clear about one thing. There are ethical and theological presuppositions. To the ethical presuppositions belong absolute truthfulness and respect for the conscience of the other party. To the theological presuppositions belongs clarity concerning the things in which there is agreement and those in which there is not agreement. Where these presuppositions do not exist, the Ecumenical Movement becomes a grandiose repetition of the syncretistic and unionistic movements of the past. As these did not serve the cause of truthfulness, but of untruthfulness; did not build the church, but destroyed the church—even so a false Ecumenical Movement, as we have it before us today in the World Council of Churches, must serve the disintegration of what we still have in the world today by way of Christian faith.

We state this with great sorrow over the tragedy which is taking place in present Protestant Christendom. For the issue concerns Protestantism, not the several Orthodox Churches which are associated with it simply for practical reasons. One would for once like to know what these shrewd Orientals, who in a pain-filled history have learned to interpret their canon law *kat' oikonomian*'— that is, to annul it practically wherever the life interest of the church requires it— really think about their associates in the World Council [of Churches]. They salve their consciences with their declarations concerning the absolute inviolability of their dogma and their culture, and they mean that very seriously. There is no power in the world which could rob an Orthodox Church of its orthodoxy. No sultan, no Bolshevik dictator, was able to do that. It would do the other churches good if they for once began to ponder the cause and meaning of this contention before they become upset over the inflexibility of the Eastern Church, of Rome, and of the remnants of orthodox Lutheranism.

Since they refuse to believe what a Lutheran says, we are going to let one of the Reformed tell us about the real issue. When in 1929 the State Church of

Hesse-Cassel and the faculty at Marburg celebrated the four hundredth anniversary of the Marburg debate in the spirit of Philip of Hesse[10] and of Bucer with a meeting of world Protestantism, it was the representative from Zurich, Emil Brunner, who spoke golden words concerning the unionism which at that time, as also at other ecumenical gatherings, was coming to the surface. We quote a few sentences from the report published by H. Hermelink, which today has also completely disappeared (*Das Marburger Religionsgespräch 1529/1929: Zum vierhundertjährigen Gedächtnis*, 1930):

> "The first thing which we descendents of the Reformation ought to do at this memorial celebration is this: We wish to refrain from excusing our reformers for the things which they did nor did not do here. It is characteristic of our time that it desires to establish church union, as it were, at any price. One cannot understand that the reformers, knowing what was at stake, parted in disunity. Let us not forget that the reformers did not as yet know two tricks, which we understand beautifully. One of these is the avoidance of the question of truth for the sake of peace and unity; the other is the bridging of divisive differences in matters of faith by appealing to an alleged higher unity of the spirit or of religious experience which lies above all formulations of creeds.

> "From this modern vantage point of the spirit it is indeed inevitable that one must view the controversy between Luther and Zwingli as a lamentable misunderstanding, as a lack of evangelical broad-mindedness and Christian love, which one can excuse only in reference to the circumstances of that time, etc. That we cease doing this, I say, would be the first requisite proof that we have come to understand something of the spirit of the Reformation. We do not wish to excuse them, but to thank them that they were in such dead earnest about the questions of faith, the question concerning the truth of their statements of faith. For this seriousness is nothing else than the power of the Reformation. Had they been less serious about their statements of faith . . . the break with Rome and therefore also the Reformation would never have occurred." (pp. 38f.)

> "It belongs to the *ethos* and *pathos* ["the character and feeling"] of the reformers that they could not cry out 'peace,' where there was no peace. Precisely for that reason they were reformers," thinks Brunner. (p. 41)

The same thing could be said of all periods of church history in which the doctrine of the Church was taken seriously. Never was there a greater opportunity for the Church to do missionary work than in the fourth century, after Constantine had given to the Church an empire for the purpose of evangelization. Should not

---

10 Philip of Hesse (1504–67), the father-in-law of Maurice of Saxony (1521–53), was born in Marburg. He met with Luther at Worms in 1521 and signed the Augsburg Confession, though he thought Article X on the Lord's Supper could have been milder. He convened the Marburg Colloquy in hope of bridging the gap between Luther and Zwingli (s.v. *Christian Cyclopedia*). MH

the theologians at that time have devoted all their powers to this missionary opportunity and agreed on a formula for union, as it had been repeatedly recommended (viz. the *homoios kata tas graphas*, the doctrine that Jesus Christ is "like unto the Father according to the Scriptures"), instead of being in controversy for two generations with respect to the *homoousios* (the doctrine that Jesus Christ is "of the same substance with the Father")? Had they yielded to this temptation, there would perhaps have been an "evangelization" a century later, but there would have been no Gospel, at any rate not the Gospel of Him who is our Savior because He is true God and true man.

In that address Brunner calls attention to the distance which lies between modern Christendom, including its theologians, and the issue with which the Reformation was concerned:

> It is not true, as superficial unionists' sentiment would have us believe, that we have happily progressed beyond the reformers in the matter of unity. This impression is due only to the fact that the present generation on the whole is so far removed from the issue of the Reformation that the conflicts hardly come into view at all. Our present unity is primarily a result of our distance from the issue, whereas the dissent of the reformers was a result of their nearness to the issue. (p. 41)

This, too, may with proper adaptations be applied to all periods of time. Why is it that Lutherans and Reformed in the sixteenth century could debate so profoundly, as it was done in the colloquies at Marburg and Mömpelgard?[11] Because they had a common basis from which they could proceed, namely, the unconditional authority of the Holy Scriptures. Modern Protestantism no longer knows this great common possession. For there is no unanimity as to what the Holy Scriptures, theologically considered, really are. Would that the World Council of Churches spoke out about the authority of the Bible! It would become apparent that in the Orthodox Churches, despite their doctrine of tradition, the Bible is regarded more highly than in the churches which make their appeal to the Reformation. No ecumenical council and no pope could ever challenge a clear doctrine of the Scriptures, such as that of the virgin birth of the Lord, as it is done in the churches of the *sola Scriptura*, Lutheran and Reformed. Also the great contest between Rome and Lutheranism as it is characterized on the Lutheran side by names such as Martin Chemnitz and Johann Gerhard, was possible because, despite the unbridgeable contrast, there was something which they had in common, namely, the great truths of the ancient church dogmas, which since Luther are not in dispute or controversy, "because we on both sides confess them" [SA I 4].

Only on the basis of a common, albeit very limited, conviction of faith is cooperation possible. That is generally admitted. Even the most extreme representatives of an enthusiastic ecumenism would not care to sit down together with

---

11 See Raitt, *Colloquy of Montbéliard*. MH

the Mormons or the Jehovah's Witnesses in a World Council [of Churches]. In one way or another everyone draws a certain boundary of possible fellowship. But unless the boundary is defined very accurately, cases such as the "Festival of Faith" will occur again and again. The San Francisco Council of Churches, under the leadership of the director of the Commission of Churches for International Affairs in the World Council of Churches and in the International Missionary Council, and of the member of the corresponding Commission on International Affairs in the Lutheran World Federation, in 1955 arranged a service in commemoration of the tenth birthday of the United Nations. A rabbi spoke the invitation to worship. The lection, read antiphonally by the liturgist and the assembly, consisted of statements from the holy writings of Confucianism, Hinduism, Buddhism, the New Testament, the Qur'an, and the Old Testament as the holy book of the Jews. This was followed by silent prayers, the text for each religion being printed on the program, including two for the Buddhists and one each for those believing in a supreme being and for the atheists.

Naturally no one would think of sanctioning a thing of that kind. But when even a professor of one of the most prominent Lutheran seminaries in America, who must know full well what faith and prayer mean, permits himself to be carried along to such a violation of the boundary, then we can see clearly what can happen to an Ecumenical Movement which does not rest upon a clear foundation. The fact that such exceptions are multiplying, especially in the mission fields of Asia, must sound the alarm for all Christians and all churches which have still preserved a remnant of dogmatic substance.

But the World Council of Churches has actually dispensed with a confessional foundation such as was at one time recommended in the Lambeth Quadrilateral (the Apostolic and Nicene Creeds) and adopted by the Lausanne World Conference of Faith and Order in 1927, at which the Nicene Creed (without prejudice to the Eastern Church's rejection of the *filioque*) was adopted as the common confession of the churches. The execution of this resolution proved impossible because the weight of the nonconfessional churches of America was too great. Hence the World Council of Churches, which was founded in 1948, returned to the basis of the Young Men's Christian Association, as it had been adopted in 1855 in Paris and as it had played a prominent part in the beginning of the Faith and Order Movement.

Hence the constitution of the World Council defines the "basis" in this way: "The World Council of Churches is a fellowship of churches which accept our Lord Jesus Christ as God and Savior." In the official interpretation found in the Appendix to the Evanston report (English edition, p. 306), the statement is made concerning this basis that it is "less than a confession, but much more than a mere formula of agreement." "It is truly a basis in that the life and activity of the World Council are based upon it."

Self-evidently that is not theology, but the arbitrary language of American churchmen "gone to seed," "the systematic misuse of a terminology invented specifically for this purpose." It is part of the unspeakable tragedy of the English-speaking churches that modern English scarcely still permits a rendering of the clear theological terminology of the great periods of the Church. This also explains much of the lack of clarity in the theological thinking of the Lutherans in America. Let's leave out of the account for a moment the unclear and theologically contestable formula "God and Savior" (because it does not exclude Monophysitism). This phrase was coined by dilettantes themselves. Either I confess that Jesus Christ is true God and my Savior—then that is a confession. Or I do not confess it—then it cannot be a basis for a fellowship of churches. (May we remind you that the English Bible uses "fellowship" to render *koinonia*, therefore the *communion* which we confess in the *Credo*, e.g., 1 John 1:3?) This ingenious interpretation clearly has the purpose of justifying this minimum of allegedly present common conviction of faith.

The basis is understood in that interpretation as a description of "the nature of fellowship" of the churches in the World Council. For this fellowship begins a fellowship of churches and "has a unique character, a specific source and a specific dynamic." The churches enter into relation with each other because there is a unity given once for all in the person and work of their common Lord, and because the living Lord gathers His people together. Then, indeed, the adoption of the "basis" is not a profession of its content. I can "adopt" it, even if I do not regard Jesus Christ as my God and Savior. What would the fathers of the Formula of 1855[12] have said to such an interpretation? Then one could indeed quiet the objections of the Swiss churches which honestly cannot with good conscience acknowledge the deity of Christ!

Thus it is now stated: "Each church which joins the World Council must therefore seriously consider whether it desires to participate in a fellowship having this particular basis. On the other hand, the World Council would overstep the limits it has set for itself if it should seek to pronounce judgment as to whether any particular church is in fact taking the basis seriously. It remains the responsibility of each church to decide for itself whether it can sincerely accept the basis of the Council."

The "basis" is to indicate not merely the nature but also the range of the fellowship. In this connection finally a more concrete statement is made: "By joining together, the churches seek to respond to the call and action of their divine Lord. The World Council must therefore consist of churches which acknowledge that Lord as the Second Person of the Trinity." One gains the impression that this statement was inserted in an outline of the document. It excludes the Unitarians, but why not also the liberal groups of the Quakers, and why not also the Unitarians in the other churches?

And what does it mean "to acknowledge the Lord Christ as the Second Person of the Trinity" if it is not a confession, but something "less than a confession"?

---

12   See above, the discussion of the WCC confessional foundation, p. 481. MH

The statement "Christ is the Second Person of the Trinity" is either true or false. It can be accepted as true only by faith. It is a part—indeed, the heart and core— of the Christian faith. Only as a believer can I make this statement. Outside of the confession it is meaningless, for the very terms "person" and "Trinity" must of necessity be misunderstood by nonbelievers. They do not even occur in their Christian meaning outside the Creed. But as the statement "Christ is the Second Person of the Trinity" is used here, it is intended to be "less than a confession," therefore a sort of working hypothesis.

May those who are here dealing so lightly with the names God, Lord, and Savior ask themselves whether they are not sinning against the commandment which forbids the misuse of the name of God. What are these people actually thinking about when they pray "Hallowed be Thy name"? And if one now takes into consideration what kind of a world power the World Council of Churches has become, and how through its large and small meetings, its education undertakings, its literature, and its subsidiary organizations, which are already making the claim in many countries to be the representatives of non-Roman Christendom, it influences the churches, we need not be surprised that the relativizing of Christian truth, the destruction of all dogmatic Christianity, and the disintegration of the confession are constantly making headway. It is a tragedy of church history that a movement which was born out of the deepest need of a torn Christendom, and out of the desire for true unity of the Church, should end in the destruction of the common substance of faith and doctrine which still existed in the era of the divided confessional churches.

5

We have spoken of the fate of confessionalism in the Reformed and Anglican churches, as well as in the present-day Ecumenical Movement, not to criticize others, but to diagnose the deadly disease which has also seized the Lutheran churches. Of course, the situation is not this, that we in the face of the nonconfessional nature of other churches could utter a confident, "Here is the Lord's temple" on the basis that we still have a Confession, and a very solid one, the Book of Concord of more than 1,000 pages. And if we do not have the entire Book of Concord, then in every case we have the Augsburg Confession, the Unaltered one, self-evidently. It cannot be praised too highly.[13]

In his above-mentioned essay, Karl Barth quotes a hymn of praise which a convinced Lutheran of the nineteenth century, or someone who considered himself a Lutheran, composed:

Sichere Kirche unsere Kirche,
Mauer um sie, Heil und Wehr,

---

13 Sasse is referring to those Scandinavian churches and their daughters which had accepted only the Augsburg Confession as their confessional basis. MH

Augsburgs siegendes Bekenntnis,
Wie ein Bollwerk um sie her.

Our Church, the Church secure,
Walled about by salvation and defense,
Augsburg's conquering Confession
As a bulwark all about her.[14]

One does not know what is worse in this verse, the poetry or the theology. It is an involuntary caricature of the Lutheran faith, but from this distorted picture we recognize the danger which threatens our Church. It is the danger that the firmness of our convictions may become a false security, the assurance of genuine faith a type of *securitas* (the false security) against which Luther, during his whole lifetime, contended with such earnestness. It may be that the "comforting and most necessary" article of faith concerning the Church, which was given us *ne desperemus*, "so that we may not despair" [Ap VII–VIII 9], as the Apology puts it, may become a false faith in the Church, a faith in my Lutheran Church, pride in the great or small church organization to which I belong. Here is the *ecclesia pura* ["the pure church"]; "Here is the Lord's temple!"

In the publication of one of the large "middle-of-the-road" Lutheran churches in America, we could read (1955) in one of the enthusiastic reports what Luther would say if he had come to the city where the great convention was taking place, if he had seen the beautiful Lutheran church edifices, the prospering congregations, the impressive meetings and church services, the great charitable and evangelistic endeavors, the well-organized financial system—in this connection the enthusiastic reporter even mentioned the name of Tetzel [1465–1519]. So that is what has happened to "my Church"!

Certainly these are all very beautiful and necessary things and we do not wish to minimize the faith and the love which lie behind such works and meetings, behind these devoted congregations. But we believe we know what Luther, with his characteristic clarity, would have replied to such talk about "his Church," he, who was of the opinion that lightning has a preference for striking church steeples[15] because in no house, not even in a brothel, such grievous sins are committed as in churches. But his human—only too human—church patriotism is to all appearances ineradicable.

Certainly we are all happy when Christians in all parts of the world, also such as belong to other denominations, begin to get interested in Luther and Lutheran doctrine. We can only rejoice if in America people who until now have

---

14 I have provided a new translation of the hymn to better reflect the original verse. MH

15 "Your only reason for praying is that you are obliged to say so and so many prayers and this you intend to do in full. Little wonder, then, that thunder and lightning frequently set fire to churches when we make the house of prayer into a house of mockery by calling that prayer in which we bring nothing before God and desire nothing from him!" (*Von den guten Werken* [*Treatise on Good Works*, 1520], Aland 761, WA 6:204–76, cited here from AE 44:67). MH

belonged to no church or who in great disappointment turn from modernist churches and find the way to Lutheranism. And we rejoice with all our hearts that people in all parts of the world who have been instructed in Luther's catechism are conscious of their Lutheranism. We salute every indication of desire for genuine worldwide fellowship among Lutherans. But then to let pride over the 60 or 70 million nominal Lutherans in this world and the increasing influence of the Lutheran churches upon public life, to let our joy over the reception given to Lutheran bishops by the last emperors and kings who still exist in this world, by presidents and mighty foreign ministers, move us to intone hymns to the Church according to the melody of *Sichere Kirche, unsere Kirche* ("Our Church, the Church Secure")—that would be completely un-Lutheran! Where such longings arise in small or great church leaders—the smallest ones seem to be in special danger in this respect—one must remember that the word "Lutheran" in our Confessions occurs only at one place, namely, where the Apology, Article XV, complains about the opponents: "That dear holy Gospel they call Lutheran."

The Augsburg Confession has no intention of presenting the distinctive doctrines of a particular church which distinguishes it from other particular churches, but it desires to confess the faith of the true Church of all times. That unforgettable champion of true Lutheran unity, Michael Reu [1869–1943] of Dubuque, especially in the last years of his life, while preparations were being made for the Lutheran World Convention planned for 1940 in Philadelphia, again and again pointed out the true meaning of the Seventh Article of the *Augustana* regarding the unity of the Church.

According to it, the unity of the Church does not consist in general agreement concerning the Gospel and the administration of the Sacraments. The Catholics and the Baptists also have such agreement in their own way. The *consentire de doctrina evangelii et de administratione sacramentorum* ("agreement regarding the doctrine of the Gospel and the administration of the Sacraments") [AC VII 2] is commented upon by means of the text which in the case of the *Augustana* is no less authentic: "That the Gospel be preached harmoniously with a clear understanding of it and the Sacraments be administered in accordance with the divine Word."

If we take note of this, then, we shall understand that the Confessions do not have a particular Lutheran Church in mind, but the one holy catholic (universal) and apostolic Church which lies hidden in visible Christendom. Then church patriotism, pride over one's own confessional Church, which is only a substitute for the real Spirit-wrought faith in the *Una Sancta* (one holy Christian Church), will cease. Then there will no longer be that horrible misunderstanding of the creeds and denominations as more or less justified expressions of Christianity, as forms of religious life, whose form one can describe and which one can arrange in "families" according to their similarities (e.g., the "family of the Lutheran Churches"). Then also the "branch theory," which has penetrated into Lutheran Christendom from the Anglican Church (the view according to which a few [Orthodox, Roman Catholics, and Anglicans] or all particular churches together form the *Una Sancta*) is possible.

One can only be horrified when he reads the statement in Lutheran church constitutions that this particular church is a "part" or a "member" of the one holy catholic (universal) church. And it becomes completely impossible to see in the *Una Sancta* a distant goal, which we must achieve through the union of all the churches, and to see in such union of all Christians into one great visible organization the fulfillment of the prayer of our Lord: "That they all may be one." What kind of apostasy from the true faith this is becomes evident from the well-known statement of William Temple: "I believe in one holy catholic Church and sincerely regret that at present it does not exist." (By the way: Whether one says "I believe the Church" or "I believe in the Church" makes no real difference. The Greek text of the Nicene Creed has "in"; the Latin text does not have it.) Only the Lutheran faith in the *Una Sancta*, and the humble refusal to glorify our own Church and our own Confessions flowing from it, enable us to answer the question whether Lutheranism isn't also infected with the disease of deconfessionalization and whether, if this should be the case, the possibility exists that it can be healed. To the first question we must answer yes.

We must not make the mistake of comparing the theory of our own church with the practice of others, so that the good which we find in ourselves would shine all the brighter against the dark background which we find in others. Certainly, in theory we still "have" the Confessions. We still pledge our pastors upon these Confessions with the *quia* of conviction. But is that not perhaps an anachronism in many churches, perhaps also in the highly conservative ones? Do our candidates really *know their Book of Concord*? Do our pastors still know it? And what about our bishops and church presidents who before God have the tremendous responsibility of preserving the true doctrine in their Church?[16]

Isn't it a fact that the Lutheran Churches which are using the English language do not even have a reliable English text of the Confessions? The edition of Jacobs is full of mistakes and antiquated. The *Concordia Triglotta* is better, but also its text needs revision. Above all, it is not proper, as we have already pointed out, to translate the *Augustana* from the Latin alone, as is done in the *Apology*, without considering the German text. But the texts alone will not do it

---

16 "It appears to me to be the decisive question for all of Lutheranism whether 'the turn of the Spirit from subject to object,' which began after the World War, will be fulfilled in the future [after this war]. To this above all it is important that our theologians again become humble students of the Confessions, as Luther remained a lifelong student of the catechism. I attempt in my lectures and courses ever and again to lead students into the fundamental study of the symbolical books. The *Augustana* and the Apology and the Large Catechism must be our breviary. For this we make use of free working fellowships in which the range of theology is talked through using something like Schlink's [*Theology of the Lutheran Confessions*] book to work through the texts. I am delighted you also treasure Schlink's book so highly" (Sasse to Leiv Aalen, October 6, 1942; in the Harrison Collection). MH

either, though they are of special importance in America, where the knowledge of German and also of Latin has declined to strongly in contrast with the nineteenth century. Is it not true with respect to Lutheranism of the entire world that the pledging upon the Confessions threatens to become what the subscription to the *Thirty-Nine Articles* means in the Anglican churches? What should a Swedish candidate think of his pledge when he knows that he is receiving his office at the hands of a bishop who received his consecration with the cooperation of Anglican bishops and will together with Anglicans consecrate other bishops? How can a pastor in Sweden or Denmark take the Seventh or Tenth Article of the *Augustana* seriously when his Church practices *communicatio in sacris* (pulpit and altar fellowship) with the churches of England and Scotland? For all these are not exceptional cases, for each of which apology is made individually, but symptoms of a development which one may observe in all Lutheran churches, not only in Germany and Holland, and in the young churches in the mission fields, but also, even though in a different form, in the conservative churches in America. For there the validity of the Confessions is indeed still taken very seriously, and unions are still rejected, but the truly definitive documents are nevertheless the new confessional forms such as the *Brief Statement*, which for Missouri and the other churches of the Synodical Conference has gained such a great importance because they fully believed themselves to be of one mind with respect to the Book of Concord.

But does the doctrine of justification in the *Brief Statement* actually agree completely with that of the ancient Confessions? Has not also conservative Lutheranism definitely gone along with the developments which are pressing for new confessions? Certainly it can become necessary to reformulate or also merely to clarify the true understanding of the Scriptures and of the old Confessions. But that can only be done on the basis of the Confessions if these with their "we believe, teach and confess" are still to express the great consensus in which we stand with the orthodox Church of all times. Most assuredly that is the will and conviction of the churches of the Synodical Conference. But the question arises whether reference to the Confessions is not infrequently made as to something self-evident, something which no longer needs to be discussed.

The full seriousness of the situation for the Lutheran Church as a confessional Church becomes clear in the question of the Lutheran World Federation. The fathers of the old World Convention, the generation of confessing Lutherans such as Morehead [1867–1936], Knubel, Hein, Reu, Long [1882–1948], to mention only these, would never have dreamed that such a thing as the present World Federation would ever emerge out of their efforts, though the theologians of the Missouri Synod predicted just that.[17] In the "Declaration of the

---

17   See Francis Pieper's introduction to the first issue of *CTM*, "Ecumenical Lutheranism," in *At Home in the House of My Fathers*, ed. and trans. Matthew C. Harrison (St. Louis: Concordia, 2011), 668–81. MH

World Convention concerning Its Confession" (Copenhagen, 1929), they stated that the confessional basis of the World Convention was for them as well as for the convention an "actual" confession, the "testimony of firm and unchanging adherence to the faith of our fathers." But this "unconditional" adherence to the faith expressed in the *Augustana* was no longer possible in the Lutheran World Federation, even though the inquiry of our Australian Lutheran Church received the *bona fide* answer that the confessional basis was to be understood in this sense.

The change which had taken place when the old generation had died out and the leadership was transferred to Sweden was too profound. In these letters we have often spoken of the broad-mindedness which was displayed in the reception of a church which (like the Church of Indonesia [HKBP])[18] either did not have the confessional basis (the *Augustana* and Luther's catechisms), or understood them only in the sense of historical membership in the family of the Lutheran churches, not in the sense of binding the public doctrine to the Confessions (Brazilian Church Federation), or that of churches which grant Communion fellowship to all Protestants and are therefore *de facto* united (Italy, England), or even of a church such as that of Pomerania, which combines unconditional loyalty to the Church of the Union with membership in the [Lutheran] World Federation, of which it is a member.

These historical facts are highlighted by the relation between the World Federation and the *World Council of Churches*. It is no accident, but a demonstration of the insoluble connection between both organizations, that they have their headquarters on the same property in Geneva. As the Lutheran World Federation in its constitution considers it one of its tasks "to foster Lutheran participation in ecumenical movements," therefore the participation of the Lutherans in ecumenical movements—and that for all practical purposes means the World Council of Churches—so the World Council, according to its constitution, is to establish "relations with denominational federations of worldwide scope." The leading men of the World Federation at one and the same time occupy leading positions in the World Council, the administrative offices in Geneva work hand in hand in a friendly manner, and, if we are correctly informed, common devotions are conducted.

Of course, no member church of the Lutheran World Federation needs to belong to the World Council of Churches. But now that the last large church in the World Federation, which until this time did not belong to the World Council, the American Evangelical Lutheran Church (of Norwegian origin) voted with a two-thirds majority to join the World Council, and now the smaller churches which with it and the American Lutheran Church are likewise entering into the "merger of the center," there will remain, with the exception of a few very small and not fully organized missionary and diaspora groups numbering a few

---

18   See above, Letter 27, "Worldwide Lutheranism after Hanover," pp. 163–81. MH

thousand souls, only one church of the World Federation which does not yet belong to the World Council. That is the United Evangelical Lutheran Church in Australia, numbering about 40,000 souls. Whether it will be able to maintain this position remains to be seen. Thus, though their organizations remained separate, the World Federation and the World Council have grown together in a way which makes the Lutheran World Federation a Lutheran branch of the Ecumenical Church. Perhaps the next generation, which has been totally trained in the spirit of the Ecumenical Church by Geneva, will ask why the organizations must remain separate.

It is a problem which exists in a different form in Germany between the EKiD and the VELKD (The Evangelical Church in Germany and the United Evangelical Lutheran Church of Germany). One cannot, on the one hand, join with the VELKD (the United Evangelical Lutheran Church of Germany) in giving assent to the Lutheran Confessions in their positive and negative statements and thereby establish the church boundary with respect to the Reformed and United churches, and then together with the EKiD (The Evangelical Church in Germany) destroy this boundary again by granting to it the right as a "confessing church" to judge doctrine and to invite the Lutherans to give ear to the errors condemned by them as "to the testimony of the brethren." That cannot be done, and especially not if one belongs to both organizations. Even Bishop Lilje ought to recognize that as leading bishop of the VELKD (the Evangelical Lutheran Church of Germany) he cannot pronounce the *damnamus* ("we condemn") against false doctrine which he as representative chairman of the council of the EKiD (The Evangelical Church in Germany) must recognize as "the testimony of the brethren."

Exactly the same is true with respect to the relation of the Lutheran World Federation and the World Council of Churches. It is impossible for me to "adhere unconditionally" to the Confessions of the fathers and at the same time to relativize them in the manner in which it is being done in the World Council. It is impossible for me as a Lutheran to give testimony concerning Christ as the hope of the world together with those who do not believe in the second coming of Christ. But if it is said that the message of Evanston [1954 Assembly of the World Council of Churches] is no confession, then one can only remind people with the answer once given by Karl Barth in Munich to Bishop Meiser as the latter put this question to him with respect to the deplorable confessional declaration at Barmen: "Is it not true, Professor, that the Declaration of Barmen was merely a theological declaration and not a confession?" The answer was: "You confessed it that time, Herr Bishop, did you not?"[19] The extent of the relativizing

---

19 On the full story of the Bethel Confession (predecessor of the Barmen Declaration) written largely by Bonhöffer (1906–45) and Sasse, and the struggle at Barmen, see Lowell Green, *Lutherans Against Hitler*, pp. 159–98. Green offers a penetrating critique in a chapter titled "The 1933 Bethel Confession: A Lutheran Criticism of Nazism": "The Bethel Confession clearly rejected anti-Semitic racism. One would seek in vain for such a statement in the vaunted Barmen Declaration, which contained little that

of the Lutheran Confessions in the Lutheran World Federation is evident from the simple fact that it practically made the attitude of the World Council of Churches in the matter of its "basis" its own. It (the Federation) must leave it to the individual member church how it understands the obligation to the Lutheran Confessions.

6

We believe we know that many a leader in the Lutheran World Federation is not happy when he observes what is becoming of Lutheranism in the world. Everyone who knows him will grant that a man such as Dr. Lundquist[20] feels the tremendous responsibility which he is bearing—though the executive secretary of such an organization is legally only the executive officer of the legislative body. Nor will anyone question that Dr. Schiotz,[21] the president of the Evangelical Lutheran Church, made his decision to recommend the entrance of his Church into the World Council of Churches only after most serious consideration, as a decision of conscience.

In general, however, one will have to say that here, as in the entire Ecumenical Movement, just as in the political mass movements of our time, not personal but transubjective forces are at work. There are mass psychoses not only in the political world but also in the Church, only that in the latter they are even more dangerous. Nor are there any ecclesiastical or theological reasons for a Lutheran Church to join the World Council of Churches. There are only excuses with which one ingeniously endeavors to justify that step. The most favorite rationalization is that Lutheranism dare not bury the talent which has been entrusted to it, that it has a confessional and missionary obligation toward the rest of Christendom, and that its testimony will not be heard if it is given on the outside. One must be "on the inside" to be heard. That is exactly the same logic with which Anglican, Methodist, and Baptist pastors seek to justify their membership in the lodge. As one cannot testify against the lodge in the lodge, just as little can one within the World Council of Churches give a testimony against the Council as it is today and as it will remain in conformity to the law according to which it began.

Sufficient testimonies of the Lutheran faith have been given in the Ecumenical Movement. That, among others, also the representatives of the United Lutheran Church did in Lausanne in 1927.[22] They even distributed special reprints of the

---

spoke against the anti-Jewish stance of Nazism. In this respect, Barmen was a sorry substitute for Bethel" (*Lutherans Against Hitler*, 176). MH

20 Carl Elof Lundquist (1908–65) was executive secretary of the LWF (1951–60) (s.v. *Christian Cyclopedia*). MH

21 See above, p. 329 n. 27. MH

22 Sasse's official report lists Holmes Dysinger, dean and professor of theology, Western Theological Seminary of the United Lutheran Church, Fremont, Nebraska, United Lutheran Church in America; W. H. Greever, professor of ethics, apologetics and

Confessions. Ten years later the representatives of this Church participated in a common Communion in Edinburgh. And again thirteen years later the president[23] of this church opened the National Council of Churches of Christ in the USA in order to emphasize the "oneness in Jesus Christ"—the Lutherans prided themselves over the fact that they were able to have the word "essential" eliminated through negotiation, but it appeared again immediately in the first communication to the American people. Besides, "what difference is there between unity and essential unity"—which exists between Anglicans, Reformed of all shades, Disciples, Lutherans, Quakers, and the Salvation Army? Who was the subject and who was the object of missions in this case? Who instructed whom? What did the Quakers learn from the Lutherans? Did it ever happen that any non-Lutheran Church recognized our doctrine of the sacraments? And how can anyone imagine that the Lutherans could reform the World Council [of Churches]? They will remain a hopeless minority there, which, in addition, is weakened by the differences in its own midst.

Is that really burying one's talent if one does not enter into every fellowship of that kind? Did Luther bury his talent when he refused the hand of fellowship to Zwingli [at Marburg in 1529]? Did the apostles do it when they refused to fellowship with the false teachers? We all wish to confess. We would also in humility instruct other fellow Christians and, wherever possible, learn from them. But to enter into fellowship in which truth and error are as a matter of principle placed on the same level in order to accomplish this end, that would be a denial which renders every confessing word illusory. Thus there will be Lutherans who feel compelled to decline absolutely the invitation to join the World Council of Churches and who likewise cannot belong to the Lutheran World Federation as long as it indicates through its involvement with the World Council of Churches, as well as through its own actions and communications, that it does not take seriously, and perhaps with the best of intentions cannot take seriously, the Lutheran Confessions, which are its doctrinal basis.

---

symbolics, Lutheran Theological Seminary, Columbia South Carolina, United Lutheran Church in America; Augustus Steimle, pastor, Church of the Advent, New York City, United Lutheran Church in America; and Rev. M. G. G. Scherer, secretary of the United Lutheran Church in America (*Die Weltkonferenz* [1929]). We think it fitting to rescue the names of these faithful men from an otherwise forgotten moment in history. "In Lausanne 1927 I have worked together with the delegates of the ULCA and others, later in the committees of the Lutheran World Convention with men like President Knubel, Drs. Reu and Long. What causes me the gravest concern is that fact that our American brethren have obviously forgotten the differences between a Lutheran Church and a Union Church" (Sasse to LCMS President John Behnken, March 1, 1958; copy in the Harrison Collection). MH

23 If the calculation means 1950, the man in question is Franklin Clark Fry, president of the ULC (1945–62). His predecessor, F. H. Knubel (president 1918–44), wins frequent praise from Sasse. The NCCCUSA was formed in Cleveland in 1950 by a merger of several previously existing ecumenical organizations. MH

And nothing in the last years has so served to clarify the position of Lutheranism and the true unity of the Church as did the manly resolution of Missouri not to join the Lutheran World Federation.[24] The Lutheran World Federation ought to sing a *Te Deum* in Minneapolis [at the assembly scheduled for 1957] for this clear confession which in the long view was the greatest service perhaps even to it. For now the world, which already saw the Lutheran Church being absorbed into the creedless Ecumenical Church, knows that there is still a church, or are still churches, which are unwilling to surrender their doctrine, which are not of a mind to abandon the fundamental dogmas of the Christian faith to Rome. That was also a strengthening for many Reformed people who were completely isolated in their churches. It was for them a revival of the hope that God still has ways and means to preserve the old churches of the Reformation from being totally pulverized between Rome and sectarianism. It was an encouragement to do everything in our power to work for the preservation of the Lutheran Confessions.

But what can and must we now do? Let me in conclusion add a few words in answer to this question. The first thing which we have to do is to understand the situation in which the Lutheran Church finds itself today. We must see clearly, and we must pray God that He teach us to understand the times. It is one of those times of the Church when the *casus confessionis* ("a case of confession") [FC SD X 1] has come, when not merely the confession of the mouth but also confession by deed is demanded of us. As we had to confess our faith in the days of Hitler in Germany and silence constituted denial,[25] so the time for remaining silent has come to an end for the rest of the faithful Lutherans today if we do not wish to become deniers of the truth. This is true particularly in America, where Lutheranism is being drawn into the stream of nationalism.

The second thing we have to do is repent. How could it ever come to this in the Lutheran Church? Where were we in the great hours of temptation? Why has confessionally loyal Lutheranism failed so? Why in the days of Hitler did it leave the confessing to others? Where was the voice, the warning voice of our American

---

24　See Sasse, "Missouri and the Lutheran World Federation" (n.p., n.d.) [July 31, 1958?], typed mss., 22 pp. Huss number 58–03. See also "Concerning the Nature of the Lutheran World Federation" (n.p., n.d.) [June 1963?], mimeographed, 3 pp. Huss number 63–04. MH

25　Sasse was editor of the *Kirchliches Jahrbuch*, the general annual for all Protestant churches in Germany, in 1932. He published the first open churchly rejection of the Nazi party platform, particularly the Aryan paragraph (24). See Green, *Erlangen School of Theology*. For a detailed account, see also Feuerhahn, "Hermann Sasse as an Ecumenical Churchman," 68ff. In a letter of September 29, 1933, Sasse wrote to Hodgsen from Erlangen, stating: "Besides I lost a part of my usual income because I cannot bring out this year and perhaps will not in the future bring out the *Kirchliches Jahrbuch für die deutschen evangelischen Landeskirchen*." Apparently the Nazis sought to harass Sasse by investigating the racial lineage of his wife, Charlotte. A document of February 18, 1935, is noted by Feuerhahn: "Reimöler: Aryan lineage of Mrs. Sasse established." See Feuerhahn Chronology. MH

brethren, against Barmen and its untruthful and un-Lutheran "confession," against the EKiD of 1948, against the World Council of Churches of that year?

Doubtless it was in many cases primarily a matter of noble discretion. There was no desire to mingle into the affairs of other churches. They wanted also to exercise Christian patience and to wait and see how things would develop. But on that account they often neglected to speak when the time for speaking had come. There also existed a theological uncertainty, at times also a lack of the gift of discerning the spirits. We all, the entire Lutheran Church, must repent. To this day every renewal of the Church has been born out of repentance, not out of accusations raised against others, but out of the genuine *mea culpa, mea maxima culpa* (the confession of sin: "My fault, my own most grievous fault!"). It is also well to consider that in the language of the New Testament the same word (*homologein, confiteri*) signifies the confession of faith and the confession of guilt.

The third thing which is demanded of us is faith and prayer. We believe that God also can revive sick churches, dying churches, to new life. In our ordination vow there occurs the beautiful statement: ". . . and never to give up a soul as lost." As we are to give up no soul in our congregation, no soul which has been entrusted to us, as lost, so we should give up no church as lost. At the beginning of the nineteenth century the Lutheran Church according to human judgment seemed to be dead, even as it seemed in general as though the Christian faith had perished. Then God granted that wonderful revival on which basically even now lives everything that remains of Christianity in the world. He granted this revival to all churches in all countries, not only to Lutheranism. Who knows what, when God's winds blow, may still emerge out of the Christian faith of other churches, which today is so deteriorated! God also can put our churches to shame by that which He does in other churches.

But whatever He may do, He does it in answer to prayer. Luther's mighty prayer—that is the way his contemporaries in the year following his death regarded it—rescued the Church of the Reformation during the severe crisis in which it seemed doomed. Again, the revival of the nineteenth century was in answer to the prayers of the "quiet ones in the land" [Ps. 35:20],[26] of the seven thousand who had not bowed their knees before the Baal [1 Kings 19:18] of reason, just as even today there still exist the unseen people of God who do not worship the Baalim of our times.

The fourth thing that is demanded of us is love, concerning which many say that it is so frequently lacking among Lutherans. Not the false love which cries peace where there is not peace [Jer. 6:14] and thereby also denies to the soul of the neighbor that peace which surpasses all human reason!

We mean the true love of the New Testament, the love which can also use the sword (Matt. 10:34ff.), the love of John which says no to heresy (1 John 4; 2 John

---

26 "For they speak not peace: but they devise deceitful matters against them that are quiet in the land" Ps. 35:20 (KJV). MH

6ff.). Even when we must speak the clear, unambiguous no to many things which occur in the Lutheran churches of the world and in Christendom generally, and particularly when we have to say it with Lutheran clarity, we shall not want to cease loving those people whose errors we have to reject for the sake of the truth and with whom we therefore cannot have a *communicatio in sacris*, a pulpit and altar fellowship, even if they call themselves Lutherans.

The fifth thing we must do in order to understand the Confessions again is to study the Scriptures. As the Lutheran Church was born in the study of the exegete and preacher, in the interpretation and proclamation of the Word of God, so every renewal which has been granted to it has come out of immersion in the Scriptures. It is not true that the theologians of the nineteenth century discovered and "renewed" the confessional writing and then renovated the confessional Church on the basis of romantic feelings. On the contrary, the renovation was simply the rediscovery of the living content of Scripture, of the Gospel of the Crucified and Risen One, the living experience of justification. That is acknowledged generally by Vilmar in Hesse, and Goehrke and Knak in Pomerania, by Thamsius and Harless in Franconia. "Not till now," writes Harless, "after I, at the hand of the Scriptures, have experienced and recognized the nature of saving truth, did I turn to the confessional writings of my Church. I cannot describe the surprise and emotion with which I found that their content conformed with that of which I had become certain out of the Scriptures and out of the experience of faith." That is the way in which people become Lutherans. It is no indication of soundness of our church that in so many Lutheran faculties, exegesis (interpretation of Scripture) is the weakest subject and the most important biblical-theological works of today are written in other than Lutheran churches.

The sixth thing we must learn in order to become Lutherans again is that we must do serious work in the history of dogma and in dogmatics. Certainly in this respect, the situation is much worse in other churches, as, for instance, the Anglican, not to speak at all of other denominations. That which is written today in the field of systematic theology in Protestantism is, in comparison with that of other periods in church history and with the work of the Roman Church (with a few exceptions, like Karl Barth) amateurish. There is in America a more or less intelligent philosophy of religion, such as that of Niebuhr[27] and Tillich,[28] but it is not theology in the strict sense of the word.

---

27 The American theologian Reinhold Niebuhr (1892–1971) wrote on ethical and social problems. A professor at Union Theological Seminary (New York), he was influenced by Barth and Emil Brunner. For a generation his "Christian realism" exercised an influential critique on American social and political institutions. See *ODCC*, 1153. MH

28 Paul Tillich (1886–1965), like Sasse, served in World War I as an army chaplain. In 1933, he left Germany and became a professor of philosophical theology at Union Theological Seminary (New York). He sought to answer the questions of culture in terms of existentialism, ontology, and Jungian philosophy. See *ODCC*, 1622. MH

But what about us? What a paucity of truly good theological literature! This is something which we who have the task of training young theologians by means of the English language know best. What is truly important is the Luther research going on in Germany and Scandinavia. But it, too, is only in its initial stage, in which it is unable to contribute much to dogmatics, to preaching, to the life of the Church, because it becomes too thoroughly mired in the purely historical and selects from the mass of material only that which pleases modern man in this era of existential philosophy. Is it scientifically justifiable to be compelled to read presentations of the theology of Luther in which Luther's doctrine of the Sacraments is treated only in passing or not at all (e.g., the posthumous work of Johann von Walther, *Die Theologie Luthers*, 1940)?

In the future we shall have to do our theological work in a much different manner in order to understand our Confessions anew. Nor dare we leave theology only to the professors, but we must give thought to the fact that in the Lutheran Church every pastor in his own right must be a theologian. A theologian, as we know, is not merely the representative of a professional science, but he is one who speaks God's Word in the sermon and in his cure of souls and who carries on that praise of God which the ancient Church also called "theology."

Let us never forget that the word "confession" has still a third meaning. *Confiteri* does not only mean the confession of faith, not only the confession of sin, but at the same time and always the praise of God. Not without good reason did Luther upon occasion count the *Te Deum* among the confessions of the church. A true confessional church is a church which in the midst of the distress of this world and in the midst of its own distress does not cease to sing: *Te Deum laudamus, te Dominum confitemur* ("We praise Thee, O God; we acknowledge Thee to be the Lord").[29]

✑

Affectionately yours in the faith and confession thus understood, honored brethren, and with best wishes for a blessed New Year,

Your
Hermann Sasse

---

29 The topic of the nature of confession had long occupied Sasse's thought and work. See "The Church's Confession" (1930), trans. Matthew Harrison, *Logia* 1, no. 1 (October 1992): 3–8. Huss number 056. MH

Person Index

Aalen, Leiv (1906–83), 60n, 237n, 262, 263, 398n, 492n
Adam, Karl (1876–1966), 151
Agricola, Johann (1499–1566), 426n
Alexander (pope, r. 105–115), 441
Althaus, Paul (1888–1966), 46, 193, 248n
Ambrose (340–397), 147, 160, 215, 218, 282, 300
Amsdorf, Nikolaus von (1483–1565), 156
Anacletus (pope, r. 76–88), 441
Andreä, Jacob (1528–90), 43, 277
Anselm of Canterbury (ca. 1033–1109), 71
Antichrist, 25, 96, 101, 102, 103, 104, 105, 106, 107, 108, 109, 110, 114, 115, 190, 198, 240, 259, 298, 343, 414, 430, 433n, 447
Antiochus Epiphanes (ca. 215–164 BC), 102
Anton, K., 157
Aristophanes (446–386 BC), 314n
Aristotle (384–322 BC), 28, 206, 218, 221, 257, 282, 284, 286, 288, 393, 394
Arius (d. 336), 297n
Arseniew, Nikolaus von, 358
Asmussen, Hans (1898–1968), 76, 77n, 110, 196, 267, 351
Athenagoras (fl. second century), 209
Attila ("The Hun," 406–453), 34
Atzberger, 104
Augustine of Ancona (Augustinus Triumphus, 1243–1328), 109
Augustine of Hippo (354–430), 34, 35, 73, 86, 154, 203, 206, 211, 212, 213, 215, 216, 217, 218, 219, 220, 221, 222, 223, 242, 257, 282, 283, 300, 301, 381n, 435n, 436, 445, 452, 453, 454, 455, 456, 459, 460, 471n
Aulén, Gustaf (1879–1977), 252, 257

Bach, Johann Sebastian (1685–1750), 393, 395
Bachmann, E. Theo., 251n
Baier, Johann Wilhelm (1647–95), 27
Bainton, Roland, 367, 368
Barth, Karl (1886–1968), 20, 28, 46, 52, 76n, 77, 134, 140, 144, 165, 182, 183, 199, 222,

225, 251n, 252, 264, 265, 266, 270n, 284, 313, 323, 351, 353, 394n, 478, 479, 480, 481, 482, 489, 495, 500
Basil the Great (ca. 330–ca. 379), 282, 341
Baur, Ferdinand Christian (1792–1860), 36n, 347
Bea, Augustin (cardinal, 1881–1968), 111
Behnken, John William (1884–1968), 24, 49, 69, 96, 116, 137, 180, 182, 204, 335, 353, 367, 399n, 404, 423, 450, 473, 475n, 497n
Bell, G. K. A. (1883–1958), 332n
Bellarmine, Robert (cardinal, 1542–1621), 43
Bengel, Johann Albrecht (1687–1752), 59n, 398
Berengar of Tours (ca. 1010–88), 302, 456, 459
Berggrav, Eivind (1884–1959), 328, 347, 349
Bernadette (1844–79), 343, 432
Bessarion (1403–72), 303
Besserer, 155, 156
Beto, George J., 5n
Beza, Theodore (1519–1605), 43
Bezold, C., 341
Bezzel, Hermann (1861–1917), 59
Billerbeck, Paul (1853–1932), 208
Bismarck, Otto Eduard Leopold von (1815–98), 114, 477
Boleyn, Anne (1501–36), 372n
Bonaparte, Napoleon (1769–1821), 408
Bonaventure (1221–74), 292
Bonhoeffer, Dietrich (1906–45), 496n
Boniface VIII (pope, r. 1294–1303), 374n
Bonner, Campbell, 361
Braun, Thomas, 338
Brent, Charles (1862–1929), 59
Brenz, Johann (1499–1570), 426n
Brightman, 187, 341
Brown, 251n
Brunn, Friedrich August (1819–95), 313, 377
Brunner, Emil (1889–1966), 28, 265, 485, 486, 500n

Brunner, Peter (1900–1981), 193, 194, 251n, 467, 468
Bucer, Martin (1491–1551), 82, 174, 182, 191, 192, 372n, 459, 462, 485
Bugenhagen, Johannes (1485–1558), 156, 228
Bulgakov, Sergei (1871–1944), 342
Bultmann, Rudolf (1884–1976), 37, 61, 84, 262, 265, 273

Caecelian (d. ca. 345), 297n
Cajetan (Tommaso de Vio, 1468–1534), 219
Calhoun, Robert L., 347
Calixtus, Georg (1586–1656), 43
Callimachus (310/305–240 BC), 281n
Calov, Abraham (1612–86), 125, 260n
Calvin, John (1509–64), 28, 56, 57, 85, 165, 170, 189, 191, 193, 195, 253, 326, 367, 372, 377, 397, 400, 456, 480
Carloman, 300n
Casel, Odo (1886–1948), 361, 466, 467
Caspar, Erich (1879–1935), 440
Catherine of Aragon (1485–1536), 372
Celestine I (pope, r. 422–432), 142
Celsus (fl. second century), 211
Cerularius, Michael (patriarch, r. 1043–1058), 297, 302, 307
Charles (Charlemagne, ca. 742–814), 297, 300, 381, 430
Charles V (emperor, r. 1519–56), 369n, 370, 371, 372n, 426n
Chemnitz, Martin (1522–86), 42, 150, 242, 474, 486
Chomjakov, Aleksej (1804-60), 434
Chrysostom, John (ca. 345–407), 146, 147, 148, 152, 188, 223, 282, 283, 290, 341, 452
Chytraeus, David (1531–1600), 158, 160
Cicero, Marcus Tullius (106–43 BC), 394
Clement of Alexandria (ca. 150–215), 211, 437n, 444n
Clement of Rome (bishop, 92–101), 188, 209, 215, 438, 440, 441, 442, 443
Cohn, J., 282
Constantine (emperor, r. 305–337), 34, 35, 297, 430, 439n, 485
Cooper, Anthony Ashley (1801–85), 64n
Copernicus, Nicolaus (1473–1543), 281, 282, 286
Cranmer, Thomas (1489–1556), 372
Cumont, Franz (1868–1947), 290
Cybele, 459
Cyprian (ca. 200–258), 156n, 196, 356, 443
Cyprian, Ernst Salomon (1673–1745), 176, 198, 391, 392, 393
Cyril of Jerusalem (ca. 315–ca. 386), 160, 363n

Cyrill, 304
Dannhauer, J. K. (1603–66), 10n
Darsow, 96
Darwin, Charles (1809–82), 432
Davidson, Randall Thomas (1848–1930), 315
Deissmann, Adolf (1866–1937), 320n, 420n
Dell, 79
Dibelius, Friedrich Karl Otto (1880–1967), 52, 71, 178, 261, 313, 380n, 384
Didymus the Blind (ca. 313–398), 301
Diestelmann, Jürgen, 231n
Dietrich, Veit (1506–49), 284
Dionysius the Areopagite, 456
Dionysius the Great (patriarch, 190–265), 304
Dioscorus (d. 454), 38n
Dix, Gregory (1901–52), 160
Doehler, 116
Döllinger, 338
Domitian (emperor, r. 81–96), 208
Donatus (fl. ca. 354), 298n
Dornseiff, 242
Drach, G., 138
Drews, 230
Dysinger, Homes, 497n

Edward VI (king, r. 1547–53), 446n
Edwards, Jonathan (1703–58), 345n
Eichhorn, Karl (1810–85), 377
Eisenhower, Dwight D. (1890–1969), 230
Elert, Werner (1885–1954), 102, 125, 126, 127, 175, 248n, 252, 281n, 345, 350, 351, 353, 390, 394n, 404, 405, 406, 416
Elizabeth I (queen, r. 1558–1603), 372, 446n
Engberding, H., 341
Engelder, Theodore (1865–1949), 29
Engels, Friedrich (1820–95), 164n, 316
Ephraim (ca. 306–373), 301
Epiphanius (ca. 315–403), 210, 301
Erasmus, Desiderius (ca. 1467–1536), 86n, 419, 435n
Eratosthenes (276–194 BC), 281
Erdmann, 231
Eusebius (ca. 260–ca. 339), 210, 317n, 441, 444, 461
Eutyches (ca. 380–ca. 456), 38n
Evaristus (pope, r. 97–105), 441

Farnese, Alexander. See Paul III
Felix of Aptunga, 298n
Fendt, E. C., 79n
Ferdinand (emperor, r. 1556–64), 369, 373
Ferdinand II (of Aragon, 1452–1516), 370n
Feuerhahn, Ronald, 320n, 376n
Fisher, Geoffrey Francis (1887–1972), 61, 402

Flacius, Matthias (1520–75), 156n, 235, 259n, 260n, 434n
Flavian, 304
Fleisch, D. Paul (1878–1962), 332
Fortunatus, 445n
Frank, H., 157
Franklin, Benjamin (1706–90), 64
Franzmann, Martin, 312
Frederick III (1515–76), 458n
Frederick William I, 391n
Frederick William III (r. 1797–1840), 25n, 427n
Frederick William IV (r. 1840–61), 427
Fredric (deacon of Rome), 297
Freytag, D. Walter (1899–1959), 326
Friedrich, J., 338
Fröhlich, D. Richard, 327
Fry, Franklin Clark (1900–1968), 69, 178, 204, 309, 330n, 350, 423, 497n
Fuerbringer, O. A., 330n
Fürstenau, H., 376

Gensichen, H. W., 400
Gerhard, Johann (1582–1637), 27n, 43, 221, 229, 243, 260n, 460, 474, 486
Gerhardt, Paul (1607–76), 25
Germanos, Strenopoulos (archbishop), 201
Giacometti, Z., 376
Goebbels, Joseph (1897–1945), 313
Goehrke, 500
Goethe, Johann Wolfgang von (1749–1832), 459n
Gore, Charles (1853–1932), 60, 483
Gottschalk (ca. 804–ca. 869), 381
Grabau, Johannes Andreas August (1804–79), 246, 398n, 419n
Graebner, Theodore Conrad (1876–1950), 16, 335
Graff, P., 228
Grass, Hans, 157, 158, 160
Gratian, 445
Green, Lowell, 248n, 497n
Greever, W. H., 497n
Gregory I ("The Great," pope, r. 590–604), 213, 220
Gregory VII (pope, r. 1073–85), 297n
Gregory of Nyssa (ca. 331–ca. 396), 282, 283
Gunkel, Johann Friedrich Hermann (1862–1932), 265n, 284

Hallesby, 262
Hamann, H. P., 3
Hardt, Tom, 366n
Harless, Gottlieb Christoph Adolf von (1806–79), 249, 260, 396, 477, 500

Harms, Hans-Otto, 227, 228, 233
Harnack, Adolf von (1851–1930), 32, 36, 40, 53n, 83, 94n, 249, 253n, 259n, 306, 441, 454
Hartenstein, K., 320, 321
Heckel, Theodor, 60n
Hecker, I. Th. (1819–88), 246
Hegel (1770–1831), 432n
Hegesippus (second century), 441
Heiler, Friedrich (1892–1967), 37, 137, 140, 141, 340, 341, 428
Hein, Carl Christian (1868–1937), 60, 180, 493
Heitmüller, Wilhelm (1869–1926), 90, 260n, 265n
Helvidius (fl. fourth century), 340
Henry IV (emperor, r. 1056–1105), 297n
Henry VIII (king, r. 1509–47), 258, 372, 376, 429, 446n
Hermelink, H., 485
Hippolytus (ca. 170–ca. 235), 298n
Hitler, Adolf (1889–1945), 47n, 112, 164, 196, 232, 234, 308, 344, 345, 351n, 379n, 380, 382, 427, 498, 499
Hodgsen, 251n, 498n
Hoen, Cornelius (d. 1524), 80
Höfling, Johann Wilhelm Friedrich (1802–53), 228, 229
Hofmann, Johann Christian Konrad von (1810–77), 94n
Holl, Karl (1866–1926), 8, 52, 235, 248n, 253, 367, 397
Hollaz, David Friedrich (1648–1713), 26, 220
Homer, 436n
Hooft, Willem Adolph Visser 't (1900–1985), 274
Hopf, Friedrich Wilhelm (1910–82), 179, 237n, 278, 352
Horton, W. M., 417
Hugh of St. Victor (d. 1142), 454, 460
Humbert of Silva Candida (d. 1061), 297
Hunnius, Aegidius (1550–1603), 132, 160
Hus, John (ca. 1370–1415), 106, 382n
Huß, Hans Siegfried, 237n
Hyginus (pope, r. 136–140), 441

Ignatius (patriarch), 300n
Ignatius of Antioch (d. ca. 112), 93, 304, 340, 440n
Ihmels, Ludwig Heinrich (1858–1933), 59, 330, 350
Irenaeus (ca. 130–ca. 200), 209, 304, 439, 440, 441
Irving, E. (1792–1834), 348n
Isabella I (1451–1504), 370n

Ivan, 307

Jacobs, 252, 492
Jansen, Cornelius (1585–1638), 471n
Jeremias (patriarch, 1536–94), 43
Jeremias, Joachim (1900–1979), 90
Jerome (ca. 345–420), 211, 216, 219
Joachimsen, Paul (1860–1930), 370
Johansson, Gustaf (1844–1930), 60, 448
John VIII Palaeologus (emperor, r. 1425–48), 303n
John of Damascus (ca. 675–ca. 750), 290, 301, 358, 455
Jonas, Justus (1493–1555), 144, 148, 455
Jones, Eli Stanley (1884–1973), 62
Jordahl, Leigh, 223n
Josephus, Flavius (ca. 37–ca. 100), 214
Julian ("The Apostate," emperor, r. 361–363), 211
Jülicher, Gustav Adolf (1857–1938), 89
Julius II (pope, r. 1503–13), 107n
Justin Martyr (ca. 100–ca. 165), 185, 229, 285, 466

Kabafilas, Nilos, 303
Kant, Immanuel (1724–1804), 28, 136, 257
Karlstadt, Andreas Rudolf Bodenstein von (ca. 1480–1541), 80
Kattenbusch, 302
Kavel, August Ludwig Christian (1798–1860), 9
Kawerau, G., 157
Kempis, Thomas à (ca. 1380–1471), 456n
Kepler, Johannes (1571–1630), 281
Kierkegaard, Sören (1813–55), 257, 399
Kleine, H. F. de, 171
Kliefoth, Theodor Friedrich Dethlof (1810–95), 11, 260
Knak, Joachim Karl Friedrich (b. 1806), 500
Knolle, Theodor (1885–1955), 153
Knox, Ronald, 281
Knubel, Frederick Hermann (1870–1945), 250, 251n, 334, 400, 493, 497n
Köhler, Walther, 81, 82, 86, 87, 88, 184, 447
Kolde, Hermann Friedrich Theodor von (1850–1913), 248, 370
Köstlin, G., 107
Krafft, 238n
Kramer, Fred, 5n
Kretzmann, P. E. (1883–1965), 16, 26, 29, 130n
Krodel, Karl, 237n
Krüger, Gustav (1862–1940), 265
Krummacher, Friedrich-Wilhelm, 60n, 118

Leibniz, Gottfried Wilhelm von (1646–1716), 197
Leiper, 54
Leisegang, Hans, 208
Lenin, Vladimir (1870–1924), 111
Leo I ("The Great," pope, r. 440–461), 34, 35
Leo IX (pope, r. 1049–54), 302n
Leo X (pope, r. 1513–21), 107, 114
Leo XIII (pope, r. 1878–1903), 303, 340, 372n, 376, 446
Leo of Ochrida (bishop), 297
Lepsius, Johannes (1858–1926), 356
Lieberg, 230, 231, 233
Lietzmann, Hans (1875–1942), 91, 92, 365
Lightfoot, 280
Lilje, Hanns (1899–1977), 52, 111n, 163, 177, 178, 204, 313, 325, 328, 348, 445, 471 495
Link, Wilhelm, 206
Linus (pope, r. 67–76), 441
Loewe, K., 157
Löhe, Johann Konrad Wilhelm (1808–72), 10, 59n, 68n, 94, 142, 174, 225, 232, 238n, 240, 247, 273, 279, 349, 377n, 396, 397, 419n, 476
Lohmeyer, 90, 193
Long, Ralph Herman (1882–1948), 493, 497n
Löscher, Valentin Ernst (1673–1749), 197, 393
Lucarius, Cyril (1572–1638), 455
Lundquist, Carl Elof (1908–65), 3, 32, 162, 489
Luther, Martin (1486–1546), 6, 8, 9n, 10, 12, 13, 14, 15, 18, 20, 26, 27, 28, 29, 30, 40, 45, 51, 56, 59n, 63, 66, 68, 71, 72, 75, 77, 78, 79, 80, 81, 82, 83, 84, 85, 86, 87, 88, 89, 92, 94, 95, 96, 104, 105, 106, 107, 108, 109, 110, 111, 113, 114, 115, 119, 121, 122, 123, 124, 126, 127, 133, 134, 136, 137, 141, 144, 145, 146, 147, 148, 149, 152, 153, 154, 155, 156, 157, 158n, 159, 161, 166, 167, 169, 170, 171, 172, 173, 175n, 176, 178, 179, 184, 185, 186, 189, 190, 191, 192, 193, 194, 198, 199, 202, 203, 206, 213, 219, 221, 222, 223, 228, 229, 230, 241, 243, 246n, 247, 252, 253, 256, 257, 258, 259, 260, 268, 269, 271, 272, 277, 278, 279, 280n, 283, 284, 287, 289, 291, 292, 296, 304, 305, 307, 310, 321, 322, 323, 324, 325, 328, 337, 340, 345, 346, 351, 353, 362, 367, 368, 370, 371, 372, 373, 376, 388, 389, 390, 391, 393, 394n, 397, 398, 400, 412, 414, 419, 429, 430, 433, 434, 435, 439n, 447, 452, 454, 455, 457, 458, 459, 461, 462, 463, 464, 465, 469, 477, 478,

479, 480, 483, 485, 486, 489, 492n, 494, 497, 499, 501

Major, Georg (1502–74), 434n

Mani (Manes, Manichaeus, ca. 216–ca. 277), 435

Manning, Henry Edward (cardinal, 1808–92), 439

Marcion (ca. 100–ca. 160), 38, 298n

Marcus Aurelius (emperor, r. 161–180), 306

Marquart, Kurt (1934–2006), 223n

Martin, 295

Martinsen, T. Paul, 225

Martyr, Peter. See Vermigli, Peter Martyr

Marx, Karl (1818–83), 164n, 316, 343, 432

Mary (queen, r. 1553–58), 372, 446n

Maurice of Saxony (1521–53), 485n

Maximus the Confessor, 304

Mayer, Frederick Emanuel (1892–1954), 293

McKenzie, Douglas, 251n

McPartland, John, 408

Medici, Giovanni de'. See Leo X

Meiser, Hans (1881–1956), 204, 405, 406, 424, 495

Melanchthon, Philip (1497–1560), 28, 65n, 107, 124, 125, 126, 140, 148, 156, 157n, 158n, 280n, 325n, 391, 394, 434n, 445, 455

Melhausen, 427

Melito (d. ca. 190), 361, 362, 363, 364, 365

Menander (342–291 BC), 314n

Meyer, Heinrich (1904–78), 326, 328

Meyer, Lawrence, 293, 334, 474

Michael III (emperor, r. 842–867), 300n

Michael IV (emperor, r. 1034–41), 297n

Michelangelo (1475–1564), 210

Michelfelder, Sylvester Clarence (1889–1951), 70

Miltiades (d. 314), 210

Möhler, Johann Adam (1796–1838), 386, 432, 434, 435, 436, 428, 429

Molitoris, 379n

Montanus (fl. second century), 210

Montini, 342

More, Thomas (1478–1535), 372, 373

Morehead, John Alfred (1867–1936), 493

Moses Amyraldus (1596–1664), 345

Mott, John Raleigh (1865–1955), 315, 320n

Mowinckel, Sigmund Olaf Plytt (1884–1965), 467

Mueller, E. F. K., 479

Muhammad, 430, 435, 436

Mühlenberg, Henry Melchior (1711–87), 256

Müller, Karl, 118

Müller, Ludwig (1883–1945), 427

Mundinger, Carl S., 8

Mussolini, Benito (1883–1945), 112

Mützelfeld, Karl (1881–1955), 450

Naumann, Charlotte Margarete. See Sasse, Charlotte

Naumann, Martin, 312

Neander, J. A. W., 253n

Neill, Stephan Charles, 350, 418

Nelson, E. Clifford, ix

Nelson, Olof H., 78, 79

Nestorius (d. ca. 451), 38, 298n

Newman, John Henry (1801–90), 376, 426, 427, 432, 434, 436, 482

Newton, Isaac (1642–1727), 281

Nicholas I (pope, r. 858–867), 303

Nicolaus of Oxerne (d. 1382), 282n

Niebuhr, Reinhold (1892–1971), 20, 500

Niemöller, Martin (1892–1984), 46, 321n, 330

Niesel, W., 144

Nikon (patriarch, r. 1652–58), 302n

Noack, F. W., 251n

Nommensen, Ludwig (1834–1918), 175, 322

Novatian (third century), 297n

Nygren, Anders Teodor Samuel (1890–1978), 63, 178, 329, 330

Oecolampadius, Johannes (1482–1531), 86, 87, 89, 184

Oesch, 384

Oldham, Joseph H., 320n

Olevian, Caspar (1536–87), 458n

Origen (ca. 185–ca. 254), 211, 219, 301, 306

Osiander, Andreas (1498–1552), 140, 372n, 454

Osiander, Margaret, 372n

Otto I ("The Great," emperor, r. 962–973), 430

Otto, Rudolf (1869–1937), 467, 468

Oxnam, Garfield Bromley (1887–1972), 61

Pacelli, Eugenio. See Pius XII

Palmer, Edwin J. (1869–1954), 59, 319n, 411

Pantaenus (d. ca. 190), 444

Parker, Matthew (1504–75), 446

Parsch, Pius (1884–1954), 471

Pauck, Wilhelm (1901–81), 251n, 367

Paul III (pope, r. 1534–49), 114

Paul of Samosata (third century), 440n

Pelikan, Jaroslav (1923–2006), 28, 367

Pepin, 300n

Peter of Amalfi (archbishop), 297

Peter the Great, 304

Peterson, Erik (1890–1960), 194

Petri, Ludwig Adolf (1803–73), 396, 397

Pflug, Julius von (1499–1564), 426n

Philaret (Vasili Mikhailovich Dorzdov, 1782–1867), 456

Philip of Hesse (1504–67), 485
Philo (ca. 20/30 BC–ca. AD 50), 207, 208, 209, 211, 282
Photios (partiarch of Constantinople, r. 858–867), 300, 301, 302
Pieper, Francis (1852–1931), 27n, 28, 160, 182, 251n, 393, 394, 494n
Piepkorn, Arthur Carl (1907–73), 139, 428n, 474
Pinsk, Joh., 342
Pius I (pope, r. 140–155), 441
Pius IX (pope, r. 1846–78), 109, 369, 376
Pius XI (pope, r. 1922–39), 142, 340, 343, 372n
Pius XII (pope, r. 1939–58), 56n, 96, 114, 142, 151, 190n, 303n, 338, 360, 374, 375, 386
Plank, Max (1858–1947), 286
Plato (ca. 428/427–347 BC), 206, 282, 284, 286, 292, 314n
Pliny the Younger (61–ca. 112), 104, 188
Plotinus (ca. 205–270), 211n
Polack, William Gustave (1890–1950), 8
Pörksen, Martin, 330
Porphyry (ca. 232/233–ca. 304), 211, 215, 218, 220
Prenter, 4, 162
Preus, Herman (1896–1995), xn, 53n, 75, 203, 226, 242, 262, 279
Preus, J. A. O (1920–94), 53n, 111n, 330n
Preus, Robert (1924–95), 53n, 394n
Preuss, Hans (1876–1951), 106, 107, 157, 405
Procksch, Otto (1874–1947), 405, 406
Ps.-Justin, 209, 210
Ptolemy (ca. 90–ca. 168), 281, 282n
Pusey, Edward Bouverie (1800–1882), 483

Quenstedt, Johann Andreas (1617–88), 27, 220

Rad, Gerhard von (1901–71), 467
Radbertus (785–865), 381n
Ranft, J., 434
Reim, E., 33n
Renan, Joseph Ernest (1823–92), 290
Rengstorff, Karl Heinrick, 405
Reu, Johann Michael (1869–1943), 124, 179, 225, 251n, 321, 334, 349, 401, 491, 493, 497n
Ritschl, Albrecht (1822–89), 36, 53n, 63n, 125, 164, 249, 252
Robinson, John (ca. 1575–1625), 480, 482
Rocholl, Rudolf (1822–1905), 236n, 477
Rockefeller, 272
Rose, 240
Rosenberg, Alfred, 266, 313
Rottman, Hans, 404, 406

Rouse, Ruth, 350, 418
Rufinus (ca. 345–ca. 410), 219

Salazar, 382
Saliger, Johann (Beatus, d. after 1571), 157, 160
Sandegren, Johannes (1883–1962), 330
Sasse, Charlotte, 374n, 420n, 498n
Sasse, Wolfgang, 473
Schaftesbury. See Cooper, Anthony Ashley
Scheeben, Matthias Joseph (1835–88), 104, 195, 337
Scheibel, Johan Gottfried (1783–1843), 9, 395, 396, 477
Schelling, 432n
Scherer, M. G. G., 497n
Schiotz, Fredrik Axel (1901–89), 329, 330
Schlatter, Adolf (1852–1938), 266
Schlatter, Theodore, 266n
Schleiermacher, Friedrich Daniel Ernst (1768–1834), 52, 53, 63, 164, 209n, 252, 253n, 348n, 398
Schlink, Edmund (1903–84), 65, 126, 202, 339, 346, 347, 492n
Schlünzen, 167
Schmidt, K. D., 38
Schmidt, S. (1617–96), 10n
Schmidt, S., 111n
Schmitt, Alois, 290
Schmucker, Samuel Simon (1799–1873), 18, 245
Schreyer, Paul, 198n
Schuh, Henry Frederick (1890–1965), 79n, 350, 423
Schulz, 406
Schwiebert, 367, 368
Seeberg, Reinhold (1859–1935), 235
Selnecker, Nikolaus (ca. 1528/1530–92), 148
Semler, Johann Salomo (1725–91), 26
Seneca ("The Elder," ca. 54 BC–ca. AD 39), 436n
Serapion (d. after 362), 160
Servetus, Michael (ca. 1511–53), 372
Sieck, Louis, 116, 251n
Sigismund, Johann (1572–1619), 377
Simon the Just (ca. 300 BC), 431, 437
Sixtus (pope, r. 115–125), 441
Söderblom, Nathan (1866–1931), 140n, 328n, 447
Solovjov, Vladimir Sergeyevich (1853–1900), 303, 304
Spener, Philipp Jacob (1635–1705), 10, 391
Stählin, Gustav (1900–1985), 177, 268, 405
Stählin, Wilhelm (1883–1975), 78n, 140, 141
Stalin, Joseph (1878–1953), 112, 307

Stauffer, Ethelbert (1902–79), 405
Steimle, Augustus, 497n
Steiner, Rudolf (1861–1925), 140, 141, 459
Stephan, Martin (1777–1846), 8n, 398n
Stephen III (pope, r. 752–757), 300n
Stoll, Christian, 237n
Stolz, John, 116, 424
Strossmayer, Josip Juraj (1815–1905), 304
Swainson, C. A., 341

Taft, 348
Tanner, Adam (1572–1632), 132
Tappert, Theodore Gerhardt (1904–73), 225, 394n
Teigen, Bjarne, 156n,
Telesphorus (pope, r. 125–136), 441
Temple, William (1881–1944), 59, 378–79, 428n, 492
Tertullian (ca. 155/160–ca. 220/230), 211, 439
Tetzel, Johann (1465–1519), 489
Thadden-Trieglaff, Adolf Ferdinand von (1796–1882), 350
Thadden-Trieglaff, Reinhold von (1891–1976), 350, 418
Thamsius, 500
Theodore of Mopsuestia (ca. 350–ca. 428), 188
Theodoric (ca. 454–526), 304
Theodot of Studion, 304
Theophilus (d. ca. 181/186), 210
Theophylact (1055–1107), 148
Thiersch, Heinrich Wilhelm Josias (1817–85), 347
Tholuck, Friedrich August G. (1799–1877), 249n, 253, 397
Thomas Aquinas (ca. 1224/1227–1274), 3, 42, 136, 147, 159, 221, 272, 282n, 283, 288, 292, 376, 409, 456, 465, 470
Tillich, Paul (1886–1965), 459, 500
Tixeront, 444
Torquemada, Juan de (1388–1468), 382
Trajan (emperor, r. 98–117), 104, 306
Troeltsch, Ernst Peter Wilhelm (1865–1923), 53n, 105n

Ulfilas (Ulphilas, ca. 310/313–381/383), 317
Ursinus, Zacharias (1534–83), 458n

Vajta, Vilmos (1918–98), 271, 272, 277
Van Dusen, Henry (1897–1975), 420
Vermigli, Peter Martyr (1500–1562), 372n
Victoria (queen, r. 1838–1901), 315n
Vilmar, August Friedrich Christian (1800–1868), 10, 105, 108, 260, 270, 396, 409, 416, 476, 484

Vilmar, Jacob Wilhelm Georg (1804–84), 396, 397, 500
Vincent of Lerins (d. before 459), 436
Virgil (Publius Vergilius Maro, 70–19 BC), 212
Vogel, Heinrich, 279
Vulgarius. See Theolphylact

Walther, C. F. W. (1811–87), 8, 9, 10, 11, 12, 13, 14n, 20, 27n, 30, 160, 182n, 186n, 197, 246n, 247, 258, 260, 273, 377n, 394n, 398
Walther, Johann von (1876–1940), 253, 494, 501
Warnshuis, A. L., 320n
Weiser, 467
Weiss, J., 265n
Weizsäcker, C. F. von, 287
Wentz, A. R. (1883–1976), 256, 447
Whitefield, George (1714–70), 345n
Wichern, Johann Hinrich (1808–81), 416
Wiederaenders, Roland, 10n
Wigand, Johannes (1523–87), 158
Wiggers, J., 157, 160
Wilamowitz-Moellendorf, Ulrich von (1848–1931), 314
William of Champeaux (ca. 1070–1122), 454n
William of Ockham (1285–1347), 80
Winter, Roy L., 247
Witte, Max (1909–55), 231, 385, 386
Wittenberg, Martin, xiv
Wobbermin, 251n
Wolferinus, 155, 156
Wucherer, Johann Friedrich (1803–81), 238
Wulfila. See Ulfilas
Wycliffe, John (1320–84), 106, 456, 459
Wyneken, Friedrich Conrad Dietrich (1810–76), 397–98

Young, Wm. L., 19

Zahn, Theodor von (1838–1933), 94
Zankov, Stef., 456
Zenzelinus of Cassanis (d. ca. 1350), 109
Zinzendorf, Nikolaus Ludwig von (1700–1760), 262
Zoellner, Wilhelm (1860–1937), 59, 60n, 350
Zwingli, Ulrich (1484–1531), 28, 79, 80, 81, 82, 83, 84, 85, 86, 87, 88, 89, 92, 124, 156n, 170, 182, 189, 190, 191, 192, 253, 271, 323, 324, 328, 340, 372, 389, 390, 400, 456, 459, 462 485, 497

Scripture Index

OLD TESTAMENT

Genesis
222, 279, 282, 283, 284,
288, 289, 290
1 288
1:16 283
2:7 290
3:5 ....103, 287
11:1................295
17:11...............456

Exodus
361, 362
12:11..............89
12:46..............89

Numbers
27:18..............443

Deuteronomy
5:1 467
5:2 468
34:9 443

Joshua
10:13 207

2 Samuel
1:18................207

1 KINGS
317n
19:18 499

2 KINGS
317n

Nehemiah
8–10 438

Job
289

PSALMS
289, 467n
2 363
35:20 499
50:14..............149

51:19 149
60:11 15
77:19...............86
77:20..............86
124:2...............15

Song of Songs
134

Isaiah
11:4................102
25:8................216
40:8 36
53 ....90, 363
53:6................238, 241
55:11 460
60:17..............438

Jeremiah
6:14 499
11:19..............363
17:5 403
23:25 209
30:2 207
36:2 207

Ezekiel
4 468
5 468
13:2 208

Daniel
11 107

Joel
2:28...............100

Amos
5:18 ....100, 161, 360
7:14 ....208, 217

Jonah
3:4 217

Micah
3:3 364

6:5 416

Malachi
1:11 187
1:14...............187

APOCRYPHA

4 Ezra (Esdras)
14:22..............207
14:25..............207
14:40..............207

Tobit
11:4...............132
11:9...............132

1 Maccabees
12:9...............214

NEW TESTAMENT

MATTHEW
266n, 359
6:6 199
6:24...............113
10:19 222
10:32..............278
10:34..............499
11:4................160
11:5................100
13:33..............90
16 442
16:15 63
16:19 388
18 442
18:18 ....388, 445
18:20..............160, 174, 191,
422
21:12–17.........218n
23 443
23:8................443
23:10..............443

23:15...............7
24:14...............100, 464
24:24...............108
26 173
27:9...............219, 222
27:46...............38
28:19...............461
28:20...............174

Mark
  91, 92, 359, 464
10 173
10:14 173
11:15–18.........218n
14 173
14:22...............148
15:25...............218
16:18 29

Luke
  359
1:1 ....207, 210
1:38...............338n
2 84
4:18...............160
4:23...............69
13:3 165
14:23...............375
18:16 173
19:45–47.........218n
22 173
22:19...............145, 150

John
  89, 92, 93, 103, 191, 357,
  359, 362
1:1–14.............228
1:14..................46, 103, 463
2:14–16 ....218n
3:5 84
3:8 428
5 93
5:17 289
5:25...............102
6 ....79, 83, 92, 93,
  127
6:1–13.............92
6:31...............457
6:51...............83
6:51–58.........84
6:53...............93

6:54 100
6:55–56 92
6:63...............88
9:4 30
10:35...............207
14:26...............93
15:1...............89
15:11...............365
15:26...............93
16:12–13.........430
16:13 93
16:14 431
16:20...............365
16:22...............365
17 30
17:1...............383n
17:17...............120, 207
17:21 ....120, 351, 387
18:28...............359
19:14 218
19:34...............84, 457
19:36...............89
20 442
20:19...............186
20:21...............439, 443
20:22 ....388, 428
21:24...............210

Acts
  222
2:16...............100
2:17 464
2:38...............461
2:46 365
4:12...............346, 417
7 ....222, 357
10:48...............143, 229, 461
13:1–3.............444
13:3 444
14:23...............439
17:23...............285
18:26...............401
19:5 461
21:10 468

Romans
  188, 440
1:2 214
1:19..................287

1:19–23 453
2 ....395n
3 402
6:1 359–60
6:2 100
6:4 ....190, 191, 457
12:1 149
12:2 307
15:4 ....132, 133
16 17
16:16 ....187, 188
16:17 ....17, 135, 188, 399

1 Corinthians
  188, 220
1:10 135
1:13...............461, 468
1:14...............143, 229
1:17...............229
1:18–25 221
1:21 221
1:22–23.........209
1:23...............468
1:30...............152
2:2 468
2:8 468
5 360
6:19 190
10 ....91, 362, 452
10:1 ....457, 461
10:11...............100, 457
10:16 ....77, 91, 158, 173,
  175, 186, 285, 387, 390
10:16–17.........91
10:17 ....91, 186
10:18 149
10:18–21 453
11 ....91, 452
11:7...............173
11:19...............298
11:23 ....91, 437, 464
11:24 145
11:26 ....92, 100, 145, 147,
  153, 464
11:27–30.........91, 92
11:29 83
12:13 ....387, 457
13:10 134

14 452
15:3.................91, 437, 464
15:4.................466
15:23.................102
15:55.................216
16 17
16:20.................187, 188
16:22.................17, 188
16:23.................188

2 Corinthians
3:6 218
6:14 188
11:30 250
13:4 468
13:12 187
13:14 188

Galatians
437
1:8 462
3:1 468
6:14 250

Ephesians
275
4 ....135, 386
4:4 ....190, 321
4:4–5.................386
4:14 414
5:25–26 151

Philippians
2:10.................387
2:10–11...........351
3:21 190

Colossians
1:11.................456
2:12–13 457

1 Thessalonians
5:26.................187

2 Thessalonians
2 103
2:3 ....101, 102, 108, 111
2:4 103
2:8 102

2:9 101

1 Timothy
3 442
4:14 444
5 442
5:17 444
6:20.................66, 298, 437

2 Timothy
1:6 ....442, 444
2:19 437
3:16 ....207, 214

Titus
3 269
3:5 456
3:9 298
3:10.................269
4:10.................66

Hebrews
29, 362
1:2 ....100, 194, 464
6:2 443
7:27.................78
9:12.................78, 194, 467
9:26.................194
9:27.................467
9:28.................194
10:10 78
11:3.................285, 288, 393
13:10 149
13:15 149
13:16 149

1 Peter
360
2:5 ....149, 150
2:9 150
5:14 187

2 Peter
1:4 37
1:19.................207, 214
3:3 100
3:3–9.............101

1 John
1:3 ....188, 488
2:18.................101, 102, 298
2:22.................101
4 499
4:1 ....66, 93, 298
4:1–7 188
4:2 190
4:3 103
4:12.................222

2 John
6 499–500
7 ....101, 298
9 188
10 ....269, 298

Revelation
98, 100, 188, 290, 441
1:6 150
1:7 387
1:9 161
1:11.................188
2 416
3 416
3:20 161
4 100
5:12 357
12:10–11 357
13:8 ....194, 468
14:6.................464
19:15 102
19:20.............102
21:4 290
22:18.............188
22:18–19 437
22:20 ....17, 100, 188